NORMAN VINCENT PEALE

A New Collection of Three Complete Books

NORMAN VINCENT PEALE

A New Collection of Three Complete Books

A GUIDE TO CONFIDENT LIVING

STAY ALIVE ALL YOUR LIFE

THE AMAZING RESULTS OF POSITIVE THINKING

WINGS BOOKS
New York • Avenel, New Jersey

This omnibus was originally published in separate volumes under the titles:

A *Guide to Confident Living,* copyright © 1948 by Prentice-Hall, Inc., copyright renewed 1976 by Norman Vincent Peale.
Stay Alive All Your Life, copyright © 1957 by Prentice-Hall, Inc., copyright renewed 1985 by Norman Vincent Peale.
The Amazing Results of Positive Thinking, copyright © 1959 by Prentice-Hall, Inc., copyright renewed 1987 by Norman Vincent Peale.

This edition contains the complete and unabridged texts of the original editions. They have been completely reset for this volume.

This 1996 edition is published by Wings Books,
a division of Random House Value Publishing, Inc.,
40 Engelhard Avenue, Avenel, New Jersey 07001,
by arrangement with Simon & Schuster, Inc.

Wings Books and colophon are trademarks of Random House Value Publishing, Inc.

Random House
New York • Toronto • London • Sydney • Auckland
http://www.randomhouse.com/

Printed and bound in the United States of America

Library of Congress Cataloging-in-Publication Data

Peale, Norman Vincent, 1898–1993
    [Selections. 1996]
    Norman Vincent Peale : a new collection of three complete books.
        p.   cm.
    Contents: A guide to confident living—Stay alive all your life—The amazing results of positive thinking.
    ISBN 0-517-14671-1
    1. Success—Religious aspects—Christianity. 2. Peace of mind—Religious aspects—Christianity. 3. Business ethics. 4. Conduct of life. 5. Christian life. I. Title.
    BV4598.3.P392   1996
    248.4—dc20   95-18750
                                                                              CIP

10   9   8   7   6   5   4   3

CONTENTS

INTRODUCTION

Dr. Norman Vincent Peale was a man of extraordinary character and kindness. He had great insight into human nature and showed relentless interest in, and love for, every manner of man and woman. He saw the good in all people and had a remarkable ability to bring out their best.

Dr. Peale was a man of virtually two centuries. In certain passages, his material reflects his times, and yet his philosophy is timeless. His writing and beliefs offer much of value to today's readers.

Readers may be surprised to discover that much of what has become popular in today's alternative health circles was advocated by Dr. Peale in the 1940s and '50s. He was talking about harmonizing the body, mind, and spirit decades before "holistic" health became a buzz word for the '90s. He advocated meditation, visualization, and affirmation—and used those terms specifically. Above all, he showed how these techniques could be incorporated into the Christian life style.

Regardless of the words you use or the religion you profess, the underlying principle of Dr. Peale's work remains the same. Indeed, his success in life demonstrated the power of his beliefs: Think positively and accomplish greatly!

A GUIDE TO
CONFIDENT LIVING

TO MY CHILDREN
Margaret
John
and
Elizabeth

INTRODUCTION

OVER A CONSIDERABLE period, the author has had the opportunity to work with large numbers of people facing modern problems in the heart of America's greatest city. He has conducted a consultation service in the Marble Collegiate Church on Fifth Avenue, New York, to which hundreds of people every year come for help and guidance. The staff consists of ministers, psychiatrists, physicians and social psychiatrists.

The author has evolved a specific technique designed to lead people to personal happiness and success. This method has worked for the many who have put it into practice. Its efficiency has been amply demonstrated; it has been tested and found satisfactory by hundreds of people. It has produced amazing results in the personal experience of many. It has indeed proved a guide to confident living.

Yet the principles of happiness and success to be presented in this book are not new. They were not created by the author but are as old as the Bible. In fact they are the simple principles taught in the Bible. If the techniques possess any uniqueness, it lies in the effort to show HOW to use these principles in a practical and understanding manner suited to modern men.

The book may seem repetitious at times. That is because it is a text book of a formula. It hammers on one basic procedure and repetition is the master of studies, as the classic saying goes. Reiteration is essential in persuading the reader to practice; to try and try again. If water wears away a stone, so does emphasis, even at the danger of repetition, wear away our apathy toward self-betterment.

This book is not theoretical. It contains the detailed description of a technique of living that can lead those who definitely put it into operation to success and happiness. The book is written with one primary purpose: to state and demonstrate a simple, workable technique of thinking and acting that has revitalized the lives of thousands of moderns. The important substance in the book is the how-ness. It tells you HOW you can acheive your most cherished desires.

This book presents in simple outline those formulas which make life work successfully. Each chapter deals with an aspect of the unified theme of the book, namely, HOW . . . to be happy and successful. The tested method is applied to some of the basic causes of unhappiness and failure: tension, fear, inferiority, wrong thinking, and other mental handicaps.

Not every factor in successful and happy living is discussed, for that is neither possible nor necessary. The formula is applied to enough factors, however, to teach the reader *how* to use techniques which are applicable to all situations. The method is sufficiently developed to show the reader what he wants to know—how to be happy and successful. This book is offered as a guide to confident living.

NORMAN VINCENT PEALE

CONTENTS

1

A NEW-OLD WAY TO
FREE YOUR POWERS

A YOUNG AND HIGHLY trained physician sometimes writes an apparently curious prescription for people afflicted with the maladies described in this book: fear, inferiority, tension and kindred troubles. His prescription is—"Go to church at least once a Sunday for the next three months."

To the surprised and mystified patient to whom he has given this astonishing prescription, he explains that in a church there are a mood and atmosphere containing healing power that will help cure him of the troubles I have just mentioned. He further asserts that he does not particularly care whether the patient listens to the sermon. Church going is of value if a person merely sits quietly, yielding himself to the mood and atmosphere of the church. This modern physician reports that amazing benefits have come to his patients as a result of this practice.

A woman, a long-time friend of the doctor's family, was the type of patient who goes from doctor to doctor, never giving heed, never putting into practice the advice received. Finally she came to this doctor and he told her frankly, "I don't want your case." When she asked him why, he replied, "Simply because you will not do what I tell you."

She begged and insisted and promised faithfully she would do as he prescribed, but still he demurred. In a final plea she said, "I have the money to pay for your services and how can you as a doctor refuse my case?"

So he consented on one condition: she must do exactly as he prescribed without argument and with full cooperation. He even made her sign a paper to that effect.

The reason she was in such a nervous condition was because her sister had married the man whom she wanted to marry and she hated her sister. Her entire personality was simmering and the hate poisons were unsettling her to such an extent that her whole system reacted and she had actual symptoms of sickness. The doctor gave her some medicine because he knew that was what she wanted—the first day pink, the second day white pills.

Finally one day the doctor wrote the prescription described above.

When she looked at it, amazement overspread her countenance and she snapped, "That is the silliest thing I ever heard of. I won't do it. What are you anyway, a doctor or a preacher?"

The doctor took out the paper she had signed and said, "You must do it or I am through with your case."

Grudgingly she followed directions. Some time elapsed before any benefit was apparent because of the antagonisms in her mind, but presently even she began to yield herself to the healing atmosphere and curative mood present in a service of worship.

One day to her surprise and despite her antipathy, she found herself interested in the sermon. She followed it keenly, discovering to her astonishment that it was common sense. It appealed to her tremendously. Her interest grew, she became docile to the ministrations of the physician and presently, due to this wise combination of medical practice and religion, resentment went out of her and health came in.

"So you see, my prescription works," said the doctor. In this case he also prescribed religious reading. Gradually the idea of Christianity as a technique and a scientific mechanism designed to overcome the problems to be treated in this book began to dominate her mind. Today this woman has a firm grip on life and is a well person, not only physically but emotionally and spiritually, for it was in the latter areas of her life that the poison was being generated.

Another doctor has on several occasions sent patients to my church. These people are not physically ill but are so filled with fears, anxieties and tensions, feelings of guilt, inferiority and resentment that, like the woman described above, they are properly called sick.

He sent one man who had not been to church in years and when the doctor told the man to go to church, the patient resisted, saying, "I detest sermons."

"Go to church anyway," the doctor said, "and don't listen to the sermon. Take cotton along if you wish and put it in your ears when the sermon begins. But there is one thing I want you to do. In that church every Sunday morning and evening they have a period of quietness, which they call 'the period of creative silence.' The minister will suggest that you yield yourself to this quietness and open your mind to the recreative power of God which has the power to permeate the soul, bringing benign and healing influence. The minister will be entirely correct in saying that and it will be a medicine far better than anything I can give you. It is the only way I know out of your difficulties. Therefore that is the medicine which I prescribe for your condition."

This man followed directions and the doctor reports that now he, too, is listening to the sermon. In fact, he finds himself intensely interested in the church. He never dreamed it would make such an appeal to him. A definite change for the better is beginning to come over him.

"By giving these patients the advice to go to church, I am utilizing a technique that works in many maladies. I have learned that in treating a human being we must consider the whole man and deal with him as something other than a mechanism or organism, for man is more than a bundle of chemical reactions. I believe," said the doctor, "that faith plus science properly correlated can do tremendous good."

An explanation of the phenomena described by this physician lies in the effectiveness of group therapy. Psychiatrists and psychologists not only utilize consultation and psychological treatment in working privately with individuals, but under certain circumstances they also make use of group treatment for several patients at one time. In such circumstances the counselor is working with people who have a common background in personal counseling. They are therefore familiar with the usual procedures and know how to cooperate fully.

In the instance of a service of public worship, the minister who during the week is a private counselor, attempts to bring to bear upon the members of a large congregation similar techniques for applying spiritual power except that now he uses group therapy. His congregation is composed of many types. Some are present because they realize their need of help. Others need help but are not conscious of it. Still others are present merely out of habit. Others may be present because they unconsciously seek some satisfying answer to the vague dissatisfactions of their minds.

In a large congregation, while there is a wide diversification of interest, it is also true that there are only a few basic human problems. It must also be taken into consideration that people are people regardless of who they are or what their backgrounds may be. There are certain deep universal appeals to human interest and to these human nature always responds. There is no force equal to religion in its power to touch and to satisfy basic needs. For this reason the personal religious counselor and the religious practitioner of group therapy have an opportunity enjoyed by no other scientist in the field to reach to the depths of human nature and thus bring healing strength, peace and power.

May I outline my own practice? The above mentioned theories began to develop in my mind some years ago as the number of persons with whom I was privately counseling increased. I came to the ministry of a Fifth Avenue church at the low point of the depression, back in 1932. New York City, as the financial center of the nation, was profoundly affected by the depression and I soon became aware of the fear, anxiety, insecurity, disappointment, frustration, and failure everywhere at hand. I began to preach on these themes and stressed how faith in God could give courage and wisdom together with new insights for the solution of problems. Advertising such topics in the press brought large congregations to hear these discussions. Soon my schedule of personal interviews was more than I could possibly handle and long waiting lists developed. Recognizing my lack of specialized knowledge, I turned to a highly competent psychiatrist, Dr. Smiley Blanton, for help and thus began the counseling clinic in the church.

Soon I began to notice in the congregation scores of people with whom I had counseled personally. It was then that the thought came of carrying over from the interview room to a big congregation the same technique of spiritual treatment we were utilizing in personal consultation.

One technique used in the service of public worship which has produced amazing results is the period of directed quietness. Attendance at Quaker meetings had taught me the value of creative silence. In meeting with the Friends, I derived great personal benefit such as lowering of tension, strength over fear and mental clarification which helped me in one or two instances to the most astounding solution of problems. The Friends, of course, have the advantage of long years of training in the tradition of silent meditation. We in the churches generally have never developed expertness in utilizing quietness in worship. Protestants as a rule do not practice complete quietness but inevitably have a background of music. I began to interject complete silence but did it gradually and only occasionally; it proved so effective that now if I omit it for one service many people are sure to protest.

The technique which we employ was described in a pamphlet issued by the Marble Collegiate Church Sermon Publication Committee:

> Picture the church filled to overflowing by a great congregation numbering more than 2000 people. The sunlight is streaming in the great windows, illuminating the sanctuary and falling softly upon the worshipping multitude. The church interior is a combination of gold and soft reds, with red brocade cushions and back rests in the mahogany and white colonial pews. Around three sides the great balcony swings.
>
> The front of the church is not in the form of an altar, but a small platform on which are placed three large, stately chairs, against a backdrop of rich red velvet. At the left of the platform is a beautiful lectern on which rests the great pulpit Bible. Towering above and behind the backdrop is a great nave which carries out the gold decoration. Here sits the choir. Dr. Peale is seated in the large center chair, his associates on either side.
>
> Following the reading of the Scripture, a deep hush settles upon the congregation. Dr. Peale arises, steps to the front of the platform and with nothing between himself and the congregation he speaks somewhat as follows: "We have come here this morning because God is in this place and we want to make contact with Him. This greatest of all experiences possible to human beings is best accomplished through silence. It is possible for every person in this Church to now establish a close contact with God that he shall be recreated. Remember the words of the Scriptures, 'In Him we live, and move, and have our being.' As long as we are 'in Him' we are in the flow of God's power and strength. Peace and power are ours. But sadly we become detached from

this flow. We do not live 'in Him' and thus accumulate fear, anxiety, negative thinking—everything that causes failure. Let us, therefore, practice now a moment of absolute silence. I suggest that you allow your body to assume a relaxed position in order that tension may go out of you. Perhaps you may wish to close your eyes to shut out the world. In this moment of silence, the one thing you must not do is to think about yourself or any of your problems. Instead, think about God for one minute and conceive of Him as now recreating you. Let us retire into a vital and vibrant period of creative meditation."

So saying, a deep silence falls upon the congregation. If there has been any coughing up to this point, it ceases. The only sound you can hear is the swish of automobile tires on the Avenue outside and even that seems far away.

It is not a dead silence, for there is aliveness and vibrancy in the air. There is always the spirit of expectancy that something great is about to happen. Sometimes this silence lasts only for sixty seconds. Sometimes longer, but people become lost in the silence. It is as if God, Himself, touches their minds with peace.

Presently in a very quiet voice, Dr. Peale breaks the silence by saying: "Come unto me, all ye that labor and are heavy laden, and I will give you rest." And he also adds, "Thou wilt keep him in perfect peace, whose mind is stayed on thee." He stresses this latter verse, emphasizing that for the period of quietness the minds of the worshippers have been fixed not upon their troubles but upon God. And because of that firm fixing of their minds upon the Eternal, God has sent His peace to them in that period of silence.

Scores of people report that the most amazing benefits have occurred to them in this quiet period.

I am convinced that in the vibrant and healing silence which falls over a great congregation when the suggestion is emphasized and accepted that God is present and that Jesus Christ walks the aisles to touch human beings, actual power is being released.

We know that the universe is filled with power, that the very air is charged with it. Only a short time ago we discovered atomic energy. Other forms of energy which shall subsequently be developed may even be greater. Cannot we then assume that in this dynamic universe there are spiritual forces all about us ready to play upon us and to recreate us? The New Testament definitely assures us that spiritual power is a fact. Christianity is more than a promise of power. It is power itself. The New Testament declares, "As many as received him, to them gave he power." Again it states, "Ye shall receive power, after the Holy Spirit is come upon you." All of which means that when an individual conditions his mind to the illimitable spirit of power which fills the universe, it shall fill him also.

The New Testament tells us that Christianity is life, not a way of life, but life itself. It is the essence of life. It is vitality and vibrant energy. Christianity is, therefore, more than a creed or an idea. It is a throbbing, pulsating, vibrant, creative energy even in such manner as the sunlight is energy, only infinitely more so. It is a deep therapy which can drive to the heart of a personality or of society (which is an amalgamation of individual personalities) in breaking down infection centers, building up life centers, transforming, endowing with new energy—in a word, recreating. "In him was life; and the life was the light of men." "In him," that is in Christ, is life (vitality). "In him" is creative energy and this creative energy is the tremendous dynamic power of life itself.

We do not half realize the tremendous power with which we may make contact when in church. But when we drive deeply into Christianity, as in a service of worship such as described, and gradually yield to the atmosphere, we become relaxed in body, mind and spirit. The hymns, the choral music, the reading from the Bible, the quiet, unhurried mood all conspire to conditioning the mind for the period of silence. When by a conscious act of will one turns his mind to God, fixing his thought upon the divine source of power and energy; then in such manner as if he had turned a switch and electrical contact had been made, spiritual power begins to pass into him.

I call attention to a network of wires which draw electrical energy out of the universe. This power illuminates the church. It operates the pipe organ. It controls the heating unit. By means of thermostatic control of this power, the heat flow comes and goes as needed. Electrical energy operates the loud speaker system to carry the service to overflow auditoriums in the same building. The entire structure is a network of wires which constitute in themselves the medium over which power flows. Isn't it a reasonable assumption that such a building where many minds are unified in concentration on the same objective is also a great reception center for power far greater than electricity? Two thousand mental and spiritual antennae draw spiritual power to this congregation and this power enters the minds, bodies and souls of those who have become attuned to this mystic yet real force.

Another central factor of Christianity employed in spiritual therapy is the thought of light. It is interesting to observe the frequent references to light in the New Testament. It is usually related to new life. Men have discovered the extraordinary healing properties of light in healing.

Judged by its healing effect, Christianity possesses the same quality. The Bible tells us that in Jesus Christ is life and this life is the "light" of men which can heal and transform them so that they themselves are filled with new and recreated life.

In applying group therapy in services of public worship, many individuals are exposed to creative light energy in a spiritual sense. I want always to be on the side of common sense and factual realities. A crank is abhorrent to me. I believe always in being truly and completely scientific and rational in religious faith and practice. This does not mean, however, that one must be bound by materialistic science. Christianity, as will repeatedly be pointed out in this book, is itself a science. I positively believe, therefore, that if a man will go to church and attune himself to the mood and atmosphere and if for one minute of silence he will turn from the negative and destructive thoughts that agitate his mind and, if truly relaxed in body and in soul, he will affirm faith in God, he thereby opens himself to the recreative power that flows constantly through the universe.

After such a service, I received a letter from a very rational and intelligent woman:

> I want to tell you how much your services mean to me. It is an inspiration to attend a service in the Marble Church and I feel that it is to those services that I owe the fact that I am well now.
>
> For five years I have had attacks of insomnia and a nervous breakdown. Last fall I returned to my position after being ill all summer. In desperation I thought I would try to work again.
>
> After six weeks of every day being a misery, and after three times offering to resign, I went to a service in the Marble Church. You had the silent prayer before which you told the congregation how to pray and how to cast out all worry and how to let the mind receive the power of God to take over worries. The sermon was along the same line.
>
> I went out of church feeling much better. I prayed often for help and guidance and on Wednesday of the following week, I suddenly realized that I felt all right and I have been so ever since. I began to enjoy my work. After a few weeks I began to sleep without taking any medicine. At your church service I found the clue for curing myself by your showing me how to let God help me.

This woman came to church a defeated, baffled, disorganized person. Apparently she was of that mental and spiritual quality which enabled her to become sufficiently childlike and naive to follow with faith the suggested procedures. The tremendous power of faith came to the forefront of her mind and faith is the contact point with God's power. As she sat in church relaxed, yielding and believing, the healing light of God began to encompass her. It proceeded into her life by its deep therapy. It took away the sense of strain. Her nerves relaxed. It penetrated into her mind, deep into her tortured and tormented being. It reached the spot from which her trouble was coming. It spread throughout her mind a healing radiance and she was changed.

A friend gave me an excellent definition of a competent church service: "The creation of an atmosphere in which a spiritual miracle can take place." Tremendous things happen to personality under such circumstances when the mood is auspicious.

I heard a charming young woman say that she was sitting rather indolently in the congregation when the preacher shot out these words, "God has the power to take an ordinary person and make him extraordinary if that person will yield himself completely to the power of God."

This struck her with great force, so much so that it revolutionized her thinking. A change begin to take place in a personality hitherto ineffective and she became one of the most amazing persons I have ever known. She developed unusual charm, superior leadership abilities and such an infectious spiritual life that scores of people have been changed by contact with her. With all of this, she is a person of rare personal qualities, having all of the gifts and graces of a modern woman. In any group, she is "the life of the party."

A man wrote me following a service of worship. His trouble was mental confusion. He was in New York for a conference which involved the future of a business. A heavy investment was involved in the negotiations. All day Thursday, Friday and Saturday he and his associates struggled for an answer but without results. This man was wise enough to understand that a sustained tension of mind instead of producing clarification tends toward continued bafflement. You have to break the tension of thought sometimes and relax your mind to get an idea through. So that Sunday he came to church and heard the minister suggest that all problems be dropped from the mind for one minute and that everyone turn his thoughts to God. This businessman had never previously heard this procedure advocated but the logic of it appealed to him and he followed precisely the directions given. He was an expert in his business and he had come to church on the assumption that the church provides expert spiritual treatment, so he followed directions expecting results and he got results.

He states that all of a sudden like a spotlight moving across a dark theater to light upon some particular object on the stage, itself blacked out, the answer to his problem stood out in his mind distinct and completely formulated. Unquestionably the sustained thought which he had given to his problem throughout the previous days had been formulating an answer in his mind but the releasing of the answer was accomplished by relaxing his mind through spiritual therapy.

Take another man, one prominent in the financial life of New York. He asked me to visit his firm in the Wall Street district where I found a very prosperous and important business being carried on under his direction. After showing me his interesting offices and describing his outstanding work, he made this surprising statement, "Most of the people who work for me are making more money for themselves and this business has attained new heights all because of something that happened to me in your church."

He had come to church one Sunday morning and had fully entered into the spirit of the service. His mind, which is very active and alert, became attuned. Of a sudden into his mind flashed an idea. It was a complete outline of profit sharing that would allow certain people to go far beyond their existing salaries. He immediately put this plan into operation with the result that not only does each person participating in the plan make more money, but the firm has gone away ahead of any previous records. The best place on earth to get a new and workable idea for your business is in the type of church service described in this chapter.

Such amazing power can thus be generated that we hear often of people's lives being completely changed, sometimes instantly, in church services. Undoubtedly the reader has read stories of dramatic conversions which have been validated in the subsequent life of the individual for long years even to the day they die. The explanation of these phenomena is that these persons made contact with a power developed through mood and atmosphere and faith that at the proper conjuncture affected the individual so tremendously that previous habits were broken, the individual becoming as the New Testament graphically says, "A new creature: old things are passed away; behold, all things become new."

The congregation of my own church over a period of several years has been trained in this technique. However, this congregation is composed at every service of hundreds of visitors, many of whom find this procedure entirely new. They, too, report that when they yield themselves in full cooperation to the spiritual force to which appeal is being made, amazing results are obtained.

Not long ago I attempted to apply this therapy to a large congregation in a Southern city before which I had never spoken. The members of this congregation were totally unacquainted with this form of Christian procedure. I was preaching on the text, "Hear, and your soul shall live." I stated that "to hear" means more than merely to listen with the outer ear. The word has a deep content, implying the complete enthrallment of the mind to the presence of God. I pointed out that it means to hear not alone with the ear but also with the very essence of the mind. I explained that "to hear" means to believe that something is being said that has the power to drive to the center of your nature and release you from any crippling thing which may dwarf or frustrate your personality.

I asked the members of this large congregation to conceive of God's power as flowing through the church and playing down upon them. I urged each person during one minute of silence to turn from every problem in his mind and to listen intently not to me, the speaker, but to Jesus Christ and to practice "hearing" His words, "Come unto me, all ye that labor and are heavy laden, and I will give you rest."

I ceased speaking and stood still while a deathlike hush fell upon the vast assemblage. Afterwards a man came to me and stated that he had attended church for years but that even so his mind continued to be filled with fears and worries and that since boyhood he had suffered from a lack of confidence in himself. "All my life," he said, "I have been inwardly and emotionally bound up and though I have become fairly successful, it has been despite myself rather than because of it. I have suffered inner conflict all my life but," he asserted as he looked at me with an expression of incredulity on his face, "during that moment when you asked the people to really listen, I became completely lost and enthralled. When it was over I came to, but in the moment that I was lost, I found myself. I feel as if some power has rushed through me carrying out with it that which has troubled me for years. I believe that at last I am free."

What had happened to him was simply that he had made contact with a force so great that it permeated the controlling areas of the mind and made him over. This power, namely, God, created him in the first place and that power is always present to keep recreating us if the contact is not broken but is firmly maintained. When it *is* broken, fears and defeats surge in to dominate the personality; if the contact is reestablished, these destructive elements are flushed out and the person again begins to live. In this case the operation seemed to be instantaneous, as it often is. Sometimes it requires cultivation over a period, but always it marks the recreation of the individual.

We shall proceed to outline a simple but workable technique for successful living. As stated in the Introduction, nothing is offered here on a theoretical basis. Every principle in this book has been worked out in verifiable laboratory tests. These principles will work when they are worked. Confidence in these teachings is based on the fact that they had been developed out of the lives of real people, not once but many times. They have the effect of law because they have been proven by repeated demonstration. Let me drive home this fact: *If you will utilize the principles of faith stated in this book, you, too, can solve the difficult problems of your personality. You, too, can really learn to live.* It is not important what church you attend—Protestant, Catholic, or Jewish—nor does it make any difference how much you have failed in the past or how unhappy your present state of mind. Regardless of how apparently hopeless your condition may be, if you will believe in the principles outlined in this book and seriously start to work with them, you will get positive results.

I urge you to consider carefully the amazing things that often happen in church and suggest that you submit yourself not only to the private therapy of faith but to the astounding effect that group therapy may have upon you.

But to attend church successfully, skill is required. Worship is not a hit or miss affair. There is an art to it. Those who by study and practice become expert in church going master one of the greatest of all skills, that of spiritual power. That you may learn to go to church efficiently, I suggest the following ten rules to guide you in mastering the art of church going. Consistently put these rules into practice and one of these days the great thing may happen to you.

1. Think of church going as an art, with definite rules to follow, an art you can acquire.

2. Go regularly to church. A prescription designed by a physician to be taken at regular intervals is not effective if taken once a year.

3. Spend a quiet Saturday evening and get a good sleep. Get in condition for Sunday.

4. Go in a relaxed state of body and mind. Don't rush to church. Go in a leisurely manner. The absence of tension is a requisite of successful worship.

5. Go in a spirit of enjoyment. Church is not a place of gloom. Christianity is a radiant and happy thing. Religion should be enjoyed.

6. Sit relaxed in the pew, feet on floor, hands loosely in lap or at the side. Allow the body to yield to the contour of the pew. Don't sit rigid. God's power cannot get through to your personality through a tied-up body and mind.

7. Don't bring a "problem" to church. Think hard during the week, but let the problem "simmer" in the mind over Sunday. God's peace brings creative energy to help in the intellectual process. You will receive insight to solve your problem.

8. Do not bring ill will to church. A grudge blocks the flow of spiritual power. To cast out ill will, pray in church for those you do not like or who dislike you.

9. Practice the art of spiritual contemplation. In church do not think about yourself. Think about God. Think of some beautiful and peaceful thing, perhaps even of the stream where you fished last summer. The idea is to get mentally away from the world, into an atmosphere of peace and refreshment.

10. Go to church expecting some great thing to happen to you. Believe that a church service is the creation of an atmosphere in which a spiritual miracle can take place. Men's lives have been changed in church through faith in Christ. Believe it can happen to you.

I could summon scores of people to testify to the great things that happen in church to change people's lives. However, one stands out unforgettably in my mind. Early one Monday morning I received a telephone call from a gentleman who asked if I had received the card mailed to the church the night before. We have in our pews simply worded cards upon which an individual may register his desire to begin practicing the spiritual life.

This man stated that he had signed a card the night before and urged me to come to see him at once. He was so insistent and it apparently meant so much to him that I left my office and went to see him. I found that he was the controller of a large business organization. He was surrounded by all of the accoutrements of an important man and occupied a spacious office. He was a quiet, dignified man, one of the most impressive personalities I have ever known.

"Something has happened which has changed everything and I simply had to talk to you about it at once because it happened in your church last night."

He then launched into the story of his experience, talking in a quiet manner, though intense excitement was evident beneath the surface of his calmness. "I am not a church man," he asserted. "In fact, rarely have I gone to church over the past twenty years. I have been too busy, or at least I thought I was. For some few years now I have had the feeling that something is lacking, yet I seemed to have everything—money, position, friends, influence and power; but you know how it is, how sometimes your food just doesn't taste right. Well, life did not taste right to me. The flavor was not as fine as when I was younger. I have lived a fairly decent life and there is nothing dramatic in what happened to me in the way of turning from sin, for I really have no sins of a very serious nature. It was just that my life doesn't thrill me any more—that is, until last night." Then he began to recite the same old story of tension, fear, irritability, antagonism, as characteristic of his daily trouble. These things he apparently did not consider as sins but they were the root cause of the dissatisfaction with which he had been afflicted.

"At any rate," he continued, "I happened to be walking down Fifth Avenue last night and passed your church. The topic on the bulletin board attracted me and I decided to go in. I came in late and the only seat I could find was in the rear of the balcony. The first thing that surprised me was that the church was filled. I did not think that people went to church any more, especially on Sunday night but then, you see, it has been a long time and I know very little about churches.

"I found myself yielding to the mood and atmosphere of the place. It was homey and friendly. A feeling of satisfaction began to come over me and I really had a peaceful feeling too. In your sermon you were driving home the point that if anybody in that great congregation had anything bothering them, that they could have the matter settled if they would turn their minds to God. I imagine that is a crude way of expressing what you said, but that is the idea I got. You were very positive in your assertion and illustrated your sermon by the stories of people who had done that and to whom something great had happened. I was intensely interested in those stories and suddenly I became aware that what had happened to those people was what I wanted to have happen to me. You then stated that there was a card in the pew upon which one could register his desire to have this happen.

"I took that card in my hand but could not bring myself to sign it. But I put it in my pocket and went back to my hotel, went to bed and to sleep. In the middle of the night I was suddenly wide awake. It was shortly after three A.M. I struggled to go to sleep but a strange excitement seemed to possess me, and I arose and sat in my chair. The memory of the church service came back and suddenly I thought of the card. I laid it on my desk and re-read it. As I did so I knew that I must sign that card. I found myself praying. I signed the card.

"Then I felt that I must mail it at once to you, so I put on my bathrobe and walked down the hall to the mail chute and stood there holding the card. For a moment I hesitated. It was so strange that I, Bill———, should be doing such a thing. Had I suddenly become emotional! Had I grown old? Was I turning to religion in my old age, but fifty-six isn't old, is it?

"Then I opened my fingers and dropped the card. For just a second I could see it flash down the mail chute and then it was gone."

He turned a very intense gaze upon me. "The minute I dropped that card, something happened to me. I became inexpressibly happy." Saying this he dropped his head on the desk and to my surprise began to sob. I am always embarrassed to hear a man cry and I simply sat still and let him sob. Finally he raised his head and without even apologizing said, "It seems that my whole life all of a sudden is broken up and I am so happy that I wanted you to come over here at once so that I could tell you about it. From this time on I know the answer to all my problems. I have found peace and happiness."

This gentleman lived for three years after this time, but always I shall remember him as one of the greatest personalities I ever knew. He went to church and something great happened to him which changed everything for him.

And this same thing happens in churches everywhere every Sunday, or for that matter whenever a church service is held. Put yourself in the way of it—it can happen to you.

And now—an important reminder—fix this thought firmly in your mind until it dominates your consciousness: *You do not need to be defeated by anything.* Your life can be a great experience. The methods and techniques suggested in this book will work *if you work them.*

2

DON'T KEEP YOUR TROUBLES TO YOURSELF

AT A RAILROAD STATION newsstand my attention was drawn to an extensive display of magazines and books dealing with the common problems of living.

"I notice you have a great deal of this literature for sale," I commented to the salesgirl.

"Yeah," she slangily replied, "and I'm tellin' you that kind of stuff sure does sell."

"More than murder mysteries or movie magazines?" I inquired.

"Yeah, more than all of those, and they even outtop the love stories. Believe me," she declared, "this self-improvement or self-help literature is what we count on to pay the profits of this business."

"What is the reason?" I asked.

"The answer's easy," she replied. "The poor things (referring to her customers) are all tangled up. There are so many things they want to get away from, mostly themselves, I suppose." Then she paused. "I guess they're looking for someone to release them from all their troubles."

One learns not to be surprised at wisdom from unexpected sources. An observant salesgirl daily serving the public may develop shrewd insights into the ways of human nature and the needs of human beings.

As I walked away, her wise words rang in my ears: "The poor things are all tangled up. They are looking for someone to release them from all their troubles."

Of course, it is a very large order but somebody has to perform this function of release for modern people. To meet the situation, a whole new profession has developed, that of personal counseling. It is not in the strict sense new for there have always been men who have dealt with personal problems. However, it is only within recent years that it has become a specialized undertaking. Human beings of late seem to have developed higher tension, greater nervousness, deeper fears, profounder anxieties and more severe neuroses and complexes. It is one of the marked characteristics of our time. Some antidote being positively required, the personal counseling service has been developed. It is performed largely by psychiatrists, psychologists, clergymen, social workers, and of course physicians.

It must be borne in mind that the beneficiaries of this new profession are not people of distorted mental life or pathological persons. The profession's primary function is to keep normal people normal. Counseling is basically preventative rather than curative, but it is also curative. It deals with the common fears, anxieties, hates and guilt reactions of everyday people. Modern man is beginning to realize that primarily it is in his thoughts that his happiness and efficiency are determined; he is learning that the condition of his emotional health indicates whether or not he shall have peace, serenity and strength. And mental, emotional and spiritual health are essential to success in living.

Experts in personal efficiency know that to be successful in business, or in any kind of work, it is necessary to be a well integrated, well-organized personality. Men fail not alone because of laziness or lack of ability, but there are deeper causes of failure in the mental attitudes and emotional reactions. In most instances the average person does not understand these reactions and their fundamental influence upon all his actions. The trained counselor helps a person to know himself, to understand why he does what he does. He teaches a person to analyze his motives, his objectives and his reactions. If it is a good practice to go to your dentist, or to your physician periodically, it is equally wise to go to your spiritual advisor for regular checkups. When you begin to feel troubled and your personality seems to be disorganized, go to your counselor and frankly tell him what is troubling you. He may be able to release you from these unhappy factors which make you one of that vast number whom the salesgirl characterized as "poor things, they are all tangled up."

Through an example, I can make plain the scientific attitude that underlies religious counseling. A man, who was a victim of nerves, came for an interview. His mind was in such a panic that he could no longer do his work. He occupied an important position but had completely lost his grip. He was not suffering a nervous breakdown but was moving rapidly toward that condition. His doctor told him frankly that he had no medicine for him except sedatives. He recommended that he see a psychiatrist, but as the patient was leaving the office, the doctor reconsidered. "Maybe you had better see a minister," he advised. The thought had just flashed across the physician's mind that perhaps this man's trouble was in the sphere where the minister practices.

"In a certain sense," said the physician, "ministers are also doctors. That is to say, they are physicians of the soul and it is often the troubles of the soul that make us sick in mind and spirit and sometimes in the body as well."

The patient came to see me. He was not a member of my church, nor had I ever met him. Indeed I knew nothing about him whatsoever. After a brief discussion, it became obvious that he needed to make a confession which I encouraged him to do. After he had cleansed his thoughts completely, and he had plenty in his mind to make him sick, I asked, "Why didn't you see your own minister about this?"

"Oh," he said, with a shocked expression, "I know him too well."

"What do you mean, you know him too well?" I asked.

"Why," he said, "you see, he is a close friend of mine. Our families have dinner together every so often. His children know my children, and why," he added rather lamely, "he is my pastor. He would be shocked to hear these things."

"You always try to put your best foot forward with your pastor, is that it?"

"Why, certainly," he replied, "that is what everyone does with his minister. You just don't want your minister to know anything bad about you."

"You are not very friendly with your doctor, I take it."

"Why, of course, the doctor is as good a friend of mine as the minister."

"Has your doctor ever operated on you?" I asked.

"Oh, yes, twice."

"Then your doctor knows you inside and out. There is nothing about you that is hidden from him, is there? But you are not embarrassed before him, are you, when you go out to dinner. You do not think as you watch the doctor across the table that he is sitting there saying gleefully, 'Ah, I have seen that fellow's insides. I know just what they look like.' Of course, the doctor has no time to keep your insides on his mind. It is a professional matter with him. He sees you as a patient and in such interviews he is largely the scientist, though, of course, he has a personal interest in you. When he is with you socially, he thinks of you only as a friend, not as a patient. He has a right, in the periods of social and friendly intercourse, to be relieved of his professional duties which require him to think of people's ills and their insides.

"So," I continued, "surely you do not think that when the minister goes out to dinner with you, that he is sitting across the table saying, 'Ah, I remember what he told me about himself. I know something he did. I know all about his moral and spiritual insides.' What is true of the doctor is also true of the minister. He, too, wants to enjoy friendly relationships when he is socially engaged. He sees so much of the pain, trouble, and evil of life that when he finishes with his interviews he wants relief from all of it; therefore, he has trained himself to cast them out of his mind.

"Remember that the minister is also a professional man. When he is dealing with a human being in the relation of pastor and parishioner, he is applying all of his spiritual, psychological and scientific knowledge. He is entirely objective, viewing the person whom he is interviewing as a patient to whom he must apply a cure. When later he meets that same person socially, the chances are that what he was told in the interview never enters his mind. I know from experience that people have come to me six months or a year after I first interviewed them and I could not for the life of me remember a single detail of their story.

"That is only natural," I pointed out, "because I see a great many people and could not possibly burden my mind with all the details of everything that everybody tells me. I would have a nervous breakdown if I tried that. The minister who counsels with people, cannot in the very nature of the case keep such matters in his mind."

Personally I do not even keep a "case history." No written records are made. The interview is completely confidential. If a person returns for counseling and previously related facts are not recalled, it is necessary for the individual to retell the story to freshen my mind regarding the problem.

There is also in the relation of the minister with his parishioners the background idea of the father and his children. The Catholic church emphasizes that the priest is the spiritual father and the church the great mother of mankind. The priest as father represents the mother church which exercises care over her spiritual children. Protestants have never held this concept but that which is told to a minister is kept, of course, in complete and sacred confidence. There will never be even the slightest breaking of any confidence reposed in him as a pastor. The minister also acts for God in his sacred capacity as spiritual shepherd of the congregation.

It is important to think of the minister as a scientific person to whom one can talk as freely and as confidentially as with a doctor. His true position in the community can be called that of a scientist of the spiritual life, especially trained for his particular function. He has as much right to "hang out his shingle" as any other scientifically trained man, not for the practice of medicine, for never would he infringe upon the function of the medical healer, but for practice in his own sphere; he should be looked upon in the community as a skilled, well-trained scientific man—a shepherd of human souls, a physician of personality.

A prominent physician, Dr. James H. Means of the Massachusetts General Hospital, and Professor of Clinical Medicine at Harvard University, said, "The patient, when he is sick, should send for his minister as quickly as he sends for his doctor." Therefore, do not think of the minister merely socially. Do not overly emphasize the sacred or pious character of his calling. Do not be embarrassed to frankly tell him everything. He has heard of and probably has dealt with every problem and every sin that you may mention. There is nothing you have ever done or can do that has not at some previous time come before him as a human problem. He does not become shocked nor does he lose his regard and respect for you for he has a deep and philosophical understanding of human nature. Despite whatever evil you may confess to him, he is trained to see the good in you and help you bring it into dominance. He will give you understanding kindliness and will aid you with all the skill at his command.

Many people today are learning to think of a minister in this manner and the results of this newly established relation are encouraging, even amazing. The consultation service has become an integral part of the Protestant ministry. Psychological and psychiatric knowledge is being widely employed. Ministers, of course, do not infringe upon the prerogative of the duly accredited psychologist or psychiatrist, and are exceedingly careful never to go beyond their own knowledge. Ministers are, however, setting apart office hours when members of their church or anyone in the community, for that matter, may come to consult them. Ministers moreover are discussing simple, basic human problems in their sermons with the result that people are becoming increasingly aware that these pastors are truly what their titles indicate: men who understand human beings and who know how to relieve them of their troubles, thus making it possible for them to live effective lives.

Many young ministers nowadays are taking courses with psychiatrists, psychologists and physicians, not that they expect to have medical degrees, for few ministers would desire that, but in order to better understand why people do what they do. Obviously the solution of many problems goes deeper than medication or surgery. Perhaps these pastors are better qualified than those of previous generations to exercise the gifts bestowed by the Great Physician for their scientific knowledge of faith as a therapeutic is probably more extensive.

In some instances ministers have organized a staff in their churches upon which outstanding medical men, psychiatrists, psychologists, and social workers are glad to serve on a clinical basis, or in an advisory capacity.*

In view of this service readily available to modern men and women, it is possible for any person to secure relief and release from the troubles weighing on his mind. So don't keep your troubles to yourself. See a counselor qualified to help you. Go to your minister as you would to a doctor.

I realize that this advice runs counter to a rather common but false heroism. People say, "I always keep my troubles to myself." This is usually said with the assumption that such an attitude will be commended. Being close-mouthed about trouble is frequently considered very long-suffering and strong. Under certain circumstances it is commendable and under still other circumstances it is heroic, even inspiring. All of us have known people who have been compelled to suffer pain for years, and who

---

* In the Marble Collegiate Church on Fifth Avenue, New York City, of which the author is the minister, the eminent psychiatrist, Dr. Smiley Blanton, conducts a clinic in which he is assisted by three other psychiatrists, a psychologist, and a social psychiatrist. It is one of the pioneer religio-psychiatric clinics in American churches.

have done so with a glorious spirit, never even allowing pain to show upon their faces. They have not distressed their loved ones and their friends by constant reference to their suffering.

On the other hand, some people seem to develop into whiners and complainers. They are victims of self-pity, thinking constantly about themselves. They do not keep their troubles to themselves and they should learn to do so. They want everybody else to keep their troubles for them, and people do not like to be the repositories of other people's troubles. Ella Wheeler Wilcox well says:

> Laugh, and the world laughs with you;
> Weep, and you weep alone.

But the policy of keeping your troubles to yourself can be dangerous. There is a sense in which the human personality must have release from itself. A person cannot forever bottle up within himself the guilt, the problems and the adversity which have affected him. To use a crude phrase, it is advisable to get some things "off your chest." Perhaps the word "chest" in this common saying is wisely used because it would seem to have reference to the heart. The heart has been traditionally considered the center of emotional life.

In more classic phraseology, Shakespeare gives the same advice, "Canst thou minister to a mind diseased, pluck from the memory a rooted sorrow, raze out the written troubles of the brain, and by some sweet oblivious antidote cleanse the bosom of the perilous stuff that lies upon the heart?"

Inner release is a necessity faced by every human being. The heart must be relieved. It is a dangerous policy to carry things too long, else they turn inward upon you. So don't keep your troubles to yourself. Get them straightened out by someone who knows the art and is skilled in counseling. People who do follow this suggested procedure, who turn to their minister, their rabbi, or priest, or psychiatrist or psychologist, or other well qualified counselor, or even to some wise and understanding friend, receive profound benefit. Often they receive complete relief from their troubles.

The counselor draws up and out of the mind the ideas and thoughts which have been causing trouble and admits new and healing thoughts. It is impossible to drive out a thought, just by being willing to do so. If by force of will it is ejected momentarily, it comes rushing back into the mind when the pressure is removed or when the guard is down. The only successful and permanent method is to supplant destructive thoughts with good ones, diseased thoughts with healthy ones. To accomplish this the counselor employs specific techniques.

In our interview room a man piteously described his condition. He happened to be a banker in a small city, an influential man in his community. He was a man of unquestioned character and was held in high respect.

"I simply do not understand it," he said. "I live a decent life and try to help people in many ways, but I am unhappy. In fact," he concluded, "I am miserable."

Investigation revealed an inner state of conflict. He was filled with fears and anxieties and there was not a little hate and resentment in his mind. It seemed when we started him to talking that there were more people than even he imagined in his town who irritated him and whom he detested. He had a strong desire to get even but his stern religious training had helped to sublimate much of this antagonism. However, he had not cast it out. He had merely forced it inward where it was creating pressure as steam will when bottled up.

He poured all of this out hesitantly at first, but in a torrential flood as he finally let go of himself and the restraints of embarrassment and self-consciousness were eased.

I listened patiently. The important thing was not what I should advise, but that he should tell everything. In other words, he must get it all out. A complete mental catharsis was required.

How should I advise him? To pray! Yes, but he had been doing that all of his life. To read the Bible! Of course, but daily he had made it a practice to read the Bible. Perfunctory religious words would not suffice. Plainly it was necessary to attack his situation in a simple and yet fresh and original manner. It is my belief that the Christian religion has not been made simple enough, even for educated men of his type. We should learn that the really effective way to make religion a useful tool is to cast it in simple thought forms and work out its techniques in very lucid and simple procedures. It should be made graphic, even picturesque, and a new slant given to lift it out of the dull and lifeless formality which often renders it impotent.

So I said to this man, "Would it not be a fine thing if we could reach down into your mind and take out all of those thoughts which have put your brain into such a turmoil and tumult?"

"You have no idea how wonderful that would be," he declared.

Pursuing the idea, I said, "Wouldn't it be great if a surgeon could take a knife and cut a hole in the top of your head, then take an instrument and go down in and scrape all those ideas out? He might then take one of those instruments such as a dentist uses to blow air into a cavity and blow it all around inside your head to be sure that no vestige of those diseased ideas lurked there. Then when it was all cleaned out, the physician would close up the top of your head."

Then I reminded him of that wise insight in the Bible which says that even if we got the devils out and cleaned the house, they would come trooping back. Therefore it was obvious that he would have to do more than merely to empty his mind and sweep it clean; otherwise the expelled thoughts would, by reason of their long habitat, return and take up their abode in the house which they had been forced temporarily to vacate.

Continuing this rather curious spiritual treatment, I said, "When your head would be all cleaned out, before the physician should close it up, perhaps I as a minister would also be present and I would open the Bible and pick out of it some of those great verses about faith, forgiveness, kindliness, and drop them down into your mind—just cram your brain full of them. Then let the physician close up the hole in the top of your head and clamp it down. Those new ideas in the form of Bible texts would soak into your mind and permeate it, creating a healing influence so that finally you would be changed completely."

He sadly shook his head, laughing as he did so at the oddity of this therapy, and said, "Isn't it too bad that can't be done? It is just a pity."

We sat quietly considering the matter, then I asked, "Why can't it be done?"

"But how?" he demanded. "You can't cut a hole in the top of my head."

"We do not need to do that. There are already two entrances into your brain—your eye and your ear." Therefore my professional advice to you is to go home, take a New Testament, and underline in red every verse that you think you need and commit them one by one to memory. For a time even give up reading books and magazines and only glance at the paper. Concentrate on filling your mind with verses from the Bible. Fully occupy your mind with these healing thoughts so as to prevent the destructive thoughts you have so long harbored from continuing to live in your mind. Concentrate on expelling destructive thoughts by the powerful and creative thoughts taken from the Bible. These words from the Scripture are very powerful and will curette the diseased thoughts out of your mind in due course.

"Then," I said, "go to church and really listen to what is said. Listen beneath your conscious self, eagerly reaching out for vital words and sentences and thoughts. Sincerely meditate upon them and conceive of them as dropping deeply into your brain.

"Thus you will have admitted healing thoughts by the two entrances to your brain which are available to you, namely, your eye and your ear. So the actual hole in your head is not necessary. When you feel a hate thought or a defeat thought coming into your mind, immediately turn to these words and ideas which you have assembled. Say them over quickly. Repeat them again and again. Persevere in this practice and you will soon change the character of your thoughts entirely. Flush out your brain and refill it with healing power."

The banker did as directed. Being a man of considerable mental strength, he was able to apply a simple procedure. Only minds great enough to be simple can benefit by a procedure like this one. Please remember that the greatest of all thinkers, Jesus Christ, said that unless you "become as little children"—you cannot get results.

The banker tells me that as a result of this simple procedure, the whole character of his life is changing, but he warns, "When I let up, those old ideas try to sneak back, but I do not let up and with every passing day I get more and more control. I have found," he concluded, "that by changing my thinking, by putting into my mind the great ideas of my religion, that I can literally force out destructive thoughts. It was a battle at first," he admits, "but the power of faith can overcome any opposition and gradually I am winning the peace of mind which I have sought."

I have found that such simple techniques and procedures often secure extraordinary results. A general contemplation of religion and a formal observance of its forms, while doubtless stimulating and inspiring, is not always sufficient to cure the deep maladies of the soul. The application of specific remedies in some such simple form as suggested in the foregoing incident is often required to bring full relief.

To the reader who may be surprised by the "curious and unusual" procedure recommended to the banker, the best answer is that it worked. It has been my experience, even with the most intellectual and sophisticated persons, that when Christianity is reduced to precise formulas and is applied in simple techniques or devices, it "works" in an amazingly successful manner.

If, as I believe, the minister is a spiritual doctor, he must be in a position to suggest practical spiritual prescriptions.

In counseling, two basic human problems seem constantly to recur. One is fear and the other is guilt. Fear is treated elsewhere in this book, so I shall not discuss it here.

Sin, or a sense of guilt, has a peculiarly damaging effect on the personality. It may be best described as a wound. Guilt cuts deeply into the emotional and spiritual nature. At first this personality cut may not cause suffering and one may feel that "he has got away with it." However, if, like the history of some physical diseases, the development is slow, nevertheless the time comes when this guilt malady begins to cause trouble; all of a sudden it may "break out."

Tension increases, nervousness becomes a problem, curious obsessions develop. One man with whom I worked always had to go back to try the door. Another man washed his hands constantly after touching things. Perhaps like Lady Macbeth, he was trying to wash out a spot which did not exist on his hand but which certainly did exist on his mind. Frequently the obsessions are much deeper and result in acute suffering. The mind becomes unsettled, the emotions are thrown out of gear, and one is desperately unhappy and ineffective.

One cause of this phenomena is that guilt is an unclean wound. Sorrow, for example, is a clean wound. It pains deeply but being clean the wound heals according to the process of nature. A clean wound in the flesh heals without difficulty. A tree hit by lightning generally heals over its wound, but the effect of guilt or sin is quite another matter. Being unclean the restorative and curative process cannot be completed. Guilt festers and becomes an infection center; as in the body, so in the mind and the spirit. The personality always and automatically makes the effort to protect itself. Nature strives to isolate an infection center, but in the case of guilt it cannot be done. In youth and even in the strong middle years, its injurious effects may be in part at least halted but with the declining vitality of advancing years and the heavier burden of responsibilities which comes with maturity, resistance declines and the long-held infection of guilt rushes out to dominate the entire system.

Sometimes you hear of men breaking down, having heart trouble, too-high blood pressure, abnormal tension. A vague, unaccountable dissatisfaction tends to spoil their happiness. Not always, of course, is a sense of guilt the root of such difficulties, but in personal counseling we find that it is the cause or at least a contributing factor in a large number of cases.

This particular generation does not seem to like to admit the fact of sin. Some people have gone so far as to say that sin does not exist, but saying so does not make it so. In my opinion one of the profound causes for the nervous tension of this era is that it does not recognize and properly deal with the suppuration of guilt long lodged in human minds. It may also be that the enormous social sins of our time are sapping the mental and emotional health of modern men.

Yes, it is indeed strange and sinister this sense of guilt. You think it won't make any difference and so you take it into your system and presently it begins to throw off what amounts to a "poison," judging by the reaction of the personality. This "poison" gets into your thinking and soon you say to yourself, "I don't seem to be happy. I don't enjoy things any more. I am nervous. Everything has a bad taste. What is the matter with everybody? What is the matter with me?"

Of course, this isn't an actual physical poison but poison is the best word I can think of to describe the unhealthy and deteriorating secretions that flow from a sense of guilt. It has been well established that nervousness or anger or hate can stimulate secretions in the body and disturb the proper functioning of the physical system. Guilt can affect human beings in a similar fashion. Prominent physicians have proven the theory that hate and resentment cause definite physical trouble and there are many laboratory records available in support of these facts. You simply cannot allow the poison of guilt to remain in your mind and at the same time be happy and efficient.

This was illustrated by the case of an officer in the air force who came for an interview. After many missions he was shot down in a raid over some oil fields in Europe. He suffered battle fatigue and shock. He was sent back to a hospital where he was given the splendid treatment which our air force hospitals provided. Still he did not fully recover. Happiness, a grip on life, normal and emotional health eluded him.

Finally the doctor in charge turned him over to the chaplain and through the chaplain he came to our consultation clinic.

In the interviews which followed it came out finally that prior to entering military service, the boy had committed a sex sin. He had attempted to rationalize it on the basis that he was going away and might never see the young lady again. They had planned to be married but circumstances did not permit it at the time and it was hoped that the marriage might take place after the war. However, passing time made both parties feel that it was not wise to consummate the marriage and besides other persons had entered in to complicate the relationship. The boy explained it to himself by a process of rationalization, which is obvious and all too common, but it is a fact that you cannot fool your subconscious mind though you may delude your conscious mind. The mind always tries to save one's face; therefore, the conscious mind is not to be trusted under such circumstances. In the subconscious mind, however, the sin is held and seen for what it is. The mind had attempted to bury it, to isolate it, but it began to fester and finally it was brought out as the cause of the continuing emotional sickness of this young officer.

"Son, your trouble is not in your body," so we told him. "Really it isn't even in your mind. It is in your soul. It is in your moral and spiritual nature." The psychiatrist corroborated the diagnosis.

The boy, being a very alert and intellectually objective young man, recognized the validity of the analysis. He was willing to submit to spiritual treatment, the essence of which was simply that he get the sin forgiven. As soon as he did this (and his attitude was profoundly sincere), the most remarkable change came over him. He quickly became released, happy, even gay, and exuberant. He had such a burst of energy and enthusiasms, that those who knew him were amazed, and no wonder, for a heavy load resting upon his soul had been lifted. Rapidly he returned to health and at the present time is very successful in the job he took after being discharged from the service.

It was difficult at first to persuade the boy to tell the counselor the whole story. This reluctance was not particularly due to a sense of shame, but because he had been led to believe that what we call "sin" no longer has the effect that older generations believed it possessed. His social set had been emphasizing for a large part of his developing years that the thing he did was not really wrong. In fact, he attempted to argue with us that it was not wrong, but nineteen hundred years of Christian civilization had made his subconscious mind know that it is wrong. Therefore his subconscious mind reacted in a manner that was not affected in the slightest by what his particular generation thought about it. Had he followed the beliefs which had been accepted by his conscious mind, he would today be one of those who are wrecked by life. The subconscious is not always your enemy. Indeed it may be your hope as is proved in this case.

In dealing with guilt, the counselor often encounters the strange difficulty that while an individual may feel that he has received the forgiveness of God, he is unable to forgive himself. This is largely due to the fact that the mind has become conditioned to the presence of the guilt complex. There is a curious reluctance in the human mind to let go of guilt no matter how unpleasant. Strange indeed is the mind. It wants freedom and yet hesitates to take freedom when freely offered. It wants to be delivered and yet frequently will not take deliverance when it comes.

I have often noticed that a person who completely confesses guilt and derives the tremendous relief which that confession provides, will presently return and desire to confess the matter all over again and repeatedly.

A man came to see me who confessed a sin and experienced deep relief, but he kept coming back at intervals to confess again the same sin in identical detail. Finally I said to him, "You are having an awfully good time, aren't you?"

"I always feel better after I have confessed this," he replied.

"You may feel better temporarily, but soon your mind begins to take back the guilt. Your mind does not believe that it can be free. It reasons that such deliverance would be too good to be true. Your mind governed by habit is slow to accept the idea that you can be delivered from the domination of the guilt complex. So presently you feel about as badly as you did before you first came to me. But having experienced the release of confession you return to secure once more a temporary peace of mind."

I pointed out to him that he must learn to forgive himself if he expected to break this recurring circle of defeat. In his mind he must forgive himself and take freedom. Instead of the circle which led him from spiritual imprisonment to release and back again, he must walk straight ahead and away, not back around the circle.

I then told him that he must never confess it again to me or to any other person, but on the contrary he must repeatedly say to himself, "Thank God, I am through with that and I intend to remain through with it."

"So," I said to him, "go ahead and confess it to me once more, but this must be the last time it shall ever be spoken."

When he had finished, I said, "Now, that is the last. I will never listen to it again and I strongly urge you never to tell it to another person." I felt sure he would not confess to another because he had a hard enough time telling me the first time. I had become a kind of spiritual father to him, a releasing agent, but if he was to be cured, he had to make a transference beyond me to God and to his own mind. He had to accept forgiveness from both God and himself. Repeated confession indicated he had not really surrendered his guilt.

It was several months before I found his name again on my appointment book. When I entered the interview room, he stood up and with a vigor I had never previously noticed about him, he literally crushed my hand with his handclasp.

"Well, my friend, what is on your mind this time?" I asked.

Quickly he replied, "Don't you worry. I am not going to confess that matter again. I just came in to tell you that at last I am through with it. I only want to tell you that the very minute I decided the whole matter was finally cleared up, that God truly had forgiven me, then I did as you suggested, I forgave myself and at last I walked away from it. It seemed to drop away and I actually have left it behind."

Then he added, "I have committed to memory that passage of Scripture that you gave me and what a wonderful thing it is. It really works: at any rate, it has for me."

The passage from the Bible which I gave him is this, "Forgetting those things which are behind and reaching forth unto those things which are before, I press toward . . ." (Philippians 3:13–14.) So, don't keep your troubles to yourself. But once having told them to a competent counselor and been forgiven by God, and having found release, then forgive yourself and turn your back definitely on them. Fill your mind with hopeful, helpful and positive thoughts. Have faith and go forward. Don't look back. March straight ahead for always life lies straight ahead—never backward. Press forward.

Once in my counseling work I had a unique experience in this connection. A little, white-haired old lady came to see me. She was obviously under great distress. She had a very sweet face, one not unlike Whistler's immortal portrait of a mother. As the series of interviews progressed, I found myself more and more drawn to the conclusion that it was a guilt case. It seemed unlikely in view of the gentleness and beauty of her personality, yet I realized that a competent physician of the soul must explore every possibility. Therefore with exceeding diffidence I raised the question whether in her experience she had acquired a sense of guilt, whether she had committed a sin, or, what is more subtle, whether she thought she had done so.

It turned out that the last was the answer to the problem. She related that as a young girl of about eighteen years of age she had been very much in love. She had been raised in a strict Christian home and her ideals of personal conduct and personal purity were very high. The young man with whom she was in love was a bit more flexible in his morality and it seems that they verged on the commission of a sex sin. His insistence to yield to his false moral reasoning was considerable. She assured me however that she did not yield to him but, she said, "Here is the terrible thing about it—I desired to do so. It was only after the most awful battle with myself that I was able to resist it."

Now, she said, "I read in the Bible 'That whosoever looketh on a woman to lust after her hath committed adultery with her already in his heart.' So I saw at once my guilt. I had not performed this act, but it had been my desire, therefore I was just as guilty as if I had done so. All my life long," she concluded, "I have lived a clean, righteous life, but in this I sinned and it has haunted me and I know that when I die, I will be damned," so concluded her pathetic story.

I pointed out to her that we cannot govern the thoughts that come into our minds. In the words of an old saying, "You cannot keep the birds from flying over your head, but you can keep them from building nests in your hair." I explained that actually what she had done was to achieve a great moral and spiritual victory. I told her that she had met the enemy on the battlefield of her life and after a terrible battle had destroyed him and that rather than condemn herself she should thank God that she had the inner strength to win this struggle. But it was to no avail. The idea of guilt so long held could not be that easily dissipated.

Finally I did something which is perhaps not regular in Protestant practice, but it was effective. I asked her to remove her hat and I had her kneel at the altar of the church. Standing behind the altar, I said to her, "You recognize me, do you not, as a minister of the Church?"

She said, "Yes."

"As a minister of the Church, do I stand as a human representative to you of God?"

"Yes," she said, "you do."

"Do you believe that God will forgive you of any wrong and take the burden of any guilt off your mind, and do you now confess your wrongdoing and trust in Jesus Christ as your Saviour?"

"Yes," she said, "I sincerely believe, and I do put my faith in Christ."

I then laid my hand upon her head. I was touched by this and I can yet remember my hand resting upon her snowy white hair. She was at least seventy-five years old, perhaps as good a woman as ever walked the earth, a saint though she did not know it. I then said to her, "In the name of Jesus Christ, who alone can forgive sins, I declare that by His power you are forgiven for any wrong. Go and sin no more," and I added, "Forgetting those things which are behind, and reaching forth unto those things which are before, I press toward . . ."

After a moment or two of quiet prayer, she stood up and looked at me. I have often seen glory on human faces but never more resplendent than that on her face. "I feel so happy. I think it is gone," she said simply.

She lived for four years after that and several times she said to me,

"Why didn't I go to somebody long years ago and have that thing taken away?"

She learned the value of not keeping her troubles to herself. She found that anyone can be released from his troubles.

3

HOW TO GET RID OF YOUR INFERIORITY COMPLEX

"THERE IS ENOUGH atomic energy in the body of one man to destroy the city of New York," says a prominent physicist. We read these words with surface understanding but let us try to press them deep into our minds and realize them. There is enough power in *you* to blow the city of New York to rubble. That, and nothing less, is what advanced physics tells us.

That being so, and it is undeniable, why have an inferiority complex? If there is literally enough force in you to blow up the greatest city in the world, there is also literally enough power in you to overcome every obstacle in your life.

Pythagoras was absolutely right. "Know yourself," he urged. That includes knowing your powers. When you do know yourself and realize tremendous power within yourself, you will then know that you do not need to be a defeated person—defeated because you are beset by a false feeling of inferiority.

Quite possibly you often do feel defeated. Depression settles over you, bringing the disheartening feeling that there isn't much use in fighting on. Probably everybody is tempted to sink into this dull and gloomy attitude occasionally, but not everybody yields to it. Those who accept the idea that they are defeated usually *are* beaten; for, as a famous psychologist says, "There is a deep tendency in human nature to become like that which you imagine yourself to be." Believe you are defeated, believe it long enough, and it is likely to become a fact—even though "there is enough atomic energy in the body of one man to destroy the city of New York."

But notice: people who achieve happiness and success are those who when they tend to sink into a depressed mood shake it off by refusing to accept the idea of defeat. They refuse to entertain the thought that situations and circumstances, or their enemies, have them down. They know it is the *thought* of defeat that causes defeat, so they practice thinking positive thoughts. Indomitable thoughts, thoughts of faith surge through their minds. They train their minds to think victory. As a result they gain victory.

Basically the inferiority complex—habitually feeling inferior to others—arises from wrong thinking acquired either in childhood or as a result of later experiences. An inferiority complex may be defined as a system of emotionally toned ideas ranged around one central idea—disbelief in one's self.

Symptoms of an inferiority complex may be recognized by the way you tend to compensate; that is, by the method your subconscious mind uses to make up for inferiority feelings. If we look briefly at certain types of compensation, we shall gain a comprehensive idea of how disbelief in one's self influences human behavior.

There is the type of personality which over-asserts itself. The victim, instead of walking, struts. He is pompous. When he talks it is likely to be in a loud voice. When he discusses any subject, he gives the impression of knowing all there is to know. You say, "How conceited he is!" Not necessarily. It might be more accurate to say, "How sick he is." Beneath his pompous assertiveness he has a profound feeling of inadequacy. His overbearing attitude is the way his mind unconsciously seeks to make up for the inferiority feeling. He is not deliberately or consciously doing this. It is the unconscious effort of his mind to save face. It is his subconscious mind over-asserting itself.

In contrast, but from the same cause, there is the underassertive type. For example, you sometimes meet a man on the links who plays golf very well, but always acts supermodest. He says, "I would like to play, but I'm out of practice and am poor at best. I'm not at all a good golfer." To get him to play you have to coax him. The queer twist here is that the man is egotistic over his humility. A normal person will say, "Sure, I'll be glad to play," and will play the best game he can with relaxed naturalness.

Still another form of compensation is that in which a person manifests an inferiority complex by an infantile reaction.

Years ago I worked in a newspaper office in a certain city where I encountered a woman who illustrated this type. She came bristling into the newspaper and actually complained because she did not get her picture in the paper in connection with a society function. After she left the office the city editor said, "I don't understand that woman." That isn't all he said, but that is the part that is printable. At the time I did not understand her, either, but I think I do now. As a baby every time she dropped her rattle, somebody rescued it at once. When she cried for anything she got it. When she became an adult she expected the world to continue to baby her. She is still essentially a baby, with a strong sense of inadequacy. She retreats into an infantile manifestation of inferiority.

The inferiority complex sometimes takes a curious turn. A deep inner feeling of inadequacy may manifest itself in an unreasonable desire to dominate. A person who in infancy was over-dominated may in adult life over-compensate by himself seeking to dominate others. This person may not, indeed usually does not, recognize this cause of his own attitudes, nor do others with whom he is associated. In any abnormal emotional situation, among other possible causes that of hidden inferiority may wisely be explored.

A woman came to interview me because, as she put it, she "could hardly live any more."

"I am surrounded," she complained, "by people who are constantly in turmoil. I must have peace or I'll go mad."

Her home, she said, was "bedlam"—in upheaval all the time. Everybody in her home was nervous—it was a high-strung, tense household. "Why," she fumed, "it's just awful." She said she was so high-strung she couldn't sleep. In short, she declared, an intolerable situation.

I asked her to bring her husband to see me, thinking perhaps he might be the cause of this turmoil, but he proved to be a meek, mild-mannered little man. He sat quietly while she did all the talking. Obviously he was a defeated personality. He would even look apprehensively at her before speaking, then speak timorously.

I decided to persuade the members of the family to go away from home one after the other, calculating that if the turmoil ceased in the absence of any one of them, the one who went away was, by a process of elimination, the cause of the upheaval. That seemed a simple way to work things out. The children went away first, one after the other; then the husband went off, but nothing happened to change the situation, which remained as tumultuous as ever.

Finally I asked the wife to go away for a while.

"Well," she replied, "I don't think that will solve it. If I go away, who will take care of the place?"

"Never mind that," I said. "You just go away. How long have you been married?" She told me, and I said, "Any wife who has been married that long deserves a vacation. Go away somewhere for two weeks."

She went away for a fortnight. When she left home everything calmed down. It became quiet and peaceful. Although some of the household tasks were not done efficiently, it was a place of peace and quiet.

"How are things?" I asked the husband.

He whispered, "Wonderful—great." Looking furtively about, he confided, "Everything is marvelous."

After two weeks the wife returned and came in with her husband to talk with me. I said, "We have made an experiment. We sent the three children away one by one and nothing happened. We sent the husband away; nothing happened. We sent the wife away and everything became peaceful."

"Yes," she admitted, "that's what they say." After pondering for a moment, she asked reflectively, "You don't suppose I could be the cause of it, do you?"

At this her husband came to life with magnificent assertiveness, and said, "Yes, Mary, you are the cause."

She turned to him and snapped, "You keep out of this—I'll decide for myself."

"What is my trouble?" she asked.

I liked her; she was honest. She knew the fault lay within herself, and she wanted the answer. When the mechanism of inferiority was described in the light of her reactions, she recognized the accuracy of the diagnosis. She was unconsciously over-compensating for domination she had suffered in childhood. Her mind took this method of trying to escape from a deep inferiority feeling.

She asked for guidance in correcting her personality faults. A definite and detailed plan of spiritual technique was outlined for her. She was a forthright character, and she put it into practice, with the result that the situation was completely rectified.

One day she wisely observed, "Perhaps the best way to change a situation is to change yourself."

Know yourself—change yourself—that is very important. But there is an even deeper factor in eradicating inferiority, and it is to be found among the vast psychological riches of the Bible. Among the possible methods, one of the best and surest is the formula contained in the words, "If God be for us, who can be against us?" (Romans 8:31.)

That formula has incalculable potency. If you believe what those words imply, you will develop faith in your own powers. Furthermore, you will discover that faith releases forces which come powerfully to your aid.

Let me give you a graphic illustration of the manner in which this formula works.

In Cedar Rapids, Iowa, I met Arthur Poe, one of the famous six Poe brothers who played football at Princeton around the turn of the century. The Poes are probably the most famous football family in American athletic history, for all six of the brothers were stars of the first magnitude.

That night in my speech in Cedar Rapids, I emphasized at some length the power of positive thinking, and asserted that practice of the techniques of faith makes it possible for a person to overcome difficulties. Positive thinking was outlined as a cure for the inferiority complex.

After the meeting a man introduced himself as Arthur Poe. He said, "You are right about the power of positive thought, and my own experience has proven to me conclusively what real faith can do. Without it I would have had a terrible inferiority complex."

When he went up to Princeton as Poe Number Five, having been preceded by four great football brothers, he, too, wanted to carry on the family tradition. He went out for football and made the freshman team. But late in the season he suffered a very severe injury to his leg. The doctors told him that he would never again be able to play football. Naturally, he was heartbroken. Throughout the winter and summer he nursed his leg, but the verdict held that he was through with football.

Finally, at his mother's suggestion, Poe adopted the mental attitude of putting the matter of his injured leg in the hands of God. He developed the capacity and skill of having faith. He practiced mentally accepting the formula, "If God be for us, who can be against us?"

"As a result," he said, "I played football at Princeton."

I looked up the athletic record of Arthur Poe at Princeton, and found that when he said, "I played football at Princeton," he was engaging in magnificent understatement. He did play, and with such brilliance that the memory of his athletic exploits still has the power to thrill old Princetonians, and others of a later generation who hear the story.

It was November 12, 1898. The big Princeton-Yale game was in progress. No score had been made. Princeton was being forced back toward its own goal line. Yale, marching down the field, apparently could not be stopped. But Durston of Yale fumbled; and a boy whom they said could never again play football scooped up the ball. Shaking off Yale tacklers, he started to run. He forgot about his leg. He ran like a sprinter. Down the field he went, as fleet as a deer—thrilling, inspiring. Ninty-five yards, the length of the field, he ran, crossing the goal line ten feet ahead of the nearest Yale man. Arthur Poe, running on a leg that was supposed to be incapacitated, beat Yale singlehanded. The final score was 6–0.

On November 25, 1899, Yale and Princeton were again battling for supremacy. It was the last thirty seconds of play. Suddenly the ball shot in the hands of Arthur Poe. He fell back as if to kick, but nobody expected him to kick, for with that bad leg he had never before attempted it. Everybody expected him to run, but he did not have time to run. It was kick or nothing. Arthur Poe drew back, dropped the ball; his toe caught it, and in a beautiful arc it sailed across the goal post, touching the ground just as the whistle blew, and Princeton won by a single point.

Arthur Poe did not tell me this story. When I read the account I have just summarized, I remembered the conviction in his voice as he said that all his life long he had practiced the principle that a man can overcome any obstacle by a simple faith in God.

How easy it would have been for young Poe to have developed an inferiority complex! He could easily have been thwarted in his ambition to play football, and, what is worse, he could have gone through life defeated by an inner sense of inadequacy. He refused to accept an inferiority complex. Arthur Poe got rid of it before it took root by the simple expedient of intelligently employing his religious faith.

The victim of the inferiority complex always tends to think he is defeated. Thinking so helps to produce that outcome. But the mental attitude of putting up a fight gets results, especially when you have developed and regularly practiced the thought pattern that you have an invincible ally. Say it this way, "If God be for me, who can be against me?"

Do you recall the immortal and ancient parable of the two frogs who fell into a jar of cream? The top of the cream was quite a distance from the opening of the jar. The frogs tried to leap out, but could not make it. They struggled, they stewed, they fretted, they did everything possible to get out, all without success.

Finally one frog assumed a negative attitude. He began to think defeat thoughts, and the acids of futility started to spread through his mind. He became a pessimist. He said to himself, "I know I can't get out of this jar of cream, so why should I wear myself out trying? I have to die, anyway, so why not get it over; why not die in peace?" In despair and resignation he sank into the cream and died. His epitaph was, "He died of an inferiority complex."

The other frog was made of sterner stuff. He had a different training and background, and evidently came of a long line of dauntless frogs. He was a positive thinker. He said to himself, "Sure, I may die, but if I do I shall go down with every flag flying. But I shall fight my way out of this if it is humanly [I suppose that should be "froggily"] possible; and if in the end I can't make it, I shall die proudly in the glorious tradition of the ancient and honorable frogs."

With this he went at it with all his vigor. He swam around, he thrashed about, he beat the cream and made a great stir. As a result, gradually he began to feel solid footing under him and his activity churned the cream into butter. Finally his legs, whipping like little pistons, got traction, and he leaped victoriously from the jar, the contents of which had now turned into solid butter.

Religious faith puts fight into a man so that he develops a terrific resistance to defeat. Obstacles no longer awe him. He uses obstacles as stepping stones to cross over from failure to success.

Fortitude and faith are the words. That is what keeps a man going when he seems defeated. Believe that if you put your trust in God and keep at things with unremitting energy and intelligence you, too, can build a solid foundation beneath you upon which you may mount up to victory. Therefore, train your mind never to accept the thought of defeat about anything. That verse from the Bible makes an unbeatable inspiration in any situation: "If God be for us, who can be against us?" Hold it habitually in mind and it will train you to believe in yourself by constantly reminding you that you have extra power available.

I have put a religious slant into the curing of inferiority for one reason only: *Christianity is entirely practical.* It is astounding how defeated persons can be changed into victorious individuals when they actually utilize their religious faith as a workable instrument. I am so sure of this that I unhesitatingly assert that I have never seen anything that can really down a person and keep him down if that person definitely and intelligently practices his faith. There is no situation which I have ever seen—and as a minister I've seen plenty—in which faith in God will not help.

In a hard spot, practice saying over and over to yourself, making the statement personal, "If God be for *me*, who can be against *me*?" This practice will eventually cause acceptance by your mind of the powerful thought that your inadequacy is relieved by greater force. Practice saying this formula and keep on saying it; perseverance will get results. Faith is a vital medium for recreating strength, hope and efficiency. It has a strange therapeutic and recreative effect. I could cite many cases in support of the preceding sentence, but the following incident is typical of them all.

A soldier came home from overseas minus a leg. The amputation following battle wounds shocked the boy's mind deeply. He lay on his bed neither smiling nor speaking—just staring at the ceiling. He would not cooperate in learning to wear an artificial limb, although others around him were doing so. Obviously his problem was not his physical body but was in his mind and spirit. So deep was his acquired inferiority that he had completely given way to defeat.

It was thought that a period of time at his own home might help bring him out of himself and assist in lifting his depression. He came of a well-to-do family, and at home he had every attention. In fact, his family overdid it. He was tenderly lifted into his bath, he was hovered over and coddled in every conceivable manner. This is understandable, for everybody wants to show love and appreciation for a boy who has sacrificed himself for his country.

However, the doctor realized that they were making a permanent invalid of the boy. Accordingly he placed him in a convalescent hospital. An effort was made to help him to help himself, and to give him a normal attitude toward the problem of himself but with no success. He continued to lie on his bed, indifferent and uncooperative.

One day the rather baffled and exasperated young doctor said, "I have got to be hard on the boy; I hate to do it, but somehow I must break through this wall around him. He must cast out this inferiority psychosis if he is to recover to normal living."

He said, "Soldier, we are not going to pamper you any more, or carry you around. You have got to be awakened, boy. We can do nothing for you until you open that mind of yours. We all feel sorry about that leg, but other men have lost legs in battle and they have carried on with good spirit. Besides, a man can live and be happy and have a successful career without a leg or an arm or an eye." The doctor pointed out how people are able to adjust themselves, and how so many have done astounding things.

This talk did not move the boy in the slightest. Finally, after many days of attempting to open the closed mind of his patient the doctor quite unconsciously did a peculiar thing, something which amazed even himself.

The doctor was not a particularly religious person, and up to this point had seldom, if ever, mentioned religion in his practice. However, this day in sheer desperation the doctor literally shouted at the boy, "All right, all right; if you won't let any of us help you—if you are so stubborn that you won't even help yourself—then, then—why don't you let God help you? Get up and get that leg on; you know how to do it."

With this he left the room.

A few hours later it was reported that the boy was up, had on his artificial leg, and was moving around. The doctor said that one of the most thrilling moments in his medical experience came some days later when he saw this boy walking around the grounds with a girl friend.

Later when the soldier was discharged from the hospital he came in to see the doctor. The physician started to give him some suggestion, but the boy said, "It's all right, Doc; I remember the medicine you gave me that day. And I think with that prescription I can get along well enough."

"What prescription?" asked the doctor.

"Don't you remember the day you told me that if I could not do it myself, to let God help me? Well, that did something to me. I felt sort of different inside, and as I thought about it, it began to come over me that maybe I could do it—that maybe I wasn't finished after all."

As the physician related this story he sat tapping his desk with a pencil in a thoughtful manner. "Whatever happened to that boy I cannot explain; the process eludes my knowledge. But I do know that in some spiritual manner that boy was released. His mind changed from a state of inner defeat to one of personal power." He hesitated, then added, "There seems to be a very great power in religious faith when it is practiced."

And he is right. Use your religious faith and you do not need to be a defeated person. It will recondition your mind from negative to positive reactions. It makes possible what formerly seemed impossible. This is the mechanism which explains the Biblical statement, "With men things are impossible, but with God all things are possible." When you mentally live with thoughts of God, your inferiority changes to power, impossibility changes to possibility.

In fact, that brief statement of ten short words from the Bible which I have quoted several times can absolutely revolutionize your life. "If God be for us, who can be against us?" Strong, sturdy words these. With these ten words of power you can stand up against any human situation and not be defeated.

*   *   *

In ridding oneself of an inferiority complex, the techniques at hand should not be underrated because they are simple. The purpose is to change the thought slant. Inferiority is a malady of the thoughts, and any device, however simple, that changes the pattern of thinking may be employed.

A young man came to see me who said he was having a nervous break-down. He did not look it; he was a vigorous, healthy person. He was a bit on edge, however, and obviously high-strung. He was not having a nervous breakdown, but was trying to imagine himself into one. He sat in my office reciting one by one the "enormous" difficulties he was then experiencing. I made a few suggestions of an optimistic character, but he immediately leaped upon them and began to tell why they couldn't be done. He was expert in advancing objections. He was what I once heard a businessman refer to as an "obstacle man"—a man adept in finding obstacles. He leaped on these suggestions of mine with such vigor and alacrity, such condemnatory skill, that he almost convinced me that everything *was* against him.

Finally, I said to him: "It is a shame that life is treating you so badly and that you are a failure. It is too bad, too, that you are breaking down and going to pieces; I feel very sorry for you."

He looked at me in amazement, and then he all but got out of his chair; he sat on the edge of it. There was a flash in his eyes and a flush on his face. His whole manner became aggressive.

"I am not a failure," he snapped. He threw back his head with the air of saying, "I can do things."

Indeed, he then did everything but call me names, and I looked admiringly at him and said, "Wonderful! That's wonderful!

"If you would get up each morning and talk to yourself in the mirror just as you are talking now," I advised, "you would convince yourself that you have strength and power and possibilities within you." I actually urged him to stand before a mirror and talk to himself in just that fashion, and to say out loud the ten tremendous words, "If God be for us, who can be against us?"

He actually did just that! His wife told me she was never so amazed as to hear her big, strapping husband talking with himself in the bedroom, standing before a mirror saying to himself, "You can do things. You have brains. God is with you. If God be for you, who can be against you?" She walked in on him and found him thus, to his embarrassment.

That man now has a grip on himself. When I meet him, as I do occasionally, he says, "It is all due to a text—yes, a text." While the text helped, of course, so had the simple procedure which he practiced. It was designed to get his mind to thinking the idea contained in the Bible text.

It works when you believe it—and practice it. He learned the secret of driving off his inferiority complex by employing a practical formula.

* * *

The simple but effective technique of faith described above is greatly needed today, for everywhere human beings are afflicted with the inferiority complex. The feeling of inadequacy or inferiority is a widespread deterrent in personality development. It may well be that the rise of inferiority of a personality problem is due to the decline of religion among the people. If there is a connection between the decline of religion and the prevalence of inferiority, then the remedy is plain: revive religious faith and inferiority feelings will diminish. The spiritual principles suggested here are not theoretical. It is a proven fact, demonstrated in case after case, that religious faith properly applied can rid people of the inferiority complex.

Those ten words from the Bible contain the basic solution to the inferiority complex. They represent one of the greatest, if not the greatest, spiritual and psychological facts in releasing personality; namely, the thought of God's presence with *you*. Practice believing that God is with you and you will get to believing that nothing *can* be against you. By a subconscious procedure the sense of inferiority and inadequacy gradually give way to one of confidence and faith.

Fear and faith, as previously pointed out, are the two greatest powers competing for control of the human mind. Inferiority and inadequacy on the one side; faith and effectiveness on the other—that is the issue. But never forget that faith is stronger than fear; adequacy is stronger than inadequacy.

Repeat those ten words of reassurance a half-dozen times every day; let them saturate your mind. When you face a critical or difficult situation, practice saying to yourself, "God is with me; I can meet the crisis that I now face."

I have a friend, a successful businessman named Jerry Henderson, who practices this technique, and I am indebted to him for a very striking story of its efficiency. You will see by this story that I have not made exaggerated claims.

Henderson was in the Canadian Rockies at Lake Louise to climb and to ski with a party of friends. Shortly before, one of the most famous ski masters had been killed in a heavy avalanche and the suggestion of danger was potent.

Henderson's party went with their guide to climb White Eagle peak. They climbed all morning, and by noontime had surmounted five thousand of the nine thousand feet they had set out to climb. At this point the guide told them that they had to cross a transverse valley lying before them. The sides shot down at an angle of forty-five to fifty degrees.

"Do not call or whistle or raise your voices, for it might start an avalanche," the guide warned. Since hearing of the death of the ski master all had been impressed by the danger of avalanches.

The guide took from his pack a big ball of red yarn. He cut off fifty-foot lengths and gave one to each skier.

"Tie this around your waist," he said. "If an avalanche starts, shake off your skis, throw away your poles and start swimming just as if you were in the water. This will tend to bring you to the top. If the avalanche buries you, the end of this red yarn will protrude and we can find you."

In the party was a girl in her twenties. She looked down at this steep declivity and thought of the possibility of an avalanche, and she became very frightened. She began to whimper and cry, and said to Jerry Henderson, "I can't do it. I'm terrified. I simply can't do it."

He did not feel any too blithe about it himself, but Henderson believes in and practices the ten great words. He takes the position that one need not fear if God is with him; that one can reasonably count on God to see him through whatever comes.

He turned to the trembling, hysterical girl and said quietly, "The Lord has watched over you throughout your life, hasn't he? You believe that, do you not?"

"Yes," she sobbed.

"Well, then, can't you trust Him to take care of you for the next twenty minutes?" he asked.

A remarkable change came over the girl. She made the descent beautifully, taking her place in the long graceful line as each skier followed the other about forty yards apart. She made the descent with exultation. She had achieved a marvelous sense of victory over herself. She learned that there is a secret through which one can get rid of an inferiority complex.

Try simple religious practices. They work. You can be rid of your inferiority complex.

4

HOW TO ACHIEVE A CALM CENTER FOR YOUR LIFE

HIGH TENSION is a prevailing American malady. The adult who has not apprehensively watched the doctor take his blood pressure is in the minority. Glance at the obituary columns of the daily papers, and note how often the cause of death is high blood pressure, angina pectoris, and other hypertension afflictions. Many "strokes" have excessive tension as a contributing, if not a root, cause. For multitudes of high-strung, nervous people life is constant and unrelieved strain.

A well-known physician says: "We know how to control the germ-caused diseases: typhoid, scarlet fever, diphtheria, smallpox, and tuberculosis. But the degenerative diseases which come about because of the age of the individual plus wrong living habits, too much work, strain, stress, too little rest and relaxation, are the troubles which are mowing down so many of our valuable people forty years of age or more.

"Worry, fear, strain, overwork, under-rest, excesses in sex, nicotine and alcohol, wrong diet, overweight; all may bring your blood pressure to dangerous heights."*

Apparently Americans have always been more or less of this tense type. A French writer came to this country in 1830 to study the American, whom he classified as "a new breed of man on the earth." The French visitor noted the restless aggressiveness of our people.

"The American," he complained, "is so restless that he has even invented a chair, called a rocking chair, in which he can move while he sits."

If this French observer could see us now he would surely be forced to revise upward his conclusion, as the tempo has mounted.

A Scotch physician analyzes us. "You Americans," he concludes, "wear too much expression on your faces. You are living with all your nerves in action."

A primary factor in tension is mental disorganization. The helter-skelter mind always feels overburdened. A disorderly mental state means confusion and, of course, tension. Such a mind rests lightly upon problems

---

* M. A. Mortenson, M.D., in *Battle Creek Sanitarium News*, Vol. 13, No. 3.

which it never decides. It skips nervously from one presented problem to another, never arriving at a settled conclusion, in fact, not even grappling seriously with the issue involved. Thus deferred decisions accumulate. The result? The mind gives up and cries desperately, "I am swamped"— simply because it is not organized. It is cluttered up and *seems*, therefore, to be overwhelmed. Note the emphasis, *seems*.

The mind in this situation reacts somewhat like the body in shivering. One shivers when passing suddenly from a warm to a cold area; the body attempts to accommodate itself quickly to the sudden change in body temperature. It has been estimated that as much energy is expended in a half-minute of shivering as in several hours of work. This results in depletion of vigor. In a similar way, shivering in the mind depletes its force when one fails to practice the fundamental principle of mental organization.

Get the calm selective ability to take up one thing at a time and concentrate upon it. Deal finally with it, if possible, before passing to the next matter.

In my office we receive a heavy daily mail covering a wide variety of matters. We operate on the policy that every letter gets an answer. I used to come to my office and find a formidable pile of letters—and be dismayed. Contemplating the labor of thinking out replies to those letters, my mind would inwardly (and sometimes outwardly) complain, "Oh my, oh my, how can I ever get these letters answered?" It was the "I am swamped" reaction. But I learned that the way to answer letters is to answer them as they arrive. A letter unanswered for two weeks has answered itself.

There is only one way to work down a pile of letters. Pick up the first letter, decide upon an answer, and dictate that answer at once. If information not immediately obtainable is required, dictate a memorandum pertaining to it and put the letter in the proper receptacle. If additional study is indicated, place it in a receptacle for pending matters—but don't let them "pend" too long. Handle the letter in some way. Do not put it down indecisively, only to pick it up aimlessly again and again. If you follow this ineffective course, the letters will pile up until your desk is a nightmare, and your mind will fight back with the cry, "I can't stand it—this strain is too much." Then your mind will tell you that you are unequal to your job, and if you keep at this procedure too long you may have a nervous breakdown.

When you organize your mind, a sense of power will come to you, and you will soon wonder at the ease with which you can handle responsibilities. Your capacity for work will increase; so will your pleasure in what you are doing. Strain and tension will subside.

A careful and consistent cultivation of a relaxed mental attitude is important in reducing tension. Americans are inheritors of the Horatio Alger tradition: "strive and succeed." The author is an apostle of hard work, of the good old American principle of creating your own wealth and position by means of your own abilities and efforts. But there is a sense in which it is a mistake to try too hard. Effortless ease is the procedure best designed to achieve superior results with the least strain. Athletes know that trying too hard throws them off their timing. The fine coordination which characterizes the great men of sport is attained by the principle of "taking the game in stride." They do not go into the game to make a record, or get the headlines, or to become stars. They play the game for the love of it. They are alert, they think of the team rather than themselves. They play the game with naturalness and so to the full extent of their ability.

The sports writer, Grantland Rice, reports a conversation with Joe Gordon, then of the New York Yankees, in which the famous player told of an experience in World Series baseball. In his first World Series, Gordon said he was "tied up" all the time. "I wanted to make a great record and hit the headlines. As a result I became tense and rigid and did poorly." In the next series Joe Gordon was wiser. He decided to forget he was playing in a World Series. He determined instead to play ball just as he had on the sand lots, "because it is the grandest game in the world," and to have a good time playing. This released the tension in his mind, and therefore in his nerves and muscles. He became a natural player. As a result he made a much better record in the second series; in fact, he was one of the stars.

In a World Series game, "Dizzy" Trout was on the mound for the Detroit Tigers. He wore glasses. He had been ill and without practice for two weeks; and it was so damp before the game that he couldn't limber up his muscles and get relaxed. And yet he had to go into a World Series game before 42,000 fans in a hostile city and pitch. That demanded calmness, and he had his own way of securing it.

When things got tense, as they did quite often, he simply took off his glasses and wiped them painstakingly, while 42,000 people watched expectantly and the batter at the plate fidgeted. Then he put on his glasses, and began pitching, and one by one the Cubs struck out.

There's calmness for you! Some wag remarked that all of the Chicago Cubs would wear spectacles the next season.

Whatever your work may be—writing books, teaching children, running a business, cooking for a family, working in a factory, plowing a field, or preaching sermons—give your job your best; work hard, slight nothing, take everything in your stride; stay relaxed. Don't try too hard for effect; do not strain for success. Do your job naturally, because you like it, and success will take care of itself.

I learned this basic truth from a red cap in a Chicago station. I was on my way to speak in a city in Western Illinois, and had three "important" calls to make in Chicago between trains, but my train from New York got later and later. I paced the corridor and fumed and fretted. I worked myself into a fair-sized dither. Finally the train rolled into the grimy, cavernous terminal. With ill-concealed impatience I waited for the porter to get the bags onto the station platform. I was the first man off, and luckily secured a porter, as I had two heavy bags.

"Please bring those bags quickly," I directed. "I am in a terrible hurry."

I started at high speed down the platform. Conscious that he was not following, I turned impatiently. "Come on, I'm late." But there stood the porter calmly looking at me.

"Where you steamin' for, brother?" he asked me. "That ain't no way to make time." Then he said, "Just walk on ahead and I'll come along, and there won't be two minutes between us." I slowed down as admonished and walked along beside his truck. He turned and said, "I'se livin' de relaxed life. . . . Take it easy, boss," he advised. "You can do a lot in a short time if you just go along easy at it. Besides," he concluded, "you'll live longer."

"Thanks, my friend," I said, rather humbly. "I happen to be a minister, and I will preach this idea to my congregation. Do you go to church?"

"Yes, indeed, suh, I sure does; and" (here he finished me completely) "I tries to practice what I hear there."

So I slowed down, made my calls, and had time to spare, but I was tired before I got started. Much of the energy needed for the day had been nervously dissipated by tension. Relaxation is best secured by remembering that "Easy does it." Practice using the light touch and you will be surprised to find that success comes easily.

It is important to maintain a constant intake of energy. A National War Fitness Conference held during World War II days was attended by educators and representatives of the armed services who came together to discuss recreation. The value of games and calisthenics was emphasized, but the conference surprisingly declared that the best recreation is to go to church. Recreation means *re-creation*, they explained.

By going to church and practicing the technique of spiritual living, one can establish contact with the basic flow of energy which we call God's power. The New Testament says, "In Him we live, and move, and have our being." This means that God does not create a man and then abandon him to get along as best he can on his own. He makes it possible for a constant re-creation or renewal to take place. By utilizing methods of contacts which are known to be effective, spiritual energy renews power in the soul, the mind, and the body. The electric clock is automatically rewound by the current flowing through the universe. In similar manner people are revitalized who maintain a close spiritual contact. It is the natural way to live.

Mrs. Thomas A. Edison described her husband to me as "Nature's man." "He could work long and hard," she said, "then lie on his old couch and immediately go to sleep. He would relax completely and sleep soundly. When he awakened he was instantly wide awake and refreshed."

The inventor did not find it necessary to woo sleep or to fight his way back to an awakening. Thomas Edison seemed to be carried along by some flow of power.

"Never," said Mrs. Edison, "was there any disunity of mind, never obsessions or impeded flow of energy. He was like a child in God's hands; Nature's man. Perhaps this was one reason God could pour all those wonderful ideas through his mind."

It appears that the wizard of Menlo Park was in harmony with the universe, and therefore the secret places were unlocked for him. Edison "lived and moved and had his being" in the source of never-failing energy and adjusted personality.

The thought that a human being can sensitize and tune his personality so that he can be the beneficiary of an automatic renewal of power is of such importance as to merit experiment. I know a businessman whose imperturbability, inner peace and poise are impressive. Yet he confesses that his major problem was tension. But he discovered a workable technique for living without tension.

"I need to be renewed at least two times a day," he explained. "I retire into my private office at eleven o'clock each morning just when one begins to have a let-down feeling and spend two minutes in meditation. Again at four o'clock, the time of the late-afternoon energy lag, I repeat the same process."

This two-minute period of meditation does not take the usual form of prayer. This man does not consider his problems during this period, but instead "thinks" about God. He dwells upon thoughts of God's peace. He affirms God's presence. He conceives of spiritual strength as flowing into his being. He reports that these four minutes per day result in so marked a refreshment that it amounts to a complete renewal of energy in body and fresh clarity of mind. He declares this daily practice to be far superior to "pick-me-ups" previously relied upon.

A young officer had been shot down on his thirty-first bombing mission. His plane cracked up, and so did he—not physically, but emotionally. The crash, plus the strain and tension of his job, put him into a serious nervous state.

"It's how I feel inside that makes it so hard," he explained. "I'd almost rather have lost a limb than to feel all the time like a volcano about to blow up. I feel as if I would burst into a hundred pieces, and there are times when I want to scream—to shriek. The worst of it is I can't sleep, and when morning comes I think, 'How will I ever get through this day?' I'm certainly shot." He concluded with this pathetic statement, "I'm sick of myself. I don't like living with myself any more."

No one could blame the poor fellow. He was drawn taut, like a stretched rubber band. He could not relax, or rest. There was no peace in him. Little wonder he felt about himself as he did.

I assured him that he could work out of this condition. I happened to know of some medicine that could help him, and told him about it.

"Do you pray?" I asked.

"I try to, but it's hard thinking of the words. My mind wanders and I get nervous," he replied, "so usually I end up by not praying very much." When asked if he tried to read the Bible, he stated that any kind of reading was impossible; he could not concentrate. It "got him all tensed up," he said; made him want to shriek.

This boy was in a bad state of nerves. However, his trouble was not in his body, but in his mind. Nervous states, tension, inner turmoil, are usually not caused by any physical damage, but rather by disorganization of thoughts. Of course, I realized it would be of little value to say, "Cheer up—you'll be all right. Have faith and pray." He needed to know "how" to do that.

I gave him the following advice: "When you go to bed tonight, practice relaxing. Raise your arms and let them fall limply by your sides. Repeat this three or four times. Think of your entire body as being filled with peace. Close your eyes lightly and think of the tension as going out of the eyelids. Try relaxing the eyelids by thinking of them falling shut limply, somewhat as your arms fell by your sides.

"Then lying relaxed with lights out, say, preferably out loud, or quietly under your breath if with others, the simple words, "The Lord is my Shepherd."

"Conceive of these words," I urged, "as a medicine which permeates your mind, sinking into the subconscious as you sleep; conceive that this medicine is extending its healing benefit through the entire body and deep into the soul." I suggested also that he repeat this process before arising in the morning.

The young officer tried this prescription; he really worked it, and it did him a vast amount of good. The old peace has now returned, the strain is gone. Remember—the trouble very likely is in your thought. Thoughts may be healed the same as a cut finger, only the medicine isn't iodine and salve; it's a much more effective healing agent—it is the thought of God's peace, His presence and power. It takes a thought to heal thoughts.

Sometimes our personal attitudes cause inner tension. A man told me that he would willingly trade his annual two-weeks vacation from his job for a two-weeks vacation from himself. Unfortunately that cannot be. We have to live with ourselves whether we like it or not, so the best course is to get so we can like it.

A friend of mine used to have a terrible time with himself. Everybody irritated him. He came into New York on a commuters' train each morning, and the people on the train got on his nerves. Much of the news he read in the paper made him mad. He was filled with resentments, not merely against people he knew, but also against people he saw, and people about whom he read and never saw. He ate his breakfast in a busy and crowded restaurant in the city, and the people there got on his nerves. "What's the matter with people nowadays?" he complained.

He finally discovered that it wasn't the people at all; that it was himself who was causing the irritation and tension. He really did not hate other people basically; he hated himself. He was a sensitive and sore personality, a bundle of antagonisms organized around one central antagonism, namely, his own dissatisfaction with himself. Of course, he derived no pleasure from living with himself. He was a personal civil war.

There are many people like this, poor souls; but there is an answer to this unhappy condition. This man found it. He could not change himself. There is not much point in trying that. So he asked God to change him. He then began practicing Christ's attitude toward people. Presently he found that people and things didn't irritate him any more. He found himself actually beginning to like people. People seemed different, but actually *he* was the one who was different. Naturally when one has good will he exudes it unconsciously, and this in turn brings out good will in others. At any rate life became different because he was different. Now he enjoys life because he enjoys himself. He eliminated the irritable drive of tension.

The foregoing experiences suggest the importance of definite exercises in reducing tension. The habitual practice of tested methods gets results. Some prescriptions for the healing of tension are medical, others psychological, others spiritual; and still others, perhaps, partake of all three.

Following is a simple "prescription" which I, and hundreds who have tried it, have found to be very effective.

Some years ago I was heavily borne down by the pressure of work, and fell into that frantic attitude of mind common to those who try to do too much in too short a time, or who at least have the notion that they are so doing, which is just as bad. The result was that I lost the capacity for sound, restful sleep. After tossing for several hours I arose about three o'clock one morning in an acute state of tension. Instead of reclining in a relaxed attitude, I had been lying in bed doubled up, as if expecting that at any moment the bed would collapse and precipitate me onto the floor. My mouth was dry; I was restless and hot. I went into the library. I picked up several books, but none of them interested me. What book is interesting under such circumstances? I stomped restlessly about, finally stopping at the window which I opened. I put my head out and looked up and down Fifth Avenue.

It was raining, and the rain fell upon my head. I turned my face up to the rain, which fell cool and refreshing upon my face. It ran down until presently I could taste it and smell it. It occurred to me then that among all the things of this world which change, one thing never changes, and that is the taste and smell of rain. Even falling through the murky skies of Manhattan, it tasted and smelled just as it did years ago in Ohio; I remembered the old rain barrel at the corner of my boyhood home on a rainy day in May, when great pools where one splashed with bare feet formed under the trees. It gave a momentary sense of peace and refreshment to reflect upon the changelessness of the rain.

Finally I sat down in an easy chair and picked up a little pamphlet. Leafing carelessly through it, I read:

"You are restless, you are tense. You are anxious and nervous. You cannot sleep."

"How in the world did you know that?" I cried in astonishment.

I continued reading. The writer said, "Practice a simple method for overcoming tension."

The pamphlet, which has long since disappeared (it contained little of value except the germ of an idea), suggested physical, mental and spiritual exercise which proved valuable. It being early in the morning, and having nothing else to do, I decided to try the suggestion offered. The method, later developed by additional experimentation, follows:

First of all, relax the body. To do this allow your head to fall back against the head rest of your chair. Let it drop back easily, not in any sense rigid, but as though the head were falling off your shoulders. Then stretch out your feet as far as possible, and push your toes beyond that, as far as you can extend them. Raise the arms and let them fall limply and naturally by the side. Allow your hand to fall upon your knee, like a wet leaf on a log. What is more relaxed than a wet leaf on a log!

Sit loosely in the chair with every muscle relaxed, allowing the chair to bear the full weight of the body so that if the chair were removed the body would fall inertly to the floor.

After the body has been relaxed, relax the mind. We have a marvelous gift which we call imagination. By imagination one may transport himself hundreds of miles over mountain and sea, and return in the fraction of an instant. It is the true magic carpet. By it you can take a vacation trip without paying for a ticket or moving from your own home.

Imagine that you are, for example, in the north woods, peacefully sitting with your back to a tree. The atmosphere is redolent of pine and cedar and hemlock. All is quiet, save the natural sounds of the forest. Before you is a lake, its blue waters unruffled, except for the occasional leap of a fish. Looking through the trees you can see in the far distance great mountains, lost in a mystic haze of blue, shouldering out the sky. The sunlight is falling mellow and warm upon the earth, splashing down through the trees and dancing on the water of the lake.

Following this method of relaxation, I found I was attaining not only a sense of rest in body, but also a pervading calmness of mind. The mind was being relaxed by taking it away momentarily from the problems agitating it and rendering it incapable of rational functioning and collected thought. This had been accomplished in just a flashing moment of time.

A quick turning of the mind in prayer while engaged in the busy activities of the day is like that. You do not need to go apart and kneel down to pray, although the posture of humility is helpful. Simply turn your thoughts to God. In so doing you are opening your mind to Him. He will do the rest.

The third and final element in this process of relaxation is the relaxation of the soul. The method is simple. Relax the soul by the exercise of spiritual thinking. Fix the mind on God. Think of God in whatever terms He is most understandable to you. People have many differing conceptions of God. When the name of God is spoken different minds instantly form varying pictures. But think of God in terms of His kindliness, His watchful care, His compassion and understanding.

In relaxing the soul, say to yourself words from the Scriptures which express peace and God's care. Among them use this verse from Isaiah: "Thou wilt keep him in perfect peace, whose mind is stayed on Thee."

Most people suffer tension because they keep their minds stayed or fixed, not on God, but at the far lower level of their personal troubles and anxieties.

Repeat quietly to yourself other healing passages: "Peace I give unto you: not as the world giveth, give I unto you. Let not your heart be troubled, neither let it be afraid." And again, "Come unto me, all ye that labor and are heavy laden, and I will give you rest."

The words of old hymns are often helpful such as the line from "Lead, Kindly Light"—"So long Thy power hath kept me, sure it *still* will lead me on."

God has watched over you in the past. He can be depended upon to do so now and in the future.

As a result of this experience I quickly felt the desire for sleep. I was rested in body. Muscle and nerve relaxed. I was conscious of worries being lifted from the mind, and tension passing. There was a sense of peace deep within.

This process is not intended merely to induce sleep, but is a formula which may be employed in the busiest part of the most active day. Nor is it escape from active responsibility. It increases the capacity for active work. Power is derived from quietness.

Edwin Markham has a wise line: "At the heart of the cyclone tearing the sky is a place of central calm." The cyclone derives its power from a calm center. So does a man. Out of relaxation comes driving energy. Power is generated in and derived from a calm center.

Practice will reduce the time needed for this exercise, until it will require only a moment. By such technique, modified or expanded to suit your own personality, you may find complete relaxation and learn to live without tension.

5

HOW TO THINK YOUR WAY TO SUCCESS

"WHERE DO YOU get your successful ideas?" I asked a famous businessman. We were in his library.

"Upstairs in a little room," he answered. "Would you like to see it?"

He led me to a small room furnished with only a table and two chairs. Simple yet exquisite drapes hung at the windows. On opposite walls were two pictures. One showed the Matterhorn capped with snow; the other pictured a swiftly flowing, sun-speckled trout stream, rushing over smooth stones and into deep pools. "Both pictures," he said, "represent peace. One portrays peace immovable, the other peace movable. Both aspects are necessary to the proper contemplation of peace," he remarked.

On the table was a pad, several pencils and a Bible.

"Here is where I get my ideas," he said.

He explained that his method is to come home from his office well in advance of the dinner hour and shut himself in this little room. There his privacy is never disturbed. He seats himself in an easy chair and consciously and deliberately relaxes his body. He does this by placing his feet firmly on the floor, raising his hands and letting them fall limply two or three times, saying as he does so, "My arms are dead, my arms are dead." He does the same with his feet, lifting them up and letting them drop. He also relaxes his eyelids by allowing them to fall a half dozen times as inertly as possible. This technique, he said, is quite effective in eliminating strain.

Next he reads from the Bible, selecting passages dealing with quietness, serenity, peace of mind. He knows where to find these quickly and I noticed that they were underscored. His favorite quotation is, "Let this mind be in you, which was also in Christ Jesus." (Philippians 2:5.)

"It is possible," he asserted, "to experience the quality of mind Christ had and to possess to a degree His insights and clarity of understanding."

The next procedure is to write down the particular problem upon which he wanted insight. It may be a business problem, or some personal matter, or a domestic quandary. Every factor pertaining to the problem is put down on paper. "Writing down an idea tends to clarify it," he declared. He quoted Themistocles, "Speech is like the cloth of Arras opened and spread abroad; whereas in thought it lies as in packs." When he has put down on the paper everything he can think of in connection with the problem, he then studies and considers it, weighing and analyzing it.

The final procedure takes the form of a prayer somewhat as follows: "God, I feel relaxed in body and in mind. My little mind is not big enough to understand the intricacies and ramifications of my problems. I have tried to study this problem. I now ask you, God, to give illumination, insight, and understanding that I may take the proper course."

Having done this, he said, "I leave the room and put the problem out of my mind. I then spend the evening reading or conversing with friends. The answer may come in the midst of a conversation or I may be awakened in the night with the answer clearly in mind. Sometimes I may have to repeat this process several times, but," and he emphasized this with great earnestness, "whenever I have practiced this method of thinking, the right answers to my problems always come. The answer has not always been what I expected or wanted, but the answer I have received has been the right one when judged by the ultimate results."

This man had discovered that the ultimate in the art of thinking is the spiritual touch. He had learned how to think creatively. His emotional, spiritual and intellectual energies joined to deliver ideas that were sound and practical.

We need to cultivate practical techniques of thinking, for the power to think is one of our greatest faculties. Your life, or mine, is not determined by outward circumstances, but by the thoughts that habitually engage the mind. You create your own world by your thoughts. It has been said, "A man is what he eats." A deeper truth is, a man is what he thinks. The wisest of all books says, "As he thinketh in his heart, so is he." As a man thinks habitually in his conscious and subconscious mind, that is what he becomes.

Marcus Aurelius, wisest man of Rome, said, "Our life is what our thoughts make of it." Ralph Waldo Emerson, wisest American, said, "A man is what he thinks about all day long." Obviously a person thinks about many things in the course of a day. Beneath all of these thoughts, however, is one basic or primary thought. Into this fundamental thought, all other thoughts are drained, and from it, take their color and content.

For example, some people allow fear to become their primary thought. Fear usually begins as a thin trickle of worry across the mind. Repeated over many days, it becomes habitual until it cuts a deep channel across the consciousness. Every thought a man, to whom this has happened, thinks— about his family, about his business, about his health, or about the world—is colored by the basic and primary thought of fear and comes up tinctured with anxiety and insecurity. No matter how he resists the persistent thought of fear, he cannot escape it. He is what he thinks about all day long; he is a man of fear.

To counteract this condition—substitute a different and stronger basic thought. The only primary thought that can successfully oppose fear is faith or the positive thought. Only faith is stronger than fear.

But what is the technique for developing faith? It is to affirm the positive thought. Faith, too, begins as a thin trickle across the mind. Repeated, it becomes habitual. It cuts deeply into the consciousness until finally (to use a crude figure) you have two basic channels of thought—one of fear, and one of faith. But fear can never defeat faith. As you deepen the channel of the faith thought, the channel of the fear thought finally dries up. The faith thought overflows and becomes the deep, flowing, primary thought of the mind. Then every business, about your family, about the world is touched by the thought of faith and comes up bright, resplendent, optimistic and positive.

As a result of your new and positive caste of thought, you will learn to believe in yourself, in your country, and in the future of mankind. You will now have a deep, positive conviction that life is good. Shadows which once frightened you and obstacles which once defeated you flee away and are overcome. Physically you may be the same person, but mentally you are living in a different world. Actually you are a different person because you are thinking differently. You are what you think about all day long. But your thoughts now give you power and are leading you to happiness and success.

A thought, properly employed, possesses a healing property. Physicians today are emphasizing "psychosomatic" medicine; psycho—of the mind, and soma—of the body. They study the effect of thought or emotion upon physical states. For emphasis, a physician once said that he would have little trouble in getting most of his patients well if only he could cut off their heads during convalescence. And, in fact, chemical and organic conditions would frequently adjust themselves were it not for the effect of improper thinking. I would argue that every individual should have a regular check-up on his thought processes. A wise man has bodily check-ups to keep himself in physical health. Why not check-ups for mental health? The mind is surely as important, if not more so, than the body, for the body is largely regulated by the mind. Get your mind checked up.

The church may serve as a kind of re-conditioning center where a person can submit his mind for an overhauling and get it put back into order. Contrary to a popular misconception, psychiatry does not deal with pathological cases, but may be defined as a science which helps to keep normal people normal. The cure is often effected by the simple application of spiritual and psychiatric treatment.

A New York City businessman came to our church clinic. He was a successful man holding a rather important position. By an extraordinary summoning of his energies, he was able to keep going. His expenditure of nervous energy was immense. He felt depleted in energy and had little strength and no zest. His mind was haunted by interlocking obsessions.

"What do I need?" he asked.

"Mental conditioning," I replied.

"What is mental conditioning?" he asked in some surprise.

"It is a process to freshen up the mind," I explained.

He told me that he was "no good until eleven o'clock in the morning." "I have an awfully hard time getting up, and when I do, I am disagreeable and unhappy until about eleven. Then I manage to perk up and do pretty well for a few hours."

"What time do you get up?" I asked.

"Around nine. I have a wonderful wife. She serves my breakfast in bed."

"Now isn't that sweet?" I said. "She comes in and says consolingly, 'How are you, sweetheart,' doesn't she?"

"Yes," he said, "how did you know?"

"And what do you do?" You groan, 'Oh, I feel so terrible!' Then she puts her soft hands lightly on your brow, and says, 'That's all right, sweetheart, you just lie there and I will bring you up some breakfast.'"

"Yes, that's what she does. Isn't that wonderful?"

"You haven't a wife. She is acting like a mother, babying you," I said.

"The doctor says there is nothing wrong with me except my mind," he continued. "He says I'm a victim of self-pity as a result of wrong-thinking."

"Your doctor is right," I said. "You need to have your mind re-conditioned. I suggest that you pray and ask for strength—then believe that strength is being given you. Tomorrow morning when your wife comes into your room and asks how you are, give her a crisp, healthy answer. Say to her, 'I feel new strength—through God's help I know I'm all right.' Then get out of bed, and go singing in to shave."

"She would die of a heart attack," he said.

"Get downstairs," I continued, "and eat breakfast at the table. Get started to your office by nine o'clock." I thought it ought to be eight-thirty, but I didn't want to be too hard on him.

"That wears me out to think about it," he said.

"It's your thoughts that wear you out," I explained. "But you won't be tired if you conceive of God's energy as being yours."

I did not see him for quite a while. Then one day I met him on the street.

"Do you remember that mental conditioning business you told me about?" he asked. "Well, all the way down the street that day I thought, 'That man Peale is a fool. Mental conditioning—affirming I feel fine; of all the crack-brained notions.' Then I got to thinking maybe I really was not as bad off as I had been assuming. A few mornings later I was certain I felt better and decided to try out your suggestion. My wife came in and said, 'How are you?' 'Fine,' I answered, 'marvelous!' I leaped out of bed, swept her off her feet, kissed her and set her down hard, and went singing in to shave. You never saw such an expression on anybody's face. And—I had a good day and have been practicing your idea ever since. When a negative thought tries to sneak into my mind, I affirm that God is flooding my mind with peace and strength. I have found that when you affirm it, you have gone a long way toward having it."

People develop defeatist habits of thought which make them miserable. Their happiness is frustrated by their thinking. Things will be different when you think differently. When depressing thoughts come to mind, literally say, "You old, depressing defeat thought—get out of my mind. I can defeat you. I affirm that God's strength is in me." Actually talk back to your thoughts. At all costs conquer defeatist thinking, otherwise it will conquer you.

Get your mind renewed and life will be different!

An industrialist discovered the truth of this. He underwent a physical examination and the doctor said, "There is nothing wrong with you that cannot be cured by a new mental outlook on life." He charged plenty for this prescription and well he should, for it was sound advice. The industrialist went to his minister. He got his thinking changed—got the worry and fear thoughts out. Rid of the thoughts that were poisoning his mind, he is now a new man. He learned to think his way to success and happiness.

It is very important to keep the thought processes in good condition for in your mind are all of the paraphernalia needed to build your career. Keep your mind free from confusion and all the creative ideas you need will be yours. Your mind will deliver them to you if you keep your intellectual equipment well regulated.

An important factor in the achievement of success is the art of original and creative thinking. The average person does not trust his own mind to create for him the ideas which he needs. Business firms are beginning to realize the importance of creative thinking and in some instances have actually employed men for the sole purpose of thinking. They are not research men, but thinking men. Their job is to study the business, fill their minds full of it and then trust their minds to deliver fresh and creative ideas.

Dr. Glenn Clark quotes the late Arthur Brisbane to the effect that there are many positions in this country which will pay a salary of fifty thousand dollars a year for thinking creative thoughts. These jobs go begging, he says.

It is said that John D. Rockefeller, Sr., once employed a man at twenty-five thousand dollars a year whose job was to sit in a swivel chair and think up new ideas for the business. A jealous person complained to Mr. Rocke-feller, "Why do you pay that fellow twenty-five thousand dollars a year for swiveling around in a swivel chair and staring out the window?" Mr. Rockefeller said, "If you can think up as many good ideas as he does, I will give you twenty-five thousand dollars a year and a swivel chair." Do not conclude, however, from this incident that every man who swivels around in a swivel chair is worth twenty-five thousand dollars a year. Many are merely engaging in intellectual free wheeling.

May I at this point inject a homely parable? A man was hard pressed for money and he prayed and asked the Lord to give him some. The Lord, in His kindliness, heard the prayer coming up from earth and called one of his angels and said, "That poor fellow needs money. Send some down to him."

The angel returned and said, "Lord, I have looked through the vaults of heaven and can find no money. We have only that which 'neither moth nor rust doth corrupt, and where thieves do not break through nor steal,' but while we have no money, we have some wonderful ideas and insights. Shall we send some of those down to him?"

The man had continued to pray and he showed great faith and the Lord was delighted and said, "Yes, open the windows of heaven and pour out so many insights and ideas that he will have more than he needs."

And so it happened that everybody said, "What a creative, ingenious, resourceful mind this man possesses." This parable is as sound as the good earth on which we walk.

If you do honest and thorough intellectual work, the next step is to relax your mind, trusting it to sort the material and deliver insights and solu-tions to problems. The best kind of thinking is that which is done uncon-sciously after conscientious study and preparation. Professor Brand Blan-shard, professor of philosophy at Yale, and former President of the American Philosophical Association, tells us that great writers employed the art of unconscious thinking. He describes the method of several.

"Stevenson, when he had a story to write, would block out the plot and then leave the detail to his 'Brownies,' the little people who worked during sleep in the hidden places of his mind. Henry James has described how, in writing *The American*, he took his main idea and 'dropped it for the time into the deep well of unconscious cerebration,' where it went on to take form and substance. Milton, for long periods, would brood over a theme and write nothing. But during these 'droughts,' as he called them, the springs were forming beneath the surface and suddenly, in the middle of the night sometimes, he would call for his daughters to catch, from dictation, the torrent of verse that came welling up. People used to wonder at the pulpit fertility of Beecher; he once preached daily for eighteen months without missing a day; and his sermons were powerful ones. But he has left it on record that the work was largely unconscious. He kept a number of themes ripening at once in the cellers of his mind; a week or so before the sermon was due, he would select one that was well along, consider it a while intently, then commit it again to the cellar. On the morning of delivery he would find that it had germinated into a large mass of relevant ideas which he would then order and put down at tremendous speed.

"Nor is it only in art and letters that unconscious thinking has been used; it has solved some of the knottiest problems of the sciences.

"Thus Gauss had been working on a theorem in arithmetic for four years, after which 'as a sudden flash of light the enigma was solved.' But he explicitly adds that he was unable to see the thread he must have followed in reaching this end result.

"I have found," says Bertrand Russell, "that if I have to write upon some rather difficult topic, the best plan is to think about it with very great intensity—the greatest intensity of which I am capable—for a few hours or days, and at the end of that time give orders, so to speak, that the work is to proceed underground."*

Here is an example that could well be added to Professor Blanshard's list. Mr. Robert G. LeTourneau, famed industrialist and world's largest builder of earth-moving machinery, has the genius to invent very complicated machinery. On occasion during World War II, the government ordered certain types of machines, as, for example, one able to pick up broken planes. It was needed quickly. Mr. LeTourneau and his assistants went to work on it but were getting nowhere. The solution did not come.

It happened to be prayer meeting night and Mr. LeTourneau is never absent. He said to his assistants, "I am going to prayer meeting. Perhaps the solution will come while I am in the meeting." He put the problem entirely out of his conscious thought, went to the prayer meeting where he fully gave himself to the spirit of worship. Before the meeting was over, the entire machine was pictured in his mind. He had only to go back and set down the blueprint.

One of the outstanding practical thinkers in American business is Beardsley Ruml, often referred to as America's number one idea man.

"Ruml's method of tackling problems is to sit in a chair and do nothing. He has advised executives who have problems on their hands to lock themselves up, sit in a chair, and do nothing for at least an hour a day. It is essential for apprentices at musing, that there should be no newspapers or other reading matter around to break the spell. Ruml spends much more than an hour a day in sessions of this kind. With his mind released from ordinary influence, he can command wider vistas of fact and theory than when methodically studying a subject.

"He has described the mental condition in which he gets his ideas as 'a state of dispersed attention.'

* Brand Blanshard, *The American Mercury*, December, 1945, p. 693.

"Although information helps, it is not necessary to know everything about a problem, according to Ruml, in order to tackle it in reverie, or waking-dream fashion. He thinks nothing of letting his subconscious mind wander through regions in which his knowledge is very rarefied. His farm plan is an example of an idea picked out of remote space; Ruml was profoundly ignorant of the farm problem at the time. He is highly educated and has investigated many subjects, but he is not a typical scholar. He reads comparatively little. His career tends to vindicate the old philosopher Hobbes, who said, 'If I read as much as other men, I would know as little as they do.'

"Ruml doesn't proceed from premise to conclusion or follow any known logical method in inventing his plans. He doesn't seem to hear voices or receive messages. His faculty is usually described as clairvoyance or intuition, two unsatisfactory words which fail to throw much light on what actually goes on in his mind."*

In one industry a "silent room" has been set aside for executives where without books or other paraphernalia they may have solitude to practice the art of creative thinking.

Dr. Frederick Kettner, authority on youth training, considers the practice of creative silence a vital part of education. Silence brings about remarkable changes in young people. He makes the unique suggestion that the architecture in the modern age should include a "silence" room in each home where man can figuratively wash his brain and heart. Many modern homes include a "rumpus" room, primarily intended for the children. Judging from current domestic situations, it would seem that there are altogether too many "rumpus" rooms in homes. We need more "silence" rooms.

A successful sales manager says it isn't necessary to have a room in which you may go apart; one may practice the art of retirement into mental quietness even in the midst of confusion.

His method is to remove his glasses and put his hands over his eyes for a half minute. In this half minute he deliberately thinks of a peaceful scene, such as the place he fished last summer, or a mountain view. Having allowed this picture to flash into his mind, he then says quietly to himself the following words, repeating the sentence several times, "Peace is flooding my mind, my body, and my soul." He declares that he feels peace flowing in upon him by the act of conceiving it as doing so. He turns to his work with the feeling that a refreshing of his thought processes has taken place. Dullness and haziness lift and energy and new perceptions are given him.

An outstanding investment banker in New York told me that he considers the reading of the Bible the most valuable method of clarifying and stimulating his mind. He goes to his office in the financial district at

* Alva Johnston, *The New Yorker*, February 10, 1945.

seven-thirty in the morning and spends the first half hour reading the Bible. He then has fifteen minutes of quiet meditation after which he says he is ready for the day's work. He is an accomplished linguist and some days reads the Bible in French, other times in Spanish, claiming that the differing emphases given by these languages, add to his insights.

Recently he went to another city on an important banking mission. For two hours of his journey he studied business reports affecting the negotiations. For the next hour, he said, "I read St. Paul—mark you, not merely for spiritual values, but primarily for the stimulation of my mental processes. Finally I had fifteen minutes of relaxing prayer and meditation, after which I went to sleep. Upon arrival at my destination I did not try to sell the people anything they did not want or need. I merely laid all the facts before them as I had thought them out. I then returned to New York. Two days later I had on my desk a large amount of business." Had no financial results materialized he would have been satisfied with the knowledge that he had done all within his power.

"You really think that this practice has clarified your thinking?" I asked.

"I do not think it, I *know* it," he answered firmly.

PRAYER—THE MOST POWERFUL FORM OF ENERGY

EARLY ONE MORNING I arrived at the Grand Central Station in New York and took a taxi to my home. The driver proved to be a very happy and friendly man.

"You're up bright and early this morning," I commented.

"Oh!" he replied, "I am here every morning at this time; that is, every morning except Sunday."

"And what do you do on Sunday?" I asked.

"Why, what do you suppose?" he replied. "I go to church." He stopped for a traffic light. "That isn't the whole of it," he said. "I sing in the choir also. I like the old hymns, don't you?"

Upon my agreement, he suddenly offered, "Would you like me to sing a hymn for you?"

This was astonishing, but one learns to expect almost anything in New York, so I said, "Yes, I would like to hear you sing." At this he broke into one of the old hymns, which he sang in a clear tenor voice as we rolled down Fifth Avenue.

When he had finished I complimented him, and then asked, "Have you a good minister in your church?"

"A good minister!" he exclaimed. "We have the best in New York and I don't mean maybe!"

This pleased me, for I always like to meet a man who is enthusiastic about his minister. Just then he went past my own church at the corner of Fifth Avenue and Twenty-ninth Street.

"There is where I go to church," I told him.

"Is that so?" he replied. "Do you have a good minister there?"

"Well," I said, "only so-so; you see, I happen to be the minister my-self."

This unexpected information nearly caused him to run up on the side-walk.

"I guess I took in too much territory back there," he said.

When we arrived at my home we chatted for a minute.

"I'll tell you why my minister means so much to me," he said. "I haven't always been a taxi driver. I had a good business once, but it went down in the depression. I knew that God had a plan for me, and He didn't fail me. My minister got me into the taxi business. He said, 'Bill, running a taxi is the same as operating any business. If you give good service, if you are friendly, if you treat people right and trust in God, you will get along, and you'll have a good time doing it.'

"My minister told me that every morning when I went over to the garage to get my cab, *before I started out*, I was to bow my head over the wheel and dedicate my day's work to God and to people. That may sound pious, but I want to tell you that I have made a good living. What's more, I have had a wonderful time, and I am very happy; happier than I have ever been before."

I say without qualification that here was a man who combined good business practices with his religion, and was a success in life. I haven't the slightest doubt that this man has by now gone on to greater things, because he has the philosophy that works: trust God, work hard, put your business in God's hands, and serve people.

This taxi driver utilized a procedure which one of the world's foremost scientists, Alexis Carrel, highly recommended. He said, "The most powerful form of energy one can generate is prayer. Prayer, like radium," he continued, "is a luminous and self-generating form of energy."

Alexis Carrel, whose political aberration does not vitiate his scientific knowledge, made that astounding statement to a generation that is perfectly familiar with power in its most dramatic forms. Yet, points out this scientist, the most powerful form of energy one can generate is not mechanical, electronic or even atomic energy, but prayer energy.

Most of us are novices in prayer. Many seldom pray, some do not pray at all. There are, generally speaking, three ways in which men get what they want and need: (1) by work, (2) by thought, (3) by prayer. The first two are used every day. The third is greatly neglected.

Why? Probably because work and thought are obvious factors of our everyday experience. They are common, everyday things, while prayer is associated with something different, with special forms and postures. It has been made a sort of Sunday-go-to-meeting thing remote from our daily lives.

This elimination of the prayer factor from man's experience is a tragic omission. It compels us to bear the entire weight and burden of life. Little wonder men break down, or fail to achieve the best possible. Through spiritual procedures we may make contact with a tremendous source of strength. Greater strength may be generated by prayer than by the thoughts of the brain or the working of the hands. Let me repeat: the most powerful form of energy one can generate is prayer energy.

The connection between men and the universe may be far more subtle and profound than we may think. We are part of nature and of God, and to truly succeed in life one must harmonize himself with nature and God.

A brilliant woman recovered from a long and serious illness and went to Florida to recuperate. She went to Daytona Beach, one of the most beautiful beaches in the world. During her convalescence it was her custom daily to lie on the beach to get the sun. No one was near her. Alone in the midst of nature, she practiced deliberately turning her mind toward God. She prayed deeply.

One day she became acutely conscious of the deep silence of nature. She felt strangely attuned to the world. The quietness was such that to her astonishment, she could actually hear her own heart beat. She began to count those beats. She noticed the rhythm, steady and undeviating. She was listening to the beating of her own heart as it sent the life-blood coursing through her body.

As she lay listening to her heart beat, she turned her eyes and looked through the beach grass near her, washed clean and fresh by the tides. Her eyes selected one particular blade of beach grass. She watched as it was moved slowly and gracefully to and fro by a gentle breeze. She was amazed to discover that it moved with virtually the same rhythm and beat as her heart.

Then her eyes lifted to the sea. Sprinkled with sunshine like myriads of diamonds, sparkling in the sunlight, it rolled majestically inward in long foamy curlers upon the clean sand. Her mind suddenly became alive to the amazing fact that the beating of the waves upon the beach was also in rhythm not dissimilar to the waving of the grass and the beating of her heart. She became aware of one fundamental rhythmic harmony. Then came a realization that she was at one with nature, that she was a constituent part of its inner harmony. This thought caused all loneliness and fear to leave her mind. Now she knew that she was in tune with God, that God's healing forces were flowing through her bringing back bodily health. This brought a deep peace and feeling of renewal.

"I shall never be afraid of anything again," she declared. "For now I know there is a power by which life can be recreated. I know the secret of attuning to that power." It is a medium through which the close connection of man to God is achieved.

To be efficient in prayer you must learn the art of praying. It is a mistake to think that the laws of efficiency do not apply to prayer. Obviously skills are required in the operation of all power. It is not reasonable to assume that no skill is required in the exercise of the greatest power of all. Yet in mastering the art of prayer it is only necessary to follow certain simple principles. You do not have to go to college or technical school to become an expert in this field.

The first step in learning to pray is just to pray. You can read every book ever written about prayer, and you can attend innumerable discussions on prayer, but still the only way to learn to pray is to pray.

As a young man I took lessons in public speaking. Some time later I met one of the greatest orators of that period and asked him, "How does one become proficient as a public speaker?"

"By speaking," he replied. "Learn the art by practice. Speak every time you get a chance. Keep doing it. Keep practicing constantly, seeking to improve yourself."

That advice applies to all efficiency. It is important to study the rules and techniques of anything you want to master, but in the last analysis you learn by doing.

How much time each day do you spend in prayer? I have asked that question of many people and have arrived at the conclusion that about five minutes per day is the probable average. Some pray more than that; some less—most people probably less.

Let us try a little arithmetic. The average person is awake about sixteen hours a day. That means he has 960 minutes at his disposal. If he uses only five minutes to pray, it means that he is praying only one half of one per cent of his waking hours. There was a time during prohibition days when according to an act of Congress one half of one per cent of alcohol in a beverage was legally declared to be non-intoxicating. This percentage is non-intoxicating in religion also. Raise the daily percentage of time you spend in prayer if you expect to experience its power.

Again I quote Alexis Carrel: "When we pray we link ourselves with the inexhaustible motive power that binds the universe. Pray everywhere; in the street, in the subway, in the office, the shop, the school, as well as in the solitude of one's own room or in a church. True prayer is a way of life. Today as never before prayer is a binding necessity in the lives of men and nations."

A practical plan is to practice utilizing spare moments that would otherwise be aimless. I know a young woman who lives in Brooklyn and works in Manhattan. She formerly spent the fifteen minutes required for the subway journey by just sitting and staring at the advertisements around the car. Then one day she hit upon the expedient of closing her eyes and reciting quietly to herself the Lord's prayer and a few verses of scripture. She would pray about her work for that day and also pray for various people. Having a rather witty way of expression, she told me that the distance between her home and her office was "three Lord's prayers and three Twenty-Third Psalms." Thus she gets in thirty minutes of prayer each day on the subway. Out of these thirty minutes during which she formerly reshuffled her worries, she now draws inspiration for a singularly happy and useful life.

My friend, Frank Laubach, a famous educator, utilizes time spent in a bus to pray for his fellow passengers. He fixes his eye on each one in turn and prays for him or her. People who know him have commented on the amazing manner in which this radiation of love and goodwill changes the atmosphere of a bus. Laubach picturesquely says he just sits in a bus and "swishes love all over the place." One day a sour-faced man sitting in front of him to whom he had said nothing suddenly turned around and growled, "What this country needs is a religious revival." Apparently this kind of praying is contagious. If you do no more than make some of your otherwise aimless minutes prayer minutes you will soon notice new strength and joy welling up within you.

Prayer responds to law as does any science. Learn these laws and practice them and you will inevitably get a definite result. One of the primary laws of prayer is simplicity. Make your prayers simple and natural. It is not necessary to use stereotyped phrases and words. Talk to God as to a friend.

I learned a great deal about prayer from my grandmother. She lived in a little town in the Midwest, in an old-fashioned house, typical of that region. There was a romance about the old-fashioned house. My grandmother's heating plant was a wood-burning stove. One side of you was warm and the other side freezing. Never in her lifetime did she have modern refrigeration. Her butter and eggs were placed in a crock outside the door. She was a strong, simple, old-fashioned woman.

My brother and I used to spend our summers with her. She took us over from our parents. After supper (dinner was the noon-day meal in those days) she would read to us by a kerosene lamp. Her concave lenses sat rather far down on her nose as she read stories to us.

Then she would take us upstairs to bed. It was a great high-posted bed laid with handmade quilts, and had an old-fashioned featherbed mattress in which we would sink so far that only our ears protruded. She would put the lamp on a stand and kneel by our bed. On her knees she would talk to the Lord, as to one with whom she was well acquainted and—as I see it now—to reassure us.

"O Lord," so her prayer ran, "I hate to put these two little fellows away off here in this bedroom. When I take this light away it is going to be very dark, and they are so little. They may be scared, but they do not need to be, because You are here, and You are going to watch over them all through the night. You will watch over them all their life long too, if they are good boys. Now, Lord, I ask You to watch over the pillows of these little fellows this night."

Then she would take the lamp, the glow fading upon the wall as she passed from the room. Her soft footfalls died away as she passed down the steps. On stormy nights, especially when the wind would howl around the house, my brother and I would huddle together in that big bed. I used to look up in the darkness and in imagination see a great, kindly face looking down on my pillow. I have always thought there was something magnificent about that prayer, "Look down upon the pillow of these little fellows."

My grandmother said, "Remember, God is not some Oriental potentate sitting upon a throne; He is your friend; He is right by your side. Talk to Him in simple, plain language, telling Him what is on your heart, and He will listen to you."

Make your prayers simple. If you are sitting at your desk and you do not know what to do about some matter, do not call your partner, because he may not know, either; but call in a greater Partner. Merely say, "Lord, I am stuck with this business problem. You know more about this business than I do; tell me what to do." If your fears and anxieties are heavy, talk to God about them in simple fashion. Then do your best and leave the rest to Him. Quit worrying about the things. God's love will protect and defend you. Trust Him, work hard, think straight, and things will come right.

In learning this art we need to recognize that prayer is a very simple thing. We have, perhaps, made it too stilted and formal. A professor under whom I studied was one of the most God-like men I ever knew. I learned much about prayer from him. I liked to hear him pray in college chapel. When he prayed I surreptitiously watched him. His lifted face lighted up—an outward reflection of an inner light. His hair, what there was of it, was snowy white. To his students, he was a human and practical saint whom we loved. Though now he is gone, we who studied under him shall never forget him. His name was Reverend Doctor George H. Butters, D.D., Ph.D., LL.D., but to his students he was "Daddy" Butters. Even in the classroom we sometimes called him "Daddy," but he never minded that.

He used to tell us that he had a difficult time with his wife in the matter of prayers. It seems that his wife was what he called a "rigid Christian," who believed that the only way to say one's prayers at night was to kneel down by the bedside. Sometimes it got very cold in the New England town where he lived, and his wife was a fresh air enthusiast! When bed-time came, the wind would be whistling through the room, impelling one to get ready for bed in a hurry. Mrs. Butters throve on the cold, and when she discovered that her husband had crept into bed, she would quietly, but firmly ask, "George, have you said your prayers?"

"No, my dear," would come the meek reply. "I am saying them in bed."

"George, you get out of bed and say your prayers in a proper manner."

Obediently but painfully he would slip out of bed, down to the cold floor, the cold wind whipping across his bare feet.

"On those occasions," he commented, "My prayers were short and to the point."

I remember his telling this in one of the most dignified churches in the city of Boston, to the delight of a distinguished congregation; real people always like a human being for a preacher. To "Daddy" Butters God was a friend. God was with him when he sat down to lunch. He was with him at his desk, in his office, when he rode on the train—He was with him everywhere. He talked about God as we would talk about a good friend. His entire cast of mind was that of one who lived with God. Life to him was itself a prayer. But he was never a kill-joy. I think of him as one of the happiest, most genuine, down-to-earth human beings I ever knew.

People who have this simple contact with God have power. No matter how much difficulty, hardship, pain, tragedy and futility may come to them, they rise above it magnificently.

It cannot be over-emphasized that an important technique of prayer is to do all you can, then leave it to God. Put your hand to your problem with force and vigor, fully utilizing your own brain and effort; then put it into God's hands through prayer. A prominent New York physician recently told me that while this idea sounds simple, it contains a very profound and vital truth. He found this out from a critical experience, for he was taken ill and had to undergo a very serious operation. As a physician, he knew that the mortality rate for this particular operation was alarmingly high, that the chances for coming through were slight indeed. Naturally this realization caused him to be very greatly disquieted. His professional career was at the peak. He wanted to live.

He decided to practice prayer. He had secured the best scientific earthly help obtainable. Having done all that he could possibly do, he then simply put the matter in God's hands. He calmly rested himself upon God's will and wisdom. He told the Lord he did not want to die, that he wanted to live. He told the Lord that he had the best doctors available; that now having done all that any human being could do, he was willing to leave the outcome to Him. However God wanted it to be, he was willing to accept.

He reports that immediately a sense of peace came into his mind and with it confidence. He said he felt inwardly that it would be all right however it turned out. He went into the operation with every human and divine force, free and unimpeded. He regained his health, and today is back at work every day performing one of the most difficult and skillful operations known to the medical profession.

A businessman in New York learned by practice the value of prayer in his business activity. "In the morning," he says, "I am usually the first to reach my office. I ask God to guide my efforts during the day, and I thank Him in advance for answers to my prayer. Before starting out to interview prospective customers it is my practice to pray by name for each man. I do not pray that I may make a sale, for emphasis upon self-interest tends to break the circuit. It would be dictating to God who may not want a sale made on that particular visit, or on any other visit for that matter. I merely pray for my customer as a person and ask that God may bless him in all his problems.

"The result," he continued, "is that I meet my customers in an atmosphere of friendliness and confidence. I have often noted that we are strangely attuned. Moreover, I have been privileged to help people whom otherwise I would never have contacted. This procedure lifts business above money-making to the plane of human understanding. Of course, it results ultimately in material blessings, not through any mysterious process but simply by being right with God and man. I am able to keep calm and handle each problem as it arises, and in strange ways overcome difficulties which in former years would have floored me completely." Let us turn from this successful businessman to a San Francisco woman who was in despair.

By accident this woman heard a radio talk by the author—a talk dealing with the simple and practical techniques of prayer. She wrote as follows:

> This is my story—as briefly as I can put it—a big story to put in a few words.
>
> In the summer of 1943, one afternoon I turned on the radio—something I seldom if ever do during the day. My next impulse was to turn it off when a sentence caught my ear. I waited for the next sentence and so on till I found myself sitting down by the radio and listening.
>
> I always called myself a Christian, prayed, etc. but for the first time in my life something happened. That afternoon I first heard you, I was in the depths of despair. Things were going from bad to worse until it seemed involuntary bankruptcy was confronting me. Real estate salesmen seemed powerless. From that very afternoon I got a new grip—a new way of praying, I guess. I feel I was led, literally led, step by step to the office door of a woman broker across the Bay, whom I had never even heard of before. She took hold of the properties with vigor, even developed new qualities in them. It would take pages and pages to give you the story.
>
> But, and here is the next great step. I have always had a desire to make designs. I talked very hard to God—asked him to show me definitely what to do. I received word that a two-yard drapery length of mine which I had sent to an International Textile Exhibition had received the first award. This has led to wonderful contacts with some of the best and most reliable firms. They wanted my designs. I am relating all this modestly, with reserve and deep sincere thanks to Our Lord and Father. It is a sample of the way the impossible becomes possible when God is the partner.

People who practice the simple techniques of prayer secure guidance to an unusual degree. They are directed in their activities and contacts by an invisible but definite power. In meeting situations and in dealing with people, they acquire remarkable skill. I do not, of course, believe that there is anything magical in prayer, but from my experience I do feel certain that insights, leads, and illuminations are given to people who habitually practice an attitude of prayer, in which they become amenable to divine guidance. I have seen enough indications of the validity of this statement that I accept it as a scientific injunction, to wit: Yield your mind with its problems to an attitude of prayer. Be willing to accept not what you want or what you think ought to be, but affirm that you will be led in the solution of your problem. The result will be that over a period of time you will clearly see the outlines of a pattern which you, yourself, did not conceive.

John G. Ramsay, Public Relations Representative of the United Steel Workers of America (C.I.O.), told me about a mutual acquaintance who spends one hour each day in prayer. Ramsay smiled and said, "I could not do that. I get enough suggestions from God in two minutes to keep me busy all day long." John Ramsay says that he gets guidance and direction for his daily work from these two minutes of prayer. Here is an example he relates.

"Some months ago I sat down at a table for four in a dining car. Three other men were already seated; as I later discovered, none was acquainted with the other. They all seemed gloomy and depressed. As I do not like to eat a meal in such an atmosphere, I began a conversation which I hoped would lift their spirits. Soon we were talking animatedly—mostly about religion.

"After we finished dinner, one said to me, 'I'd like to talk with you for a few minutes.'

" 'Certainly,' I replied, 'let's go into the lounge car.'

"The Lord must have wanted this conversation to be held, for even though the train was crowded two seats, side by side, awaited us. My new companion told me that when he left home as a boy, his father enjoined him never to allow more than ten minutes to elapse upon a train before talking to the nearest person about his religious life.

" 'On my first train ride,' he said, 'I was seated next to a burly fellow. I kept my eye upon my watch until ten minutes had passed; then, scared to death, I blurted out, 'Are you saved?' I got the rough answer you might expect, and for twenty years I have never spoken to another man about religion.

" 'Today,' he continued, 'you got three men, none of whom had met the other, to talking about religion naturally and interestingly in a couple of minutes. What's your technique?'

"We chatted for some time and, as he rose to leave, he introduced himself as vice president of a certain steel company; then he asked me my name and business.

" 'I am John Ramsay,' I replied. 'I am an organizer for the United Steel Workers of America, and it is my job to organize the employees of your company.'

"Despite differences in point of view, we established fellowship and understanding based upon our common religious faith. I have never thought much about my 'technique,' except that it is to try to live a God-centered life."

This book emphasizes scientific spiritual principles which have been demonstrated in the laboratory of personal experience. Principles of guidance, of prayer, of faith, of simple trust, of relaxation, are presented not as theory, but as the Q.E.D. of actual test. Everything in this book is factual.

Whatever your problem, no matter how difficult, you can release spiritual power sufficient to solve your problem. The secret is—*pray* and *believe*. Even though it may be hard to believe, do it nevertheless. Simply believe that Almighty God will give His power to you. Pray and mentally yield yourself to God's power. Do this by affirming that you have not sufficient power within yourself and that, therefore, you are willing to put yourself completely in contact with spiritual force. The basic secret of the Christian religion is not effort or will power, important as they are. The secret of Christianity is faith. The only struggle it urges you to exert is the effort to believe. The art is to learn to have faith. When you have done so you become a channel through which divine power flows. It flows through *you*. You then have all the strength you need to meet any situation involving you.

As an illustration, here is the personal experience of a man who was "through." From brilliant success he plunged downward; then, at an age when many men retire, he came back. Here is a story that will thrill many—told in the man's own words.

"For upwards of fifty years my life was like a song. Then, for four years I never smiled. I had a lovely wife, three fine sons and a beautiful home. In business, mine was what people call a success story. At forty-seven, I was a Lieutenant Colonel in World War I, in charge of millions of dollars of supplies. At fifty, I was president of a large oil company. At fifty-eight, I was a close associate of one of Wall Street's leading figures. I was on top. Life was good, and I believed that although trouble might come to others, it would not come to me—well, just because it couldn't.

"Suddenly, all went wrong. I was one of the spectacular wrecks of the depression. I lost everything—my personal fortune, the home I loved, quickly, followed by the death of my wife, my idyllic companion for thirty-three years. To climax all my troubles, I was taken with encephalitis, a form of the dread sleeping sickness.

"After many weeks, I was pronounced cured, but there were scars in my emotional system.

"I was looked over by some of the best men in the medical profession, who said, 'Nothing is wrong with you.' I knew there was but, as I look back now, I see that my trouble was not in their line. So I went from neurologist to neurologist, from osteopath to osteopath, from diet faddist to diet faddist. Steadily I lost weight, gained in irritability and became more and more of a trial to my family and friends.

"When I returned to business I got no better; I became a neurasthenic and a hypochondriac of the worst sort. Nothing that anyone said to me that could have been helpful, made the slightest impression. I thought constantly of my troubles, which I sought to unload upon other people. In street-cars I told my woes to anyone who would listen—friend or stranger.

" 'John,' said a friend to me, after I found a new life, 'do you remember an afternoon when I rode uptown with you on the subway? You talked all the way about your illness and your troubles. Finally, I told you I had an engagement, and left the train at Fourteenth Street, just to get away from you.'

"I know now, but didn't then, what a pest I was. The way I carried on, I was the only man in the world who had any troubles. I was resentful and venomous, and I cursed everything in general. Each morning, upon waking I asked myself, 'How in the name of God can I go through with another day?' I found myself hoping that some morning I wouldn't wake up. One day I sat in a hotel lobby, a farewell letter in my hand, deliberating from ten in the morning until late afternoon whether to leap from a top-floor window. I know now that my real trouble was not with my body but with my spirit.

"During this time I made two half-hearted ventures into realms of thought control and of religion. They had helped others, but my faith was weak. My attitude was: 'Well, God, I don't believe You can do anything about this situation, but let's see You try!'

"And to myself I said, 'This requires a miracle, and the days of miracles are past.' Nothing came of these ventures, of course, because there was no faith. But four years after I was stricken, the light of health and happiness dawned upon me in such a way that it could have been only God-directed.

"I was walking down a narrow street, carrying a cane which I used to think I needed, when I inadvertently struck a man who was passing me. Turning to apologize, I found him to be a genial person with an office in the same building with me. He asked me to call, which I did. I found him to be an ardent believer in the power of religious faith. He urged me to put my life in God's hands, to surrender all my troubles to Him and to practice thinking about God instead of myself.

"I was taught to pray and to have faith. This was the turning point in my life.

"It was pointed out to me that my thinking was all wrong; that the first thing I had to do was clear out my mind. (As a man thinketh, so is he.) This is the stuff I cleaned out of my mind! Self-pity, ill-will, fears and other evils. No wonder I was sick. This was the first real mental catharsis I had ever known and it was effective because it was done on a spiritual basis, under the direction of an understanding man.

"After this mental cleansing my friend began to feed my mind on simple, spiritual, wholesome food. I was given a course of reading lessons in spiritual truth. I was shown how to read the Bible. I discovered that the main part of the know-how is just to read it. I purchased one of those Bibles in which the words of Jesus are marked and also I read the Psalms. After reading I would sit quietly, with the thought that these words were passing through my mind like medicine.

"This person also taught me how to use my mind positively rather than negatively. Instead of dwelling mentally upon my troubles, I learned to affirm, in my own mind, that God was helping me at that very minute. Gradually this idea took possession of me. I found that one does become what he affirms he is when he does it in God's name.

"I practiced living with Christ in my mind, often talking to Him as though He were right with me (I know He is). My mind was flooded with a healing sense of peace. I felt myself becoming a new man, fulfilling one of the greatest and truest of all Bible texts: 'If any man be in Christ, he is a new creature: old things are passed away; behold, all things are become new.'

"This new-found power changed everything. I recovered gradually the zest I once had for work. A friend said to me. 'You are yourself again; it's a miracle!'

"Only God could have done this to me and shown the inner reservoirs of peace and strength which are in me now. Within a year God had helped me to become one of the big producers of my company. In succeeding years I have done an annual business of more than one-half million dollars. I claim no credit for this—merely mention it to show what God can do. This may sound materialistic, but it isn't. I cite it only to show the return of strength and power inwardly.

"Some months ago I met the head doctor of one of the big psychiatric clinics I once attended. He asked me how I was. 'Fine,' I replied. 'I've found something which really helped me.' Then I told him of my recovery. 'Well,' he observed, 'we work along the same line, except for excluding the religious element.'

" 'Yes,' I told him, 'that's what's the trouble with it.' Although the clinic was the last word in psychiatry, it was not until I found 'the religious element' that anything happened to me."

The man of this story discovered and put into practice the laws governing prayer and as a result was remade.

Now to sum up. Learn to pray correctly, scientifically. Employ tested and proved methods. Avoid slipshod praying. To guard against perfunctory praying, here are ten rules for saying your prayers. They have proved to be an effective, workable discipline of prayer.

1. Set aside a few minutes to be alone and quiet. Relax body, mind and spirit by turning the thoughts away from problems and fixing the mind on God. Think about Him in the way that is most natural.
2. Talk to God simply and naturally, telling Him anything that is on your mind. Do not think you have to use formal words and phrases. Talk to Him in your own language. He understands it.
3. Practice talking to God as you go about the business of the day. On the subway or bus, or at your desk, close your eyes for a moment to shut out the world and have a word or two with God. This will remind you of His presence and give you a sense of His nearness.
4. Affirm the fact that God is with you and helping you. That is to say, do not always beseech God for His blessings, but affirm the fact that He is now giving you His blessings.
5. Pray with the thought that your prayers reach out and surround your loved ones with God's love and care.
6. Think positive, not negative, thoughts when you pray.
7. Always state in your prayer that you are willing to accept God's will, whatever it is. Ask him for what you want, but express your willingness to take what He wants.
8. In your prayer simply put everything into God's hands. Pray for strength to do your best, and with confidence leave the rest to God.
9. Say a word of prayer for people who do not like you or have treated you badly. This will help them and release tremendous power in you.
10. At some time during every day say a word of prayer for this troubled world, for our country and for a lasting peace.

Then—*believe* that your prayers will be answered. "What things soever ye desire, when ye pray, *believe* that ye receive them, and ye shall have them."

7

FORGET FAILURES AND GO AHEAD

ONE OF THE MOST important of all skills is that of forgetting. It is said that a man is what he thinks, or what he eats. A man is also what he forgets.

I am not straining to be paradoxical when I say that to be happy and successful you must cultivate the ability to say to yourself—forget it! It may not be easy, neither is it as hard as you think, but—one thing is certain, you must learn to forget.

Memory is one of the greatest of our faculties. The ability to retain information and experience is of vital importance. But it is a more subtle art to be able to cast out of the mind—or at least from a commanding place in it—failures, events, unhappy things that should be forgotten. It is a great skill to be able to be selective and say, "I will hold this in cherished memory. This other I shall cast from me." To be efficient, to be happy, to have full control of your powers, and to go ahead successfully, you must learn how to forget.

Anyone who deals with personality problems in an intimate way is bound soon to become aware of the importance of forgetting. In dealing with people one finds that their problems really center around a few simple propositions—fear, guilt, selfishness, self-centeredness, and the inability to forget.

I know a top executive, who has risen by hard effort and marked ability to an important position, but he will not hold it unless he learns to forget. He is a man of considerable rigidity and wants everything to be just so. His wife died recently. He thinks of her as the finest person he ever knew. But she was rather carefree, while he was rigid.

Perhaps she wasn't quite as good a housekeeper as she might have been, and that annoyed him. Now she is gone and he remembers only his criticisms. He comes home at night and sadly says to himself, "I would willingly have everything out of place if only I had her back." He is haunted by remorse, by regret, by the memory of little complaints he made.

I told him that where his wife is now, in the greatness and vastness of the eternal life, these little things do not matter. All that matters is the greatness of her love for him. If she could, she would tell him so. I warned him that if he does not learn to forget, then the heavy burden of regret will deteriorate him. She lived her life. She knew that he loved her . . . For this man the future of his life depends upon whether he can put these regrets in the past and go forward.

Repeatedly in personal counseling one encounters this tragic inability of people to forget. A curious case is that of a man who cannot write when he gets nervous. When he goes to a hotel to register, his fingers refuse to function. He says that he deliberately goes to the end of the line so that everybody may register ahead of him. He does not want anybody to see him make "this awful signature," with fingers that do not function properly.

I suggested that he go to a hotel, get at the head of the line, and in a loud voice that everybody in the lobby could hear shout, "Gather 'round, gather 'round, see the worst signature in the United States." That might help free him from this crippling inhibition. To overcome the nervousness of his fingers, he must break a long line of memory that goes back to the past, to childhood.

When he was a small boy, his father suffered a muscular accident that destroyed the ability of his fingers to write. The father became horribly self-conscious about it. He told the boy about it so often and so impressed it upon the boy's mind, that although there was, of course, no organic injury to the boy's fingers, there was what amounted to an injury to the mind. Long memory reaches out and puts its inhibitions on the fingers of the boy, now a man. It is a startling illustration of how a deeply held thought reaching far back in memory can render a man ineffective.

But it is necessary to develop skill in the art of forgetting. I have emphasized that the Bible is the wisest of all Books. The Bible contains the formula for forgetting: "This one thing I do, forgetting those things which are behind, and reaching forth unto those things which are before, I press toward the mark . . ." (Philippians 3:13–14). This formula contains the secret of how to forget and go ahead.

"This one thing I do." The man who said this was resolutely disciplining his thoughts and controlling them. At the precise minute a man determines to control his thoughts, he is on the way to self-mastery. Usually our thoughts control us. The first step in forgetting is the simple determination to forget; to turn your back on something by reaching out to the things that lie ahead. Practice that thought pattern and you can break the hold of unhappy memory.

Mrs. Peale was at a meeting out on the plains of the West, representing one of the denominational boards of our church, of which she was president. People came from miles around to this meeting, and all stayed for a church dinner. There had been a drought and much privation among the farmers of the plains. She sat across the table from a hard bitten, old

North Dakota farmer—a shy man with big, rough hands. She tried to interest him in conversation but he did not respond.

So finally she asked him, "How are the crops this year?"

"The crops, well, I guess there aren't any crops this year," he replied. She asked, "How is that?"

"Well," he said, "first we had grasshoppers—they ate up nearly everything. Then came a dust storm that destroyed what was left. But I was lucky. I got in five per cent of my crop, but my brother, who lives near me didn't get in anything."

The devastation was so awful that she sat awestruck and finally asked, "How do you feel about that?"

"Oh," said he, "I don't think about it any more. You see—I aimed to forget it."

This farmer had not enjoyed the benefit of the schools or other advantages, but for years he had gone to a little church on the plains. The winds swept against it, the snow piled deep around it in winter. It was seared by the heat of the summer, and the rains of the spring and the autumn beat against it. It had rough, wooden benches and old worn hymn books, but there he heard some very wise words, "This one thing I do, forgetting those things which are behind, I press toward the mark." The old man had found it a solid philosophy in disciplining the mind. He "aimed to forget." He may have lost that one crop but he saved himself.

Of course, some people can do that by force of will, but most people are not endowed with any tremendous power of will. It is very difficult to eject a thought by merely saying, "Be gone." Often such an attempt only tends to fix a thought more firmly in the mind. One must be more subtle. The secret is to substitute thoughts. *Expel one thought by substituting a more powerful thought.*

I have had some interesting correspondence with a doctor in the Midwest. He uses his religion soundly and skillfully in the practice of medicine. He told me about the ailments of some of his patients (no names, of course) and asked, "As a spiritual doctor, what would you prescribe in these various cases?"

He has one patient whose employer was unjust to him and dishonest as well. The doctor is satisfied that the facts are true and that the employer is as represented—cruel, unkind, dishonest, although he stays within the limits of legality. As a result of his ill-will toward the employer, the patient developed a peptic ulcer. The doctor says the ulcer is primarily caused by his disturbed state of mind. The hate thoughts, the revenge thoughts, the ill-will thoughts have made him sick.

He says, "The problem is to change the patient's thoughts if the ulcer is to be cured." The patient must change his thinking about his employer. He must stop secreting the poison of resentment. I cited the case of another man who became miserable through being resentful of people.

One day he was reading the Bible and saw the statement, "Vengeance is mine, I will repay, saith the Lord." "Well," he said, "if the Lord is willing to bother about these resentments, I will let him take care of this man who has mistreated me. The minute I shifted the responsibility of getting even with the fellow over to the Lord, and off my shoulders, I felt a hundred per cent better."

The Lord, in due time, will indeed "take care" of the person who has mistreated you. Why not follow this good advice and let God handle the matter? Do not waste your time in carrying thoughts of ill will toward somebody, because those thoughts do not hurt that somebody; they hurt only you. They may give you peptic ulcers.

Oftentimes a person will agitate you in order to annoy you. Knowing that you are annoyed, he is happy or at least thinks he is. I advised the doctor that he suggest to his patient this idea about mentally shifting the responsibility of resentment over to God. I suggested further that he persuade his patient to try the most subtle form of retaliation: namely, that he pray for the man who had mistreated him and thus set spiritual forces flowing back toward him; in short, conquer him by love. This is the most scientific of all reactions to an ill-will situation. As you affirm goodwill toward an enemy your mind will tend to forget and so gain relief. Shift the emphasis of the mind and master the art of forgetting.

Long held grudges, deep seated hates, form impenetrable obstacles to the flow of power through a personality. It is difficult to eliminate ill-will with its poisonous effects from the mind by merely being willing to do so. It is not quite that simple in the case of an habitual mental attitude.

The secret, as indicated, is to use a reverse method. Try to pray for the person you do not like. I realize that this may almost seem hypocritical, though it is not, but it is a method that will work. In so doing, you are setting against the corrosive effect of a grudge the only force more powerful than hate, namely, good-will or love. Long established poisons secreted by ill-will are dissipated by the curative force of good will.

Even the striving, however feebly, after an attitude of good will toward another person helps one to forget mistreatment. Many people are ruining their efficiency, making themselves miserable and in fact destroying any possibility of a happy future, simply because they will not forget insults, slights, or unfairness.

A man came to me with the complaint that "he simply had to get some peace inside of him." He could not sleep nights. He was nervous and tense. He snapped at people. Naturally, everybody steered clear of him.

In our church clinic we went over his attitudes, his daily schedule, and his general practices of thought and action. All checked well except one thing. He had what amounted to almost a hatred for certain competitors in his particular business. It happened that most of these men were of another race and religion and there was some prejudice mixed up in the matter, but mostly it was merely personal conflict, jealousy, ill-will and unforgiveness.

I assured him he could be cured if he would follow the spiritual prescription I would give him. He replied that he would follow it, but almost broke his promise when the prescription was outlined. "For the next two weeks," I said, "you are to pray twice a day for each of your competitors by name. You are not to pray for yourself at all during this period. You are to pray that each of these men shall do a bigger business this year than you do."

"Why," he shouted, "that would be a big lie."

"Not in the mind of your true self," I replied.

"You must get rid of the attitude of mind that is defeating you," I said. "You must learn to forget, and the only way to do it is to pray yourself into good-will if the poisons of ill-will are to be eliminated."

Grudgingly he promised to carry out this procedure, and he did. He reported afterward that for the first week it was a very painful process.

"Imagine it," he said, "my praying and asking that those good-for-nothing high binders should go past me in business. But what do you know! As I kept at it, one day when I was praying, of a sudden I felt better inside. I felt light as a feather and happy and experienced such relief as you have no idea."

"The pain that was inside of you, has it left you?" I asked.

"Yes," he replied, "It was just like a great wave of peace coming into me."

Now, months later, he tells me that he has even learned to like the men he formerly hated. He had a block that was causing a lessening of power in his mind. Had he kept on with this hatred, he would probably have become a sick man. Many people would find if they would honestly trace it back in their minds that much of their nervousness, irritability, even physical ills are caused by personal conflict and hate that they will not forget. In the instance of this man, his emotional sickness was healed by employing a powerful spiritual antidote, and as a result he became happy and efficient. He learned to forget and so he was able to go ahead.

One should not only "forget those things which are behind," but also "reach forth unto those things that are before." There should always be the idea of forward moving—moving away from a situation which one desires to forget. I know a wealthy widow, a gracious and lovely lady. Like many people who trust other's honesty and kindness, she was fleeced out of a large sum. She lost thousands of dollars, and futilely she asked again and again, "Why did I do it?"

She had to learn to think of her experience as money well spent, for she learned a lesson. "It is worth fifty thousand dollars to you to learn that all kinds of people exist in the world, so take your lesson and walk away from it a wiser woman," I commented. Walk away from things that are over and past and cannot be helped. Reach forth to the things that are before. Take your lesson—make yourself wiser. Avoid useless post-mortems on past mistakes. Forget them and go ahead.

My friend, Grove Patterson, Editor of the *Toledo Blade*, and one of the greatest editors in America, says that he was a frequent victim of his own post-mortems. He would lie awake nights trying to figure out why he did this or that, or didn't do it. But he found a solution. Not being able to do anything about it, he just forgot it by saying, "So what!" This, says Grove Patterson, induces a strange tranquility. Of course it does, for it relieves the mind of the foolishness of carrying past actions which for good or ill are done.

Whatever has happened, it makes no difference what, there are only two things to do: (1) do everything that you reasonably can about it; (2) then practice forgetting it. Walk away from it in your thoughts. Conceive of it as lying back there growing ever more dim against the horizon as each day carries you farther from it. Unless you do this you will hamper your efficiency. If in addition to present problems, you pile high on your memory past actions that are now outdated, you will go staggering through life under an impossible load.

A high-ranking Army officer came to my office. He paced the floor, he wept. He was a big, fine looking man, and he apologized for weeping. I went out of the room and said, "Go ahead, cry it out." When I returned he said, "My life is ruined."

He had been drinking considerably.

"I tried to forget it by drinking," he explained, "but couldn't so I went out and got into a taxi and said to the driver, 'Take me to a church.'"

"What church?" the taxi driver asked.

"Any church," the officer replied.

"Catholic or Protestant?" asked the driver.

"Protestant preferably, but any church, take me to a house of God," was the man's reply. And the taxi driver brought him to our church.

"Well," I asked, "what is the matter?"

"I was never cut out for this military business," he explained. "I hate it with all my heart. I am a farmer and all my life I have loved growing things, I love life, I hate the destructiveness of war. I have seen it all, I have been through the most terrible experiences, things I shall never be able to forget," he replied.

"What is the main thing you won't forget?" I asked.

He replied, "One American soldier had shot another and I sat on the court and we voted him death. As long as I live I shall never cease to see the face of the kid, when one of his own American officers read the sentence that he was to die. I shall never forget his face."

This man obviously faced deterioration unless he could properly learn the art of forgetting.

"You thought you did your duty, didn't you?" I said.

He replied, "Yes."

I continued, "The boy is dead, isn't he?"

"Yes," said he.

"You can't bring him back," I told him. "You as a representative of the sovereign rights of a nation passed judgment upon him. It was part of your duty as a soldier."

I said, "My friend, it is done. Why don't you look at that face that you say you will never cease to see and say, 'Son, I want to live for you as I live for myself, and in the long years that are to come, if there is anything wrong with the whole military system, I will do my utmost to correct it. I will live for your country and mine and the things for which you died.' "

The act had been irrevocable. He could not go back and restore the boy to life. This officer had to walk away from it, whether it was a mistake or not. The cure consisted of forgetting that which was past, and also of reaching forth unto the things that are before. He picked up his hat, there was a look of peace on his face and he said, "I see it. I have something greater than I realized to live for."

He asked and received forgiveness for any wrong done. Now he must forget the things that are behind, weave any mistakes into the pattern of life, discipline his thinking by bringing into the mind spiritual thoughts of God's purpose, and walk away from the mistakes (if such they are), having learned wisdom from them.

My friend, Dr. Smiley Blanton, an eminent psychiatrist, once stated to me that in his opinion the wisest psychiatric statement ever made was the words from Ephesians, "Having done all, stand." These words were uttered many generations ago by one of the most astute minds history has ever produced, a man named St. Paul. Dr. Blanton said that he has read practically everything in the field of psychiatry and that there is nothing to equal the wisdom and insight contained in these few words, "Having done all, stand."

The psychiatric, curative value of St. Paul's statement is based on the simple process—do the best you can. Do all you can. Give a proposition or a problem or a situation all the energy both physical and mental of which you are capable. Leave no stone unturned. Exercise all your ingenuity and efficiency, then realize there is nothing further that you can do about it; therefore, there is no use fretting, worrying, or engaging in mental post-mortems; no use rehashing or going over the situation. You have done all you can do, therefore *stand*; that is, do not allow yourself to be upset, trust God and trust what you have done. It will come out the way it ought to come out if you will just leave it alone.

When Henry Ford was seventy-five years old, he was asked the secret of his health and calm spirit. "Three rules," he answered, "I do not eat too much; I do not worry too much; if I do my best, I believe that what happens, happens for the best."

The fact that religious people, that is, genuinely religious people, learn this art almost by second nature, is one of the reasons why the practice of religion is so vitally important.

I saw a very interesting and unforgettable demonstration of this truth in a railroad station in a large city during wartime. The gateman, a huge fellow, let some soldiers through the gate when the train came in before he allowed the civilians to pass through. A humble mother clung to a young soldier, to the boy's obvious embarrassment. She was making quite a demonstration of her grief, which apparently she was unable to control. The son gently, but firmly, was trying to get away from his mother, for unconsciously he realized that she was approaching hysteria. As he passed from sight through the gate, she sank against an iron rail and sobbed bitterly. Indeed, she all but screamed.

I was standing near by and noticed that as the crowd moved through the gate, the gateman was watching her closely.

Presently he left his post and went over and spoke to the woman. A change seemed to come over her as he talked. He assisted her to a seat. Her sobbing ceased and she leaned back, calm and relaxed. Then I heard him say as he left her, "Remember now what I told you."

My curiosity aroused, I engaged him in conversation. "I watched you handle that woman, and if I am not too inquisitive, I would like to know what you said to her."

"Oh," he replied, "I didn't say anything."

"I am sure you must have said something very helpful," I coaxed, "for obviously it had its effect upon her. I would be interested in knowing just what you did tell her."

"Well, I will tell you. It is this way. I saw that she had lost her grip, so I just went over and said to her, 'Listen, Mother, I know exactly how you feel. I have been through it myself. Lots of people have, but you have just got to forget these things. I don't mean that you are going to forget the boy, but you are going to forget your fears.' Then I just added, 'Put your faith in God and He will see both you and the boy through.'"

A bit surprised, I asked him, "Are you a religious man?"

"What does it sound like?" he asked.

This man was wise in the ways of human nature because he was a student of spiritual techniques. He realized that this woman needed to know how to forget her fears that she might go ahead. He knew how to apply mental and spiritual therapeutic. She, on the other hand, was able to receive his guidance. In each of them faith was an active quality. Thus the mental adjustment was made which gave her power to go ahead. Her mind accepted the sane and sensible proposition that "having done all" she could "stand."

Adversity and failure may become obsessions which freeze the mind, thus preventing new ideas from gaining entrance. One must be able to forget adversity and failure and go forward. If a person will keep his mind fluid, new insights and ideas will come.

I know a man and his wife who discovered how to perform this very important feat of forgetting in order to make progress.

This gentleman was a partner in a business which suffered a disastrous fire and he emerged from this tragedy all but ruined financially. It broke the spirit of both the man and wife. The wife sat home and worried about it, and he went out and worried about it, futilely tramping the streets. "Why did this have to happen to us?" they bewailed again and again. They simply could not forget it, and not only were they failing to recoup but they were both getting into a highly nervous state.

In fact, the wife worried so much that finally they sent her off to a sanitarium. While she was in the sanitarium she stumbled on a new idea of praying. She discovered that it is not effective to pray frantically and in an attitude of desperation, for in so doing the mind is not receptive. Fear has closed it against any fresh concept. She learned to pray in a relaxed manner. She definitely practiced relaxing her body before beginning to pray. She relaxed her mind by giving the entire problem into the hands of God. In her prayer she said that she and her husband were ready to do anything that God wanted them to do, if He would show them.

After a few days her mind took a strange turn. She began to think of some pot holders she had made. The idea of these pot holders kept coming into her mind. They were simple little things made out of cloth, merely little pot holders that she had sewed herself. They constantly kept coming into her mind as she prayed. Finally in her prayer she said, "Lord, what is that you are trying to tell me about these pot holders?" She declares that the Lord seemed to say to her, "Go home and start making pot holders."

She felt this so keenly that she did go home and started making them. Her husband, a great giant of a fellow, sat in the kitchen and helped her. One day to his amazement he sold the whole lot of them to the purchasing agent of a chain store who said, "These are wonderful pot holders. We will take all you can make."

They went on making pot holders and then she thought of some other things to make. She was very handy. She began to make other little knick-knacks which her husband sold to the store chain. To sum it up, they finally built a plant and at the present time have about four hundred employees making a great array of the most interesting and useful articles.

This woman's discovery of a new and simple technique of prayer did two things for her. First, it released her from failure by teaching her how to forget; and in the second place, having freed her mind of the creeping paralysis of this developing obsession about the past, she got an insight which changed everything and opened up a successful future.

This woman had to face a crisis. Usually we think of a crisis as a dangerous something that we wish we did not have to face. Perhaps when our civilization is older we may acquire some of the timeless wisdom of the East. The Chinese word for crisis has two characters. The first character means "danger." But the second character means "opportunity." And there you have it: a crisis is a danger point and an opportunity too. It all depends on whether you can forget the failures and mistakes and look expectantly to see in your situation, however unhappy it may be on the surface, the unexpected values and great opportunity it may contain.

8

HOW TO BE FREE FROM FEAR

"THE COMMONEST AND subtlest of all human diseases is fear," says a distinguished physician.

A well-known psychologist declares that fear is the most disintegrating enemy of human personality.

Obviously these scientific men are referring not to normal but to abnormal fear. Normal fear is both necessary and desirable. It is a mechanism designed for our protection. Without normal fear a person cannot be a well-organized personality. He would be lacking in ordinary and sensible caution. Normal fear prevents us from taking chances, from doing hazardous and foolish things.

But the line of distinction between normal and abnormal fear is very finely drawn. Before one realizes, he may step across the line from normal fear into the dark and shadowy regions of abnormal fear. And what a terror abnormal fear is! It disturbs your days and haunts your nights. It is a center and source of complexes. It tangles the mind with obsessions. It draws off energies, destroys inner peace, blocks power. It reduces one to ineffectiveness and frustrates ambitions. Abnormal fear is the poisonous well out of which dismal unhappiness is drawn. It makes life literally a hell. Many are they who suffer from this grievous malady. How pathetic and pitiful they are—the unhappy victims of abnormal fear.

But you can be free from such fear. Abnormal fear can be cured. In this chapter we shall outline a cure that will work if you will work it.

A doctor, in boyhood, developed a fear psychosis. It grew upon him until by the time he entered medical school it was drawing off the energies of his mind so much that it was only by Herculean efforts that he was able to do his work. It put an abnormal strain on his energies which left him weak and ineffective.

With great expenditure of nervous energy he finally graduated and went into internship still carrying his heavy burden of fear.

Finally, unable to stand it longer he consulted one of his medical teachers and said, "I must be rid of this terrible burden of fear or I will have to give up." The older physician, a wise and kindly man, directed the young student to a Healer who, as he cleverly said, "keeps office in the New Testament."

"I followed my teacher's suggestion," he declared, "and that Physician gave me a medicine which made me well."

And what was this medicine? It was not a liquid in a bottle, nor was it compounded as a pellet, but it was in the form of words. It was that potent combination of words called a Biblical text. "For God hath not given us the spirit of fear; but of power, and of love, and of a sound mind." (II Timothy 1:7.)

"I *took* those words," said the young doctor. "I allowed them to sink deeply into my mind. By a process of intellectual and spiritual osmosis, their healing potency penetrated and infiltrated into my mind and in due course deliverance came, followed by a strange sense of peace."

It is remarkable what a few words can do when they are the right words. Dr. Edward Trudeau, famed pioneer in the treatment of tuberculosis, who himself succumbed to that disease, gained strength by repeating several times daily the word "acquiescence." He would say it slowly, allowing its great meaning to sink deeply into his mind. Dr. Paul Dubois, Swiss psychotherapist, who had to struggle against obstacles, practiced saying the word "invulnerability."

I have observed the strange power in a similar use of Bible verses. The Bible advocates this practice, for it says, "If you abide in me, and my words abide in you, ye shall ask what ye will, and it shall be done unto you." (John 15:7.) That is to say, if a person *abides* (meaning a long-term, habitual, mental immersion) in communion with Christ, and allows Christ's words to *"abide"* (that is, to linger as a permanent thought in the mind), he will develop such a potentiality of power that life will flow toward him rather than away from him. He will be released and his powers function efficiently. Law then operates in his favor rather than against him, for now his changed thought pattern has put him in harmony with law or truth.

If you are troubled by fear, I suggest that you too "take" these healing words, "For God hath not given us the spirit of fear; but of power, and of love, and of a sound mind."

But what is the "medicine" that is compounded in these words? One of the words is *power*. What power? The only power that can counteract fear is the power of faith. Faith is ordinarily thought of as theological, as the acceptance of a creed. We also think of faith as an intellectual proposition, an assent to an idea. But there is another meaning to faith. It is something alive and active. It is a vital substance like sunlight, like the violet ray, like the growth of our beings. Faith is not only theological and intellectual, but also acts as a medicine. That is to say, it is a healing property for the mind, the soul, and often the body as well.

How is medicine taken? Ordinarily through the mouth or by injection into the blood stream, but there are other entrances through which medicine may be inserted. One is through the eye. For example, pick up the Bible and read some of its great words. A reflection is made on the retina of the eye. This image changes into the form of an idea: a positive idea of faith. The idea passes through the mind until it arrives at the infection point caused by fear. There it throws its healing influence around the center of infection. It drives off infection and finally through the therapeutic operation of a spiritual idea the diseased idea is cast from the mind. One, therefore, has taken medicine (a healing agent) through the reading of the Scriptures. A powerfully healthy idea has driven out an unhealthy idea.

Again, you may take spiritual medicine through the ear. Go to church. Hear the Bible read. Listen to the sermon. Sound waves fall upon your ear and are admitted into the brain in the form of a spiritual idea. By a similar process the healing idea makes its way to the diseased center and engages in battle with the fear thought. By reason of its superior power, faith drives fear out and takes possession.

The mind having been cleansed, the center of infection heals rapidly until a normal condition again prevails. This may be a curious way of describing the effect of faith in the mind, but this concept of faith as a vital healing agent has worked for so many that its validity is proven.

The world is filled with worried, anxious people, who are made so because of the thoughts they habitually think. If such people will practice the creative idea of religious faith, allowing it to dominate their minds, everything can become different. Many people have been healed of the debilitating influence of fear through no other means than a new concept of faith entering their minds.

A prominent businessman came for an appointment. "Do you think I am losing my mind?" was his question.

"You look rational enough," I replied. "What makes you think you are losing your mind?"

"Because I cannot make the simplest decisions," he replied. "Throughout my business career I have handled matters of large importance and have made decisions affecting vast sums of money. But now the simplest and most seemingly unimportant decisions cause me no end of struggle. When finally I make a decision, I am haunted by the possibility I have decided incorrectly. As a result I am filled with fear. Perhaps my inability to make decisions is caused by my fear. Anyway I seem to be afraid of everything. I have been sitting in the balcony of your church on Sundays and am interested in the idea of faith as a healing property.

"Throughout my life when I have been sick physically, I have gone to doctors and they have given me prescriptions. Now I am not sick in my body, but I believe I certainly am sick emotionally and spiritually. I am slipping badly. Can't you give me a spiritual prescription?" he asked.

"Yes," I replied. "I can give you a spiritual prescription and if you will take it faithfully, you will get well."

"That is what I want," he said, "and I will faithfully practice it."

I gave him the following "prescription." When you awaken in the morning before you arise, completely relax yourself. Stretch your arms out as far as possible, then allow them to fall limply on the bed. Do the same with your legs. Also practice opening and closing your eyes by letting your eyelids drop laxly. Relax your fingers. Then conceive of your entire body as being inert, yielded to the bed. Completely let go. Allow all the tension to go out of you. (This method of relaxation was more fully described in earlier chapters.)

When you feel that you have accomplished this, close your eyes and pray. "God, I am going to get up now and go to the office. You are going with me, for you said, 'I am with you always.' I shall not be afraid all day long because you are with me. I shall have some decisions to make, but you will be with me, helping me, and the decisions will be made satisfactorily because you will be there to guide me."

"Next," I said, "go to your office and after lunch lie down, if you have a place to do so. If not, lean forward on your desk. Put your head on your hands. Again relax the body and having done so, pray saying, 'Lord, we had a wonderful morning together. We made some decisions and they are good decisions because you were with me. We are forgetting them now and I am not afraid, for you are with me.' "

Finally, "Go to bed at a reasonable hour. Before you get into bed, throw up the windows, fill the room with fresh air, take a half-dozen deep breaths, inhale and exhale deeply, slowly. Deep breathing has a powerful effect in reducing tension. Then get into bed and again practice the formula of relaxation."

"What about saying my prayers? I always say them on my knees by my bed," he complained.

"Well," I replied, "evidently the kind of prayers you have been saying on your knees haven't been doing you much good, so we will change the method of your prayers. I believe it is a good thing to kneel down to pray for the spirit of adoration is stimulated by the act of kneeling, but it is a mistake to become so stereotyped in your method of prayer that the freshness goes out of it. Try another method for awhile, if only for the sake of variety."

"That is wonderful," he said, "I always wanted to pray in bed but my wife would never let me because she said I would go to sleep before my prayers were finished."

"God would understand that," I said. "It isn't so much what you say as that you think of Him. He knows what is in your mind anyway.

"Get in bed and relax. Then close your eyes and pray, 'Lord, we had a great day together. I wasn't afraid because you were with me all day long.

We made some decisions and they must be all right for you helped me make them. Now you will be with me in the darkness to watch over me. The decisions are made. We shall let them stand, and we shall have a great time tomorrow.'

"Then turn out the light and repeat these words, 'He giveth his beloved sleep.' Then go to sleep. Don't be afraid of anything."

On a sheet of paper I wrote "Spiritual Prescription" and outlined the above described process. A man with a great brain has the ability to be simple. I have never seen a first-class mind that could not be naive, simple, and even childlike. An intellect that cannot react simply is not a first-class mind no matter how profound a man may appear to be. This gentleman had a first-class mind.

"Take that prescription three times a day for two weeks," I said. "Then come back and see me."

Today he is a well man. His mind is clear. He is not afraid. He is in perfect control and is having the time of his life helping other people. He says he cannot understand how he lived so long and missed this "simple and wonderful secret."

Some time later I met an important executive of a large organization. He pulled from his pocket a little paper on which was written "Spiritual Prescription."

"Where did you get that?" I asked, and found that our friend had given it to him. This executive commented, "It worked for him and I was greatly impressed. It works for me also."

You do not need to be haunted by fear. Your religion can help you. It acts as a medicine, releasing power in your mind, the power of faith which drives away fear.

That the technique of faith eliminates fear many can testify. "The first time I jumped from a plane," a paratrooper told me, "everything in me resisted. All there was between death and me was a piece of cord and a little patch of silk, but when I actually found out for myself that the patch of silk would hold me, I had the most marvelous feeling of exultation in all my life. I wasn't afraid of anything and the release from fear filled me with exquisite delight. I really did not want to come down; I was actually happy."

Fear defeats us because we are unwilling to put our trust in what we regard as an ethereal thing, namely, faith in God, but like the paratrooper, when we leap out, trusting to faith, we find that this mystic and apparently fragile thing actually holds us up.

This is an important truth but I must confess that it took me years to learn it and even longer to be willing to practice it. Strange how we can have at hand the formula that can mean so much, yet we will not take this attitude: "I will do all that I can do about any problem. Beyond that I shall trust in God and know my faith will hold me up."

The second ingredient in the medicine against fear is love. Love is one of the most misunderstood and misused words in the English language. Hollywood and current fiction have made of it a sticky, even questionable sentiment. It has been made synonymous with sex. But love is not that at all. It is a strong, dominant, curative emotion or force. It is the power by which we make transference to other people and through which they help us. It is also the power by which we make transference to other people and through which they help us. It is also the power by which we make transference to God, through which God loving us, gives us strength and power. "Perfect love casteth out fear," because perfect love is complete trust.

Love is the natural, naive, basic relation that a human being should have with God. When he does, he can move through this world unafraid. He believes that someone is with him who loves him. He knows that he can trust this someone to protect him and watch over him.

If you really want to know how to live, associate with children. If you have none of your own, borrow some. There are times when I would almost be willing to lend you my three, but I would want them back very quickly, for I would become very stodgy without them.

When our first child arrived, I was afraid to touch her, thinking she would break to pieces. I know now that they are not as fragile as they seem and have been convinced that a little rough treatment helps them. I was not quite so fearful of our second child. He was a little tougher than his older sister, but it was not until our third baby came that I was really released.

I found great pleasure in tossing her high in the air. I did not toss her so far that I couldn't catch her, but she always seemed to enjoy being tossed. As I threw her up, she would take a breath, and then as she came down, she would snuggle into my arms and laugh like a rippling brook, and then cry, "Do it again, Daddy." I became amazed by the fact that apparently she had no fear. Children are said to have two basic fears, fear of falling and fear of loud noises, but she had no fear of being tossed. I think it was because instinctively she knew that the person tossing her loved her; therefore she trusted him. "Perfect love casteth out all fear" in her, so she yielded herself to the fun and was perfectly relaxed.

One of the wisest things ever said was when Jesus Christ advised us to have the attitude and mind of little children. Our so-called "smart" sophistication has just about ruined us emotionally. It may be one reason for the tension, "nerves," and breakdowns of our time. Form a simple love for God as a kindly Father who will take care of you. If you learn to love Him, you will learn to trust Him and then you will not say to yourself with terror, "I wonder what is going to happen? How will I ever get through this thing?" Trust God, believing He will see you through. This is a simple dogma of Christianity but it is one of the most neglected and unused. Develop a simple childlike trust in God and see how your problem of fear clears up.

It might be a good idea in church to take up not one collection, but two. Very large baskets might be used for the second collection, the ushers bringing them down the aisles. The people might be asked to put not money but their fears in these baskets. When all the fears had been gathered up, let the ushers bring these baskets to the altar. They would be so heavy now that the ushers would stagger under them, but what sense of release would be in that congregation! Only one song could be appropriately sung, "Praise God from whom all blessings flow." The released congregation would sing with such fervor that the very roof would tremble.

But do you know what would happen after the benediction? The people would start out and then one by one with sheepish grin they would turn and come back to the basket in which each had placed his fear and fish around until he had found it. People are so used to their fears that they would feel homesick without them. People become such victims of fear that they are afraid to walk away from them.

But when a man habitually affirms, "I love God, He has been good to me and I can trust Him, so I am going to put my fear in His hands and walk away from it," that man will find release.

If you are worrying about something, practice this little formula before you start out tomorrow morning. Stop for a minute and say, "God is with me. He loves me. I can trust Him. So I will do my best and I won't be afraid." You can depend upon this to work, after you have practiced it for a few days. Make this an automatic procedure and it will release a tremendous power against fear in your personality.

The final ingredient in the medicine for the cure of fear is a "sound mind." Obviously the reason we have fears is because we develop an unsound or tangled mind. The unsound mind develops in various ways. It often begins in childhood when parents unconsciously implant their own fears and anxieties in the child's mind.

It also develops from the breakdown of morals so widely prevalent today. People get the idea that the Christian moral code no longer prevails and that they may violate it with impunity. They learn to their sorrow that what we call sin is, in reality, a wound in the mind. Sorrow, for example, is a clean wound. It hurts, it cuts deeply, but it will heal because there is no infection in it. But sin is an unclean wound. It is a foreign substance invading the mind and the mind tries to close around it but it cannot; it becomes infected.

A man may carry this guilt through youthful years and even into middle life, but all the time like a suppurating tooth, it sends infection into his emotional system. Men will sometimes break down and attribute the disaster to overwork and it may be that, but often the real cause may be the infection-drain of a sense of guilt. Out of this state of infection rise the ghosts which haunt a man's mind. These ghosts fill him with fear and his mind becomes so tangled with obsessive notions, reactions and impulses that everything is tinctured with fear.

It is really a very pathetic thing when one allows a foreign substance to enter one's mind. If you were to open up a fine watch and push a pebble into the works, people would think you were demented. Yet people do an equally destructive thing to their minds. It has got so that if anyone tries to dissuade people from committing this offense against themselves, he is termed an old fogy or mossback.

I have observed over a period of years in the religio-psychologio clinic of our church that a very large number who come to us for treatment are people afflicted with a sense of guilt. It is curious how many of those who come are on the young side of life, that is, under forty. Fear is their main trouble. Often the basic cause is that having departed from moral living they have become victims of a sense of guilt. The end of the process is such a tangle of emotional reactions that St. Paul's implication of an unsound mind is not far from the facts.

They are afraid that they will be found out. They are afraid of the future. They have lost confidence in themselves. They are afraid of other people. They have become victims of blind, unreasoning, fundamental fear. They have a psychosis. They throw the lie right back in the face of the unsophisticated novice in life who tells them that they must be "emancipated." There is only one way to be emancipated and that is through the discipline of spiritual morality. Follow that and you will not be afraid of man nor the devil. Your mind will be sound, stable and rational.

How is the "unsound mind" cured? Analysis often-times is helpful. When you understand why you react in a certain way, improvement often begins at once. Self-knowledge leads to self-improvement. The practice of spiritual formulae is helpful. One of the great needs is for people to know the "how" of practicing the spiritual life. People are urged to pray, but are not told exactly how to pray. We are urged to have faith, but are not instructed in the precise and workable procedures of faith. Our forefathers worked out techniques which were satisfactory to them. We need now to relearn the simple ABC's of how to put the curative principles of faith into operation.

In an attempt to meet this need the following incidents may serve as a suggested practice. These represent two simple "spiritual devices" which were employed successfully in the cases of two people who appealed for help . . .

There came to our church clinic a successful New York businessman who was haunted by fear. The strain was breaking him down, and he knew that he must find a cure for his fears.

He had started attending church, which he had not done for a long time. Then he came for an interview. He described attitudes and actions which certainly had infection qualities in them. He thoroughly cleansed his mind by confession. He received forgiveness, but his fears had continued for so long that he could not let them go. God had forgiven him, but he had difficulty forgiving himself.

He called upon me about every fortnight. I told him there was nothing to be afraid of. He would leave with his mind at rest, but two weeks later the fears would return and he would be back again. I finally said to him, "You fail to get rid of this state of fear because you are always asking God to remove it, yet not believing that He is doing so. You are an expert asker, but a poor receiver. What good do you accomplish by asking continuously, yet never practicing the art of receiving?"

I quoted the Bible statement, "Ask, and ye shall receive, seek and ye shall find; knock, and it shall be opened unto you." I pointed out that the word "receive" quickly follows the word "ask"; that the word "find" follows hard upon the word "seek" and "shall be opened" comes closely after the word "knock."

The plain meaning, I explained, is that we are to ask, then have such simple faith that we shall immediately receive.

Here is a clear law: have faith, ask God for something, believe that you will receive it. My caller said that he understood, but had never done it that way.

Then we hit upon a device. I asked him to put his watch on the table before him and, keeping his eyes on the watch, to pray for two minutes, asking God to take his fear away. He objected, "How can I pray with my eyes open?"

"Do you always pray with your eyes shut?" I asked.

"Certainly."

"Well," I observed, "your prayers with your eyes shut apparently haven't done you much good. Don't be stereotyped. Try praying with your eyes open."

Rather sheepishly he kept his eyes on his watch and for two minutes asked God to remove his fears. When the two minutes were up, he said, "Amen."

"Now," I directed, "say another prayer for two minutes, but this time thank God for doing what you asked: namely, for taking your fear away."

"Why!" he exclaimed. "Has He taken my fear away?"

"You asked Him to, didn't you?" I said. "According to the formula, your fear is gone—if you will let it go. You must make up your mind to accept the great thing God has done for you. So, for the next two minutes thank Him."

This was three years ago. Recently I saw the man again. "I'm away ahead of you," he boasted. "Nowadays I ask God for only one-half minute to help in solving a problem; and I thank Him for three and one-half minutes."

"Do you still use the watch?" I asked in surprise.

"Of course! You told me to, didn't you?"

The watch was merely a symbol, I explained. Symbol or no symbol, he said that he was going to "stick to the watch." I may add that those who doubt this as good religious practice might recall the Biblical injunction, *"Watch* and pray."

If you do not find help in your usual religious practices, why not try such a simple formula as I have described? Simplicity is the essence of spiritual power.

A second incident illustrating spiritual techniques for the elimination of fear is the story of a young woman who telephoned me one day during wartime. Her husband was overseas, and so sure was she that something would happen to him that she had a bad case of nerves amounting almost to panic. She was in New York, away from relatives and friends; having no one else to turn to, she appealed to me as a minister. "What shall I do?" she kept repeating. "It would kill me to lose my husband."

"How old are you, young lady?" I asked over the telephone.

"Twenty-six."

I thought I heard a child's voice, so I asked, "Have you a youngster there?"

"Yes, a two-year-old girl," she replied.

"Is she upset and worried like yourself?"

"Why, of course not!" she answered.

"How do you explain her lack of nervousness?" I asked.

She hesitated. "Why, because she's only a baby. Besides, she has me, her mother, with her. I suppose she just puts her trust in me and lets me do the worrying."

That gave me an opening to suggest one of the simplest cures the Christian faith offers for worry. "Have you an easy chair close by?" I asked.

"If so, please draw it up to the telephone and sit down."

After a moment she reported that she had done so.

"Now put your head back," I directed. "Relax your body and take three deep breaths."

For the first time, she laughed a bit, then asked dubiously, "Shall I really?"

"I suppose it does sound queer," I admitted, "but three deep breaths taken in and completely exhaled relieve tension."

"Next," I continued, after she told me she had followed these directions, "take your little girl on your lap. Now, make a transference; try to think of yourself as a child in relationship to God. As your child puts her trust in you, her mother, so may you, by concentrating upon it, put your trust in your Heavenly Father. Put your husband—put all three of you— in God's care. Practice this simple procedure until peace comes to your mind."

She promised. After church the following Sunday a young woman came up to me and said, "I'm the one who telephoned you about being nervous. I tried your method, and it works. I have control of myself now and I know I won't get panicky again."

Then she added, "I always thought religion was a vague sort of thing— just something you believe in. I'm beginning to see that it really works."

Don't settle down to live permanently with your fear. If you do so you will never be happy. You will never be effective. There will be no success and happiness for you. Remember there is a cure for fear. Say confidently to yourself, "Through God's help and the application of simple techniques, I will be free from fear." Believe that—practice it and it will be so.

9

HOW POWER AND EFFICIENCY CAN BE YOURS

EVERY NORMAL PERSON wants a feeling of power. Not power over other people, for that is a disease and abnormality. But every normal person wants power over circumstances; power over situations; power over fear; power over weakness; power over themselves. And . . . everyone can have that power.

Everyone desires to be efficient; everyone desires to perform with skill. Efficiency is an element in power. Without it there can be no grip or mastery. There is great satisfaction in being able to do a thing well. To see a game played well, to hear a song sung expertly, to watch a skillful actor on the stage, is a source of happiness. It is not so much the game itself, or the song, or the action on the stage. It is the delight in witnessing a perfect demonstration. Even a commonplace thing done well gives a glow of satisfaction not only to the person who performs it but to all who witness it. This truth was recently brought home to me at a luncheon.

The service was by an old-fashioned butler, a master at his art. He had composure, a quality which is always to be admired. He was not in the least flustered as the average waiter or waitress seems to be these days. He took his job in his stride deftly and with gentility. Lingering after the luncheon, I said, "I want to congratulate you. I always like to watch a man who knows how to do his job. I admire the master of any art and I have seen one today in you."

He was pleased and said, "Beg your pardon, sir, it *is* an art. I learned it in England, sir, in the old days."

Let us take it for granted you want, like this superb butler, to be efficient. You can be efficient! How? Upon the answer depends to a large degree your success and happiness. And the answer is—seek to become expert in the practice of your religious faith. There was a time when a reader at this point would explain, "Here is where we go from common sense to theory." There is an old and false notion happily disappearing in this country that anything religious is theoretical—that it just doesn't fit into practical life. But intelligent people nowadays realize that Christianity is not a Sunday-go-to-meeting thing, remote from practical living, but a scientific, usable technique.

A prominent advertising man said to me, "There will be a definite upsurge of religion in the postwar era."

"Why?" I asked.

"Because," he replied, "after every great war, perhaps due to the dislocations incidental to war and the necessary readjustments, there is always a widespread desire for self-improvement. The best ways to improve yourself are by the application of either psychology or religion, perhaps by both of them. Psychology, in my opinion, however, does not go deeply enough; therefore this postwar generation will learn that efficiency, the ability to handle people and to get along, the ability to do things well, is a product of practical religion."

This advertising expert went on to tell about a large account that he had handled for several years. It was a course in beauty culture for women, which he had prepared by employing outstanding authorities to write booklets on various phases of the subject. One pamphlet told how to take care of the body; another how to eat properly; another how to use cosmetic preparations. The course was designed to release the inner charm and beauty of the feminine personality. This course together with a kit of cosmetic articles had been sold to more than a quarter of a million persons. Now a new advertising project had come his way, and he was discussing it with me.

The new project was to teach men how to be effective. The client was a clothing house, and a series of pamphlets was under preparation, each teaching a man how to be his full self and completely release his personality. For example, a famous athletic director was writing a pamphlet on exercise. Another expert was writing on how to wear clothes properly—how to know what shirt goes with a certain suit, and how to select a well-matched tie. Another pamphlet had to do with methods for approaching a customer, how to sell one's self, how to sell a product.

But the crux of the matter, said the advertising man, "is to teach our customers how to think; how to release the deeper spiritual self."

He concluded with this pregnant statement, "It is impossible to create an efficient man unless he has some kind of spiritual experience. Without this experience the thing that gives him the final touch of power is lacking."

There was a time when Christianity was generally regarded by the average person as theoretical and having no relation to practical everyday affairs. The advertising expert I have quoted is the refutation of this notion. Men who really think now know that Christian principles are the most skillful, most necessary principles in developing successful and efficient men and women. It is being demonstrated that no other system is so completely designed to give skill, power and efficiency to modern people as the simple principles of the Bible.

Here is further proof. A prominent periodical wrote up the "amazing" career of a successful business woman. What made her success all the more remarkable was the fact that she had had no previous business experience. So she had been asked to outline the principles upon which she had built her business. When she submitted the article, the publisher exclaimed, "This is astounding. These ideas are unique. Would you mind telling me where you got them?"

She smiled and said, "I guess you are not very familiar with the Bible. My article is practically a rewrite of the twelfth chapter of Matthew, verses 20–26."

The most antiquated man in America is the rare gentleman who still gets off the old canard that religion is something for Sunday only. That remark stamps him as belonging to the horse-and-buggy era.

Probably the reason so-called practical men think of Christianity as theoretical is because they regard it entirely as theology or philosophy. It does fulfil itself in these fields, but Christianity may also be thought of as a science. In fact, it is an exact science, for it is based on law as is any science. It is the science of personal and social living. Learn its laws and you will always and invariably get equivalent results.

It is rather crude to think that the only law existing in our universe is that which governs material things. We are constantly finding new applications of power in the universe and each new one is, as are all the others, regulated by law. The latest, of course, is atomic power. The average man scarcely knew this form of power existed, yet it has released such force that he is aghast. It is interesting to recall that years ago the famous scientist, Steinmetz, said that the greatest scientists of the future would be those who would chart and explain spiritual laws.

The New Testament has always been regarded as a distinctly religious book and it is that, but it may also be thought of as a formula book of spiritual science. It contains procedures by which anybody who intelligently applies them can develop power in his mind and personality.

So we have available a spiritual science equally as great, perhaps greater, and more valuable than the laws of chemistry, physics, electronics or atomics. In a power plant an eminent engineer once described to me a powerful dynamo. He commented on the amount of energy this dynamo could generate, but as we walked away he said, "It may sound queer, but you and I can generate more actual energy by means of faith and prayer than that dynamo can produce. I mean that too," he added firmly.

It is a fact that Christianity is a power mechanism. St. Mark says:

> For verily I say unto you, That whosoever shall say unto this mountain be thou removed, and be thou cast into the sea; and shall not doubt in his heart, but shall believe that those things which he saith shall come to pass; he shall have whatsoever he saith.

Therefore I say unto you. What things soever ye desire, when ye pray, believe that ye receive them, and ye shall have them.

Putting those words into present-day speech, what do they say? Just this—if you have faith, not a great deal of faith, just a little real faith, not any larger than a grain of mustard seed, which is quite small, then you shall say to "this mountain," that great rock-like obstruction that lies across your pathway, always defeating you, "be removed," and it shall not only be removed, but shall be cast into the sea (i.e., swallowed up out of sight). And if you shall not doubt this in your heart—that is, shall not have a negative attitude about it in the subconscious—but shall simply believe, whatsoever you ask shall come to pass.

A psychiatrist of undisputed standing stated that one of the most powerful forces is released through a formula in Matthew which reads, "All things, whatsoever ye shall ask in prayer, believing, ye shall receive." He offered it as his opinion, based on long experience in his profession, that when a patient's mind is conditioned in terms of this scriptural verse, the most amazing changes can and do take place. "Faith," he said, "possesses a tremendous healing property and power producing force."

Regarding such passages from the Bible as those which I have indicated and others, there are various attitudes you can take. You may say, "I don't believe it, it is just not so." Of course, you have a right not to believe it, but it is doubtful if you have a right to dogmatically assert it is not so. In so doing you are setting yourself against the most reliable ancient document known to mankind. It forces us to take a choice between whether to believe you or the document. In the face of the religious belief of many distinguished men of science, the dogmatic statement that the Bible is not so is both unimpressive and unconvincing.

Another attitude one can fall into is a passive one. You may say, "I do not understand it, I do not disbelieve it, but it is beyond me and therefore I will not use it." That, of course, simply means that a person does not avail himself of power he could employ.

Probably the most sensible attitude is to assume that maybe it is true; that perhaps here is a law not perfectly understood, but one which many people have demonstrated will work. Perhaps it is wise to accept the workability of the law, deriving from it what power and efficiency one can gain, hoping later to penetrate into a deeper understanding. Matters of religion should be approached in the experimental attitude of a real scientist.

I spent an afternoon not long ago in the home and laboratory of the late Thomas A. Edison. Mrs. Edison showed me mementos of the distinguished inventor, unquestionably one of the greatest geniuses of all time.

Mrs. Edison said to me that after World War I, Mr. Edison told her that in the next war the great lack would be rubber. He stated that the chances were that our rubber supply would be imperiled, if not cut off—

which revealed astounding foresight in itself. Realizing that it would be important to develop domestic sources of rubber, Edison began his experiments. In his painstaking and thorough manner, he examined innumerable plants in the hope of finding rubber. Finally he gave orders to his associates to take sickles and go out in the New Jersey meadows and cut down all the plant varieties they could find. The specimens were laid on tables and painstakingly examined one by one. Finally Edison discovered in the well-known and commonplace goldenrod the latex which he was seeking. At first he produced five per cent of rubber, later ten per cent, and then fifteen per cent. This was the experiment upon which he was working just before his death. When death interrupted his labors, he had released rubber from the goldenrod up to the point of fifteen per cent.

The lesson to be drawn from the example of Edison is this. Some people approach spiritual laws with the rational and factual attitude of the scientist and find at first a small percentage of truth which results in a degree of power. Those who keep on operating the law, investigating and working with it, increase the percentage and as they do so, there is released into their lives mentally, physically and spiritually an increasing power and efficiency which gives them a grasp and mastery far beyond other people, especially beyond those who just dogmatically assert, "There is nothing to it."

Years ago Emerson said there are unexplored chambers of the human mind which some day will be opened to release unrealized spiritual powers. A French psychiatrist says that there is another element present in the mind beyond the conscious and the subconscious. This element he terms "the superconscious." The characterization is interesting. Perhaps it was to this "superconscious" that Christ referred when He said, "If you have faith . . . nothing shall be impossible unto you." When His disciples commented upon the greatness of the works which He was doing, He said, "Greater works than these shall ye do." We read that "He marvelled because of their unbelief." That is to say, He was astonished that people who had such potential power would not release it. It is entirely likely that in you is locked up all the power and efficiency you need. Evidence gained in thousands of cases indicates that the only sure way of releasing it is to become expert in the faith mechanism described in the New Testament.

Captain Eddie Rickenbacker discovered this principle years ago. He himself told me about his discovery. In an automobile race he was coming down the home stretch with his throttle wide open. Due to his sensitive "feel" of the mechanical workings of his automobile, he became aware that something was wrong. At the rate of speed at which he was traveling, this might spell distaster. He says, "A momentary tremor of fear crossed my mind, but . . . I lifted up my mind." He relates that a feeling of exultation passed through him. It was an overwhelming and absolute conviction that he could bring that machine in, not by his hands, but by the power of his mind.

He doesn't say this boastfully, but explains that at the time he told nobody of it for fear nobody would understand. Today, however, Captain Rickenbacker explains we are better acquainted with the law of psychokinetics, the power of the human mind over conditions, circumstances, material things. Indomitable mastery and control over adversity or opposition is exercised by the mind when the driving energy of faith is released.

I am confident of the scientific workability of faith in developing power and efficiency, for the same reason that any scientist knows that a formula will work, namely, he sees it work and gets results.

In my scientific laboratory (the Marble Collegiate Church of New York) we had a member, a business executive, who became enthusiastically convinced of the techniques of faith. He had not been a long established church man and became interested in the church only because he was "sold" on the idea of Christianity and its formula of faith. "I think you have got something there," he declared. Because as he put it, "there is something to it," he joined the church and was regular in attendance, enthusiastically practicing spiritual techniques.

One afternoon he telephoned saying, "I must see you right away about an important business matter." One might think it curious that a business-man would see a minister about a business problem, but when you get right down to it, most business problems are problems in which persons are involved. The minister deals with persons and therefore he can be a scientific adjunct to anybody interested in business research.

My friend, who represented a specialized business in New York, came in and said, "Here is my problem. We have a competitor in the middle-west and this competitor employs the star sales executive of our industry. This man has forgotten more about the business than the rest of us know about it. Our competitor has discharged him, however, for the third and last time. I would like to employ him."

"Why don't you?" I said.

"Because," he replied, "there is a catch to it—he is an alcoholic. My president won't take him on because he says there is no hope for an alcoholic. I have continued to urge my president, however, because I believe we can cure him. I have heard you talk from the pulpit about faith and I am sold on the idea that if we have faith, nothing is impossible, so I have finally convinced my president, and he has told me he will give me one month to get this man cured and if we do, I can have him on my sales force."

"Do you realize what you ask?" I said, and then I explained to him what the scientific authorities say about alcoholism. I showed him that it is scientifically regarded as a disease, one of the most serious that can attack a human being, the usual end of which is either the insane asylum or death, or both.

"I don't know anything about that," my friend insisted. "I only know that the Bible says that if you have faith—'nothing is impossible unto you.' I take that as meaning alcoholism also," he concluded firmly.

"Does this man go to church?" I asked.

"No," he answered, "he doesn't. Not very often at least."

It so happened that a church supper was scheduled for a night or two later and I asked if he thought the alcoholic would come to that supper.

"Yes, I think he would," my friend replied. "I know he eats."

So I met this man. Later the alcoholic came to my office. He said, "Now listen, Doctor, Mr. V. is very much interested in me. He is an awfully nice fellow. But don't waste your time on me. There's no use trying to do anything with me. This thing has got me. I'm licked, completely licked."

He told me he was forty-five, and had two boys and a lovely wife. He had an engaging personality and a brilliant mind.

"You say you are licked?" I asked him.

"Yes, absolutely—completely washed up," he said.

"That's marvelous," I replied. "You are sure that you have no strength of your own?"

"No, I'm all through. Sometimes I feel if I could only get free, if I only could . . . the things I could do! But the minute I think I am free, drink knocks me back and it has knocked me back too many times. Don't waste your time on me."

"My friend," I said, "when you tell me that you have no strength of your own, you are at the beginning of deliverance, because now you are ready to say, 'Having no strength of my own, I put my life in the hands of God with faith.' In so doing you will get strength, all you need."

"Do you think I have a chance?" He looked up with wistful eyes.

"Yes, I certainly do."

"All right," he said, "I'll do whatever you say. What do you want me to do?"

"Let's start," I suggested, "by your going to church twice every Sunday for the next month."

"Oh!" he groaned; but he agreed to do so.

I wrote to Mr. V. as follows:

Yesterday I had a very satisfactory talk with Mr. C. Our discussion was exceedingly frank.

I found him absolutely honest, and it pleased me that while he admitted his weakness and did not seek in any sense to minimize it or hide it, at the same time he was not unduly derogatory of himself. Sometimes there is a tendency for a man to run himself down completely, which means that his self-respect has run out. He simply, honestly, faced with me the great weakness of his character, and convinced me that it is his definite purpose to eradicate drinking from his practice.

He told me that he has made one discovery which he would never admit before—namely, heretofore he has gone a considerable period of time without drinking, but always believed that he could take one drink and control the matter at that point. Now, he says, he has learned that he must not drink at all, that one drink inevitably leads to more. This is pleasing, because it is extremely difficult to get an alcoholic to the acceptance of the fact that he must not drink at all. The biggest delusion in the mind of the alcoholic is that he can drink moderately. With men who are alcoholically inclined there is no such thing as moderation. Therefore I believe that real progress has been made with this man. He stated that his contact with religion had not been very close, but that now he has seen that religion can be a practical power in a man's life, and agreed to follow certain ideas which I laid down to him and which he found in my books. He also is going to associate himself with Alcoholics Anonymous.

I believe he has definitely started up the road which leads to complete sobriety. I have weighed this carefully and I would not give this as my opinion unless I felt that he honestly means business. I think he does, and I assure you that I shall do all in my power to help him.

Incidentally, I think you have used extremely good judgment and common sense in the way you have approached this matter.

The next Sunday morning I looked down and there was my friend, Mr. V., on the end of the aisle. Next to him was the alcoholic, and then Mr. V.'s wife. Mr. V. came up after the first service and said, "Now, Doctor, for a while forget about the rest of the congregation and preach to this man. We have to get him cured. I need him in my business."

I confess that I almost did. He was there regularly, listening carefully. It was very impressive: two businessmen trying to settle a business problem as a human problem.

One Sunday night about three weeks later, I was preaching on the text, "What things soever ye desire, when ye pray, believe that ye receive them, and ye shall have them," and outlining the power of affirmative faith. I found myself saying, "If there is anybody in this great congregation defeated by anything, no matter what it may be, if he will now believe that the power of God is being released in his life and if he will, as our heads are bowed, raise his hand as a sign and symbol of his acceptance of this power, I declare that he will now receive it" . . . which was an astounding thing to say, but I said it. We would get more astounding results from Christianity if we were not timorous about believing in it.

About fifty hands went up all over the congregation. To my astonishment I saw this man's hand go up. After the service this man came up to me, shook my hand, and went away, but indirectly I heard he was doing well. Later he told me that when he put up his hand "something happened to him." A feeling came over him such as a man experiences when after a long illness suddenly he realizes that he is well. The urge to drink did not come back. The desire *completely passed away*.

To complete this narrative, I insert the correspondence that documents this working partnership of business and religion in the problem of alcoholism.

From letter of Mr. V. written to me:

> I know you are interested in Mr. C. and of developments in connection with our program together.
>
> I was unusually impressed and gratified to receive a letter from Mrs. C. which has reference to Mr. C. and I am sure you will be happy to read some extracts from it, and so I quote them below:
>
> "He certainly is a changed man and I am sure it is due in a large measure to contacts with you and members of your family. I do my very best to keep up the good work while he is home. He is so sincere it is very easy to do. I've gone to church all my life and have brought the boys up that way too—but Mr. C. certainly taught me a great deal about the power of faith and I'm very grateful."

You can imagine how thrilled I was to get this word from the wife of this alcoholic and my delight in the success attendant upon our efforts was increased when I received the following letter from Mr. C.:

> I know you will be interested in the success that has rewarded our efforts of the past several months. The final result is my appointment as General Manager of the ——— Company. At the next meeting of the Directors of the Company I am to be elected Vice President, also.
>
> Nothing approaching this was contemplated at the outset. The sequence of things that led to it, even now, seems unbelievable. I am indeed awed. They didn't just happen and certainly were far beyond my planning. I know He answered my prayers, and yours, also those of Mr. and Mrs. V., and Mrs. C. Even my two youngest boys, ages eight and ten, included in their nightly prayers 'Special prayer for Daddy.'
>
> But better than all this I now have a firm hold on myself. I am sure I have the complete and simple faith to which you refer in your books and sermons. My mind is at rest and I know peace and happiness again. You can readily appreciate what it means to my wife and three boys. It has been no effort to avoid my old weakness. I seem to have found a substitute—faith.
>
> I find it difficult to adequately express my gratitude. The change dates from the time I first attended your church and had the opportunity to talk to you personally. Then the high spot that Sunday night in your church when on your suggestion I raised my hand in the way of public acknowledgement of God and put myself in His care. To me that was tremendously impressive.
>
> Many problems will be facing me—perhaps the biggest in my business experience. I approach them with complete confidence and with the knowledge that unlimited power and help are always available to me.

When I received this letter I knew that a healing had taken place. Even as medical science is able to develop an immunity against certain forms of disease, so it is possible by the application of spiritual techniques to change emotional and mental reactions so that a person becomes as the New Testament so picturesquely expresses it "a new creature: old things are passed away; behold, all things are become new."
So I wrote to Mr. C.:

> You have found the secret; by faith you have accepted God's power and He has given it to you.
> May I suggest that you form habits of prayer in which you constantly affirm to God that He has given you this strength, and thank Him for it. Pray not only in the morning and the evening, but get in the habit of turning your mind to God frequently during the day. Also, I suggest that you form the habit of reading the Psalms in the Old Testament and Matthew, Mark, Luke and John in the New Testament. Read a chapter every day if possible. These suggestions are to build up in your mind a consciousness of God's presence and His power. This is part of a definite spiritual technique which is very valuable.

This story of the alcoholic goes from one climax to another. A year and a half later in one of my letters I told him that I never failed to pray for him and that I was very much interested in having reports from him from time to time. To this suggestion he wrote me the following tremendous statement of his experience.

> I am humbly grateful because you still remember me in your prayers. It is my firm conviction that that has helped me through very difficult situations. I am referring to the many problems of business today, not my old difficulty. That is a closed book. It is now a year and a half since I even had a drop of intoxicating drink. It has not even been at all difficult. Surprisingly enough, I have never once been tempted. I am confident I won't be. This just could not have been if I had not attended Marble Collegiate Church, met you and had that first talk with you. You pointed the way that changed everything for the better. My spiritual highlight was in your church one Sunday night when the congregation sat with heads bowed and eyes closed and I responded with others in raising my hand, putting myself unreservedly in God's hands. All of this is written in complete sincerity.

At the end of a year and a half he declared that he had *never even been tempted to drink alcohol*, that the cure was still operative.

Nearing the end of two years, he called on me in my office. He told me that he was on his way to the middle-west where his company had recalled him and had made him Vice-President for the Dominion of Canada. As he sat across from my desk I asked him, "Have you ever had the desire to take alcohol since that night?"

His answer was, "Not the slightest desire."

Some people might call this a miracle. Anybody who knows the true meaning of the disease of alcoholism is well aware of the astonishing thing which happened in this case.

However great a recovery this is, it is not a miracle. This man had made contact with a spiritual law. He was changed by the operation of this law. He discovered a basic power in the universe just as truly as the man who released atomic energy. This power is so great that it burned out of his mind every vestige of the disease which was destroying him. He discovered and put into operation the law of faith.

But the story goes on and arrives at one of the great factors in the cure of alcoholism; the urge to help someone else get cured. Mr. C. writes:

> I have a purchasing agent with plenty of the very same difficulty I had. I have been trying to help him over a period of several months with considerable but not complete success. I have talked to him many times—got him going to church—given him many of your sermons and books to read, and have tried to pray for him regularly. So far I haven't been completely successful in convincing him that he can't do it for himself but to let God do it for him.
>
> You can still feel proud of the job you did on me. It is fast approaching three years now since I have had a drink. I am much safer than any man who never touched a drop. But beyond that and more important, you showed me the way to build religious faith and trust that means more to me than all else. I have a long, long way to go but I really believe I make some little gain each day. In a very humble way I try to help others do the same. You know it is rather convincing to others when an old sinner like myself tries to show the way.

I do not relate this story on the supposition that you, the reader, are an alcoholic. My purpose in telling this story is to point out that if faith can revitalize and remake an alcoholic, it can assuredly give you power and efficiency.

All around you at this moment is divine healing energy. The very atmosphere is charged with it. If you will practice faith, you can be healed of ill-will, inferiority, fear, guilt, or any other block which impedes the flow of recreative energy. Power and efficiency are available to you if you will believe.

10

HOW TO AVOID GETTING UPSET

"THAT FELLOW BURNS me up." The speaker was flushed of face as his fist crashed on the table. "I'm sick of that fellow's name in the newspaper. I'm all burned up inside."

That's a picturesque and exact description of the inward condition of that man. A seething cauldron of agitated emotion, he was truly burning up on the inside. A human being cannot forever stand resurgence of such agitation. Every day we hear of people who become ineffective or "break" and in many cases it is simply because they allow people or situations to "burn them up."

One important rule for being happy and successful is—don't let things agitate you. This is vital.

A doctor once told me what he had prescribed for a businessman who complained that his nerves were "all frazzled." "You don't need to be agitated or upset. Practice your religious faith," he suggested.

"Do you get many such cases, and is that your usual prescription?" I asked.

"Yes," he replied, "I have noted a pronounced rise in the number of emotional and nervous problems. Many patients become ill simply because of inability to overcome prolonged agitation. But, except in cases where a definite physical cause exists, my belief is that the average person need not be agitated or nervous if he will take the medicine you parsons hand out."

This wasn't the first time this idea had been presented to me. About twenty years ago I took my mother to a prominent heart specialist in Boston. After a thorough examination he leaned back in his chair and looked quizzically at my mother and said, "Mrs. Peale, are you a Christian?"

My mother had been a minister's wife for a good many years and an active church worker. This question startled her.

"I try to be," she replied.

"I am afraid you are not working at it very hard," the doctor said, "and there is very little I can do for you. I could prescribe some medicine but beyond palliative effects, I honestly do not believe it would be of value. I suggest that you definitely practice the technique of trust, calmness and faith which you find in the New Testament. Do that and I think you will get along all right," he said.

Today we know that an important step toward emotional and physical health is to believe in and practice your religion. Religion contributes to physical and emotional health because it deals with mental states and attitudes. Many human ills, as explained many times in this book, derive from improper thinking.

People often say that their nerves are "all shot to pieces." This is usually not so; very seldom are their nerves actually damaged. The nerve is simply a telephone wire from the brain to a given part of the body. What a person means when he says that his nerves are "all shot to pieces" is not that there is anything wrong with the actual nerve, but that the thoughts which stimulate the nerve are disturbed. These agitated thoughts make it impossible for the brain to send orderly and controlled impulses to the nerves so that contrary and uncertain messages go out over the nerve wires. The brain is in confusion because the thoughts are in confusion. Thus the nervous system tends to be in disorder. As a result one feels nervous, tense, tied-up and agitated.

Nervousness is primarily derived from the thoughts we think. Learn to think orderly, controlled, disciplined, calm thoughts and you will not be tense or agitated. In view of these facts it is more and more evident that the chief cure for the prevailing tension and agitation of this era is a return to religion.

I met a friend, a minister, whom I have not seen in several years. I had heard that he had suffered a nervous breakdown. But now he seemed robust and looked the picture of health. We sat in his library one winter day before a cheerful fire. He stretched out his long legs, leaned back in his chair and asked, "Have you ever given thought to the relationship of religion to the art of resting? Our religion," he continued, "has been so concerned with morals and ethics, both matters of the greatest importance, that many have failed to realize the tonic effect of faith. Why," he exclaimed, "it is amazing what religion can do to cure tension, heal worried and anxious thoughts, and give strength for the stresses and strains so prevalent today."

"You must have found something," I prodded him.

"I surely have. A couple of years ago I had a nervous breakdown. I went to a hospital and was put through all the tests. My energy had gone. I was weak and listless. Finally the doctor in charge of my case gave me his diagnosis." (It was an experience not unlike that of my mother's previously described.)

"We have analyzed your case, Reverend Doctor So and So," he said, "and we have decided that if you practiced Christianity, you could get well." Astonished, my friend demanded, "What do you mean?"

"I suppose you never read the New Testament," continued the doctor.

"Of course, I do," protested the minister.

"Oh, I see," pursued the doctor. "You read it but you do not believe it."

"I do believe it," shouted the minister.

"Well, then let's put it another way—and come now, admit it—you don't really practice its teaching of faith and trust, do you? I know you practice its morals and ethics, but you do not practice your religion in your thought life. Put into mental practice these principles: 'Take no thought for the morrow' or 'Let not your heart be troubled'—'Fret not thyself'—'Come unto me, all you that labor and are heavy laden, and I will give you rest.' "

It began to dawn on my friend what this wise and kindly doctor meant. Quietly he said, "I see what you mean and you are right. I *will* practice my faith in my thoughts as well as in my actions."

"It's really a great medicine—the greatest tonic of all," said the physician.

There sat my friend that day of our visit, two years later, well and strong. His wife who sat by smiled and said, "I told him that for years, but he would not pay attention to me but went on wearing himself out and becoming a bundle of nerves."

"Well, I'm cured all right," he continued, "and now I'm urging people to practice the gospel for the sure release it will give from tension and fear. I urge them to take the greatest medicine of all."

A friend of mine, manager of one of the largest hotels in America, had been commenting upon what he said this country needs, namely, "to get back to the simple principles of religion."

"Why," he said, "if we don't do it everybody is going to crack up. I move about in the lobby of this hotel a good deal and one learns a lot just by watching people. All you have to do is just to stand and watch people use the revolving doors and you will see what I mean. Why, for some men the whole day is spoiled if they miss one section of that door."

"You mean it annoys them to miss one complete revolution of the door," I remonstrated.

"No, sir," he said, "it used to be that but now they are so tense, it upsets them to miss just one section. Something must be done or we are all going to be nervous wrecks."

The results of such tension are clearly evident. Pick up any newspaper any day and count the causes of the deaths reported. If you get past fifty today you may live to a ripe old age. High blood pressure, heart failure, maladies of hypertension, these are the sickles that the old man with the long beard uses to cut men down in their prime these days.

It is understandable how men break under strain. In the manufacturing of automobiles the severest test is to drive the car at high speed over a smooth concrete pavement. It would seem that the toughest test would be over a rough road, but on the contrary, high speed over smooth pavement sets up high frequency vibration which more quickly indicates hidden weaknesses. High tension and agitation in a human being vibrate those hidden weaknesses which cause him to break.

Caruso had a dinner trick which used to delight his fellow diners. He would hold aloft between his thumb and forefinger a fragile glass with a long stem. He would sing the ascending scale and sound a high note repeatedly. The glass would shatter into a hundred pieces.

If high frequency vibration or tension thus affects an automobile or a glass, think what it can also do to our highly organized human personalities and bodies.

In his book, *Release from Nervous Tension,** Dr. David Fink explains the process. He calls attention to "the interbrain." "Nerves," he says, "control all of our organs. These nerves are grouped chiefly in one part of the nervous system, and this part of the nervous system is the central control that normally should keep our hearts and stomachs and lungs working in harmony with each other. This nervous center of our emotional life is called the interbrain. Sometimes it is called the thalamus or hypothalamus. The interbrain is the seat of the emotions: love, hate, fear, rage, jealousy, etc."

Dr. Fink quotes Dr. Harvey Cushing as stating that "emotional storms coming out of the interbrain can cause ulcers of the stomach, palpitations of the heart and other maladies."

The interbrain, says Dr. Fink, "sits in the driver's seat." He explains its working. "Above the interbrain is the forebrain, sometimes called the cerebrum. The forebrain which occupies most of the space within your skull is the part of your nervous system that analyzes, thinks, decides. It lets you know just what is going on in the world. It is with your forebrain that you read your newspaper. Your forebrain interprets the general situation and sends its findings to the interbrain for action and feeling. The interbrain reports the situation back to the forebrain in terms of elation or depression. When you feel calm or happy or sad or depressed, or when you have the jitters or nervous indigestion, you know it because your interbrain has told your forebrain just how it feels."

Dr. Fink sums up, "To enjoy good health you must first get right with your interbrain."

Perhaps a man who was sent to me by a physician was having interbrain trouble. Over the telephone this physician said, "I am sending a patient to see you. Physically there is nothing wrong with him. All he needs is to get his nerves converted." Perhaps he should have said, "He needs to get his interbrain converted." "Show him how to put his trust in God and he will not be so jittery and upset," concluded the doctor.

---

* David Fink, *Release from Nervous Tension*, (New York: Simon and Schuster, Inc., 1943).

* * *

A diffused and general application of religion will not necessarily help to overcome tension. No reader should jump to the conclusion that if one goes to church next Sunday, all will be well. I certainly advocate going to church next Sunday and every Sunday, but it is essential to do more than sporadically rush into a church in a desperate manner. I know people who have gone to church for years who are still pathetic victims of tension and agitation. The failure lies in the fact that they have never learned how the simple and practical techniques of Christianity may be applied to tension and agitation.

A man who is sick doesn't rush into a medical library and start desperately reading. He sits down with the doctor. The doctor examines him and out of his knowledge of those medical books and long years of practice, writes the patient a prescription and gives simple advice to apply to his particular malady. The patient takes the prescription to the drug store. He does not think he will be cured by subjecting himself to the aroma of all the medicine in the store. The druggist fills the prescription, giving him a specific medicine. He writes specific instructions on the bottle or box— "Take three times a day as directed." Religious practice should follow similar procedures, diagnosis, and specific application of formulae.

A man came to our church clinic complaining of severe nervousness. He was a manufacturer and was under great stress. He drummed his fingers on my desk as he talked.

"Why are you drumming your fingers?" I asked.

"I didn't even know I was drumming them," he replied in some surprise.

"Well," I suggested, "don't drum your fingers. Just let your hand rest on the table in a limp and relaxed manner." I saw that he was sitting rigidly on the edge of his chair, so I urged, "Sit back and relax."

"In what other ways does your nervousness manifest itself?" I inquired.

"I worry about my business all the time. Every time I am away I worry whether my house is going to burn down or something happen to it. I worry about my wife and children, wondering if they are going to get hurt."

I gave him a prescription, a little formula to practice. "Just say to yourself, 'Let my house burn.' Is your house insured?" I asked.

"Yes, it is."

"Well," I continued, "say to yourself, 'let it burn.' Also say, 'I put my wife and children in God's hands, He will take care of them.' You must learn a simple technique, you must have the naive genius to follow the greatest of all thinkers who told us that the answers to life's problems lie in childlike or simple attitudes."

He said, "I'll try."

"Good," I said. "Imagine that Jesus Christ is actually by your side.

When you start worrying, stop and say, 'Lord, you are with me; everything is all right.' When you go into a restaurant even if you are with somebody, pull up a chair unostentatiously and imagine that Jesus Christ sits in that chair. When you walk down the street, imagine that you can hear His footfalls, feel His shoulders, see His face. When you retire at night, pull up a chair by the bed and imagine that Jesus Christ sits in that chair. Then before you turn out the light have a word with Him and say, 'Lord, I'll not worry, for I know that you are watching over me and will give me peace.'"

"Oh," he protested, "that sounds foolish."

"It is merely a simple psychological device to make you feel the presence of Christ and I have had a great many people use it with excellent results," I explained.

He came back to see me not long ago. He did not drum his fingers. He sat evenly in his chair, there was no nervousness. There was a new look on his face. "You feel better?" I suggested.

"Yes, I do; yes, I do." He hesitated, then said, "I should like to say something to you. You know that business about Christ sitting in chairs, and walking with me?"

I said that I recalled my advice.

"Well," he said rather hesitantly, "do you know I honestly believe there is something to it—I believe He is there actually."

He is right. There is something to it.

Another man who came to my office agreed with this finding. He told me that he could not sleep. He was quite haggard, and obviously at the breaking point.

"The trouble is my mind is too agile," he complained. His education was largely scientific, with degrees from an engineering school. He was a man of brilliant mentality, but his mind operated too rapidly for his emotional make-up and did not synchronize with his living.

This discrepancy in my visitor reminded me of the incident of the city man who went out to the country and watched a farmer who was sawing a log with long, even, measured strokes. This city fellow said impatiently, "Here, let me saw the log." He started in with slow, measured strokes, but before long accelerated the tempo. The stroke went crooked, the saw caught.

The city man said, "I guess I didn't do so well, after all."

The farmer replied, "It's because you allowed your mind to get ahead of the saw."

Tension causes men's minds to get ahead of their emotional nature—and dislocation of a perfectly synchronized and correlated personality results. That was true of the man who had come to see me.

I asked him to practice a simple spiritual device. "When you go home and go to bed tonight, put a chair by the side of your bed. Imagine that

Christ sits in the chair, and when you get ready to go to sleep, look over toward the chair and say, 'He giveth his beloved sleep.' Then make it personal—'He giveth me (his beloved) sleep.' Believe that Christ will be there watching over you. Then turn out the light and go to sleep."

He said, "I'll try. But it's only imagination, because Christ couldn't be there."

"Try believing it just the same," I suggested.

He told me later that for the first four nights nothing happened, and he had just about decided it was a "crackbrained notion," as he put it. "But," he continued, "the fifth night I had a wonderful sleep. And," he paused, "I believe that Christ's presence is more than imagination—it is a fact."

The last time I saw him he said that he still puts the chair by the bed. Of course, he is resting too heavily upon the symbolism of the chair. But if he can get results by pulling up a chair, it's all right, for back of it is one of the most powerful, one of the most effective, one of the profoundest of all ideas, the idea, namely, that God is with you and that no harm can come to you, that you need not be afraid of anything.

The devices for eliminating agitation need not be involved. One is to practice taking a detached attitude toward irritating things. Practice lifting your mind above the confusion and irritation around you.

One way to do that is to form mental pictures of great hills or mountain ranges, or the wide sweep of the ocean, or of some great valley spreading out before you. Get a mental picture of the stars serene in the heavens, or of the moon sailing high on a clear, calm night. One can do this while busy at a job. Hang these pictures on the walls of your mind and think about them habitually.

The practice of detachment helps one to remain quiet, peaceful, controlled in the midst of the little tempests of this life. Let me tell you of a few people and the devices or techniques they have successfully employed to overcome agitation.

Just before Christmas one year my wife took me shopping. I always try to avoid it, but so far have never yet been able to get through a Christmas season without having to go shopping. She took me to a crowded store, and the counter where we wanted to purchase some articles was the most crowded of all. It was literally besieged by women. To my embarrassment I was the only man in the crowd.

I noticed the salesman. He was a tall, easy-going, young fellow who wore the button indicating honorable discharge from military service. He had a very relaxed attitude even though he was being called on all sides. He gave his attention to the one customer whom he was serving at the moment. It seemed that she had bought three articles, and I was standing close by when he tried to add up the cost. She had her eyes glued upon his pencil as he added the column, and you were conscious of a stiff and suspicious attitude on her part. Perhaps this confused him, for he added the column incorrectly, and I was struck by his wholesomeness when with a boyish grin he said, "What do you know? Didn't add it right, did I?"

"No, you didn't," she snapped. Dutifully he tried it again, appealing to me meanwhile to help him. Despite my clumsiness in mathematics, we managed this time to get the column correctly added.

Then he flashed her a radiant smile so warm that it thawed even the iciness in her face, and he handed her the package with the statement, "I am a poor mathematician, but believe me, you have got some fine articles there for Christmas. I hope they are going to make the people for whom you have bought them very happy. Merry Christmas!" And with that he turned to the next customer, who happened to be myself.

I discovered that he had been employed recently by a large advertising firm. Before putting him to work they sent him out, as he put it, "to get acquainted with the great American public." He certainly was in a place where he could get acquainted with the public all right and I asked, "How do you like it?"

"Oh," he said, "I like it all right; only why is everybody so mad? They storm around my counter from all directions, and they all seem to be mad. I don't know what they're mad about; I doubt that they know themselves. They are buying Christmas presents to make people happy, and yet they're all mad. But," he added, "I've got a secret; I just don't let it ruffle me. I flash a big smile on 'em and treat 'em nicely; it breaks them down—every last one of them."

This young fellow had hit upon a technique for not being agitated. If he holds that throughout his life, he will be a successful man. He got relaxed, gave his attention to one customer at a time, and "flashed a big smile on 'em." In other words, he had mastered the skill of being detached. Thus irritation had no power over him.

Robert Louis Stevenson made a wise statement: "Quiet minds cannot be perplexed or frighened but go on in fortune or in misfortune at their own private pace like the ticking of a clock during a thunderstorm." That is really a discerning bit of wisdom.

I have a little old farmhouse in the country—a place over one hundred and fifty years old. We have some old things around that house, including clocks. There's something fascinating about the ticking of a clock, especially in the quiet of the night. One of those old clocks is in the dining room. One day we had a violent hurricane. The great maples seemed almost to bend double under the driving winds. The rain beat upon the windowpanes. The very beams of the house seemed to creak.

But the old clock acted as if there were no storm at all. "Tick tock, tick tock," it said calmly. If the clock had been a modern human being, it would have speeded up its tempo as if to cry excitedly, "Isn't it a terrible storm? What shall we do, what shall we do?" But the clock was measuring time which is rooted in the center of the stars. It was measuring decades, generations, eons, not merely excitable little minutes. So, it just went on, "at [its] own private pace."

A man who has cultivated "the peace of God which passeth all understanding," does not get agitated by the little storms of life. His life is rooted in something eternal so he goes on "at [his] own private pace like the ticking of a clock during a thunderstorm."

The late William Jennings Bryan, one of the greatest orators of our time, had this art perfected. Years ago a friend of mine was with Bryan all one summer. He slept with him in country hotels. He even slept with him on benches in country railroad stations. One night they lay down on a couple of baggage trucks somewhere in the Tennessee mountains as they waited for a train. At this time a certain newspaper was pounding Bryan unmercifully. My friend was wrought up about it. That night he said, "Mr. Bryan, why is it that you don't get worked up and mad and excited about the attacks this newspaper is making on you?"

"What newspaper?" asked Mr. Bryan.

"Why," said my friend, "don't you know?" And he named the paper.

"Oh, that one—well, you see, I never read the papers that attack me. I only read the others. The papers that attack me do not seem to me to be logical," concluded Bryan with a chuckle.

You may say Bryan's was a closed mind? Not at all. Bryan felt that he was right in the positions he was taking. He did his best and after that just went on "in fortune or in misfortune . . . like the ticking of a clock during a thunderstorm." Had he read the papers that attacked him and allowed himself to become irritated, the next thing he might have done would have been just what they wanted him to do. They wanted him to fight back angrily, knowing that "whom the gods would destroy, they first make mad." Bryan was a religious man. He had the peace of God inwardly. His enemies could not get him off center.

Gandhi also practiced this formula. At the age of seventy-five, the Indian nationalist leader said that he planned to live another fifty years. He said his plan to reach the age of a century and a quarter included an abundance of humor, balanced diet, avoidance of all stimulants, adequate sleep, deliberate refusal to be annoyed, disturbed, angered or upset, resignation to the will of God, and prayers twice daily.

I have a friend, a public figure who is often attacked quite violently. He never shows agitation. "I don't understand you," I said to him one day. "I should think you would sometimes get disturbed because of what they say about you."

"It doesn't bother me," he said.

"Why not?" I asked.

"I have two never failing sources of peace," he replied. "One, the short stories of Tolstoy; the other, a Book known as the New Testament. Do you know," he said shrewdly, "it is a funny thing about this business of speaking unkind things, of speaking ill about a person. Point your finger at me," he said. I did so. "Now, what are the other three fingers doing? Pointing back at you, aren't they? You see I win three to one." Incidentally that is a good trick to employ the next time somebody says a mean thing about you. Somebody points one finger at you but three accusing fingers point back at him.

The person who is organized and calm and controlled in his mind by habitual practice of the formula of faith can live without tension. The secret is to develop the art of detachment, the ability to live above agitation.

One of the surest methods for overcoming agitation is to put yourself in contact with the re-creative process of nature. All nature is constantly being re-created. Every spring we see it demonstrated. The trees, flowers, and grass are attuned to the flow of that energy which is ever present in the earth. When a man is created, he is not set off by himself to run down like a clock that had been wound up. He is more like the electric clock which constantly rewinds itself by being connected with automatic and constant energy.

The process is described in one of the most astute and remarkable statements in the Bible, "In Him (that is, God) we live and move, and have our being." (Acts 17:28.) That is to say if you keep in continuous conscious contact with God in your thought and actions, you have life and energy and fullness of being.

This may be done by reminding yourself daily that "In Him I am living, in Him I am having new energy, in Him I am realizing the fullness of my own being."

Take time every day to affirm that the re-creative process is taking place in you, in your body, in your mind, and in your spirit. A new feeling of aliveness, eagerness, and vitality will come to you by following this simple practice.

A doctor telephoned me and said, "I have a patient for whom I can do no more. He thinks the wrong kind of thoughts. That is your field," the doctor concluded, "and if you will take him over, I will send him down."

I asked the doctor what he would suggest that I could do for his patient, and he answered, "Teach him to think differently. I suggest that you persuade him to commit scripture passages to memory until he fills his mind so full of these healing ideas that the other and destructive ideas are expelled. Of course, you know that you cannot force an idea out of the mind by being willing to do so, but only by putting in a stronger idea can you displace a thought that is causing damage."

I was impressed that an up-to-date physician would make such a simple and yet apparently wise suggestion and determined to try it with the man. The patient was a resident of Westchester County and was engaged in business in New York City. He had "New Yorkitis," a disease that is a combination of anxiety, haste, tension and panic, all rolled in one. "New Yorkitis" literally shakes people to pieces. It is a product of the high tempo of metropolitan life, and thus not limited to New York City.

Every morning it was this man's habit to come into the city on the 8:29 train which he barely caught after dashing from his house at 8:28. On the train he read the paper, and got madder and madder at what he read. Before he was in the city, he was in a rage. In the evening he would go out on the 5:19, which he caught at 5:18¼. Again he read the paper and again he got mad. As a result he was not far from the end of a pretty frayed rope.

He was disgusted when I suggested that the doctor and I both thought the cure lay in committing scripture passages to memory. "So you want me to go back to the primary department," he sneered.

"Yes," I said, "you may have some formal and ethical religion, but as far as knowing the simple techniques of applying the Christian faith you just don't know how, so we have to start you again with the ABC's."

I explained how our plan would supply new ideas and would gradually expel the agitated thoughts and spread a healing balm of peace and quietness through his mind.

He had a good brain and he got the idea; the simplicity and logic of it appealed to him. He agreed that he would carry out the "prescription." As suggested previously, a great mind has the capacity to be simple; in fact, a mind that cannot be simple is not a first-class brain. This is why the greatest Teacher said that if we want to become expert, we must "become as little children," that is, simple, naive, artless.

This man did as directed and one day about six months later the doctor telephoned and said, "Our patient is cured. He has control of himself now. His mental outlook is changed and he feels better in every way. I am again impressed by the amazing re-creative power of simple Christian practice."

Sometime later I made a speech in Buffalo before a large audience. It was a hot night and I spoke with vigor. Afterward I shook hands with several hundred people. A man tapped me on the shoulder and said that I had barely time to get my train. He rushed me through the city at "breakneck" speed, skidding around corners on two wheels, arriving finally with a great flourish in front of the Lackawanna Station, his brakes screeching.

Carrying two bags, I dashed through the gates which I heard clang behind me as the conductor called "All aboard." I threw my bags on the platform and pulled myself aboard as the train started. I was out of breath, panting and actually shaking. The car was crowded. There was no place to sit down, and the only thing to do was to get into my lower berth. Still highly keyed up from the experience of the preceding two hours, I lay in my berth.

Suddenly I became aware of a pain in my arm and around my shoulder.

This disturbed me. Then it seemed that my heart was beating too fast. Foolishly I tried to take my pulse. It appeared to be running about twenty beats too rapidly. The thought came that people die in Pullman berths and I thought, "Wouldn't it be terrible to die here in this berth?" A possible newspaper headline, "Minister dies in berth," flashed across my mind.

Then I remembered the suggestion that one could quiet oneself by reading. Unfortunately the only reading material I had was a book on the foreign policy of the United States which obviously was not designed to fill the mind with peace. Then it occurred to me that if the prescription I gave to the man from Westchester County worked for him, why wouldn't it work for me too? "Practice what you preach," I said to myself.

So I said quietly to myself a number of scripture passages. Then I recalled that some psychologist had said that it is more effective to verbalize aloud any statement designed to affect the mind, so I began to recite these scripture passages out loud. What the man in the upper berth thought of this, I do not know. But I lay there reciting all the scripture verses I could recall which dealt with quietness, peace, faith.

Presently I began to feel quieted. Drowsiness came over me, and a deep sense of rest seemed to spread throughout my entire body. The next thing I knew it was morning and I was in Hoboken. The route of the Lackawanna railroad is tortuous through the mountains of Pennsylvania, but I slept soundly and had to be awakened by the porter.

It was a rainy, dismal, raw morning, not designed to lift the spirit. However, as I stood at the prow of the ferry boat, crossing the river, I noticed the seagulls diving and gliding and it came over me that I had never seen such grace and beauty. I had never observed the loveliness of seagulls before, but now I thought I had never seen anything so exquisite as the graceful way in which the birds slipped down the wind. Suddenly it occurred to me that everything seemed wonderful and then I realized that I had never felt better in my life. I had a feeling of health, energy, vitality, and aliveness that was positively exhilarating. I felt deep happiness bubbling up. I caught myself saying, "It is wonderful to be alive," and I eagerly looked forward to the responsibilities of the day. As a matter of fact, I never had a better day in my life.

I became aware that unconsciously I had discovered a law, one of the greatest of all laws, namely, the formula for the re-creation of a human being through the practice of faith. It is a law that can revolutionize your life. It can make the whole world different because it can make you different.

11

HOW TO ATTAIN MARRIED HAPPINESS

HAPPY MARRIED LIFE is possible to those who will apply to themselves a few simple, common-sense principles. The "complications" said to destroy so many modern marriages are not inevitable. In truth, the marriage problem has often been made too involved by the "experts." I have counseled with married couples for a good many years at the heart of America's greatest city, and as a result I am convinced that many marriages which are at what seems a breaking point can be firmly and permanently held together by the application of the principles outlined in this chapter. These principles are not advanced as theoretical propositions. They are stated as the laboratory result of working with hundreds of couples in the confidential relation of a spiritual advisor.

The function of a counselor is not to consider the problems of dispute between a husband and wife and attempt to sagely settle them out of some superior wisdom. Even were he able to exercise perfect judgment and contribute the soundest possible advice, still in most cases, the cleavages which cause the dispute would remain. When a marriage comes to the point of serious disagreement, it probably cannot be settled entirely on the basis of logic or judicial discussion. Some positive treatment must be given to the basic causes which have thrust a husband and wife into warring camps, one against the other.

I am not much concerned about a moderate amount of disagreement or even bickering, for it is not unnatural that a certain amount of conflict should exist between human beings living in close proximity. I have never been impressed by the statement often made that a husband and wife have lived together for, let us say, forty years, and never had a cross word. Ignoring the question of whether the assertion is true, it still remains that it would be a rather dull existence for two people to live together on such an insipid plane that there never would be any argument. A good, robust difference of opinion strenuously engaged in is not bad for human beings provided they never let the sun go down on their wrath. If they carry over from one day to another accumulated irritations arising from personal disagreement, serious division may ultimately develop. Battle the issues out if you must but get them settled and forgive any sharpness before you go to sleep for the night. Let the passing of each day witness an unanimity of spirit, regardless of the divisions of opinion which may have occurred during the day.

While it is the custom of this day to rationalize most marriage failures on the basis that the partners were not by nature adjustable to one another, the fact remains that most could have adjusted had they taken the situation in hand and corrected a few simple faults. For example, one of the most basic drives in human nature is the craving to be appreciated. No less a person than William James so declares.

William James was one of the most distinguished scholars in American history. Considering the importance and extent of his works, he may be regarded one of the greatest minds to be developed on this continent. He was an eminent philosopher and was one of the early pioneers in the science of psychology. In one period of his life, William James had a long and protracted illness, in the course of which a friend sent him a potted azalea, together with words of personal appreciation. In making reply to his kindly gift, the distinguished philosopher-psychologist said it had reminded him of an immense omission of which he had found himself guilty in writing his immortal work on psychology. He had discovered to his chagrin that he had omitted from his textbook the deepest quality of human nature—namely, the craving to be appreciated.

Let husbands and wives get that fact fixed in their minds and never forget it. Indeed they should constantly remind themselves that *every person craves to be appreciated*. Govern yourself accordingly and you have nipped much married trouble at its root.

And now down to cases . . .

A young woman, obviously in great mental distress, came to consult me. She was seriously considering leaving her husband, she said.

From her story it soon developed that all she needed was a little ordinary appreciation. Some more profound authority might call it affection but to me it seemed simpler than that.

I talked with the husband who said, "Oh, she would never leave me."

"Don't be so sure of that," I said.

He looked stunned. "Why, she could not do that. What could I ever do without her?"

"Did you ever tell her that you couldn't do without her?" I asked.

"Why, no," he answered, "I don't like that kind of talk and besides she knows it anyway."

"She may know it, but she wants to have it told to her just the same."

"Why?" he said.

"Don't ask me why," I replied. "That is just the way of women." (But it isn't only women; all of us have the deep craving to be appreciated which William James spoke about.)

"Have you by any chance brought her flowers or candy lately?"

He was a huge, clumsy-looking fellow.

"Now, wouldn't I look fine lugging home flowers? I would look like a fool, me carrying flowers," he snorted.

"Just the same," I replied, "my professional prescription in this situation is to invest in some flowers and tell her you cannot get along without her."

Grudgingly he agreed to do it and, as it later proved, that attitude was all that was needed. It broke up the growing coolness between them, dissipated misunderstanding, and stimulated the original strong affection that basically existed between them.

I realize that this may appear to be oversimplification, and I am aware that in serious marriage disagreement, this may not be effective, but in the early stages simple appreciation is one of the most important of principles relating to married happiness.

Great issues develop from small beginnings. A lack of appreciation which reveals itself in commonplace things may grow until it becomes a very great divisive factor. It may even come to be an almost insurmountable barrier.

A case was brought to me by a wife who traveled several hundred miles to talk about her marriage which she said was crumbling. In fact, she and her husband had been living apart for some time, but there was sufficient desire on the part of both to hold the marriage together to cause them to agree to meet in New York and to visit our church clinic to lay their problems before us.

The couple were in their mid-thirties. Of good families, they were college graduates and were extraordinarily intelligent people. It developed that the man had engaged in several extra-marital affairs which he brazenly and rather cruelly described in the presence of his wife, since at that particular point I was seeing them together. He later attempted to impress me with the fact that one woman with whom he had developed what he called a "beautiful love affair" and whom he had described as a paragon of virtue, was, as he finally admitted, not quite so classic in her purity.

In private conversation with the husband I asked him to be objective, to lay aside emotional reactions as far as possible, and tell me what he thought was the reason he and his wife first began to drift apart. To my astonishment he opened up a vigorous tirade against his wife on the basis of her alleged poor housekeeping, plus personal dowdiness. His complaint was that she did not think enough of him (that is, did not appreciate him enough) to properly care for the home. It seemed that she enjoyed going out with "the girls." These girls were her college friends and they had together developed a craze for bridge playing. It was their habit to gather in some convenient place for lunch and play all afternoon. This happened several afternoons each week.

Late in the afternoon she would dash home and throw together a few things, ending up with an obviously improvised dinner. Often the beds were not made until time to retire. The clutter which normally accumulates in a home was allowed to remain. This, he said, was more than he could stand. "I may be fussy, but when I come home, I think I have a right to find the place at least straightened up, a decent meal on the table and certainly the beds made."

I found it necessary to remind him that when he married this woman, he did not hire her as a housekeeper. I pointed out that he made a contract to live with her not as a man with a housekeeper but as a man with his wife, that they were supposed to become as one, sacred partners for life. I also pointed out that the two little boys had nothing to say about being brought into the world by him in partnership with his wife, and that he was simply the breaker of a contract, giving no thought to the two boys or to his own sacred agreement, but thinking only of his own comfort and nicety of his life.

The discussion revealed that he still had a strong attachment for his wife though there was considerable acidity in their relationship.

Later in talking with the wife I noticed that her petticoat showed. Her hair was rather frazzled. She was basically a nice-looking lady but no care had been exercised in her dress. I asked her if she liked housekeeping. Her answer left no room for doubt. "I positively hate it," she declared. One chief trouble with her husband was that he didn't make enough for her to have a maid, she complained.

I pointed out to her that when they were married, there was nothing in the marriage contract about her having a maid. Furthermore, I told her she was young enough to work hard in the home, and that hard work would do her good. I asked her if she went out with the "girls" and she said she "certainly did." I raised the question why once a week wouldn't be sufficient for her bridge parties with "the girls." I also politely suggested that she make the beds the first thing after breakfast and pick up the newspapers and sweep the place out. I told her that while I was no housekeeper, still I knew that if she would budget her time and activities, she could do up the place in no time at all.

She wanted to know why a minister from whom she expected some spiritual counsel laid all this stress on how she fixed her hair, on why she didn't pull up her petticoat, and on being a better housekeeper. I replied that those matters seemed to be the trouble points.

He had a "few" deficiencies which he admitted and with which we dealt. The interviews ended by mutual pledges that the simple principle of appreciation would be applied and that these obvious deficiencies would be corrected.

Inasmuch as this chapter may be read by persons whose marriage has ended in divorce, I want to say something to help them adjust to that situation. Often such an experience may result in a severe shock to the personality. It can wreck one's life and totally blot out happiness. But there is an answer to even this tragic situation, as the young woman discovered who wrote the following very moving letter to the author.

I want to tell you that your book* has saved my life and reason, and brought Christ Jesus into my tortured brain and starved soul and breaking heart. I certainly needed Him as much as any other human being alive. You have also saved me from a nervous breakdown.

My background was religious, but when I got to college I dropped all interest in anything but the pleasures in this material world, and I guess I have been practically an atheist since, believing only in the Golden Rule. If I had only had a personal faith and lived by it I can see that my life would not have been in the turmoil that it has been.

When I was twenty-five I was married, happily for five years, and had one son—when I was thirty my husband deserted me spiritually for a young girl of nineteen—I tried for ten years to keep my home together, not knowing what else to do or where to turn—he stuck to her for five years, during which time I was so afraid of him I didn't dare make an issue of it. If I had only gone to a man of God who could have helped me! After that we never found each other, and hardly spoke, and in 1946 I was so exhausted with his mental cruelty that I gave up and got a divorce in order to save my brain and spirit.

Later I found out that he was engaged to this same girl, and in the flash of an eye all my old love came back—it was as if the agony of ten years didn't exist—and with my love came emotions of hatred, revenge, jealousy and rage—a sickening fear made me physically ill so that I couldn't eat or sleep, and I became weak and dizzy—by the fourteenth day I knew I would have to call a doctor, although I knew that a doctor couldn't cure my fear and breaking heart. I was pacing around the room, and said to my sister, "I've got to get some help from somewhere." On trying to get my mind off my terror I picked up a copy of your book—as I started to read, somehow I felt better—the chapter on fear helped me so much, and somehow all of a sudden I seemed to feel safe—and as if I wasn't alone—then like a rushing torrent it came over me—this is the answer—the blessed Lord Jesus—where have I been all these years of nightmare, fear, agony and destruction of spirit? Then I read your marvelous sentence, "Christianity is not a creed to be recited but a power to be tapped." And I remembered the Bible verse—"Fear thou not, for I am with thee." These two thoughts stayed with me, *power* and *reassurance*—I talked with my sister about it, and as I looked into her beautiful blue eyes, filled with love and compassion and tears, I knew I had found HIM.

After that I was able to eat and sleep, and while those dreadful thoughts of desire for murder, bitterness, grief and heartache kept coming back, I would look to heaven and keep my mind on Christ's love and sacrifice, and in the past month they have gradually disappeared. I have been praying constantly for grace and goodness, reading the Bible a great deal, and my mind is healed. Aside from that I feel that I have discovered something marvelous, which will

* "The Art of Living."

sustain me through whatever life brings in time to come. And I see my husband, not as a heartless brute, but as an unhappy and desolate man, also looking for comfort and help all these years, and now trying to find it in another woman's arms instead of in the right place. This thought has helped to take away the bitterness, and left in its place a feeling of compassion, and a sincere wish for his happiness. I know that if he can ever find God he will come back to me, because we had a wonderful love, and we both love our son dearly. I have no way of helping him, except through prayer, as he is very bitter about the embarrassment of the divorce, and will not see me, but perhaps God will show him the way, if it be His *will*—if not I know I can carry on, and will be useful to my boy and others.

Another principle of basic importance in preserving married happiness is to decide how much you love your children. The husband of a famous Hollywood motion-picture actress said to me when some of the press agents of Hollywood first suggested his wife's divorce, and I might say even instigated it (though without deliberate intent), that there could be no divorce because, he exclaimed, "we have the baby and can we cut the baby in two?"

His expression is well taken, for that is exactly what frequently happens to the children of a broken home. They are not cut in two physically but they often are emotionally. Out of a long experience in a religio-psychiatric clinic, I can state that many of the adults with whom I have worked on the matter of divided personality or inner conflicts, or haunting fear and inferiority attitudes, were made so because they were the children of broken marriages. Instead of selfishly thinking of themselves, let parents give thought to the future of their children. The sense of responsibility ought to have some weight with people of character. Perhaps if parents actually knew what their children think, it might help them to avoid some mistakes which wreck home life and cause agony. In the last analysis the children are of first and final importance to a man and wife; that is, if husband and wife are real people. When a child comes to a couple, he is of more importance than their own personal "happiness" (this word used in the Hollywood manner).

One day years ago a young boy came to see me. He was fourteen or fifteen, and was very nervous. He was on the verge of tears. As he clasped and unclasped his hands the blood came and went at his knuckles.

"I must talk to you," he blurted out. "I can't talk to my mother nor to my sister. I haven't anybody to talk to. I must talk to you."

"Go ahead, son, what is it?" I said. "You can talk to me. Tell me anything that is on your mind."

"Well," he said, with great hesitancy, "I want to ask you—is—is—is my dad all right?"

"What do you mean, son, is your dad all right?"

"I mean," he stammered, "is he straight? What they say about him isn't so, is it? Please tell me the truth," he demanded.

"I admire your father very much. I do not know anything bad about him. What is on your mind?"

"Well," he said, "at school they kind of laugh at him and whisper—they have got him mixed up with some woman. Oh, gee, that isn't so, is it?"

The boy was obviously brokenhearted and suffering intense agony. So I said to him, "I don't think so, son, but even if it is, you have to act like a man."

"Shall I tell my mother about it?" he asked, "or shall I go to my father?"

"No," I answered, "don't tell your mother and you can't talk to your father about a thing like that. Just pray for him and keep on believing in him. Keep on loving him and having faith in him."

I did nothing about it for a few days but it troubled me. I did not want to believe it either but I began to have my doubts, so I thought it was my duty to see this father. Naturally he was very angry and told me it was none of my business. That attitude I expected.

I said to him, "I only came to you because of this boy of yours. I just want to tell you how your boy feels." I told him of my interview with his son, and said, "You are going to lose this lad if you are not careful. Your name is being tossed about in a way that humiliates the boy. You can get mad at me all you please but I am just warning you. You had better give it some thought. Do you want the boy or the woman?"

He did not answer but sat at his desk, sullen, angry, face ashen, trying to control himself.

A few days later he came to me and said, "Well, I guess I had better get it off my chest. Yes, it is so. I really did not want to do it, but I did. Now I am in it and I am caught. I guess I'm a dirty dog and I hate myself. My wife is the finest woman in the world." Then he turned to me with a look of fear and almost fiercely said, "My boy doesn't believe this story, does he?"

"Not now," I answered, "because I told him it wasn't so. At the time I really did not think it was."

"Well," he answered, "what can we do about it? We've got to do something."

"There is only one thing you can do about it," I said, "and that is quit it; quit it right off. Break with it instantly and then decide to lead a different life. That is all. Just quit it and get straightened out."

One Sunday about six months later I received this family as members of the church. They stood in front of the altar, the father, mother, sister, and the boy. I do not know to this day how many of them ever knew the story. They never mentioned it to me, but I have never seen anybody happier than that boy that day. I can see his face yet as he stood there struggling to keep back tears, but his smile! It was like sunshine through rain.

That was years ago. The boy is grown up now and is a man in his own right. The sister is married and has her own family and the father and mother are at home alone but they are living together in deep happiness. Their hair is turning gray now, but strangely enough every happiness and joy and success has come to them. Theirs is a religious home and they are very proud of their boy and you should see how proud he is of them, especially of his father who obviously has always been and is now and ever shall be his idol. The boy has turned out to be a great success in life, a magnificent personality, but had that home broken up, I am convinced it would have broken him also. Marriages that break very frequently break the children, and there is no escaping this fact. One can never live that guilt down. It will haunt one in the subconscious mind. It will sour "happiness." It is something to think about as one strives toward married happiness. Think seriously about this matter and perhaps you can solve your differences.

As might be expected, this author believes that personal religion and religion in the home is the best of all answers to the problem of married happiness. The author is joined in this belief by psychiatrists, social workers, judges, and others whose occupations bring them into contact with marital problems.

And well we should be concerned for during the year 1945 there was one divorce for every three marriages in the United States. This compares with a rate of roughly one to six before World War II and one to nine just before World War I. In some communities there are now as many divorces as marriages.*

A Philadelphia newspaper recently carried a symposium on the alarming divorce situation. During the particular week under discussion the Marriage Bureau issued 533 marriage licenses, and for the same period the courts handed down 236 divorce decrees. The newspaper stated, "You don't have to be a viewer-with-alarm to get excited over statistics like those. Something is happening to the sacred institution of matrimony, not only in Philadelphia but all over America, for the divorce rate is skyrocketing everywhere. Attribute it to post-war social upheaval, if you will, or blame it on Hollywood influence. The fact remains that an astounding number of couples today do not look upon marriage as the permanent affair our parents and grandparents did."

The newspaper called upon two distinguished judges of the city, both of whom have passed on thousands of divorce cases, to express their opinion

---

* The figures are by the Commission on Marriage and the Home and by the Executive Committee of the Federal Council of the Churches of Christ in America as quoted in *The Christian Advocate* for March 20, 1947.

on the subject. After analyzing the various reasons for divorce, one judge said, "I blame it primarily on a lack of religion. Where there is no religion, there is no civic or social responsibility. Where there is no social responsibility, there is no family responsibility, and lacking that everything goes out of the window."

The other judge stated, "Overindulgence in alcoholic beverages is a cause of disagreement in a large percentage of divorce cases that come before my court."

Apparently also many businessmen hold the same opinion regarding the value of religion, first in preventing and second in settling marriage difficulties. The head of personnel of one of the largest businesses in America telephoned me one day saying, "I have a young man and his wife here in my office and I wonder if you would be good enough to talk with them. This young man," he explained, "has been working for our company as head of our branch office in another city. Recently he has plunged into rather serious trouble. We here at the home office under the circumstances must remove him as our representative in that particular city. In fact, we had it in mind to discharge him, but before doing so, because of his wife, we would like to give him another chance. We are unable to decide whether we are justified in giving him another opportunity. Before arriving at a final decision my associates and I are requesting you to interview this young couple and give us your reaction."

This prominent personnel man brought the young husband and wife to my office for the interview.

"Well," I asked, "what is the trouble? I am here to help you, so tell me all about it."

To which the young man replied, "I had to come to New York to see the big bosses. They wanted to see me."

"What about?" I asked.

"Well," he answered, "things weren't going so well."

"Why not?" I queried.

"I got into trouble," he replied.

"What kind of trouble?" I asked.

His wife then spoke up, "Go on and tell him."

"Well," he said, "in our business we have a great many young women. I did wrong."

I said, "With one of the girls?"

He confirmed my suspicion and continued, "They called me up here and said it had created such a scandal they would have to let me go. I brought my wife along with me. At the office they said that I was a bad influence and that I had lost my discipline in the organization. They are now deciding whether to give me another chance in a different branch in some other city. I don't know what ever made me do it, but I told them I was going outside and tell my wife. They said that was my responsibility. I went out and told her. It was a terrible experience but I told her all about it."

"How long ago did you tell her?" I asked.

He said, "A half hour ago."

"Well, what did the officers of your firm say then?"

"They sent me over to see you," he replied.

I turned to the wife, "Is there anything more you want to know?"

"Yes," she answered, "I want to know if this is the only time."

"Yes, it is the only time," he replied.

But I didn't believe him and said, "You had better tell us everything, get the whole business straightened out right now, let's get it over with. Tell us of every time. This operation has to be performed, so let's get at it."

To which he earnestly replied, "That is all. I pledge to you before God that this is the only time I have been unfaithful to my wife."

I then turned to the young woman and said, "Is there anything more you want to ask? Ask every question now because before you leave this room, I want you to promise me you will never ask him another question about it. Your mind must not dwell on this thing for your own future happiness and your future relationship with each other."

She asked a few questions and he answered them fully.

I then asked him, "Do you want to be a good man?"

He replied, "I do with all my heart."

I then asked, "Do you love this girl?"

His answer was firm. "Yes."

I then asked her, "Do you love him?"

She countered with, "I find it difficult to say yes. But down deep I do."

I then suggested that we pray. Without my instructing them to do so, they went down on their knees. I said to the husband, "You pray." He looked at me despairingly but I reiterated, "Go on, you must pray." There was a long, long silence, and then he started to pray, slowly, hesitantly, with great embarrassment and then all of a sudden with a veritable gushing out of everything that had been pent up in his mind. It was a complete purging of the soul. It moved me profoundly, but not half so much as when she started to pray. She fought with her inmost soul before my eyes; in the hearing of my ears such a battle of faith I had never heard before. That broke me up even more.

When the atmosphere cleared and they stood up before me in one of the most primitive and basic human relationships, they looked each other straight in the eye and searched each other's eyes. It seemed to me that they stood so for minutes and that my presence was quite forgotten. Then she said to him, "If we have faith in God and in each other, we can build again."

Before they left my office I had to say to this young wife, "I have met many great people in my time, but I want to say to you, young lady, that you are one of the greatest human beings I ever met." And to the boy, I said, "You ought to thank Almighty God that He gave you such a woman as this." Her words have haunted me ever since—for it is the great answer to all such problems—"If we have faith in God and in each other, we can build again."

In this situation faith gave the wife sufficient control to hold her steady in a terrific crisis into which without warning she was plunged. It also enabled the young husband to be entirely honest with himself, a ruthless honesty which precluded any attempt at rationalization. He had done wrong and he knew it and he said so quite frankly. His faith had provided him with a sharp perception of the exact line of demarcation between good and bad. He did not debate with himself or with his wife or with me whether he had done right or wrong. He knew. Many people who flounder in such a situation do so either because they do not know what is right or wrong or else they attempt to dispute the matter not only with others but, what is more tragic, they dispute it with themselves. Religious faith gives you a clear knowledge and understanding. You just *know* what is right and what is wrong. In the vernacular, "You don't kid yourself."

So being honest with yourself you get to the bottom of the trouble at once. The Christian faith of these two people also helped them to believe that no matter what had happened, it could be put behind them; that having cleared the matter up, they could build again. Such people having a deep faith realize that there are no hopeless situations. He is a wise man who builds up some real faith for himself against crises which may come.

I cannot advocate too strongly that marriages be built upon spiritual foundations. One of the wisest statements ever made is that solemn assertion in the Bible, "Except the Lord build the house, they labor in vain that build it." (Psalm 127:1.) This statement is from the Book which reveals more precise knowledge about people than any other book in history. It simply states a solemn and irrevocable fact that you cannot build a successful marriage upon any other basis than the principles of love, beauty, forbearance, mutual respect and faith taught by Christianity.

It is very significant when you think about it that the old-time American families had family prayer in the home. Until recently, family prayer was one of the characteristic features of happy American home life. The divorce rate has climbed ever since people generally gave it up. This fact seems to be more than a coincidence. Marriages were consecrated in prayer. Husband and wife prayed together and had grace at the table. When the children came, it was made a family prayer period. It did something to people. It taught them how to live together and it kept them free from those mistakes which destroy marriage. Unconsciously over the years it built up character, a sturdy kind of character which molded a great free people and preserved their institutions of freedom.

Over a period of years I have found that when you can get a couple to pray together from the very day they are married, the surest preventative to marriage difficulties has been found. I would go so far as to say that I do not know of a single couple who have practiced this who have not had happiness in marriage. It will restore married happiness to people whose marriages seem to be entering upon difficulties.

Here is a convincing illustration. A young woman came for an interview. She was quite distressed and told me that her married life was rapidly approaching the breaking point. I gathered from what she said that the fault was largely her husband's. The counselor, however, must always keep balanced, remembering there are always two sides. Finally we made her feel that perhaps she had some responsibility about the situation. Her husband, it seemed, was given to violent outbursts of temper and profanity. She pictured him as a very irritable man with whom to live. I asked if there was any religious atmosphere in the home and she acknowledged that there was none at all.

"Oh," she said, "my husband does talk a great deal about God, but not in the way you mean."

I outlined to her my theory that when a husband and wife pray together, they lift their problems above bickering into a region where quarrels fade away and where peace and understanding endure.

"Do you ever return thanks at the table in your home?" I asked.

"No," she replied, "when I was at home with my mother and father as a little girl they had grace at the table. I did learn a little prayer of grace from my father, one that he often used, but since we have been married, we have never prayed together and have never returned thanks at the table, although we are members of a church." (They never went to church except at Easter.)

"Why not begin the practice?" I asked. "When you sit down to dinner tonight, just say to your husband, 'Jim, I sort of feel I would like to return thanks. Do you mind?' Do not be strained or self-conscious or pious about it, just do it and then start talking about something else."

She seemed very doubtful and hesitant but finally agreed to apply this prescription to their matrimonial situation. Later she told me what happened. Her husband solemnly sat down to the table and glumly started to eat. She said softly, "Jim, I sort of feel like I would like to return thanks, do you mind?"

Astonishment spread over his features but he said nothing. This went on for two or three nights. He listened to his wife's voice in prayer. Perhaps he detected a tone he had not heard in a long while. One night he growled, "Who is the head of this house anyway? I am going to return thanks myself."

Presently it got so when in discussing their problems, it seemed quite natural to pray about them. The atmosphere of the home gradually changed. Bickering and argument waned and both the husband and the wife have told me that it is next to a miracle the way in which this simple practice provided the basis for happy married life.

In a certain American city a man said they had one of the most beautiful suburbs in the country. He insisted that we drive out to see it. His appraisal was correct; two or three hundred acres of the most beautifully landscaped terrain were dotted by lovely homes, each one architecturally picturesque. The residents of these homes were the leading younger married people of the city; leading, that is, from the standpoint of position and money. The man waxed enthusiastic over these houses, particularly about the fact that they contained the finest home bars that he had ever seen. It appeared that each home owner vied with his neighbor as to who could have the most attractive bar in his house.

I asked if these people were churchgoers, to which he replied with surprise, "Oh, no, very few of them go to church, except Easter maybe."

I asked if their parents had been church people.

"Oh, yes, almost without exception, the former generation were religious people."

"Well," I asked, "did their fathers and mothers have bars as nice as these bars?"

"Oh, my, no," he said, "they didn't have bars."

"That is strange," I commented. "I can't imagine any well regulated household not having a bar!"

Then I inquired as to the marriage status of these people—whether there were many divorces among them.

"Of course," he replied, "most of them have been divorced. In fact, only three or four are living with their first wife or first husband." Then he whispered surreptitiously, "There are lots of goings on around here that wouldn't look good in print."

"Pretty risqué, if you ask me," he confided.

I do not want to exaggerate but one wonders if we have arrived at the time when the family altar has given way to the family bar. In moments of sober reflection every American must ask himself what is going to happen to the country that substitutes the family bar for the family altar? Is there any relation between the break-up of the family and the entrance of liquor into the family in this dominating manner? The reader must decide this question for himself on the basis of the evidence, "Which will hold a marriage together and develop children of character—the family altar or the family bar?"

Many so-called expert solutions of marriage difficulties are offered today. Innumerable articles are written on "What is happening to marriage." Everybody is becoming intensely concerned about the break-up of the family. America was built upon certain institutions, principally the home, the church and the school. If the home collapses, what will happen to American civilization? Cicero said, "The empire is at the fireside."

Basically there is one principle for married happiness and the establishment of an enduring home and that is an atmosphere of religion in the family. Whatever your religion may be—Protestant, Catholic, or Jewish—put it into practice in your home. It is amazing how the difficulties that make for marital and family unhappiness will disappear.

A marine engineer who had been to sea for twelve years married a young widow who had one son. He had never been compelled to adjust to any family or business situation. The wife, widowed at twenty, had for ten years carried on her husband's business in a man's world. She supported herself, her son and her mother by this business. The mother lived with them in a tiny apartment and worked in the office of her daughter's business.

The young widow met the marine engineer in a service club during the war. They were quickly married but for the first six months never had more than two days together at a time, these being when he was in port. The war ended and they started life together. He began to take over the business which she owned and had operated. He moved into the already overcrowded apartment. In fact, he was moving into a new world in every way. Both the husband and the wife were high-grade people but adjustments seemed so difficult that people said, "It can't be done." The couple, too, were becoming sure that they had made a mistake. They were fed up, regretted the marriage, and were at the breaking point.

During this time they attended church regularly. They became interested in a young married couples' group at the church. One day they frankly shared their problems and defeats with another couple who from experience had learned how spiritual faith can remake and enrich marriage. This other young couple challenged them to stop the practice of constantly looking at the problems in their situation and in each other that caused or aggravated the condition and instead to start definitely asking for God's help.

They were also challenged to honestly examine themselves, to see what was wrong in their own attitudes, and to deal positively with resentments and fears. They began to replace these faults with understanding, patience and faith. They were urged to seek spiritual changes in themselves, and thus through changing themselves to change the situation.

They admitted they had tried everything but God; they had even been to a psychiatrist. The idea of God as a personal friend and positive factor in the situation, the idea that He would be concerned with the details of their lives, was entirely new to them.

They joined the other young couple in praying audibly and asked that the above change take place. They "surrendered" themselves to God's will. One week later in a small group they related that a miracle had happened and indeed their personal appearance confirmed it. They seemed to be completely released and obviously were in love in a deeper way. New confidence came to the husband which immediately affected and changed his business contacts, resulting in an amazingly fine order. New joy radiated the personality of the wife.

They began at once to practice in the home morning and evening prayer periods during which they asked for answers to the daily problems that confronted them. Both prayed audibly. They instituted the practice of a quiet period during which they said they were listening for God's guidance. They adopted the practice that when a business problem confronted them, instead of each belligerently telling the other what ought to be done, they sought jointly in prayer to find the Christian way to deal with it.

When problems arise with the teen-age boy, the wife's son, they sit down with him and all three read from the Bible, pray together and seek the best way to meet the problem. There is no longer division or jealousy in their decisions with the boy but instead an attitude of teamwork prevails, all three of them being on the "home team." This couple are so completely filled with this new spirit that they positively believe it can solve any problem. They are constantly and eagerly helping other couples who have missed domestic peace, enlightening them on the marvelous way in which it can be obtained. They are sure they have a formula which will guarantee to any husband and wife the enjoyment of married happiness.

Proceeding inductively from our clinical case histories, let me close with a few simple and practical procedures for creating a spiritual atmosphere in the home:

1. Get in the habit of saying a pleasant thing as the first words you speak in the morning. Say something of a happy and constructive nature. That will set the mental and emotional tone for the day.

2. Everybody in the home should get up five minutes earlier and utilize those extra minutes for silent prayer—*everybody* at the table for this period. Then let one member of the family offer a few words of prayer. This serves to control the usual hectic start of the day's work.

3. Find one of the early morning religious radio programs which seems helpful. *Sit down quietly* and listen to it.

4. Say grace at lunch. If the wife is alone, let her have a quiet moment of meditation thanking God for her family and asking for guidance.

5. At dinner, say grace. Make a rule that no problems, worries or resentments shall enter into the table conversation. Make anyone who so offends drop a nickel into a bank.

6. At the close of the meal let one member of the family read a few verses of scripture. Vary this occasionally with an inspiring poem or a stimulating paragraph from a spiritual book. Let the one who prays thank God for the other members of the family by name.
7. Don't get glum when you do this. A sour expression does not denote religion. Gaiety does.
8. Take the whole family to church on Sunday and sit together in a "family pew."
9. Keep good religious literature on the home reading tables.
10. Keep a Bible on your night table and drop a few great texts into your mind before going to sleep. Psychologists say that what you think about in the last five minutes before sleep has a deep effect on your consciousness. Thank God for all the blessings of the day. Then as you turn out the light, repeat these words: "He giveth his beloved sleep." Then believe that God is giving you deep and refreshing sleep and it will be so.

Write it above the fireplace in every home and engrave it on the mind of every husband and wife in the land—"EXCEPT THE LORD BUILD THE HOUSE, THEY LABOR IN VAIN THAT BUILD IT."

12

HOW TO MEET SORROW

WHY SHOULD A BOOK on success and happiness contain a chapter dealing with the technique of meeting sorrow? The obvious answer is that sorrow cannot be escaped. Sorrow is a great shock and its effect on anyone, one way or another, is profound. It may make one a bigger and finer person, or it may cloud the mind and dull the spirit. It may dissipate enthusiasm and destroy incentive. In short, one must know how to meet sorrow; how to summon courage and carry on. What can a person in sorrow get hold of that will preserve the values of his life?

The late Ernie Pyle, famous war correspondent, wrote a moving story of his walk on the beaches of Normandy late on the afternoon of D-Day. The sand was strewn with the personal effects of American boys, who early that morning had landed in a history-shaping invasion. Scattered about were touching little personal keepsakes, snapshots, books, letters. Beside the body of one boy he found a guitar, and by another a tennis racket. Touching thought—American boys going into battle, even then irrepressible tourists as in the days of peace, taking along tennis rackets and guitars.

Alongside the body of one lad, he saw half buried in the sand an issue Bible. Ernie Pyle picked up the Bible, walked a half a mile with it, then walked back and laid it down where he found it. "I don't know why I picked it up," he said, "or why I put it back down."

Perhaps he thought vaguely he would send it to the parents of the boy to comfort them. Perhaps he returned the Bible to the spot where he found it because dimly he felt that the boy having died in this faith, the Book ought to remain forever with him.

Whatever his reasons, the incident suggests that in the solemn questions of life and death, there is only one Book that has the answers that satisfy our minds and give understanding and comfort. People gain great victory over sorrow by means of their faith.

I sat with a prominent businessman in his beautiful home. His wife was dead and he was in deep grief. About his house was all that wealth could provide of beauty and loveliness. Costly rugs were on the floor, exquisite pictures and hangings on the walls. But what did it all matter? A beloved wife was gone and a man whom I knew to be a strong leader in the business world was broken with grief.

What he told me in the intimate friendship of that hour of sorrow was impressive. He was a man of somewhat austere mien with no outward evidence of sentiment in his nature—a typical aggressive and efficient businessman of the sort that compels respect and gains dominance. Within his home, however, he was dependent, leaning upon his wife who had been almost a mother to him. He was shy about social contacts, and much preferred to remain at night quietly in his home reading, his wife knitting, or reading, at the opposite side of the table. Like many men of similar type, he was a boy never quite grown up, but putting on a strong front before the world.

"I've found something in religion that I never felt before," he said quietly. "Last night I knelt by my bed as usual to pray. I've done this every night since I was a boy. When I was married forty years ago," he continued, "my wife and I agreed to pray together every night. We would kneel by the side of the bed and she would pray out loud. I couldn't do that," he explained, "and anyway she was much better at it and I always felt God would listen to her."

Rather shyly he said that he would hold his wife's hand as she prayed. Like two simple-hearted children they were. God must have looked with delight upon them, judging from the way he blessed them.

"Well," he went on, "we did that all these years and then—then God took her away, and last night I knelt alone. Out of long habit I put my hand out for hers, but it was not there. It all came over me then how I missed her and loved her, and I wanted her so badly I could hardly bear it. I felt as I did long ago when I was a boy and was scared and wanted my mother. I put my head down on the bedside and I guess for the first time in my life I really prayed. I said, 'O God, I've heard about people really finding you and I believe you do help people. You know how much I need you. I put my life in your hands. Help me, dear Lord.' "

He looked me full in the face, and his eyes were filled with wonder as he said, "Do you know what happened?" His words came slowly. "Suddenly I felt a touch on my hand, the hand she always held. It was a strong, kindly touch, and I seemed to feel a great hand take my own. In surprise I looked up, but, of course, could see no one. However all the pain seemed to go out of my mind and peace came into my heart. I knew that God was with me and would never leave me, and that she is with me too." So he concluded with determination in his voice.

This man had discovered a basic fact taught by Christianity; that fact is that *what seems to be death is not death at all.* Apparently Jesus Christ did not think of death as we think of it. As he stood by the body of a little girl, he said, "Weep not; she is not dead, but sleepeth." When He came to the bereaved household of Lazarus, He informed them, "Our friend Lazarus sleepeth; but I go, that I may awake him out of sleep." It would seem that death to Him is a condition of sleep. In His teaching actual death is something more sinister than physical death. He teaches that the body is only a temporary house for an eternal soul. Apparently death in the mind of Jesus Christ means death of the soul. He said, "The soul that sinneth, it shall die." "The wages of sin is death" (i.e., for the soul). Historically as civilizations become pagan they tend to increase emphasis upon the body as the ultimate value. The teaching of Christianity, however, is "Be not afraid of them that kill the body."

In His thought, what we call death does not in any sense affect the continuity of the individual's life. The New Testament contains a magnificent passage which describes the state of our deceased loved ones; "They shall hunger no more, neither thirst any more; neither shall the sun light on them, nor any heat. For the Lamb which is in the midst of the throne shall feed them, and shall lead them unto living fountains of waters: and God shall wipe away all tears from their eyes." (Revelation 7:16-17.)

That is one of the most comforting passages ever written. They shall hunger no more. What hunger? Hunger of the body? Mental or spiritual hunger? Whatever it is, they shall hunger no more, but will be satisfied. Nor shall they thirst any more. Perhaps thirst is a more poignant description than hunger for it is a deeper anguish when experienced. The point is that our loved ones have their deepest longings and yearnings completely satisfied.

The passage also indicates that their life shall be so full and beautiful that it can only be described by the loveliness of fountains of living waters. And "every tear shall be wiped away from their eyes."

After my mother's death, as I relived our life together, I remembered one lovely Sunday afternoon when together we saw the famous fountains of Versailles. Like myriads of diamonds in the sunlight, the fountains played to the delight of my mother.

She was a very great traveler and visited many countries. She was, in truth, a connoisseur of beauty. One rainy night she fell into ecstasy as she contemplated a ferry boat running between Manhattan and Hoboken. She commented in ecstatic tones on its romance and charm, on the mystery of the river, the night and the rain and the boat with its lights in the mist.

After she passed away it gave me comfort to think of her as being taken by God's hand and hearing him say, "Come unto me, I will show you more marvelous fountains than those you once saw at Versailles." I am sure that she eagerly followed. I can almost see the dancing fountains reflected in her eyes. It is not difficult to think of God as wiping tears from her eyes. As she loved to travel and used to write enthusiastically that she was having a glorious time and only wished we could be with her, so I believe that though she is out of sight at present, she is having a time of great happiness. It would not be fair to her to want her back from that land of ineffable charm. I can imagine her making mental notes of places of beauty and she probably says to herself, "When my husband and children come here, won't it be a delight to show them these beautiful places which I have found and enjoyed?"

A veteran nurse says: "It has always seemed to me a major tragedy that so many people go through life haunted by the fear of death—only to find when it comes that it's as natural as life itself. For very few are afraid to die when they get to the very end. In all my experience only one seemed to feel any terror—a woman who had done her sister a wrong which it was too late to right.

"Something strange and beautiful happens to men and women when they come to the end of the road. All fear, all horror disappears. I have often watched a look of happy wonder dawn in their eyes when they realized this was true. It is all part of the goodness of nature and, I believe, of the illimitable goodness of God."*

Do not hold on to your loved ones in your thought. Release them, let them go. You do not lose them by so doing. You hamper them with your dark and dismal thoughts of grief. They have earned the joy and delight which they are now experiencing. Do not spoil it for them.

I visited a little old-fashioned country burying ground one winter day with a friend. This man had met with outstanding success but he told me that when his mother died he felt that life was not worth living. He did not marry until late in life and had spent his earlier years in great devotion to his mother. His happiest experiences did not consist in the attainment of some sought-after ambition, but were the pleasure of going home and telling his mother about them. When she died, and this was no longer possible, he said that life seemed to lose its meaning. There was nothing to work for any more. He was somewhat bitter and found himself constantly seeking his mother out in his thoughts and resisting the idea that she had passed from him.

As we stood in this little burying ground, he said, "That is the way I felt until one day I came to this place." He had shown me a little crossroad store that had been operated by his father, and after the father's death, by his mother. "She was a frail little woman," he said, "but her sparkling black eyes never showed any defeat. She had little education and few opportunities. She had to work hard to bring up her little family. As a small boy I saw her drag heavy bags of sugar across the floor of the store. She would pull and I would get behind and push.

"Then came the night before I went away to college. She took me into her room and, reaching under the mattress, pulled out four crumpled ten dollar bills. 'I have saved them for you,' she said. 'Take them, go to college, work hard and become a fine, outstanding man.'"

* *Getting the Most Out of Life*, an Anthology from *The Reader's Digest*, p. 116.

He said, "I shall never forget those crumpled bills resting in her little hands. I noted how worn her hands were and it touched my heart.

"So, when she died, I did not want to live. But one day I stood in this cemetery and looked at the old familiar hills capped with snow. It was all very peaceful and the stark beauty of the world in the cold winter sunshine gave me a sense of eternity. I prayed, using the same words that she used to use. All at once I had a peculiar feeling of peace and inner quietness. A thought came that had never previously occurred to me. It was that I was not being fair to my mother. She had worked hard and now for the first time she was free of labor and toil.

"All her life she had read about heaven. I could still hear her voice singing, 'There is a land of pure delight.' She was one of those simple Christians for whom earth was a preparation for heaven, and I was not allowing her to enjoy this heaven for which she had labored and toiled, and of which she had dreamed. So, standing in that little cemetery I spoke out loud, 'Mother, I am going to let you go, have a good time, you have earned this joy.' As soon as I said that, I had peace in my heart. It was as if she actually came and stood beside me and said, "Thank you, my son, you understand. I will wait for you and meet you across the river. Meanwhile my spirit will often be near you.'"

There is a natural wistfulness regarding the state and condition of our loved ones, when they have passed from this life. We have no exact information but there is sufficient reason to believe that our loved ones who died in the faith are in the kindly hands of God.

It must be a beautiful place to which they have gone. We know *nothing* about it, of course, but we do have intimations. When that great wizard of the natural sciences, Thomas A. Edison, came to die, it was noticed that he was attempting to give a message. His physician, bending low, heard Mr. Edison say faintly but distinctly, "It is very beautiful over there."

A minister told of being with a dying man. The family gathered in his room felt it must be dark going through the valley all alone, so they lighted all the lights that the dying man would not be afraid of going into the dark. Of a sudden at midnight he raised his head on the pillow, and with a look of surprise said, "Put out the lights. Can't you see, the sun is up."

I knew the meteorologist in a certain city. He had held his position for forty years. For four decades he had charted the weather and had studied natural laws. He was by instinct, training and experience, a rational and a scientific mind. He was also a man of deep religious faith. His son was not a religious person in a formal sense. When the father came to die, he suddenly turned to his son, who sat by his bedside, and said, "Bill, I see the most beautiful place. It is beyond description and . . . in a window is a light for me." An expression of great peace and happiness came over his face and he said no more.

When the son related this incident, I asked him, "What do you think your father actually saw?" His reply was characteristic of the scientific attitude of both father and son. "What do I think my father actually saw? Why, there is no doubt about that. He never reported anything he did not see or test or know. He saw what he said he saw."

"Could it have been an hallucination?" I asked.

"Not at all," he replied. "My father had not the type of mind to have an hallucination. He saw something and reported it precisely as was his custom with all data," said the son. "I am absolutely sure of it."

We must seek our information about the after-life from the only source that is thoroughly reliable, one that has stood the test of time. To the question, "What is the state of our loved ones after this life?", the Bible suggests the answer: "Blessed are the dead which die in the Lord." That means, "Happy are the dead who die in the Lord."

It is difficult to associate happiness with death. Death for us is the ultimate tragedy. But can anything in God's plan be a tragedy? Tennyson said, "Death is the bright side of life." Robert Louis Stevenson, when death came to him, said, "If this is death, it is easier than life." One wonders in the light of such statements and certain experiences whether death is the tragedy we think it is. We cannot believe that God, in transferring a man from one form of life to another, would make of it a tragedy.

A news reporter had to undergo a serious operation. As it was performed under local anesthesia, he had all his faculties about him, and was able to note and record his experiences. He decided he would go into this experience as a reporter, describing each step. If he came back from the edge of death, he would have a great story to tell. He found himself sinking. He came to a point where he did not want to come back. The pull was to go on. It was such an entrancing aspect of peace and beauty that every element in his nature urged him forward. It was reported afterwards by the doctor that he had a sinking spell. Then, by an act of will, he said, "I must return, I must fight off this allurement." With great reluctance he returned to normal life again, but said he would never again have a fear of death.

The process of birth holds some suggestions of the protection we may experience at the end of earthly life. An infant, snuggled up under the mother's heart in the pre-natal days, is surrounded by warmth and protection. If he could reason, the baby might say, "I don't want to be born; I don't want to go out of this world into that other world. I am happy here; I am afraid of birth."

In his pre-natal existence, he might regard birth as we do death, as the end of one certain experience and the beginning of another uncertain one. Then he is born. Looking down at him is the kindest and sweetest face in the world. He is cuddled in his mother's loving arms. There he is held and protected, fed and loved. God made it that way.

So after many years, when a man comes to die, need he be terrified at the prospect or death—or, if you please, of another birth? Should he fear to pass from this world into the next? If he had love and protection when first he came to this earth, may he not assume he will have the same as he enters the next life? Can we not trust the same God to take care of us in death as He did in birth? Will His attribute of love so quickly change? It would not be like Him.

We should learn to think of death as a natural part of our total experience. Let me relate the story of a woman who deeply understood this truth. She was past middle age when she came to see me. "I have a hard problem for you," she said. "Three of the best physicians in New York have told me that I must undergo a serious operation not later than Monday morning, and that this operation may mean my death. The doctors told me frankly, because I asked them for the truth."

She had the quality of personality that could take the truth, no matter how grim. "About a year ago," she continued, "I lost my son in the war." She showed me his picture, then said, "I ask you, sir, if I die as a result of this operation on Monday, will I see him again?"

She looked me squarely in the eye, searching intently for any indefiniteness or evasiveness. I looked directly into her eyes and told her: "It is my positive belief, based upon what I know of Jesus Christ, that you will see him again."

"How soon will that be after I go?" she asked.

"I wish I could say," I replied, "but if your son were in a foreign country and you went to see him, you would make for him as soon as the ship landed, wouldn't you? You will find him. It can't be long, for love can never lose its own."

She said, "I have a husband and a daughter. If I live, I will be with them. If I die, I shall see my son."

I said, "Yes, you are in a very fortunate position. Regardless of what happens, you still have all your family."

"God is very good," she said slowly.

When she stood up to leave, I took her by the hand and could not help saying, "You are one of the greatest personalities I ever met."

Quietly, rationally, simply, she was getting ready for a journey. When she left me, she went to a photographer and had her picture taken. Later I saw those photographs and there was a light on her face. Next, she saw her lawyer and even made arrangements for her funeral. Then, quickly and in complete peace, she went to the hospital, where she submitted to the operation. Despite the best skill of modern science, she passed on. Today, I believe, she is with both her son and her loved ones.

I cannot prove this. Long ago I got over the idea that you have to prove everything. The man who disagrees cannot disprove it. Although perhaps as yet the superiority of faith cannot be proven scientifically, yet we may reasonably consider our faith as a logic which goes beyond so-called scientific knowledge. It is the deep logic of human intuition which, in the final analysis, is an ultimate source of truth. What we feel inwardly in the logic of experience, in the flash of intuition, is true especially when millions of human beings in every generation so think and so "feel."

We live in a generation during which death has visited households as never before. Only recently death's sinister touch was on battlefields all over the globe. Death lurked beneath the sea and hid behind every white cloud. His message daily came through the mail into thousands of homes. His solemn voice came over the telegraph wires, in the form of a little yellow envelope containing a message which said, "The United States Government regrets to inform you that your son . . ." Then there was the shutting of a door, a stifled sob, and many an American family repeated an experience known throughout the history of our country. Death ruled the world. Even in days of peace, death is always present.

But remember this—death never wins. Write across the skies, blazon abroad that every man may hear the great and abiding faith which rises above the roar of battle, above the smoke and tumult of pain and suffering, above death itself as expressed in the lilting victorious words which have survived the centuries: "I am the resurrection, and the life: he that believeth in me, though he were dead, yet shall he live."

That is the fact we need to know: life wins an everlasting and glorious victory over death.

During the late war the chaplains went with the troops to the very front. This accounts for the high casualty rate among chaplains. Catholic, Protestant, Jewish chaplains, they were in danger with the boys.

When a boy lay wounded or dying on the field, perhaps the first man to bend over him was the chaplain. The Christian chaplain wore on his helmet a little white cross—the Cross of Christ. The first thing that the eyes of the wounded man would see was the white cross on the helmet just above him. One thinks of a boy struck down, feeling death approach. Perhaps a terror wells up within that he wouldn't admit to anybody. A wave of homesickness and loneliness comes over him. He would give anything to see the face of his mother, or his wife, or the face of his sweetheart, or feel the touch of the hands of his little children. He would like once again to see the sunlight falling on the old hills of his native land. He would like to see the sparkle of the Hudson, the Ohio, or the Mississippi, but that is all very, very far away, except that it is printed in his heart. He is dying far from home and loved ones.

A kindly face bends over him. He sees on the helmet the cross and something responds in his heart. The Church is here. The faith has followed him. The tie that binds still holds and the everlasting arms are beneath him. Then the chaplain, out of the kindness of his heart, puts his hand under the head of the dying boy, perhaps strokes back his hair just as his mother would have done, and says, "Son, listen, you remember these words, don't you, boy? Believe them. Believe them with all your heart: 'I am the resurrection, and the life: he that believeth in me, though he were dead, yet shall he live.'"

The boy listens, peace comes into his heart. His eyes grow hazy. Earth recedes; the face grows dim, the voice fades. For just a moment he is crossing a valley. And then almost more quickly than it takes to tell it, suddenly everything is bright around him and there is a glorious light and a radiance more wonderful than anything he has ever seen or known.

He looks up in happy surprise. There is a face above him, but it is another face, stronger, more kindly, even than the other face that he saw through his pain. Again he sees a cross, but this time it is shining in light and he hears words like rippling music, tender words, words of triumph and faith and the voice that utters them is the voice that formulated them long ages ago, "I am the resurrection, and the life." The voice says to him, "You have found it, my boy, you have found it. I am with you as I said I would be. That man over on the earthly side of the river was my representative and he pointed you the way to cross over. You are here now with me and all is well."

It is not unreasonable to believe that in this universe, which is both material and spiritual, our loved ones who have gone from us are not really very far from us.

Many people report that when least expected they have had a definite feeling of the near presence of loved ones.

A man whose rationality I respect told me that for the first three weeks after his father's death, he suffered profound grief. "But," he said, "one day all of a sudden that grief lifted. I had a very serious problem to solve, and I almost felt that my father was there helping me to solve it. I got the touch of his mind. I felt his presence. I could not be grief-stricken longer, for it unmistakably came over me that he was near to me."

He asked if I felt he could believe that experience to be real, and I told him that I thought so.

I have found some help in an illustration used by Stewart Edward White in his book, *The Unobstructed Universe*. When the electric fan is in motion at high speed, it is possible to see through the thick blades. Mr. White makes the point that ours is an unobstructed universe, meaning that those who have passed into the spiritual world are merely living in an area of higher frequency, or a different frequency than that in which we dwell. They are near to us but we cannot see them. Man has a psychic nature governed by the laws of the spiritual universe. Thus intuitions, insights, spiritual apprehensions are not unnatural or bizarre, but are normal experiences. They are flash-overs from the spiritual world which is correlated to our own. Why they come, we do not know, but it is very dangerous to assert dogmatically that they are not real. The most likely fact is that they represent a fundamental reality in our universe, namely the indestructibility of the spirit and the deathlessness of the human soul.

I should like to conclude this chapter by relating an experience with a brokenhearted Gold Star mother. Shortly after the close of the war *The American Magazine* published a pathetic letter written by Mrs. Frank C. Douglas of Blytheville, Arkansas, in which she told how her son's death in battle had shaken her faith. I was so moved by her letter that I immediately wrote an answer, not only to her, but to all mothers everywhere who had known this crushing experience.

The American Magazine has given permission to insert here my answer to Mrs. Douglas, which it published in the issue of April, 1946. My letter was preceded by an editorial note.

> In a recent issue of *The American Magazine*, Mrs. Frank C. Douglas of Blytheville, Ark., told how her son's death in battle had shattered her faith in the power of prayer. Since the publication of her letter, more than 3,000 readers from all over the nation have written to offer her advice and comfort. From all these letters Mrs. Douglas selected several which she found to be especially helpful. Among them is the following letter from Dr. Norman Vincent Peale, minister of the Marble Collegiate Church of New York, noted writer and radio speaker. Dr. Peale's letter is published here in the hope that it will also be of help to others.

> Dear Mrs. Douglas:
> If we could always keep our loved ones alive through the exercising of faith, there would never be any death. There has to come a time when, after God has spared them time and time again, He cannot spare them longer. It is given to all men to die. Some die in youth. Others die in old age. Some die in time of peace as a result of accident or disease; others die in time of war. I think one must assume that whenever a man dies, his life's work has been accomplished on this earth. In the thought of God, years as we measure them are as flashing seconds to Him. It makes no difference whether a man lives twenty years or eighty years, when he has finished his work here he is promoted to that higher realm of the spirit which we call heaven.

> Really, it is a high honor that some men can finish their life's work at an early age, while others in the sight of God apparently do not do so well, and they have to stay here longer until they finally work it out.

> It is a fact that we poor human beings think so deeply in earthly terms. God does not place the same valuation upon earthly existence that we do. He said, "Be not afraid of them who kill the body, but rather those who may destroy the soul."

> Of course, this is little comfort to one who looks and longs for a beloved face and figure. But if we are thinking spiritually rather than in an earthly way, we do not lay so much importance upon the life of the body.

You have been a woman of faith. You say your son had faith. This meant that you were both in the will of God. You were harmonized with His will and purpose. I would think, then, that you ought to assume, which I am sure you may, that your son being yielded to God, His will was done.

God in His answers to prayer often says "Yes." Sometimes He says "Wait." Often he says "No." In any case, His will is done, and true faith is to believe that what has happened has happened for the best. If one does not take that attitude, he is setting his personal desire against the wisdom of God. Oftentimes we confuse with faith merely that which we desire.

I should like to ask you, in the deepest possible kindness, do you really think you have lost your son? Let me tell you a little story.

Recently I sat in the home of two good friends whose son had died in France. Two photographs were on their library wall. One was of the father in the uniform of World War I; the other was of the 20-year-old son in the uniform of this war.

In the intimacy of friendship they talked tenderly of their son. "He always whistled," the mother said. "Far down the street, when he came home from school as a little boy, you could hear him whistling, and as he grew up he whistled. He would come dashing into the house whistling, and toss his coat and hat at the hall hatrack; and both would catch the peg and hang there. Then he would run up the stairs whistling. He was a gay spirit."

They told humorous incidents; and, in that intimate way of friendship, we were laughing—and occasionally the laughter would be through tears. Suddenly, the mother said sadly, "But we will never hear him whistle again."

Strange as it seems, at that moment I had an indistinct, but nevertheless real, feeling that I had "heard" the boy whistle as we talked. It might have been the mood we were in, yet I prefer to believe differently; but as she said, "We will never hear him whistle again," I found myself saying, "You are wrong about that"—I hesitated—"I had a feeling that right this minute he was whistling in this room."

The father—a sturdy, unemotional person—spoke up quickly: "Strange that you should say that; I had the same feeling myself." We sat hushed and awed. Ingersoll's great line passed through my mind—"In the night of death, hope sees a star, and listening love can hear the rustle of a wing."

In the faith that God will give you peace and understanding, I am—Cordially yours—Norman Vincent Peale.

13

CHANGE YOUR THOUGHTS AND YOU CHANGE EVERYTHING

CHANGE YOUR THOUGHTS and everything changes. Your life is determined by the kind of thoughts you habitually think.

If, however, your thoughts do not change, you will follow your old life pattern as the following story shows . . .

A hotel manager told me that a Barbers' Supply Association held a convention in his hotel. This organization had a very enterprising publicity agent. He went down to a poor street in a bad section and found the most unpromising specimen of human nature he could locate—an unkempt, unshaven, drunken, sad creature. This down-and-outer was taken to the hotel where they gave him a haircut; dressed him in a good suit of clothes; gave him nice linen. They decked him out in a rakish looking overcoat and cane and spats. When he emerged from this refurbishing, he was a marvelous example of the barber's art. Meanwhile, they had photographed every process of this transformation, and each photograph appeared in the daily newspaper. It was hailed as a first-rate publicity stunt. Everybody was amazed at what the barbers could do, with the help of the tailors, in making over a man. The hotel manager was impressed. After the convention his interest in the man remained.

He said to him, "By a strange set of circumstances you have been made into the form of a gentleman, and lifted out of the slums. Now your great opportunity is at hand. I am going to give you a job in another hotel which I operate, and I am going to back you, and we are going to make a successful man of you. When will you go to work?"

The man replied, "Suppose we make it tomorrow morning at eight o'clock."

A doubt crossed the mind of the hotel manager, but he agreed. The doubt came back at eight o'clock next morning when his man did not show up. Nor did he appear all day. So the manager, following a hunch, went down to the same street from which the man had come and after a search found him dead drunk, sleeping on some newspapers in an alley, his fine clothes rumpled and soiled.

The hotel manager said that it was a most disillusioning experience. "The barbers may be able to clean him up on the outside, but you can never make anything out of a man until you also change him on the inside," and he added ruefully, "I wish I could have had him just a little longer, for the thing that was wrong with that man was his thought processes. Maybe if I could have had him a little longer, I could have changed his thinking and so have changed him."

To make amends for his depressing story, the hotel manager told me another.

"I have somebody to counteract the man who reverted to his old thoughts," he said. "It is Jimmy, the elevator boy and bellhop. He was sent to me by a church school for delinquent boys. He was a bright lad, greeted everybody politely, was always courteous. He worked hard and had good moral habits. One day the boy came to me and said, 'I am going to get married. Will you be the best man?'" So this big hotel manager was best man for a bellhop, which was just like him.

He became interested in the boy and one day said to him, "Jimmy, you are an unusual fellow. What makes you this way? You have something that is missing in a good many boys. What is that something?"

Jimmy answered, "Oh, I don't know unless it is what they did for us down at the school."

"Well," he asked, "what did they do for you at the school?"

The boy replied thoughtfully, "Oh, I don't know unless it is that they got us to thinking—kinda religious—I guess that's it. They got us to thinking kinda religious."

Of course Jimmy has gone ahead. He discovered that life is what your thoughts make it. He learned to think "kinda religious."

A man's world is not primarily made of the circumstances that surround him. The kind of thoughts he thinks determines the exact kind of world in which he lives. You are not what you think you are, but what you *think*, you are.

The wisest men of all time have said this. Nineteen hundred years ago there lived a Roman Emperor by the name of Marcus Aurelius. He has been called the wisest man of the Roman Empire. On his long marches and military campaigns, he sat by his campfire writing his thoughts. These thoughts were gathered together in a book called *The Meditations of Marcus Aurelius,* one of the greatest heritages from antiquity. And one of the greatest things that this wise man said is this: "Your life is what your thoughts make of it."

The wisest man who ever lived in the United States of America, some people say, was Ralph Waldo Emerson. And he said, "A man is what he thinks about all day long."

And the wisest of all Books declares, "As a man thinketh in his heart (i.e., as a man thinketh in his subconscious mind), so is he."

What you think, what you have been thinking over a long period of time, what you are going to think in the days ahead will determine precisely what you are and the kind of world you live in. What you think determines what you become.

Change your thoughts and you will change your world. Change your thoughts correctly and everything will change into inner peace, happiness and personal power.

"Be ye transformed by the renewing of your mind." (Romans 12:2) No wiser thing was ever said. You can transform yourself, the world in which you live, your home conditions, your business conditions, in fact your whole life, by a spiritual renewing of your thoughts.

This book advocates a formula of living that assigns large importance to the power of our thoughts in changing the conditions of our lives. The secret, as Jimmy, the bellhop, said, is to think "kinda religious." Normal spiritual thinking can so change a person's life as to make everything different.

Thought patterns which have been traced over a long period of time are difficult to modify. Wrong thinking becomes habit and habitual procedures resist change. Fortunately in Christianity we have a phenomenon called "spiritual experience." It is a process by which God's power accomplishes in our minds, sometimes instantly, what laborious, tedious, correction would require months to achieve. This is not to say that all spiritual experience is instantaneous. Often, indeed more often, it is a process of growth and progressive development. In whatever way spiritual experience occurs, it is a method superior to psychological discipline and is more effective and certain of permanence. This comparison is not to be interpreted as minimizing the value of psychological discipline, a value I readily grant.

Condition your mind to spiritual change by practicing spiritual thinking. Read the Bible regularly. Commit its passages to memory, thus constantly feeding your mind material which will remake its attitudes. Know spiritually minded people and experience the gradual mental change which results from spiritual conversation. Subject your mind to the atmosphere in which spiritual experience occurs; go to church regularly. Get your mind into the habit of prayer. Think about God and Christ at every opportunity. Persevere until you find yourself enjoying this plan of disciplining your thinking. In this process you are changing your thought pattern, making it possible for spiritual experience to change everything for you.

The great change may come when least expected. I was in a certain city one day and between engagements went into a large downtown bookstore. The head sales person was a very pleasant little elderly lady. We got into conversation and she told me she had been in that store for a great many years.

"I would like to ask you a question," I said. "What type of book has the greatest sale today?"

"Oh," she said, "the answer to that is easy. It is books dealing with self-improvement and books dealing with religion." Then she volunteered the opinion that the highest form of self-improvement literature is religious writings.

Naturally I was interested to know that the general public was buying this type of literature, and then she commented, "The most unlikely type of people seem to be buying religious reading. They aren't what you would call saintly people but they are young folk, every-day people, all kinds, business people and for the most part men. Would you like to hear of an interesting incident that happened here recently?" she asked.

Assured of my interest she said, "One day not long ago a tall, lanky soldier came into the store. He was over six feet and as thin as a rail. Yet he was whistling exuberantly, with total unconcern for the presence of others; just whistling out of a heart that was obviously overflowing with joy. 'My, my,' I exclaimed, 'somebody is certainly happy.' He gave a broad grin and replied, 'I sure am, ma'am, I sure am happy. I have just come back from overseas. I was in a German prison for a long time and I lost forty pounds.'

" 'I don't see anything in that to make you so happy,' I said.

" 'Oh,' he said, 'you don't understand, so I will tell you.'

" 'In that prison we had very little to read. Anything in print that came our way was devoured by the boys. One day there came into my hands an old, worn, dog-eared copy of a religious novel that was widely read a few years back.'

"He said, 'Back in the United States I never would have looked at this book. I never went to church or anything, for I always had the idea that churches were dull, stuffy places, and they never would get me inside of one, except maybe on Easter.'

"This book was the story of how everybody who came under the influence of Jesus Christ had wonderful things happen to them.

" 'Well,' he said, 'ma'am, I read that book and all of a sudden something wonderful happened to *me*. I believe Jesus Christ is alive now just the same as He was in the Bible story times, for as I read this book, I am sure He touched me. Suddenly quicker than I can tell you about, I felt happy inside of my heart and everything changed. The whole world became different. Why,' he said, 'I was set free before the American army came. I was set free from myself, which was the greatest prison I was ever in.

" 'So,' he continued, 'I finally got back home and was reunited with my wife and she is a wonderful girl, the prettiest and sweetest there ever was, but'—he hesitated—'she is lacking something. She is heavyhearted and dull. In her mind she is pessimistic and negative. Life for her is just a hard dragging kind of thing. She is not happy. So, ma'am, I have come down to this store to get a copy of that book and I am going to read it to her in the hope that she will get what I got. I want the same thing to happen to her that happened to me.' "

What *had* happened to him? That a tremendous change had taken place in him is obvious. At the precise moment when his emotional and mental attitudes were favorable, a book able to vitally affect his thoughts came into his hands. So a spiritual experiene took place and everything changed.

Other people arrive at a similar condition more gradually. They definitely set out to practice new habits and attitudes. They systematically seek help from religion and presently they, too, become aware of change in outlook, in personal relations, and in the strength and power which is theirs. It is manifested in their daily lives. Happiness comes and also a grip and mastery over circumstances.

They say of a man who knows where he is going and how to get there that he is "on the beam." This means he has reduced the element of error and is closely approximating the center of truth or efficiency.

Another common statement is, "He has something on the ball," meaning he has the skill. He has the slight extra turn. He knows how to do it.

Another such statement is, "He is in the groove," meaning he is going right straight down the center to the mark. He has mastered the matter. All of this may seem quite remote from religion, but it isn't. The Bible is very wise. It says, "Seek ye first the Kingdom of God, and his righteousness; and all things shall be added unto you." What does that mean? Simply, seek skills in God's way of doing things. Seek God's *rightness* (the word righteousness indicates "rightness," skill, genius, the slight hair's turn that makes everything different). Seek the rightness which God teaches and you will have the skillful touch. Therefore, where you have failed heretofore, you will now acquire skill.

The pity is that a lot of people go through life blundering, failing, struggling along, never quite obtaining or achieving, when all can be different if they will learn and practice the simple principles of Christianity. Then things instead of being subtracted from them will be added unto them. Instead of life slipping from their grasp, life will flow toward them. Nothing can break them down, nothing can overwhelm them, nothing can destroy the peace, happiness and usefulness of their lives.

Another factor in the process by which changing your thoughts changes everything is the practice of the psychology of joy. If one expects to live a happy life, he must first practice thinking happy thoughts. If, as has been stated by wise men, our life is what our thoughts make of it, then it follows naturally that a joyful existence is predicted upon joyful thinking.

It is not likely that aimless thinking or the occasional and vagrant joyful thought will produce this effect. One must deliberately set about thinking happy thoughts as the normal slant of his mind. Discipline yourself daily to the practice of thinking thoughts of joy instead of succumbing to gloomy and depressed thoughts.

People manufacture their own unhappiness by the kind of thoughts they think. They may possess every factor which conceivably makes for happiness but miss a pleasant and useful existence because their thoughts have fallen into habitual gloominess or negativism. People easily develop the habit of thinking negatively. They form a thought pattern of depression and failure. As a result they feel mentally, emotionally and physically depressed.

Instead of practicing the psychology of joy, people who fail practice the psychology of pessimism. Their minds become filled with shadows and as a result life generally is full of shadows. Remember this important truth about your life—there is a definite tendency in human nature to become what you habitually think and practice. Set yourself, therefore, deliberately to be a joyful personality in your thinking. Obviously this will require practice. It will be very difficult at first as it always is when you try to overcome old mental habits. Everything in the mind resists the abandonment of a mental habit. But if you persevere and take your mind by the scruff of the neck, if one may use such a figure, tyrannizing over it, determining to control it, you will finally accomplish your purpose and your mind will yield to your new determination.

When Jesus Christ said, "These things have I spoken unto you, that my joy might remain in you, and that your joy might be full," he was stating a truth so potent, so electric, so profound that the man who ignores it misses the greatest aid to success and happiness. This truth can absolutely free a human personality. Psychologically we know that joy is a freeing and releasing agent in the mind. Joy can even make you feel better physically. It can help unlock your muscles. It can release energy. In short, it has the power to make you efficient, to get your whole personality, body, mind and spirit coordinated. Joy helps you to function efficiently. If the psychological effect of joy were better understood, it would be deliberately and enthusiastically practiced by every intelligent person.

William H. ("Little Bill") Miller,* one of our great athletic coaches, says that one of the best ways to become an athlete is to develop the psychology of joy. He was teaching a man to play golf. According to Coach Miller, the most important factor in golf is relaxation, the complete ease and freedom of muscular coordination, the absence of tension. And one way to get that, he insists, is to develop an inner spirit of joy.

Miller was once having trouble in teaching a man because the pupil was very tense and tied-up. To counteract tension, the coach said, "Joe, before you make your next shot, imagine that somebody has just told you the most uproarious joke you ever heard. Laugh heartily; then before you

---

* Author of *How to Relax* (Scientific Body Control).

finish the laugh, turn around, give no thought to the technique, just swing your club, strike the ball. Have no concern about where it goes, just laugh and hit it." The man did so and the ball sailed straight as an arrow down the fairway. The coach explained, "The joy welling up within him set Joe's mind free." When the tension dropped out of Joe's mind, it dropped out of his muscles. His whole being became coordinated through the therapeutic of joy. He became a unified personality and the stroke was natural with the result that it was good.

On another occasion Miller was teaching a girl to play tennis. Her techniques were correct, but still she was not a successful player. The coach said, "Let's sing as we play."

Rather self-consciously she started to sing. But when she got into the rhythm of the song, strangely enough she discovered it was the rhythm of the game. She forgot herself, lost herself. Her strokes fell into natural form and she struck the ball properly as she sang. She became released, and being filled with joy played excellently.

Learn the skill of living. Practice your religion. Think joy, not gloom.

One marvels at the astute wisdom of Jesus. Today the great scientific thinkers of our time are only beginning to learn principles which He taught two thousand years ago. Think of it, twenty centuries ago He told us that the psychology of joy releases people. Now in this modern age psychiatrists, athletic coaches, students of the human mind, are just beginning to recognize the truth of these teachings. He was the first to instruct us that when a person feels his thoughts with spiritual joy, it sets free creative abilities and makes for happiness and success.

This thing called spiritual experience plus the practicing of the simple techniques of the Christian faith produces the thought changes which make for happiness and successful living.

Let me call as witnesses several different types of people who have experienced the change of thought and life outlined above.

At a dinner party, I sat beside a famous actress. Two other ministers sat at our end of the table. One of these ministers was an elderly man and had been one of the most eminent clergymen in the United States. The other minister is known round the world, a great and eloquent orator. The older minister is the best story teller I have ever heard, bar none. Had he gone on the stage, he would certainly have been a famous comedian.

The second man was also a capital story teller. I chimed in with my own poor little stories. One story after another by three ministers—a sort of ministerial "Can You Top This?"—kept the party in an uproar. Had there been a "laugh meter," it would have registered high scores.

Finally the famous actress shook her head in wonderment and said, "I never heard anything like it. I have been in all kinds of parties, and in the most sophisticated night spots, but I never met three such gay lads as you ministers."

She looked sharply at us and asked, "You haven't had anything have you? Personally I can't get that happy until I have had several."

I started to say, "Of course not," when the elderly minister intercepted me and replied, "Yes, we have had something. Yes, madam, we are intoxicated."

His face was so radiant and his eyes so alight that she understood and said softly, "I know what you mean." She understood that Christ so completely releases people from dwarfing, crippling thoughts and emotions that life never grows stale.

Some years ago I spoke to several hundred young people at a convention. They were a gay and happy crowd, a rakish looking lot too. Judging by their outlandish attire, I thought, "This is certainly a sophisticated crowd." I found that I was right; they were sophisticated. Sophistication means worldly wise. Supposedly, a sophisticated person is one who knows what it is all about, and how to get happiness out of life. He knows his way around. On the other hand, certain bored, cynical pagans you see yawning around are not truly sophisticated. They are not worldly wise, because they have missed happiness. A truly sophisticated person is one who is smart enough to find out how really to be happy. Therefore, although some may be surprised to hear it, a sophisticated person is a spiritual person.

I never encounted such an eager audience as this group of young sophisticates. They anticipated ideas before they were half uttered and at anything humorous, before you made your point, they were ahead of you and roaring with laughter. They were alert, vibrant, a crowd of the most released people I have met.

One of these boys later said in his slangy jargon, "I used to run with a pretty fast crowd but I never began to enjoy life until I got in with this gang," indicating the crowd by a wave of his hand. Then he shook his head and said, "That bunch I used to go with was a bunch of saps—honestly! I only wish I could make them understand how to really get a kick out of life."

"How *do* you get a kick out of life?" I asked.

He looked at me and, absolutely without embarrassment, replied, "Why, get Christ into your heart, that's the way to get a kick out of life."

Usually when people start talking about religion they get a funny look on their faces and act embarrassed, but this boy shot his statement right out as normally and naturally as you please.

Something of this nature happened in my church recently. This church is located in the heart of New York City on Fifth Avenue and the young people come from everywhere in the United States. A young broker from Kansas City came to New York "to do the town," as he said. He stayed at a hotel near the church. He started uptown, headed for the night clubs, but as he passed the church he saw a sign. Something about it stopped him. It announced a young people's affair that was going on that evening. Back in Kansas City, he was a church man of sorts, and he thought, "I shall just go in here and see what a young people's meeting in a New York City church looks like, and maybe I can give them a few pointers back in Kansas City."

He intended to stay only for a few minutes, but found such a spirit of radiant happiness that it captivated him, and he stayed all evening. He had a mid-western breezy style and ability to get acquainted. As a matter of fact, even an iceberg would have acquired a genial glow of warmth from that crowd. He played around with them all the weekend, and then went back to Kansas City.

When he left he said, "What do you know? I came to New York on business and to do the town, and I got a greater thrill in this church than I ever could have found on Broadway or in the night clubs. I never did get up to the bright-light district. I found all the bright lights I needed right down there in the church."

By changing your thoughts you can also change situations and changing some situations is a requisite to success and happiness. You can develop an almost incredible power that will help you in crises where otherwise you would surely fail. We put too much dependence upon methods other than those of a spiritual nature to give us force and strength. We have not yet learned to believe in the astounding power of spiritual force. The sun quietly and without a sound can accomplish what all the bedlam of the machinery of the world cannot do. Quiet spiritual thinking establishes contact with spiritual energy and thus endows the man who practices it with super-human strength.

On an early morning train running from Cedar Rapids to Chicago, I happened to meet the famous Negro singer, Roland Hayes. He occupied the seat across from me in the parlor car. We had what was for me, at least, one of the most stimulating conversational experiences in my life. The talk turned to religion, the consuming interest of Mr. Hayes. Without question, he is not only one of the truly great singers of our time, but one of our noblest spiritual geniuses as well. He has sung before presidents and kings, and before acclaiming audiences in many lands, but he remains a simple, unaffected disciple of the King of Kings.

He told me that it is his custom as he begins a program to stand quietly for a minute by the piano as the vast audence waits. He closes his eyes and prays saying, "Lord, as I sing, please blot Roland Hayes out. Let the people see only Thee."

"I believe," he explained, "that when I do that sincerely, I become a channel through which God's spirit flows to move and lift the hearers." Critics have long been impressed by the deeply spiritual quality of Mr. Hayes' artistry. Undoubtedly it is accounted for in part at least by his devout attitude. Singing, to him, is primarily a method by which people may be lifted spiritually.

Roland Hayes told me a story that morning on that rushing train that will live with me forever as an illustration of the power of the spirit over any force in this world.

In a certain town late at night, he was set upon by four policemen who manhandled him without the slightest justification. Their attitude was brutal, bordering on the sadistic, and they gave full expression to their hatred not for him alone but for his race. Here was one lone and defenseless Negro at the mercy of four white men unrepresentative of, and a disgrace to, the white race.

"Didn't you get angry and fight them back?" I asked.

"How could I?" he replied. "I was no match physically for even one of them. But I *was* a match for them in another way and so was able to overcome them. I brought to bear a power that no evil can stand against."

"What did you do?" I asked with intense interest.

"I retired into God-consciousness," he replied. "I just prayed for the spirit of Christ to flow through me into the hearts of these misguided men. As I thus exercised spiritual thought-power, suddenly I had a feeling of being lifted up high above this hatred and I looked down upon them in compassion and pity. One policeman raised his pistol with the intent of hitting me with its butt. While his arm was raised a curious and bewildered expression overcame his face. Slowly his poised arm dropped. He had been stopped by the tremendous power of the spirit, by God-consciousness."

Later Mr. Hayes was invited back to that town by the Christian-in-spirit members of that community. He returned as guest of honor at a great tribute meeting. Messages came from the President of the United States and other distinguished citizens.

As the train on which we rode roared through a snowstorm, I sat awestruck before the spiritual power of this man, for his story was told with a complete absence of self. At times his voice was so low I could scarcely catch his words. I, who try to preach Christianity, sat as a very imperfect student in the presence of a master of the spiritual life.

Roland Hayes had discovered and demonstrated a spiritual method that proved extremely practical. By long practice he had become a master at it and therefore was able to summon the energies of his mind in a crisis. Not being practiced, perhaps we would fumble this skill at first. But if you will discipline and train your mind, seeking constantly to bring it into harmony with the mind of Christ, you, too, in your hours of difficulty will be able to summon a power against which nothing can stand.

Happiness and success therefore depend strangely upon our ability to free our minds to work for us. Anything that inhibits the flow of spiritual energy through the mind tends to defeat us. Men allow their minds to become shackled in many ways—by self-pity, by anxiety, by self-interest, by lust, by greed. Charles Dickens spoke wisely when he said, "We bear the chains we forge in life." We prevent ourselves from attaining our heart's desire by the cruel manner in which we hamper our own minds.

In this book we have tried to outline many of the ways in which the mind can become untangled. Psychiatric science is of great assistance. In our Psycho-Religio Clinic at the Marble Collegiate Church, the distinguished psychiatrist, Dr. Smiley Blanton, and I have worked painstakingly on the problem of eliminating the tangles from people's minds. Sometimes it is a long, slow, tedious process. It is often effective, I am thankful to report. There is great effectiveness in the joint operation of Christianity and psychiatry. However, we have learned to rely upon another factor that cures the mind as a surgical operation oftentimes cures organic trouble that has not yielded to long treatment. Perhaps I can best explain this process by applying to it an old and often misunderstood term. This term, however, is the best possible explanation. The term is "conversion," and I take that to mean the inflow into the mind of spiritual power with such potency and therapeutic effectiveness that the mind is completely changed. There is a phrase in the New Testament which is very graphic and which portrays what takes place in this process. "If any man be in Christ, he is a new creature: old things are passed away; behold, all things are become new." (II Corinthians 5:17.)

That is to say, change your thoughts (spiritually) and everything changes. A newspaper editor told of experiencing this process in his struggle with fear. This man, born in Canada of French-Canadian parents, came into the world with a withered leg. From earliest infancy he had to wear a brace on his leg. As he grew, he found that he could not compete with the other boys. If he couldn't run or play or climb trees as a little lad, how could he climb the ladder of life later on, he reasoned.

Thus the poisonous fear began to come into his thought and finally fear created a brace on his mind, even as he had a brace on his leg.

But the father said, "Son, don't worry about that leg of yours. Someday I am going to take you into the cathedral and there before the great altar, God will heal you."

The great day came. Both father and son, dressed in their best clothes, went reverently into the church. They came down the aisle of the cathedral hand in hand, the boy looking about wonderingly, his little withered leg thumping along.

They knelt at the altar. The father said, "Son, pray and ask God to heal you." They both prayed. Finally the boy lifted his face. His father was still in prayer. Then the father lifted his face. The boy said in later years, "I have seen my father's face under many circumstances, but never before had I seen such unearthly beauty as was upon his countenance in that moment. There was a light resting there. It was the reflected exultation of the true believer. There were tears in the father's eyes, but beyond the tears and shining through was the dazzling sunlight of faith. It was a wonderful sight, my father's face," the boy said.

Then the father put his hand on the boy's shoulder and said with deep feeling, "Son, let us give thanks to God. You are healed."

The boy was profoundly impressed. He stood up and then he looked down and there was his leg, the same as before. They started down the aisle, the little withered leg thumping along as usual. The lad was deeply disappointed. They came almost to the great door of the cathedral, then the boy said, "I stopped dead still, for all of a sudden I felt something tremendously warm in my heart. Then I seemed to feel something like a great hand pass across my head and touch me. It was as light as eiderdown but I can feel it to this day, the delicacy and yet the strength of the touch. All of a sudden I was wondrously happy and I cried out, 'Father, you are right, I have been healed. I have been healed.' "

Boy that he was, he was wise enough to know what had happened. He said, "God had not taken the brace off my leg, but He had taken the brace off my mind." God is great enough to heal a withered leg, if it is His will, but perhaps it is a greater thing to heal a wounded mind, a mind which carries the brace of fear. To strike off that brace, to set free the mind so that never again should it be bound and hampered by abnormal fear or any other enemy of success and happiness surely is one of the greatest things in this world. With the mind set free your thoughts change and so—everything changes.

STAY ALIVE
ALL YOUR LIFE

✳

"May You Live
All the Days of Your Life."

—Jonathan Swift

To my wife
RUTH STAFFORD PEALE
with appreciation
for her wise advice,
enthusiastic support,
and constant helpfulness
in the writing of this book

TO THE READER, DEAR FRIEND

I APPRECIATE your interest in this book. It was written with you in mind. Its purpose is to help you enjoy a more satisfying life. I like to think that by reading and, more important still, by practicing the suggestions the book contains, you will have a greater sense of well-being, increased vitality, and a keener interest in living.

This desired result is achieved through applying certain simple formulas. But these are not easy. There is no easy road to a happy life. But neither is that goal impossible.

I believe the Lord intends us to be filled with energy and enthusiasm; to have dynamic health of body, mind, and soul. Vibrant life is surely God's intent. We can come to no other conclusion if we read the Bible. Life glows from its pages. One of its most characteristic statements says, "I am come that they might have life, and that they might have it more abundantly." (John 10:10)

This volume goes further than my previous book, *The Power of Positive Thinking*, in emphasizing how to achieve well-being, vitality, enthusiasm and effectiveness in life. My former book outlined how to *think* positively about your problems. The present volume attempts to show you how to put these positive thoughts into *action*, and by believing and having faith in their power, succeed in achieving what you want out of life.

I am sorry that I cannot promise all the answers. Who can? But some of the answers to effective living are outlined here. I base this judgement upon the experience of many who live by the principles described in this volume, and some of whose inspiring stories are mentioned. I sincerely trust that through this book you, too, will learn to live dynamically and happily all your life.

I wish to express appreciation to my daughter, Margaret Ann Peale, for her valuable secretarial assistance in the preparation of this manuscript. Acknowledgment is made to *Guideposts Magazine*, Carmel, New York, for permission to quote from various articles.

NORMAN VINCENT PEALE

CONTENTS

HOW TO USE THIS BOOK TO
HELP SOLVE YOUR PROBLEMS

Publisher's Note: This short section has been specifically designed to aid you in solving some of the difficult problems you face in the course of your daily social, business and personal life. It will also refer you to specific chapters in the book where more detailed help is available.

Below you will find a number of such problems stated. Along with each is a brief comment by Dr. Peale on the subject and a reference to a particular section in the book where the problem is fully discussed by him. We hope this special section will prove useful to you in suggesting solutions to some knotty problems, and that you will look to this section whenever you feel the need of Dr. Peale's help.

• *How can I stop worrying about things I can't possibly do anything about?*

"The basic secret of overcoming worry is the substitution of faith for fear as your dominant mental attitude. Two great forces in this world are more powerful than all others. One is fear and the other is faith; and faith is stronger than fear . . ."

See Chapter IV, "Kill Worry and Live Longer," page 218.

• *I get keyed up so often and cannot seem to relax. Is there anything I can do about this?*

"The Biblical prescription for energy calls for 'waiting' upon the Lord . . . The secret of a continuous powerflow is in adjusting yourself to God's controlled pace and tempo. Synchronize your thinking and living with God's unhurried timing . . . The absence of tiredness depends upon being in the natural rhythm of God."

See Chapter VII, "Stop Being Tired—Live Energetically," page 256.

• *I've always thought peace of mind was a good trait. But lately I've been hearing that it just "lulls" people into a false sense of security. Is peace of mind really a valuable thing to acquire?*

"A great value of peace of mind is that it increases intellectual power.

The mind is efficient only when it is cool—not hot. In a heated state of mind, emotions control judgement, which may prove costly. Power comes from quietness . . ."

See Chapter XII, "Peace of Mind—Your Source of Power and Energy," page 315.

• *Why do I so often seem to be wrong about things? Is there some formula for not making so many mistakes?*

"A successful life depends upon developing a higher percentage of wisdom than error. Then you will do fewer things wrong and more things right. In improving your right-decision percentage, the knowledge of *how* to make a decision is very important. And more and more people are learning that the highest percentage of right decisions is attained when spiritual methods are employed."

See Chapter VIII, "Learn from Mistakes—and Make Fewer," page 271.

• *How can I control my temper and keep from flying off the handle when frustrating things happen?*

"A rudimentary fact that many miss is that there are some people and things in this world that you just have to get along with, and no amount of resistance or railing will accomplish anything except to increase your frustration . . . A quiet and urbane philosophy . . . is most important in eliminating frustrated feelings."

See Chapter III, "How to Conquer Your Frustrations and Be Creative," page 205.

• *I am a moody person; how can I develop a more positive and happy outlook on life?*

"Your mind may try to block you in your desire to become a joyous and harmonious individual by telling you that 'thinking doesn't make it so.' But thinking CAN make it so and often does, if at the same time thinking is implemented by diligent effort and by scientific and persistent practice."

See Chapter X, "Your Life Can Be Full of Joy," page 291.

• *How can I be expected to accomplish things that I feel are beyond my limitations? Maybe I'm not as smart or talented as other people?*

"The amazing untapped power you have within you is of a force and quality that you cannot fully comprehend. Therefore, do not let yourself be a victim of the dismal concept of self-assumed personal limitation . . . Even if your ability, training and experience are less than other's, you can compensate for almost any lack by dynamic enthusiasm."

See Chapter II, "Enthusiasm Can Do Wonders for You," page 191.

• How can I conquer boredom and that "half-alive" feeling in regard to my daily work?

"Put animation into your daily work. Your life's vitality can be increased by taking an immense pleasure in all that you are doing. Practice liking it. By this attitude tedium and the distinction between labor and pleasure is erased . . . you will get enjoyment out of your activity because aliveness stimulates the sense of excitement."

See Chapter VI, "You Can Have Life If You Want It," page 246.

• What is it that makes me so tense at times and what can I do about it?

"Tension can and does have deeper causes than pressure and hard work. Tension may arise from old and seemingly buried feelings that originally caused hurt and may have deepened into resentment. We seldom put two and two together to see the connection between our present tension and old antagonistic attitudes . . . but you should explore this possibility . . ."

See Chapter IX, "Why Be Tense? How to Adjust to Stress," page 285-286.

• I can manage to handle the "little" things in life, but I'm just afraid to tackle the big ones. Can you help me?

"I believe that when you plan something big you are actually thinking the way God intended men to think . . . Big faith equals big results. Big dreams, plus big thinking, plus big faith, plus big effort—that is the formula by which big things are done . . . and by which big difficulties are overcome."

See Chapter V, "You Can Have Power Over Your Difficulties," page 233.

• I constantly doubt my ability to accomplish the things in life I really want. How can I fight this self-doubt?

"Every individual forms his own estimate of himself and that basic estimate goes far toward determining what he becomes. You can be no more than you believe you are. Real belief helps to make your faith come true. Belief helps stimulate power within yourself . . ."

See Chapter I, "The Magnificent Power of Belief," page 181.

- I *wish I could believe in a life after death, but I can't. Is there any proof of immortality beyond what religion teaches?*

"One of the most significant facts about modern thinking is the new conviction that the universe is spritual. The old materialistic conception is fading . . . Current scientific investigation seems to lend support to our intuitions and faith. Recently an eminent scientist expressed his personal belief that the soul theory has been proved according to the minimum standards of science."
     See Chapter XVI, "Live Forever," page 366.

- Is *it really true that emotions can cause sickness, and, if so, what can be done about it?*

"A real cause of ill health is ill will. Having allowed ill will to accumulate and its inevitable accompaniment of guilt to clog the mind, naturally your vital powers are depressed. Sick feeling results. The cure of this condition is good will . . . This may be accomplished by a shift in the attitude of love and the healing qualities which it generates."

     See Chapter XIII, "How to Feel Well and Have Vibrant Health," page 332.

- How *can I rid my mind of depressing thoughts?*

"Study your thoughts, write them down on paper and analyze them, whether they are creative or destructive . . . replace every weak thought with a strong one, each negative thought with a positive one, a hate thought with a loving one, a gloomy thought with a lifted one . . . You will find this literally a magic formula."

     See Chapter XI, "Lift Your Depression and Live Vitally," page 309.

- How *can I cope with my problems when I feel so alone in facing them—so alone that I lose confidence in solving them?*

"There is a text in the Bible that is so powerful it can change your life . . . 'If God be for us, who can be against us?' Personalize these words so that they apply directly to you . . . Now bring a picture into your mind of God facing your obstacles. Can they stand against God . . ?"

     See Chapter XIV, "Self-Confidence and Dynamic Achievement," page 339-340.

- How *can I have faith in life, or even in God, when I am so frequently distracted by pain?*

" . . . faith becomes an instrument for getting insight into the fundamental meaning of suffering and for bearing it. Even as pain may be removed by faith, so it may be endured by faith."

See Chapter XV, "Living Above Pain and Suffering," page 352.

1

THE MAGNIFICENT POWER OF BELIEF

"Every individual forms his own estimate of himself and that basic estimate goes far toward determining what he becomes. You can do no more than you believe you can. You can be no more than you believe you are. Belief stimulates power within yourself. Have faith in faith. Don't be afraid to trust faith."

ONCE, WHILE I was dining with friends in a Southwest Texas hotel before giving a lecture, a man entered the restaurant and asked for me.

In the conversation he startled my friends and me by saying, "I came to this town a bum." Noting our bewilderment, he continued, "I mean it—a bum, a hobo." This statement was so unbelievable, considering the obviously fine person who spoke, that we listened intently.

He told us that back in West Virginia, a few years before, he began drinking heavily. He lost one position after another, each new job being further down the economic scale, until finally he hit bottom. Dirty and unshaven he shuffled the streets, only halfheartedly looking for work which he did not get. Finally, in desperation, his wife left him. Homeless, broke, and defeated he left town and aimlessly "bummed" west. He slept in haystacks, barns, and alleys. Meals were begged from door to door.

One day a kindly lady gave him a handout on her back porch and stood watching him wolf it down. "You look like a nice young man," she observed. "You shouldn't be in this condition. I am going to give you something which can change your life if you will use it."

She went into the house and returned with a book. "Read this," she said. "Do what it says and you can be a useful person again."

Our friend shuffled on west with the book in the pocket of his ragged coat. Having nothing else to do and much time on his hands, he read every word of it dozens of times. Often, to escape the winter cold he would go into libraries and there read his book.

Gradually, its simple message began to penetrate his dark thoughts and permeate his consciousness. "Get in harmony with God, change your thoughts and your way of living; believe and succeed; through faith you can; believe you can, and you can." So ran the emphasis of the book.

Finally, by practice, he learned to pray and to have faith. He sincerely tried the spiritual technique suggested and the change began. Presently he came to this Texas town where he had been told a certain man would give him a job. "As I approached his home a beautiful young woman was sweeping the walk. Will you believe it when I tell you that she is now my wife?" he asked with a smile.

He worked at a number of small jobs, each better than the last. Then he felt a desire to be an accountant, having a liking for figures and some experience with them in the pre-drinking days. One day a company dealing in pipe for the oil fields asked him to figure a job estimate. He had never undertaken so complicated a proposition, but he prayed for guidance, studied hard over the problem, and finally figured costs quite accurately. This was a remarkable achievement considering his lack of experience. From then on he went steadily forward and became successful as a person.

Finishing his remarkable story he pulled from his pocket the soiled and ragged book which he had carried on his wanderings and tenderly laid it on the table with the remark, "Anybody can do as I did, and most will not have as far to rise. The secret is, have faith, believe, and practice."

This man's experience demonstrates a law which is stated succinctly in the dynamic and creative teachings of Jesus Christ. "If thou canst believe, all things are possible to him that believeth." (Mark 9:23) As you train your mind to believe, defeat tendencies are reversed, and everything tends to move out of the area of the impossible into that of the possible.

First, become a believer in God, not merely academically, but believe confidently in Him as your guide, and actually practice spiritual principles. Second, believe in yourself, in people, and in life itself. Have a sincere desire to serve God and mankind, and stop doubting, stop thinking negatively.

How do you have faith? Simply start living by faith, pray earnestly and humbly, and get into the habit of looking expectantly for the best. This type of thinking will presently cause an actual reversal in the flow of your life, for life is always in a state of flow one way or the other. Failure factors will move from you and success factors, by a magnetic attraction, will move toward you. The dynamic and positive attitude is a strong magnetic force which, by its very nature, attracts good results.

This, of course, does not mean you will get everything you want. When you live on a faith basis your desire will be only for that which you can ask in God's name. But whatever you should have, whatever is good for you will be granted. There is no limit to what God will give to those who practice His laws.

By success, of course, I do not mean that you may become rich, famous, or powerful for that does not, of necessity, represent achievement. Indeed, not infrequently, such individuals represent pathetic failures as persons. By success I mean the development of mature and constructive personality.

Through the application of the principle of constructive thinking you can attain your worthy goals. The natural outcome of living by creative principles is creative results. *Believe and create* is a basic fact of successful living. You can make your life what you want it to be through belief in God and in yourself.

Frank Lloyd Wright, the famous architect, who has been called one of the most creative geniuses of all time said, "The thing always happens that you really believe in. And the belief in a thing makes it happen. And I think nothing will happen until you thoroughly and deeply believe in it."

The Biblical law, "According to your faith be it done unto you," (Matt. 9:29) expresses the truth that the extent to which you receive God's blessing depends precisely upon the degree to which you believe.

Many illustrations of the operation of this principle might be given. For example, a woman told me that for years she depreciated herself as "the plain one" of four sisters. The other three so-called more charming sisters had always told her she was plain and unattractive and she came to believe that untruth.

Then one day a friend said, "But you are not plain. Try picturing yourself as the sincere and attractive person you are. Charm," she continued, "is not procured from a bottle. It comes from right thinking and radiant living. So, decide what you want to be, then paint a picture of yourself as being that. Humbly believe that, with God's help, your picture of yourself will come to pass."

This friend asked her a direct question, "What do you really want from life? You will need to answer that question specifically, before you will have any chance of getting it." It was a wise question, for goals are never reached unless they are first specifically formed in the mind.

"If you really would like to know," said the other with embarrassment, "I want a husband and children and a good home." (Her sisters, all married and having homes of their own, had assured her that she was too plain and could never hope for marriage.)

"Do not be embarrassed by such a normal desire," said her friend. "To accomplish this worthy goal hold a mental picture of the home and husband and children you want. Then put the wish in God's hands to give or to withhold. If it is His will, He will grant it. Ask Him to develop your personality in preparation for wifehood and motherhood. Ask God to make you beautiful, charming, and good."

This woman painted and held her mental picture, affirming it by unremitting perserverance into reality, and this Cinderella story came true.

Some people complain that only the gifted or the accomplished may

successfully employ these creative techniques. Such thinking is a dangerous form of rationalizing failure. The more jealousy one has in his nature
the more critical he is of those who have accomplished things.

If you are critical and mouthing negativisms it could be that your own
failures are caused by a mixed-up, hate-filled mind. A sign of mental
health is to be glad when others achieve, and to rejoice with them. Never
compare yourself or your achievements with others, but make your comparisons only with yourself. Maintain a constant competition with yourself. This will force you to attain higher standards and achievements. Do
not defeat yourself by holding spiteful or jealous thoughts. Think straight,
with love, hope, and optimism and you will attain victory in life.

A demonstration of these facts is described in a letter I received several
years ago from a man who applied them in a difficult situation.

> Dear Dr. Peale,
>
> A week and a half ago I was ticket collector and doorman at a theater in the
> Bronx. Then the boss told me business was slow and I was laid off. In my
> heart and soul, however, I had no fear because faith had entered into my life.
>
> In a week my money was about gone, and I still had no job, so I went to the
> New York State Employment Service and filled out an application for a hotel
> job. I pictured myself getting a good job. A day later the man called me and
> gave me a good job at a hotel for more money; $42.00, when I had only been
> getting $27.56.
>
> Now, I learned all this in the Marble Collegiate Church by going to the
> services on Sunday. My life is improved and I am improving. My life is turn-
> ing to light, and goodness, and the darkness of ignorance is being blotted out
> of my life. I know how to get ahead and keep going. I love the church and I
> will help the church out as much as I can and I am going to give the church
> one dollar every Sunday.

He loves the church and he wants to give to God. Why not? The
church taught him the great secret of positive faith, which opened new
vistas of hope for him. This man, lacking in education and struggling on a
poverty level, had nevertheless become sensitized to that electric atmosphere that develops in church when spiritual power is released. He listened to the message about getting in harmony with God and learning to
live by faith.

He believed that message and practiced it. It did not free him from
difficulty. It was never promised that it would. But that message did give
him the know-how and power to handle his difficulties and master them.
The validity of his experience is attested by the fact that, having received,
he wanted to share with God. It is a subtle and important fact that if we
seek spiritual values only for ourselves they will turn dead in our hands;
but when we receive and give, they replenish themselves.

I have seen transformations in people, under the influence of spiritual power, that are almost unbelievable. I have watched people come to the church as one sort of person and depart altogether different. In church creative living techniques are taught and specific methods are outlined for using dynamic principles to overcome failure, cast out fear, and heal sorrow. Something may happen to you in church that can completely change everything in your life for the better. You will be very wise, indeed, if you get alerted to the possibility.

To the Marble Collegiate Church every Sunday come people of all creeds, or no creed. Among them are old and young, sophisticates, the poor, the rich, the mighty, and the defeated. They are all there, mixed with the happiest crowd of people you ever saw, people whose lives have been changed. You should hear them sing. Their enthusiasm is infectious. They have a happy religion, because it is to them the symbol of victory over themselves and every wrong and defeating thing that previously took the joy out of life. Dynamism is in the very atmosphere.

Let me tell you about another man who, like our theater doorkeeper from the Bronx, found the answer; only this man was a banker. Spiritual laws are not respecters of persons. They are available to all who will believe and practice and live on a spiritual level.

I stood with this banker one summer Sunday outside a small, country church where we had both been worshipping. "What a great place the church is," said Bill. "If people only knew what they can get in church, they would flock there by the thousands." (Perhaps that is why immense throngs are now pouring into churches every Sunday.)

He was speaking of something he knew to be true through personal experience, the surest of all verifications. Several years before he had been president of a bank but, due to a feud, he had been ousted and found himself, at fifty-two, with no job. His first reaction was one of panic, for he had two children in college and other financial obligations. He was flooded with hatred for the men responsible for his dismissal. Finally he yielded to the sinister despair that he was finished.

It was at this point that he came to church, desperately looking for a way out. He heard about the simple, dynamic, creative principles of faith. Then Bill and I had a conference. How could religious faith help him, he wanted to know.

I said, "First you must empty out all that hate. Pray for those men. Ill will corrodes the soul and impedes the channel through which spiritual and creative power flows."

"That is hard," he said, "but I'll try."

"Then," I said, "fear must come out. Put your problems confidently in God's hands and believe that He will guide you."

He followed these directions and continued to practice this new way of thinking even though things grew much worse. His finances actually got so low that he was forced to resort to blueberry picking to buy groceries.

This would be enough to discourage most men completely, and previously it would have done so for him, but his new faith was working in him. He felt strangely peaceful and was able to see the creative values in his hard experience.

"Formerly my wife and I were so busy we became almost strangers to each other. Picking blueberries on opposite sides of a high bush helped us really to know each other. Her smile, the loveliness of her soul, the wonderful things she said, and the loyal way she stood by me built me up. We found God and each other in a blueberry patch," he said tenderly.

Today Bill is head of a small town bank, but more important, he is a constructive factor in his church and community. And when people consult him about business matters he goes further and gives them some helpful thoughts on how to believe and succeed. In his own practical way he gives people the simple, dynamic, creative philosophy of Jesus Christ.

One thought you must always hold is that you can attain a higher level for your life. Few people realize their real possibilities. Many believe that "ordinary" persons must remain ordinary all their lives. That concept is false and a slander on human nature and on the God who created you. One of the chief functions of spiritual truth is to reveal and release the extraordinary possibilities in so-called "ordinary" persons. Personally, I do not believe any human being is ordinary. I like the statement of Dr. Harold C. Case, President of Boston University, that "The spirit of democracy is to believe everyone into greatness."

Why do some people seemingly have the touch of failure? Why do things go so wrong for them, and so often? Why do they experience an ever accumulating series of irritating frustrations, their projects and plans so frequently going badly? In most cases, analysis reveals that ineptness is inherent in the individual, rather than in the circumstances. If things continually go wrong for you, perhaps the psychology of wrongness is in you and should be corrected.

Do not waste time complaining about conditions or about other people. Honestly face the possibility that your thinking may be wrong; that your trouble may be within yourself. It isn't that you lack ability, but rather that your mental slant and approach is tinged with failure thoughts and, naturally, failure follows. Also, your attitudes may be harsh, critical, and unfriendly toward other people, with the result that they withdraw from you without themselves understanding the reason. In subtle ways a lack of personal inner harmony is quickly reflected in inharmonious personal relations. And your relationship with other people is profoundly important to your own successful living.

It is also important to emphasize that a basic factor in successful living is not how much you know or how hard you work, although neither is to be minimized. The most important factor is what you believe and how sincerely you believe it. This law was stated by William James, one of the greatest thinkers in American history, who said, "In any project, the important factor is your belief. Without belief there can be no successful outcome. That is fundamental."

At a high school commencement a large banner stretched across the stage proclaimed the class motto in huge letters, "They Conquer Who Believe They Can." High school graduates who go into the world with that truth printed on their minds, will do something constructive, provided they continue to hold the concept. Whatever your goal, you can attain it if you believe you can and then keep on believing even when it is hard to believe.

This truth is so dynamic that even the most unlikely persons often demonstrate its power. For example, a janitor's helper in a big city railroad station had a job pushing a mop. At forty-five he was only a mop-pusher. It would seem that a man so situated would not have any great future.

However, there was a railroad conductor, a man of faith, who came in and out of that station. He liked this mop-pusher and one day said to him, "You ought to have a better job than this."

"How?" the man asked dully. "I have a wife and three children and an aged mother and I never had any education; and besides, a man can't get ahead like they once did in this country. Those days are gone forever." So he mouthed the cynical, negative philosophy we have heard so much in late years.

But the conductor made him believe in his country and himself and reminded him of all that God can do with a person who is surrendered to God's Grace. He painted a picture of something better, until that picture began to form in the man's mind. This set in motion dynamic forces that stimulated events. One day the conductor told him that in a near-by town a man wanted to sell a hamburger stand. He inspired the mop-pusher to go and look over the opportunity.

When he arrived in that town he found the price asked for the hamburger stand was three hundred and fifty dollars, and our prospective restaurant man had but twenty-five in cash to invest. But now he had something worth more than money. He had positive thoughts. He had developed real faith, and the sustained visualization of a better opportunity had already made his personal reactions dynamic. With this fresh, new quality of mind he was unwilling to accept defeat. So, carefully and prayerfully, he considered the situation and submitted to the owner a proposition that he purchase the place without down payment, but agreeing to pay, within a year, the sum of five hundred dollars. Ordinarily the owner would have impatiently brushed aside such an offer, but something in the spirit of this man impressed him and he accepted. Then this man arranged with the grocer and butcher for the daily purchase of supplies on credit, with the stipulation that they be paid for each morning from the previous day's receipts.

From that desperate beginning the erstwhile lethargic and defeated mop-pusher worked, believed equally hard, and today owns a very nice restaurant. Printed on his menus are these lines which nourish the spirit of his customers as his good food strengthens their bodies.

> *If you think you are beaten you are;*
> *If you think you dare not, you don't;*
> *If you want to win but think you can't*
> *It's almost a cinch you won't.*
> *If you think you'll lose you're lost;*
> *For out in the world we find*
> *Success begins with a fellow's will;*
> *It's all in the state of mind.*
> *Life's battles don't always go*
> *To the stronger and faster man,*
> *But sooner or later the man who wins*
> *Is the man who thinks he can.*

"I can do all things through Christ which strengtheneth me," (Phil. 4:13) is the statement of a spiritual law, which expresses the result that comes when a believing person establishes a real working partnership with God.

It is most important to have faith in faith itself. Cultivate the conviction that, as you think constructively in terms of faith, you can successfully handle any situation that may confront you. Emerson warned that "no accomplishment, no assistance, no training can compensate for lack of belief." The late Mr. Justice Cardozo of the United States Supreme Court said, "We are what we believe we are."

Every individual forms his own estimate of himself and that basic estimate goes far toward determining what he becomes. You can do no more than you believe you can. You can be no more than you believe you are. Real belief helps to make your faith come true. Belief stimulates power within yourself. Have faith in faith. Do not be afraid to trust faith.

The parents of a sixteen-year-old boy entered him in a preparatory school which they could scarcely afford, but they wanted their son to have advantages they had not enjoyed. The boy appreciated his opportunity and determined to justify it. He set his heart on winning the scholarship prize to compensate for his parents' sacrifice. He worked diligently and began to ascend to dizzy heights of scholarship that he had never attained previously.

Up and up went his marks—80, 85, 90. He had never received such grades and, like a person climbing a high place, became frightened at his own achievement. Then came a destructive thought. "This scholastic level is too high for me. I am out of my depth. I cannot hold this standard." Thus, he began to doubt and to disbelieve. Soon his mind accepted his lack of faith in himself. Then, since his ability was no longer challenged, his mind closed up and he could not seem to remember his lessons as well. The quality of his work fell off. Soon he was doing poorly in his studies and his marks declined. He became very discouraged and was even ready to quit.

"But one night," said he, "I opened my Bible in the hope of some encouragement, and happened upon the verse which said, 'With God all things are possible.' (Matt. 19:26) That made me think, 'My parents believe in me and, for a while, I was able to get high marks. Since I did that well once, why couldn't I do it again. I believe that God will help me.' All of a sudden," he said, "I knew that I could do it." And he did do it. His grades crept up again. He became top boy in scholarship. When he recovered faith in faith his personality focused and power flowed through.

So, practice every day the act of casting all doubt out of your mind. Never settle for anything less than all that you want to be. Perhaps you are getting older and you say to yourself, "I have done all I will ever do; I have reached my limit." Never say that. Never entertain such an unworthy or false thought. You are not entitled to write yourself off as through. Do not impose self-created limitations upon yourself. Keep on believing as long as you live and your effectiveness will be prolonged.

Academically and theoretically most people believe that God helps people, but not always do they actually seek that help in specific situations. "What can God do in this particular instance?" they ask dubiously. Let us answer that negation with the question, "What can't God do?" Thousands of sincere people have demonstrated that, through faith, a power and wisdom beyond all human ingenuity may be brought to bear upon specific situations.

When Bob Richards, world's champion pole vaulter, received an award as the amateur athlete of the year he was asked by reporters for the secret of his athletic powers. "I owe my achievements to the power of the Lord," he replied. When the athletic sportswriters interrogated him further he explained, "Oh, don't get the idea that some metaphysical power comes down as I start to vault, and lifts me over the bar. It isn't that way at all. When I speak of the power of the Lord, I mean the psychological influence which He exerts over all those who search their souls and find there the strength to perform wonderful things."

So conclusive is all the evidence that spiritually constructive thinking can determine the outcome of our lives that an intelligent person cannot wisely ignore this scientific law of living. First, get your life right in terms of God's laws. Be a dedicated person. Next, be sure your goals are spiritually sound. Then, think success, believe in success, visualize success and you will set in motion the powerful force of the realizable wish. When the mental picture or attitude is strongly enough held it actually seems to control conditions and circumstances.

An example is that famous story of a tense moment in a World Series baseball game some years ago between the New York Yankees and the Chicago White Sox. In the fifth inning the score stood 4 to 3 in favor of Chicago with Charlie Root on the mound for Chicago. At the plate stood the mightiest batsman of all time, Babe Ruth. But the pitcher did not fear him, for Ruth had hit a home run in the first inning and surely that was the only home run he had in his system for that day.

The pitcher put the ball straight across the plate. Babe Ruth held up one finger in derision. Straight as an arrow the second ball came whizzing across. Ruth held up two fingers of derision. Pandemonium reigned. Was it possible that, like the mighty Casey, he would strike out in this crisis? Then Ruth did a strange and almost contemptuous thing. He raised his finger and pointed straight across the fence to indicate where he proposed to hit the ball.

The pitcher went into his windup and sent the ball once again whistling straight across the plate. There was a sharp crack and in a beautiful arc the ball sailed straight and true just where Ruth had pointed over the fence. It was an electric moment, an unforgettable episode in the history of American sport.

After the game somebody asked Babe Ruth, "But suppose you had missed that final strike?" A look of genuine surprise overcame the Babe's face. "Why," he said, "I never even thought of such a thing." Which may be precisely the reason he did not miss the ball.

This illustrates a profound law; namely, that when you take into your mind the thought of impossibility, you tend to create the conditions of impossibility. Prior to the formation of such a negative thought your entire being, body, mind, and spirit, works as a unity in perfect harmony. The powerful positive forces of the universe are flowing through your personality. But when you change the cast and slant of your mind so that you hold the idea of the impossible, you tend to block off in yourself the continued flow of co-ordinated power.

As a result the fine balance of personality is lost. You become rigid and tightened up. The easy flow of harmonious power is interfered with. In the case of a baseball player his all important timing is affected just enough to make that fraction of a difference whereby the bat will pass over or below the ball rather than meet it squarely. Similarly, in your life skill will be lacking when the doubt idea becomes uppermost.

I am not sure that positive thinking extends to fishing, but I witnessed what seemed a demonstration. I went fishing one day, in the inland waterways at Sea Island, Georgia, with two men and my daughter Elizabeth, then about eleven years old. None of us were catching anything except Elizabeth, who hauled in two fish.

"How come, honey?" I asked. "Our lines are in the water right alongside yours and yet we catch nothing and you've got two."

She looked at me with a twinkle in her eye. "Oh, Daddy," she explained as she pulled in another, "I practice positive thinking."

The army engineers corps has a suggestive motto: "The difficult we do immediately—the impossible may take a little longer." Since God and you form a strong combination and "with God all things are possible," then it may be assumed that God and you can do the impossible even if it does require a little time. Make that the dominating thought of your mind— God and you are undefeatable. As this thought takes real hold of you then things which heretofore you considered impossibilities will move into the area of the possible.

Though these assertions may perhaps seem extravagant, nevertheless, the principle works when you believe and practice it as countless persons have demonstrated. The secret of course is daily to practice filling your mind with possibility thoughts. Continue until belief firmly takes hold of your mind. One simple method for doing this is to avoid saying, "I don't believe I can do it," and instead affirm, "Perhaps I cannot do it alone, but God is with me and with His strength I can do it." Affirm in this manner a dozen times a day until your negatively trained mind accepts the positive point of view. Remember, always, that you can if you think you can, and do not allow doubts to clog your mind.

I had an appointment for luncheon in Washington and, having a short time to wait, went into a pleasant garden adjoining the hotel. This garden has a fountain with a bird bath. A few elderly ladies were taking the sun.

I noticed a young sparrow perched on the edge of the bird bath. All the other sparrows came down, got themselves a drink, gave themselves a bath, then flew away, but he remained hesitant. Then two or three of the women came up and said, "What's the matter with the poor little thing?" One said, "I think we had better take him into the house; there is something wrong with him."

But a man standing nearby said, "Let him alone. What do you want to do, destroy his self-confidence?"

"But," they argued, "the bird is sick."

"No, he is not sick," said the man. "He is just getting a start in life; leave him alone."

I became very interested and watched carefully. Finally the sparrow got up enough courage to fly a few feet. His mother and father came around and encouraged him and all his relatives gathered around and urged him on. I watched him learning to fly and marveled at his spirit. It was an object lesson in perseverance and confidence.

That evening, by curious coincidence, I happened to read in my paper a letter to the Editor about a robin which had hurt its wing. "Even though his wing droops," the writer said, "the robin sits up in an old cherry tree and sings. But," he added, "I am worried about his wing, what shall I do about it?"

The Editor answered, "Let his wing alone. A robin's wing is of gossamer texture proportionately stronger than much material of greater density. And," he continued, "remember a good, old doctor named Mother Nature. If you refrain from applying human methods to that wing, the robin, because he has no academic knowledge to hamper him, will have faith enough to let his wing droop until nature restores its strength.

"The robin," he continued, "is wiser than humans because, not knowing so much about the difficulties of life, he does not become discouraged. In this the robin is helped, without doubt, by his lack of human intelligence." Then the Editor concluded with this penetrating observation: "In the case of the robin, the channels of immortal help are not blocked by thought."

It is true of people no less than robins that the inflow of Divine power is blocked by thought, negative thought. Our failure lies in not being naïve enough to practice the power of faith. Perhaps the importance of this quality of naïveté explains why the greatest of all Teachers emphasized the value of becoming as a little child, since by the childlike attitude we are able to have faith and not doubt. It is indeed a searching thought that we may block the channels of immortal help by wrong thinking. You may know so much about your difficulties that your mind can see nothing but those difficulties. Too much emphasis upon difficulty will fill you with complete defeatism.

The head of a sales organization told me that one of their salesmen reported it was impossible to do any business in a particular section of the city where he was working. A baseless legend to this effect had developed and he accepted it. So, he was defeated before he began. A few setbacks and he just knew that sales were impossible in that area.

The company then transferred him out of town and put another salesman into his territory without informing the new man of his predecessor's defeatist ideas about that particular section of the city. The new salesman's first report showed more business out of that area than from any other. He had the advantage, actually, of an unworked section and, due to his lack of a defeatist feeling toward that area, proceeded to make the most of it. The new salesman had success simply because he did not know there was supposed to be no business in that section. Doubt did not have opportunity to affect his sales.

The principle of believe and succeed is no bright and easy panacea. Certainly it is not advanced as a method for gaining material things. And it is difficult to master. But it is an amazing formula for achieving goals, and for overcoming failure.

That this dynamic thinking is closely related to the basic truths of this world is demonstrated by the fact that it sets powerful forces in motion which stimulate accomplishments in even the most difficult circumstances.

People who insist upon failing tell me that while these principles may work in easy situations they do not apply in difficult ones. But just remember that the Bible, from which these creative ideas are taken, was not written for easy situations. Its teachings were meant to apply under the most difficult conditions.

Some years ago I met a couple who told me "how poor" they were. They reiterated this dismal complaint several times in that one conversation. They had two attractive young daughters whom they wanted to send to college. They were hard working, upright people, but were very negative. They emphasized, repeatedly, how little they had and that their girls would doubtless be denied a college education for that reason.

"I have read your philosophy of positive thinking," said the father, "but that is not for us, only for the more fortunate. Tell me how I can send my girls to college by thinking positively. My wife is a college graduate. I'm not, but our greatest ambition is to give our girls this advantage. But how can we?"

I started figuring some way to get the money for them, but the father quickly said, "I don't want money from anybody. I want to do it on my own."

I admired him for his independent attitude and said, "Let's start by affirming now that, by the help of God, the girls are going to have a college education. Repeat the affirmation daily. Believe you will be shown how to make your faith a reality.

"The second step," I continued, "is to paint a mental picture of your daughters receiving their diplomas. Hold that picture firmly in consciousness. Establish it as a fundamental thought in your mind, your wife's mind, and in the girls' thoughts, also. Then, put the picture in the hands of God and go to work.

"You will need to work hard, think hard, and believe hard. Adopt the principle of believe and succeed. Believe and picture constantly that the college graduation already is an accomplished fact in the projected scheme of things."

He grasped this concept and began to shift from his defeatist "poor" thoughts to a thought pattern of creative accomplishment. Not only did his daughters graduate from college but, also, the economic level of the family has risen. These people have become dynamic and vital and are making a real contribution to their church and community.

Asked to explain these accomplishments the father declares, "I simply learned to believe. I kept on believing at all times even when everything seemed most difficult." And he added, "I also got busy and worked instead of wasting time and energy in complaining and feeling sorry for myself."

By such a sound formula of thought and action he was able to meet difficulties and, instead of being defeated by them, they merely helped strengthen his faith. His belief put him in harmony with the law of supply and, as a result, new and creative sources of support opened.

Another example of the creative power of belief is the experience of my friend, Dr. Frank L. Boyden, famous headmaster of Deerfield Academy, one of the finest of American preparatory schools. When Dr. Boyden came to the school years ago its future was precarious due to inadequate financial support. Today it has a beautiful campus, outstanding plant and equipment, and a superior faculty.

I asked Dr. Boyden how he created this splendid school from such unpromising beginnings.

"Well," he replied, "I think the banks in our town had their doubts. Probably they felt many times like writing us off; yet, whenever I needed help it was always available. I just kept on believing that we would come through." And he added, "I believe in the law of supply. When everything seems to be against you, even when there seems little hope, fill your mind with faith, do your best, work hard, and put the results in the hands of God. If sincerely you endeavor to do God's will, the law of supply will operate and it will supply your needs. This school was built upon the spiritual law of supply."

Of course the plus to that formula is Dr. Boyden's own dedicated personality and amazing understanding of boys. And not least in importance was his willingness to work hard and give his best. When this is done the law of supply operates effectively.

Any human being can do more with his life than he is presently doing. To begin with, you must desire to do so. The second step is to surrender yourself to God and live by His will. Then take God as your spiritual guide and partner in life. Next, pray without ceasing and have faith always. Be sure to hold positive pictures of achieving worthily and unselfishly. Finally, expect the cooperation of events, work hard, and think creatively, forget self, keep a heart full of good will, hold no resentment. And always remember—with God's help you can if you think you can.

How to Believe

1. Believe.
2. As you train your mind to believe, everything tends to move out of the area of the impossible into that of the possible.
3. Never compare yourself or your achievements with others, but make your comparisons only with yourself.
4. A sign of mental health is to be glad when others achieve, and to rejoice with them.

5. Failure lies in not being naïve enough to practice the power of faith.
6. Make your life what you want it to be through belief in God and in yourself.
7. Start living by faith, pray earnestly and humbly, and get into the habit of looking expectantly for the best.
8. Get your life right in terms of God's laws.
9. Be sure your goals are spiritually sound.
10. Think, believe, visualize success.
11. Keep on believing as long as you live.

2

ENTHUSIASM CAN DO WONDERS FOR YOU

"When you cast out pessimism and gloominess and cultivate the attitude of optimism and enthusiasm, amazing results will be demonstrated in your life. Even if your ability, training, and experience are less than others', you can compensate for almost any lack by dynamic enthusiasm."

ARE YOU an enthusiastic person? Do you eagerly anticipate each day? Are you excited about life? If not, then at all costs get real enthusiasm into your personality, for enthusism can do wonders for you.

My own mother was one of the most enthusiastic persons I ever knew. She was alive to her finger tips even though forced to cope with physical difficulty a large share of her life. She got an enormous thrill out of the most ordinary events and happenings. She had the ability to see and enjoy romance and zest in everything.

She travelled the world over. Years ago in China, during a revolution, she complained that she encountered so few bandits. Once, when her party was halted by fierce-looking brigands, she seemed actually disappointed that they did not kidnap her and her companions and cause some thrilling international incident.

I recall an experience with her one very foggy night while crossing from New Jersey to New York on a ferry boat. To me there was nothing particularly beautiful or interesting about the fog, but my mother excitedly cried, "Norman, isn't this thrilling?"

"What is thrilling?" I asked rather dully.

"Why," she enthused, "the fog, the lights, that ferry boat we just passed. Look at the mysterious way its lights fade into the mist."

Just then came the sound of a fog horn, deep-throated in the "heavy-padded whiteness" of the mist. That phrase, "heavy-padded whiteness," is my mother's, and I thought it particularly picturesque. Her face was that of an excited child. Up to that moment I had no feeling about that ferry boat ride except that I was in a hurry to get across the river; but now its mystery, romance, and fascination began to penetrate even my dull spirit.

She stood by the rail and eyed me appraisingly. "Norman," she said gently, "I have been giving you advice all your life. Some of it you have taken, some you haven't; but here is some I want you to take. Realize that the world is athrill with beauty and excitement. Keep yourself sensitized to it. Never let yourself get dull. Never lose your enthusiasm."

Wherever in the great beyond she is today, I am sure she is having the time of her life. Being what she was and is, she is as enthusiastic over there as she was here. I determined to follow her advice and have practiced keeping enthusiasm alive. Therefore, I can assure you from personal experience that it does wonders for you.

Ruth Cranston in her *Story of Woodrow Wilson* says: "Woodrow Wilson's classes at Princeton were the most popular ever known in the history of that University, and they were far from being snap courses. Year after year the students voted Wilson the most popular teacher. And the reason, he radiated enthusiasm.

" 'He was the most inspiring teacher I ever sat under.' 'He made everything he touched interesting!' 'There was about him an aliveness, an enthusiasm that was infectious.' Such were some of the comments of his students, though he was lecturing on subjects that could be obtuse and dull: international law and political economy."

The president of a large company states: "If I am trying to decide between two men of fairly equal ability, and one man has enthusiasm, I know he will go farther than the other because enthusiasm acts as a self-releasing power and helps focus the entire force of personality on any matter at hand. Enthusiasm is infectious; it carries all before it."

That, of course, is understandable, for a man with enthusiasm gives the job his full potential. He throws everything into it. Enthusiasm is constantly renewing and releasing him, bringing all his faculties into play, utilizing his best.

Those who do the most and the best in life invariably have this quality of enthusiasm. So amazing are the achievements of such persons that it may be said that optimism and enthusiasm can actually work miracles in people's lives.

Emerson, considered by some to be the wisest man who ever lived in the United States, is an advocate of enthusiasm. "Nerve us up with incessant affirmatives," he says. "Do not waste yourself in rejections nor bark against the bad, but chant the beauty of the good" When you cast out pessimism and gloominess and cultivate the attitude of optimism and enthusiasm, amazing results will be demonstrated in your life. Even if your ability, training, and experience are less than others', you can compensate for almost any lack by dynamic enthusiasm.

In the light of this, how foolish to accept the depressing and uninspiring doctrine of personal limitation. If asked how far they can go and how much they can do, some say, "Not very far and not very much. You see," they negatively explain, "I am not as gifted as others." To that assertion I would answer by a question and a statement: "How do you know you have limited ability? You do not know that for certain; you have merely accepted the concept, and by so doing, have actually limited yourself."

As a matter of fact, the amazing untapped power you have within you is of a force and quality that you cannot fully comprehend. Therefore, do not let yourself be a victim of the dismal concept of self-assumed personal limitation. Without being immodest you can and should be enthusiastic about yourself. Remember what William James, one of America's greatest psychological thinkers, said about your possibilities if you practice belief: "Believe that you possess significant reserves of health, energy, and endurance and your belief will help create the fact." Such is the power of dynamic and enthusiastic faith.

Many persons are paralyzed, not in their limbs, but in their thoughts. They have sold themselves on a constricted view of themselves; but such self-appraisal is a false opinion of their own personality. Most people underrate themselves. To counteract the crippling effect of such downgrading of yourself, practice optimistic enthusiasm about your own possibilities. When you vigorously reject the concept of personal limitations and become enthusiastic about your own life it is astonishing what new qualities will suddenly appear within you. You can then *do* and *be* what formerly would have seemed quite impossible.

An outstanding example of the infectious power of enthusiasm to bring out new capabilities was demonstrated by the old Boston Braves when, by transfer of franchise, they became the Milwaukee Braves. In Boston, the team had been drawing small crowds, had no support, stirred no enthusiasm, and did very poorly their last season in that city. Then they were transferred to Milwaukee. It had been fifty years since Milwaukee had boasted a Big League Baseball Club and the enthusiasm of the citizens for their new team was positively unbounded. They crowded the ball park, twenty to thirty thousand for each game. All Milwaukee, it seemed, took the Braves to their hearts, were proud of them, and wanted them to win. Indeed, all believed they would.

As a result, that former seventh-place team played as never before. A newspaper article stated that one could sit in the stands and actually feel optimism, confidence, and faith flowing from the spectators into the players. The same team that finished in seventh place one year, pushed almost to the top of the League the next year, and has been one of the most dramatically successful teams ever since.

They were the same men as before; the same, yes, but with a difference. They were now experiencing and drawing upon a new power, a power sparked by enthusiasm. And that power worked miracles by releasing abilities hitherto unrealized. They were now superb athletes, whereas before they had been ordinary, faltering, and defeated.

You, too, can draw on new power. If you are now defeated by your weaknesses, your tensions, your fears, and your inferiorities, it is only because you have never taken into your mind this glorious, radiant quality of enthusiasm. While the change to this new quality of life is not easy, no profound change in character ever is, yet the method is clearly and simply defined. There are two steps, psychologically and spiritually sound, which you can take to increase your enthusiasm. One is to change the character of your thoughts, the other is to revamp the existing pattern of your attitudes. This is best accomplished by practicing the basic principles of religious faith and psychological understanding.

Enthusiasm cannot live in a mind filled with dull, unhealthy, destructive ideas. To change this condition, practice deliberately passing a series of enthusiastic thoughts through your mind every morning. Look in the mirror and say something like this: "Today is my day of opportunity. What fine assets I have—my home, my family, my job, my health! I have so many blessings. I will do my best all day and God will help me. I am glad to be alive." Repeat this same thought-conditioning technique as you retire at night. This daily process of ridding your mind of gloomy and depressing thoughts which, of course, are profoundly unhealthy and self-defeating, is very important since your prevailing pattern of ideas can affect your whole impact upon life. Unhealthy thoughts can make you unhealthy. Defeatist thoughts can defeat you.

I hailed a taxicab in New York City on a sunshiny morning, saying in merry fashion to the driver, "Good morning. How are you?"

He looked at me wearily and answered coolly, "So what?"

Despite this chilly response I persisted, "Sure is a great morning!" He glanced at me again, "I don't see anything great about it. It's going to rain after a while and the weather's going to get bad."

"Well, what is wrong with rain?" I asked. "Good old rain."

But that didn't affect him either. There was another man with me who kept calling me "doctor," so after awhile the taxi driver turned to me and said, "Say, doc, I've got some pains in my back. I feel terrible."

"A young fellow like you shouldn't have pains," I replied. "How old are you?"

"Thirty-five," he answered, then added plaintively, "What do you suppose is the matter with me?" Apparently he took me for a Doctor of Medicine.

"Well," I replied thoughtfully, "I think I know what you've got, although I am not accustomed to practicing in taxicabs." Continuing the physician fiction I said, "I think you have psycho-sclerosis."

"What's that?" he demanded with a startled look.

"Did you ever hear of arteriosclerosis?" I asked.

"Yes," he said doubtfully, "I guess so."

"Well," I explained, "that is hardening of the arteries. Perhaps, instead, you have hardening of the thoughts, psycho-sclerosis, and it can be very serious."

"What can I do about it?" he asked apprehensively.

"Well, I have been riding with you in this cab for only a few minutes, but your gloomy and pessimistic thoughts and expressions would depress any passenger, to say nothing of yourself. Perhaps if I rode with you very much I would develop psycho-sclerosis, too!"

By this time we had reached the Marble Collegiate Church, my destination, and I got out and said, nodding in the direction of the church, "I'm not the kind of a doctor you are thinking of. I'm what you might call a spiritual doctor and while I do not want to preach to you, I believe spiritual treatment would help you." I then explained various spiritual treatments, mentioning the method of passing happy and enthusiastic thoughts through the mind, indicating my belief that such practice might help reduce his pains. I did emphasize that he should see his physical doctor as well. The taxi driver was quite bewildered by the diagnosis that his trouble might be mental and spiritual, but a look of understanding came over his face and he said, "I get you. You think I am feeling badly because I am thinking badly."

"Yes," I agreed, "that is a good way to put it. I have known that to happen, and if I were you I would really go to work on my thoughts. Get your mind full of enthusiasm and optimism." I invited him to consult our counseling experts at the church clinic, which he did; and to attend services, which he also did. He was given religious and inspirational literature to read, study, and practice and he proved a cooperative "patient" in psychological and spiritual therapy.

The practice of enthusiastic ideas and attitudes may come hard to an individual whose tendencies veer toward automatic negative reactions. The development of an instinctively enthusiastic outlook begins with a positive affirmation, as previously described, even though at the start that may run counter to actual feelings. The very use of the affirmation itself commits one to the positive attempt and when real effort is made to affirm enthusiasm however feeble it may be, a start is made toward becoming an enthusiastic person. Success depends upon resolutely keeping at it until the positive pattern of enthusiasm takes firm hold. I must reiterate that the formula I am advocating is not easy, but if you try and keep trying, you will get wonderful results.

How this method changes conditions by changing individuals is illustrated by the case of a man who telephoned me from a hotel in a nearby city one night. "I just don't know what to do," he said desperately. "I can't sleep I'm so discouraged. In fact, I'm just about sunk. Tomorrow afternoon at three o'clock I have to meet the greatest crisis of my whole business life," he went on gloomily, "and if things don't go right tomorrow, I'm finished." In addition, he said, "I've just received word that my wife is ill and may have to go to a hospital and all in all, I'm in such a bad way that I thought I would phone you. I hope you don't mind."

I assured him that I didn't mind and then said, "No doubt you have survived many crises and you will get through this one, also. You seem awfully tense," I suggested. "I imagine you are sitting in your room hunched over the telephone, clutching the receiver very tightly, and your free hand is probably clenched too. Am I right?"

"I guess you are," he mumbled.

"Well, please hold the receiver loosely and unclench the other hand." Then I asked, "Is there an easy chair in your room?" He replied that there was. "Well, pull it up, sit back in it, stretch out your legs, put your head against the headrest of the chair, and talk to me easy-like."

I detected that he was slightly bewildered by all this. Finally, he said, "O.K., I'm sitting in the easy chair. My head is resting on the chair back."

"Now," I said, "put your feet up on a desk or another chair." He sort of laughed at that one and said, "O.K., you've got me pretty well eased up now."

I then explained that it is very difficult to force a creative idea up from the subconscious as long as the surface of the mind, the conscious part, is in a rigid state. "You must get yourself relaxed so that the fresh and vital thoughts which you need can come through. What have you been thinking about lately?" I asked.

"Mostly about myself, of course. What else is there to think about?"

I suggested that he shift his thought emphasis from himself to other people, that he cease projecting inwardly, and start cultivating an outgoing attitude. By this he would bring to bear the subtle spiritual law that, as you give yourself, you find yourself. He happened to have a passing knowledge of the Bible and was aware of the law to which I referred. For your information it is stated in the following words: "For whosoever will save his life shall lose it: and whosoever will lose his life for my sake shall find it." (Matt. 16:25) And let me add, it is one of the most subtle laws applicable to human experience.

Then I asked, "Have you done anything unselfishly for anybody lately?"

"No, I haven't," he admitted. "I've been too tied up with my own anxieties."

"All right, tomorrow morning, first thing, go to the Salvation Army, in person, and ask them to give you the name of some needy person. Then go and personally do something for him. By that means you will start forgetting yourself. In fact, you will get better results if you do something for several people. Make a real sacrifice. Go out of your way to get interested in somebody and help him; then note how much better you feel. That will prove a releasing device and will get life to flowing properly. But remember, you must not do these things for what you may get out of it, but rather you must try to have a sincere desire to help other people.

"Then," I continued, "after we stop talking immediately start offering a prayer of thanksgiving. Stop asking, and start thanking. Give thanks for everything you can think of—all positive factors of good that are yours; and continue to offer thanksgiving. It might help to list them all on paper.

"Next, put the problem of tomorrow in the hands of God and confidently believe that He will give you a good night's sleep. Then tomorrow go into that interview, peacefully and confidently, believing that you are being guided by God, and that God is with you. Conceive of Him as actually taking charge of the situation, guiding you in what you shall say. Meanwhile, calmly think everything through in a constructive manner. Above all," I concluded, "be optimistic and enthusiastic—no gloom, no negativism, only faith and gladness. Practice this technique and I am sure things will go well."

It was several weeks before I heard from him. Then he telephoned to say that while everything had not turned out exactly the way he wanted, he was now convinced that the outcome had been for the best. He was amazed by the manner in which the situation had clarified.

"I have certainly learned my lesson," he said. "I have discovered that gloominess and depression destroy creative capacity and therefore block off the ability to handle things. I realize that I still must do a powerful reconstructive job on myself. But I have been practicing enthusiasm and already it has made such a difference in me that I am going to make enthusiasm a habit. And," he added, "I have adopted as a policy your suggestion about doing something for somebody every day. Believe me, you've got something there."

He concluded with this observation "I wonder why I never realized before that Christianity really works as a practical program."

To sum up the formula he used:

1. Practice calmness and quietness.
2. Do something every day for somebody.
3. Pray with thanksgiving.
4. Flush negatives out of the mind with enthusiasm and optimism.

A good Bible text to repeat everyday is "O give thanks unto the Lord; for he is good." (Psalm 106:1) Never doubt that the creative power of enthusiasm will do wonders for you. It is a powerful factor in the art of living dynamically all your life.

Enthusiasm also has a powerful effect on well-being. A noted New York State physician said, "People can actually die because they lose their enthusiasm. The physical organism cannot handle the mental attitude of uselessness." Recently I asked a physician to appraise the psychological advantages of optimism over depression, and this was his answer: "Depressive thoughts, habitually held, increase the possibility of infection by at least tenfold. Optimism, real faith, and enthusiasm taken together, are powerful agents in burning out infection. I have noticed that people who maintain a confident attitude show greater healing power in the presence of sickness and disease. Enthusiasm is one of the greatest sources of health." So said the physician.

That this is a practical fact is illustrated in a letter from Mary Alice Flint. Ten years ago, she says, she was habitually tired and lacking in energy and enthusiasm. Today she is spiritually vigorous and physically well. In my opinion she and her husband Maurice Flint are two of the most spiritually influential persons I know. She is a vital and vibrant personality. She says she can work all day without tiring. After returning from a recent trip where she held meetings and talked to customers in the stores where the jewelry which she and her husband manufacture is sold she wrote this dynamic letter:

"My trip was terrific and stimulating. It gave me some fresh new ideas. I used to spend a lot of time dreaming of the things I would like to do, but I never went so far as to dream of the things that have actually come about in the last few years.

"Whether I have been reborn or only released, I do not know. But I do know that at my age, when my energy should be waning, I have experienced a renewal of strength beyond anything I ever had before. The marvelous part of it is that I know, so long as I am needed to do the work God intends me to, this strength will continue. If this isn't one of the modern miracles, then it is mighty close to it.

"My husband and I realize that the source of this revitalizing is in God and in enthusiastic faith in Him."

Every day this woman passes through her mind, by a process of prayer, meditation, and surrender of self, a series of enthusiastic faith thoughts. This has revamped her whole slant on life, renewed her interest in living, brought out the best in her personality, and has given her a flow of energizing health, both spiritually and physically.

A second effective way to develop enthusiasm is simply to act enthusiastic until you become so. It is a psychological fact, often demonstrated, that you can be freed from an undesirable feeling by assuming the exact opposite feeling. For example, if you feel afraid, you can make yourself courageous by acting courageous. If you are feeling unhappy, by deliberately acting happy you can induce happy feelings. In similar manner, if you are lacking in enthusiasm, by simply acting enthusiastic you can make yourself enthusiastic.

A fascinating illustration of a man who demonstrated this principle is told in the first chapter of Frank Bettger's book *How I Raised Myself from Failure to Success in Selling*. This one chapter is a classic in the techniques of enthusiasm. Bettger was playing baseball on the Johnstown, Pennsylvania team. Though young and ambitious, he was fired from the team on the grounds of being lazy. Bettger knew that he was not lazy, only nervous. The manager explained that if he expected to get ahead he would have to put more enthusiasm into his work.

Finally, the New Haven team gave him a tryout. He said: "My first day in New Haven will always stand out in my memory as a great event in my life. No one knew me in that league, so I made a resolution that nobody would ever accuse me of being lazy. I made up my mind to establish the reputation of being the most enthusiastic ball player they'd ever seen in the New England League.

"From the minute I appeared on the field I acted like a man electrified. I acted as though I were alive with a million batteries. I threw the ball around the diamond so fast and so hard that it almost knocked our infielders' hands apart. Once, apparently trapped, I slid into third base with so much energy and force that the third baseman fumbled the ball and I was able to score an important run. It was all a show, an act I was putting on. The thermometer that day was nearly 100°. I wouldn't have been surprised if I'd dropped over with a sunstroke the way I ran around the field.

"Did it work? It worked like magic. Three things happened: 1. My enthusiasm almost entirely overcame my fear. 2. My enthusiasm affected the other players on the team, and they too became enthusiastic. 3. Instead of dropping with the heat, I felt better during the game and after it was over than I had ever felt before."

Bettger says his greatest thrill came the following morning when he read in the New Haven newspaper, "This new player Bettger has a barrel of enthusiasm. He inspired our boys." Then the newspapers began calling him "Pep" Bettger, the life of the team. It is an exciting demonstration of the power in acting enthusiastic.

The significant fact is that two years from the time he was discharged by Johnstown, he was playing third base for the St. Louis Cardinals and had multiplied his income 30 times. "What did it?" he asks. "Enthusiasm alone did it. Nothing but enthusiasm."

Later, when he went into life insurance, he put into effect the same principle of demonstrating enthusiasm and became an outstandingly successful man in that field.

Walter Chrysler stated a powerful truth when he declared: "The real secret of success is enthusiasm. Yes, more than enthusiasm, I would say excitement. I like to see men get excited. When they get excited they make a success of their lives."

So, to become enthusiastic, practice deliberately forcing yourself to act enthusiastic. By this procedure you can actually become enthusiastic. In a short time you will no longer need to force enthusiasm as it will become natural to you.

Real enthusiasm, not the synthetic or assumed kind, the enthusiasm that bubbles up from deep inner sources, is spiritual in nature. The word "enthusiasm" is derived from two Greek words, "en" and "theos," meaning "God within you," or "full of God." Therefore, you will have enthusiasm, force, and power to the extent that God is actually present within you. God gave you life; God can and will renew your life. When you get out of harmony with God, life declines, vitality ebbs, and then enthusiasm leaks away. When enthusiasm is low, vitality, energy, and power are also low.

Therefore, get full of God and your enthusiasm will rise and as it does, you will experience new vitality, energy, force, and effectiveness. Always remember that enthusiasm was built into you by Almighty God in an original creative process. And God not only creates, He also recreates unless, by living in a nonspiritual manner, you interfere with His natural renewal processes. But if you keep in harmony with God, recreative enthusiasm and vitality will continue to renew you indefinitely.

Enthusiasm is an important factor in the vibratory pattern of life. The entire universe being in vibration, it is important to be in harmony with the vibrations that come from God. At this very minute you are being bombarded by millions of vibrations. You are receiving vibrations from people and objects surrounding you. They strike upon you and unconsciously you respond to them. It is important to cultivate sensitivity to positive vibrations from God, the source of your life.

There are varying grades of vibrations. For example, on a rainy day you get different vibrations than on a sunny day. People have vibrations, too. Some people leave you cold, and others make only a moderate impression upon you. And then you encounter people who are surcharged with vibratory power. They thrill and captivate you, they fascinate you, move you, draw you to them.

I attended a high school play, a very good one. Everybody in the cast was excellent, but there was one boy who appeared on the stage for not more than three minutes. He was a slight boy of about sixteen, and yet he was a bundle of dynamic vibration. What he will be at twenty-five is not hard to imagine, for that boy has the Divine gift of vibratory transmission. He swept in upon the stage so briefly, and yet he lifted and captivated the audience. Days later I was still under the spell of that boy who was surcharged with enthusiasm and, therefore, was in harmony with the vibratory powers of the universe.

So, to have enthusiasm affirm, and believe as you affirm, "I am now in harmony with the spiritual vibrations that flow from Almighty God. I will now live as though I have enthusiasm. I do have enthusiasm. I am now in God's vibration flow and am receiving enthusiasm from God." You can demonstrate to yourself by practice the absolute reality of such affirmation. This technique is practical because it works. Deepen your faith, affirm enthusiasm, forget yourself, serve God and people, and you will attain new and higher levels of life. And you will have deeper satisfaction.

When the power of enthusiastic faith is constantly maintained you will have a perpetually fresh interest. Life will never get old or stale. You will become and remain vital and effective.

We sometimes hear people complaining: "There is no future for me in this business or in this town. Everything is against me." Such complainers actually make their own unhappy situations. What you picture tends to actualize in fact if you hold the picture long enough, continuing to emphasize it. Such people do not realize what great things would happen in their lives if they would quit complaining and saturate their minds with creative enthusiasm.

People who go ahead constructively in life are those who pour boundless enthusiasm into what they are doing. They never minimize their work or opportunities but on the contrary, they take hold enthusiastically and, therefore, stimulate the forces of successful accomplishment.

Recently, while recording radio talks I became aware that the engineer with whom I was working, Hal Schneider, seemed to get an unusual thrill out of his work. He kept stimulating me with his own enthusiasm. I was helped by his enthusiastic spirit. It seemed to draw me out of myself. After the recording and while he was gathering up his equipment I said, "You really like your job, don't you?"

"I sure do, I love it," he replied, and at my urging proceeded to tell me about himself.

He came of a poor family that lived in an under-privileged section of New York City. His first job was that of elevator boy in an apartment house. It was not much of a job, but he never thought of it that way. It spelled opportunity to him and he gave his whole self to it with enthusiasm. He was ambitious to do something with his life and he said, "I tried to become the best elevator boy they ever had."

But his real ambition was radio engineering. He studied that subject in his spare time. He was most enthusiastic and haunted the radio studios until finally he got a small job. But that job was not a small job to him. He went at it so enthusiastically, studying and thinking and working, that in due time he became one of the National Broadcasting Company's top engineers. In fact, he was good enough to get the assignment of traveling with General Eisenhower during his 1952 campaign.

"On that train," he said, "I wonderingly reminded myself that I was that poor little elevator boy. And here I was, actually putting a famous General, now candidate for President of the United States, on the air. I just couldn't get over it, I was so thrilled.

"But my greatest experience came," he said, "after the General was elected. It was at a huge meeting in New York City. Thousands were present and the whole nation was waiting to hear what the new President would have to say. It was a tremendous moment.

"There stood the President ready to speak, and there I was ready to put him on the air. The President waited at the podium. They were a bit slow coming through with the cue. I stood for fifteen seconds with my finger poised and you could hear a pin drop in that big auditorium. Then all of a sudden it came over me, think of it, even the President of the United States could not begin until I pointed my finger and gave him the go-ahead. Sure I love this job, it's full of thrills." He glowed with the enthusiasm that made him a top-flight engineer.

This man's experience proves once again that any job may become more than a job when you have the imagination and the enthusiasm to make it so. This young man had enthusiasm within him and he let it come out. So can you. You want your life to be different, you want to rise above humdrum routine. You want to render a real service. You can have it different, but you do not need to change your job in order to change your life. Just change yourself. Change your thoughts and attitudes. Become enthusiastic and the old job will become a new one, and your life will fill up with power. In this way you will start up the path that leads to greater things.

I have seen the combination of enthusiasm and prayer do so much in the lives of so many that I must write with enthusiasm about what enthusiasm can do for you.

I can tell you with enthusiasm, soundly based on the facts, that every idea, every suggestion, every technique described in this book will work. I have seen them operate in the lives of hundreds of people. Therefore, you can, with confidence, believe in the practicality and workability of the principles which are presented in this and other chapters.

One man who achieved a rebirth of enthusiasm through these methods was formerly a sleepy, dull salesman. As a result of his lethargic thinking and uninspired work, he was living from hand to mouth. When he heard about the achievements of other salesmen, he could always tell you wherein their methods were wrong. The habit of criticizing other people who are doing constructive things in life is one sure sign that basically you are a failure. At heart you are not very big, and no man is a true success unless he is big at heart and generous. Whenever you find yourself criticizing others in this way, it would be wise to make a thorough and honest analysis of your jealousies and resentments.

This salesman had sold nothing in many days. He was constantly telling his wife of the mistake he had made getting into selling in the first place; he didn't like it, he didn't like people, people didn't like him. Whenever he went into an office to see a prospect people froze. So ran his dismal complaints.

One real asset which this man had was a wise and spiritually minded wife. She did not argue with him, but instead, with positive faith, prayed for him. She prayed and believed that guidance would be given. When you ask for God's help and at the same time negate your prayer by doubting that you are going to get it, your prayer will be answered by denial. How could the answer be otherwise, for obviously the real prayer is one of doubt.

But this wife prayed with positive faith that her husband's native enthusiasm and ability would be reasserted. Finally, she persuaded him to pray with her. Their joint prayer took the form of an affirmation that their life was being renewed and they visualized a change as taking place within them.

This kind of praying always has an effect, and one morning the husband said to his wife with a new firmness, "Let me pray this morning" and this was his prayer: "Lord, fill me with enthusiasm for my product (naming it). Fill me with enthusiasm for all the good I can do through my work."

That may seem a strange prayer, but remember the selling of that product was his work in the world, his livelihood; that is to say, his life. Through prayer, he had gotten the creative idea that the purpose of selling a good product is not only to make a living but primarily an opportunity to serve God and man. He went out that day in an outgoing and self-forgetful frame of mind, his emphasis shifting to a sincere interest in the people he called on.

That very day he sold two small orders. Day and night he continued to affirm creative enthusiasm. Naturally he did not change all at once; people seldom do. They sometimes make spectacular and instantaneous reversals, but personality change is usually gradual. But his new attitude gradually reshaped him until he became one of his company's most effective producers. "I am a man of only average ability," he told me, "but I have discovered that when an ordinary man believes enthusiastically in God and in his work and in people, he can do his job in an extraordinary manner." And how right he is!

The application of enthusiasm to occupations which seem drab and uninspiring often proves the magic touch that turns the ordinary into the extraordinary. Any aspect of life is only as drab as you conceive it to be, only as commonplace as you think of it. But you can, by your thoughts, lift it out of drabness, out of the commonplace, and cause it to be extraordinarily worthwhile. It all depends upon how much enthusiasm you generate and sincerely maintain within your mind and how spiritually dynamic is your motivation. A real sense of purpose plus enthusiasm will enhance your job, whatever it may be.

Successful living may be measured by the extent of your enthusiastic participation in life. I watched a football game on television. Two men in the backfield of one team were dynamos of enthusiasm. Everywhere the ball went, there they were. They seemed to cover the entire field, so eager and fast and enthusiastic were they. Their extraordinary effectiveness was explained by a simple fact—they were filled with enthusiasm. They gave it all they had.

If you are not getting on as well as you would want—and we should never be satisfied regardless of achievement—try giving more to your work, to your family, to your church, and to your community. Notice how the giving of yourself draws people to you. One of the surest of all truths is that life will give you no more than you give it. Go all out for life and it will go all out for you.

Enthusiasm carries all before it. Enthusiasm can do wonders for you.

Enthusiasm is so important that I wish to conclude this chapter by summarizing some steps which will help you to cultivate this essential quality.

1. Look for interest and romance in the simplest things about you.
2. Enlarge your view of your own God-given capacities. Within the limit of humility develop a good opinion of yourself.
3. Diligently practice eliminating all dull, dead, unhealthy thoughts so that your mind may be freshened up and capable of developing enthusiasm.
4. Daily affirm enthusiasm. As you think it, talk it, and live it, you will have it.
5. Practice daily relaxation to keep your mind and spirit from getting tired. Enthusiasm is a characteristic of the vigorously alert.
6. Act enthusiastic, for as you act you tend to be.
7. Allow no sense of guilt to take the luster off your spirit. It's the greatest of all causes of ennui.
8. Keep the creative channel open between God and yourself, remembering that enthusiasm is "entheos" meaning "God within."
9. Keep spiritually virile and alive.
10. Give all you've got to life and it will give its greatest gifts to you. It will never grow dull.

3

HOW TO CONQUER YOUR FRUSTRATIONS AND BE CREATIVE

"There are levels of the mental life to which no exasperation or frustration can ascend. And peaceful thinking brings you to that mental level where nothing can bother you unduly."

To LIVE with dynamic aliveness all your life you will need to keep from feeling frustrated. And, of course, you can.

People react curiously and quite differently to frustration. A California woman, exasperated by her inability to keep her house in a neat and tidy condition, decided to get rid of the place. So she set it afire and burned it to the ground. That was her startling way of coping with frustration.

A man returned home after an absence of twenty-five years. He had walked out, a quarter of a century earlier, because his wife was a nagger and he couldn't take it any longer. His wife said she was glad to have him back and he found her much quieter than before. That was his way of dealing with his frustration.

A business executive, fifty years old, was found dead at his desk, revolver in hand. He left a note explaining that tension and exasperation were "driving him mad," and he could stand it no longer. So he simply blew his brains out. That was his way of meeting frustration.

One evening in a hotel lobby, I encountered a man who was quite intoxicated and noisy. Knowing him, I was aware that he had a well-developed inferiority complex which usually kept him quiet, even shy, when sober. But liquor always transformed him into a rather unpleasant extrovert.

"I suppose you wonder why I'm drunk," he demanded. "Well, I get so exasperated it drives me crazy. When I get drunk I forget my frustration, for a while at least."

"Does frustration return after you sober up?" I questioned.

"Sure, always. Perhaps I should stay drunk all the time." That was his method of handling his frustration.

When frustrated we may not burn down our houses, walk out on our families, shoot ourselves, or become alcoholics; but in many subtler ways we allow frustration to dominate us and destroy our happiness and effectiveness.

Obviously, none of the above methods is an adequate answer to frustration. What then is the answer? One very good method is simply to do the best you can about everything, and then do nothing further. If you rush feverishly, doing your work with tense anxiety, never feeling that anything is finished, you arouse the hot and irrational emotion of frustration. Try substituting cool emotions by emphasizing deliberateness and organized efficiency. Quietly affirm that you are doing all you can. Practice entertaining quiet thoughts, rather than excited thoughts or hot thoughts or nervous thoughts. Picture yourself as "pouring" coolness on your heated tension. This, of course, is easier said than done, but you can do it by just doing it.

My good friend, the famous psychiatrist Dr. Smiley Blanton, author of the important book *Love or Perish*, declares that St. Paul's statement, ". . . and having done all, to stand," (Ephesians 6:13) is one of the greatest of all methods for healing frustration. That is to say, when you have done all you can do, just stop; do no more, let the matter rest. There is nothing further than can be done, so do not do anything further. Leave it with God. Let Him handle it from there on.

When you cease your nervous and feverish efforts to do more than you can or need to do, calmly realizing that there must come an end to anxious concern and nervous effort, then you will be delivered from the disorganizing effects of frustration.

I met a New York businessman on the veranda of a resort hotel. I had known him for years as the hard-driving type, and had rather formed the opinion that he was an over-tense, frustrated individual. But here he was sitting with his feet on the porch railing, hat pulled down over his eyes, just sitting.

Somewhat astonished I said, "I'm very interested in seeing you relax so efficiently."

"Well," he drawled, "I was about as frustrated a person as you could find, but I learned to get over it. And it's quite simple; I just decided to do all I could about everything, and when there is nothing more to do I just don't do it."

In modern language, he was agreeing with St. Paul's antifrustration technique. Relieved of frustration he could relax effectively, and have adequate and well directed energy when it was needed.

A second procedure for avoiding frustrated feelings is to practice peaceful thinking with the objective of making it your permanent mental slant. And this is an acquirable ability. The curative effect of peaceful thinking on frustration is illustrated by the experience of a woman who overfrequently consulted her doctor. And she always got around to talking about her daughter-in-law, habitually using the phrase, "She is driving me crazy.

I simply cannot stand her." This monotonously reiterated statement of annoyance with the younger woman was not unlike a record needle stuck in a groove.

The doctor noticed that she had developed a peculiar physical symptom, that of moving her head constantly from side to side. He suspected that his patient's trouble was caused by some deep frustration, which he shrewdly felt was tied in with hate. He pointed out to her that there was nothing she could do about the marriage of her son to the young woman; that her daughter-in-law was, in fact, her daughter-in-law and that she would just have to learn to get along with her.

A rudimentary fact that many miss is that there are some people and things in this world that you just have to get along with, and no amount of resistance or railing will accomplish anything except to increase your frustration. Therefore, the quiet and urbane philosophy of accepting persons and situations, and of learning to think about them peacefully, is most important in eliminating frustrated feelings.

Such was the philosophy the doctor outlined to this woman. As a prescription he gave her what he called a "therapeutic formula," not in the form of medicine but rather a medicinal mental pattern. He assured her that, by the "injection" of peaceful thoughts into the depths of her mind, she could overcome her frustration and perhaps, also, the physical symptom of the nervous head movement. His instruction was simply to repeat over and over many times daily these affirmative words: "God is giving me peace." In addition, she was to speak about her daughter-in-law in a kindly fashion as frequently as possible each day.

Improvement did not come easily, but after some days of this "spiritual medication" the head motion noticeably lessened and finally ceased altogether. Her spirit of frustration diminished gradually, and in due course she was able to accommodate herself to her daughter-in-law. The doctor presently tells me that he believes a genuine good-will relationship is developing between the two women. This skillful and effective religio-medical healing of frustration was brought about by the acceptance and practice of peaceful thoughts, accompanied by elimination of hate.

Another doctor tells of a young man who was constantly saying, most explosively, when anything annoyed him, which was often, "That burns me up." The doctor pointed out that the expression used by this patient was, in fact, a true picture of his inward state, both emotionally and physically.

The young man was running a persistent fever of approximately 100°, and at night he suffered cold sweats. The doctor at first thought these symptoms might indicate tuberculosis, but upon further analysis concluded that they were due to a "burning frustration." This physician, who is very accomplished in applying not only *materia medica*, but healing thought therapy as well, suggested to the young man that he go regularly to church. He directed him to a church where the therapy of quietness is an integral part of the worship service.

The first result was a profound feeling of quietness experienced by the patient. As he grew more skillful in the practice of quietness, he saw clearly that the chief values of his life were being lost in the hectic intensity of uncontrolled emotion. The healing therapy of spiritual peace presently got through to his mind. The doctor reports that in time he learned to apply spiritual technique to his everyday problems; and gradually the temperature became normal and the night sweats ceased. The therapy of applied quietness, penetrating to the deep center of his frustration, had a healing effect.

We need quietness as we need food and water, as we need sunshine and restful sleep. And we do not half appreciate the cumulative effect on our frustrations of peaceful thoughts deliberately employed.

I addressed the annual convention of the National Automobile Dealer's Association in the civic auditorium at Miami Beach, Florida. The audience consisted of some five thousand men engaged in one of the most competitive enterprises in America. And since the meeting came at a time when this particular industry was under considerable economic pressure, there was, in that group, not a little concentrated tension and frustration.

That morning, before going to the auditorium to give my speech, I was in my hotel working on a manuscript, and ideas were not flowing too well. In fact, at that moment I had to deal with some personal tendency toward frustration. Finally, I became aware that the mounting tension within me was blocking the flow of creative ideas. So, I relaxed in my chair and looked out at the beach where the sea was washing softly on the sandy shore and the ocean breezes were moving gently among the palm trees.

Have you ever noticed the utterly relaxed and graceful manner in which a palm tree lies over against the wind or moves with its motion? If you get the chance it might pay you to study palm trees for their secret of real relaxation. Their fronds move with a dignified sweep and rhythmic gracefulness and there is complete absence of rigidity.

I left the room and went to the beach which was deserted at that hour and location. I was alone with the sea and the sky and the winds and the sun and the palm trees. I sat with my back against a tree and looked at the sky which Emerson so aptly called, "the daily bread of the soul." As I listened to the deep roar of the sea I began to feel quiet, relaxed, and peaceful. What healing there is in the sea, sand, sun, and wind! As I watched and listened and communed with nature and with God, the frustration feelings left me.

Then I went to the auditorium to speak to the Automobile Dealers. The two speakers who preceded me told how difficult it would be to get business that year. They described all the trouble that was in store for the dealers, and you could sense the deepening gloom and frustration in that great crowd of American businessmen.

When my turn came to speak I felt moved to ask how many of them in the four days they had been in convention at Miami Beach had gone apart and communed with the great ocean that lay before them and which dominated their environment. I told them of my experience before coming to the meeting and quoted a verse from Masefield's poem:

> I must go down to the seas again, to the lonely sea and the sky,
> And all I ask is a tall ship and a star to steer her by.

I suggested that each man go down to the sea, preferably alone, and spend a little time with the sky and with the vast waters and with God. While making this suggestion, I noticed that a curious hush fell over that great audience. I believe we could all sense a deep and healing power. These men, important to the economy of our country, needed strength from a deeper source.

On the plane coming north I met a man who said, "I was sitting in that convention nervous, exasperated, frustrated. I heard you make that statement about your experience by the sea and it appealed to me. So, after the meeting I went to a lonely spot on the beach. I did not even take my wife along. I walked along the shore and observed the sandpipers running near the edge of the water. I picked up some shells and listened to the roar of the sea. I sat there a long time watching twilight come and the long shadows fall across the waters."

He hesitated, then continued with some embarrassment, for obviously he was deeply moved. "I happened to remember that story in the New Testament about Jesus being on the sea with His disciples and how they were frightened by the storm and He quieted the sea. And I remember particularly where it said, 'And there was a great calm.'

"Suddenly I felt peaceful and quiet. It was one of the most moving experiences of my life. So, I have come away from that convention, not discouraged, but with hope and optimism; I know that I am going to have a good year not only in selling, but in living as well." It was evident that he had experienced a spiritual, mental, and even physical rejuvenation.

Frustration is a combination of heat and stress; and the healing of heat is coolness and the healing of stress is peace. When one receives deeply into his being such an experience as this, he can thereafter work with vigor and energy. He will no longer work in a feverish and tense manner, plagued by exasperating frustration. There are levels of mental life to which no exasperation or frustration can ascend. And peaceful thinking brings you to that mental level where nothing can bother you unduly.

In overcoming frustration, another important technique is to desire and practice emotional control. I emphasize desire because one must first decide, honestly, very honestly, whether he really wants emotional control. People often say they do, but really they do not want it at all. They do not want to give up the "luxury" of letting themselves go emotionally.

I was watching a baseball game on television with my daughter Elizabeth, then ten years old. One of the players flew into a heated controversy with the umpire and reacted violently. "He's getting nowhere acting like that," I commented.

"Oh, yes he is," Elizabeth replied. "He certainly is getting somewhere. He's getting out of the game."

If that player could have seen himself as millions of people saw him, neck muscles distended, mouth stretched wide open, he might have regretted making such a spectacle of himself. It is curious indeed that people are actually willing to experience failure, unhappiness, even the sickness that comes from emotional upset just to have a temporary, sadistic satisfaction of flying off their control center. So, to have the emotional control that overcomes frustration feelings you must really want it, and when you do want control you can have it.

This was demonstrated by a hotel room clerk who revealed such remarkable imperturbability and self-control that he quite fascinated me. I checked into his hotel early one morning. Just ahead in the line of people waiting to register was a woman to whom he was saying that he was sorry, but unfortunately no room was available at the moment, but would be within a short time.

At this she became very irritated and began to berate the clerk in a loud and complaining tone, which could be heard by practically everyone in the lobby. Yet, never by a flicker of an eyelash, or by rising color, or by any change in tone of voice did this imperturbable clerk indicate that the conversation was anything other than pleasant. He was very kind to the woman. He explained the situation in detail. He was most patient and courteous.

Meanwhile, the waiting line was growing. Finally grumbling, still obviously annoyed, and with a rather crude parting shot or two, the woman turned from the desk after being assured by the clerk that she would be accommodated satisfactorily.

When my turn came to register I could not help commenting, "I observed this incident with interest and I admire your emotional control."

The clerk smiled and said, "I believe in the principles you teach, and I try to practice them for they really work."

I knew there was an interesting story back of this man's attitude, and later sought him out. He told me that formerly he had been very easily upset. This weakness had brought him humiliation and failure in several instances so that he realized how important emotional control was to his success in life. And he evolved a plan for developing it which seemed most interesting.

He explained: "I learned that much irritation and frustration result from unrelieved muscular tensions. So, every morning and night I practice relaxing my muscle tensions. My method is to mentally 'feel' the healing touch of Jesus Christ as starting at my head and in turn resting on every muscle. I conceive of Him as actually removing from my mind all tension.

"Then I ask for automatic emotional control. This is important for irritation may burst through when least expected. But, if like a thermostat on a heating system, you can set your emotional check valve at a certain point and maintain automatic control, then you can be sure of yourself, no matter what the provocation. But to do this requires the arduous practice of spiritual control," he concluded.

This man was able to master such control since he knew very well that to succeed in his line of work he must do so. Therefore, he really wanted control enough to make himself work at it and finally he achieved it. Through these effective methods he was able to overcome the volatile explosiveness of frustration. I was not surprised to learn, only recently, that he has advanced well up the ladder in the hotel industry.

People who fail in life are often those who give way to annoyance, make the sharp retort, the mean comeback, and who show the irritated reaction. These supersensitive, uncontrollable people go unhappily from one job to another because they cannot get along with people. They are always in some personality clash or personal-relation difficulty.

You can become a very great asset to yourself by mastering the art of being urbane and philosophical, by always having your reactions under control, and by demonstrating inner peace through the practice of the techniques outlined in this book. And how vital this is! Doubtless more people have muffed their opportunities, perhaps even destroyed their future, by the display of irritation and exasperation resulting from frustration than for almost any other reason.

A man who was consulting me about his problem of frustration said, "I can't understand it. Anger surges up within me and before I know it I fly to pieces. Then I throw discretion to the winds and let them have it. But," he explained, "fortunately, people understand that I am a nervous type and they overlook what I say and do and everything is all right again."

But if that easy outcome were true he would not have felt the need for consulting anyone. The actual fact is that people do not understand and usually they do not overlook and basically nothing is quite the same again. People just do not like such a person and he does not have their respect or regard.

Deep exasperation is so difficult to master that, as previously stated, the only certain way to overcome this liability is through God-control of frustration. God changes alcoholics, thieves, liars, and cheats. The reason these types are changed, many times, and the emotional cripple is not, is that the latter is less likely to admit defeat. But God can change people whose trouble is uncontrolled emotion just as He changes individuals with moral defeat.

There is a waiter who works on a train which I take occasionally for a long, overnight trip. He and I are good friends. I will never forget the first night I met him. He served me, along with several others, and I watched him; he had a glowering look on his face.

As I paid my check he leaned down and asked me, "May I come and see you after awhile?"

"Sure, come along," I replied.

And when he was off duty he came and sat with me in my compartment. "I don't know how much longer I can hang onto this job, Doctor," he said, and I could read desperation in his face.

"What is wrong?" I asked.

"I am getting so everybody annoys me," he said. "I keep myself under control, but one of these days I am going to bust out and ruin myself. I want to know what to do."

"What is your problem?" I asked.

"Well," he said, "I'm in the dining car and along comes one of these fellows who is always throwing his weight around, and he says, 'Come here, Boy.' Now, I ask you, am I a boy? I'm fifty years old!"

"Remember," I said, "we are all boys until the very end. And there are people," I continued, hoping to help him lift his problem from the emotional to the intellectual plane, "who want to compensate for their own feeling of inferiority by depreciating somebody else."

"There's another kind of trouble," the waiter continued. "I'll bring a man his order just the way he's written it down on that piece of paper, and he'll say it isn't what he ordered. According to the rules I have to say, 'Yes, Sir, I'm sorry, Sir,' and take it back." The waiter showed me his tray which he had brought with him. "Look at that tray," he said. "One of these days I'm going to crown one of those people with it." But his voice was milder than his words.

"Let us talk about the man who calls you 'Boy.'" I really went to work on that waiter's problem; I could see it was serious. "He is an infant. Back home he doesn't amount to much and so he actually has a deep inner sense of inadequacy and tries to compensate for it by assumed extrovertish actions. Be sorry for him. Think of him as you would of a child and let it go at that.

"And that fellow who complains about the order you have brought him. Instead of hitting him over the head with your tray, I'll tell you something you can hit him with that will really get results."

My waiter friend became very interested. So I told him about Frank Laubach and his spiritual genius for shooting prayers at people. "You will get so that the person at whom you are shooting prayers will turn and smile at you," I assured him.

My friend was really thoughtful and promised, "I'll try."

At breakfast next morning I watched him. He looked at me over the head of a complaining dowager he was serving, and winked. When he passed me he leaned down and whispered, "I've got to shoot more 'n one prayer at her before she starts smiling."

And here is proof of my thesis that we must try to understand people instead of being irritated by them. This same woman stopped me in the vestibule of the car before I got off the train and asked me to pray for her. "I am going to Miami for the funeral of a loved one," she said.

When I had the opportunity to tell my waiter of this he said, soberly, "I guess you never know the trials and troubles of people." He had made a good start in his war with irritation. "In your patience" you shall possess your soul, when, like the hotel clerk, you are master of yourself; when, like this waiter, you start shooting prayers instead of striking back.

From the standpoint of both efficiency and health it is extremely important to keep frustration and emotion always under control. In his famous bestseller, *How to Live 365 Days a Year*, Dr. John A. Schindler points out that we have within our system the greatest of all health forces, the power of good emotions. The "medicinal" value of good emotions cannot be overestimated. Good emotions make us well, bad emotions make us ill.

Dr. Robert C. Peale says, "The greatest and most efficient pharmacy is within your own system. But so far we have not learned to regulate our mental and emotional reactions in order to make the maximum use of it."

This means that the elements for healthy living are within you. It only remains for you to keep yourself in harmony with them. God gives us what we need, but it remains for us to learn to use these gifts.

A neurologist states that in his personal practice frustration is a predominate cause of many cases of nervous breakdown. "People become so frustrated," he says, "that personality cannot stand the pressure and gives up."

Doctors tell us that anger disturbs the rhythmic action of the small muscle fibers of the stomach and the intestines, causing a spastic condition in the intestinal tract. It can raise the heart rate as high as one hundred sixty and the blood pressure from a normal one hundred thirty to over two hundred. There have been many cases of strokes under anger, caused by a burst blood vessel in the brain due to a sudden jump in blood pressure. If you carry a low grade seething anger in the form of resentment it can actually create a disturbance of the glandular secretions with an accompanying disorganization of the body chemistry. It is understandable, therefore, why the Bible advises, "Let not the sun go down upon your wrath." (Ephesians 4:26) Flush out of your mind the bad emotions: anger, fear, and hate, and you can develop definite feelings of health and vitality.

If you are not actually made ill by frustration, it may at least be reflected in loss of energy and tiredness. A man worked in an industrial plant under a foreman who mistakenly thought the best way to command respect was to bark orders in a top sergeant tone. And in other ways the tough foreman humiliated and annoyed his workmen. Each day this employee came home so nervous and fatigued that he thought of asking for lighter work or transfer to another company. His doctor found no physiological reason for his fatigue. Then the surly foreman was replaced with a more reasonable man who enlisted the cooperation of his workers, and treated them with consideration.

Almost at once this employee had a complete change of reaction and could work without tiring. Obviously, his exhaustion had been caused not by eight hours' toil, but by a seething annoyance and frustration caused by his boss's manner and attitude.

The Bible, having the greatest number of those good thoughts which lead to good emotions, is therefore a source of prescriptions for healing frustration. Practice committing to memory some of its many therapeutic or healing passages. An excellent one is this: "In your patience possess ye your souls." (Luke 21:19) Patience is a very great word, implying maturity, urbanity, and mental health.

As you grow in patience you will react not merely with your feelings, but with your intelligence. You will not respond with uncontrolled emotion, but rather, your motivation will be on a spiritual basis. In this way, you will become a person of philosophical and patient control. You will not easily be upset as are some who have not mastered this spiritual skill.

I watched a man trying to put through a telephone call. He got the busy signal several times. What did this great business executive do? He slammed the receiver down so hard that it bounced off the hook and slapped against the side of his desk. It was an exhibition of plain unadulterated infantilism. The man's face was red, his breath came hard, doubtless his blood pressure shot up. Such a person isn't grown up. Emotionally he is still in the infantile state, but since his blood vessels are of his physical age, such emotional outbursts often develop more pressure than they can handle.

A golfer had trouble sinking his ball in the cup. With the perversity inanimate things sometimes show, the ball just would not go where he wanted it to go. Of course the trouble was not in the inanimate object, but in the man. What did he do? He coldly restrained himself until, finally, he got the ball into the cup. Then, with a look of hate, he took the ball out, placed it on the ground and drove it with his club deeply into the earth. I do not know what score he had on the next fairway, but losing his temper could deprive him of that fine sense of timing necessary to good golf shots.

Jimmy Durante, commenting on frustrating irritations says, "Dem is de conditions dat prevail." That is indeed a wise observation. Situations do just prevail, and you have to get along with them. But if you approach them urbanely, philosophically, and spiritually you will control situations instead of having situations control you.

The human mind can develop the ability to block out frustration. A doctor told me of a woman who was forced to wear a hearing aid. She hated it and constantly complained of a roaring in her ears. "I just can't stand it," she said.

"You can stand it," the doctor replied, "if you discipline your mind. You can actually train yourself no longer to hear that noise. There is a faculty in the human brain that can block out any annoyance if you determine that you want to block it out."

Naturally, this does not come easy. It requires patience and effort and time. Nothing worthwhile in this life is easy. Disciplinary action and an exercise of will are required. Keep your mind focused on irritations and you will build them up. But by focusing your mind power on blocking them out you can successfully do so.

Prayer is a chief aid in the blocking out process. Try the experiment of praying in an outgoing manner, affirming good will toward those who irritate or frustrate you, and discover for yourself that you have the amazing power of eliminating frustration.

I demonstrated this for myself while staying in a beautiful hotel at Stresa on Lake Maggiore in northern Italy. This is one of the loveliest places in Europe. The lake and the great hotel resemble an old painting, serene and tranquil. The village is a colorful riot of flowers. The placid lake stretches away toward the hazy, towering hills in a charming vista. The fascinating little island villages, which seem to float in the lake, give the illusion of being out of a medieval picture book.

I went to bed that night expecting a restful night's sleep in that idyllic spot. But the hotel is on the main road which skirts the shore of the lake, and a constant and unending stream of noisy Vespas and Lambrettas (motorcycles) turned the night into bedlam. I lay in bed listening hopefully for just one brief interlude of quietness between the racing motorcycles and strident horns, but none ever came. The noise was always either trailing off, or coming up, or bursting upon me in devastating power.

Soon I found myself getting into a state of agitation. Then I realized that I was actually getting mad at those motorcyclists. I arose and shut the windows, but the heat was more than I could bear. It was either heat, or noise, or both, for the sound was so penetrating that it came through the windows, even though they were double ones. I tried plugging my ears with cotton, but this was uncomfortable. I tossed restlessly on my bed and with mounting asperity told my wife what I thought of people who would race with open cutouts through the still night with a total disregard for people who were trying to sleep.

I gradually worked myself into a state of frustration where sleep would be quite impossible. Then it occurred to me to practice, in this situation, the simple principles of Christianity. And when one does practice, one gets results, as I demonstrated on this occasion. I decided to send good will thoughts toward the motorcyclists. Why were they riding those motorcycles? Simply to get some joy and happiness out of life. Or perhaps they were on their way to some destination that was important to them. Life, with its many interests and hopes and problems, was riding those motorcycles along that lake, lying misty and lovely in the silvery moonlight. Therefore, every time I heard a motorcycle approach, which seemed about every half minute, I prayed specifically that the person riding it would have a wonderful life, that God would guide and bless him.

I became so positively engrossed in my spiritual contact with those nice Italian people speeding along on those ear-shattering motorcycles that I forgot my irritation, the frustration left me, and the next thing I knew it was seven-thirty in the morning. Those Vespa riders did not bother me from that time on throughout my entire stay in Stresa. It is a fact, that by prayer, if you really mean it and actually believe in it, you can block out frustration.

Learning to apply a scientific attitude in personal relations also helps to overcome frustration. By scientific I mean to take an objective and impersonal attitude toward people rather than to react emotionally. When someone does something that hurts or irritates you, the scientific, objective method is to say, calmly, "Well, now let's analyze him to see why he does this." Then develop a strategy designed to correct the relationship.

For example, a man consulted me who was very upset about another man's actions. Noting that he was in a state of frustration I explained this scientific attitude and recommended its use to him. But he protested vehemently. "It is all right to talk about being scientific, but it is I who am suffering this insult. What do you think this man called me?" he demanded.

"What did he call you?" I asked.

"I hate to tell you," he answered, "it is so terrible."

"Well, never mind, tell me what he called you."

"Why," shouted the man, "he called me a skunk. He is going everywhere telling everybody that I am a skunk."

"Well now, let us apply the scientific method," I said. "Are you a skunk?" I asked him.

"Of course I'm not a skunk!" he exclaimed, outraged.

"Well then, does his calling you one make you one?" I pursued.

"Of course not," he replied. "I'm no skunk and he knows it. What he says about me doesn't make me a skunk."

"Then," I said, "what he is saying is a lie, and a lie, according to an old German proverb, 'cannot run very far because it has short legs.' So, let him keep on saying it. It isn't so and after a while people will know that you are not a skunk and they may even conclude that he is one. You will come out of this all right."

By the practice of scientific objectivity, though not without difficulty, I observed this man rise to a high level of judicial impersonality. Actually he became quieter and less agitated. Then he began to apply the objective method to himself, to discover what there might possibly be about him that made the other person dislike him so much.

As a result of his honest, objective analysis he saw and eliminated certain unattractive personal qualities. He straightened out a few things he had done that needed adjusting. He developed an outgoing friendly attitude. His ability to take criticism and hatred quietly, without fighting back, and his genuine kindliness toward his enemy, finally drew the sting out of the other's feelings and the attacks ceased. In due course a pleasant relationship actually developed between the two men. It is a simple but powerful truth that you can pray out, love out, and think out any kind of frustration. And your ability to live successfully will be immeasurably increased thereby.

TO CONQUER FRUSTRATIONS:

1. Decide that you honestly want emotional self-control.
2. Practice peaceful thinking. With practice you will find it easier, more natural.
3. Instead of letting frustration irritate you, try to understand other people objectively, what makes them the way they are.
4. Set apart a period of quietness daily.
5. Each day practice relaxing muscular tensions.
6. Before going to bed, flush out of your mind the bad emotions.
7. Look to God for help in substituting calmness for irritation.
8. Do the best you can and leave the results to God. Then it will work out for the best.

4

KILL WORRY AND LIVE LONGER

"The basic secret of overcoming worry is the substitution of faith for fear as your dominant mental attitude. Two great forces in this world are more powerful than all others. One is fear and the other is faith; and faith is stronger than fear."

ONCE, IN Los Angeles, I delivered a public lecture using as a title the subject of this chapter, "Kill Worry and Live Longer." A newspaper misprinted the title to read, "Kill Worry and Love Longer." No doubt this mistake unconsciously represented the Hollywood influence.

Upon reflection, however, perhaps the garbled version wasn't too wide of the mark. For if you kill worry you will love longer. You will love your wife and children longer. You will love life longer. Kill worry and you will live longer and love longer, either way you take it. Fortunate, indeed, is the person who has learned to live without worry.

One glorious May day Mrs. Peale and I were driving in West Virginia. We came down a wide highway to a crossroads where a little road meandered off up a valley and into the mountains. At the intersection was a sign pointing to the smaller road. Intriguingly, it read "Sunshine Valley."

I turned to Mrs. Peale and asked, "Shall we go up Sunshine Valley?"

And she answered, "Let's go up Sunshine Valley."

I am glad we made this side trip because it was there we met Tommy Martin. We left the car and sat by one of those clear, rushing mountain streams coming down out of the blue misty hills on its way to the sea. We were listening to the music of water singing over the rocks and watching it swiftly disappear under a bridge, when Tommy came into view. He was about twelve years old and was sauntering down the road wearing a slouch hat, high boots, and well-worn trousers. He was chewing bubble gum and had a fishing rod slung over his shoulder. He looked us over with level gaze and apparently liked us, for he said, "Hi."

And then he turned to me, as though to an old friend, "Haven't you a pole? Well, come on, I'll fish for both of us." He took me to where two streams met. There, he declared, the best trout were to be found. He waded into the stream, cast his line and, in a brief moment, up came a beautiful trout. As he took it off the hook, I asked whether he was using dry flies or lures.

Chewing mightily he answered, "No, just plain old worms. They're better than fancy lures." Then he explained that the trout he had just taken was a brook trout and added, "I shot a deer in these woods last winter."

I asked him one of those stupid adult questions: "How come you're not in school?" It was Thursday, after all.

He made some sort of answer which I didn't get, but it sounded vague. And that day, as I sat on the bank watching this twelve-year-old boy fishing in a sunspeckled trout stream, I fell to wondering which of us knew more about living, he or I? And I asked, "Tommy, do you ever worry about anything?"

He looked at me with big brown eyes and answered in his mountain twang, "Worry? Shucks, there ain't nothin' to worry about!" Presently I went back to Mrs. Peale, wondering if I could ever again be like Tommy Martin.

Well, of course, the truth is that adult life brings certain responsibilities which are inescapable facts of maturity. And we have to live in a world that requires much of us. But isn't it possible, no matter our lot or how heavy our duties, to retain a gay and youthful spirit? I firmly believe that it is, and a purpose of this book is to help you recapture that spirit of joy and trust.

When I say you can leave worry behind, I do not imply that you should be indifferent to human suffering or have a careless disregard for the problems of society. Indeed, the elimination of worry will help you be a more effective citizen of the world. It is very important to acquire that sense of peace and confidence which makes you so much more adequate as a person.

The word *worry* is derived from an old Anglo-Saxon word meaning to strangle or choke. If someone were to place their fingers around your throat and press with full strength, cutting off your vital supply of air, he would be doing to you, dramatically, what you do to yourself if, over a long period of time, you are a victim of worry. You block off your own flow of power. Worry frustrates your best functioning.

I hope, therefore, you can develop Tommy Martin's philosophy: "Shucks, there ain't nothin' to worry about." And there isn't—not as long as we have God. And that is for always.

The ill effects of worry are well known to doctors. A New England physician wrote me saying, "I have noted in my practice over a good many years that fear either causes or accelerates many maladies. And," he added, "the best antidote I know is simple faith."

Dr. Walter Clement Alvarez of the Mayo Clinic is reported to have said, "We little realize the number of human diseases that are begun or are affected by worry." Dr. Seward Wood, of the University of Oklahoma Medical School, in an address before the nose and throat section of the American Medical Association on the relation of worry to the common cold and to infection of the sinuses and asthma said, "One young woman patient can turn asthma on and off by turning worry on and off."

A physician asked me to see a patient who had been admitted to the hospital with seemingly genuine symptoms of a heart attack, including shortness of breath and pains in the chest. "But," explained the doctor, "I am inclined to suspect that it is not a real heart attack but rather an anxiety attack. Will you talk to him and explore the psychological and spiritual basis of his anxiety?"

After counseling, it was ascertained that the patient did, indeed, suffer from acute anxiety. I discovered that this man, now in his sixties, had committed several sex sins in earlier life. As far as I was able to determine such incidents were limited to that early period and his conduct, subsequently, had been impeccable. He had lived in constant fear, however, that his wrongdoing would be discovered.

Those old sins had created a deep sense of guilt and had hatched a flock of fears and tensions that had haunted him for years until now they actually had him back in a hospital, with symptoms of a heart attack. His illness was entirely due to these long-held anxieties. We were able to help him find forgiveness and to achieve healthy-mindedness about the entire matter. His physical symptoms gradually disappeared, and he returned to normal health. The doctor expressed the opinion that, had the guilt-worry complex continued, the man could actually have died of the physical condition which it stimulated.

Frequently you hear people say, "I'm sick with worry," or "I'm worried nearly to death." There is more truth in these statements than you might suppose, for worry can indeed make you sick and has even been known to cause death. It is a fact that by killing worry we can, in all probability, live longer and certainly live much better.

The basic secret of overcoming worry is the substitution of faith for fear as your dominant mental attitude. Two great forces in this world are more powerful than all others. One is fear and the other is faith; and faith is stronger than fear. Basically, then, the method for overcoming worry is deliberately and consistently to fill the mind with faith until fear is displaced.

Of course, normal fear is a healthy mechanism built into us by Almighty God for our protection. Abnormal fear, on the contrary, is a pattern of unhealthy thinking that is both destructive and disintegrating. It is one of the most potent enemies of personality. Abnormal fear seems to possess the inherent power to cause ill health and even disaster.

A doctor felt this so keenly that when called to a home where he found members of the family clustered anxiously and apprehensively about his patient, projecting to him their fear thoughts, he took direct action. He told them, vigorously, that they were filling the patient's room so full of "fear germs" that his healing efforts were valueless. To dramatize his concern, the doctor threw the windows open wide. A strong gale whipped the curtains straight out. "I've got to fumigate this room of fear germs," he explained brusquely. "Unless you people start thinking faith instead of fear you are going to make it very hard for me to help. As that strong wind blows through this room purifying it, let the power of faith purify your minds of this destructive apprehension. You must stop surrounding my patient with the virus of fear." This may seem a curious procedure but it was no doubt an effective way to dramatize the influence of fear in sickness.

Worry may be described as a spasm of the emotions in which the mind takes hold of a thought or obsession, clutches it spasmodically, and will not let it go. To break its hold one must gently, but forcibly, insinuate a healthier and stronger idea into the mind's convulsive grasp. This stronger idea is that of faith in God. When faith, rather than fear, becomes your obsession you will master worry.

And how does one fill the mind so completely with faith that fear will be displaced? It is not easily done. One method is to read books about people who have overcome their fears. Do not read about weak, disorganized, and mixed-up people except as it may show you how to find constructive answers. Much fiction today deals with unhappy, blundering, conflicted, and defeated people. Many current novels contain the pathetic accounts of those who have never found themselves, who really do not know what life is all about. These books have the air of sophistication, but actually they are not sophisticated at all. The word sophistication means worldly wise, to know your way around. The unhappy characters in these books are certainly not very wise, judging from the astonishing lack of solution they demonstrate.

But tremendous stories are available about people who have overcome every manner of difficulty and fear by applying the skills of faith. Saturate your mind with such biographical material and it will help recondition your life and free you from worry.

An important technique is to fill your mind with the fear-eliminating words of the Bible. There is an enormous power in the words of the Scriptures. The Bible says, "If ye abide in me, and my words abide in you, ye shall ask what ye will, and it shall be done unto you." (John 15:7) Read and study the Bible, underlining every passage that has to do with faith. Assemble a great collection of such passages and, each day, absorb at least one into consciousness. That is best done by committing it to memory. Repeat the passage many times during the day, conceiving of it as dropping from your conscious into your unconscious by a process of spiritual osmosis. Visualize your unconscious as grasping it and fully absorbing it into your personality.

The following day commit and absorb another faith-passage in the same manner. At the end of one week, seven life-changing passages should have become a definite part of your mental equipment. On the seventh day, go over the seven verses you have absorbed. Meditate on each one, seeking to understand their deeper meanings.

You now have seven powerful faith concepts lodged in your mind, any one of which is well able to overcome fear thoughts. At the end of a month you will have received into consciousness thirty passages of faith and hope and courage. If you truly absorb these and live by them, you will definitely gain control over worry.

Still another method is to make use of freshly conceived and un-hackneyed symbols which may, in themselves, seem extraordinarily simple, but which have the power to direct the mind into new attitudes of faith.

In a radio talk I used the phrase, "Trust God and live a day at a time," and some weeks later received from a woodcraft company an attractive sign upon which, in raised letters, were these same words, "Trust God and Live a Day at a Time."

Accompanying was a letter which said: "I heard your radio talk. My business was going badly and I was filled with overwhelming fear and anxiety. I had come to believe that success in my little business was absolutely impossible; but when you used that phrase, 'Trust God and live a day at a time,' it struck me forcibly. So I had it made up in wood and placed it at the foot of the stairway in my home. Every night on my way up to bed I would look at it and affirm, 'Trust God and live a day at a time.'

"I said over those words the last thing before falling asleep. It helped to put the day behind me. Then I would ask God to give me a good night's sleep. In the morning, coming down to breakfast, that sign would remind me to trust God and live that day only. I felt more peaceful and confident.

"Presently I began to take the attitude that just one day was all I had to worry about and so I would give that day all I had of faith and effort. I began to believe that God would be with me all that day. And He was, too." The letter concludes by saying, "My business isn't out of the woods yet, but it is on the way and I see light ahead."

By the practice of this simple device, this hitherto worried man changed his outlook and his motivation from one of fear and anxiety to one of faith and hope. I find it helpful, also, for I placed the sign in my office where I can see it daily.

Another technique for destroying worry is to set against it the contrary attitude of boldness. Obviously, the worrier is not a bold person; but boldness can be cultivated. This again is not easy, but nothing worthwhile can be attained without persistent effort. The first step is to start thinking in terms of boldness. Undertake some constructive thing that frightens you; but think boldly about it.

Picture yourself as boldly attacking and overcoming your fears. Picturized concepts in the conscious mind will, if reiterated, impress themselves deeply within the subconscious. But assumed boldness must not be mere cockiness. It must be soundly based on faith as expressed by the words, "Fear not: for I am with Thee." (Isaiah 43:5) By this method of boldness your fear will disintegrate, for it cannot long maintain itself in the atmosphere of spiritual courage. Emerson advises, "Do the thing you fear and the death of fear is certain."

Steel yourself, by an act of will, to do that which you fear, whereupon you will discover that the feared thing is not as strong as you thought it to be. My dear friend, the late Grove Patterson, one of America's greatest newspaper editors, said, "When a man has quietly made up his mind that there is nothing he cannot endure, his fears leave him." We need to emphasize the importance of will power, for in many it has become flabby. It can become strong through use, however; so use yours.

Boldness will reveal to you that you are stronger than you have imagined. Fear will diminish and courage rise in direct proportion to the effectiveness with which you put boldness into effect. Practice first, the bold thought and second, the bold act. This will stimulate supporting spiritual forces that will enable you to overcome fear.

The well-known writer Arthur Gordon contributed an article to *Guideposts* magazine which I regard as a classic in the literature of overcoming fear:

"Once when I was facing a decision that involved (I thought) considerable risk, I took the problem to a friend much older and wiser than myself. 'I'd go ahead,' I said unhappily, 'if I were sure I could swing it. But . . .'

"He looked at me for a moment, then scribbled ten words on a piece of paper and pushed it across the desk. I picked it up and read, in a single sentence, the best advice I ever had: 'Be bold—and mighty forces will come to your aid.'

"It's amazing how even a fragment of truth will illuminate things. The thought my friend had written was inspired by a book, I discovered later, by Basil King.* It made me see clearly that in the past, whenever I had fallen short in almost any undertaking, it was seldom because I had tried and failed. It was because I had let fear of failure stop me from trying at all.

"On the other hand, whenever I had plunged into deep water, impelled by a momentary flash of courage or just plain pushed by the rude hand of

* The Conquest of Fear.

circumstance, I had always been able to swim until I got my feet on the ground again.

"Be bold—that was no exhortation to be reckless or foolhardy. Boldness meant a deliberate decision, from time to time, to bite off more than you were sure you could chew. And there was nothing vague or mysterious about the mighty forces referred to. They were the latent powers that all of us possess: energy, skill, sound judgment, creative ideas—yes, even physical strength and endurance in far greater measure than most of us realize.

"Boldness, in other words, creates a state of emergency to which the organism will respond. I once heard a famous British mountaineer say that occasionally a climber will get himself into a position where he can't back down, he can only go up. He added that sometimes he put himself into such a spot on purpose. 'When there's nowhere to go but up,' he said, 'you jolly well go up.'

"The same principle works, less dramatically but just as surely, in something as commonplace as accepting the chairmanship of some committee, or even seeking a more responsible job. In either case, you know you'll have to deliver—or else.

"Some of the mighty forces that will come to your aid are, admittedly, psychic forces. But they are more important than physical ones. It's curious actually, how spiritual laws often have their counterpart in the physical world.

"A college classmate of mine was a crack football player, noted particularly for his fierce tackling although he was much lighter than the average varsity player. Someone remarked that it was surprising that he didn't get hurt.

" 'Well,' he said, 'I think it goes back to something I discovered when I was a somewhat timid youngster playing safetyman. I suddenly found myself confronting the opposing fullback who had nothing but me between him and our goal line. He looked absolutely gigantic! I was so frightened that I closed my eyes and hurled myself at him like a panicky bullet . . . and stopped him cold. Right there I learned that the harder you tackle a bigger player, the less likely you are to be hurt. The reason is simple: momentum equals weight times velocity.'

"In other words, if you are bold enough, even the laws of motion will come to your aid." So concludes Arthur Gordon's inspiring article.

But since fear is composed of shadows and ghosts it tends to become sinister and overpowering. Boldness helps to project the light of truth through the fog which fear creates in the mind. Then, by common sense and complete realism, you know that fear is, very largely, the product of fevered imagination.

So the method is first, get a clear, straight view of your fear. Second, meet it boldly, head on; and third, with God's help resolutely have done with it.

A friend told me that for years he was a confirmed worrier. "But one New Year's Eve," he said, "I was scheduled to go to a party and had an hour of leisure before I was due to leave for that event. So, the year's end being an appropriate time for taking personal stock, I decided to write on paper all my worries so that I could adequately appraise them."

He found that he was able to remember his worries of that particular day, December 31st, and also December 30th, 29th, and 28th; but he had a less clear definition of his worries through the preceding week. And he could scarcely recall what he had worried about back in November. By the time he had worked back as far as September he found that his worries were just a hazy jumble in his mind.

"I was so disgusted," he said, "at this proof of the foolishness of worry that I rolled that paper up in a ball and threw it hard against the wall. It caromed off and appropriately lodged in the wastebasket. Then," he continued, "I asked forgiveness for being so lacking in faith. God had watched over me in the past; I knew I could count on His watchful care in the future. I decided I would more diligently live the life of faith. I became more diligent in analyzing any new worry as a result of these tactics. Worry is no longer a problem," he concluded. This man saw his fear for what it was; he stood up to it, and so he defeated it.

In this incident please note the emphasis upon diligence. It reminds me of an interesting remark by my friend Walter Annenberg, publisher of the Philadelphia *Inquirer*, "Diligence is entitled to a come-back." It is a virtue Americans once valued very highly. Today, no less than formerly, real achievement is impossible without it. And diligence is important in eliminating personality defects.

So, stand up to your fears, diligently do the thing you fear, and in this manner kill your fear. Some years ago I addressed a dinner meeting at which another speaker was a United States Senator who surprisingly claimed that he "hated to make a speech." He was a huge, athletic man and in his early days had been a prize fighter. He told me that one reason he entered public life was because he feared making a speech and he realized that as a public man he would be forced to make speeches.

"I wasn't afraid of the man I faced in the prize ring," he said, "but I was afraid of standing before a crowd and trying to talk to them. So, I just had to learn to make speeches because I was not content to live in fear of something." Senator Warren Barber did the thing he feared and so he put his fear to death. Incidentally, he became an accomplished speaker.

I repeat, fear is a conglomeration of sinister shadows, and a shadow has no substance. It is usually only a magnified reflection of something very small. That is why, in standing boldly up to a fear, you often find it inconsequential. An illustration of this truth comes to my mind which, I am sorry to say, does not reflect particular credit on the author. On our honeymoon my wife and I went to a delightful, but isolated cabin in the North Woods of New York State. A friend who had kindly offered us the use of this cabin said, "You should go off alone with your bride so that you can get to know each other." Well, my wife learned some things about me which were not very inspiring.

We arrived at the cabin, deep in the woods, after dark. I built a fire while my wife cooked dinner. Meanwhile, I sat by the fire and read the newspaper. It contained the report of a murder in Utica, not many miles distant, and stated that the killer was loose in the North Woods. The fearful thought flickered across my mind, "I hope he doesn't come near our cabin."

After dinner we sat before the fire. For a supposedly quiet retreat that cabin was one of the noisiest places imaginable. Creaks and rattles and thuds sounded all about. I tried to be gay, but it was forced. My wife was enjoying herself to the fullest, for she had no fears whatsoever. Finally I heard a noise that sounded like a step on the porch. Then shuffling sounds, and another step. Cold chills ran up and down my spine. "Could it possibly be the fugitive murderer?" I thought with a chill. But I had to act like a man before my bride.

"Don't be afraid," I said blusteringly. "I'll handle this."

She looked at me questioningly. "Who's afraid? What's the matter with you?"

"There is someone outside," I explained, "and the only thing to do is to walk right out there and face him. So, here goes."

I walked over to the door, stood a moment pulling myself together, then jerked it open violently and there—sat a little chipmunk, looking at me with a twinkle in its eye.

I told this story one night when I sat with the late Wendell Willkie at a dinner of the Ohio Society of New York. His comment was, "All my life I have discovered that when I stand up like a man to the things I am afraid of, like your chipmunk, they shrink into insignificance."

This is not to say that everything you fear in this life is chipmunk size. Some fears are substantial. But you can handle the real ones more efficiently when you are not afraid of them. Always remember that in fear your mind unnaturally increases the size of an obstacle. With boldness based on faith, even if there is a real difficulty, it will remain its own size and not be inflated; and you can handle it.

The deep unconscious fears which were, perhaps, planted in your mind in childhood can likewise be killed when you apply the cold light of reason and take a firm attitude toward them. Unconsciously, parents project their own fears, and children, like sensitive antennae, pick them up. Your present fears may have their roots in your childhood experience. When the original source of your fear is determined it is easier to eliminate it. Always remember, in dealing with fear, that it may owe its existence to some old, vague memory, and has no present substance.

I remember hearing of a strange fear developed by a farmer's horse. As a young colt it was driven past a dark stump. The horse shied at the stump rather violently. Every time, thereafter, that the farmer drove past this stump the fright was reenacted.

The farmer rooted out the stump and planted grass on the spot so that no vestige of the stump remained. But still, every time the horse passed the spot, he shied.

The farmer, a wise man, drove the horse around and around this spot, over it and past it and through it until the horse knew there was nothing there and was able finally to pass the place without fear.

We, too, shy in fear at shadowy remembrances, the meanings of which have long faded into the past.

As a child I often spent the summers at the home of my grandfather. He was a good and kindly man, but his fears unconsciously affected me. In closing up the house at night he would lock the door, shake the doorknob, walk away, then return and try it again. He would start up the stairs, then go back and shake the knob a third time. It was a ritual from which he never deviated. Doubtless it was a compulsive neurosis that if he did not try the doorknob three times "something" would happen. My grandfather was one of the finest human beings I ever knew, but this practice indicated a fear psychosis.

Years later I became aware of a curious tendency to re-try doorknobs myself. But when I gained insight into the origin of this tendency I was cured of it. One night I was alone in my apartment in New York City. When I came home late that evening the doorman informed me that I was the only person sleeping in that huge fifteen-story apartment house that night. I turned on all the lights and was very conscious of the silence. I went around and locked all the doors. As I locked the main door I shook the doorknob, walked away, came back, shook it a second time and walked away. I started back to try the knob for the third time, impelled by an old childhood impulse buried in the subconscious.

But suddenly I realized that a long memory out of my early childhood was reaching out to control my present actions. Therefore, I stopped by the door and said, "Oh, no Grandpa, I love you, but I will not try this doorknob a third time. I've locked the door. It's locked. There is nothing to be afraid of. Everything is all right. I hereby break this long, shadowy, hitherto-unrealized hold of an ancient fear."

See your fears for what they are; then stand up to them and kill them. But in doing this you must have, not bravado, but faith. Nor is it a vague kind of faith; it is a strong, substantial faith in God. Only faith in God can kill your fear. The ultimate technique for ending worry is to bring God into every fear situation. No fear can live in the presence of God. The deeper your faith in God becomes, the less power fear will have over you. The Bible outlines the process, "I sought the Lord, and he heard me, and delivered me from all my fears." (Psalm 34:4)

A demonstration of this truth is the experience of J. Edgar Hoover, Director of the Federal Bureau of Investigation. One would never think that a dynamic personality of proven courage would have had a struggle with fear; but all men do.

Mr. Hoover told me, very sincerely, "I lost my fear in the power of my Lord." I liked the way he stated the matter. It is indeed a most powerful method for overcoming worry; lose your fear in the power of the Lord.

The power of faith is not intended, however, merely to free you from something, even from fear. The power of faith is a positive technique for developing your power to live efficiently. Worry has a stultifying effect upon mental aliveness. But when worry is cast out, then the mind, with fresh vigor and sharpened insight, can effectively function in developing creative ideas.

John M. Fox, President of the Minute Maid Corporation, movingly tells of his battle against worry and the tensions which affected him when he was starting his great new industry. He formed the first frozen juice concentrate company and directed it to its present dominant position in the concentrate field. But when he entered the business it was small indeed. In a public speech I heard Mr. Fox say:

"I should like to tell you of an experience I had during the early days of the company. Our problems had become seemingly insurmountable. Working capital had fallen to a zero level, sales were nonexistent, the frozen food industry, generally, was on the verge of going broke.

"At this juncture I decided to attend the Canners Convention in Atlantic City. This was a mistake. Misery loves company and I found a plethora of company that year on the Boardwalk.

"My stomach began to ache—I worried about the stock we had sold to the public—I worried about the employees we had wheedled away from secure, well-paying jobs. I went to sleep at night, eventually, worrying, I woke up early in the morning worrying, I even worried about the sleep I was losing.

"My family lived in Atlantic City so I was staying with them. Besides, it saved the hotel expense which we could ill afford. One day I was asked by my father to accompany him to a Rotary Club lunch. I had little stomach for this, but I knew Dad would feel hurt if I refused.

"My unhappiness with the decision to go to the Rotary lunch deepened when I saw that the speaker was to be a minister of the Gospel. My gloom was so abject that I was in no mood for a sermon. This minister was Dr. Norman Vincent Peale. Dr. Peale announced that his subject would be 'Tension—the Disease that is Destroying the American Businessman.'

"From the first words he uttered it was as though he were talking only

to me. I knew I was the tensest man in the audience. The formula he gave
for relaxing and putting aside worry I would like to repeat.

"First, you relax physically. This is done by stretching out in bed or in a
comfortable chair. Then you methodically and carefully concentrate on
relaxing each part of your body. Start with your scalp, then your face, your
neck, your shoulders and so on down until you are as loose as a pan of
ashes.

"Second step—you relax your mind. You recall a pleasant incident in
your life: a vacation, your honeymoon, a play, a book, anything that brings
into your mind's eye a pleasant scene.

"Then finally, you relax your soul. This for most of us businessmen is a
little tougher. But it can be done by renewing your faith in the Lord. You
get right with God. You check your fears and worries with Him. He can
handle them much better than you can. You do this in prayer. If you know
no other prayer, the age-old children's one will do quite well, 'Now I lay
me down to sleep, I pray the Lord my soul to keep.'

"The first thing you know you'll be fast asleep. I know because, in
desperation, I tried it out that very night I heard Dr. Peale tell about it. It
not only worked, but I awoke the next morning refreshed and renewed
and convinced we would work out of our jam some way. We did."

Scarcely have I seen an audience so deeply moved as were those five
hundred businessmen at the New York luncheon who heard this dynamic
industrial leader give sincere testimony to the power of faith to overcome
worry in a practical situation.

Finally, may I remind you that victory over worry is not a complicated
process. A long held fear pattern is not quickly or easily changed. But
change is not impossible. I do not want to over-simplify the method but,
actually, it is as simple as to take your worries to God, leave them with
Him, and then go about your business with faith that His help is forthcoming.

George A. Straley tells about the sexton of a big city church who was
puzzled, for every week he had been finding a sheet of blue-lined note
paper crumpled into a small wad lying in a corner of the same rear pew.
He smoothed out one of the little wads of paper and it had several pen-
ciled words: "Clara-ill, Lester-job, rent."

After that the sexton began looking for the paper wads weekly and they
were always there after every Sunday morning service. He opened them
all and then began to watch for the person who sat in that particular
corner of the pew.

It was a woman, he discovered, middle-aged, plain but kind-faced, unas-
suming. She was always alone. The sexton told the pastor what he had
observed and handed him the notes. The pastor read the cryptic words
with furrowed brow.

The next Sunday he contrived to meet the woman at the church door as she was leaving and asked her kindly if she would wait for him a moment. He showed her the notes and inquired gently about their meaning.

Tears welled in the woman's eyes. She hesitated and then said softly, "You'll think it's silly, I guess, but I saw a sign among the advertising posters in a bus which said, 'Take your worries to church and leave them there.' My worries are written on those pieces of paper. I write them down during the week, bring them on Sunday morning, and leave them. I feel that God is taking care of them."

"God has taken care of them," the pastor said softly. "Please continue to bring your worries and troubles to church and leave them here."

On his way out of the church the pastor paused to pick up the freshly wadded note that had been left that particular morning. Smoothing it out he saw that it contained three words, "John—in Korea."

So, to be rid of your worries, simply take them to God and leave them there.

I once asked my readers to send me techniques for overcoming worry which they had tested and found helpful. One came from a distinguished professor of English Literature in one of our oldest universities. She had used this simple but very sound method for many years with great effectiveness. She writes:

My dear Doctor Peale: You ask us to let you know how to control worry. Here is my method. At night before going to bed, I sit in a covered straightback chair, let my hands drop over the arms of the chair, and relax my whole body. Then I say the following, each three times:

> *Tranquility, serenity, quietness*
> *Peace, Faith, Love, Joy.*

> *I have the habit of happiness.*
> *I have the habit of expecting the good.*
> *I have the habit of never giving up.*
> *I have the habit of patience.*
> *I have the habit of trusting the living God.*
> *I have the habit of helping others.*

If I find myself getting stirred up about anything during the day, I say,

> *The tendency to brood and fret*
> *Never solved any problem yet.*
> *Worry is a rocking chair*
> *That never takes me anywhere.*

Sincerely use the methods outlined in this chapter and throughout this book and you can kill your worry and live longer—and better—and happier.

How to Handle Worry

Worry may be described as a spasm of the emotions in which the mind takes hold of a thought or obsession, clutches it spasmodically, and will not let it go. To break its hold one must gently, but forcibly, insinuate a healthier and stronger idea into the mind's convulsive grasp. This stronger idea is that of faith in God. When faith, rather than fear, becomes your obsession, you will master worry.

Picture yourself as boldly attacking and overcoming your fears. Picturized concepts in the conscious mind will, if reiterated, impress themselves deeply within the subconscious.

5

YOU CAN HAVE POWER
OVER YOUR DIFFICULTIES

"When you get into storm, use the panorama philosophy, the big view. Then you will know it will not last forever. With faith in your heart you can ride it out."

THE PRESIDENT of a small steel company made a curious comment: "Your business and mine aren't too different." Since I am a minister, the remark seemed incongruous. But his explanation made sense: "I make steel for people, but you put steel into people." It is indeed true that faith does put steel into you, enough to give you power over your difficulties.

This chapter is designed to show how, by the help of God, you can overcome your difficulties and live a vital and victorious life. Never settle for less. You do not need to. When the full strength potential within you is mustered you have sufficient power to deal successfully with any difficulty.

In Greece, I heard an interesting story about Alexander the Great who conquered much of the world. Unhappily, he did not conquer himself. According to the story, Alexander slept every night with the story of Ulysses under his pillow; his purpose no doubt being to drive deeply into his consciousness the unconquerable spirit of that immortal figure.

Of course it is not necessary, actually, to sleep with the Bible under your pillow. But if you fill your consciousness with the great words and tremendous faith of the Bible, you will become conqueror of all your difficulties. Indeed, the Bible states this truth in so many words, "Nay in all things we are more than conquerors through him that loved us." (Romans 8:37) This filling of your mind with big thoughts of faith conditions you to look big at life, at yourself, at your problems. And as you develop big attitudes you can then look down upon your difficulties, seeing them in true perspective. Then they no longer seem overwhelmingly formidable and you can master them.

Through a recent experience I have become more than ever aware of the importance of thinking big. To complete this book I rented a chalet or cottage on a mountaintop in Switzerland and here I have been living for some weeks. Around the Lake of Lucerne, which lies before my house, are

four noble eminences: the jagged heights of Pilatus, the towering cone of
the Stanserhorn, the gentler slope of Rigi, and the brooding heights of the
Burgenstock. It is atop the Burgenstock, one of the most beautiful places
in Europe, that I am writing.

From my rear windows I see immense snow-capped mountains rising
tier on tier, an incredible vista of peaks: the majestic Finsteraarhorn, the
noble Jungfrau, the stately Eiger, and the towering Mönch, its precipitous
face covered with fresh snow which fell last night to add to the eternal
drifts already deep on its summit. From these white-clad mountains, scin-
tillating waterfalls leap, and cold, blue-gray rivers race with incredible
speed to the sea.

The view from my front terrace is a little gentler, dominated as it is by
the Lake of Lucerne. But there are enormous mountains, a half dozen
lakes, the picturesque villages of Küssnacht, Vitznau, Weggis, and one
larger city, Lucerne. At night the lights of the famous city on the
Vierwaldstättersee gleam like jewels.

Day after day this vast panorama calls out to one to think big. Perhaps
that is why God makes panoramas. You cannot squint at a panorama. Your
eyes, trying to accommodate to the vastness of the view, must open wide
to take it all in. Instead of seeing life through a slit, you begin to look big
at it. Unconsciously, the vast world makes you stretch in an effort to
adjust to your tremendous environment. Thus you tend toward that big-
ness which potentially is within all of us, even as it is in nature.

Living with a panorama helps develop that big philosophy that overcomes difficulty. For one thing, it teaches you that the circumstances of
life at a given moment are not necessarily permanent, they only seem that
way. On our mountain top, when the weather is fair, you have no assurance that it will continue so, for often in the far distance storm clouds can
be seen gathering over the enormous peaks. And you know that in all
probability the storm will shortly hurl itself upon you. But, being able to
see it from the vantage point of the panorama, you have time to make the
necessary preparations to meet it.

Then the colossal storm breaks with heavy clouds, rolling fog, dashing
rain, and thunder reverberating down the gorges of the Alps. But often,
even in the midst of the storm's tumult, you may see, far away, through a
break in the clouds, a green mountainside bathed in sunlight. And you are
encouraged that soon there will be fair skies again.

Often people tell me, "I have nothing but trouble; everything goes
wrong; I am surrounded by difficulties." But the philosophy of the panorama reminds you that all storms pass and, more important, that you are
big enough to live with them while they last.

And you need not be discouraged, for storms or difficulties are limited
in extent and they do pass. Fair weather always comes. This is a required
philosophy for living courageously in this world. All men who deal with

natural phenomena are aware of the ephemeral shifting of storm and sunshine.

I came home one time on a ship sailing from a Mediterranean port. Soon after Gibraltar the Captain invited us to the bridge. It was a glorious morning, sunlight shimmering on the water and blue skies overhead. We had just passed through the Gates of Hercules, with Africa on the left and Spain on the right. The surge of the Atlantic made you realize you were out of the Mediterranean and on the ocean, but the sea was calm and the day radiant.

"How is the weather ahead, Captain?" I asked.

He laid a chart before me. Pointing to it he said, "Over there is a hurricane called Flora. We are traveling at twenty-two knots in a westerly direction. Flora is traveling seven knots northerly. If the speed of the hurricane does not change I compute that we will meet it early Friday morning."

"You mean we will be on the outer edge of it?" I asked hopefully.

"No," he told me grimly. "We shall go right through it."

"Why do we need to meet it?" I asked. "You've got a fast ship. Why not go around it?"

"I would lose two days," was his answer. "It would throw me off schedule. But do not be concerned, the hurricane is only about a hundred and fifty miles in area, and on the other side there is beautiful weather. Besides, we have a ship that can ride it out."

Early on Friday I was practically knocked out of my bed. I rose and gazed at the black vastness of the ocean. Believe me, Flora was a tempestuous lady! The violence lasted until around two o'clock Friday afternoon when we began to run out of the storm. By midnight the moon was shining and the seas were calm.

Next day the Captain said, "I have always lived by the philosophy that if the sea is smooth, it will get rough; if it is rough, it will get smooth. But with a good ship you can always ride it out."

So it is with life, isn't it? When you get into storm, use the panorama philosophy, the big view. Then you will know it will not last forever. With faith in your heart you can ride it out. There is fair weather ahead. See life big. Don't let your thinking deteriorate into little thoughts. Live on a big scale. Look big at life.

These reflections remind me of a great personality whom I knew years ago and who left an unforgettable impression on me. He was Harlowe B. Andrews of Syracuse, New York, one of the most rugged and yet gentle characters I ever knew. He was one of those very different human beings whom God makes now and then.

As a young man, I often went to him for advice. One day he said something which I have used to good advantage ever since. "Norman, the way to handle difficulty is very simple: think big, believe big, pray big, act big." Then he added, "God can make you bigger than your difficulties."

That dynamic and utterly sound statement constitutes a sure method for getting power over your difficulties. Think big, and powerful forces are released. For example, the great United Nations building in New York City was built in what had been a slum and low-grade business district. It was one of the creative dreams of William Zeckendorf, whose projects are all immense ones. He operates on a huge scale of thinking. Recently I heard him say in a public address, "My experience has been that only the biggest plans are really easy." How true that is, for little plans have no lift or dynamism.

I was impressed with that philosophy, for I believe that when you plan something big you are actually thinking the way God intended men to think. And the reason you get big results is that a super-power potential is back of big concepts. When you project a big thought you must necessarily put big faith and big effort into it. Such faith and effort generate dynamic creative power. Moreover, to support a big idea you must give it all you've got. That, in itself, exerts extraordinary force. Those who plan little, uninspiring things have little faith, little enthusiasm, and it is not surprising that little comes of them. Little faith equals little results. And, conversely, big faith equals big results. Big dreams, plus big thinking, plus big faith, plus big effort, that is the formula by which big things are done; and, I might add, the formula by which big difficulties are overcome.

Select some big goal, some big objective, some big dream. Then hold it in your mind, dedicating yourself to it, no matter how many difficulties oppose you. By big thinking, which is really a form of God-thinking, you can surge past all difficulties.

In the office of a beautiful store in a western city I sat with the proprietor, an old friend of mine. He had come to that city many years before with his bride and only fifty dollars in capital. His first shop was so small he called it a "hole-in-the-wall." This later developed into a good-sized store. Then, due to circumstances largely traceable to a disloyal partner, he lost his business.

"I took stock," he said, "and decided I must not give in to discouragement. When I added up my assets they looked pretty good; in fact I was in a more advantageous position than when I started originally. I still had my wife and, this time, I had a thousand dollars instead of fifty. Also, I had a lot of experience and a deepened faith. So, I began again and built this new store. I have a simple formula," he concluded, "God, faith, big thinking, Helen, America, and work."

A mighty strong combination, isn't it? Believe, even though it may be hard to believe, that there are creative values in your difficulty. The usual, undisciplined tendency is to focus the mind only on negative factors. That is a decidedly wrong slant of thought. The wise method is to walk calmly around a dark situation, hopefully looking for any possible chink of light—and it is an unhappy situation indeed, where there isn't some faint flicker. Look at your problem in a creative and positive manner and you will find bright opportunities which you have not thought of. Never think negatively. Be realistic, face all the facts, but always look on the hopeful side.

A man telephoned to tell me of his "bad" situation. "I'm calling you for encouragement," he explained. "I thought you might pray with me over the telephone."

"What seems to be the trouble?" I asked.

"I run a furniture business," he said, "and selling is slow in our area. I've got to persuade more people to part with more money. Perhaps I bought a bigger inventory than I should carry."

While he was talking I was thinking and praying, too. If you pray when faced by a problem, really pray and believe, you will get an answer. So, out of my prayer came this thought: "Your attitude should not be to 'get people to part with their money.' Rather it should be to help them. The purpose of business isn't merely to get money from people, but to render services to people. Take Mrs. X," I said. "Maybe Mrs. X. wants a chair and hasn't the money to buy it. So, she stands outside your store and looks in your window at the chair and wishes she might have it. You stand inside and look out at her and wish she would come in and buy it." And the merchandise doesn't move and so both Mrs. X. and you are unhappy about it.

"That is just the way it is," he said.

"Think first of helping Mrs. X. And to do that you must get to know her and her family; study her needs. Do not think so much about putting her money in your pocket as about putting your chair, that she needs, into her home. Pray about a way to help her have the furniture she requires. Do this with all your customers. Think of them as people needing your goods instead of yourself needing their money. Find ways of helping them overcome their difficulties, and you will overcome your own in so doing. And," I added, "if you will go around your community spreading joy and faith and trying to help people, instead of merely thinking about yourself, the Lord will bless you and you will turn over that inventory and have a wonderful time living."

"Where did you get these ideas?" he asked curiously.

"From the greatest of all experts," I said.

"Who is he?"

"Just take it from me," I said. "I got it from Him."

"I get you," he replied. "You mean just practice Christianity."

Some weeks later he telephoned again. "I want to report," he said. "I have turned over enough of the inventory to be in the clear. I never went out among people before, but now I am getting to know them and I find some mighty nice folks. And I want to tell you about something wonderful that happened to me. I found one husband and wife who were on the outs with each other. At first we talked about furniture. Then their marriage problem came into the conversation, about whether they should get furniture, for maybe they would split up.

"So what do you think I did? Believe it or not I just sat down and prayed with them. First time I ever did such a thing in my life. That seemed to make them feel better. And before I left I sold them two chairs instead of one. They paid what they could and they now have the chairs, but best of all, I believe they have a new spirit; they wouldn't have bought the chairs if they weren't going to stick with each other. I'll keep close to them for I believe we can hold that couple together."

This man learned, indeed, to think big about his business. He found that the furniture business and human problems and religion are closely related. By thinking big he got the creative idea of forgetting himself and helping others. His own difficulties were overcome in the process.

You may regard your work as dull and unromantic, but actually it is made that way if the person who works at that job becomes dull. Try this experiment. For one day think no drab thoughts about your job. Look deeply into its possibilities. Think big and exciting thoughts about it. I believe that just one day of this will surprise you, and if you continue the experiment you will find that even the most seemingly common occupation is not without its thrill.

Charlie Franzen was one of the best carpenters I ever knew. Running his hand lovingly over a paneled room which he had just completed, he remarked, "I would rather work with wood than anything in the world." He thought big about carpentry and learned to meet his difficulties, and he had plenty, too.

Any useful type of work can be just as big as you want to make it. And you can make it big by thinking big about it. For example, there is my friend, Charlie Horan who operates a grocery store in Pawling, New York. For years Charlie worked for a grocery chain in that little village. Then, the company closed the store and Charlie had to make a big decision. He knew the grocery business thoroughly, but it was not without trepidation that he decided to venture in a store of his own. Accordingly, he opened the Horan Superette, and I went in to wish him well. "I hope I can make a go of it," he said. "I know there will be problems, but I'll give it all I've got."

We went into his back room and had a little prayer, asking that he would be granted success and that through his business he could render a service to people. Competition came in the form of a brand-new, shiny, modern supermarket, but Charlie Horan thought big, wished the best prosperity to the supermarket, and went on filling his own little store full of faith, happiness, and big thoughts. And so, despite all difficulty, his business developed.

Difficulties make no difference, really, when you think big about them and, in effect, think above them. That is the way a combat pilot gets the advantage, by coming up and over his opponent. In the battle of life marshal your spirit to take a high position that will enable you to look down upon your difficulties. Then you see them in realistic size and know you are bigger than they are. You can overcome them because you get above them in your thinking. It is easy to think little, but avoid doing so for it can make you little. Always think big.

A black boy said to me glumly, "I can never amount to much in this country."

"Why not?" I asked.

"You ought to know," he answered.

"You are healthy, aren't you?" I asked. "And smart?"

He grinned and agreed.

"You have a good mother? A good father?"

He nodded.

"Let me feel your muscle."

He rolled up his sleeves and grinned again when I congratulated him on his well-developed muscles.

"And you have a wonderful smile." I added this item to his assets.

"But I am black," he objected.

"So is Ralph Bunche, who used to be a janitor," I reminded him. "So is Jackie Robinson. So is the President of the Borough of Manhattan, Edward R. Dudley." And I went on to mention others. "Your thinking is twenty-five years behind the times, son. Then it was more difficult for black men and women, but some of them did mighty well, all the same."

I told him about a small black boy at a county fair. A man was blowing up balloons and letting them float up into the sky to the delight of a crowd of children. The balloons were of all colors. "Do you suppose that black one will go as high as the rest?" the black boy asked.

"Watch," the man said, "and I'll show you." He blew up the black balloon and it went just as high as the others. "You see, sonny," he told the boy, "it isn't the color that determines how high they go, but the stuff inside them that counts."

I added for my young friend, "If you will get self-doubt out of your mind, and rid yourself of the inferiority complex you are nursing, and believe that God will help you, and then if you give everything you have to whatever you do, you will get along all right."

I fully realize that many people have very difficult problems. But when you stop thinking negatively about your problems and obstacles and start doing something constructive about them, you will come through. The help of God, positive thinking, a desire to serve others, and the willingness to work are all you need. If you believe you can do it, you can. Think big.

I heard of a boy who badly needed a job. There was a good job advertised and he started out early that morning to apply for it, but when he got to the address given he found twenty boys waiting in line ahead of him. Still that did not stump him.

He scribbled a hasty note, folded it, and handed it to the secretary of the man doing the hiring. He told her it was important for her boss to see it at once. She was convinced by his manner and took it to her employer.

It read, "I am the twenty-first kid in line. Don't do anything until you see me." Here, obviously, was a boy who was alert, eager, imaginative, and self-confident. Naturally, he got the job.

Henry Kaiser told me that when a new project is started in his organization they give it to a man who knows all the difficulties yet is enthusiastic about it. The man who says, "It's a great idea, but I doubt that it can be done," doesn't get the job. The assignment goes to the man who says, "It's a great idea; I will have the time of my life doing it."

Some people are vibrant with life and filled with energy and dynamism. They think big. Others, however, are dull, lethargic, and pessimistic. They have not learned how to think and live dynamically. If you belong in this second group, make up your mind, today, that you can live a full and abundant life. Start now by putting into practice the policy of thinking big about everything.

Praying big prayers is of tremendous importance in gaining power over your difficulties. God will grant big things if you ask for them and are big enough to receive them.

You must have faith if prayer is to do big things for you. And if you are not getting answers, it may be that your prayers are not big enough. Do not pray little prayers—pray big prayers. You are praying to a big God. Perhaps He knows that a small prayer is backed only by small faith, and the Bible tells us He rates our sincerity by our faith. Perhaps He also rates our capacity to receive by our faith. Ask for right things, and ask right. Ask with faith, and pray big.

You want health? Pray for it. You want financial security? Pray for it. You want happiness in your home? Pray for it. You want a life filled with abundant joy? Pray for it. You want to do something worthwhile in life? Pray for it. Pray big prayers and you will get big answers.

One of the suggestions given by my old friend Mr. Andrews was to act big. Thinking big about difficulty reminds us that it is not without value. Channing Pollock, the famous playwright, once said an interesting thing to me, "Men and motor cars go forward by a series of explosions." Even as a motor car cannot fulfill its true function apart from a series of internal explosions, just so a human being cannot really go forward unless propelled by rightly directed and controlled difficulties. You can permit the explosions of difficulty to tear you to pieces and destroy you. Or they can become your motive force. The secret of successful living is to control and use the power which difficulty releases into your personality.

It has been demonstrated countless times that difficulty leads people to the greatest thing in life, that is, if they have the inner strength to stand up to difficulty. Jack Fleck, 1955 United States Open Golf Champion said, "Before I could win I had to learn to lose. I had to weave my bad breaks into the pattern of my golf." This man, who had to learn to lose before he could win, was the man who defeated the great Ben Hogan to win the championship.

Perhaps even more dramatic is the story of another holder of the same championship, Ed Furgol, who, as a boy, suffered an accident which made one arm eleven inches shorter than the other. By sheer perseverance, courage, and faith he became champion. When asked who might succeed him as title holder, several names were mentioned, but he shook his head, saying, "No, none of them will ever be champion, they haven't been hungry enough." That is to say, none of them had suffered enough difficulty and opposition and therefore had not developed the rugged vitality necessary to win through gruelling competition to attain the top honor. Difficulty is not at all a bad thing, unpleasant as it may be.

More than twenty years ago Hartly Laycock was banker in the Midwest. Then came the great depression and at age sixty he was without money and without a job. He walked the streets of Chicago. His only training was banking and banks were closing every day. Anyway, no one wanted a man past forty.

He prayed for guidance. Then "something" strange happened. One day in the want ads "something" caught his eye. It was the advertisement of an old Florida Hotel for sale at a sacrifice.

"Something" said to him to write the owners and ask about it. But he couldn't imagine being in the hotel business, so he kept looking for a job. But he found that he was continually thinking about the hotel. He called and asked the price, a sum far beyond his slim resources. He hadn't even a hundred dollars left.

He prayed again and said, "Lord, You brought that advertisement to my attention. I know nothing about the hotel business, but am willing to try it, though I haven't the money it will take." He raised a small down payment and had the hotel. But the paint was peeling off, the floorboards were rotten, it was filled with cobwebs, there wasn't a stick of furniture or a piece of carpet in the place.

"Lord," he asked, "why did You ever get me into this?"

And the Lord seemed to say that things would work out all right. There were lots of headaches and years of work, but that hotel was booked solid last season.

My dynamic friend, now eighty-two, discovered that when you believe and pray and are willing to be guided you get amazing solutions to difficulty.

So, to overcome difficulty, pray big, believe big, and act big.

One of the greatest American singers is Marian Anderson, who says in *Guideposts* magazine, "Failure and frustration are in the unwritten pages of everyone's record. I have had my share of them. We were poor folk," she continues, "but many people were kind to me. A group of well-meaning friends hastily sponsored me for a concert in Town Hall in New York. But I wasn't ready, either in experience or maturity.

"On the exciting night of my first concert I was told that Town Hall was sold out. While waiting in dazed delight to go on, my sponsor said there would be a slight delay. I waited five, ten, fifteen minutes. Then I peeked through the curtain. The house was half empty. I died inside.

"I sang my heart out, but when the concert was over I knew I had failed. The critics next day agreed with me. I was shattered within.

" 'I had better forget all about singing and do something else,' " I told my mother.

" 'Why don't you think about it a little, and pray a lot, first?' she cautioned."

But Marian Anderson was so crushed in spirit that for a whole year she brooded in silence, refusing every invitation to sing. Her mother kept gently prodding her, saying, "Have you prayed, Marian? Have you prayed?"

"No, I hadn't prayed. I embraced my grief. Then, from my torment I prayed with the sure knowledge there was Someone to whom I could pour out the greatest need of my heart and soul. Slowly I came out of my despair. My mind began to clear. Self-pity left me.

"So, one day I came home unaware that I was humming. It was the first music I had uttered for a whole year. When my mother heard it she rushed to meet me and put her arms around me and kissed me. It was her way of saying, 'Your prayers have been answered.' For a brief moment we stood there silent. Then my mother said, 'Prayer begins where human capacity ends.' "

Marian Anderson stood up to difficulty, prayed and acted big, and the result was one of the most glorious voices that the American people have ever heard. But it was developed out of difficulty.

There is a curious yet certain law that if you expect difficulty and hold such expectation deeply in your mind, the expected difficulty may actually materialize. Perhaps it is because people who take a defeatist attitude never give themselves whole-heartedly.

But other people burst into life's problems with the irresistibility of dynamism. With boundless enthusiasm and confidence they give all they have and difficulties seem to fade away. What you do with life depends upon the enthusiasm and vitality which you give to it.

Branch Rickey tells a marvelous story in *Guideposts* magazine about a baseball game that occurred many years ago when he was managing the St. Louis Browns: "There is nothing else like it in the record books anywhere. There was a player on my team by the name of Walker, a man who had all the physical qualities to be a great player. During the game Walker hit what should have been a home run and was thrown out at third.

"Walker's slow start to first base, as he watched his hard line drive fall between the left and center fielders, cost him twenty feet. Next, he lost another thirty feet making too wide a turn around first toward second base. Then, seeing the elusive ball still going, (the left field fence was down for repair) he slowed to a jog trot. This easily cost him still another fifty feet, and he was now one hundred feet behind schedule.

"Suddenly the ball struck some object, a board or stone, and bounced back into the hands of the surprised centerfielder, a boy by the name of Al Nixon. Nixon's quick turn and his strong arm brought the throw toward third. Walker, seeing that a play could now be made on him, put on a great burst of speed. He made a fall-away slide to the right and into the very hands of the third baseman. Walker actually tagged himself out.

"Exclamatory groans came from our bench. One chap in disgust kicked over the water bucket, and another threw a bunch of bats helter-skelter into the air. In discussing the play later, however, everyone agreed that if Walker had not made any one of four mistakes—the slow start from home plate, the wide turn at first, the walking trot around second, and the slide to the wrong side at third—there could have been no play upon him. And, if he had made all four correctly, he would have scored a home run standing up.

"The baseball records tell of another player, one dynamically alive. Detroit came to bat in the last half of the eleventh inning, score tied, two men out, nobody on base, and a player named Ty Cobb facing the pitcher.

"Cobb got a base on balls and then scored the winning run without another ball being pitched. By sheer adventure and skill he forced two wild throws by St. Louis infielders. His daring at first base, his boldness and skillful turn at second, his characteristic slide ten feet before he reached third, his quick co-ordination following his slide—all brought about four 'breaks' in his favor. He made what amounted to a home run out of a base on balls.

"What is the difference between Cobb and Walker? They were about the same age, weight, height, and running speed. Walker had a stronger arm than Cobb and more power at the bat. Only one rose to unparalleled fame. Cobb wanted to do something so much that nothing else mattered; Walker punched the clock," says Branch Rickey.

And I might add that Ty Cobb probably never even gave difficulty a thought. He loved the game, he gave it all he had, and he developed, thereby, an enormous power over difficulty. Walker, on the contrary, was psychologically ready for difficulties to interfere with him, and they accommodated him, as they always will if you are mentally conditioned to them.

I have been teaching positive thinking for years and, as a result, many people write telling me how they and others have overcome difficulty by applying principles of faith, big thinking, big praying, big acting. One particularly inspiring story is that of Ike Skelton.

Not too many years ago Ike Skelton was a normal, healthy youngster. Then, suddenly, at twelve years of age he was stricken with infantile paralysis. The disease left his arms dangling helplessly by his sides. His legs recovered satisfactorily and he could function otherwise, except that he could not move his arms.

Yet this boy entered Wentworth Military Academy with one burning ambition—he wanted to make the track team. The coach told him kindly, "Why, son, you can't run without your arms. You need them as much as your legs."

Nevertheless, Ike Skelton kept at it. He trotted around the track all season, but he didn't make the team. He continued to run the following season, and each succeeding year but he couldn't make the grade competitively.

Finally came the last big track meet of his school career, the one with Wentworth's arch rival, Kemper. The boy begged the coach to give him a chance in the two-mile run, the most gruelling event in the meet. Finally the coach broke down and did. "Go out there and run," he said, "but promise me you won't be disappointed." Then the coach fastened his arms to his sides so they would not get in his way and started him in the race.

The crowd had eyes only for this strange runner. When the race was over, the students surged down from the stands and lifted him enthusiastically upon their shoulders. There wasn't a dry eye in the crowd.

Had he won the race? Not at all—he came in last. But he came in, and that is the important fact. While he didn't win that race, he is winning the most important race of life through his demonstration of an undefeatable spirit. At the University of Edinburgh as an exchange student, he became one of the popular men there. Later he made a brilliant record in law school and is now in a successful law career and getting a start in politics.

What enabled this boy to overcome his difficulties and live confidently and successfully? Karl Menninger, the psychiatrist, pointed out that men do not break down because they are defeated, but only because they think they are. So don't think you are. Think big, believe big, pray big, and act big. To this add work and struggle. That is the formula for gaining victory over your difficulties.

* * *

Remember:
You are not defeated, though it may be you think you are.

By the help of God you can overcome your difficulties and live a vital and victorious life. Never settle for less. You do not need to. When the full strength potential within you is mustered you have sufficient power to deal with any difficulty.

Think big; and powerful forces are released.

Believe big; faith and effort generate dynamic creative power.

Pray big; God will grant big things if you ask for them and are big enough to receive them.

Act big; only the biggest plans are really easy.

6

YOU CAN HAVE LIFE
IF YOU WANT IT

"When your interest and appreciation are widened to include the whole great world, life becomes even more fascinating. Interest, projected outside yourself, has the power to force even hardship, suffering, and pain into the background. The more vital your interest, in others and in the world, the more certainly you can live triumphantly over your own difficulties."

WHAT DO you really want? What do I want? What does everybody want? Of course, the answer is we want life. And what is life? It is vitality, energy, freedom, growth, dynamism. It is a deep sense of well-being. It is the elimination of all feelings of deadness and desultoriness. It is to be fully vital and vigorous. It is a useful participation in worthwhile activities. It is the satisfaction of creating something, giving something, doing something.

Unfortunately, many people do not have a quality of life that squares with this definition. They are filled with gloom and apprehension. They suffer fear, discouragement, and frustration. Their spirits have been sapped of vitality; they are lethargic and apathetic. It is terribly tragic to die while you live. It is almost as terrible to be asleep when you should be wide awake. And it is quite unnecessary.

Your life is meant to be fully alive. You are designed to have vigor of body, mind, and spirit throughout your years. In studying life, as I observe it in many persons, I have been amazed by the infectious and magnetic quality it sometimes demonstrates.

I gave a talk on the same platform with a man who was advertised as "The Greatest Speaker in the United States." Such designation is perhaps extravagant, no matter to whom it is applied. But this man did, indeed, prove to be an excellent speaker. He exerted an astonishing magnetism. The temperature in Tennessee that day was nearly one hundred degrees. Yet, late in the afternoon after three other men had spoken, he held his crowd spellbound.

Although his speech was extraordinarily well delivered, what made him outstanding was his projection of an alive personality. He transmitted life to people who were hot and tired; he inspired them so that they forgot they were hot, and as they listened they were no longer tired. He was alive; and they, too, came alive.

Later, at dinner, I studied him. Then I understood. He had one of the brightest pair of eyes I have ever seen in a human being. "I know your secret," I said suddenly. "You are one of those alive-eyed people."

"What do you mean, alive-eyed?" he asked in surprise.

A personnel manager told me once, I explained, that he hires men by the kind of eyes they have. "I look over their application papers and their past record and experience. But those questionnaires are really a minor consideration with me," he said. "If a man's eyes are dull, I don't want him. And," he added, "all too few applicants have the alive-eyes which I am seeking and which, in my opinion, mark a dynamic personality." Ever since that conversation I have almost hesitated to look into a mirror.

Your spirit can stay alive through long years if you keep your mind and heart alive; and if your spirit is alive that very fact helps to keep the rest of you toned up. That is what we really want, isn't it, to be alive in every element of our being?

A person should be so eager about everything that, actually, he can hardly wait for morning to get started again. Life should be perpetually fascinating. We are designed to have enthusiasm, freshly renewed every day. The human spirit was never constructed to run down. It is we who allow that to happen. And it is a great pity.

In saying that you can have perpetual enthusiasm I certainly do not mean you should become a flippant or superficial person who falsely assumes that everything in this world is sweetness and light. We know that such is decidedly not the case. The world is full of sorrow and trouble. But it is also full of the overcoming of sorrow and trouble. And an effervescent spirit of joy and enthusiasm can help in making possible a better life for everyone.

One way to have that quality of life is to get outside yourself. People who live within themselves lose that vital something which stimulates verve and excitement. As a matter of fact, many are actually ill as a result of nothing but self-centeredness. When you lose yourself, letting your personality flow outward, your life takes on creative joy and even health. Half dead, listless, desultory people everywhere could find the vital life they really want by the very simple expedient of practicing self-forgetfulness.

A few years ago in Florida I met a man who haunted the doctor's office in a big resort hotel. He thought he was sick, and indeed, he acted so. His chauffeur brought him south in a big car and he had three nurses on round-the-clock duty. He asked to see me, when he heard I was in the hotel. The first thing he said when I entered his room was, "I feel terrible," and he kept repeating it at intervals throughout our short call. He showed many symptoms of despondency, depressiveness, and extreme list-lessness.

The hotel doctor is a close friend, and when I spoke about this man he said, "He isn't well, but medicine alone won't cure him. If you could help him overcome self-preoccupation and give him a good dose of outgoing Christianity it might even make him well."

I decided to see what I could do toward applying the suggested therapy. As we were seated on the porch of the hotel I noticed an elderly woman trying to pull a chair into position. The chair was too cumbersome for her to handle and it became hooked under a railing. I suggested to the "sick" man that he help the old lady with the chair. I said, "I think it will actually make you feel better."

He groaned and put up a protest, but I insisted and, complainingly, he went over and helped her extricate the chair; then he put it into place for her. She gave him a nice smile in return. He came back, sank in his chair beside me and said, "Do you know, believe it or not, I got a kick out of that."

"When you do something helpful for another person you always feel better," I said and I reminded him of what Jesus Christ said: "He that findeth his life shall lose it: and he that loseth his life for my sake shall find it." (Matthew 10:39.)

"I have heard that all my life, but I never thought of it as a healing procedure," he said thoughtfully. I explained that we can become physically sick through a process of selfishness that poisons our thoughts and drains off our life force. "You see how good that simple little act made you feel? Imagine how you would feel if you become outgoing in bigger things."

About a year later I returned to the same hotel and happened to see a man striding down the corridor toward me. The thought crossed my mind that here was a vigorous person. I was engrossed, however, in other matters and was about to pass him when he grabbed my arm. Then I recognized him, but he was so different. Health and energy actually seemed to radiate from him.

"I am glad to see you so much better," I commented. "Where are your nurses?"

"Oh, I don't need nurses," he said. "I'm a well man."

When I asked him to explain the change, he said, "It was caused by a very simple act which you asked me to perform." And he reminded me of the experience on the hotel porch when he helped the elderly woman. "That little service made me feel so good that I began looking for other opportunities to do something for people, just little things. Then I found a few bigger services to render. One thing led to another until, strangely enough, I began to feel so much better that, finally, I came to the day when I saw myself. I got a clear view of how I was actually destroying my life by self-centeredness. But living in a more outgoing manner has made me a healthy man," he declared.

That case is an illustration of how, by self-centeredness and overpreoccupation, you may unconsciously retreat from dynamic living. But when you project yourself outside yourself, you may thereby regain a normal mental, emotional, spiritual, and even physical condition. The final result is often a sense of complete well-being.

You can allow the cares, troubles, and difficulties of this world not only to cloud your mind and depress your spirit, but actually to limit life within you. By an accumulation of anxiety thoughts and trouble thoughts the personality languishes inwardly and presently transmits its lethargic condition to the physical body, so that one gets to feeling tired and below par.

No doubt there are people everywhere who, while perhaps not physically sick, actually suffer real symptoms due primarily to ingrown thinking. They have actually depleted the life force within them. Like the man in Florida they need only to take stock of themselves and to see themselves as they are. The next step is to get insight into what they can become. Then, they need to do a reconstructive job on their thinking. By eliminating destructive thoughts they can really begin to live with dynamic force and very great joy.

It is a truism to say that all of us have problems, troubles, and hardships. That of course is the way life is. There is no such thing as easy living. Life can be difficult, even hard. But it does not need to be so difficult or so hard that you cannot live with a joyous sense of strength. I hope, therefore, you may believe that, by the help of God, you can have what you deeply want; namely, a life of vitality and joy.

In developing dynamic life another factor is to put animation into your daily work. Your life's vitality can be increased by taking an immense pleasure in all that you are doing. Practice liking it. By this attitude, tedium is eliminated and the distinction between labor and pleasure is erased. Being alive in the fullest sense you will get enjoyment out of your activity because aliveness stimulates the sense of excitement.

Take my good friend Branch Rickey, an extraordinarily inspiring personality. In baseball for over fifty years he has produced some of the greatest teams in the history of the sport. For many years with St. Louis, then with Brooklyn, and Pittsburgh, he may fittingly be called the great man of baseball. The Editor of our *Guideposts* magazine, Len LeSourd, visited spring training camp the year Mr. Rickey had been in baseball for half a century. He asked, "Mr. Rickey, tell me your greatest thrill in baseball in a half century."

Rickey lowered his big eyebrows and his eyes flashed. "My greatest thrill? I haven't had it yet."

There is a man vibrantly alive. In spite of all his great thrills, the greatest is always yet to be, perhaps tomorrow, perhaps next week, maybe even next year. Always ahead, always in anticipation.

One night I attended the circus with a good friend of mine, Beverly Kelley, who held an important position in that organization. He was so busy that he could spend only part of the evening with me in his box. I observed his keen delight in acts going on in the rings. "Beverly, how long have you been with the circus?" I asked.

"Twenty-seven years," he replied.

"Well," I asked, "do you like your job?"

I shall never forget his reply. "Norman," he said, "it's a hundred percent better than working."

That answer is a classic. Enthusiasm and eagerness can make any job thrilling. Love your job. If you do not like it now, learn to like it. Study it, analyze it, see its possibilities, believe in it. One way to do this is upon awakening every morning say to yourself, "I have a fine job and I am going to enjoy working at it today." Affirm in this manner day by day until, gradually, your mind accepts and makes permanent the attitude expressed. This practice will generate zest and dynamism. Your entire reaction to your life by this method can undergo revitalization. And when you revamp your attitude toward your work, in effect you revamp your life, for basically your work is your life.

Still another way to add to the dynamic quality of your life is to cultivate interest in everything. A famous philosopher once pointed out that aliveness is measured by the number of points at which we touch life. A person having one hundred interests, let us say, is twice as alive as one who has but fifty interests. Depth of interest, often referred to as a consuming interest, is also a measure of aliveness.

And you can make yourself interested when you try. To make a start simply begin thinking interesting thoughts. Also, practice being interested in people and events, even if it requires an act of will to do so. If you really work at this, your interest will become actual and you will then discover that you are developing an interesting life. To the degree to which you cultivate an interested attitude you will create a life full of zest and vibrancy.

I have a very satisfying hobby, that of collecting people. Some people collect china, others collect stamps. I once knew a man who collected clocks. But I collect people. This hobby adds greatly to the joy I get from life, which I assure you is considerable.

For example, there is my friend Nino. I collected him several years ago. He has a long Italian name, but his nickname is Nino. He drove us for three weeks, from Naples to Venice, to St. Moritz, to Geneva. Another summer we drove with him from Stresa to Venice to Rome to Sorrento, and a score of beautiful towns and cities in between.

At first I was a bit uneasy with Nino. His English was broken and my

Italian practically non-existent. But by drawing upon some French and German as well as English we understood each other very well. I liked his sunny smile and glorious disposition and we got along famously. Once I said, thinking I was extending to him the highest possible compliment, "Nino, why don't you come to the United States to live?"

"Oh, Doctor," he said, "I know that is a very nice country, but why should I leave my beloved Italy?"

"I don't know," I said nonplussed, "it is just a suggestion."

Then he began describing Italy to me, the glories of its towering mountains and blue lakes, the warmth of its soft, golden sunlight. He had me almost dreaming of a villa in Florence or a house in Capri or a cottage under the eternal snows of Cortina d'Ampezzo.

When we separated at the end of the trip we vowed we would meet again and travel many hundreds of kilometers together in the years to come. I collected Nino and added him to my precious assortment of friendships.

Then, I collected a little girl in Damascus, a dirty little girl of about six. I met her outside the ancient walls of that famous city. She looked me over with a level gaze from deep, dark eyes; then gave me a fragile, wistful smile, the sweet and innocent smile of childhood. She did not ask me for anything. I said "Hello," to her in English, and I am sure it was an "Hello," in Arabic with which she responded. She understood my smile and I understood hers. I have heard sociologists describe refugees of all races and nationalities and have listened to innumerable statistics about them. But they were only statistics to me. Now, every time I hear of a refugee I see that little girl outside the old walls of Damascus with her deep, dark eyes and wonderful smile. Perhaps I shall never see her again, but I collected her and her sweetness filled me with joy and added to the vibrancy of my life.

Because human relationships touch life in its deepest meaning is the reason we are taught to love people. When we truly learn to love them we are getting very close to satisfying life's deepest desires. To prove that, notice the warm glow in your heart when you take an outgoing interest in other persons.

Then, when your interest and appreciation are widened to include the whole great world, life becomes even more fascinating. Interest, projected outside yourself, has the power to force even hardship, suffering, and pain into the background. The more vital your interest, in others and in the world, the more certainly you can live triumphantly over your own difficulties.

Not long ago my father died. He was eighty-five years old according to the calendar, but measured by zest and interest and kindliness he was always young. I never knew anyone who loved life more than he did, or who got more out of living. Whenever I think of life at its vibrant best I think immediately of Dad. Shortly after his death I received a letter from Dr. Clarence W. Lieb, an old friend of the family, a retired physician now living in California, but who was a distinguished doctor in New York City. Twenty years ago I had taken my father to him because of his then critical physical condition.

"I am saddened," Doctor Lieb wrote, "by the news of your father's death. He lived much longer than his physical condition of twenty years ago promised. I am confident that it was his fine mind and superb spirit which added greatly to his longevity. It was my privilege to have served him professionally. I bless his memory."

Charles Clifford Peale was a minister for many years, but before that he was a physician. His intellectual curiosity and his mental vitality were tremendous. He read prodigiously and was able to master and explain books and other material which many people, including his son, had great difficulty in comprehending. The late Fulton Oursler once told me that he read Du Noüy's *Human Destiny* four times before he could condense it for the *Reader's Digest*. Of course, Fulton Oursler did a masterful piece of work with that book as he always did with any writing. But he said that my father helped him greatly, having mastered the difficult book so thoroughly that his explanations were amazingly clear and cogent.

My father was the type of man who would never give up and he did not permit his sons to give up, either. He always told us, "The Peales never quit." When I was writing my book *A Guide to Confident Living*, which later became a bestseller, I became discouraged with my work and literally threw it away. My wife rescued the manuscript, gave it to my father, who found a publisher for it.

He loved to speculate about the world and everything in it, the stars and man and God. He reveled in philosophy. He loved all of nature and, strangely enough, became one of the greatest amateur authorities on snakes. Even after arthritis crippled him so that he could hardly use his hands, and a series of strokes confined him to a wheel chair, he could always think, and think he did. He became interested in astronomy and studied the heavens from his wheel chair.

He was one of the finest conversationalists I ever knew and discussed the greatest questions with charming wit and inspiration. People loved to sit at his feet and listen. He put the touch of glory on everything he handled intellectually.

Finally, the day came when a new stroke took away his speech and he could no longer form words. The last thing he ever said to me was "I am studying heaven. Scientists say, 'It's in the Milky Way . . .' Tonight, look at the Milky Way."

Following his death the doctor came from the room and said, "The light of reason was in his eyes until I closed them." How my father would like that statement. Charles Clifford Peale lifted himself above his physical difficulties by a mighty upthrust of courage and spirit and mental alertness and faith. And it was that which kept him alive for twenty years past his time, as the doctor of medicine declared.

Crippling limitations of pain could not dim the happiness that welled up in him. He lived alertly in the mind and in the spirit and in the soul, and so life never lost its fascination for him. He genuinely loved and was interested in every kind of person. Crippled though he was, he was alive to the very moment of his physical life's ending and I believe that he still lives, passing from life unto death, but to life again, because within his glorious personality he was always alive. He found the answer to the deepest desire of the human spirit which is life that triumphs over all difficulties.

To have dynamic life it is also necessary to make provision for adequate intake of inspiration. Inspiration is as necessary to your well-being as is food and drink. Without it life may of course be maintained, but it will lack the motivation that gives it meaning. Your aliveness may be determined by the degree to which inspiration is present in your mind.

The relation of inspiration to well-being is illustrated by a case in which a physician asked a pastor to see a patient of his. The doctor explained that this patient had been complaining of having no life or zest. His enthusiasm had vanished; he "just didn't feel good."

The doctor stated that he had made the usual tests, finding nothing physically wrong; yet the man continued to complain that he felt badly. It was at this point that the physician telephoned the pastor to enlist his aid.

"Really, I have no medicine to prescribe and surgery is not indicated. But you and I know that men get sick in spirit and depressed feelings can often manifest themselves in bodily ailments. I suggest that you give this man a good shot of inspiration. Give him an injection in the spirit. Get his soul toned up. Inspiration," concluded the doctor, "means to be in-spirited, or to have spirit put into you. And since spirit actually is life, without it this man cannot be well and vigorous."

Over a period of time the minister was able to get the man reinspired by teaching him to pray and to master creative faith. The doctor telephoned some weeks later saying, "The patient is much improved. It just shows what a good shot of inspiration will do."

Your supply of inspiration may indicate how healthy, how dynamic, how vital you are. Real inspiration is a widespread need of people today. So many have no lift or buoyancy of spirit. If this is true of you, possibly your lack of inspiration may very well explain your lack of satisfaction with life.

How do you get this re-creative inspiration? Of course travel, music, art, stimulating friends, and good books contribute to inspirational living. Perhaps nature, in all its varying moods, is second only to the spiritual as a source of life-stimulating inspiration. At least if affects me in that way and at this very moment I am receiving a good "shot" of inspiration.

I am writing these lines at midnight far above the Arctic Circle. Our ship is passing among the amazingly beautiful fjords of Norway. Though the hour is nearly one o'clock in the morning it is as bright as mid-afternoon. I have never seen anywhere such a dramatic demonstration of light and beauty. It is incredible, unbelievable. The nearby and far off mountain peaks are covered with snow and there rests upon them ethereal and unearthly light. Drifting clouds of soft blue-gray are rifted here and there by lighter pastel shades, soft colors made by the reflection of a midnight sun. As far as the eye can see, in a great encompassing circle, loom enormous giants of mountains, eternal bastions of rock, pushed up long ago from these vast seas here at the top of the world.

One wonders at such a time and place and in the presence of such beauty if, in a deep and inexpressible sense, this may not be a basic meaning of life itself. Perhaps the ultimate end of human existence is in being able to respond to the beauty, the everlasting peace, the glorious wonderment of the mystic world itself.

Nature provides inspiration, not only in such magnificent and tremendous demonstrations of beauty as I see this mid-June night in the Arctic, but as is also portrayed in some quiet meadow in New York State or in Ohio or in the deep South. But in whatever form we may find it, a purpose of inspiration is to stimulate us to greater living. Thus the objective of inspiration is to assist in overcoming your weakness, your sickness, and your inner conflicts.

The fundamental meaning of life, then, is to learn how to live. And that is possible only by finding God, for God alone can satisfy your deepest desire. As Augustine said, "Our souls are restless until at length they rest in Thee." And Tolstoy, who tried everything in his restless search for inner peace, at last found the answer which he expressed in these words, "To know God is to live."

Dr. Viktor Frankl, Professor of Psychiatry at the University of Vienna, told me that many in Europe today are ill simply because life has no deep meaning for them. That is no less true in our country, also. Dr. Frankl practices what he calls "logo-therapy," healing by God. He feels that many unhappy, dissatisfied people can be healed by finding life through God-centered thinking. God is the source of vital life, declares this famous psychiatrist.

We may not realize that God is our deepest desire. I have seen many men unhappily and restlessly, even blunderingly, search for their basic desire, looking for it in the wrong places and therefore missing it until, finally, they did find it in God. That is the reason God has become so popular now-a-days, and that is why churches are packed to capacity. That also explains why millions are reading religious and inspirational literature. This restless longing for God, this desire for life, has stimulated the great spiritual resurgence of modern times.

I was scheduled to speak before a convention of businessmen. The man who served as my host was one of the most extraverted, thoroughly outgoing, and likeable individuals I had met in many a day. Extremely popular with everybody, he radiated happiness, geniality, and a definitely dynamic quality.

Something I said in my speech got him to talking and he said, "I was a restless, dissatisfied, and very unhappy man. I haunted doctors' offices because it constantly seemed that something was wrong with me, or at least I was afraid it was. If an associate developed any kind of sickness I contracted the same thing, in my mind, at least, and would rush to the doctor.

"I guess I was sick psychologically as well as spiritually and I was really low in spirit. I got drunk a great deal and lived a pretty wild life, I must admit. I see now that, actually, I was trying to find a way out of my misery and I tried every angle. Of course, I was going at it in the wrong way so I felt no better and got no answers.

"Then, a young minister, a regular fellow, came to our community and I liked him immensely. He was an old college football star and a real athlete and a man's man in every respect. We played golf together and his game was every bit as good as mine, maybe better. After a game we would go to the clubhouse and I would start drinking again.

"The minister stuck with me, however, for I think he really liked me. Presently, I got so I could talk with him in plain language, and I poured out all my conflicts. And believe me, brother, there were plenty of them.

"One afternoon, coming back from the country club, the minister was driving and he turned out into the country. I asked where he was going.

" 'Oh, I want to drive out of town for a while'," he replied vaguely.

"Presently he stopped beside the road and turned off the engine. He looked at me and said, 'Bill, I have listened to you for a long time and I have been studying you and I am going to give it to you straight. I can tell you how to find what you are looking for, how to get over your conflicts, how, really, to be something and somebody.'

" 'The trouble, Bill, is that you're fighting God. You are a smart man and you should know that what you want, down deep, is God. If you don't know it, I'm telling you now. I think you will find out if you are honest about it. And I know you will be that, for I've always found you a square shooter. If you will quit fighting God and let Him come into your life, He will solve your conflicts, He will bring your divided personality together and give you peace and health and happiness. He will make you one of the greatest fellows who ever served Him.'

"I laughed when he said that, but I got to thinking about what he told me. I thought about it for several days and decided he was right. That minister helped me to find God."

I was deeply moved by the way that man looked at me when he said,

"Everything that minister promised that God would do for me He has done. And now I am trying to do something for God. At last, I have what I really wanted all along."

He had, at last, discovered how to live.

Eight Rules for Keeping Vital

1. Admit that you want to feel wholly alive. Everyone does.
2. Realize that life is full of the overcoming of sorrow and trouble.
3. Get outside of yourself.
4. Live in the present.
5. Put animation into your daily work.
6. Seek inspiration: in books, friends, music, art, travel.
7. Interest is a measure of aliveness.
8. "To know God is to live."

7

STOP BEING TIRED—
LIVE ENERGETICALLY

"A constant flow of energy develops when you hold such thoughts as hopefulness, confidence, positiveness, and good will. When your mind is dominated by thoughts of this character, a high level of vigor results."

AN ADVERTISEMENT pictured a man of about fifty years, slumped in a chair, head in hands, face showing abject despondency. The caption read: "Have You That Gray Sickness—Half Awake, Half Asleep—Half Alive, Half Dead?"

A pathetic aspect of life today is the astonishing number of tired and weary people. Many give the impression of crawling through life on their hands and knees.

But you can live without tiredness or fatigue. You can maintain energy and vitality. Surely our Creator meant us to live with continuous vigor, for the entire universe is charged with renewable energy. Since energy maintains itself steadily in the natural world, we must believe it was also meant to do the same in your life and mine.

In my house are two clocks. One is an eight-day type which I wind every Saturday night. But there are some Saturdays when I forget, or am away, and on Monday or Tuesday it stops. The other clock is electric, and because it is attached to the continuing energy in the universe it never runs down.

You can attach yourself to the continuous flow of God-powered energy through definite techniques of faith, right thinking, and sensible living. By such practice you may possess an unbroken supply of energetic force and never suffer from the "Gray Sickness."

A prominent personality returned to his boyhood home to find relief from heavy burdens and there took his life, in a sad ending to a notable career. An editorial writer, in commenting, said, "He was a tired man. He went home to rest, but apparently had forgotten how to rest." Then the writer added, "Unhappily, many of us seem to be in the same pathetic situation. We do not know how to rest."

Indeed it seems that many have no snap, no verve, no vibrancy. The

CDT's have them in their grip: Cares, Difficulties, Troubles. The conflicts and confusions of the world have seemingly invaded their minds. Such people are tired, weary, and even old before their time. They need to be connected to the illimitable energy-renewing power in God's universe.

A method for doing this is illustrated by an experience in a Midwestern city. In a shoe shining parlor I noticed that the chairs were more comfortable than such places usually offer their patrons. A man entered and, with a sigh, sank down beside me. "I don't particularly need a shine," he said, "but I get so tired that I come here now and then to rest in these easy chairs."

He was a friendly-looking man of early middle age, so I said, "You shouldn't be tired, a young man of your age."

"Oh, I'm not so young," he said. "I'm fifty-three." Then he added, "I sometimes wonder whether I know how to rest. Do you?"

We discussed the subject and presently left the place together. Standing outside, as we continued the conversation, I said, "May I give you a suggestion about resting? Please don't think I'm a busy-body or trying to preach to you, but really I do not think you are tired in your feet. Your weariness is probably centered in your mind. So the cure is to refresh and re-stimulate your thoughts. One simple technique is to repeat to yourself a half-dozen times every day, until it deeply penetrates your consciousness, the familiar Bible passage: 'But they that wait upon the Lord shall renew their strength; they shall mount up with wings as eagles; they shall run, and not be weary; they shall walk, and not faint.' (Isaiah 40:31) And there is another: 'My presence shall go with thee, and I will give thee rest.'" (Exodus 33:14)

"I know the first one," he commented, "but am unfamiliar with the second."

I repeated it. He thanked me and, watching him walk away, I felt that I could see him straighten up. He turned, smiled, waved to me, and disappeared into the crowd. I never saw him again. Perhaps I never shall. No doubt he wonders who gave him such curious medicine; but I was merely acting as an agent of the Great Physician, who teaches that we do not need to be weary or suffer fatigue, that we can have continuous energy of body, mind, and soul.

We are at last realizing that health and religion, scientifically used, are closely related. We are now learning the important truth that one's physical condition is determined to a considerable extent by his emotional and spiritual condition. The emotional life is very profoundly regulated by our thought pattern. Hitherto, people have rather generally accepted the notion, long current, that at middle age vital energies must begin to decline, and that one must thereafter carefully conserve himself in order to keep going until his older years. We have more or less passively accepted the inevitability of aches and pains and general deterioration which advancing years are expected to bring upon us. Sometimes, with a kind of pious attitude, we have ascribed these physical conditions to God's will, accepting a state of decline with resignation.

Personally, I do not believe this point of view is valid. It is my conviction that we can go on living with aliveness, and the secret of so doing lies in a dynamic religious philosophy. The outstanding concept of the Bible is "life." Jesus said, "I am come that they might have life, and that they might have it more abundantly." (John 10:10) If you fully practice the creative and recreative principles of Christianity you can live with vitality long past the period of life when energy is supposed to have gone by.

Have you not observed some people who live to a great age, but still have adequate energy and impressive vital force? How are they able to overcome deterioration? Their sustained vigor is simply because they have achieved harmony with the basic sources of vitality and energy, having adapted their thought patterns to dynamic faith and enthusiasm. They have demonstrated that by eliminating hate, worry, and tension, and by the application of simple rules of hygiene and mental health, they can avoid tiredness and have continuous energy.

The secret of a continuous power-flow is in adjusting yourself to God's controlled pace and tempo. Synchronize your thinking and living with God's unhurried timing; God is in you, and if you go at one rate and God at another, you will tear yourself apart. The maintenance of energy, the absence of tiredness, depends upon being in the natural rhythm of God.

This identification of the personality with that even tempo and rhythm basically inherent in life is one of the surest ways of eliminating destructive fatigue. Constant excitation of the emotions, plus over-stimulation by hurry and hecticness, draws more heavily upon the supply of energy than our naturally stored-up resources can resupply. But when you synchronize yourself with the harmonious flow of energy at the normal rate at which it moves when measured in God's natural world, you will then be living on the emotional level which God intended. And when you do that you are not likely to break down. On the contrary, you will have steady power.

A woman executive had over-driven herself without regard to her diminishing energy supply. Her reserves depleted, she was unable to fight off an infection. Due to lack of physical recuperative resources she was forced to leave her work for a lengthy period of convalescence.

She went to Daytona Beach, Florida, and it became her habit, every day, to go to a quiet spot on the beach and lie on the warm sands in the sunshine. After some days of this relaxation, she began to notice a curious phenomenon. From where she lay she idly watched the beach grass waving gracefully in the gentle breeze. One day her eyes chanced to single out one particular blade of grass and she was struck by the fact that it seemed to sway in a definitely rhythmic movement. She found herself beating this rhythm as one follows a musical score.

Presently, as she listened to the roaring of the surf upon the sand, she became aware that it, too, had a rhythm, and that, though on a different level, it was essentially at the same rate as the waving of the beach grass. This curious discovery fascinated her and she found herself looking and listening for rhythm in the natural world about her. As she lay with her ear close to the ground to pick up its low-keyed, harmonious sounds, she became aware of an easy but continuous flow of rhythmic energy throughout all life.

The climax of this recuperative experience came, however, the day she happened to detect her own heart beat. She became fascinated in feeling it throb as she lay with her ear in a certain position on the sand. In one illuminating moment the realization came to her that the rhythm of her heart beat was at one with the rhythm of the waving beach grass and the surging sea and the myriad sounds all about her. She experienced the electrifying consciousness that she was identified with the rhythmic and harmonious flow of nature itself. She sensed, as never before, her personal harmony with the energy of Almighty God, who is the source of all creative and re-creative power.

This was followed by the exhilarating and comforting realization that hereafter, if she kept herself steadily in harmony with the tempo and the time-beat of God, she could work and produce and carry heavy responsibilities without loss of energy. In this experience she discovered the priceless secret that when one lives at God's tempo he need not be tired and can have all the energy his responsibilities require.

If you inharmoniously build up stresses, you are bound to lose power and energy. But, by living in harmonious rhythm, you reduce stress and automatically renew energy and vitality. So, "They that wait upon the Lord"—that is, accommodate to the basic pace of life, shall indeed "renew their strength" and remain energetic. To know what this "basic pace" is, live with God in the mind awhile and you will find it.

And never forget that continuing energy is exceedingly important to your success in life. Emerson says, "The world belongs to the energetic." Keep that truth in mind as you study men, or read history. Achievement and usefulness do indeed belong to those who keep alert and vital through long years. And remember always the important fact that the truly energetic are those who have disciplined their minds to avoid conflict and stress. And they have also learned to keep their thinking zestful and enthusiastic.

We must realize that much, perhaps most, tiredness originates in the mind. We become tired when our thoughts tire. If you wish to maintain energy it is a dangerous practice to complain, using such statements as: "I am tired; I have too much to do; I am swamped; I am worned out." Such weariness-thinking and negative-affirming tends to transmit itself to the subconscious mind and actually reproduces itself in tired reactions.

The muscular organization of the body has much more potential resiliency than we realize. An experiment was made in which an arm muscle was blocked off from the brain impulse. That muscle was then stimulated for several consecutive hours and continued to react without any evidence of tiredness, demonstrating that muscles can continue functioning almost indefinitely. The nerve block was presently removed and the patient was then told that the arm was tired. This suggestion rather quickly took affect. The muscle itself began to feel tired and presently ceased to function with the same tone.

An authority on the heart is reported to have said that "the toughest muscle we have is the heart muscle. During a normal lifetime it produces enough energy to lift a battleship fourteen feet out of water." But even the heart muscle can lose its resiliency and suffer loss of effectiveness through the destructive power of wrong thinking. Fear, resentment, fretting, frustration, tension—all such unhealthy thoughts, if long held, have repeatedly demonstrated their ability to undermine the vast strength of this most powerful muscle, with disastrous results.

We must emphasize, as previously stated, that much tiredness, perhaps the major part, originates in the thoughts. But a constant flow of energy develops when you hold the type of thoughts which feed and supply vitality; such thoughts as hopefulness, confidence, positiveness, and good will. When your mind is dominated by thoughts of this character, then recreative forces are stimulated by the spiritual harmony they develop. A high level of vigor results.

Generally speaking, fatigue is not caused by work, even by what we think of as overwork. When men break down from what they call "overwork," the real cause is likely to be the result of extra heavy weight on the emotional-spiritual mechanism; burdens such as anxiety, grudges, or tension. Such fatigue is more often the result of a let-down or sagging of the thought-tone. If your mind holds a picture of yourself as tired it will not be long before your muscles and nerves will accept the thought. They, too, will become tired. The mind will have effectively transmitted a concept of fatigue to the muscles.

You can demonstrate this to yourself by observing how an infusion of some new and overwhelming interest into your thoughts can suddenly dissipate weariness and give you new feelings of energy and aliveness. A friend who has a sixteen-year-old boy wanted to raise his son in the traditional American fashion of making him get out and work. So, at the father's insistence, the boy unenthusiastically got a job in an industrial plant for the summer vacation, his working hours being from eight o'clock in the morning until four in the afternoon.

One evening, when the boy came dragging wearily home from a job which did not interest him and against which he was mentally resisting, his father said, "Bill, the grass needs mowing, and will you please do it right away."

"Oh, gee, Dad," the boy protested, "I worked hard in the plant all day long. I am just about ready to drop. I'm all in."

"I'm sorry, son," said the father. "But if you don't mow the grass I'll have to, and I'm sure you don't want to see your poor, old father struggling around that lawn, do you?" So the boy plodded wearily along at the grassmowing job, building up the thought that it was an overwhelming task. His tiredness deepened as a result.

Presently a vision of loveliness, also age sixteen, appeared, carrying a golf bag. "Come on, Bill," she said, "let's have a game."

Suddenly Bill was galvanized into energy. "Just wait until I finish mowing this grass," he replied; and he did that lawn in nothing flat. He played golf until dark, missed his supper, and then danced until midnight. Obviously Bill's muscles were not really tired. It was only in his thinking that he was fatigued. When an interest seized his mind that was stronger than the tired ideas, his body responded, since it was filled with potential energy that was not being used.

A mother who had worked hard all day sank into bed, groaning, "I'm so tired my bones ache." She fell into a deep sleep. But in the night her youngest child cried piteously. She rushed to the crib, found its face burning with fever, and called the doctor. She sat by the child throughout that entire night, showing no evidence of tiredness, until finally the crisis passed. Her muscles had been tired, but even more tired had been her mind. When consuming interest seized her mind, her body became alive and alert.

Of course, there is such a condition as healthy, physical tiredness. After working hard all day to fall into bed and sleep gives a delicious sense of rest. That is plain, normal, healthy tiredness from physical effort. A night's rest will restore energy in such cases. There is also a tiredness that may arise from physical illness. To cure this is the function of the doctor of medicine. But there is also a deep fatigue that is mental and emotional in origin, and for this there is another form of "medicine."

Manifestly, this refers to no concoction in a bottle or in the form of a pill. It is rather a medicine in the form of right thinking and right living. It is the freeing of the mind from unhealthy attitudes. Of course it stresses the giving of healthy treatment to the physical body, but primarily this medicine is the constant intake of creative energy through prayer, faith, good will, and selflessness. It is the positive affirmation of God's activity in the re-creative process.

Practice daily the dynamic principle described in the words, "For in Him we live, and move, and have our being." (Acts 17:28) Hold the belief that, since God created you, He is continually re-creating you as well. The identification of yourself with God, pictured in the Scripture statement, means that you may actually live in His vast energy. This explains why the most genuine and wholesome Christians are so vibrantly alive.

This is a practical and powerful law of vitality. Use it and you will be surprised by the manner in which your vigor and energy are stimulated. The use of spiritual techniques will also help you to eliminate overdrive, overworry, overpressure. And, of course, you cannot have real energy unless they are eliminated.

In this process it is important to practice thinking *alive* thoughts. By conditioning your mind with thoughts of aliveness you tend, actually, to be alive. The more you do this the more alive you will feel.

Think tiredness, affirm tiredness, and presently you will become tired. Think energy, affirm energy, and gradually you will come alive. Alive thinking reproduces itself in aliveness. And the more you demonstrate aliveness, the more energy and vitality you will have.

When your mind shifts into a vitalized pattern of thinking, it starts at once casting off debilitating thoughts such as fear, hate, and other conflicted attitudes. As they empty out, thoughts of zest and enthusiasm surge in to take their place. In this way tiredness is arrested and a definite reenergizing takes place.

The eager, zestful mind does not become tired in the sense of becoming fatigued. Therefore avoid growing tired in your thoughts and attitudes. Keep your interest and eagerness in every aspect of life at a high level. The tonic effect of so doing will be felt in definitely increased vitality, both of mind and body.

I cannot stress too strongly the importance of a daily emptying out of all tired thoughts and a deliberate day-to-day filling of the mind with fresh, dynamic concepts. A specific time should be set aside every twenty-four hours for this mind-drainage or mind-emptying process. Personally, I use a fifteen-minute period at retiring time. My own method is to empty the mind, even as I empty my pockets before hanging up my suit of clothes. Another way of expressing it is to undress your mind even as you undress your body. You would not jump into bed with your clothes on. But many people go to bed with their minds full of unhappy stuff, and wonder why their sleep is restless and why they are tired the next day.

A tailor once suggested that clothes will look better and last longer if all articles are removed from the pockets at night. Therefore, before retiring I empty my pockets of items such as knife, pencils, money, memoranda, and arrange all of them neatly on the dresser. I drop into a waste-basket as many as possible of the slips of paper, memos, and various accumulated items. This act gives a sense of things finished and their disposal removes the burden of them from my mind.

It occurred to me one night, while in the process of pocket-emptying, that it might be beneficial to "empty" the mind as I empty my pockets. Throughout the day we tend to pick up a miscellaneous collection of irritations, regrets, resentments and anxieties. If permitted to accumulate, these clutter the mind and become a disturbing factor in consciousness. I developed an imaginative process whereby I visualized "dropping" these mental impedimenta into an imaginary wastebasket. This gives a sense of relief from mental burdens, and makes it easier to go to sleep. The mind, being thus relieved of energy-depleting factors, is able to relax and enjoy restful renewal.

This procedure helps me to awaken refreshed and with energy replenished. This technique has also worked in similar fashion for many to whom I have suggested its use. Since it tends to remove strain and stress from the mind, it has proved generally effective in reducing tiredness. It has proved to be an efficient method for draining off the poisons of fatigue and for maintaining a high level of vitality.

As to the filling of the mind with dynamic concepts, the practical program for maintaining continuous energy suggested by my friend the late Lawrence Townsend is extraordinarily effective. Lawrence Townsend was one of the healthiest, happiest, least-old, old men I ever knew. At ninety-one he stood lithe and straight and was quite muscular. He never required glasses. He was vigorous, witty, and alert until almost the day of his triumphant departure to the other side, where surely he is having a wonderful time, even as he did here.

He had a distinguished career in the United States foreign service, at one time serving as Minister to Austria. He and his wife were intimate friends of leading figures in many countries. They were frequent guests of Their Majesties, the late King George V and Queen Mary.

Lawrence Townsend stands out in my memory as one of the greatest demonstrations of continuing energy I have ever known. He ate heartily, yet made it a policy to leave the table with an "unstuffed" feeling. He took a balanced diet with minor emphasis on sweets and starches, and extra stress on fruit and vegetables.

He retired early at night but made no fetish of this any more than of diet. If he wanted to stay up later, he did so, but he believed in the old truism, "Early to bed, early to rise, makes a man healthy, (perhaps) wealthy, and (certainly) wise." He rose early and took setting-up exercises, followed by a stimulating bath and brisk rubdown, administered with a rough towel. He then spent fifteen minutes reading the Bible together with selections from inspirational writings. Having washed his body, he declared it an equally important health principle to "wash" the mind and soul.

He spent some part of each day working with his hands. He was a rather expert carpenter and cabinet maker. He believed in "the therapy of handwork," holding to the view that such activity, employing as it does brain centers and muscles other than those commonly used in sedentary work, relieves strain and pressure. Also, he found that preoccupation with such occupational therapy tends to reduce anxiety, which he regarded as a most insidious, tiring factor.

At some time during the day, weather permitting, it was Mr. Townsend's habit to retire to a sun house, which he had personally constructed. In the roofless structure he would disrobe and take a series of physical exercises, followed by a sun bath and a period of relaxation. Then he practiced "emptying" his mind of all "thought poisons," following which he "poured" into his mind the healthiest, happiest, and most dynamic thoughts he could assemble.

Standing tall in the sunlight, he voiced aloud the following creative affirmation, and conceived of that which he affirmed as happening, even as he spoke: "I breath in pure, beautiful positive thoughts of God and Jesus Christ, which entirely fill my conscious and superconscious mind, to the total elimination of all negative, impure, enviable, uncharitable thoughts of hatred and malice, which, with God's help, I dismiss completely from my conscious, unconscious, and superconscious mind."

While Mr. Townsend's program and method may seem a bit extraordinary, yet his conquest of the aging process, and his amazing energy at ninety-one years of age, demonstrated conclusively the validity of his method. I have suggested his technique in many speeches and radio talks and not a few persons have practiced it with excellent results. I have myself made use of Mr. Townsend's re-creative technique and feel certain that, if you will practice it, and persevere, you, too, can develop energy and vitality greater than you have ever previously experienced. If you are willing to pay the disciplinary cost required, you can, I believe, master tiredness.

Another treatment is to utilize fractional moments of busy days to prevent "fatigue pockets" from forming in the mind. A good method is to vocalize energy-insinuating Scripture passages while driving your car, waiting for a bus, or in any interim period. While doing this, hold a mental image of those creatively spiritual truths as activating an unhindered energy flow. This play, followed over a period of time, will tend to prevent old, worn, tired attitudes from forming unhealthy mental deposits in the personality. Some physicians have suggested that such unhealthy thought accumulations may cause actual physiological changes which can adversely affect your general health condition.

Of course, a final technique for eliminating tiredness and living with continuous energy is to learn how to throw off responsibility and enjoy untroubled sleep. This is a skill which can be learned. One man who complained of being a poor sleeper came to our clinic for counseling. His daily and nightly habits were analyzed and it was discovered that, after he retired, it was his custom to take pad and pencil and make a series of notes about what he was going to do the next day.

He planned out tomorrow, making an outline of each matter he expected to handle, and prided himself on this "efficiency" method, regarding it as a unique procedure. He kept a pad and pencil on his night table and would often reach for them in the darkness, adding additional memos that his restless mind supplied. He related with pride how he had mastered the skill of writing legibly in the darkness. Oftentimes, upon awakening in the morning, he would find numerous memos which he had made during the night.

Why couldn't he sleep? Why was he tired all day? Simply because he was taking tomorrow to bed with him. We, too, believe in efficiency. We respect the principle of "Plan your work and work your plan," but there is a time and place for all things; and in bed, ready to go to sleep, is certainly not the time to plan the next day. In fact, if you are going to bed at eleven o'clock it is not efficient to do any tomorrow-planning later than nine o'clock. Do no planning later than eight P.M. if you are going to retire at ten o'clock. This interval of two hours will give the plans time to pass from the surface of the mind, where they agitate, to the deeper levels, where they become creative.

If, in your sleeplessness, apprehensions of the next day disturb you, simply remind yourself that God has helped you through every day you have lived heretofore, and that tomorrow will be no exception. Slowly repeat aloud the following lines of an old and familiar hymn, "So long Thy power hast blest me, sure, it still will lead me on." This will convince your unconscious of God's continuing care, and a comforting, relaxed feeling will come. Go to sleep using the conscious thought and affirmation that whatever you may be called upon to handle the next day God and you will be able to do together.

The secret, then, of continuous energy is, through whatever techniques serve you best, to "empty" the mind of thoughts and attitudes which cause tiredness. Then go on to complete the renewal process by "filling" the mind with such thoughts as will channel in to you the re-creative energy of God's dynamic universe.

Following are some suggestions for overcoming tired feelings and maintaining energy:

1. Through your thought and faith, keep attached to God, the source of all energy.
2. Avoid the gray sickness: half awake, half asleep, half alive, half dead.
3. Realize that energy sags when your thoughts sag, so vigilantly keep your thinking alert.
4. Think of yourself as a child of God, a constant recipient of His gifts of boundless health, energy, and vitality.

5. Avoid the concept of "growing old and feeble." Picture the youth-fulness of your spirit as resisting the aging process.

6. Empty your mind every night as you empty your pockets. Before going to bed forgive everybody, naming those forgiven. Leave the past in the past, and believe that God watches over you as you sleep.

7. Slow down and keep the even rhythm of God.

8. Train your mind to block off worry and frustration, two attitudes which siphon off energy.

9. Affirm that God's constantly renewing energy flows through your being giving you sufficient vitality to live effectively.

8

LEARN FROM MISTAKES
—AND MAKE FEWER

"It has been said that history turns on small hinges. So do peoples' lives. Over a period of time you make a series of decisions, each seemingly of little consequence. Yet, the total of these decisions finally determines the outcome of your life. A successful life depends upon developing a higher percentage of wisdom than error."

THE YOUNG MAN slumped in my office chair. "What's the use?" he said dejectedly. "I'm a flop. Once I had lots of hopes and plans, but that's a laugh now. Everything has gone hay-wire for me. I've flubbed everything by my stupid mistakes. Nobody will ever believe in me now." So ran his slangy defeatism. He fell silent, then sighed, "And that isn't the worst of it, I guess I've lost faith in myself."

At twenty-nine he had been dropped from a good firm for making a serious mistake in a responsibility assigned him.

"Why did I do it?" he cried in miserable futility. "I had the chance of a lifetime with that firm. I've blown the best opportunity I will ever have. Why did I do such a stupid thing? What's the matter with me?"

"Better fall back on the old philosophy," I reminded him, "and 'Don't cry over spilt milk.' "

Who doesn't make mistakes! But the greatest error of all is to let any mistake destroy your faith in yourself. The only sensible course is to study and analyze why you made the mistake. Learn all you can from it, then forget it and go ahead. Figure on doing better next time.

It is very important, in life, to learn how to make fewer mistakes. For example, I told this young man about that day, years ago, when a rookie batter just up from the Minor Leagues made three extra-base hits off the great pitcher, Christy Mathewson. The young player was elated; he had all but knocked the old master from the box. As he strode triumphantly to the club house after the game, a veteran player fell into step alongside him. "Did you carefully notice what balls Christy threw you?" he asked.

"Oh, no," flippantly replied the youngster. "I paid no attention. I just hit 'em."

"Well," replied the other, "you can be sure Christy will remember. He made a mistake in the pitches he gave you today, but he won't make that same mistake again. He'll remember, and he won't let today's bad time get him down, either."

According to the story that batter never again got an extra-base hit off Mathewson. The famed pitcher carefully analyzed his mistakes and learned profitable lessons from them. Perhaps his technique for dealing with mistakes helped build his amazing career.

I made another suggestion to this young man who, because he had made a mistake and lost a good opportunity, was so deeply discouraged. I told him that years ago I was a newspaper reporter for an outstanding editor, my old friend, the late Grove Patterson of the *Toledo Blade*. Mr. Patterson's editorials were human and kindly and wise. I happened to have one of them on my desk and read it to this dejected young man.

The editorial is called "Water Under the Bridge," and here are a few lines from it. "A boy, a long time ago, leaned against the railing of a bridge and watched the current of the river below. A log, a bit of driftwood, a chip floated past. Again the surface of the river was smooth. But always, as it had for a hundred, perhaps a thousand, perhaps a million years, the water slipped by, under the bridge. Sometimes the current went more swiftly, and again quite slowly. But always the river flowed on, under the bridge.

"Watching the river that day the boy made a discovery. It was not the discovery of a material thing, something he might put his hand upon. He could not even see it. He had discovered an idea. Quite suddenly, and yet quietly, he knew that everything in his life would some day pass under the bridge and be gone, like water. And the boy came to like those words, 'under the bridge.'

"All his life, thereafter, the idea served him well and carried him through, although there were days and ways that were dark and not easy. Always, when he had made a mistake that couldn't be helped, or lost something that could never come again, the boy, now a man, said: 'It's water under the bridge.'

"And he didn't worry, unduly, about the mistakes after that, and he certainly didn't let them get him down—because it was water under the bridge."

When I finished reading that sensible piece the young man sat silently, lost in deep thought. Finally, he pulled himself erect. "O. K." he said, and there was a new tone in his voice. "I get the idea—one mistake or a dozen mistakes can't lick me. I'll get it back—my faith in myself." I am glad to report that he successfully wove that mistake into the pattern of his very useful life.

In dealing with a mistake tendency which can plague you and get you into a lot of trouble, it helps to develop the psychology of rightness. Much error content can build up in the mind; but it is also possible to build up a rightness content. Two powerful forces are truth and error. These are constantly at war with each other, both in society and in the individual. If your mind is filled with error, then error tends to become assertive. If permitted to dominate, naturally, it will cause you to perform error. You will think incorrectly, will get the wrong slant, arrive at wrong conclusions, and make wrong decisions. Your net result will be a general, over-all mistake pattern.

If, on the contrary, your mind is filled with truth, you will be conditioned by rightness. You will have correct slants, will reduce the mistake average, and things will tend to come out right. It is as simple as that. The matter seems well expressed in a passage from the Scriptures: "And ye shall know the truth, and the truth shall make you free." (John 8:32) And, indeed, the truth will set you free from many things, including the psychology of error.

The error tendency occasionally erupts in seemingly abnormal ways into the orderly, conscious mind. Sometimes we are driven by deep impulses which we do not understand and which, actually, are shrewd attempts of our own unconscious to hurt us. One of these impulses may be the will to fail, the strange desire to inflict punishment on oneself for perhaps a guilt feeling or some other inner conflict. It is difficult for the rational, conscious mind to accept such "queer" doings as a plausible explanation of the mistakes we make, but we must realize that the unconscious mind often acts in a seemingly irrational manner, though actually it is not irrational.

A factory manager consulted our counseling clinic about a girl employee who had started making mistakes in operating a rather complicated machine. No other worker on a similar machine had such accidents, and previously this girl had been a precise and accurate operator. In studying the problem we made an investigation of the home situation and discovered that the young woman lived with her elderly father, a querulous, whining, demanding old man. He allowed his daughter no social activity, apparently wanting her entirely at his service. He was filled with the acids of self-pity and constantly reminded her of "all I did for you as a child," insisting that "it is your turn to do something for me."

She served his breakfast and prepared his lunch before going to work. Upon returning from the plant she did the breakfast and lunch dishes in addition to getting dinner. The father indolently sat around all day, never turning a hand. Throughout the evening he complained and criticized. The girl became very resentful and increasingly had the thought of escape. Then, the fact that she entertained such thoughts which she construed as disloyal, gave her a feeling of guilt. The guilt feeling created a conflict.

Finally, her subconscious transmitted to her conscious mind, in effect, the message, "I will come to your aid. I will get you out of this." The mistakes her fingers performed, as she worked at her machine, actually resulted from the effort of the subconscious to injure her and thus free her from an intolerable situation. The mistakes made by this young woman came from inner conflict, a mixture of guilt, resentment, and frustration.

Our psychiatrists explained this psychological mechanism to her. She was shown how to take an objective and dispassionate attitude toward her father. Insight was given into her own reactions and her father's as well. She was encouraged to be firm and kindly, yet to be master of her own life.

She had become rather dowdy in appearance. Our counselor suggested such obvious improvements as neater dress, a hair-do, and a facial. Then she was urged to join an active young adult group in the church.

Some weeks passed and, as she became a happier person, the mistakes ceased, and her former efficiency returned. She got on better with her fellow workers. In fact, within a year she met a young man at the church and they were married. Now they have a baby boy and the grandfather, who dotes on the child, has lost much of his self-pity. A more constructive life has come both to this father and daughter as they corrected the disturbed psychological status of their lives.

One of the best correctives of destructive error tendencies is simply to increase your spiritual understanding. This builds up truth and reduces the error content in your mind. Daily saturate your thoughts with the power-packed faith of the Bible. Develop effectiveness in prayer. Learn the art of spiritual meditation. Subject every question to spiritual testing and make no decisions that do not jibe with the best ethical insight.

One specific method for eliminating error and bringing truth into a practical situation was taught me by a hotel manager. When I registered at his hotel I was told by the clerk, "Our manager wishes to see you and has asked me to bring you to his office when you arrive." So, he sent my bags up to my room and I went into the manager's office.

"I have been waiting for you," he said. "I have a difficult problem to handle and want you with me while I decide it."

When he told me the nature of the problem, I said, "I'm sorry, that is entirely out of my field. And I don't believe in giving advice about something of which I know nothing."

"I don't want advice," he protested. "I want you to join me in bringing truth to bear on my problem. My technique for doing this is to empty my mind completely and let spiritual truth 'pour' into me." And he added, "I have discovered that this is always more effectively done when two persons whose minds are attuned pray together. Two empty minds," he explained, "furnish a better intake channel for truth." I let the "empty mind" reference pass and joined with interest.

At his direction we sat quietly and he prayed aloud, somewhat after this fashion. "Lord, we now empty our minds of all error, all preconceived notions, all misconceptions, all stupidity, all ineptness." He paused and we sat in silence for fully two or three minutes, conceiving of the mind-emptying process as taking place. Presently he continued. "We now fill our minds with truth. It is coming into our thoughts and taking possession of our minds. We are now receiving the right answer to our problem. Since we are being filled with truth we will get a true result." So went his very original affirmation.

Then he gave thanks for the help he felt he was then receiving. Concluding his prayer he declared, with absolute confidence, "The right answer will come."

I was astonished at this extraordinary technique, and awaited the result with interest. And the answer he got was a good one as subsequent results proved.

Upon concluding the error-emptying and the truth-filling process we again sat in silence for a minute or more. Finally he asked, "What answer did you get?"

I was a bit doubtful of whether I had "gotten" anything, but I did have the clear impression that I should ask this question, "Is the matter you have under consideration a right thing? Are you sure you are ethically sound in the proposition?"

It was a random shot, or at least I felt that it was, but I was later certain I did "get it." He gave me a queer look, a combination of embarrassment, and relief. "I was afraid you would say that, and yet I am glad for, frankly, I will have to admit that I have been trying to do a wrong thing. I have been attempting to tell myself it's O.K., but I see clearly that my mistake lies in always trying to do what I want to do rather than to discover what I ought to do, and then do that. That is the reason I have gone off the beam so many times. Now I clearly see the right course and will follow it."

I was so interested in the wisdom and practical value of this method of receiving guidance that I have practiced it myself. And the method holds up under testing.

"I have always had to deal with a tendency in myself to make mistakes," the hotel manager later explained. "I fumbled several excellent opportunities until, finally, I came to realize that these mistakes were coming from within my basic mental structure. In an effort to correct myself it occurred to me that the surest way to eliminate error would be to displace it with its contrary quality, truth. Then I began to seek for truth in an effort to change my mistake patterns. By experimentation I found that as I deepened my understanding of spiritual truth, I could actually reduce my mistake tendency. Now I am doing much better in my decisions, though, of course, I have much to learn. At any rate, my home-made method has proved a valuable formula," he concluded.

If you constantly fill your mind with rightness, seeking always to know

God's guidance, your mistakes will decrease in number and importance, since your basic wrongness will be proportionally reduced. The following daily affirmation has proved helpful: "I am a medium for God's truth. God's rightness is now flowing into my mind. I am now developing perception and insight." Such affirmations stimulate a mental clean-up and help eliminate wrong thought patterns.

To perform with efficiency one must develop wisdom and skill in right thinking. The wisdom of God is perfect. Therefore, if you become a "medium" through which God's wisdom flows, you will receive guidance and direction that will amaze you. I believe we can actually bring the wisdom of God to bear upon our personal decisions and, in so doing, greatly reduce our mistakes.

Of course, there is a right and wrong way to do everything. There is a right and a wrong way to sing, a right and a wrong way to swing a golf club, a right and a wrong way to bake a pie. There is also a right and a wrong way to live. Living is a science, based on definite laws. If you do not cooperate with its laws life can go very badly. When you learn those laws and live within them your life will be wonderful.

A concrete suggestion for living in harmony with those laws is to spend not less than fifteen minutes every day applying selected spiritual thoughts to everything in your life that is not going well. By selected thoughts I mean the application of everything you know about prayer, about faith, and about God. In a spirit of prayerful sincerity bring those selected spiritual thoughts to bear upon your faults and errors. Repeat this process until you are thinking spiritually about the particular matter that needs improvement. This practice will modify your attitudes, making them increasingly right, which will tend to result in right outcomes.

People who habitually think about their daily problems according to God's laws will, in time, develop something of God's skill in solving those problems. Your former mistake tendency will then shift to an efficiency pattern of thinking and doing.

Thoughtful people today are definitely applying Christianity to personal, business, and social problems as the method best designed to develop the highest degree of effectiveness. And the motivation for this widespread spiritual practice is not a desire to get ahead or make money. Indeed, such a debased use of spiritual principles would surely defeat its purpose, being in itself the application of error. The vast number of people today who live by spiritual techniques are sincerely motivated by the urge to use their lives and abilities to the fullest extent in creative activity. God put into you the desire to amount to something and to be a vital factor in the world. Those who minimize the importance of making something of themselves actually do violence to the creative objectives of Almighty God.

A businessman who has greatly reduced his mistakes always applies one simple test in arriving at a decision. "I simply ask myself, is it ethically right; is it absolutely fair to all concerned; is the decision based, not upon who is right, but upon what is right; and finally, will it do the most for the most?" This gentleman says, "Whether the problem relates to ten thousand dollars or ten dollars, unless what you do is honest, unselfish, and right it will not, in the long run, turn out right. And," he added, "more often than not, if it is wrong, it will not even be a long run."

Many people fail simply because they make too many wrong decisions. It has been said that history turns on small hinges. So do people's lives. Over a period of time you make a series of decisions, each seemingly of little consequence. Yet, the total of these decisions finally determines the outcome of your life. A successful life depends upon developing a higher percentage of wisdom than error. Then you will do fewer things wrong and more things right. In improving your right-decision percentage the knowledge of how to make a decision is very important. And more and more people are learning that the highest percentage of right decisions is attained when spiritual methods are employed.

There was a time when so-called practical people did not realize the importance of prayer, guidance, and insight in solving daily problems. But they have learned that there are subtleties and imponderables in every issue that may well be determinative in making decisions, and these can best be dealt with through spiritual procedures.

While vacationing at the beautiful Mountain View House at Whitefield, New Hampshire, a favorite retreat of mine, a man telephoned me long distance about a personal problem.

"I have a very important decision to make and cannot afford to make a mistake. Will you help me?" he asked.

When I inquired why he thought I could help he explained that he had read in a newspaper column of mine about a man who telephoned asking for help in making a decision, and that the decision turned out to be a good one.

"Evidently you told that other man the right thing to do. Now, I want you to tell me," he said.

"I cannot tell you what to do," I said. "I have no such wisdom. Every human being must make his own decisions. But what is the problem?"

"I am plant superintendent in a steel mill," he explained, "and I have been offered the superintendency of a larger plant. Where I am now employed I have charge of personnel and that is my chief interest. In the plant which is offered me I would not be in charge of personnel, although there would be other advantages. But," he added, "I do not like the vice-president to whom I would have to report in that other organization. So, I am in a quandary."

"It seems," I said, "that a very important negative must be eliminated. You are holding a spirit of ill will toward the vice-president. To be sure of a right decision I suggest, first of all, that you definitely pray out this destructive negative. You can never get a positive answer when your mind is emphasizing a negative; so, you will need to pray it out. Also, never try to think with your emotions. The brain is for thinking, and only a cool and utterly rational thought and prayer process will bring about a right decision."

"That is a new angle to me, Doctor," he said. "I am not much of a religious person."

"Religion," I answered, "is a scientific methodology for thinking your way through problems. So let us apply to this decision the key to successful problem solving. First, pray and ask God definitely to reveal to you your own abilities and how best they can be used. Then, pray that all hate shall be taken from you. You must pray with an attitude of good will for that vice-president. Third, pray that you may receive God's guidance and believe that you will."

"But," he said, "I must make this decision by nine o'clock Monday morning."

"Today is only Thursday," I said. "That gives you four days to pray and get mentally conditioned to receive the truth. You must keep all nervous hecticness out of this matter."

"But the deadline for decision is coming fast," he reiterated, "it crowds me."

"Keep your thoughts off deadlines and practice being calm and relaxed. Pray for mental peace. Place your problem confidently in God's hands. Leave it there, with faith, and you will have your right decision Monday morning at nine o'clock."

I could hear him sigh. "It will give me high blood pressure to let it go that long," he complained.

"Don't worry," I counseled. "Practice the spiritual process of developing rightness and you will have your answer in time."

On Sunday I telephoned him, just to be sure he was doing all right.

"Yes," he said, "I am following your suggestions. But the answer has not yet come. How will I know when I have God's guidance?"

I told him of my friend, the late J. L. Kraft, famous cheese manufacturer, who said that he prayed about a matter until he felt that he had prayed enough. Then he believed that whatever came up in his mind and held there like a steady light was the answer to the problem prayed about.

Some days later a letter arrived from this man who had telephoned. "The answer came just as you said," he wrote. "Clear as a bell, I got it. I have accepted the other job. I talked with the vice-president in an openminded attitude and I think we can get along O.K."

There was a sequel to this incident which suggests a subtle point in avoiding mistakes and making right decisions, and which underscores the importance of deciding things spiritually. There may be hidden in any decision the real end to which your life is being directed by higher wisdom. The alternatives which we face in any given decision may seem to be the whole question at issue, but frequently there is something else which does not show. And this something else can be the most important matter. If you could ascend to some great height which would afford a view of the whole future landscape of your life you could recognize and know the best things, and choose them. But since we cannot see very far ahead, we must take each step with all the wisdom we can muster, and have faith that we will do that which is right for us.

For example, the man who asked for advice over the telephone, and who received guidance through a practical spiritual formula, was more accurately directed than he realized. A later letter from him describes an unforeseen development that probably would not have materialized had he not followed the spiritual method for avoiding mistakes. I quote his letter in full.

"Dear Dr. Peale: Perhaps you will recall my distressed phone call to you during the latter part of June when you were in Whitefield, New Hampshire. My company had offered me a change of job, which would have put me under the supervision of a man in whom I had no confidence. The new opportunities offered by this change were overshadowed by distinct disadvantages, and the decision was far from being clear-cut.

"Your prayer with me over the phone did calm my anxiety considerably, but it was your return call on Sunday afternoon that gave me the help I needed. At that time I had not yet reached a decision, but was feeling more composed than when we first talked. You stated that I should not become alarmed, but have complete faith that God would provide the right answer at the required time.

"Well, sir, it worked just that way. I called my boss on Monday morning and spoke quite freely. I accepted the new job, but told him I thought I should have my head examined because I liked the personnel work I had been doing, the people with whom I was working, the location, and the man I was reporting to. However, I felt that the new job had greater opportunities, and therefore I would accept it. His reply was 'That's interesting.'

"That was Monday. On Friday he called back and said that the remark I had made about liking personnel work came to mind when they were reviewing the problem of selecting someone to head a development group which would operate on the West Coast. Because this work would closely parallel that which I had been doing, they thought I would prefer it.

"I made a hurried trip to the West Coast for an interview, was accepted, and moved out here last month. It is a big job, but with God's help I know I can do it successfully. It is true that if you have complete faith in the Lord He will provide a way."

You see? This man thought he merely had two jobs to decide between, but there was a third alternative hidden in the situation which had not yet materialized. Through his right thinking, that job moved into focus as the actual answer to his problem. God has greater things in store for you than you think. So, think God's way and let Him give you His greater blessings.

This is a dynamic and mysterious universe and human life is, no doubt, conditioned by imponderables of which we are only dimly aware. People sometimes say, "the strangest coincidence happened." Coincidences may seem strange, but they are never a result of caprice. They are orderly laws in the spiritual life of man. They affect and influence our lives profoundly. These so-called imponderables are so important that you should become spiritually sensitized to them. Indeed, the more spiritually minded you become the more acute your contact will be with these behind-the-scenes forces. By being alive to them through insight, instruction, and illumination, you can make your way past errors and mistakes on which, were you less spiritually sensitive, you might often stumble.

It is true that a spiritual conditioning of your mind to the Divine purposes which underlie your life will help you to make fewer mistakes. It is helpful to go into a church and sit quietly in meditation and spiritual concentration for fifteen minutes every day. If going to a church is inconvenient, the same quiet period may be observed in your own home or office. During this period talk your problem out as in actual conversation with God. Conceive of your mind as open to receive impressions and insights. Believe that you are receiving guidance. Indicate your willingness to follow faithfully whatever insight impresses itself forcibly upon your mind. At first you may not get clear direction. You will need to adjust to a spiritual type of thinking which will presently make you keenly sensitive to guidance. Not only from personal experience, but from results obtained by the many who have tried this method with success, I assure you that it is one of the most effective of all procedures for reducing mistakes.

Several years ago I struggled with a problem for days. I asked advice and went over the matter again and again, but the solution evaded me. I was about to force a decision prematurely, which is a mistaken thing to do, when I was invited to a Quaker meeting.

This meeting was held in the living room of a home and not more than ten persons were present. Except for some simple directive thoughts on the technique of meditation we sat in complete silence for forty-five minutes. During the first half of the period I was physically uncomfortable, being unused to sitting without some kind of activity or speaking.

Then I tried yielding myself to quietness. I consciously held my problem up to God and "dropped" it into the creative and dynamic spiritual fellowship which existed in that room. Presently my mind slipped into a quiescent state. It felt rested, but fully alert and alive. A strong feeling of peace, such as I had not felt in days, pervaded my consciousness. And then, like a flash, came a clear, fully-formed answer to my problem. It was not exactly as I expected it to be, but instinctively I knew it was right. And it did indeed prove to be so.

Another, and somewhat similar experience demonstrated again the effectiveness of meditation in obtaining guidance and in avoiding mistakes. For some weeks I had been struggling with another problem to which I had given not a little thought, discussion, and prayer. I had received an answer and was satisfied that it was correct, but shortly thereafter it was confirmed in a little wayside chapel, high on the Burgenstock, one of the alpine heights on the shores of the Vierwaldstättersee in Switzerland.

My wife, our son John, and I went into this picturesque little chapel for prayer and meditation. We found there a rather plain Swiss mother and her two boys. Rucksacks strapped to their backs, they were obviously out for a hike, but had stopped for a prayer before the day's outing. One of the boys was noisy and proceeded to take snapshots, completely indifferent to our desire for quiet. Soon, a couple, talking loudly, entered, carelessly banging the door. Then they departed, as did also the mother and boys.

We sat in a welcome silence. Sunshine flooded the little church, lighting up the altar decorated with geraniums, the inevitable Swiss floral piece. Sunlight fell softly on the heavy wooden pews and well-worn stone floor. In the distance, tinkling cowbells could be heard from the charming little valley of Obburgen, lying cupped between the Burgenstock and the Stanserhorn.

Then an old man entered. I knew him to be a rich old man, but was aware that he was poor, too, since he was ill and lonely and unhappy. He bowed in prayer, breathing heavily because of his bad heart and obviously in pain from his arthritic limbs. He hobbled out pathetically.

Suddenly it occurred to me to stop praying for myself and instead to pray for the mother and her two boys, for the noisy and thoughtless couple, and for the poor, old, rich man, suffering and miserable. As I did this an astonishing thing happened. No sooner had I finished those prayers than a wave of peace and joy swept over me. With it came a profound feeling of certainty about the answer to my problem. I knew that the decision I had made was not a mistake, that it was the right thing, and that I had been spiritually guided. The shift of prayer emphasis from myself to the other people very definitely had a releasing effect upon my thought processes.

Many men whom I might name, some well known, all effective in living, utilize this method of a daily short period in a church for clearing their minds, stimulating their thoughts, and keeping themselves in contact with basic truth.

Another suggestion for developing practical rightness is to cast out the mental picture of past mistakes. Holding such failure pictures, or dwelling upon memories of mistakes may cause the error pattern to repeat itself.

The mind seems to learn a mistake habit quickly and easily. Do something the wrong way a few times and the mind tends to accept that as the proper method. Therefore, when an error has been made, the procedure is first to learn all that you possibly can from that mistake, particularly how to avoid making it again. Even a mistake may have value in teaching how not to repeat it. Second, learn specifically what the right way is. Third, practice mentally visualizing that right way until your consciousness accepts a picture of yourself as performing correctly.

The late Mrs. Charles P. Knox, head of the gelatin business bearing her name, had a thought-provoking motto on her office wall: "He who stumbles twice on the same stone deserves to break his own neck." A childhood truism advised: "Turn your stumbling blocks into stepping stones." Certainly it is the part of wisdom to mark safe routes past old mistakes. A good rule is, don't make them twice and turn every mistake to good use.

A friend of mine, a small-town merchant, opened a haberdashery shop in a building where three others, in the same business, had previously failed. He was warned to avoid that particular site, "because nobody could succeed there."

But my friend refused to accept this pessimistic appraisal. He adopted the scientific, spiritual method. First he made a careful analysis of the failure of each previous merchant. And, second, he prayed for guidance. By studying previous mistakes he was able to avoid them. By prayer he developed new approaches. Now, it is said, that his business site is the best in town. That result was gained by studying the mistake experience of the others and by tapping God's wisdom to guide his decisions.

One of the mistakes of his failing predecessors was that they did not do a primary thing important to any business, namely, to cultivate a friendly spirit in their shops. So, this man employs only clerks who have what he calls, "the gift of friendliness," or are willing to cultivate it. He holds a meeting of his entire staff every morning and opens that meeting with a brief prayer. He urges his employees to "fill the store with the spirit of friendliness." In addition, he stocks only top quality merchandise, using the most attractive modern display techniques. He makes a constant study of salesmanship and teaches this important skill to his employees. In short, he drained every mistake of the previous owners of all the know-how it had to offer. First he discovered how not to do a thing, then how to do it well; first the negative, then the positive procedure.

Finally, may I emphasize that to think right and to do things right with assured certainty it is necessary to be a right person. Error in thought and action always results directly from error within the self. And it is of little use to attempt correction of specific mistakes without first correcting the central core of error. Get yourself right. Then things will go right.

* * *

Following is a list of principles which are important in learning to make fewer mistakes. They have been formulated from real life experiences.

1. Do not pessimistically assume that having made a mistake there is no hope, that a mistake means ruin.
2. Calmly and objectively examine your mistake. Learn all you can from it. Then move away from it with a new know-how.
3. Get psychological insight into the underlying causes of your mistake-tendency.
4. Increase your spiritual understanding. This will displace error from your mind by an intake of truth through prayer and faith.
5. Do not continue to hold mental images of past mistakes for that may stimulate repetition of the error.
6. Get your personality organized and your thoughts tightened up. Effective thinking and action will result.
7. Keep your efficiency high by stopping the leakages of power caused by fear, inferiority, etc.
8. Recondition your mental equipment by a daily reading program designed to fill your mind with the constructive thoughts of men who teach truth, not error.
9. Keep studying, keep trying. Always believe you can learn to do better. Constantly seek for self-improvement. Never believe you have arrived.
10. Apply the supreme personal test of all times, "Am I a right person?" If you are "right" things tend to go right.

9

WHY BE TENSE?
HOW TO ADJUST TO STRESS

"If you are to maintain power to meet your responsibilities and to continue effectively over the long pull, you must give as much consideration to that delicate, yet powerful, mechanism known as your human personality as engineers give to their engines. You can purchase another engine, but that 'engine' known as yourself cannot be reproduced if it fails, and stress is a major cause of that failure."

TENSION IS a number one problem today. We have never had a national patron saint, officially, in America, but apparently we do have one in a practical sense. The patron saint of the British is St. George; of the Irish, St. Patrick. The patron saint of Americans must be St. Vitus. We are a nervous, high-strung, tense generation of people.

Yes, America is full of tension and yet, actually, it isn't America that is tense, for the land is just the same as it has always been: wide, sweeping prairies; huge mountains, lifting their peaks against the sky; broad rivers, lazily moving toward the sea; mountain streams, splashed with sunlight, singing over rocks. The land is still the same and the land is peaceful. It is the American himself who is filled with tension and who, deep within, longs for quietness and relaxed strength.

Apparently the prevailing tension even affects the dogs, for an Associated Press dispatch from Los Angeles (a city that is not without tension) tells of a sixty-pound Airedale dropping dead of a heart attack when two smaller dogs barked at him.

Also, all tension is not in the United States, though with our national tendency to depreciate our own country we talk as though it is. The Paris edition of the New York *Herald Tribune* recently carried a story headed, "Paris Traffic Said to Affect Policemen's Nerves, Heart." The story reads: "Many of Paris' 18,500 policemen have developed cardiac conditions as a result of the French capital's nerve-wracking traffic situation. Some 2,500 of them are absent from duty every day because of nervous exhaustion after a day's work whistling, yelling, and pointing their white sticks in Paris streets."

I noticed in the paper recently an advertisement offering "peace of mind" tires for sale. The reference was to non-blowout tires. This brought to mind a statement by a rubber manufacturer who says that his industry did not learn to make efficient tires until they were designed to absorb road shock rather than merely to resist it. The time has come for all of us to learn to relax and absorb tension rather than rigidly battle it.

Many have learned to develop inner peacefulness and live without tension. On a plane I sat with a prominent business man, a dynamo of driving energy. His daily schedule is packed to the time limit. He has many responsibilities and directs innumerable activities, but handles himself with quiet and impressive power. Asked his secret, he replied, "I simply begin and end each day calmly."

As to his method for doing this he explained, "I say to myself four statements each morning and evening; and I repeat them slowly, meditating on each. One is from Confucius: 'the way of a superior man is three-fold: virtuous, he is free from anxieties; wise, he is free from perplexities; bold, he is free from fear.' The second is Robert Louis Stevenson's advice: 'Sit loosely in the saddle of life.' The third is from the Sixteenth Century mystic, St. Theresa: 'Let nothing disturb you, let nothing frighten you. Everything passes away except God. God alone is sufficient.' The fourth statement is that familiar quotation from Isaiah: 'In quietness and in confidence shall be your strength.' " (Isaiah 30:15)

"Apparently you believe that tension can be overcome by filling the mind with philosophical and religious thoughts at the beginning and the end of the day," I observed.

"That is entirely correct," he said. "And you can underscore the word religious."

Another excellent technique for overcoming tension, as I mentioned in the preceding chapter, is the practice of silence. At some time during every day it is a good thing to observe a period of absolute quietness, for there is a healing power in silence. Go into a quiet place. Do not talk; do not do anything; throw the mind into neutral as far as possible; keep the body still; maintain complete silence. William James said, "It is as important to cultivate your silence power as it is your word power," and Carlyle declares, "Silence is the element in which great things fashion themselves together."

Beneath the tension-agitated surface of our minds is the profound peace of the deeper mental levels. As the waves beneath the surface of the ocean are deep and quiet, no matter how stormy the surface, so the mind is peaceful in its depths. Silence, practiced until you grow expert in its use has the power to penetrate to that inner center of mind and soul where God's healing quietness may actually be experienced.

A friend of mine once had a problem that had been agitating his mind for days and could not get an answer. He decided to practice creative spiritual quietness. He went alone into a church and sat for an extended period in absolute silence. Presently, he began to be conditioned to quietness. He dropped his problem into a deep pool of mental and spiritual silence and meditated upon God's peace rather than upon the specific details of the problem. This seemed to clarify his thinking and before leaving that quiet place an answer began to emerge which proved to be the right one.

Having observed the beneficial effect of creative silence in the lives of so many I felt it could be used as effectively by groups as by the individual. I became convinced that the use of spiritual silence in services of public worship might help people, not only to overcome their tensions, but to find better solutions to their problems as well.

Accordingly, in the Marble Collegiate Church moments of directed, creative quietness are observed during services. Suggestions are offered by the minister of the most effective manner in which to relax the body and induce a state of quiet receptivity in the mind. It is pointed out that spiritual silence is not desultory and apathetic, but creative and dynamic. Verses, such as the following, are spoken to create an awareness of the spiritually creative possibilities of silence: "Be still, and know that I am God." (Psalm 46:10) And again, "In quietness and in confidence shall be your strength." (Isaiah 30:15) An amazing silence falls upon a huge congregation of twenty-five hundred people. The only sounds are faint street noises, muffled by the marble walls of the church edifice. Sunlight, sifting through the great stained glass windows, falls softly upon the multitude and enhances the deep impressiveness of the moment.

Many testify to the profound effect of this corporate and cooperative practice of silence. One businessman declared that in the silent period he received an answer to a perplexing production problem of his company. It seems that he and his officers had come to New York for a conference inviting this problem. Their meetings had lasted all day Friday and Saturday, and they had met for breakfast on Sunday morning. But there had been no solution. The problem was a baffling one, and men were tired and tense. At this point our friend announced he was going to church.

The customary quiet period was held and the congregation was directed as follows: "Put your problem in the hands of God. Hold it in the conscious mind for a moment, just long enough to formulate it clearly. Then think of the problem as being solved in God's way, which is the right way. Relax, and believe that the healing peace of God is touching your mind, that the blocks which have prevented guidance from flowing through are being removed. Rest your mind and body and soul in the Lord, and let your answer float to the top of your conscious mind."

This tired and tense man followed the suggestions given. In his mind, of course, were all the facts necessary to a proper understanding and solution in connection with his business problem, but these facts had not been properly assembled and organized. Because of the tension within him the component factors of the problem did not fall into the right order. Even though his answer was potentially present all the time in his unconscious, not until he came under the influence of creative silence did the solution rise from the deeper level of consciousness and become clarified. In speaking of the experience afterward he said, "The right answer, fully formed, suddenly came up into my mind. Stress had overlaid it with a rigid barrier, and it could not get through. But spiritual silence revealed it."

Mental stress always causes the mind to be heated, and when the mind is hot it cannot deliver properly. To be fully effective the mind must be coolly rational. You must think with your mind, not with your emotions. Creative answers to all your problems are in your subconscious. You can revolutionize your life if you learn to draw on this deep inner source of power. The practice of creative silence is a method for doing so. It will stimulate into activity basic insights which God has laid up within you and which you may use for greater efficiency.

Many people are learning to overcome their tensions and achieve calm control by such spiritual silence techniques. An example is the young man who was assigned the job of dealing with the most difficult customers of his business firm. He was given this responsibility because of his skillful handling of a particularly ticklish personality situation.

His method is interesting. When preparing for a difficult interview he uses the principle of spiritual meditation. One day the firm's most difficult customer was coming in, and it was the first time he had dealt with this individual. So he went into a store room for a period of meditation and prayer. As he came out he bumped squarely into his boss. "What were you doing in there?" asked the boss, a suspicious employer who severely keeps track of the actual working time of each employee. This young man was very much on the job, but in a manner the boss, at that time, did not understand.

"I was praying and meditating in quietness," said the young man.

"Business is good," snapped the boss. "Why should we pray?"

"I have a difficult customer coming in shortly," explained the young man, naming the individual, "and I wanted to find composure and deeper understanding. I need special insight and control to handle this problem."

Naturally, the boss watched him deal with the customer, whom he knew to be a very difficult person. He observed his employee's honesty, sincerity, understanding, and firmness. Afterward he said with a grin that did not belie his sincerity, "Perhaps I had better join you in that silent prayer technique." Little wonder the young man was assigned such a responsible job. His success was in no small part due to the relaxed control he had achieved by creative spiritual quietness.

Until you learn this skill you may work under that stress which is a cause of many nervous breakdowns. If you are to maintain power to meet your responsibilities and to continue effectively over the long pull, you must give as much consideration to that delicate, yet powerful, mechanism known as your human personality as engineers give to their engines. You can purchase another engine, but that "engine" known as yourself cannot be reproduced if it fails, and stress is a major cause of that failure.

The Captain of a Pan American DC-6B airplane told me that, at take off, the full twenty-five hundred horsepower of each engine is used to lift the tremendous aircraft off the ground. But immediately upon being airborne the pilot cuts back to eighteen hundred horsepower per engine for the long climb. When cruising altitude is reached power is still further reduced to twelve hundred and, for long-range flights, to as low as one thousand horsepower. The pilot explained that it is important to use full power for not more than two minutes. Its continued use beyond that maximum is likely to harm the motors.

Obviously moments come in life when a crisis demands full use of all our emotional powers and energy, but we must learn to reduce for the steady climb and for long-distance cruising. And certainly our energies cannot be conserved if, through tension, we constantly run our "motors" at full power.

As I have indicated, effective emotional control is best achieved through spiritual means. I had a number of conversations a few years ago with a man whom I never met personally, but who kept calling me by long distance telephone, complaining of tension and exhaustion. Each time I tried to say something helpful to him, and apparently gave him temporary relief.

But he telephoned more and more frequently, and I soon realized that he was leaning on me, that I had become a kind of psychological father to him, simply because he felt my desire to help him. Since everyone must stand on his own feet and conquer his own difficulties, I knew I must effect a transference of this tense person to God, if he was to achieve permanent healing of his tension.

"Say something to me that will help me to stop being tense," he kept repeating in a kind of desperation. "The only way I can get any relief is to pick up the telephone and dial your number," he explained, miserably.

One day when he called I said, "Instead of dialing me why not 'dial a Book' which you have in your possession. It will do you much more good and save you money as well." The suggestion mystified him, and I explained that I meant for him to go to the Bible for Scripture references designed to help reduce his tension. "Whenever you cannot sleep and are filled with tension and anxiety, just 'dial the Book' and read the words of the Bible. Say them aloud, conceiving of them as penetrating to the source of your nervousness and bringing you peace." I was able, also, to arrange with a local pastor and physician to work with this man in a more personal way.

One of the passages I particularly suggested that he "dial" is the fourth chapter of St. Mark which describes the disciples and Jesus in a violent storm at sea. It will benefit every tense person to read it at regular intervals.

This storm arose while the disciples were in the ship with Jesus. They were filled with fear and made their way to the stern of the pitching vessel, only to find Jesus sound asleep, His head pillowed on His arm. Such complete relaxation was surely a demonstration of perfect physical and emotional health. They cried excitedly, "Master, carest thou not that we perish?"

He opened His eyes and looked at the frightened men. He arose and studied the lowering sky and the tumultous waters. A slow smile of understanding and kindliness came over His face. He crossed the deck, awash with the waves, and grasped the mast. Swaying there in the tossing craft, what a tremendous figure He was, His magnificent physique adding to the impression of power. He raised His right arm, and in a voice that rang out over the waters said, "Peace, be still." Then states the writer of the Gospel with the genius of simplicity, "And there was a great calm."

One wonders whether that calm was in the waves of the sea or, perhaps more significantly, in the minds of those men. Certainly it was manifested in their restored composure. Now the waves did not look at all terrifying. Little wonder that they said among themselves, "What manner of man is this, that even the wind and the sea obey Him." He can speak peace to your tension and bring calmness into your mind. It is indeed an excellent technique and a workable one, to "dial a Book."

Tension has curious sources and manifests itself in many seemingly strange ways. But it is curable when all the facts and causes are systematically assembled and analyzed, and when proper spiritual treatment is given by adequately trained counselors.

In not a few instances over the years, I have observed the close relationship of guilt to tension. A person will insist that he has lived a good life apart from "a few episodes" and, "surely it would seem that the emotional system should have long since absorbed earlier indiscretions."

But strangely, the personality seems to hold them in suspension. They fester in consciousness and pockets of spiritual poison develop. The fine balance of nerve and emotion is disturbed and a state of tension is created.

Lowell Thomas told me an interesting story about a man who visited a dentist in a New England city. A small drill broke in the patient's mouth. The dentist thought he had removed all the broken parts, but some fifteen years later the patient complained of a pain in the shoulder. An X-ray revealed a dark object in the upper arm which proved to be a piece of the drill broken years before.

In similar fashion a "splinter of guilt" may lodge in the subconscious. Later, the individual may be completely unaware of the cause of his emotional and psychological pain until a spiritual operation is performed. Then tension declines and emotional, spiritual, and even physical health returns. But pockets of poison or splinters in the subconscious cannot be cleansed or removed except by spiritual curetting.

I do not imply that tension is caused only by guilt. That is but one of a number of causes. The combination of life's pressures, its burdens and accumulated difficulties, can rest so heavily upon the mind that tension develops. One becomes nervous, high-strung, and even disorganized. Here again, the cure is a spiritual therapy which, by penetrating deeply into attitudes, can substitute inner peacefulness.

Of the many illustrations of this fact one stands out particularly. I was scheduled to give a talk in a Western city and, in the hotel lobby, met a man whom I knew slightly. He was about forty years of age, a fine looking specimen of manhood, and the picture of physical health. He introduced me to his wife, a nice-looking woman, perhaps a couple of years his junior.

I asked the man the usual question as to how he was, which was an unnecessary inquiry, for obviously he was in the pink of condition. Then I asked his wife how she was, which was a mistake, as she took me seriously and proceeded to tell me in detail how badly she felt. Her husband, who presumably had listened to this unhappy recital on many previous occasions, excused himself, asking if I would talk to her for a few minutes until he returned.

She outlined a number of ways in which she felt badly and told of her fears and tensions. One phobia was that her husband, contrary to his healthy appearance, was in imminent danger of a heart attack, as she had been told that men of his age and responsibility were "dying like flies," to quote her graphic expression. She actually told me that in the night, she would put her ear close to him to see if he was still breathing.

I had a curious feeling, as I listened, that a sort of gray veil covered her face. Actually, of course, there was no such veil, the impression probably being an emanation of her unhappy spirit. She then told me that her face constantly twitched. She further declared that her eyes burned like fire. I could see no outward indication of either twitching facial muscles, or redness of the eyes, but both seemed a real source of suffering to her. She finally concluded her unhappy recital by saying, "It is impossible to describe how tense I feel."

Then occurred an amazing happening. Since her husband had not yet returned, I suggested that we sit in the lobby. It occurred to me to ask if she believed in the actual presence of Christ. She replied that she did. I then asked if she believed, since the doctor said her trouble was largely in her thought pattern, that through faith in Christ she might be healed by the creative force of the transformed mind. She agreed to this possibility, provided she could believe strongly enough, which was, incidentally, a considerable insight on her part.

I then explained that her tension had become an obsessive, fixed idea and pointed out that the mind will hold spasmodically to such an obsession, refusing to let it go unless and until a stronger thought or good obsession is substituted. The powerful idea that we desired her mind to take hold of was that of the healing presence of Christ. So I asked her to affirm aloud, using the following affirmation, "Jesus Christ is by my side. He is touching my body, my mind, my soul with His healing Grace." While affirming this she was to visualize the healing process as actually taking place then and there.

She was hesitant about this suggestion at first, but under my urging affirmed as directed. Presently I noticed that her emphasis became more positive. She continued to voice the affirmation, but each time with a heightened fervency and it was obvious that the healing thought was gripping her mind.

As I listened I had a curious consciousness of a Presence and she must have felt it too, for she stopped and, with a look of wonder, exclaimed, "He is actually here." And then I saw a strange phenomenon. The "gray veil" seemed to drop, as if by magic, from before her face and her countenance lighted up. Her face, at that moment, was beautiful, the strained look having passed. With deep feeling she said, "This is the most marvelous experience I ever had. I feel a strange sense of peace and," she hesitated, "I feel so much better."

"What about the twitching cheeks and the burning eyes?" I asked.

With a surprised look she replied, "Why, I feel none of that at all, I am so relieved." The tension had obviously broken.

I knew that this could very well be but a temporary manifestation and cautioned her against overconfidence, but said, "Continue to use that same affirmation, practice your faith seriously, and I believe you can be a well person."

Some months later I met the husband at a convention where I was giving a talk. He said, "The spiritual treatment you gave my wife produced a most remarkable effect. As a girl she was gay and happy and had lots of faith. Everyone loved her for her wonderful spirit. Then we experienced some disappointments and difficulties. Life got a bit hard. We drifted from our spiritual moorings, and finally she got into the condition in which you met her that day. But now she has almost overcome the tension which made her miserable for many months. She is getting along fine."

The woman's change came by inserting into her mind a stronger force than her tension, namely faith, and healing resulted. It is very important to realize that tension can and often does have deeper causes than pressure and hard work. I have described how guilt causes tension and how anxiety produces a like result, as in the case of the woman just mentioned. Tension may arise from old and seemingly buried feelings that originally caused hurt and may have deepened into resentment. We seldom put two and two together to see the connection between our present tension and old antagonistic attitudes. But in any effort to eliminate tense feelings you should explore the possibility that resentment may play a part.

A young man consulted me who complained of acute tension. He was, he said, "Like a rubber band drawn taut." The tension was so strong that he felt he might snap at any time. His medical check-up, while not too good, revealed nothing serious physically. It was this high inner pressure that was troubling him most.

Both in this conversation and in previous ones, as we analyzed his background, I noted repeated references to a man with whom he had gone through school. It seemed that this boy had outdistanced him in athletics, extracurricular activities, and in scholarship. That boy was now in a rather humble position whereas our friend was head of sales for a fair-sized concern. He had forged ahead of his old rival at last, yet he still showed decided inferior feelings and resentment toward the other.

When I faced him with my belief that his tension stemmed from deep antagonistic reactions to the other man he spat out vehemently, "I have never said so before, but I hate the guy with all the strength I've got." It was a violent outburst and I encouraged him to keep on talking. He poured out long pent-up antagonisms which revealed that his whole life was actually based upon competition with the other. It was a clear-cut case of a build-up of hate and inferiority into an obsession. But hate had turned back on the hater and here he was "taut like a rubber band."

I was interested in the figure and picked up a rubber band from my desk and stretched it to its limit, holding it there. "That's me all over," he said. "How can I get over being that way?"

"I think the answer is as simple as letting go your ill will and competition. Then your personality will normalize itself like this," I said, letting go the rubber band which immediately became limp.

"That's easier said than done, that letting go," he commented.

"Yes," I agreed. "The only way is to pray the hate out and pray Him in. You will have to learn to pray for that fellow and mean it."

He sat silently, then said, "That's why I came to you. I knew you would tell me to do that. I have made myself ready to do what you suggest and I'll go at it sincerely, too. I can get it out of my system, I believe."

I asked him to offer that kind of prayer right then and there, which he did. He stated that he felt better. "It will take a good many prayers to get where I want to go with this, but I'll pray them."

He shook hands and started to leave, but turned and came back to my desk. "May I have that rubber band?" he asked. "I'm going to frame it limp so as to remind myself to be that way. Why be tense when you don't have to?"

Why, indeed . . . ?

LET THESE THOUGHTS RELIEVE YOUR TENSIONS

1. In quietness and in confidence shall be your strength. (Isaiah 30:15)
2. Be still, and know that I am God. (Psalm 46:10)
3. Thou wilt keep him in perfect peace, whose mind is stayed on thee. (Isaiah 26:3)
4. Come unto me all yet that labor and are heavy laden, and I will give you rest. (Matthew 11:28)

10

YOUR LIFE CAN BE
FULL OF JOY

"In exact proportion as you give joy you will receive joy. It is a law of exact reciprocity. Joy increases as you give it, and diminishes as you try to keep it for yourself. Actually, unless you give it you will ultimately lose it. In giving it you will accumulate a deposit of joy greater than you ever believed possible."

THE PRACTICE of joy will release your personality and set free your powers. It can even give you better health and stimulate your enthusiasm.

Dr. John A. Schindler, a physician, and Dr. Robert J. Havighurst, a Professor of Education at the University of Chicago, joint authors of a booklet having the intriguing title, *How to Live One Hundred Years Happily*, make the point that between thirty-five and fifty percent of ill people are sick, principally, because they are unhappy. Dr. Schindler, in his excellent book, *How to Live 365 Days a Year*, tells of the importance of happy thinking to sound well-being. He stresses the curative value of getting patients to lift their minds daily, if only for a few minutes, into the area of pure joy.

There is an even profounder relationship of joy to health in the opinion of a noted scientist, Dr. Clarence Cook Little, Director of the Roscoe B. Jackson Memorial Laboratory of Bar Harbor, Maine. Dr. Little is reported to have said, "Internal balance is health and internal unbalance is sickness. These bodily functions are controlled by glands that are influenced by mental health."

In the light of these statements it is not surprising that the Great Physician advises us to be joyful. "Rejoice in the Lord alway," He says, "And again I say, Rejoice." (Phil. 4:4) Of course we must not interpret His message to mean that joy is the ultimate end and aim of life. Such would certainly not be a worthy motive for living. Joy is urged upon us only for the purpose of teaching us how to be alive, how to make the most of all of the faculties with which we have been endowed, how to be released, how to be free from conflicts, how to enter into a state of harmony so necessary to being a well-ordered human being.

Joy and harmony are synonymous concepts. When you are in harmony, all elements of your life function cooperatively; you are in a rhythmic relationship with God, the world, and with other human beings. When you are in harmony your whole being, mind, body, and soul, operates as one unity. They you are at a high level of efficiency as a person. Joy and harmony are fundamental factors in effectiveness.

On a DC-6 airplane I sat with an engineer who had helped to build the engines used in those planes. It was a beautiful day and we fell to talking about the joy of swift flight. I began to develop the theory that harmony is an aspect of joyful efficiency and could scarcely get the words out before he said, "How right you are. I am an engineer, and we know that the secret of making an effective engine is the degree to which we can get harmony into that engine. Efficiency depends upon reducing stresses and resistances to the lowest ratio. The parts of an engine, when working together in harmony, actually seem to sing for joy." He paused a moment and then said, "Listen to the roar of those mighty airplane engines, each delivering twenty-five hundred horsepower. There is harmony and joy in full operation."

Prior to that time the sound of an airplane engine had been only noise to me. Now I like to listen for their harmonious functioning and, indeed, it is not difficult to conceive of those engines as alive and actually singing with joy.

But this is as nothing when compared with a human being when he becomes harmonious. Then the whole personality seems to flow in unity and with rhythmic power. The stresses and conflicts having been eliminated, or at least greatly reduced, energy and vitality are increased proportionately.

Athletic coaches are aware of the importance of joy and harmony in developing effective sports contenders. Joy is a lubricant of the mind and therefore, of nerves, muscles, heart. It flows from the thoughts to the entire being, toning one up, and making for quick and responsive coordination. Joy causes a rhythmic flow of body, mind, and soul, creating that perfect timing and attunement which results in superior skills. It also supports stamina and puts heart into one. It is pretty hard to down a joyful and harmonious person.

An oldtime baseball man traced this quality of joy and harmony in some great ball players he had known over a period of many years. "An outstanding example," he said, "was Hans Wagner, one of the greatest of all shortstops. Wagner covered the area between second and third base like a tent. It seemed that he was everywhere at every minute, his great hands scooping up the ball from unbelievable angles. It was a joy to watch him because joy seemed to flow through him. He was a happy man; he played one of the happiest games of baseball I have seen in all my experience." So declared this expert.

"No man can play a really top game of golf unless he is basically happy," said a golf professional. When I expressed surprise, he explained, "Golf demands rhythm and timing which you cannot have in your muscles unless first you have it in your thoughts. An harmonious mind will send harmonious messages through the nerves to the members of the body which function in the execution of a golf stroke. The first demand I make of my students for mastering golf is to get inner harmony through right thinking."

The golf teacher told me an interesting story about a man, whom he called Joe, who was trying to perfect his drive. But he was not doing too well. He was tense and rigid, and he overpressed. Studying him, the instructor decided that Joe, essentially, was not a happy personality, that lack of inner harmony was tightening him up just enough so that his nerve and muscular responses were ill timed and, therefore, he was not delivering effectively. He outlined to Joe his theory of joy as a lubricant and told him that his game would not improve until he became lubricated with joy. To Joe's surprised question as to how that could be done the coach asked him if he knew any songs and he replied that he knew only one, "Let Me Call You Sweetheart."

"That will do as well as any," said the coach. "I want you to walk around the tee singing, at full voice and with all of the enthusiasm you can muster, 'Let Me Call You Sweetheart." Keep singing until the hills give the song back to you in reverberating echo. Then, when I raise my finger, still singing, go into the stroke, giving no thought to the technique, for your muscles, as Ben Hogan would say, have already 'memorized' it."

It had been Joe's custom, painfully and meticulously, to address the ball. He made very certain that his feet were in the proper position, he gave great attention to the precise manner in which his fingers held the club, he kept the arm stiff, deliberately and precisely pivoted, rolled on his feet, kept his eye on the ball, followed through; he did everything exactly according to the book—except that he didn't hit the ball right.

"Now," said the coach, "your mind has memorized the technical details of a proper golf stroke. I want you to release yourself and find abandon and freedom and delight in the game itself. Your muscles will know what to do. So, when I hold up my finger, keep singing and go into the stroke with a lot of joy."

Though somewhat abashed by this type of direction Joe began singing, at first hesitantly and with embarrassment. Soon, however, he got into the spirit of the procedure and sang wholeheartedly, walking around the tee, filling himself full of joy and harmony. Finally, up went the coach's finger and, still singing, his body flowing in beautiful rhythm, Joe went into the stroke and drove the ball two hundred yards plus, straight down the fairway. No doubt all over the country readers of this book, on many a golf course, will hereafter be singing, "Let Me Call You Sweetheart." And that is all to the good, for did not the great Thomas Carlyle say, "Give me a man who sings at his work." To be efficient you must be harmonious, and to be harmonious you must be a practicer of deep and vibrant joy.

And how do you become a practicer of joy? How do you train yourself to live according to the joy technique? A first step is, simply, learn to think joy. There is a psychological law, and it is a spiritual law, too, that if you wish to live a particular way, think that way over a long period of time. If you are fearful and want to be courageous, you can do so by thinking courageously. You can become a calm person by the same method. Think persistently along the line you desire, and then begin to act on the supposition that you are just that. Act as though you felt the way which you want to feel. Do this long and sincerely enough and you will tend to become precisely that which you desire.

Therefore, every morning upon awakening, start the daily practice of joyful thinking. This may be accomplished by passing a series of joyful thoughts through the mind. Explicitly, upon awakening, say something like this: "This is going to be a fine day. I had a splendid night's sleep. I am glad that I am alive. First, I shall enjoy a good breakfast. Then I will have some happy fellowship with my loved ones before the day's work begins. And all day long I shall have the satisfying experience of being with people, of doing some good, and performing some worthwhile services."

Look out the window and note the freshness of the morning. If there is no sunshine, perhaps you will see rain; so remind yourself how fresh and rejuvenating rain is. In other words, talk yourself into being joyful. By thinking and by talking you can react a joyful state. You can become what you think and affirm. Think joyfully, talk joyfully, act joyfully and presently you will become, through your thinking, talking, and acting, a joyful person.

Your mind may try to block you in your desire to become a joyful and harmonious individual by telling you that such effort is falsely conceived, and will seek to impress you by that old saying, "thinking doesn't make it so." But thinking can make it so and often does, if at the same time thinking is implemented by diligent effort and by scientific and persistent practice. If you are determined to improve yourself, your mind must be controlled by you instead of controlling you. Presently it will adjust and accommodate itself to the changed pattern of your thinking and acting. Thus, by believing, thinking, and acting you can, in time, make of yourself a joyful person in harmony and in tune with the creative forces of life.

The person whose mind has long been packed with gloomy thoughts and with negative attitudes may find this procedure difficult at first. It may require strict discipline to train the mind to think in this new and creative pattern, but remember that nothing worthwhile comes easily. You have to work at this persistently and diligently, using great effort, finally to achieve skill.

It will help to take pencil and paper and list the joyful experiences that occur to you every day. You will be quite surprised at their number and extent, and as you continue listing them they will grow in number and in meaning. Every day, systematically, pass the memory of your joyful experiences through your thoughts. Dwell upon them, relive them, immerse your entire thought process in the most moving and uplifting experiences you ever had. Your mind will presently begin to experience pleasure in this reliving of joy, and having whetted its taste, will want to create more such enjoyable experiences. As your joyful stimuli increase in number, they will penetrate to your deep consciousness, creating in you a permanently joyful state of mind.

The power of thought-conditioning in developing joy and changing your mental state is illustrated by the experience of a man whom I met on a train going to Chicago. This man, whom I knew slightly, was, at that time, an extraordinarily gloomy and negative personality. To him everything from the condition of his health, to the state of the country was very bad.

"Isn't this a terrible train?" he growled. "And did you have dinner in the evening car? Wasn't it awful? You never get any good service anymore. I couldn't eat a thing." (Later, a man who dined with him said he "ate everything in sight.")

Then he spent a little time criticizing several people whom we both knew. "By the way," he said, "I read one of your articles in the newspaper about being vital and joyful. Now I ask you honestly, do you really mean that, and can you imagine anybody in this world being joyful as you indicated?"

"Sure I can," I said. "I am."

"But how?" he inquired, perplexed. Then he added dubiously, "You do seem to get a big kick out of living."

"The way to be joyful," I said, "is to think joy, affirm joy, believe in joy, practice joy, and give joy. For example, instead of saying, as you did, 'This is a terrible train,' say enthusiastically, 'This is a wonderful train.' As a matter of fact it is. Actually, it is a work of art, the product of scientific genius. And besides, there is a great deal of romance to it. It is a city on wheels, streaking through the night. And, as to the meals in the dining car, they are not bad at all. Get in the habit of taking an urbane, positive, and happy attitude toward conditions, situations, and circumstances as you meet them daily. Instead of thinking in terms of dissatisfaction, discontent, and gloom, as you are now doing, practice slanting your thoughts toward joy. Make a sharp mental shift in your viewpoint."

I realized that this man had practiced negativism and gloom for so long that he had become, you might say, an expert in such attitudes. However, I outlined to him the joy-producing principles and techniques described in this chapter. Apparently I became quite enthusiastic, since I felt that way, and painted for him a picture of what he could be. It came over me that I was stating exactly what, unconsciously, he wanted to be.

Oftentimes, people who talk glumly and negatively are, in a reverse manner, indicating what they would like to be; namely, the exact opposite of their expressions. At any rate, he seemed genuinely interested and promised that he would try the simple techniques outlined. Evidently these new ideas began to register almost immediately, for when we arrived the next morning in the La Salle Street Station in Chicago, the weather was hazy and overcast. I happened to leave the train just as the porter was saying to him, "I hope you had a good night."

"Oh, not so good," he replied, "but then, not as bad as sometimes." He looked around at the weather and remarked, "It looks pretty gloomy today, doesn't it?" Then he saw me. His face changed, a grin crossing his countenance. "Oh, good morning, Doctor," he said, a bit chagrined. But he spoke with a new cheerfulness. Then, with a wider grin, "Wonderful day, isn't it?" Already he was beginning to realize the power of optimistic thinking, plus optimistic affirmation.

And I know he continued to work at it, for his wife told me of his sincere efforts to change himself. His new thinking was presently reflected in his much improved attitudes and in the fact that he felt better. "It is amusing to watch my husband," the wife said. "Actually he stands before a mirror and affirms that he is standing tall, thinking tall, and believing tall. It all seems sort of queer, but it must work, for life is certainly much better for him than it used to be. And," she added significantly, "for his family as well. What does he mean by that statement, 'standing tall, thinking tall, and believing tall'?" she asked, a bit perplexed.

I explained that in my conversation with her husband on the train I had referred to my friend, William H. Danforth, for many years head of a large St. Louis industry. He wrote a wonderful little book called, "I Dare You." It was based on a boyhood experience when he was suffering from ill health. A teacher said to him, "I dare you to be healthy," and gave him a method that helped him to become so. It was simply this, "stand tall, think tall, smile tall, and live tall." Mr. Danforth pulled himself up to dynamic health by daring to believe that he could become a strong, healthy individual.

I suggest that you, too, for a moment before the day begins, take a deep breath and say, "I am standing tall, I am thinking tall, I am believing tall." This is a slight variation from Mr. Danforth, but the affirmation will pull you up straight and bring the organs of your body into natural position. It will tend to slough off unhealthy thoughts from your mind and it will pull your faith up to a new level.

I was impressed by the common sense expressed by Dr. John C. Button, Jr. in an address to the American Osteopathic Association. "We sit at breakfast, we sit on the train on the way to work, we sit at work, we sit at lunch, we sit all afternoon. Sloppy sitting is turning too many Americans into a hodgepodge of sagging livers and squashed pelvic organs. Try, frequently, standing erect to avoid indigestion, neurasthenia, chronic grouch, and a thousand and one similar ailments."

Perform that technique and you are bound to feel better and be better. The disciplinary uplifting of the body, the mind, and the soul, practiced repeatedly, definitely rejuvenates and re-energizes. It takes the sag out of the body, dullness from the mind, and strengthens the spirit to better handle the burdens that usually depress.

As I have pointed out, the development of inner joy and dynamic harmony, as in all spiritual improvement, requires practice and more practice. You can never become proficient in any skill without practice. Based on the actual experience of the many who have demonstrated the beneficial effect of these techniques, I assure you that the practicing of new joy-attitudes will, in time, bring about substantial improvement within you.

At an airport a young woman approached me, asking pardon for the intrusion but saying she wanted to ask a question.

"Do you think," she said—and there were tears in her eyes—"that a person who has messed up her life horribly can ever know joy again?"

Obviously her question called for analysis and at that moment my plane was being called. So I scribbled a sentence on a card and handed it to her. "Try that prescription," I said. "And let me know how you come out." The sentence I wrote on the card was from the Bible: "If ye know these things, happy are ye if you do them." (John 13:17.)

A good many months later a woman came up to me following a talk I had made. "Do you remember," she asked me, "giving a card with a Biblical prescription on it to a woman at an airport? Well, I am that person and I was fascinated by the words and read them over and over. 'If ye know these things' and I asked myself 'What things?' I read through quite a bit of the New Testament trying to find that verse and finally I did find it and in the reading I came to realize what it meant. I knew then why I was unhappy. I wasn't living right and I wasn't thinking right. I was filled with fear and hate. I had done things of which I was ashamed. That one sentence," she ended simply, "changed my whole life."

This lack of joy is a problem for many people today, young and old. I was interviewed not too long ago by the young editor of a high school newspaper. She said, "I want to ask you a question that all of us are interested in; how can you really be happy?"

"Let me get this straight," I said. "Are you telling me that one of the great questions to which high school students are seeking an answer is how really to be happy?"

"That's right," she said. "Dr. Peale, so many of us are all mixed up. We just want to know how to be happy."

So I gave her that same sentence: "If ye know these things, happy are ye if ye do them."

Everybody really knows what to do to have his life filled with joy. What is it? Quit hating people; start loving them. Quit being mad at people; start liking them. Quit doing wrong; quit being filled with fear. Quit thinking about yourself and go out and do something for other people. Everybody knows what you have to do to be happy. But the wisdom of the text lies in the final words: "If ye know these things, *happy are ye if ye do them.*"

It is amazing and pathetic, too, how many people go through life victims of inward disharmony. They struggle along having no gladness in them at all. Imagine not being glad you are alive! Do you wake up in the morning eager to be up and at the job? Do you have a good time all day long? If not, do you want to know how to become glad you are alive? One answer is to use the simple and completely practical spiritual and psychological principles outlined in this book and in other writings of similar nature.

Still another good technique is this: in exact proportion as you give joy you will receive joy. It is a law of exact reciprocity. Joy increases as you give it, and diminishes as you try to keep it for yourself. Actually, unless you give it you will ultimately lose it. In giving it you will accumulate a deposit of joy greater than you ever believed possible.

Recently, in a magazine, I noticed an interesting story about a television star whom I have known for some years. I remember her in the early days of her career. Then she was very negative and unhappy. Of course she was not doing very well either, for her gloomy thinking dulled the basic charm in her personality. Then she began attending church where she met some vital people whose lives had been dynamically changed. She felt this alive something that they had and she wanted it. Through their help she became a vitally spiritual person. This experience was so complete, so thorough-going that she was eager to share it with everyone. She had achieved for herself a deep personal joy and it meant so much to her that she just had to give it out to everybody.

She took every opportunity to share her joy with others, especially with the people who viewed her programs. She filled her work so full of exuberance that it transmitted itself with dynamism and charm. Strangely enough, and yet not so strangely, her advancing success kept pace with her development in joy attitudes. She became a genuine dispenser of real happiness. There was now a magnetism about her that drew people to her and, of course, to her program, and therefore increased its value. She found joy; then she kept and deepened it by generously giving it away.

To succeed in any activity, or simply to succeed as a person, become joyful and dynamic. Get filled with power, the power of joy. What I have said does not imply that the purpose of learning the techniques of joy is to attain success. But surely, every normal person wants to do the most that he can with his life, and it has been repeatedly demonstrated that joy releases personality which then becomes outgoing. New creative capacity is stimulated. Negativism and dark thoughts tend to freeze personality. By self-emphasis one actually shrinks into himself and, in so doing, loses personality force. He becomes so fearful and self-consciously tied up that he becomes clumsy and inept. As a matter of fact, such a person is disorganized and therefore is bound to be inefficient.

The best and surest of all cures for this condition is to pray for help; study the Bible to learn how to live victoriously; go to church for instruction and for fellowship that is spiritually alive; ask the Lord to become your organizing influence. Then your personality will take on new tone. It will become strong and well-directed. Christ puts people together on the inside and He is the only one who can really do it. The slang phrase "get organized" is your answer, but let God do the organizing.

I was in the washroom of an airplane. Those cubicles, as you know, are quite small. A fellow passenger kept pushing at the door, trying to get in. I said, "If you will just wait one moment . . ."

"I don't want to wash up," he interrupted, "I want to talk with you. I saw you come back here and I thought it would be a good time to have a word with you."

I leaned against one wall and he against the other in that small room. "What's on your mind?" I asked.

"I'm absolutely miserable," he said, "and I'm disgusted. I have a terribly hard time with myself. I can hardly stand living with myself. And besides, they load responsibilities onto me that are too big for me and that adds to my unhappiness."

"What is your business?" I asked.

"Oh," he said with disgust, "I'm just a peddler, a sort of salesman. But now my company is sending me out around the country to give inspirational talks to our salesmen. Isn't that a laugh? Do I impress you as an inspiring personality or able to inspire other people?" and he laughed mirthlessly. "I haven't got the ability to do this job. I've got to talk to college graduates and I never had more than a high school education myself. Why did the head office pick on me and make me miserable this way?"

Obviously he was abnormally depressed to so completely belittle himself. I looked at his dejected figure. "Would you mind standing up straight?" I suggested. He looked surprised. "Yes, I mean it," I said. "The way you stand or sit has a good deal to do with how you feel. If you stand straight you are likely to start thinking straight."

He straightened up, pulling himself erect against the wall. "That does make me feel a bit better," he commented.

"Of course it does, and I hope you will keep practicing it." I told him about the stand tall, think tall, believe tall technique. "Another thing, never depreciate your job. You said, 'I am only a peddler.' What you should say, and I hope you will say it, proudly, every day of your life is, 'I belong to one of the greatest occupations. I am a salesman. It is my privilege to deliver to people from an honest manufacturer an honest and needed product or service.' Say also, 'I am a descendant of a great breed of men. I am a trustee of the American economy and American free civilization.' Never go around saying in a minimizing fashion, 'I'm only a peddler.' Never think yourself or your job down."

Then I added, "I am sorry you work for a concern headed by such stupid men."

"Who said they are stupid?" he demanded.

"Well, they must be," I insisted, "to send you out to give sales talks."

He bridled. "My bosses never make a mistake. They are the smartest men in the business," he asserted proudly.

"Well, then, that means they believe in you and if they are as smart as you say it must be because you are worth believing in. Even though you are deficient in education they know that you use your brain, that you give all of yourself to your job, that you love your work, and that you believe in their product. They know that you have qualities that can help other people. As practical men they do not make mistakes. They know they can trust you to do a good job. This should make you very happy and you need happiness in the work you are doing, for one of the best contributions you can make to your salesmen is to transmit a dynamic spirit to them. When are you making your first sales talk?"

"This afternoon," he replied.

"All right," I said, "Let's have a word of prayer about it now. And let us thank God that He has made you a salesman and such a good one that you can help other people have the joy of being salesmen. Let us thank God that you can show them how to be more effective human beings."

So, in that washroom, sixteen thousand feet in the air, we prayed and dedicated this man and his job to God and to human service. When he returned from his trip he telephoned me. "I had a wonderful meeting that afternoon and have had good going ever since. Do you know what happened to me on that airplane?" he asked. "God put me back inside of myself." He was reorganized, inwardly, by a new thought process based on faith and joy.

The practice of the principle of sharing joy has helped to develop some of the most remarkable people I have ever known. One, for example, is a good friend whom I encountered when I arrived at Grand Central station in New York one morning. All around me on that train were business executives and expensively dressed women, all prosperous in appearance, but most looking gloomy and nervous. As we emerged from the train I saw this friend of mine and noted the genuine happiness written all over his face. This man wasn't one of the big executives, but he is a big man, perhaps more so than many of the so-called bigs. He was piling up bags, putting them on trucks, for that is his daily work. He is Ralston Young, a Red Cap.

We exchanged happiness with each other. As I left him, stimulated as I always am by his great personality, I fell to wondering why Ralston still carries bags, for I am sure he would have no trouble at all in securing a better paying job. I spoke of this to another friend who also knows Ralston. "He thinks Grand Central station is the best place to spread joy and to share his spiritual convictions," explained this man. Then he told me about a man who was quite drunk who came into the station one night and asked Ralston, "Where can I get a present for my little girl? She is eleven years old and I want to take her something."

"Why do you want to give her a present?" Ralston asked.

"Why, to make her happy, why do you suppose?" growled the man.

"Mister, may I suggest a present to make her really happy?" Ralston asked softly.

"Sure, what is it?" the man grunted.

"Just give her a sober Daddy. That will make her very happy because she loves her Daddy and would think it wonderful to have a sober Daddy."

"What do you mean, preaching to me?" blustered the other.

"I'm not preaching," answered Ralston. "I'm just thinking about your little girl. Why not take her home a sober Daddy?"

The man cursed, grunted, and swayed slightly as he followed this interesting Red Cap to his train after they had, together, purchased a little gift. That man came back several days later and hunted Ralston up. "What you said sticks with me," he said, "but I want to know why you went to work on me."

"Because I could see you are not a happy man, but want to be," said the Red Cap. Then Ralston really did go to work on him and in due course transmitted his own spiritual joy to the man. Is it any wonder that Ralston Young is a joy-filled human being? He has spread so much joy to so many people in the great station where he works, and outside of it as well, that waves of joy wash back to him from everybody, everywhere. So, for your job's sake, for your health's sake, for your mind's sake, for your family's sake, get joy. And you get joy by thinking joy, acting joy, and sharing joy.

Another technique of happiness is to saturate your mind with joy. Jesus Christ says, "The words that I speak unto you, they are spirit, and they are life." (John 6:63) This means that if you study the words of Jesus, meditate on them and saturate your conscious and subconscious mind with them until they become your dominating thought pattern, you will attain real enthusiasm, dynamism, and joy. Your spirit will no longer sag. By a process of spirit transfusion you will actually incorporate some of the vital dynamism of God into your own personality. That is bound to have a profoundly rejuvenating effect on your entire life.

There is a marked increase today in the number of joy-filled people. This is a result of the spiritual resurgence of our time. And it is also traceable to the new knowledge of spiritual techniques which so many are studying and mastering. I have been making a "collection" of people who are living joy-filled lives, and believe me they are everywhere. I have personally drawn joy from them and now, in this book, I am pleased to pass some of their joy along to you and to tell you, as they told me, how they got it.

While spending a few days in Florida, I received the following letter from a young college student up North. He had heard that I was in his home town and wrote to me as follows:

Dear Dr. Peale,

My grandmother lives in the same town in Florida where you are now staying. For years I have been saving to buy her a round trip ticket to New York because she says if she could only worship in the Marble Collegiate Church it would be the happiest day of her life.

She has inspired me for so many years and taught me that nothing is impossible with God. She had seven children and educated them all by herself. She reared two grandchildren and educated them. She sent my sister and me through school. I have seen her go to bed hungry, saying she wanted nothing so that the family could be fed.

She purchased the house where she now lives with a down payment of one dollar and fifty cents. A book should be written about her life and it is my prayer that I may be inspired by God to write it. She is an angel on two feet and has a laugh like music.

By the way, we are black.

Thank you and God bless you.

Sincerely yours.

Of course I went to call on the boy's grandmother and, as he said, she proved indeed a wonderful person. Written unmistakably on her face was the reflection of that inner light which marks a truly joy-filled personality.

When I arrived at her house, a humble little place on a dirt road, no one was at home. Just as I was about to leave I noticed an old lady coming down the road with a basket on her arm. She had a rolling gait, somewhat like that of a sailor. She was singing softly. I knew she was the woman I had come to see and waited until she reached the house. "Are you Mrs.——?" I asked.

"Land sakes, yes, honey," she said. "What do you want?"

"Oh, I just came over to see you," I said.

"Now isn't that nice of you, but why did you come to see me?" she persisted.

"Your grandson wrote me about you," I explained. "He told me you are an angel on two feet. And I just wanted to see an angel on two feet."

She chuckled and laughed in the most infectious manner. "Land sakes, honey, I ain't no angel," she said.

"And he told me your laugh was like music," I continued. At that she did laugh. And he was right, it was like music.

"That boy shouldn't be saying things like that," she said, but obviously she was pleased.

I went into the house with her and she showed me pictures of all those children that I had been told she educated. I congratulated her and told her what a highly successful human being she was. "Oh, I ain't successful," she said. "I just love 'em, that's all." And I couldn't help but love her when she said it.

Just then her telephone bell rang. I overheard her end of the conversation. "Now, honey, don't you worry," she said to someone on the line. "I'll be over this afternoon and prop you up."

As she hung up the receiver she said, "That poor rich white woman. She's having a terrible time and I've got to go over and see her this afternoon. She does take an awful lot of proppingup."

I rather liked that phrase, "proppingup." She explained that people who need proppingup do not have any faith to sustain them. "You say that white woman is rich," I questioned, "and still needs proppingup?"

"Honey," she replied, "she ain't rich, she's poor. Folks ain't rich unless their riches are inside." She gave me one of those radiant smiles, the smile of a human being who is really rich and wise, too!

She was one of the most stimulating human beings I ever met. I could not help asking, "Where and how did you get this joy?"

She chuckled. "Oh, I just love everybody," she said. "I didn't go out hunting for joy. I just love everybody and when you love people you are happy." And I could see that she meant that, too. Then she added, "But the real reason I'm happy is I have Jesus in my heart. When you have Jesus in your heart nothing bothers you, nothing discourages you. You are just happy, that is all."

Think joy, talk joy, practice joy, share joy, saturate your mind with joy, and you will have the time of your life all your life. And what's more, you will stay alive as long as you live.

So convinced am I of the importance of joyful thinking in improving life that I deliberately practice it and have worked out a simple formula to aid me:

1. I searched through the New Testament for all references to joy, and there are many. Actually, the New Testament is a joyful book and Christianity is a joyful faith.
2. I committed many of these passages to memory. By this method your mind can be reconditioned. By a process of absorption joyful thoughts tend to displace unhappy ones.
3. I repeat quite a few of these passages daily. The constant saying of a thought will change you to harmonize with it. In time you tend to become what you think and say.
4. I listed all the joyful facts of my life. This list I read frequently to remind myself of the reasons for my joy.
5. I try to bring joy to as many others as possible. It is a curious fact that you get joy out of giving it; you lose joy by selfishly trying to keep it.
6. I try to see the joyful side of life. One must see the pain of life with clear eyes, and help all he can; but there is also lots of joy, and one should see that, too.
7. I got in the habit of acting joyful in a normal and reasonable manner.

11

LIFT YOUR DEPRESSION
AND LIVE VITALLY

"Any person can change from depression to power if: first, he wants the change to take place with all of the concentrated desire of which he is capable; second, if he will go all out to get it; third, if he will practice belief with all of the mental ability that he possesses; and fourth, if he will put himself in the way of having a deep and profound spiritual experience."

BRITISH WEATHER forecasts are interesting. A typical one read: "Cloudy, rain, fog, with occasional bright intervals." That seems also a rather accurate description of "weather" conditions in many lives. It is generally agreed that we can do little about the weather. But we can control the climate of the spirit. We can increase the number of bright intervals, we can conquer depression.

Depression may be serious or mild. The marks of serious depression are a perpetual sadness, slow reaction of mind and body, morbid and bitter self-criticism. A person suffering from these would seem to need profound therapy. In this chapter, however, we refer to mild depression, which is rather widely prevalent. Some authorities say that perhaps one out of every three persons has some degree of mild depression.

Symptoms of mild depression are discouragement, loneliness, disconsolateness, feelings of inferiority, and just getting no fun out of life. Mildly depressive people are always saying, "What's the use? Things are never going to be any better. I'm a flop."

I should like this chapter to be an effective effort to "Punch holes in the darkness" of your depressive attitudes, to borrow a graphic phrase from Robert Louis Stevenson.

An effective cure of depression is the practice of hope. The more hope you build up within your mind the more quickly your depressed feelings will lift. And as hopefulness becomes a habit you can achieve a permanently happy spirit. It is best to start very simply, as simple as saying hopeful words to yourself when you awaken in the morning. Tell yourself, for example, "This is going to be a great day. I am going to feel fine all day long. I am going to do constructive things today." Then keep on talking hopefully all day long.

By saying the words, you start the process which leads to the actual fact. Through repetition the idea of hopefulness will imbed itself in your thought pattern and, if continued, will force out depression and make hopefulness your prevailing cast of mind.

"But," you may object, "you cannot actually talk yourself into something!" Of course you can. Your mental attitude is very much affected by the words you say. If all day long you say gloomy, pessimistic, and negative words, you will be gloomy, pessimistic, and negative. Saying the words tends to develop the thought. Of course, the reverse is true also; hold the thought and you will then say the words. Either way, words and thoughts have a very definite tendency to reproduce themselves in fact. Think and speak gloom and you will create gloomy results.

If, on the contrary, you speak and think hope, you will tend to bring about a hopeful outcome. You can talk yourself into any desired state of mind. Much miserable feeling is self-manufactured by how we think and speak, or speak and think. Practice hopefulness, talk hopefulness, and you will begin to feel better. Then you will begin to do better.

This does not, of course, ignore the cold, hard, realistic facts of daily existence. But hope is a powerful method for overcoming cold, hard realities. Talk hope, think hope, and you will burn out depression. Then, with clear thinking and resolute spirit you can meet difficulty and overcome it. It is amazing how a hopeful person can make things go well, whereas others are defeated by obstacles.

Life is tough, no doubt about that, but no toughness can be as tough as genuine hope. One of the toughest things in the world is a mind filled with hope. The so-called toughness of difficulty cannot stand against it. Get your mind filled, therefore, with hope and it is bound to lift your spirit.

The cure of depression also involves improved personality-tone. A spiritual tuning up is essential. The human engine must be tuned up like any other engine, if it is to function efficiently. When an airplane is about to take off the pilots tune up and test the motors to get the engines ready to lift the great weight of the ship off the runway. When our human motors are sluggish and out of tune, we lack the lifting force necessary for powerful and vital living.

We then need complete body, mind, and soul revitalization. Right eating, right exercising, right thinking, right praying, right living, these are all part of the process of tuning life up to vitality. When piano strings have lost resiliency, the piano tuner brings them back to vital tone. Renewed life tone is important to dynamic living.

My long-time friend and personal physician, Dr. Z. Taylor Bercovitz, of New York City says, "To get in tone one must get in tune." His prescription is, "Every day spend five minutes on a rowing machine and five minutes on your knees." Tune up the body and tune up the soul. Religion and medicine harmonize to give resiliency and vitality.

In this tuning process or development of personality-tone, the motivating force will come by deepening your spiritual experience. Fill your mind full of faith. Then you will have astonishing power over defeat and depression.

In Pensacola, Florida, I addressed the student naval pilots. I was given a ride in a jet airplane. What a process to be dressed for a jet ride; Mae West vest, and flares in case of disaster; then meticulous instructions about how to inflate the vest in case of a crash in the water.

They placed a shoulder harness over me and safety belt around me. They put a helmet on my head and down over my ears. My feet were placed in position, and I was told that it was very important to keep the heels on a certain catch and my finger on a release button for, if we should crash, I would merely have to press the button to be ejected from the plane. By this time a certain amount of tension had begun to rise in my mind. Then they put on the oxygen mask, pulled down the plane top and there we were, hermetically sealed in. For the first time in my life I had a bit of a tussle with claustrophobia.

"Isn't it wonderful?" the captain called back to me through the inter-communicating system.

"I never felt like this in my life," I called back, working away at my claustrophobia.

"You are in for the time of your life," he informed me, enthusiastically, "because we are going into another world."

I hoped that he meant another world in this world.

We roared down the runway at an incredible speed, then zoomed into the sky, in such a take-off as I had never experienced. "As soon as I can find a hole we will go into that other world," the Captain said.

He found it and zoom—I never knew a plane to climb so fast—five thousand, ten thousand, fifteen thousand, twenty thousand, twenty-five thousand feet. Then I saw what he meant. We were indeed in that other world. I had a sense of being suspended, motionless, in a vast and illimitable canopy of blue. There was practically no sound, only a faint hum, for we were traveling at a rate of speed that was running away from sound, running away from the world, running away from every defeat. Wordsworth's lines kept going through my mind and I said them aloud, "I Wandered Lonely as a Cloud."

Then I, too, became enthusiastic, and called to Captain "Smoke" Strean, one of the best pilots in the Navy, and my good friend, "This is wonderful! I wouldn't have missed it for the world. I feel a sense of freedom and release and uplift. Why," I said, "it's (searching for the best description of all) it's like a spiritual experience."

"That is exactly what it is," he called back, "a spiritual experience." Then he continued, "This is the experience for which we train our students." And he described it in this glorious phrase, "We lead a student step by step until at last he realizes that he is no longer earthbound."

One of the greatest facts in this life is that we, too, can be led step by step, until at last we discover that we are no longer earthbound. What experience can be greater than to have contact with a lifting force that can take us up above every depression in life. This process is very well described in a phrase given me by a good friend, Mrs. Winifred Pond, who herself has the lifted spirit. I asked her secret. "It's something I learned from a dear old woman years ago in my home down South. She used to say, 'Live over the top of things.' "

This is indeed a wise suggestion. Condition your thoughts to live over the top of things and you will constantly have that lift of spirit which will deliver you from depression.

But the elimination of depression also involves a patient, persistent, perhaps long-term, clearing away of gloomy thoughts. And this you cannot do alone. You need God to help you. A doctor in Alabama wrote me saying, "Seventy-five percent of my patients do not need the surgeon's knife, or medicine; they need God." This physician is saying that much of the illness with which he deals is due to unhealthy thoughts which habitually occupy the mind. Of course, the sick often need medicine, and sometimes need the surgeon's knife. But they also need the help of God in clearing away unhealthy thoughts. You can make yourself sick by wrong thinking and, similarly, you can make yourself well by right thinking.

Dr. John A. Schindler tells of a grocer who came to his clinic complaining of severe stomach pains. No physical ill was found, the trouble being psychosomatic. His sickness developed because a big supermarket had opened in the community where he had his independent grocery and was taking much of his business. He also had a son who was always getting into trouble. The poor man was so unhappy that his stomach pains were constant. He was sick of depression.

Twice every year it was his custom to go fishing and hunting in Wisconsin. Five miles out in the country he would stop his car and look back at his town and would still have stomach pains. But when he started his car down from the hill crest where he had paused to survey his town, the pains left him, not to return until he reached that same spot on his homeward journey.

Because he couldn't go hunting and fishing all the time to find relief, the doctors had to teach him to rid himself of his unhealthy thoughts. They lifted him to a higher level of thinking, they helped him find a new philosophy of life. As Dr. Schindler puts it, "We treated the man for gloomy thoughts and he became well."

The doctor suggests how you can prove for yourself the power of thoughts over your sense of well-being. "Go home and sit in the easiest chair you have in the house," he says, "so that you cannot blame what happens on the chair. Then worry, and think depressing thoughts for just one hour. Either you will have a crick in your neck or a pain will hit you somewhere else. Some people are susceptible in the neck; others may be more susceptible in the nose. You can even develop the sniffles by doing this," the doctor declared.

That emotion can produce bodily symptoms and actually affect you physically is brought out in William James' famous definition of an emotion as "a state of mind manifesting itself by a sensible change in the body." To refer again to Dr. Schindler, to cure psychosomatic illness he recommends substitution for the unpleasant emotions, such as anxiety, fear, apprehension, depression, and disappointment, of the pleasant emotions such as confidence, assurance, pleasant expectancy, joy, and hope. "The 'pleasant' emotions produce changes that make us feel *good*; that is to say, they are optimal changes."

A man came down from upstate to New York City one Sunday to attend Marble Collegiate Church and something really happened to him that day to relieve him of a depression under which he had lived for months.

This man received three devastating blows in quick succession: first, his business failed, largely due to a disloyal associate; second, his son was killed in the war; and third, his wife suddenly died. All this together was more than he could take. He was stunned, and groped blindly in an unreal world. It seemed impossible that these terrible things could have happened to him.

Despite all that his friends attempted to do, still he walked the streets in a daze. He had no energy, no interest, no hope. He was utterly depressed. Months went by. Then, finally, he decided to spend a few days in New York City in the hope that a change of scene might give relief.

In telling of it afterward, he recalled that on Saturday night he went to a show, one of the most popular in town. But it left him cold. It seemed dull and uninteresting. He went to a well-known night club with no better results. Sunday morning he came to church. You can never foretell what great things may happen when you go to church. The very place is filled with mysterious powers which, if properly contacted, have the potential of revolutionizing your life. Actually, one should always enter the electric atmosphere of a church with a sense of excitement and expectancy. And the more you expect, the more you will receive.

This man told me afterward that he remembered nothing said or done in church that morning. So profound was his depression that apparently he could not concentrate sufficiently to listen with the conscious mind, but his subconscious, which is ever alert, picked up something that proved profoundly recreative. The healing atmosphere surrounding him penetrated deeply into his consciousness. All of a sudden, and without warning, the dazed condition which had affected him for months passed, and he experienced an exhilarating sense of illumination.

"It was," he said, "as if a high-powered light suddenly flashed on all around me. I had a feeling of lightness, as though I was being lifted into another realm of existence. I seemed to feel new waves of life passing over me, around me, and through my very being."

He struggled for words to give expression to an experience which, perhaps, is inexpressible. "Heavy weights," he said, "seemed to be lifted, and a feeling of immense relief overcame me. I became wondrously peaceful."

He says that he walked out of that church into a real world again. But more than that, he felt surging back into his reawakened personality a sense of mental and physical vigor. He returned to his home, well on the way to becoming a rehabilitated person, and thereafter worked with zest and efficiency. Gradually he rebuilt his life.

The powers which this man demonstrated after his spiritual reconditioning were, of course, within him all the time. They had merely been buried under a heavy mass of grief, disappointment, self-pity, and depression. The dynamic mood and atmosphere in the church created a state of mind in which it was possible for spiritual power to penetrate to the control center of his personality and release him. The log jam of negative, depressive thoughts broke up and a powerful stream of new thoughts swept his mind free of depression.

This type of release does not always occur in quite so dramatic or immediate a manner and is just as valid if its occurrence is over a period of time, or even comes hard.

Any person can change from depression to power if: first, he wants the change to take place with all of the concentrated desire of which he is capable; second, if he will go all out to get it; third, if he will practice belief with all of the mental ability that he possesses; and fourth, if he will put himself in the way of having a deep and profound spiritual experience in the manner indicated. The tremendous powers of the mind are released only when the above positive conditions are present. But the most astonishing change does take place when these steps are sincerely followed.

Another illustration of the powerful spiritual process which burns off depression is that of a man who was an alcoholic for years. He had all but wrecked himself physically and financially. Formerly he had been an executive in a large commercial organization, but was now touching bottom. In a hospital he was told of a man in Brooklyn who had demonstrated unusual ability in helping people with the problem of alcoholism. This turned out to be "Bill," founder of Alcoholics Anonymous, but in those days Bill had not yet accomplished his great work.

"I went to see him," said this man whom I shall call Mr. X., "because I wanted to get well. I desired this with all the force that was within me, but

I was utterly depressed. I hoped that Bill would not talk to me about God, because I had no use for God and I was sick of hearing about this God business. So I resolved that if he mentioned God I was simply going to walk out on him."

"Bill assured me that I could overcome my trouble, 'but,' he said, 'you will have to put your trust in the Higher Power.'

" 'By that do you mean God?' I asked.

" 'Yes, I mean God,' Bill answered.

" 'I knew you would bring up this God stuff, so I am walking out. I don't want anything to do with God and if that is all you have to offer, good-bye.' "

So, Mr. X. stomped out and down the street toward the subway station at the corner. As he walked, utterly despondent, he was muttering to himself, "God, that's all they talk about. God! I'm sick of hearing about God—God—God," he muttered.

Suddenly he stopped short, blinded by an overwhelmingly bright light. It seemed to be surging up from the street. The sidewalk undulated, and all around him swirled light. This strange light shown on the faces of people passing by. It was on the buildings; it was everywhere. In a daze, he stumbled down into the subway, only to discover that this same light also suffused the usually drab transportation system in its effulgence. He felt himself caught up in it. He rubbed his face with his hands, asking fearfully, "What is the matter with me? Am I going blind? Am I going crazy?" He bolted off the train and took another train back to Brooklyn and to Bill.

Shaken, he related his experience and then asked, "Bill, tell me, what in the name of God has happened to me?"

" 'You have named it yourself,' said Bill, echoing his own words. 'In the name of God, something has happened to you. Perhaps you should get a New Testament and read about a man named Paul,' Bill suggested. 'He, too, was quite down on God. In fact, he was persecuting the followers of Christ. While on his way to further persecution there came a great light and struck Paul to the earth. That is one way God comes to people, in a burst of light.' "

From that day Mr. X. was never again defeated by his old problem. Depression lifted from his mind as the returning sun drives the fog out of the valley. He filled all of the requirements set forth in the above formula. Actually, it was only with his lips that he said he did not want God. Deep within him, he was longing for God. His lips framed the fiction that he did not want God, but his heart was saying all the time, "With all my heart I truly seek him." Mr. X. got what, in his unconscious self, he really wanted, which was God.

As for that bright light which came up all around him, obviously this brilliance was not in the streets of Brooklyn, or in the subway. The light which dawned upon Mr. X. flowed from his own mind. It was a mystic, inner light and its brilliance was by way of contrast with the shadows and dark depression which had previously inhabited his mind. A profound and revolutionary re-emergence of spiritual power, stimulated by intense mental and emotional heat, cauterized that area of his personality where defeat and depression had formerly been generated. However it may be explained, the change through which Mr. X. passed amounted to a spiritual rebirth and drove off his depression, making life altogether new.

Another effective technique for eliminating depression and getting your spirits lifted is the practice of thought replacement. Our spirits sag because our thoughts sag. We become tired and depressed in our minds. The practice of thought replacement can bring about spirit transfusion. We can pump new life-giving concepts and ideas into our minds by the use of the words of faith, which are life-giving, life-changing words. Weariness leaves and depression vanishes.

One successful practicer of the technique of thought replacement, a prominent scientist, says that his method is to replace every weak thought with a strong one, each negative thought with a positive one, a hate thought with a loving one, a gloomy thought with a lifted one. Dr. Max Morrison, who tells of this man's experience, says that by this method the scientist also stopped persistent headaches, for they too can be caused by unhealthy and depressive thinking. Study your thoughts, write them down on paper, and analyze them, whether they are creative or destructive. Then, simply go about replacing the destructive ones with positive thoughts. You will find this literally a magical formula.

I receive a very large mail from people everywhere who give testimony to the marvelous way in which the replacement of depressive thoughts with faith thoughts has brought about remarkable improvement in their lives. Following are two letters out of the daily mail bag.

"My letter will be a bit different from the ones you usually receive. I have everything to make life wonderful, good, and beautiful. God and I are very personal friends. I can do all things I love to do for others because of His blessed help. I have a fine, kind husband, a beautiful daughter, and I also enjoy a host of wonderful friends. I sing, play the piano, and give talks of a devotional nature. I pray that I am a blessing to those who need a blessing. What more could anyone ask of life than this?

"Incidentally, I am without sight . . ."

A very different letter indeed! "Incidentally, I am without sight!" Here is a woman who knows how to handle a handicap that could be profoundly depressive. She seems actually to disregard it. She fixes her thoughts on God and the welfare of others, overcomes her handicap, and so lives joyously.

Fortunately, very few of us are born sightless or become blind. But all of us do grow older—and age and its problems seem a depressant to many. The other letter from my friend, Joe Mezo, shows how a man handles the age and retirement problem, which becomes such a difficult experience for some.

"I reached the retirement age of sixty-five and, against my wishes, was compelled to retire by the bank I had been with for twenty-four years. I won't go into detail as to how I felt. This happened on a dismal and rainy night—I was walking through Rector Street, and I never felt more depressed or useless in all my life.

"Suddenly, it happened! I felt I was not alone. A voice within me said over and over again, 'God is good; God is good.' I immediately felt uplifted. Every drop of rain broke the puddles into tinseled lights. It was beautiful. I went home, greatly comforted, and have had the feeling ever since that I am looked after.

"About two weeks later I had a call from another bank asking me to organize a credit department.

"I am now sixty-nine and in good health. I feel the best is still ahead. The good Lord is giving me the opportunity, the strength, and the courage to keep on."

Here is expressed that same dauntless, positive spirit. "I feel the best is still ahead!" This man is not depressed by his sixty-nine years. He has fixed his mind on the Source of eternal youth.

Depression, of course, is an attitude of mind. You become depressed because your thoughts are depressed. How change the depressive thought? By passing through your mind thoughts of faith. This must be done consistently and with great perseverance until the faith concept takes hold. Faith is always stronger than depression and if held and practiced will ultimately displace your mind's thoughts. One of the most effective thoughts for counteracting depression is the simple concept that God cares for you and will see you through.

Many years ago, I had my own struggles with depression. At that time I lived on lower Fifth Avenue, in New York. It was my habit to walk home from church Sunday nights and, on my way, occasionally, I stopped in at a little drugstore. It was run by A. E. Russ, a fine man, kindly and wise. Now and then, when I had done poorly, I would pour my woes into his ears: What a poor sermon I had preached that night; nobody would be in church next Sunday. So ran my dismal depression.

He would listen patiently and tell me to go back next Sunday and try again. Sometimes he would come to hear me. Then, one Sunday night, when I thought my sermon had been particularly poor, I stepped into his store and said, "Mr. Russ, I am looking for a job."

"What is the trouble?" he asked.

"I guess I had better give up preaching," I told him. "I can't do it. There is no use trying. I guess I will get another job."

"What kind of job are you looking for?"

I watched him making sodas and replied with a question: "Do you need a soda jerk here?"

"Well," he said, "as a matter of fact, I am looking for someone."

"I'll apply for the job. I can start right now."

"All right, put on an apron," he directed, "and come around the counter and see what you can do." I followed instructions and, taking a seat at the counter, he ordered, "Give me a chocolate soda."

"Yes, sir," I said. I hunted around and found the right ingredients and mixed them in a glass. When I squirted in the carbonated water, I didn't get quite the head on the soda a professional does, but it looked pretty good to me. I set it down before Mr. Russ. He inserted a straw and took a long draw.

Then he looked up at me and shook his head, "Better stick to preaching."

We went behind his prescription counter and sat down. "Son," he said, "everyone in every job has his moments of despair. You are going through the same thing everyone else does." He reached into his pocket for his billfold and brought out a picture of a lovely young woman. "Take me, for example. I lost her after we had been married only three years. The light of my life went out. There was nothing but darkness and despair. Then I turned to the Bible and one day, I found a message that was like a burst of light: 'He careth for you' (I Peter 5:7) Suddenly I knew in my heart that God did care for me and that He would see me through."

That experience gave him faith which helped him to overcome his depression. And from it he learned three things which are sure cures for discouragement: first, think right; second, believe right; and third, act right.

Another friend, the famous merchant, J. C. Penney, found that the simple act of turning to God will cure depression. When I use the phrase "turn to God" I do not use it glibly or piously as an old hackneyed phrase. By it I mean, wholeheartedly, to put your faith in God. Admit that you cannot help yourself. Then believe that only God can help and that such assistance will be forthcoming. I have found it of value to say over and over this affirmation, "God is the only presence and power in my life." When God takes hold as you let go, great things will happen. Remember, the word "believe" means to lean your whole weight on.

Mr. Penney made a tremendous fortune, and then he lost much of it. He went through a tragic time. He contracted heavy debts. Finally he suffered nervous breakdown with shingles, and other distressing maladies. He was in a sanatorium, very low physically, spiritually, and mentally. One night he became certain it was to be his last on earth. He wrote farewell letters to his family. It seemed to him in his depression that everybody had deserted him. He felt totally alone, in abysmal darkness, a beaten and defeated human being.

But, to his surprise, when morning came, he was still alive. As he lay in bed, weak and depressed, he heard the sound of voices singing a hymn. He got out of bed and shuffled down the hall where a religious meeting was being held. The people were singing, "Be not dismayed whate'er betide, God will take care of you." He leaned against the door and thought, "I was reared a Christian. Will God take care of me?"

He returned to his room and in a moment of complete surrender, gave his life to God. He began to feel as if a great blanket of fog was lifted and light was coming through. In the days that followed, a deep joy welled up within him. Life and zest returned. For years now Mr. Penney has been going up and down the country, telling what God can do for human beings. He has become one of the most constructive men in the United States.

Finally, a very simple method for overcoming depression is to learn to care for people as God cares, and help to lift their depression. A basic law of human nature is that you lose your own depression by taking on that of others. Love is well termed the greatest of all virtues, because of its remarkably curative properties. Love is always a symptom of self-forgetfulness and when you love people enough to forget your own miseries and take their troubles to heart, then you lose your misery and your depression is dissipated. This is why the Bible is constantly urging us to love one another.

One of the greatest and happiest human beings I ever knew was the late Hugh M. Tilroe, for many years Director of the Department of Public Speaking at Syracuse University. He was a huge man and frequently frightened his students by his rugged manner, but he had a kind and great heart of love. A minister who passed through a tragic experience told me the sad story of how his wife, a beautiful woman but lacking in character, became involved in a cheap scandal. He came home late one night to find her note telling of her infidelity and that she had decided to leave with a man, naming a person of low reputation in a nearby city. To that moment the minister had thought of his wife as a virtuous woman. He sat shocked and numbed. In his depression he called Dr. Tilroe. "Stay right where you are until I come," Professor Tilroe commanded in his brusque voice.

He drove the seventy-five miles to the little town where this minister lived and found him still sitting at the table, his wife's note crushed in his hands. It read something like this: "I have never been any good. You are as good as gold, but I am a bad woman and everyone knows it but you. I have tried, but I'm just no good. It is better that I leave you. I only hope that God, whom you so faithfully serve, will comfort you."

Professor Tilroe roughly, but kindly, threw his arm around the shoulder of the broken man. "Pack your bag," he said, "and get into my car."

They drove through that stormy night, mile after mile, without exchanging a word. "I could see the Professor's face reflected in the windshield," the minister told me. "I felt like a little boy with his father. He was a strong, good man. His very presence comforted me." They went to a fishing cabin which Professor Tilroe owned on Oneida Lake. Opening the cabin, he built a fire, cooked some food and said to his friend, "Eat what you can, then go to bed."

"Aren't you going to bed?" asked the minister.

"No, I'll sit up for a while," said Tilroe.

The minister tossed in restless sleep, but whenever he awakened during that long night he saw Professor Tilroe in a rocking chair beside his bed. He moved only to put wood on the fire. But not until morning did they discuss the problem.

"All night long," the preacher told me, "he sat up and watched over me. He was like my mother, my father—he was like God."

You can understand why, when Professor Tilroe's time came to die, the church overflowed with a great congregation at his funeral. Many in that church had found new life through the huge, kindly man who, in lifting depression from so many, became one of the happiest men I ever knew. Throughout all his years in Syracuse University he had loved people and had given of himself to them. He said to me one time when I was low in spirit, "Think of this text: 'If ye know these things, happy are ye if ye do them.' (John 13:17) One of those things is just love people. Love and help them and you will be happy all your life, even when life is painful and hard." How right he was. It is as simple as that. The real answer to depression is love of God and love of people.

To Cast Off Depression

1. Identify the symptoms of depression.
   Serious depression: perpetual sadness, slow reaction of mind and body, morbid and bitter self-criticism.
   Mild depression: discouragement, loneliness, disconsolateness, feelings of inferiority, getting no fun out of life.
2. Practice hope. As hopefulness becomes a habit, you can achieve a permanently happy spirit.
3. Right eating, right exercising, right thinking, right praying, right living—these tone up vitality.

4. Practice of thought replacement can bring about spirit transfusion.
    Replace each weak thought with a strong one.
    Replace each negative thought with a positive one.
    Replace each hate thought with a loving one.
    Replace each gloomy thought with a lifted one.

12

PEACE OF MIND—
YOUR SOURCE OF
POWER AND ENERGY

"We do not fully comprehend what we can do with our emotions. When we control them we have power. When they control us the results are often disastrous."

BELIEVE IT or not, a New York professor is opposed to anyone having peace of mind. He says all this talk about peace of mind irritates him because it means being soothed into an easy and pallid existence.

But the professor misunderstands. Peace of mind does not mean soothing; quite the contrary. It is the source of great energy. It does not mean escape into a dream world, but more effective participation in a real world. It does not mean innocuous lulling, but a dynamic stimulation of creative activity.

A great value of peace of mind is that it increases intellectual power. The mind is efficient only when it is cool—not hot. The nervously excited mind cannot produce rational concepts or orderly thought processes. In a heated state of mind, emotions control judgment, which may prove costly. Power comes from quietness. Marcus Aurelius said, "By a tranquil mind I mean nothing less than a mind well ordered." Carlyle wrote, "Silence is the element in which great things fashion themselves together." Perhaps an even more graphic statement is Edwin Markham's picturesque line, "At the heart of the cyclone tearing the sky . . . is a place of central calm." The cyclone derives its power from a calm center. So does a man.

I knew another professor, a wise man to whom I went, greatly perturbed, years ago. "You cannot think your problem through," he told me, "with an overheated mind such as you have at this moment. You must achieve at least a measure of mental peace before we can get your thoughts to deliver a rational answer. Never trust your emotional reactions unless they are under full control."

Then he had me sit quietly in a chair. He read some lines of poetry, concluding with a few Scripture passages. Finally, after a long silence, he prayed, "Lord, touch this young man's mind with Thy healing Grace and give him peace of mind." Only then did he permit me to outline my problem. To this day I recall with admiration how he guided my thinking to a sound solution.

"Never try to think without a peaceful mind," he advised. I have since urged this procedure on others who have used it with excellent results.

Seneca, the philosopher, says, "The mind is never right, but when it is at peace within itself."

The headmistress of a preparatory school for girls tells her students, "Be still at the center of your being." She explains to the girls that "real power to meet life is developed in those deep centers of inner quietness where the soul and the mind meet God."

God evidently attaches great value to silence for He filled the world with silent places. Apparently He believes it wise for us to fill our lives with silence, too. Consider the fact that seventy-one percent of the globe's surface is water and only twenty-nine percent is land. The sea is a silent place, although not without sound; but the sound has no stridency; it is the voice of the great deep—God's silence.

Think how many cities we could have if all this water had been dry land. But, perhaps, God did not want more cities. He wanted silence more.

Great insight is stated in the Bible: "Be still, and know that I am God." (Psalm 46:10) This is to say, make room for silence in your life. It is an aid to peace of mind.

The power of silence in developing peace of mind and with it, depth of life, is inestimable. Silence fertilizes the deep place where personality grows. A life with a peaceful center can weather all storms and develop great strength. Take Lincoln for example. How may we best explain his strength, his poise, his amazing understanding, his keen insight? Lincoln matured amidst the silence of the primeval forests which whispered deep secrets to him. Perhaps we have wasted sympathy on Lincoln because of his lack of schooling. He went to school to silence, and thus grew a depth of soul and quality of mind of enduring superiority.

In this mechanical era the circumstances of our lives do not easily afford solitude and silence of this type. But we can cultivate inner peacefulness and, unless we do, we may suffer devastating stress and strain. Thoreau said, "Most men live lives of quiet desperation." If that was so in his time, how much more is it true today.

Why, then, do we write about peace of mind? Simply because all of us need it. Dante when asked what he sought in life replied, "I am searching for that which every man seeks—peace and rest." Perhaps never has modern man craved peace of mind as today. Since religion is not always presented in a manner designed to guide men to sound techniques of inner peace, millions are turning to materialistic methods for satisfying this longing. The sale of peace-of-mind drugs, for example, is assuming gigantic proportions.

I happen to be writing this chapter in Europe and have before me a copy of the *London News Chronicle* carrying a headline reading, "Are Drugs the Answer to Sick Souls." The newspaper article asks of the British people, "Are we becoming a nation of drug addicts? Have we reached the point forecast by Aldous Huxley twenty-five years ago in his *Brave New World* where all we need to do if we feel worried, anxious, or upset is to take a pill?

"Huxley called his wonder drug 'Soma.' It had all the advantages of alcohol with none of its defects: 'Take a holiday from reality whenever you like, and come back without so much as a headache. Euphoric, narcotic, pleasantly halluciant; that was Soma.'

"Now listen to our own drug manufacturers of today, extolling the virtues of their new tranquillising drugs, in their advertising to doctors: 'a tranquillising agent which places a barrier between the patient's emotions and his external problems.' . . . 'harassment and worry are replaced by an unfluctuating mood of untroubled composure.' . . . 'daytime sedation without hypnosis.' : . . 'Calms the quaking inner self.'

"Man is entering the atomic age, with his thoughts and the control of his emotions at Stone Age level. Panic keeps breaking through. Anxiety is the malady of our time. But, instead of trying to show patients how to cope intelligently with their fears, doctors are prescribing more and more dope, aided and abetted by the drug companies." So concludes the newspaper story.

In my judgment this article is excessively severe regarding doctors and drug manufacturers. Most of the physicians whom I know are suggesting either spiritual or psychological solutions. Moreover, the elements out of which drugs are compounded were created by God and it is not unreasonable to assume that their proper use is within His purposes. Where tension has a definite physical cause the use of a drug seems not improper. But most tension is, perhaps, related not to soma but to psyche, not to body but to soul.

The profound question is, shall people get peace of mind from drugs or from the Gospel of Jesus Christ? Shall they turn to that which will satisfy no longer than the effect of a pill, or shall they put their faith in that which never passes away? How can any thoughtful person, unless he is totally unconcerned with the misery of men's lives, flippantly cast aside peace of mind?

I attended a Rotary Club luncheon at Interlaken, Switzerland. At my table was a physician. I asked him whether there is as wide prevalence of psychosomatic troubles and diseases of hypertension in Europe as in our own country. "Oh, you mean the manager's disease?" he responded. He felt that anyone who must carry responsibility is susceptible to the anxiety-tension complex.

The "manager's disease" is apparently an American problem, also, according to *Time* magazine which says, "After checking the health of more than twenty-five thousand executives averaging forty-five years old, New York's Life Extension examiners found that only twenty percent were in normal health. In Chicago three doctors examined fifty-five executives under fifty years of age and found that only three were entirely free from organic disorders. Of three hundred and forty Standard Oil of New Jersey executives reporting for a medical check-up, two hundred thirty-five had something wrong and one hundred and ninety-two had ills that would materially affect their working lives. The American Fidelity and Casualty Company found that the average businessman dies six years before his time."

Perhaps this condition is one reason, among others, why so many business people today are evidencing a new interest in the teachings of Jesus Christ. And that interest is well placed, for through it they can, indeed, find peace of mind and new power to live.

In a radio talk I told about a West Coast druggist who sent me a prescription blank made out by a Los Angeles physician for a patient. It carried the usual RX insignia, meaning "take thou," and the prescription read, simply, "Be Imperturbable." The pharmacist said it was the most difficult prescription to fill that ever came to his shop. "Despite all the claims made for them," he declared, "we haven't a pill on our shelves that can guarantee the treatment prescribed by the doctor. I told the patient that he had better go to church, read the Bible, learn to pray, and live a clean life. In effect," he declared, "I told him to fill the doctor's prescription at church."

Since relating that incident I have heard from a number of bookstores that customers have presented prescriptions from doctors for books designed to help the patient find inner quietness.

In the current stress on heart trouble, peace of mind is an important healing factor. Dr. John P. S. Cathcart of Ottawa told the Canadian Psychiatric Association that his studies have convinced him that heart attacks nearly always occur at times of high emotional tension. In general, job and family stresses are the most important factors in attacks of this kind. Avoidance of emotional stress is most important. And concludes Dr. Cathcart, "A useful anticoagulant is peace of mind."

Our trouble is that we push too hard. We are an over-tense, high-strung people. We need to learn the great art of being still. Several years ago my friend, Augustus L. Bering, after watching businessmen passing through the lobby of Hotel Sherman in Chicago where he is the manager said, "It seems that if a person misses just one section of a revolving door the day is practically ruined for him." I questioned if he did not mean one complete revolution rather than one section and he replied, "It used to be one complete revolution, but has now been stepped up to one section."

Recently Mr. Bering wrote me that the situation is even becoming worse, for he saw a man actually run for an escalator, brushing him aside to make one particular landing step. After landing, he did not walk on up, but stood triumphant with an air that implied, "Well, I made it!" And wisely asks Mr. Bering, "So what?"

The wisdom of Pascal applies today no less than in his own time: "Most of man's trouble comes from his inability to be still."

In gaining peace of mind an important step is to learn emotional self-management. This quality, like everything of value, comes only to those who use their own strength to get it. Emerson says, "Nothing can bring you peace but yourself." This means you will need to muster your will to eliminate all disorganizing thoughts, such as hate or fear or superstress. In so doing, you may require a spiritual operation to eliminate diseased thinking. And such unhealthy thought patterns can be very serious, often having definite physical results.

I delivered a sermon one Sunday in an Eastern community and discussed mental peace. A woman was present who had been attending that church regularly for some years. While a good person, apparently her religion had never penetrated to her emotional control center. She had quarreled violently with a number of people, particularly with an old friend. Her mind was filled with resentment and accompanying agitation.

For some time a rash had been on her body. The doctor finally diagnosed the skin irritation as "an outward manifestation of an inward emotional irritant"; in other words, her hate had broken out.

In the sermon I mentioned that unpeaceful thoughts can make us sick, and said that those who humbly desired it could find peace of mind. I then allowed a period of silence to ensue, during which the suggestion was made that all might experience a healing of thought and emotion. I stated that in achieving this result it was essential to empty out all unhealthy thoughts and sins. This woman humbly prayed for healing, asking forgiveness for her hates and other wrong attitudes. She really meant it, too. And when you are truly sincere, prayers become effective.

She reports that suddenly she felt "a warm feeling throughout her being." Then she became inwardly peaceful and "a sort of fresh clean happiness" began to surge through her mind.

A few days later she noticed that the rash was definitely reduced. Her physician encouraged her in the belief that she had experienced a cure. Within weeks the rash was gone altogether.

This incident was checked with the physician who said, "The facts are precisely as reported," and added, "this woman had allowed annoyance, irritation, and hate to accumulate in her mind to such an extent that it actually broke out into a physical rash. I believe the curative factor was the peace of mind which she developed."

It is not often that a lack of inner peace breaks out in actual physical irritation. But it is true that your emotional and mental system, and your physical being also, may be vitally affected by unquiet conditions in your inner life. Peace of mind heals.

My brother, Dr. Robert Clifford Peale, physician and surgeon, has had remarkable success in teaching his patients the healing qualities of urbanity. Not only does he administer medicine and perform surgery when needed, but he also encourages his patients to develop a quiet philosophy of life. This has had excellent results in improved physical conditions. He says: "I believe that doctors in the future will need a deeper understanding of the mental and emotional problems of their patients in order to help them."

Another effective method for gaining peace of mind is the practice of what I call "memorized peacefulness." By this is meant the mental storing up of peaceful impressions to draw upon as needed.

I discovered this procedure, quite by accident, during a stay at Atlantic City. I looked out at beach and ocean while working at the desk in my room. It was an overcast day with alternate cloud and fog and sunshine. Circling seagulls were crying in their hoarse manner. The ocean was washing languidly upon the sand. Now and then the sun would break through and a great streamer of light would pass across the water. Then it would fade as the mysterious fog closed in again from the sea. I found the scene quite restful and closed my eyes in a moment of relaxation.

While so doing I realized, of a sudden, that I could "see" this scene just as plainly with my eyes closed as with them open. I was, of course, beholding it in memory. But, I reasoned, if I could visualize it plainly one minute after actually viewing it, why could I not do the same one year or even ten years afterward. So, I began to use the technique of memorizing peacefulness, storing up in memory scenes of peace and quietness. In times of stress, I bring them out and they pass as pictures across my mind with healing effect.

Carl Erskine, famous Brooklyn Dodger baseball pitcher and my good friend, who has developed skill in relaxation and inner quietness, uses this interesting and successful method of "memorized peacefulness."

It helped him to achieve an all-time record for strikeouts in a World Series game, when he struck out fourteen New York Yankee batters.

When I commented to Carl upon his distinguished pitching career, he made the interesting remark that he had learned much in church that had helped him to arrive at Big League success. He says, "One sermon has helped me overcome pressure better than the advice of any coach. Its substance was that, like a squirrel hoarding chestnuts, we should store up our moments of happiness and triumph so that in a crisis we can draw upon these memories for help and inspiration.

"As a kid I used to fish at the bend of a little country stream just outside my home town. I can vividly remember this post in the middle of a big, green pasture surrounded by tall, cool trees. Whenever tension builds up both on or off the ball field, I concentrate on this relaxing scene, and the knots inside me loosen up." This practice of "memorized peacefulness" is an extraordinary technique for relaxation and mental peace.

The practice of quietness in the physical body is also important. Your mental state and your muscle tensions are closely related. Note the many evidences of muscle tension within yourself: restless movement of the hands, drumming of the fingers, stroking the cheek, chair squirming, even nail biting. Some years ago, I became convinced that reduction of muscle tension would help reduce mental tension. So I began experimenting with bodily-stillness techniques in connection with spiritual practice.

One method I employ is to use the words: "Be still, and know that I am God," (Psalm 46:10) as a practical physical relaxation formula. In bed, ready for a good night's rest, I get into a comfortable position and then say: "Be still, my muscles, and know God's relaxation. Be still, my nerves, and know God's rest. Be still, my heart, and know God's quietness. Be still, my body, and know God's renewal. Be still, my mind, and know God's peace." This should be repeated several times.

John Masefield who used a somewhat similar procedure referred to it as "the getting of tranquility."

An amazingly effective method of *peacefulizing* the mind is the getting of tension out of the physical body. Incidentally, it will help you go to sleep.

Of the many other techniques for creating mental peace and stimulating your power center, I wish to single out a practice which I like to term "aggressive activation." That is but another way of saying, "Stop fretting and do something constructive about your problem." When you face an upsetting situation do not work yourself into an emotional state, but ask yourself what you can do about it and then start doing the wisest thing you can think of. It is remarkable how quickly you will begin to experience peace of mind about the matter. This attitude will deepen your mental control and help bring about a constructive solution.

An illustration of this method is the case of a woman who telephoned me from her home in the far West. "I am distressed and almost desperate," she sobbed. "I have just discovered that my husband is having an affair with another woman. She is younger than I, and more attractive.

"This has come as a terrible shock. I never suspected anything. My husband and I have worked hard for all we now have. I suppose I have become rather old and, now that he has arrived, he wants someone with more glamour. But I must try to accept it. Please pray for me that I may bear it."

"Yes," I said, "I will, but why not go further and pray that you take over again?"

"What would be the use," she said dully. "It wouldn't be dignified and besides it's all over."

"I wouldn't be too concerned about dignity," I said. "He is your husband and you love him. And besides, you should save him from himself. As for it being all over, the election isn't always decided until the last precinct has been heard from. With God's help, I would get him away from that other woman."

"Tell me what to do," she asked meekly.

"I have never met you, Madam," I replied, "so would you be kind enough to describe yourself to me? Are you a handsome person?"

"Why," she said with some hesitation, "they used to say I was one of the prettiest girls in this section."

"Don't they say that anymore?" I asked.

"Why, no," she replied. "You see, I am forty-five."

"What has being forty-five got to do with it?" I asked. "Go and take a look at yourself in the mirror. I'm sure your basic beauty is still there."

"I have lines in my face," she told me, "and I'm tired and right now, I am pretty bitter, too."

"Perhaps if you got the tiredness and bitterness out of your mind, the lines would be erased from your face, and the old charm would return," I said.

"Think of the advantages you have," I counseled. "You have a legal marriage to your husband. You have years of association behind you, and in that there is deeper sentiment than you think. You have an immense advantage over this younger person, for their relationship is not honest, but furtive, and so is on an unstable basis.

"Hold a picture in your mind of the restored relationship. Pray with compassion for this poor woman who is making the mistake of thinking there is something in this for her. Stand up to this problem.

"If it is just vitality that she has, you can have vitality too, only in a deeper sense. Pray those depressive thoughts out of your mind and attack this problem constructively."

After some weeks she wrote me, "Through God's help my husband and I are rebuilding our marriage on a strong spiritual foundation. Had we done that in the first place I don't believe this would have happened."

When this woman practiced aggressive activism and went constructively to work on her problem, she began to have mental peace. Her mind cooled from its hysterical state. And when the mind is cool it begins to function efficiently. The purpose of the mind is to think, which it cannot do when overwrought. Thus, peace of mind is of practical importance for it releases that quality of mind-power which produces constructive results.

Having peace of mind may be as simple as cultivating unemotional common sense. Just make up your mind to stop being upset. You have enough potential will power to do that if and when you really want to. I had an interesting talk with one of the most famous baseball pitchers of all time, the late Cy Young. Even in the era of iron men in baseball he was a sensation. He started in eight hundred seventy-four games and won five hundred eleven, a record that has never been broken.

Also, his record of twenty-three consecutive hitless innings stands unchallenged. In fourteen seasons he won twenty or more games. In five seasons he won more than thirty.

"During your baseball career were you ever nervous or tense?" I asked.

Cy looked at me with genuine surprise. "Why, of course not," he replied. "I wasn't made that way. And besides, what sense would there be to that?"

I asked his opinion of today's pitchers as compared with his day. He admired some current pitchers but added, "In the old days managers did not jerk them out of the game at the first sign they were in pitching trouble. In my time we just stayed in there and pitched our way out of trouble."

That is a power-packed idea. And peace of mind develops that control with which you can "pitch your way out of trouble."

With peace at the center you can handle crisis situations efficiently. Not being emotionally motivated, you can think. The power of controlled thought is immense.

An example of a man whose peace of mind enabled him to deal with a great crisis in masterly fashion is my friend F. W. Delve, C.B.E., chief officer of the London Fire Brigade. Little did Mr. Delve realize the terrible responsibility that would come to him one tragic night when twenty-five hundred fires burned simultaneously in London. It was the first great incendiary bombing and it seemed that London, like ancient Rome, might burn to death.

"We looked the situation over, and it seemed a bit bad. But we spent no time telling ourselves how badly it looked. We just took things as they came and tried to do our job. The bombing and burning continued for one hundred and twenty successive nights. We had to save everything we held dear, and so we went ahead and saved it," was his very casual explanation of one of the most astonishing defense actions in history.

When seeking peace of mind remember the importance of aggressive activation. Instead of a purely emotional reaction, do something constructive about the situation.

It is important, also, to develop slower-paced emotional reactions in gaining peace of mind. This can be accomplished by practice. One way to do this is to picture yourself as reacting calmly under every circumstance. Since we tend to become what we imagine ourselves to be this practice will, in time, give you such a habit of mental peace that it will be very

difficult to shake your composure. One man of impressive emotional control has the policy of "never getting mad until twenty-four hours later."
He scientifically analyzes an annoyance and lets its heat simmer down,
meanwhile mentally seeing himself as meeting it with control. He prays
for guidance and considers all phases of the matter in an objective, dispassionate and scientific manner. He also applies to it a benign good humor.
Almost invariably, within twenty-four hours he is able to handle the situation without anger.

We do not fully comprehend what we can do with our emotions. When
we control them we have power. When they control us the results are
often disastrous.

A friend says that his father, when irritated or provoked, instead of
flying into rage, "flies into a great calm." To have peace of mind discipline
yourself never to get mad or resentful. This, of course, is difficult. But as
stated throughout this book, important emotional victories in life are
never easy. But they are possible, and that is the vital fact. To aid in self-
discipline hold this text in mind, "When he giveth quietness, who then
can make trouble." (Job 34:29) This means that God will give you a depth
of inner peace so that nothing or nobody can trouble you.

Many destroy their peace of mind by being grievance collectors. Even if
there is adequate cause for such feelings, still, the nursing of grievance
isn't worth the emotional effort. It can only create a prickly condition in
your mind which will disturb your peacefulness and emotionally condition
your reactions. Then you are so likely to do and say things which are
bound to be ill-advised. The net result will be one of harm to yourself.
Nobody can develop upper-level personality power who allows himself to
collect and hold grievance. The only sane attitude to take toward a grievance, even injustice, is simply to forget it, skip it, let it go by. In this way
you will handle yourself with dignity and skill and enjoy the benefit of
peace of mind.

Moreover, by reacting to injury, injustice, and hostility in this spiritual
manner and with emotional control, you will develop a power that your
detractors do not have. Not only will you have the satisfying consciousness that you can absorb into the equanimity of your spirit criticism and
the attacks of jealous and unfair individuals as they come, but gradually, by
your powerful control, you will gain the understanding and esteem of all
fair-minded people.

In attaining peace of mind the ultimate method is to establish a close
contact with God. As you live in harmony with His teachings, gradually
you will build up a very strong consciousness of His presence. When that
occurs there will come to you a deep and profound peace that nothing can
shatter. Then you will be able to handle your difficulties with greatly
increased effectiveness.

Finally, many people are without peace of mind and therefore lacking in

the power to live effectively because of their sense of guilt. This is so vital
to peace of mind and power that I urge you to eliminate at once anything
that is wrong. Have a spiritual operation on yourself and get all moral
fester removed. Be absolutely honest and ask yourself the straight question, "Am I doing anything that is wrong according to the laws of God
and the teachings of Jesus Christ?" Peace of mind and greater strength
will come in as moral wrong goes out. It will be an exchange of great
advantage to you.

One morning in a dining car the steward seated me at a table for two. A
woman sat opposite. I was reading the morning paper, when of a sudden
the train, which was traveling at a high rate of speed, gave a noticeable
lurch and this woman cried out with real fear in her tone.

"Oh," she exclaimed, "that lurch. Don't you think this train is going
awfully fast?"

"Well," I said, "it does go right along, but not too fast, I am sure."

"Many more such lurches and we will be wrecked," she said nervously.

"Oh, I don't think so. This train makes this trip every night and I never
heard of it being wrecked."

"Maybe this will be the time," she said fearfully.

"Oh, I doubt it. The law of averages is with us."

Then she said, "I had a lower berth last night and couldn't sleep for
worrying because I had read in the paper where a woman out west was
murdered in a lower berth."

Next she told me she had to get home because she was worried about
her children. "Oh, I am worried about so many things."

"You have already told me three things you are worried about—the
lurching of the train, possible murder in a lower berth, and your children.
How many more fears have you?" I asked.

"Oh, I've a lot of them." Then she asked, "Why do people have so
many fears?"

"There are many reasons. Sometimes fears are projected on one by
parents, unconsciously; or perhaps people with whom you associate infect
you with their fears. Sometimes people develop fears from a sense of guilt,
some wrong they have done. There are lots of reasons." When I mentioned the one about guilt, she immediately called the steward, paid her
check and left without another word. I was troubled that I might have
offended her in some way, but could not see how, so went back to my
paper.

Later on my way through the train, I saw this woman crying bitterly. I
passed her, then returned and said, "Madam, I hope I didn't say anything
to hurt your feelings."

"Oh, no," she said, "I am just so upset."

"If I can help you in any way, I will be glad to," I replied.

She looked up at me and asked, "What are you? A psychiatrist, or some kind of a doctor, or something?"

"No, none of these. I am a minister of the Gospel. Here is my card, and when you are in New York I hope you will worship in our church."

"I no longer go to church. You see—I'm a—bad woman," she replied so quietly I could scarcely hear.

"That is all the more reason why you should go to church," I said. "The church is for bad women and bad men, as well as for good people. Why do you say you are a bad woman?" I asked.

"Why am I telling you these things?" she said.

"Perhaps God wants you to," I replied. "Maybe you had better get it out of your mind. Why do you think you are a bad person?" I persisted.

"Because I have been away with a married man, and it bothers me."

"Of course that would bother you. You see your actions are contrary to what you really are." Then I explained how moral lesion creates intense conflicts and fears. "You are suffering from an acute sense of guilt. And your guilt makes you afraid. You are sick and you need a physician. You need to be healed in your mind and soul."

"What can I do?" she asked. "I'm so unhappy."

"There is only one thing to do and that is to ask God's help. Start by immediately quitting your wrong-doing. Then ask for forgiveness. Simply tell me as a pastor that you are sorry for your wrong-doing and that, with God's help, you want to live a righteous life. You have committed sin in an acute form but you are not really a bad woman. You are a woman who is thinking and acting badly. Essentially, you are a good woman, so you are in conflict between what you want to be and what you are. Through forgiveness, God will change you. Then your fears will gradually pass and you can have peace of mind."

I gave her the name of an understanding and competent minister in her city who helped her to find new life. He counseled her; she accepted his guidance, and she is now living on an entirely different basis; no longer is she filled with fear. She has found peace of mind. With it she has gained power over her weakness. She is another of those who know the meaning of living dynamically.

I wish to conclude this chapter by giving you an excellent formula for having peace of mind. It was given me by an old friend, Fred Fuller, a prominent attorney of Toledo, Ohio. Mr. Fuller suffered a serious illness during which he had a struggle with tension and unrest of spirit. A thoughtful physician gave him a "Creed" which proved very beneficial. Mr. Fuller, who carries it on a card in his wallet, read it to me. It seems so wise and helpful that I want to make it available to you.

1. Conserve your energy, i.e. don't race your motor.
   a. Do not rush—work, eat, and play leisurely.
   b. Do not get overtired at work or play.
   c. Be moderate in eating, drinking, smoking, working—everything you do.
   d. Do not hesitate to refuse to take on unimportant, burdensome tasks.
2. Stay calm and serene. Do not fret or worry or allow yourself to become unnecessarily involved in situations fraught with emotion.
   a. The past is past.
   b. Do your best today and let it go at that.
   c. Do not be apprehensive of tomorrow—it will take care of itself—most worries never come to pass.
   d. Put your trust in God and forget all fear. He has a plan for you and in such a situation who can be against you?

You can have peace of mind and with it the power to live more effectively.

13

HOW TO FEEL WELL
AND HAVE VIBRANT HEALTH

"Even as airplane engines must be tuned up before taking off, so must a human being have a tuning-up process. The body has many miles of blood vessels and nerves to stimulate, if you want to travel in high gear. And your mental and spiritual elements also require constant attunement to keep them functioning at full potential."

STOP DYING, and start living. And live vitally all your life. Either you are growing or you are dying. That is the law of life. And the secret of growing may be as simple as making up your mind to put the accent on life as did the writer of the following animated letter:

Dear Dr. Peale,

I have been a victim of nerves and fear for over twenty years. My husband died about twenty-two years ago and I tried to take out an insurance policy, being then forty-seven years old. I was turned down. I went to my family doctor and asked him what was wrong with me, and he told me that there were a lot of things the matter, that I could expect anything, any time.

Well, I just gave up and have thought, every time I get sick, "Now I'm going to die." I have lived this dying-life for over twenty years. Finally, I remarried, thinking I should have someone to take care of me and bury me.

Now, at the age of sixty-nine, after reading your book* and memorizing the Scripture verses as you said to do, I feel wonderful and I am going to quit dying and start living all over again.

There is a woman who made up her mind to be alive and who took the first necessary step toward being alive, that of filling her mind with lifegiving thoughts. When her spirit came alive she began to feel alive and well.

One memorable night years ago I learned how faith helps in restoring life, for I saw one of the greatest laws, the law of health, in actual operation. It was two o'clock in the morning. The ringing of the telephone roused me from a deep sleep. The voice was that of a prominent physician

* The Power of Positive Thinking.

who said, "I have a case that isn't yielding to my treatment. My patient is in a crisis and I need help. Will you come immediately?"

This request startled me. What help could I give? I remember standing at the door of that home before pressing the bell, and praying for guidance.

The doctor took me into the living room and I asked, "What can I say to a patient under these circumstances? Is she conscious or unconscious?"

"Intermittently both," he answered, "but I don't want you to say anything to the patient. Remember, the Bible says that where two or three are gathered in His name He is in their midst to help. So, you and I, a minister and a doctor—two, as in the Bible's formula—are going into that room and fill it to overflowing with faith in the healing Grace of Jesus Christ.

"As her human physician, I have done all of which I am capable. But I am also an agent of the Great Physician. I treat the patient, but God must heal. Science now needs the help of the spiritual. And," he added, "you and I are partners because you, too, are a servant of God, and as such you also are charged with the responsibility of healing."

So, as a team, we entered the patient's room. The doctor sat on one side of the bed, I on the other, and each of us quoted Scripture passages. The patient was restless and feverish. I offered a prayer. The doctor prayed. I prayed again, and he prayed still another time until we both became startlingly aware of a Presence; *The* Presence. Apparently the patient did, too, for her restlessness stopped. She opened her eyes and looked at us with a very sweet smile; then she fell asleep.

We sat for perhaps an hour, praying and talking about God and His healing power. We focused an harmonious spiritual fellowship on the situation. We recounted the healing of Jesus. Presently I became aware that this spiritual conversation was actually being absorbed into the consciousness of the patient, for the change in her was marked, even to my unpracticed eye. Finally the doctor said, "The crisis has passed. She will get well."

This experience was also a turning point in my life. I was so moved that I could not sleep the remainder of the night, but walked the streets in great excitement. For the first time I began to see that I had been making a serious mistake in teaching only a highly ethical religion. I had seen a power actually at work that was beyond ethics or science. I had looked skeptically upon the supernatural. I had thought of religion, basically, as a system of ethics and theology, concerned with moral betterment and the improvement of social conditions, primarily the latter. I regarded medicine as concerned only with the cure of disease through materialistic processes.

That Christianity might have any important relationship to health had never gripped my thinking. I was a strict materialist and regarded as cranks those who related stories of healings where faith was claimed as a factor. My experience with the dedicated doctor, and other subsequent incidents, taught me that the Christian Gospel is dynamically applicable to sickness; that Jesus Christ is not only the healer of our souls, but of our minds and bodies as well.

So, for years now, I have taught that the practice of the principles of religion, in connection with medical guidance, can help you feel alive and well. Today we know that God works in at least two ways in healing people: through His servant the practitioner of medical science, and through His servant the practitioner of spiritual faith.

When we apply this joint therapy to human problems we discover that many people do not feel alive and well because their minds are poisoned by wrong thinking. They hate, they are resentful, they are tense and frustrated, they are filled with fear. That the body can be adversely affected by unhealthy thinking is generally realized today.

The Reader's Digest carried an important article entitled, "Stress—the Cause of All Disease?" in which Dr. Hans Selye, a prominent medical research scientist, outlined his theory that all disease is caused by a chemical imbalance in the body due, primarily, to stress. He bases his conclusion on the fact that the chemical balance within the body is governed, mainly, by three tiny glands: the pituitary and the two adrenals. The pituitary lies at the base of the brain and the two adrenals lie astride the kidneys.

"These three glands, together, weigh no more than a third of an ounce, and their principal job is to adapt the body to all manner of stress. If you are chilled, the arteries constrict and raise the blood pressure to produce greater warmth. When bacteria invade the body, the glands provide hormones to produce inflammation which walls off infection. In case of severe injury, they hasten the clotting of the blood, lower blood pressure to control hemorrhage, increase blood sugar to provide quick energy, decrease sensitivity to pain. It is the task of the pituitary and the adrenal hormones to combat stress and fight off any threat to the body's welfare."

But, as Dr. Selye points out, "in this hurry-up world we are subjecting ourselves to too many stresses. We hurry constantly and worry incessantly. The businessman drives himself at his office all day, then worries half the night. The housewife tries to run her home, maintain a social life, and participate in community activities and at bedtime is so jangled that she takes a sleeping pill.

"Glands attempt to adjust to the continual demands of constantly increasing stress. They pour out excess hormones, trying to keep the body going. For a while they succeed, but in the end the defense mechanism itself breaks down. As a result, arteries harden, blood pressure rises, heart disease develops, arthritis strikes. These and other diseases are all part of the stress picture."

Recently a nose and throat specialist said to me, "In your books and articles remind people of the harm they are doing to themselves by stress in the form of hate, vindictiveness, resentment, and frustration." This physician told me, further, that over one-third of his patients have ear, nasal, or sinus trouble, not for physiological reasons, but because of their resentments, anxieties and other conflicts.

He told of one man who came to his office whenever he caught cold, which was rather frequently. The doctor discovered the interesting and revealing fact that every such cold was preceded by a fight with his wife. The tissues were actually affected by changes brought on by intense emotional stress. (I am not saying that every time you have a cold you have been fighting with your wife!) The doctor declared, also, that dizziness, ringing in the ears, temporary deafness, nervous tension, and pressure may often be attributed to ill will, fear, anger, and other forms of wrong thinking. It seems that we are just catching up with the Bible which always linked disease with wrong-doing.

Dr. Karl B. Pace of Greenville, North Carolina, was recently honored as National Country Doctor of the Year. When I asked the chief cause of sickness his quick reply was, "Nerves and tension." He gave some worthwhile advice: "Live each day as it comes. Don't worry about next week. Learn to live instead of trying to get rich. Never remain angry. Begin each day by liking everyone you meet. Take a siesta after lunch to help you relax. Marital quarrels can cause your ulcers, your headaches, or other pains. If either the husband or wife would try one-twentieth as hard to make a go of marriage as finding fault with each other, you would probably have no problems. Never go to bed angry with each other. Go to church, practice your religion, and live a quiet and serene life."

Another physician says: "Many patients could have good health if they would simply practice the therapy of their religion; really use prayer and faith in their daily lives." Another doctor states: "Many of my ailing patients could be well if they would have a real experience of God." A clinic examination was made of five hundred patients. It was found that the illness of some three hundred eighty-eight, or about seventy-seven percent was traceable to psychosomatic causes. The doctor picturesquely commented, "These persons are draining back into their bodies the diseased thoughts of their minds."

Another physician believes so profoundly in the unity of religion and health that on his waiting room table he places religious books and a copy of the Holy Bible. These books are well used, according to the office secretary. Still another physician with an apt gift of expression, said, "Beat wear and tear by prayer and care."

The dynamic effect of Jesus Christ in creating health and vitality is described in a dramatic scene. He stood on a plain by the sea, the waters sparkling like dancing diamonds in the sunlight. Snowy peaks grazed the sky in the distance. A vast multitude surrounded Him as He stood tall and erect, the picture of health and vitality. They were conscious of power flowing from Him, of the emanation of a vital force.

The multitude, which surged around Him, came bringing the lame and the blind and those that were "vexed" in their minds. These people instinctively knew they were in the presence of dynamic power. They had faith and healings resulted. The Bible describes the event in these words, "And the whole multitude sought to touch him: for there went virtue out of him, and healed them all." (Luke 6:19)

We are also told that "Jesus Christ is the same yesterday, and today, and forever" (Hebrews 13:8), which means that the same power is available now if, with similar faith, we ask help. Obviously you cannot touch Christ with your physical hand as they did long ago. But there is a more subtle way to reach Him: by sending out faith thoughts from your mind to His. The outstretched hand or the outstretched thought; each expresses faith, and it is faith that releases the healing force.

The experience of a man in Georgia is typical. He writes: "For some time I have had it in mind to write you a word of appreciation for a wonderful experience that came to me when I was in the hospital with a heart condition which had been brought on by stress and overpressure.

"I felt that I would never be able to work again, for all power and strength had gone out of me. That morning you suggested something in your radio talk that started me on the road to recovery and now I am able to do my work and I feel better than I have felt for years. I still practice the thing you suggested.

"First, you asked the people in that hospital to get quiet; then to start thinking of God touching the feet and following with His healing touch over the entire body until it became a mass of the thought of God and His power to heal. I remember doing that, and I affirmed as you directed, 'Think of the hand of Jesus Christ as touching your feet and every member of your body and finally resting on your heart, and hear Him say, "Let not your heart be troubled." (John 14:27) Then feel His hand resting upon your head.' By the time I had finished that process I felt calm and confident about my condition. I got well, and ever since that time I have felt vigorous and strong." This man, in a hospital, no less than those long ago on the hillsides, reached out by faith and touched Christ and was healed.

A real cause of ill health is ill will. This malady is well named, for it is actually "sick will." Having allowed ill will to accumulate and its inevitable accompaniment of guilt to clog the mind, naturally your vital powers are depressed. Sick feeling results. The cure of this condition is good will, that is to say, "well will." This may be accomplished by a shift to the attitude of love and the healing qualities which it generates.

I was once asked to see a man who had every material thing that anyone

could seemingly want in life. He had been so abjectly catered to by everyone that if any person had the effrontery to differ, even slightly, with him
he would seethe in resentment. One associate had opposed him rather
vigorously and this tycoon had developed what literally amounted to hatred for this man whom he accused of "double-crossing him," though this
appraisal was not true.

He had dwelt upon this man's honest difference of opinion to such an
extent that he could think only evil of his business associate. This ill will
had gone on for some months. At the time I saw him he complained of a
small appetite and of not being able to sleep. His stomach was also causing
considerable discomfort. Moreover, he had developed pain, particularly in
his hands and fingers.

The doctor had diagnosed this trouble as a type that could be healed by
treatment of his emotional state. "In fact," said the man, "the doctor says
that I can get over it if I 'get myself straightened out.' "

"What do you mean, 'straightened out'?" I asked.

"I mean straightened out in my mind. But the worst thing bothering me
most is my right arm. I can't seem to raise it higher than my shoulder, try
as hard as I will, nor can I fully clench my fist. I can close it about nine-
tenths of the way, but that is as far as I can manipulate it, and I feel a lack
of force in my hand."

As we talked, a curious and repetitive emphasis came out in his speech.
As he discussed the man whom he declared had double-crossed him, he
fumed, saying explosively, "I would give my right arm if I could smash
that guy." Referring to several other people whom he disliked, he kept
coming back to that figure, that if he could only retaliate against them he
would "give his right arm." Apparently in his mind the picture of giving
his right arm was, for him, a sufficient characterization of the virulence of
his ill will.

I do not wish to press this diagnosis too far. It is perhaps almost too apt
and simple, but I made a long guess and said, "I think that right arm of
yours might actually be inhibited by hate. To feel well and vital, maybe
you'd better empty out the poisons and acids of antagonism through the
curative force of love."

"How in the world do I do that?" he asked.

"It's just this simple," I said. "Pray for that man you hate until you
actually pray out the hate and pray in love. You will have to forgive and
forget and attain for that man good will—well will—if you hope to be
well."

This man was a very forthright individual, and it was with great difficulty that I persuaded him to employ the suggested cure. But he is one of
those strong characters who goes all out for anything, whether it be hate
or love; so when he finally decided to practice love he gave full coopera-

tion. I told him that the way to get rid of hate and substitute love was, while praying for the disliked man, to try and see the good in him rather than the bad. I encouraged him to adopt an objective and scientific attitude toward his hates, thinking of them as symptoms of an illness that required treatment.

When he was convinced that he could eliminate the ill will that was making him suffer physically by praying for his enemy he began practicing this healing formula. I asked him to pray out loud to be sure he had the right approach. It was a bit amusing because halfway through the prayer he stopped and addressed the Lord, colloquially, though not without proper respect, "Lord, I'm a fourflusher and I don't really mean this prayer. I'm only doing it because I'm told to."

But I interrupted and said, "but you've got to mean it, and you must pray until you do mean it."

"O.K.," he said, "let's start praying again and I'll make myself mean it." Note that he did not qualify his intention by even saying he would try, but would make himself mean it. If I know the Lord at all I'm sure He likes honest and forthright men like this one.

He finally got to the point where he could actually pray for the other man. And then things really began to happen. Power came through. I cannot report that all of a sudden, miraculously, he raised his right arm. He had a lot of deep-lodged sin and spiritual weakness in him, and it took many weeks of this stiff curative process to drain it out, but drain it out he did.

Recently I saw him, and with a grin he said, "Look at that arm." He raised it full above his head. He chuckled and declared as he demonstrated, "I can clench my fist, too, and I could sure hit that bird now, but do you know, the funny thing is I no longer want to hit him because I really like him. We have come to understand each other. I like that fellow because I always know exactly where he stands." (That characteristic was what originally caused his dislike.)

This industrialist became a man of vital energies. He feels well and is very alive. Moreover, he has brought to his new spiritual interest the same thoroughness that gave him success in business. He reads and studies the Bible and other religious writings meticulously. He applies Christian principles in business and has become extraordinarily service-minded. He explained his reversal of attitude from his former self-centeredness by explaining: "You must share God's blessings, for you cannot keep them unless you also give them away." How right he is. People who seek God's power only for what it can do for them will be frustrated unless they become a medium through which the benefit is conveyed to others.

Still another illustration of the strange manner in which unhealthy thinking and attitudes conspire to reduce aliveness, is a case history which was reported to me by a pastor who conducts healing services with considerable success.

To a healing service came a middle-aged woman who walked with a noticeable limp. She waited for the pastor afterwards and said, "Of late this limp has developed and my doctor says there is apparently nothing he can do for me, that it must represent some hidden injury to the muscles. Will you please pray for me?"

"No," was the surprising answer of the pastor. "I will not pray *for* you, but I will pray *with* you. We will make the prayer a cooperative spiritual enterprise, not primarily to ask relief for your trouble, but to ascertain what has happened within you, spiritually and psychologically, that has manifested itself in this physical condition. We must probe for possible psychosomatic and spiritual ills." He then prayed that the woman might receive insight, and she went away. She returned to several successive healing services, and each time the pastor had a private exploratory prayer with her, asking for guidance. But still the limp continued.

Finally, after one prayer session, she said, slowly, "An idea keeps coming to mind in my prayers. It is this: my daughter and son-in-law formerly lived with me and I simply could not abide my son-in-law. I detested him, and not long ago we had a big row. My daughter took his part against me. It was a terrible experience and it left me limp in my mind and spirit. And it was not long afterward that the limp developed in my leg. It never occurred to me that there could possibly be a connection between my physical condition and my feeling toward my son-in-law and daughter. The notion is preposterous, isn't it?"

"One way to find whether there is any connection is to remove the barrier between the young couple and yourself and then see what happens in the physical problem," the minister replied.

The woman decided to go to her son-in-law and daughter and tell them she was sorry for her attitude. She said, in reporting to her pastor, "I hesitated at first, fearing they might not receive me, and I did not want to be humiliated. I continued to pray and finally, I went to their house. They were surprised and cool at first, but when I told them how sorry I was, that I hadn't acted right and wanted to correct my attitude and have their forgiveness, they were very kind. We had a genuine reconciliation and," she added, "I'm surprised at what a nice person my son-in-law really is; and he seems to like me, too, believe it or not."

As the pastor watched the woman walk from the church he had the impression that she was improved, but was hesitant to expect a seemingly miraculous result. But, after some weeks, the woman became aware that she was walking normally again. The minister tells me that physicians authenticate the case and, in fact, one remarked, "People limp in and out of my office whose basic illness is in the emotions; yes, perhaps in the soul."

Do not conclude from this that everybody you see limping around your community has had a fight with someone in the family or is filled with hate. I only cite this as an illustration of the apparent relationship between unhealthy thinking and feeling.

You can stay dynamically alive by flushing out of your mind the unhealthy attitudes which act as depressants and then by filling your mind with those creative thoughts which faith stimulates. Aliveness depends upon the penetration into the personality of a stimulating, transforming, and vitalizing faith.

Aliveness and a sense of dynamic being do not come easily. Values of this importance cannot be achieved without spiritual "blood, sweat, and tears," to use Churchill's famous phrase. It is hard to change a wrong mental cast developed over many years. Sometimes a person may have such a tremendous spiritual experience that he is changed very quickly and dramatically. But, for the most part, we must painstakingly work and practice our way to vital well-being.

An excellent suggestion for practicing aliveness was given me by a dynamic and energetic friend, Melvin J. Evans. An expert in management engineering, industrial relations, and marketing, Mr. Evans likes to describe himself as a "human engineer." His achievement in the field of personality rehabilitation through industry is outstanding. Mr. Evans maintains an almost incredible schedule of speeches and conferences in addition to regular business activities.

I asked the secret of his energetic and joyful aliveness of body, mind, and spirit. He believes it possible to develop a daily rhythm that stimulates energy and vitality. He described a recent schedule: "I have been out on conferences and lectures for two days straight. I came in on the plane at seven o'clock tonight and leave by plane again at eight tomorrow morning and for the next three days will be busy from early morning until late at night. I have been able to develop zest and energy for this activity through the following routine.

"First, every morning breathe very slowly and deeply, stretching meanwhile.

"Second, repeat the Twenty-third Psalm slowly and prayerfully, stopping after each phrase to express thanksgiving."

That is a quite interesting technique. For example, the first phrase in the Twenty-third Psalm is, "The Lord is my shepherd." After saying that, meditate on the way God has watched over you and taken care of you. The next phrase in the Psalm is, "I shall not want." After repeating those words, reflect, thankfully, that you do not lack food or shelter. Since hearing of this technique I have practiced it myself and find it amazingly effective and stimulating.

"Third, make a similar use of the Lord's Prayer, briefly stopping to be thankful after each phrase.

"Fourth, turn on the radio to a marching tune and really step out for a few moments." Mr. Evans says he used to be hesitant about suggesting this procedure until he read that Winston Churchill uses it. He puts on his bathrobe, a cane over his shoulder, and really prances around every morning.

"Fifth, stop several times every day for two minutes of prayer." Consider the potential value of this. It means twenty to thirty minutes a day of prayer, and a different kind of prayer at that, the thanksgiving, joyful type. Contrast this with your usual, depressing thoughts, not for thirty minutes, but for several hours a day. They take the life out of you. These brief prayers of thanksgiving and joy and faith will have a powerful tonic effect on you.

"Sixth, whenever an interruption comes, fill it by taking a half dozen breaths and saying a quick prayer."

This daily tune up of body, mind, and spirit may be effectively aided by spiritual reading and meditation. Supply yourself with books or booklets that are scientifically constructive in spiritual practice. I have prepared a booklet, *Thought Conditioners** which may be helpful.

Even as airplane engines must be tuned up before taking off, so must a human being have a tuning up process. The body has many miles of blood vessels and nerves to stimulate, if you want to travel in high gear. And your mental and spiritual elements also require constant attunement to keep them functioning at full potential.

When you contemplate the bad effect of years of unhealthy thinking on your mental and emotional nature, you can understand why the verve and spring goes out of you. To feel alive and well, daily revitalize your entire being with dynamic spiritual thinking, with exercise, and with the observance of the laws of health.

No one needs to go drooping and crawling through life. Jesus Christ teaches a method that makes people come alive, makes them joyous and vibrant.

When you live contrary to the truth which Christ teaches, you actually siphon off your own dynamism and drain your basic vitality. Wrong thinking and living can so undermine personality that, in effect, it may give up completely and produce nervous breakdown. It can even kill you. Dr. Charles Mayo is reported to have said, "I never knew a man to die of overwork but I have known them to die of doubt." It appears that faith is more even than creed or thoughts; it is life force. When faith declines and wrong thinking dominates, the personality sickens.

*   *   *

* May be had free of charge by addressing request to Peale Center for Christian Living, 66 East Main Street, Pawling, New York 12564.

The following suggestions may help you to feel alive and well:

1. Send for your minister even as you call your doctor when illness comes.
2. Believe in the healing Grace of Christ and affirm that it is operating in you.
3. Think of your body as the temple of the soul and treat it with respect.
4. Empty out all resentment and hate.
5. Pray for your doctor that he may have healing skill as a servant of the Great Physician.
6. Keep body, mind, and soul spiritually tuned up by daily periods of exercise and thanksgiving.
7. Visualize health and wholeness and entertain no sick thoughts about yourself or loved ones.
8. Believe that God, who creates, can also re-create, and think of the re-creative process as operating within you at all times.
9. Study and practice the spiritual rules of health contained in the Bible.
10. Remember the famous statement of Ambroise Pare, one of the most noted physicians of Europe, "Je le pansay, Dieu le guarit"—"I dressed him, God cured him."

14

SELF-CONFIDENCE
AND DYNAMIC ACHIEVEMENT

"Many people, perhaps most people, never utilize the potential strength within their own personalities. There is resident in you an immense reservoir of force; the power of the subconscious mind. Faith releases this power. Then, mental, emotional, and spiritual strength emerges which is more than enough to override your defeats."

FROM INFANTILE PARALYSIS to world champion high-jumper, that is the thrilling story of Walter Davis. It was said that he could not walk again. But his minister planted creative faith in his mind. His mother nurtured that faith, and lovingly worked over his weakened legs until he could walk and, presently, even run.

One day he saw a boy high-jumping and thought this a sport he would like to try. He did quite well at it, so decided he would become the best high-jumper in the world. What audacity faith puts into our minds!

But his legs were still weak. When he married, his wife watched his painstaking efforts to strengthen them and she said, "Walter, you must have power in your mind, too." Then she coined a wonderful phrase: "The strength of belief; with that you will have the strength you need in your legs."

Walter Davis put his wife's suggestion into practice and, eventually, it brought him a world record. In a championship field meet he cleared the bar at six feet, eleven inches, then at six, eleven and a half. The bar was raised to six, eleven and five-eighths. On his first jump he knocked the bar down; on the second jump, the same. He lay on the ground for a moment's rest and repeated to himself, "The strength of belief." He painted a mental picture of himself clearing that bar, propelled by the strength of belief. Then, before a hushed stadium, he jumped and went over the bar at six, eleven and five-eighths! The boy they said might never walk again was champion high-jumper of the world!

The strength of belief is your key to self-confidence. It will more than help you meet and overcome your difficulties and obstacles.

There is a text in the Bible which is fundamental in attaining self-confidence. It is so powerful that if driven deeply into your consciousness, it can change your life.

"If God be for us, who can be against us?" (Romans 8:31)

Personalize those words so that they apply directly to you, say "If God be for *me*." Then bring to mind a picture of all the things you think are against you. Now bring a picture into your mind of God facing your obstacles. Can they stand against God? Practice the strength of belief.

No hazard, obstacle, or difficulty need defeat you. Accept that as a fact, hold that confidence firmly in mind until it becomes reality, and you will have mastered one of the greatest secrets in this life. But this must be a humble faith in God and not bumptious faith in your own power. Every day fill and refill your mind to overflowing with that kind of faith until your thinking is thoroughly reconditioned.

Faith, the greatest power in this world, moves mountains and hurls obstacles aside. It overrides so-called impossibles. It crushes fear. It makes life vital, dynamic, and joyful. The answer to all your struggles, to all your defeats, and to all your hopes as well, is faith—wholehearted, all out, enthusiastic faith.

One of the most powerful, most valuable, most practical truths ever stated is described in the following three sentences. "If ye have faith . . . nothing shall be impossible unto you." (Matt. 17:20) "According to your faith be it done unto you." (Matt. 9:29) "If thou canst believe, all things are possible to him that believeth." (Mark 9:23)

The words of the Bible can condition your mind so that confidence and faith may develop within you. Having spent several summers in Switzerland, I have come to know that one of the great personalities of that country was the late Friedrich Frey. From peasant beginnings he became a leader in the Swiss power industry and developed a uniquely beautiful summer hotel enterprise on the famous Burgenstock. In these hotels he placed his own magnificent collection of paintings, tapestries, and antique furniture.

His son, my friend Fritz Frey, the dynamic head of these enterprises, in explaining the strong personality of his father, said, "In his early life my father was ill for a year. During this period he read the Bible through many times. What he read profoundly affected him. I believe he could walk a ridge with a precipice on either side and have absolute confidence."

It cannot be urged too forcefully that successful living depends upon acquiring confidence and this is best accomplished through the consistent and persistent practice of faith. To an amazing degree this practice will free you from your weaknesses and fears, give you a consciousness of your untapped resources, and make possible the releasing of your hidden ability. It will activate the deeper powers of your personality, and help you to develop a more effective grasp on life.

So, do not attempt to cope further with life without learning and perfecting the techniques of dynamic and creative confidence.

I make these assertions because of the great number of people who have developed confidence through the suggested techniques. They took seriously the Biblical statement, "The Lord is on my side, I will not fear." (Psalm 118:6) What more do you need than that? Only your own cooperation. So shift your thoughts from the things that are against you and focus them on the vast power that is for you. Think obsessively of difficulty and it will grow to enormous proportions and may defeat you. Change your thinking to a confidence-obsession and you will be made bigger than your difficulty. It will require a very great deal to defeat the person who actually attempts to do God's will at all times. And certainly God wills that you shall be victorious over your weaknesses.

In this book I can tell about only a few of the many whom I have known who have found the key to self-confidence. One is my friend Dr. Alfred P. Haake, an outstanding public speaker. But he was not always eloquent for, as a boy, he was so badly afflicted with stuttering that he could scarcely form a complete sentence.

I asked him how a boy who stuttered so pathetically became a competent speaker. His answer was, "When we adapt ourselves to God's laws, changes occur within ourselves that seem miraculous, but which are simply the working of spiritually scientific principles."

As a boy his stuttering made school very difficult. The boys would sometimes call him "out" in baseball games when he was actually safe, just to hear him stutter. He knew well enough what he wanted to say, but the words piled up below his throat and he was unable to organize them. He was the butt of the unthinking cruelty of his schoolmates.

One Sunday afternoon he went to a meeting at the YMCA in Chicago to hear the late Senator Albert J. Beveridge of Indiana. The Senator was himself a celebrated orator.

"Until this very day," says my friend, "I can close my eyes and see Senator Beveridge standing there with his finger seemingly pointed straight at me as he said, 'Young man, there isn't a thing in the world you cannot do if you believe you can.'"

To this unhappy, nervous, stuttering lad it seemed that the words were meant especially for him. For the first time he actually accepted the incredible possibility that he might overcome his handicap.

He told his mother about his great new hope. She was a wise woman and knew something of the heartbreak that results from over-expectation, so she cautioned gently, "Be patient, my son. If we have faith and never stop trying, some of our dreams are bound to come true."

The boy, deeply stirred, knelt by his bed that night with the first real feeling he had ever had that God does understand. Then, to his astonishment, he started to pray out loud with scarcely a stutter. It was a tumultuous outpouring of deep, inner feeling and, he says, "I felt then, and I feel now that my prayer went straight to the heart of God."

This first release gave evidence that complete victory could and would come. But no miracle happened. He still stuttered a great deal and the boys and girls continued to laugh at him; but now he was different inwardly and his mental attitude was becoming more confident. Next day he stood bravely and answered a question in class, struggling hard, but not giving up. Through all his painful efforts to speak he heard the voice of the Senator saying, "Have faith," and the voice of his mother adding, "Be patient."

He read about Demosthenes who was said to have overcome a speech impediment by speaking with stones in his mouth. For days after that the boy went to the shore of Lake Michigan, filled his mouth with stones and practiced speaking as Demosthenes did. He tried this again and again with fewer stones each day. Then he would fall upon his knees, crying out piteously, "Oh, God, please let me talk."

"God must have listened to my words and known the pain and hunger in my heart, for one day as I knelt by the Lake shore a calm came over me, and I knew I would win this battle. I was certain that my dreams would come true if I continued to believe in God and in myself."

Lots of trying followed. He took lessons in public speaking and worked and struggled, prayed and believed, and then one day he made a complete speech without hesitation, receiving applause from his audience. That was the happiest day of his life. From then on he made speeches whenever opportunity offered, and always told people how they can overcome every difficulty if only they will believe in God and so have confidence in themselves.

Many people, perhaps most people, never utilize the potential strength within their own personalities. There is resident in you an immense reservoir of force; the power of the subconscious mind. Faith releases this power. Then, mental, emotional, and spiritual strength emerges which is more than enough to override your defeats.

In the subconscious God presides with His illimitable power. If you are allowing yourself to be defeated, practice thinking confidently and focus your thoughts upon God. This inward power, this power of God within you, is so tremendous that under stress and in crises people can perform the most incredible feats. Such demonstrations should make us realize that we can overcome every difficulty in life.

A newspaper tells of a farmer's wife, a woman of only average strength, who was in the farm garage where her husband was working under a jacked-up automobile. Suddenly the car slipped off the jack, leaving one wheel resting partially over his body in such a manner that he was unable to extricate himself. No one was near to help her. Ah, yes, there was! There was God and His immense untapped power within herself.

She prayed and was guided to draw upon this vast power which emerges from within us under extraordinary crises. As this inner force flowed up within her she lifted the car almost imperceptibly, just the barest fraction of an inch, but nevertheless enough so that her husband could wiggle free.

When, later, she attempted to move the car, of course she could not budge it at all. No doubt nature sent a tremendous shot of adrenalin through her system in that moment of crisis. But beyond that chemical assistance, where did she get this power? Was it from the outside? Obviously not. That extra power came from within herself; from God within. It was a super-strength which she did not know was stored up within her. She was able to draw upon it through the combined dynamics of crisis and affirmative faith.

Another case is that of a man who was an invalid, or who thought he was, which may be quite as bad, for if you are an invalid in your mind, the consequent reactions and result are often not dissimilar to physical invalidism. One may slip into an invalid state from psychological as well as from physical reasons. At any rate, this man sat helplessly in his wheel chair, a psychological invalid.

One summer day his sixteen-year old son wheeled his father to the beach and then went in swimming. Presently, too far off shore, he was stricken with a cramp. No one was near to respond to his cries for help. The father, terrified by his son's danger, looked frantically about for assistance. Realizing the situation, crisis freed him. He sprang from the wheel chair, rushed to the water, threw off his clothes, dove into the sea, and brought the boy safely ashore.

Then he was aghast at his own action. But when no ill effect immediately occurred, the possibility began to dawn upon him that he was not an invalid at all except, perhaps, in his thoughts. He never returned to the wheel chair and ultimately became a normal person.

Whence came this sudden access of strength? From outside himself? Not at all, but rather from within where it had been waiting all the time. It is very important to emphasize to yourself that there is an enormous reservoir of power within yourself, but it is God-power and must be used spiritually and in harmony with the laws of Christ. You may draw upon this power by practicing faith in God and by humbly conditioning your life to His will. You may then be confident that the "impossibles" of life are not impossible at all. As the Bible points out "The things which are impossible with man are possible with God." (Luke 18:27)

It is also expressed in another significant statement, "For, behold, the kingdom of God is within you," (Luke 17:21) meaning God's mighty power is deep within your subconscious waiting to come to your aid when faith releases it. When you realize your inner power supply and live upon it, you will experience one of the most thrilling discoveries in this life. You will know that you have adequate ability to handle life successfully through the power of God within you.

The dramatic fact is that the very moment you decide positively that nothing shall longer defeat you, then from that instant of decision *nothing can defeat you*. If your decision is a real one, and truly God-centered, in that flashing second you take power over circumstances. You will grow in your new strength through the deepening of your faith.

As a boy I was afflicted with extreme shyness, and for years I suffered actual mental pain and agony. My shyness was so bad that I was acutely self-conscious and shrank from meeting strangers. Then, in some manner, I got the idea that I wanted to be a public speaker, probably out of a desire to compensate for my defeat feelings. While I wanted to be a speaker, yet I hated speaking, for whenever I forced myself to appear before people I suffered excruciating misery from my shyness and embarrassment.

Near the end of my freshman year in college, a professor rendered me a very great service although in the process he gave me a rough time "Norman," he said, "you might conceivably amount to something, but never as long as you are such a pathetic victim of shyness. What is the matter with you? Have you no manhood?" he asked. He really let me have it. His comments were what you might term uncomplimentary, to use profound understatement. "In fact," he said, "I am disgusted with you. You are afraid of everything. Try making a man of yourself. Use the faith you have been taught. Do something about yourself."

That sort of talk made me so mad I stomped out of his office. He was only trying to rouse me and knew he had to hit me hard to bring me out of my self-consciousness. But I walked down the hall enraged, saying to myself, "I'm going to leave this school, but I shall come back and tell that professor a few things." What I was going to tell him would make your blood run cold.

Then I started down the steps of Gray Chapel. Strangely, I recall that I came to the fourth step from the bottom and there I stopped short, for a new and revolutionary thought hit me. I can remember even yet how it struck with almost a physical impact. It was "Why don't you quit this shyness now? Why not stop it right this minute? Get through with it, and do it immediately."

And so, on the fourth step from the bottom, I asked the Lord to help me, and the Lord seemed to say, "If you really mean it, I will help you now."

And I answered, "Yes, I really mean it." The combination of prayer and faith, and being none too gently prodded by that professor, brought this decision to focus at that precise moment.

I moved down from that step across the campus, and can even yet remember the feeling of exultation which swept over me. I knew that I did not need to be a frightened, shy person any more. I realized, for the first time, that I could conquer my inferiority. Of course, I did not get over it immediately. In fact, I had plenty of struggles with it for a long time, but the process was started which led to control over this unhappy personality difficulty. In that moment of spiritual experience I gained the confidence that, with God's help, I could master my failure.

So, I say you do not really need to be defeated by anything if you make up your mind that you won't be, and if, at the same time, you do these four things. First, decide you are now through being dominated by an inferiority complex. Second, start filling the mind with an affirmative faith in God. Third, believe humbly, but strongly, in yourself. And fourth, start living in the belief that God is with you, helping you.

Lack of faith in yourself is one of the greatest barriers to the full expression of your personality. Carlyle says "Alas! the fearful unbelief is unbelief in yourself." Actually it is an affront to God when you have a low opinion of yourself, for He made you, you know.

Put your problem in the present tense. Affirm that God is *now* helping you. Affirm that you are *now* doing and acting efficiently. Affirm that, since God is *now* guiding you, your ineptitude and failures are *now* being superseded by a new keenness of mind and by a calm confidence. This may not happen in one dramatic moment, but even the gradual unfolding is dramatic.

Several years ago I met a young man who had just been made a junior officer of his company. The president of his organization is a famous businessman whose facial expression and demeanor give somewhat the impression that he is forbidding and difficult, although actually, he is a kindly person. His extraordinary physical size adds to this overpowering impression of sternness.

The young man was required, by his duties, to report personally to this president every day, which made his job a painful problem since he was an acute sufferer from inferiority and shrinking. This daily consultation with the "great" man presently assumed the proportions of a crisis, so much so that he contemplated resigning.

He explained that the effect the older man had on him was "overwhelming." "Frankly," he continued, "that man frightens me so that I find it impossible to think clearly when in his presence. I become inarticulate and awkward. If only I could overcome this terrible shyness, I believe I might handle my job satisfactorily; but otherwise, I may be forced to quit."

The answer, of course, was to start developing within his thought rational, reasonable belief in his own abilities. He needed to hold the thought that he had been appointed to his important position because his superiors had respect for his ability. Beyond that he should think of his new position as an opportunity for constructive service. Here again was that old bug-a-boo of thinking too much about yourself.

I made the following specific suggestion: "When your president summons you to his office, before you enter, stand for a moment outside his door and silently pray for *him*. Do not pray for yourself. Actually, all shy people are egotistical, their thought being painfully self-centered. To be healed, the shy person must master self-forgetfulness.

"Then," I continued, "send out good will thoughts to the man behind that door. His very reserve and pompous attitude may indicate his need for understanding, even affection. He may also need someone who is not afraid of him. Pray that you may be of help to him, believe that you will be, then enter his office with confidence and with a desire to serve." He promised to follow these directions.

Some months passed before I saw him again and then I met quite a different person. He revealed a new and quiet confidence. "How are you getting along with the boss?" I inquired.

His face lit up as he replied, "He is a wonderful person. When you get under that rough exterior he is a kindly man. I followed your suggestions and, for a while, nothing happened. But presently I began to realize that I was feeling better about the problem. Then one day the boss said something that nearly bowled me over. 'Bill, I have come to depend upon you. You are a great help to me.'

"That was the finest compliment ever paid me. For the first time I felt that I mattered in the business, that I was actually important to its success. That really did something for me. Now I get a big kick out of the job and," he added, "it is a privilege to work with that man." I noted that he said "with" rather than "for," denoting an identification and growing confidence in his own value to the enterprise. This man's attitude changed from one of self-consciousness, fear, and tension to one of relaxation, confidence, and assurance.

Every person who is now defeated by situations or circumstances, or by any feeling of inferiority or inadequacy, or any other personal weakness, must come to a precise releasing moment when, in his thoughts, he resolutely decides that he is going to have confidence.

When your conscious mind definitely accepts this thought it is then passed to the subconscious where, if firmly emphasized, it will become determinative. There must be present, however, a positive spiritual force to activate your decision. That force is a humble faith in God. It may be deepened by using such an affirmation as, "I believe that God *now* gives me strength. I believe that God is *now* helping me. I believe that God is *now* releasing my hidden powers."

Continue to affirm in this manner until your subconscious mind fully accepts that which the conscious mind passes to it. Then it will become a fact. As you maintain and strengthen faith in this manner your problems, instead of appalling you by their difficulties, will become increasingly easier of solution. Instead of being controlled by your weaknesses you will assume control over them.

Two of my most inspiring friends are Roy Rogers and his charming wife, Dale Evans Rogers, who are beloved by young Americans and older ones as well. At dinner in our home Roy told of his painful struggles with his inferiority complex, especially about talking in public. As a boy he says he was so shy that "the thought of saying anything before a class or just a few people would make me take off across the cornfields. But Dale is a mighty smart woman. My biggest triumph came when I used her suggestions about talking in public. The music part I handled without any fear, but when it came time to say a few words, I felt the same old nervous symptoms. Then I closed my eyes for just a moment and said silently, 'Lord, I'll just make a mess of things on my own. Help me to relax a little so that what I say to these people will really mean something.'

"I started to talk and found myself saying things I'd never said before. And they came out as naturally as though I was just standing there and someone else was talking. From that time I've never had more than the normal amount of nervousness."

I write so certainly about these matters for, as previously indicated, personal convictions concerning the power of faith developed out of my own painful experience with inner defeat. At the risk of making this chapter too biographical, I should like to relate another of the determinative incidents out of which this philosophy evolved. I feel justified in so doing since the point of view presented in this chapter and throughout this book developed out of hard, difficult, personal experience. And, if by recounting my own sufferings and struggles I can help other people overcome their own, the purpose of this book will be achieved. I, personally, know that the techniques of faith work, and have no doubt about it at all, for I tested them in my own experience. Thus, in urging my readers to become practitioners of creative faith, I am advocating a formula of living, the soundness of which I have good personal reason to know.

At age twenty-eight I was suddenly called to head a church situated in a large university community. Its membership consisted of professors and their families, as well as leading business and professional people. Some learned and distinguished men were regular worshippers at that church.

I came to this responsibility young and with little experience. Furthermore, I was still struggling with self-doubts, a holdover from my earlier battle with shyness. These conflicts are hard, but fortunately they do die. In my heart I agreed with the many people who prophesied my early failure. But I stubbornly determined not to fail. Unfortunately, however, I did not attack the problem in the right spirit, which was to forget self and go ahead and do the job in a natural manner. Instead, I worked ceaselessly, day and night, with tense effort, my nervous activity being largely based on fear of personal failure rather than on a humble desire to serve God.

Due to the kindly cooperation of the people and the efficiency of my associates, and perhaps to some extent to my own unremitting activity, the church program went along fairly well. But the strain of my feverish attempt to keep pace with the job began to tell. The haunting fear of failure drove me on. Soon I found myself in a highly nervous state. These hectic efforts were undermining my reserves of strength. Not only did I derive little satisfaction from my work, but I began to have a feeling that, despite all good intentions and sincerity of purpose, something fundamental was lacking. There was no lift, no spiritual power within me.

So, driven by necessity, I began to experiment with prayer in real earnest. I prayed for illumination and guidance, and presently found the solution. It came about as follows:

During this period of unhappy conflict, while traveling on a train running between Toledo and Columbus, Ohio, I was working on a sermon for the following Sunday entitled "The Secret of Power." Suddenly the thought came that the title was highly incongruous, for what did I know about any secret of power? Though I was completely sincere yet, actually, I was using only words without personal experience.

Then, strangely, I felt an overwhelming urge to pray. This proved to be one of the greatest prayers of my life. James Russell Lowell describes my experience as well as his own:

> I, who still pray at morning and at eve . . .
> Thrice in my life perhaps have truly prayed,
> Thrice stirred below my conscious self
> Have felt that perfect disenthrallment, which is God.

In my prayer I told the Lord that I was tired of my fear of failure and of being everlastingly concerned about myself. I told Him I was fed up with struggling simply to justify the confidence some people had in me, or to prove my worth to others, or to have good results for mere personal satisfaction. I told the Lord I wanted to be honest and sincere. And I deeply meant every word of this prayer.

Then, suddenly, I discovered one of the greatest of all spiritual laws, that of complete surrender. Driven by the intense pain of my conflicts, I went the full limit of surrender to God and told the Lord that if it was best for me to fail, I was willing to fail. I stated that God was free to do anything with me He wanted to do, expressing only the hope that He would get it over as quickly as possible. I told God that I put myself completely and unreservedly in His hands and would try to follow His will as He might indicate; that my desire was only for spiritual peace and strength. It was a sincere and complete outpouring of deepest desire.

I learned in that moment that when we really mean our prayers, not fractionally or halfheartedly, but completely and wholeheartedly, we receive accordingly.

The result was overwhelming and amazing. I had no sooner finished this prayer than I became conscious of deep and complete peace. It is difficult to describe the serenity that came. It was one of the few unforgettable moments of my life. Then I began to feel a strange, quiet confidence. For the first time in my whole existence, I experienced personally the meaning of spiritual victory.

I knew, then, that we may live victoriously, not because we have any power within ourselves, but because when we give ourselves to God, He gives Himself to us. It was a most ecstatic feeling of joy and wonderment.

Yet, coupled with this new and victorious feeling of release was the recognition that this was no power of my own, but was something given me. It was God's strength as He bestows it upon weak human beings. Many times since then my personal power has been very low, but that experience reminds me that, when I continue to surrender myself completely into God's hands and practice faith, I am sustained.

It is with some hesitation that I relate this experience lest pride be read into this narrative. I assure my readers that this type of experience does not lead to pride, but rather to humility, emphasizing as it does a profound recognition of one's dependence upon a power greater than himself. I tell of this experience only to say to you that whatever your condition in life, whatever difficulties you may be facing at the moment, this procedure is an absolutely certain way to gain strength and peace and victory. Practice wholeheartedly giving yourself to God, and God will, with equal wholeheartedness, give Himself to you. This is your great key to humble self-confidence.

4 Keys to Self-Confidence

1. Cultivate "the strength of belief."
2. Shift your thoughts from the things that are against you and focus them on the vast power that is for you.
3. The very moment you decide that nothing shall defeat you, from that instant *nothing can defeat you.*
4. Surrender yourself to God.

15

LIVING ABOVE PAIN AND SUFFERING

"We live in a world full of wonders. Indeed, we have seen so many marvels that scarcely anything now excites our incredulity. Can we, therefore, believe that wonders may not also occur in the area of spirit? Can they be as exactly governed by law as phenomena in the materialistic realm? The fact that we do not completely understand these laws does not indicate that such laws do not exist. Spiritual healings do not always occur; but they do occur, and one may always have the hope that he may be granted this great blessing by God."

LIVE DYNAMICALLY, enthusiastically, and with vitality, is the message of this book But some face the problem of pain and suffering and to them this type of life may seem difficult. Life can indeed be a tough, hard road when one must walk with pain. But, even so, you can make of it a creative experience.

As difficult as it is, pain is not without value. Du Noüy discerned its purpose: "Without . . . suffering . . . man does not really humanize himself nor liberate his spiritual aspirations. It is because of this that pain is fruitful. . . ."

In this chapter we will discuss effective techniques for the enduring of pain and suffering. But, on the more positive side, I want to plant the creative thought in your mind that you can rise above pain and, perhaps, even eliminate it altogether. The way you think has a great deal to do with the way you feel. And faith is the healthiest form of thought. So, instead of thinking sickness, weakness, and disease, try thinking in terms of vitality, energy, and well-being. This will require effort, of course, but many have demonstrated that such constructive thinking tends to tone up the system and greatly increase well-being.

Always hold a mental image of yourself as healthy and vigorous. Such an image, held in the mind, has a strong tendency to develop into actuality.

Also, when you pray for the well-being of others it is important to hold optimistic thoughts. While voicing the words of faith, if you visualize that person as sick instead of well, your real prayer, then, becomes an affirmation of sickness, not health. And the result is that you get what you see and believe. "According to your faith" [that is, according to the image in your mind] "be it unto you." (Matthew 9:29)

The Reverend A. H. Durham relates an incident illustrating how faith projected upon a condition of sickness sets vital forces in motion.

"About three years ago I was requested to visit, immediately, a young member of my church who was critically ill.

"I went at once and found the most frightened person I had ever seen. She held my hand in both of hers and kept repeating through her tears, 'Oh, Reverend Durham, I don't want to die.' I told her that she was the only one who was talking about death, and asked her to repeat for me the opening phrase of the Twenty-third Psalm. She replied at once, 'The Lord is my shepherd; I shall not want.'

" 'Now,' I said, 'if you could say that from your heart, and not just merely with your lips, you would not be the frightened girl you are, for you would be sure that your Shepherd is here, and that He will supply your wants.'

"Then, for about ten minutes I told her of all the comfort those words of faith could bring to a believing heart, and thus succeeded in calming her and preparing her for the prayer for her complete recovery which I then offered. Before leaving her I administered the 'laying on of hands,' using the form found in *The Book of Common Prayer* of the Episcopal Church.

"The next morning I was back at the hospital shortly before nine, but had to wait outside her room as the nurses were busy with her. Her doctor came up to me while I was waiting and said, 'Reverend Durham, some wonderful physical change has happened overnight to that patient . . . I can't understand it.'

"I replied, 'Oh, Doctor, I think she was just a very frightened girl last night.' But the doctor insisted that I was wrong, because she was having convulsions when they put her in that private room. It then occurred to me that they had taken her out of her ward and put her in that room to die without disturbing the other patients. I was glad, then, that I did not know the night before that the doctors had given her up.

"A week later as she left the hospital for her home, the nurses said, 'Well, we have seen a miracle, for we never expected her to walk out of this ward.'

"I do not believe I would have succeeded in awakening her faith in God that night if I had known what the doctors thought of her condition. Today she is well and hearty."

Had the minister known about the convulsions before he went into the patient's room he might very well have transmitted to her an image of death. Not having that knowledge to make him negative, he surrounded her with a positive faith image. That vital force turned the tide.

The problem, however, is to hold an image of health when you have full knowledge of the situation. The method then is not to concentrate mentally upon the sickness, but to see the person, or yourself, as in the flow of God's health and vitality. All creative energy in the universe flows from God and, through faith, we may draw upon it to combat sickness.

But the fact must be faced that pain and sickness may remain with one until the end of earthly life. In that event, one prays for strength to meet the inevitable with courage. Then faith becomes an instrument for getting insight into the fundamental meaning of suffering and for bearing it. Even as pain may be removed by faith, so it may be endured by faith.

This truth was brought home to me by the experience of my own uncle, William F. Peale. My affection for him is unbounded. He was a successful oil producer, a keen thinker, a strong yet kindly personality.

In his sixty-eighth year he contracted cancer of the throat and his larynx and tongue had to be removed. He suffered indescribable pain. All resources of modern medical science were employed, together with the techniques of prayer and faith.

But God's answer was that his life on earth should end. And that answer will come to each of us in due course. We must develop within ourselves the philosophy, the faith, and the courage to meet it and see it through, knowing that God never lays a burden or a pain upon us that He does not give us equivalent strength to bear it.

My uncle was not a regular church-going man, though a sincere believer. He talked very little about his religion. He had deep sentiments, but he concealed them well. His main sign of affection would be to thump you heavily in the chest, or give you a clap on the back, or do something nice for you, minimizing it at the same time. Under a rather brusque exterior, was the kindest and tenderest heart in the world.

As he lay on his bed before the operation I sat by his side. I told him how sorry I was for all that he was compelled to endure. And then I said to him, "I would like you to know, Uncle Will, that my admiration for you is more than I can ever express. Some of us talk a great deal about God and faith and the things of religion, and you say very little. But I shall always remember you as one of the greatest human beings I ever knew. I would like to ask you how you are able to stand up to this thing as you do?"

He turned to me with a very peaceful look on his face and said, "There is nothing else to do, is there? I just have to take it as it comes."

We sat in silence for a moment and then he added, "But with the Lord's help I think we can see it through."

"Would you like me to pray?" I asked. He nodded and said, "Pray like Mother used to pray long ago when she put me to bed at night."

I remembered my grandmother so well. She had a simple faith in Jesus. So, in my prayer, I prayed to Jesus: "Dear Jesus, be with Uncle Will in this operation. Help him to put his hand in Yours and not be afraid. Help him to know that You will stand by him every minute of the time. Help the doctors, too. And give Uncle Will the strength, the comfort, the patience he needs. This we ask in Jesus' name. Amen." That was the way Grandma would have prayed and he looked at me with a wonderful smile.

Then, before I left the room, I did something I had never done with him before: he was not the kind to whom you showed affection in this manner, and it wasn't the way I usually did things, either. I leaned down and kissed him on the forehead. In that hospital room I had a wonderful experience of the Presence of God in a time of pain and tragic suffering. By simply putting your faith in Him, you can get through your pain and suffering as Uncle Will did.

Also, I have known others who were not claimed by death, but whose disability became permanent and who learned to live with it in a victorious manner. In the last analysis the secret of life isn't in what happens to you, but what you do with what happens to you.

There is my friend Harry Doehla. He was a bright lad making a good record in school when, at seventeen, he was taken with rheumatic fever. He was told that he would never walk again and could never use his hands.

The word "useless" drummed itself into his consciousness. The hurt in his mind was worse than the pain in the muscles. He was in black despair.

While his parents worked in the mill he sat at home in a handmade wheelchair. One day he fell onto the floor, and lay hopeless and helpless until a passing mail carrier put him back into the chair. Then, one day, a man gave him a Bible text, "If ye have faith, and doubt not, yet shall . . . say unto this mountain, Be thou removed . . ." (Matthew 21:21)

"Well," said Harry, "mine is a big mountain, but one thing is sure, while I may be crippled in hands and legs I am not crippled in mind or soul. And I can live, not by leg power, but by mind power; not by hand power, but by faith power."

Then he "got" the idea that he might sell greeting cards. So, with his gnarled hands he painfully made his first greeting card. It took him weeks and he sold it for a nickel. That was the greatest day of his life. Later he built a successful greeting card company. "I discovered I had something in my brain greater than any deficiency in my body. I had mind-power through faith."

He wrote his unforgettable story for our magazine *Guideposts** under the title "By Wheelchair to the Stars." Harry Doehla is the fastest man in a wheelchair I have ever known. He whirls it up to his automobile, slides into the seat of his car, and drives with skill.

You see, it isn't all-important what the condition of your body is; the important factor is the condition of your mind and soul. With mental power and faith power you can weave pain and suffering into a great life.

* Guideposts Associates, Inc. Carmel, New York

Harry Doehla did; so can you. Another example is my friend Harry Moore. One tragic day he was told that he would be blind. Standing at the window of his room on the sixteenth floor of a New York hotel the thought came that in less than a minute he could end all of his troubles; he need not live with the agony and frustration of blindness.

But instead of throwing himself out the window he fell to his knees and prayed, "Dear Lord, I need You. I cannot get along without You. Help me and show me what to do."

He prayed for a long time. "All of a sudden," he said, "I seemed to feel a Presence and to hear a Voice saying, 'I am with you always.' " (Matthew 28:20)

In the succeeding years he has had a successful career of service. He is one of the best storytellers south of Mason and Dixon's line, which is saying a great deal for any storyteller. He is a radiant, victorious person bringing inspiration to all. He stood up to his pain and suffering and did something constructive about it. You never think of him as blind, at all.

Such human experiences as these I have described prove several things about life. One is that sometimes we simply have to live with our pain and suffering and physical disability. Another is that in living with it we can overcome it.

The man with arthritis may go to a doctor and be told that there isn't much that can be done about it, medically speaking, and that he will just have to live with his arthritis and get along with it the best he can. And, if he stops fighting it, and cooperates with it, the chances are that it won't bother him too much and he can live a very satisfactory life with it. That is the way life is; we have to get along with arithmetic, and with arthritis, and with other things as well.

There is an enormous power in the human spirit to rise above pain and suffering when the spirit is determined and when you plumb those deeper resources of power which have been inherently built into your system.

William James brilliantly discussed the second wind that enables us to forge past the first and even second barrier of fatigue.

Your normal energies carry you to the first barrier of fatigue. You feel that you cannot go further. But, if you project your faith and energy beyond the first conscious barrier of fatigue, you emerge into an area of consciousness where fatigue drops away and you have what Professor James called a second wind, or new access of power.

People who do the great things in life, who overcome enormous odds and difficulties, are those who go not only beyond the first conscious barrier of fatigue, but perhaps beyond even a second, as well. There is released within them what seems to be a superpower so that they perform the most astonishing feats.

An illustration is the experience of Enrico Caruso, the famous tenor, who was so ill that it was felt he could not get out of bed to sing. But he said that he must sing, and that he was determined to sing. Seven-thirty came and his manager said, "Senor, the last moment has come; you must go to the opera house."

Blinded by pain, he dragged himself from his bed and was taken to the opera house. He lay on a couch as they dressed him for his role, being too ill to stand.

Eight-thirty came and the manager said, "Senor, you must go on the stage." He pulled himself up, went to the wings. Then he forced his great will beyond the first and second barriers of fatigue and, when the cue came, rushed on stage, pouring out unforgettable melodies.

Charles A. Lindbergh, in his historic flight through the lonely vastness of the Atlantic skies, amidst drifting fogs and winds, kept his little plane going hour after hour until he became overwhelmed with the desire to sleep. If he could only close his eyes for just one delicious moment! His description of his struggle against sleep is a classic. He knew that if he gave in it would mean certain death. So, he pushed his spirit past the first barrier of fatigue, then past the second barrier, and then he became aware, all at once, of a second self. It was the emergence of power from within.

Real champions force through these barriers by sheer faith and courage. Alice Marble, former tennis champion of the world, on the day preceding the championship match at Wimbledon, strained a muscle. She suffered such excruciating pain that when she tried to raise her arm to practice her serve, she cried out in anguish. The doctor told her she might permanently harm herself if she insisted upon playing.

But Alice Marble was there to play so she went into a little room off the stadium and prayed for strength. Before beginning the game the players were supposed to curtsy to the Queen. Her opponent gave a beautiful curtsy while Miss Marble was able only to nod her head. But the Queen smiled pleasantly, nonetheless. It was with great agony that she served. At that moment she came to a pain fatigue barrier where it seemed she could go no further, but by her faith she forced beyond the barrier and lost her pain. When Alice Marble became champion she used an interesting phrase, "Prayer is my racquet."

No discussion of pain is adequate that does not consider the possibility that pain, either of spirit or body, may be a manifestation of disharmony.

One form of disharmony is ill will. I have indicated elsewhere how appropriately named is such feeling, for the will is indeed sick. This can create a form of pain quite as intense as physical pain.

Dis-ease means ease discounted. Ill will is dislocated harmony. So, when you live on a basis of ill will, your will is actually dis-eased. But your will can be made well by the healing power of good will (healthy will).

Dr. James Dale Van Buskirk, in *Religion, Healing and Health*, recounts a case history from Dr. Walter C. Alvarez of Mayo Clinic about a man who killed himself with ill will. The patient was in good health, when his father's death precipitated a dispute with his sister over their parent's property. The sister contested the father's will and won. From that time the patient could think or talk of nothing else.

It became an obsession. He detested his sister with a malignant hatred. At length he developed symptoms of illness. His breath became foul and stayed so. He began having difficulty with his heart and blood pressure. Then followed various bodily deteriorations, and before many months he was dead. "It seemed obvious," was the doctor's startling comment, "that he died of bodily injuries wrought by powerful emotion. The profound ill will generated in his system over a period of time had actually killed him."

The powerful effect of spirit on the body is generally recognized today. If the soul is sick, the body may become sick. It appears, then, that to be healthy you need, also, to be holy. The word "holy" does not mean super-pious, but derives from "wholth," an Anglo-Saxon word meaning the entire being or whole person. Spiritual harmony is a powerful resistance to that disharmony known as disease. Faith greatly helps in alleviating pain, especially psychic pain.

One way that Christ heals is by restoring spiritual harmony, both within and without the personality. And harmony is so vital to well-being that it cannot be overstressed. Harmony has a powerful influence in establishing health which may have been undermined by vindictive attitudes.

A pastor told me of a girl in his parish who took twenty-eight sleeping pills and was at the verge of death. The doctor considered her chances for recovery as slight, for she had a profound will not to live. Her father, it seems, was a mean, dominating person, and the house was filled with a spirit of tension and ill will. The girl was sincerely religious and she had a strong sense of filial obligation to her father.

But she had hate feelings toward him and, consequently, developed a deep sense of guilt. The inharmonious situation finally became intolerable to her. This, coupled with neurotic feelings of unworthiness, stimulated deep depression which resulted in the suicide attempt.

The pastor, in counseling with the family, made clear the necessity for spiritual harmony among them. Through prayer, self-examination, and forgiveness the members of this family were fused into a feeling of unity between themselves and with God. Hate was washed out and love, the most creative of all emotions, began its salutary operation. This made them ready for the act of healing faith. They surrendered the sick girl to God. They affirmed that, being God's child, His healing Grace was even then touching her. They asked for her recovery but, with love and faith, surrendered her to God's will.

Then the pastor took that formerly inharmonious family to the church. He had them kneel at the altar and pray for a deepened harmony in their hearts and in their home.

The father, who had never before prayed aloud, now offered a simple, but curative prayer. "Lord, I am a mean man. I ask You now to take all the meanness out of my heart and fill me with the harmony of Christ."

The pastor reported that the turn came in the illness of the girl at that precise moment, and in a short time she was well again. That was corroborated by the physician. "That father," declared the pastor, "is now one of the best Christians in my church. And," he added, "the home is a place of harmony and peace."

Thus, healthy thinking helps bring about healthy feelings. Never forget that there is a close relationship between faith and physical and emotional health.

A fact of comfort to the pain sufferer is that he can actually lose his pain, at least temporarily, by becoming more interested in something else. A professor who had a severe chronic sinus condition discovered that during the three hours a day he spent teaching, he was without pain. In other words, his teaching was more pleasant than pain was unpleasant.

Another man who suffers constant pain has his own method of relief when it hurts more than usual. "My back hurts," he says to his wife, "so I guess I'd better wash the car and put up the storm windows."

My own father lived with the pain of arthritis. His philosophy of pain always impressed me as extraordinarily sound.

"Learn what you can about your disease," he said. "Know what to expect. Learn to do what you can about it. Beyond that, just get along with it." One should learn, he advised, to be aware of corollary symptoms and not to worry about so-called "new symptoms," as in arthritis, for example, in which many reflex pains occur. The fact that you know what these pains are removes alarm over symptoms and actually lessens their effect. "The thing to do," says my father, "if you have arthritis, is to say, 'Well, it's arthritis, and that's the way arthritis is.' Take pain, like people, as it comes," he advised. And then he adds, "You can live a great life within your limitations."

All of which leads to the proposition that, as tough as it is, one of the most practical solutions to the problem of pain is simply to make up your mind to live with it. The effect of pain is great, very great indeed. But the power of mind, the power of soul, is greater.

Not only can the mind be made philosophical with regard to pain, but by discipline some have also cultivated stoicism (the ability to take pain without evident reaction). People who were reared from childhood to be overly conscious of pain suffer to a greater extent than those who were taught as children to minimize or ignore pain.

A neurosurgeon, who is conducting advanced research into controlling pain with supersonics, is reported to have explained that "ultra-high frequency sound waves are used to destroy pain pathways in the brain." Perhaps prayer and faith may also set in motion spiritual high-frequency waves vibrating from God to the believer to destroy "pain pathways" in consciousness.

The basic way to cope with pain is simply to pray. You have the right to ask God to take away or reduce your pain. That is what you honestly want, and any forthright and honest desire may be expressed to God. Believe that He will grant your request.

Put the pain in God's hands and leave it to Him. If it is His will that you are to bear it, God will fortify you with sufficient understanding and strength to endure it. Also, pray for the healing of other people who suffer pain. Develop the attitude of compassion toward all sufferers. As sympathy and love flow out from you, curative forces will flow in toward you.

The following letter shows with simplicity and sincerity the effective use of prayer in the experience of pain.

Dear Dr. Peale,

Eight months ago I suffered a coronary attack. I am fifty-one years old and for the past twenty years have been an athletic coach. Although I have a wonderful wife who is a good Christian, my own spiritual salvation was sadly lacking. During my illness I read your book. Then I started to read the Bible. I did a great deal of thinking, and for the first time started praying. Curiously, I found I was praying for others as much, if not more, than for myself. I continued to read your book and the Gospels and to pray.

One night, as I lay in bed, I was having a bad spell of pain. Then I decided to put everything in God's hands. As I lay there quietly praying I suddenly found myself weeping. Then a sense of warmth and light, prevailing peace and joy, seemed to flood my being, and the pain was gone.

Such complete giving of the self to God is the most effective way of gaining that inner peace and sense of Divine love that takes pain away.

In dealing with pain and suffering one needs, as I have indicated, to practice spiritual acceptance. If, after deeply spiritual prayer, the pain and suffering remain, one must then draw strength from God to live with it and to be creative about it. Never forget, however, that there is within you potential power to rise above pain and gain victory over it. And, do not neglect the possibility that through deeper and more intense prayer and faith you may finally find release.

I was impressed by a phrase used by Captain Raoul de Beaudean of the *Ile de France* when that ship arrived to help the sinking *Andrea Doria*. There was heavy fog as the *Ile de France* came up to the scene of the disaster. The Captain of the French liner said, "I gave an intense mental prayer for a clearing of the fog. In truth the fog did start lifting." The phrase used by the Captain is of utmost significance: "an intense mental prayer." Intensity of effort, intensity of faith, intensity of longing, intensity of self-giving, these are basic factors in healing by faith.

A friend told me of the following prescription written by a physician for a woman patient suffering from a severe throat and chest condition. It read "Rx—More vigorous prayer."

"Did she follow your prescription?" my friend asked.

"She did indeed," said the physician. "She was in true pain, had definite congestion and symptoms, but I could not reach the seat of her trouble for it was of the spirit."

"Did your prescription restore her to health?"

"Of body, mind, and spirit," the doctor answered.

The late Dr. Alexis Carrel who won the Nobel Prize in Physiology and Medicine gave many clinical reports on spiritual healing and significantly stated, "The only condition indispensable for the occurrence is prayer."

A thought is a force, and a good thought is a more powerful force than an evil one. Hold the following thought for it contains power: "The one who created my body will care for its failings and failures. If need be, He will heal me physically or mentally through a doctor or nature, and when doctors or nature fail He can heal me through His own power."

It might be well to define our terms. Physical healing is bodily healing through the application of medical knowledge and skill. Mental healing is healing of mind or body through the therapeutic use of psychology or psychiatry. Spiritual healing is that type of healing which is effected through other than the recognized methods of medicine, psychology or psychiatry, that is healing wrought directly through religious faith.

A minister who has had outstanding success in the field of healing through religious therapy is the Rev. Alfred William Price, Rector of St. Stephen's Episcopal Church, Philadelphia. People began coming to him with their troubles, mental, emotional, spiritual, and sometimes physical. He did his best to help them, but there always seemed some whom he could not reach. He remembers particularly one man badly crippled with arthritis and filled with bitterness, because he had been passed over for promotion in his job, a promotion he felt he deserved. Dr. Price tried to make him see that there was a strong relationship between his illness and his bitterness.

The clergyman sat one day in the pew in his church which was occupied years ago by the famous Dr. S. Weir Mitchell, great neurologist and pioneer of psychosomatic medicine. He remembered Dr. Mitchell's famous words, "It is not the body that is ill, but the mind." He turned to a Bible passage and read, "Is any sick among you? Let him call for the elders of the church; and let them pray over him . . .

"And the prayer of faith shall save the sick, and the Lord shall raise him up; and if he have committed sins, they shall be forgiven him." (James 5:14–15)

Dr. Price rose from that prayer to take up the great work of healing in the name of Christ.

He says, "God is on the side of health. Remember that God always answers every genuine prayer according to the measure of our faith. If we create the proper conditions His power will flow through us, healing every fiber, every tissue, and every drop of blood. With your spiritual imagination create in your mind a picture of the perfection in your body or mind which you crave."

"In our healing ministry," Dr. Price says, "our primary effort is to have the sick person healed in the area of the mind and soul. When this is accomplished the healing often comes as a by-product."

Gertrude D. McKelvey says that some few receive instant healing, others gradually over a longer period, and some are not healed but write of new courage to face their maladies with peace of mind.

For example, there was Mrs. J. whose hands had been so badly crippled with arthritis that she could not even move a finger.

"While I knelt at the altar a doctor's name kept coming into my mind," she told Dr. Price. "I had seen so many doctors, but I felt a strong urge to see just one more; this was God's leading."

"Did you know the doctor?"

"No," answered Mrs. J. with an expression of wonderment. "To my knowledge, I had never heard of him, and I didn't know where to find him, either. When I came out of St. Stephen's Church onto the street I realized that Jefferson Hospital was just around the corner and, strangely, I knew I must go there and ask for him.

"To my amazement I learned at the hospital that he had just finished his lunch and could see me for a few moments. He said he was glad I had come because he thought I had the kind of arthritis that he could cure with a new serum he had just learned about. He asked if I was willing to try it. I agreed, and in five weeks I was completely healed. Since then I have dedicated these hands to God's service," she concluded, holding out hands with no trace of the knotty, twisted mass they had once been.

We live in a world full of wonders. Indeed, we have seen so many marvels that scarcely anything now excites our incredulity. Can we, therefore, believe that wonders may not also occur in the area of spirit? Is it not as exactly governed by law as phenomena in the materialistic realm? The fact that we do not completely understand these laws does not indicate that such laws do not exist. Spiritual healings do not always occur; but they do occur, and one may always have the hope that he may be granted this great blessing by God.

The power of faith and prayer, taken together, constitute the greatest power available to human beings.

A sound demonstration of this power is related in this moving story written for *Reader's Digest* by Elise Miller Davis and Edward S. Zelley, Jr.

"Speeding more than 1,000 travelers homeward from New York City, the Broker, crack Jersey-shore commuter train, jumped the track, plunged down a 25-foot embankment. Coaches piled up in a tangled mass of grotesque wreckage. Here is the amazing story of one man among the injured, Bob Stout, of Locust, New Jersey.

"The Rev. Roger J. Squire, pastor of the First Methodist Church of nearby Red Bank, New Jersey, had many parishioners on the Broker. He went from house to house, lending sympathy and offering what help he could. He came to the Stout home as Mildred Stout was kneeling by the crib of her child.

"The Rev. Mr. Squire offered a brief prayer for Bob and his family. Then he went on to others. Mildred felt a little better. Tall, lanky, red-headed, Bob was beloved in the church. Both Stouts sang in the choir, and Mildred remembered that she was to sing a solo on Sunday.

"Not until 12:30 A.M. did she find him. His chart in the Perth Amboy General Hospital read: 'Possible skull fracture.' And then: 'Last rites given at 10 P.M.' Some kindly priest had done all he could.

"Next day Bob Stout sank deeper and deeper into unconsciousness. He responded to no stimuli, no tests. His condition was too critical to permit X-rays, but severe brain injury was suspected.

"Mildred stayed in his room, praying almost constantly. Wednesday passed. And Thursday. Every feeble pulse beat, every faint breath could have been the last. But, incredibly, Bob hung on.

"On Friday an eminent neurosurgeon was called in. He scheduled an exploratory operation for Sunday noon. He didn't mince words: the risk was great, chances were slim.

"Sunday morning the nurse telephoned Rev. Mr. Squire, 'Mr. Stout's wife is the only person in the world who is sure he will live. She just keeps saying, "I've put my trust in Him." '

"As the pastor began the 11 o'clock service, a line from the order of worship, mimeographed days before, caught his eye: Solo—'Trust in Him'—Mrs. Robert Stout. What he did then seemed to be dictated by a Power beyond himself. Stopping in the midst of the service, he left his pulpit and faced his congregation before the altar rail.

" 'It is 11:15,' he said. 'Bob Stout is critically ill at Perth Amboy General Hospital and soon will undergo an operation. I think Bob and Mildred would like to know we are praying for them.'

"He asked each member of the congregation to concentrate on Bob Stout, to surround his hospital bed with love and faith. Then he turned and knelt at the altar as every head bowed in prayer.

"Picturing Jesus as long ago He had gone about on earth touching the sick and healing them, Mr. Squire prayed, 'We beseech Thee to go with us now, O Master, to the hospital at Perth Amboy, to walk up the stairs, down the hall to Room 248, to enter and stand by the bed.

" 'Now, Master'—the pastor's voice faltered . . . 'lay Your hand on Bob Stout's brow and heal him!'

"An unreal moment of vast silence hung in the air.

"Then Mr. Squire rose, returned to his pulpit to continue the service. The prayer had seemed long to him, but when he glanced at his watch it was only 11:20.

"After the service Roger Squire sat alone in his study when the phone rang. Answering he heard Mildred's voice, husky with tears. 'There's no medical explanation for what happened,' she said. 'His pulse and respiration were almost nonexistent, and then . . . he just opened his eyes.'

"Instructed to report to the doctors even the slightest change, the nurse had run from the room. When she returned with a doctor, Bob was unconscious again. He was then wheeled to the X-ray room.

"There the specialist re-examined Bob. 'I honestly don't know what made me do it,' he commented later. When he gently pinched Bob's shoulder the patient responded, 'Ouch!' It was Bob Stout's first word in five days.

"The surgeon turned from the table. He sent word to Mildred that the operation was being called off. Bob's pulse and respiration improved unbelievably. He had passed a crisis and the results of trauma were receding.

"As Mildred's voice came over the wire, Mr. Squire recreated vividly the scene at the hospital. What had actually come to pass? Who could say? Perhaps miracles do happen.

" 'Just one thing more,' the pastor said, recovering his voice. 'Does anyone know what time it was when Bob first opened his eyes?'

" 'Yes,' said Mildred, 'it was 11:20.'

"Mr. Squire hung up the receiver and bowed his head."

To Live with Pain:

1. Even as pain may be removed by faith, so it may be endured by faith.
2. Hold a mental image of yourself as healthy and vigorous.
3. The secret of life isn't in what happens to you, but what you do with what happens to you.
4. God never lays a burden or a pain upon us that He does not give us equivalent strength to bear it.
5. As difficult as it is, pain is not without value.
6. It isn't all-important what the condition of your body is; the important factor is the condition of your mind and soul.
7. There is an enormous power in the human spirit to rise above pain and suffering when the spirit is determined.

8. You have the right to ask God to take away or reduce your pain.
9. Complete giving of the self to God is the most effective way of gaining that inner peace and sense of Divine love that takes pain away.

16

LIVE FOREVER

"Current scientific investigation seems to lend support to our intuitions and faith. Recently an eminent scientist expressed his personal feeling that the soul theory has been proved according to the minimum standards of science. His studies indicate that 'the soul survives the barriers of time and space.'"

WHEN MY FATHER and my brothers, Bob and Leonard, and I returned home after the funeral services of my mother we felt, as do all families, a deep sense of loss and loneliness. We sat in my minister father's study in the parsonage home at Canisteo, New York and talked about the old days when we were little boys. Our talk was about the dear old homey things, the tender experiences that bind families together by ties that not even death can shatter. We alternately laughed and cried, for life is a patchwork of smiles and tears, each emotion fertilizing and enriching the other.

Then Leonard, the youngest brother, and a capable pastor, took up the old Book, the Book that she had taught us to love and believe. He began to read aloud some of those great and eloquent passages:

"Let not your heart be troubled: ye believe in God, believe also in me. In my Father's house are many mansions: if it were not so, I would have told you. I go to prepare a place for you. And if I go and prepare a place for you, I will come again, and receive you unto myself; that where I am, there ye may be also." (John 14:1–3)

"For we know that if our earthly house of this tabernacle were dissolved, we have a building of God, an house not made with hands, eternal in the heavens." (II Corinthians 5:1)

"For this corruptible must put on incorruption, and this mortal must put on immortality. So when this corruptible shall have put on incorruption, and this mortal shall have put on immortality, then shall be brought to pass the saying that is written, Death is swallowed up in victory. O death, where is thy sting? O grave, where is thy victory?" (I Corinthians 15:53–55)

Suddenly Dad leaped from his chair, pacing the floor in great excitement. With profounder emotion than I ever heard him show from the pulpit, and he had rare power to move men and women, he cried, "If these things are true and I know they are, this message of life and joy should be shouted from the housetops."

So that is what I am doing now, "shouting from the housetops" the greatest of all messages, the glorious truth that you and your loved ones live forever.

When I told my great friend, Dr. Daniel A. Poling, about this book, its title and message, he declared, with his usual keen understanding and glorious faith that the last chapter must be called "Live Forever." And so it is.

I have not the slightest doubt concerning the truth and validity of immortality. I believe absolutely and certainly that when you die you will meet your loved ones and know them and be reunited with them, never to be separated again. I believe that identity of personality will continue in that greater sphere of life in which there will be no suffering nor sorrow as we know them here in the physical sense. I hope there will be struggle, for struggle is good. Certainly there will be ongoing development, for life with no upward effort of the spirit would be incredibly dull.

Nor is this immortality given to us cheaply. To be worthy of living forever, your soul must be cleansed and you must be in harmony with God. In the teaching of Jesus Christ death does not refer to the body but rather to the soul. "The soul that sinneth, it shall die." (Ezekiel 18:20) But the soul that has been forgiven and cleansed, will live forever.

The sign of Christianity, the cross, is a plus sign. It is not a minus sign. The Bible itself says that Christianity is a process of addition, not subtraction. "But seek ye first the kingdom of God, [that is everything that is described by the cross, the plus sign] and his righteousness; and all these things shall be added unto you." (Matt. 6:33) When life is finished here, it is not subtracted from you, but immortal and eternal life is added to you.

Some seem to want proof of this positive faith. There are few out-and-out disbelievers yet remaining in these more enlightened days. And what tremendous difficulty faces a disbeliever in immortality in having to prove his negative position.

Many years ago I read a statement by a scientist who said dogmatically, "At death the life of man is snuffed out like a candle flame." When he made that statement he was listened to with some respect because materialistic science was still riding high, wide, and handsome. But now, he would simply be asked to prove his statement. How does he know? How can he prove his remark? The answer is, he doesn't know, and cannot prove it.

On the positive side we do not believe in immortality because we can prove it, but we try to prove it because we cannot help believing it. Indeed, the instinctive feeling that it is true is one of the deepest proofs of its truth. When God wishes to carry a point with men he plants the idea in their instincts. The longing for immortality is of such universality that it can hardly be met with indifference by the universe. What we deeply long for, what we deeply feel must surely reflect a basic fact of human existence.

Such great truths as this are not believed because of proof and demonstration, but by faith and intuition. Intuition is an important factor in the scientific perception of truth. As Bergson pointed out, scientists often come to the end of verifiable knowledge, then, by a leap of intuition, arrive at truth.

Current scientific investigation seems to lend support to our intuitions and faith. Recently an eminent scientist expressed his personal feeling that the soul theory has been proved according to the minimum standards of science. His studies indicate that "the soul survives the barriers of time and space."

Exciting scientific investigation is proceeding in the field of extrasensory perception. Years ago a number of eminent scientists, among them Wallace, Myers, Royce, and James, began psychical research studies.

Later McDougall and Rhine and others developed parapsychology. This study of the "psyche" or "soul" included those phenomena with which psychology did not deal. These scientists raised the question, "Is there a spiritual factor to men?" Using the most exact methods they examined precognition (the ability of the mind to see something which has not yet happened) retrocognition (the ability to see again that which has happened in the past) and finally clairvoyance and telepathy. After innumerable experiments competent authorities have declared these findings sound from a mathematical point of view. That is they occurred more times than the mathematical percentage of chance would justify. Such investigations seem to have come close to proving scientifically that there is an aspect to man distinctly of greater permanency than his physical attributes.

One of the most significant facts about modern thinking is the new conviction that the universe is spiritual. The old materialistic and mechanistic conception is fading. Sir James Jeans declares that, "All the world is in vibration." Einstein told us, "Matter and energy are interchangeable, one and the same." Scholars, it seems, are recognizing the deep spiritual something that lies at the core of life.

I have quoted Jeans and Einstein. Now I am going to quote a cowboy. The philosophers and the scientists are not always the wisest; sometimes fishermen, farmers, cowboys, men who live with the stars and the earth may have the subtlest wisdom. This cowboy writes as follows under a San Antonio, Texas date line.

Dear Sir,

What is the thing that is spoke of as subconscious? I have used that thing all my life and I know there is something about that thing I don't understand. I have read all I have gotten a chance to on the subject. I strongly believe that it is something we can use. I believe that it has saved my life many times.

I was raised in West Texas and I spent much of my life breaking wild horses. And I know something that is called the subconscious will work on horses. I know that something travels from man to horse, and from horse to man. I have felt it on the bridle reins. That same thing will tell me which trail to take when I am lost in the mountains or on the plains. It guides me through the darkness of the night.

You may think I am crazy to make such statements, but I won't try to do anything without first asking that thing about it. And I then act quick when the answer comes.

Now, if you can see any sense to this question and these statements, will you please answer me in very simple language.

Your friend,

I like that cowboy. Living with the stars and the plains, with the mountains and with God has made him a philosopher of depth. On the trail he felt this "thing." And what is this "thing?" It is God in contact with that deathless "thing" within man.

This is a mysterious universe and within its outward forms is indestructible life. The Bible reminds us that what seems to be death isn't actually. It describes how the Lord, whom they thought dead, was alive and appeared to many. He would be seen; then He would vanish to reappear again.

These manifestations of disappearing and reappearing were designed to emphasize that while He seemed to be gone, He was not gone, but is ever near to us. Then comes the astonishing statement that we shall know the same aliveness after the experience called death. "Because I live, ye shall live also." (John 14:19) The mere fact that we can no longer see our loved ones in the flesh does not at all mean that they are not alive. They still live in this dynamic, mysterious universe even as we too shall live forever.

The day I received the news that my mother had died I went to the Marble Collegiate Church and sat in the pulpit. I did that because she had always told me, "Whenever you are in that pulpit I will be with you." I wanted to feel her presence.

Then I went into my study. On the table lies a Bible. It lay there that morning and it has been there ever since. It is old and tattered now, but that Bible will remain there as long as I am connected with the church, and then I will take it with me wherever I may go. I never give a sermon that I do not, first, put my hand on that Bible.

On that morning of her physical death I placed my hand on the Bible, in an instinctive desire for comfort, and stood looking out toward Fifth

Avenue, when all of a sudden, I distinctly felt two cupped hands, soft as eiderdown, resting very gently on my head. And I had a feeling of inexpressible joy.

I have always been afflicted with a questioning kind of mind and, even then, I began to deal factually with this experience, reasoning that it was hallucination due to grief. But I did not believe my own attempt to reason it away. Then the idea dawned that I should lift my thinking to the spiritual level and realize that in this dynamic universe, what we call death is but the change in form of deathless spirit. From that moment I never doubted my mother's spiritual aliveness.

I once wrote of this incident in a magazine article, and received scores of letters from people who told of a like experience. One physician wrote: "I was attending a man in his last illness. Of a sudden, a look came over his face that can only be described as out of this world in its beauty. He began to call by name his mother, father, brother, sister. Then he said, 'Why, Frank, I didn't know you were there.' And, closing his eyes, his spirit took flight.

"The daughter of the man," the doctor continued, "told me that mother and father, brother and sister, had been dead for years. But about his mentioning Frank, she could not understand. Frank was not dead.

"An hour later came the message that Frank, a cousin, had been killed in an accident some hours before."

They live and they will live forever as you will, also, in this dynamic universe. The conviction that this is true first gripped me years ago in a little country cemetery in Ohio. I was standing by my father's side as the body of my beloved grandmother was lowered into the grave. I felt very sorry for him that day for he was sad and so was I. I can see the preacher even yet, standing by the grave and, in memory, hear the strong, sure tone of his voice as he repeated those immortal words, "I am the resurrection, and the life: he that believeth in me, though he were dead, yet shall he live.

"And whosoever liveth and believeth in me shall never die." (John 11:25–26) Suddenly, I had one of those flashing experiences of intuitive perception and instantly, deep in my heart, knew that immortality is a true belief.

Only a short time ago, on a sun-kissed day, I came to the place where those words were first spoken. We rounded a turn in the road that winds up to Jerusalem and there on the shoulder of the Mount of Olives was the village of Bethany just as it appeared in every Biblical picture book. We came to the grave where once rested the body of Lazarus and descended to the spot from which he came forth. Later, emerging into the brilliant daylight, we stood by the open tomb and read aloud the great words. The place where we were standing must have been almost the exact spot where Jesus made that immortal statement to those grieving people.

You never know when your greatest experiences are going to come. When least expected an unforgettable moment flashes across your life with inexpressible meaning. It is difficult for me to recall without deep emotion the feeling of absolute certainty that burned into my mind at that moment that the words spoken there nearly twenty centuries ago are absolutely true. I turned to my wife and said, "On the spot where we now stand was uttered the greatest statement in the history of the world. Think," I said, "of all the grieving millions of people down the centuries who have been comforted by the words spoken here." And again I had that overwhelming feeling of their truth. "I am the resurrection, and the life: he that believeth in me, though he were dead, yet shall he live."

So, God's answer to death is life. In fact, the Bible is filled with emphasis upon life. It preaches a faith based on life, not death. The Bible constantly talks about spiritual experiences, flashing intimations, being surrounded by shining ones, the glory of a Presence, all of which is to tell us that what seems to be death only seems so, that the real fact is life eternal.

Our conception of death as a horror is surely unrealistic. Robert Louis Stevenson said, "If this is death, it is easier than life." Somewhere I read the statement of a great thinker: "Life is the dull side of death." No doubt death is only a process of passing to the other side through a very thin barrier. We need not fear it. Socrates, one of the earth's wisest men, said, "No evil can happen to a good man either in life or after death." The Biblical Book of Revelation in a marvelous passage tells us not to fear death, "And he laid his right hand upon me, saying unto me, 'Fear not . . .'" (Rev. 1:17)

It would be incredible, that a good God, acting as Creator, would make anything as horrible as the death we have traditionally pictured. Basically, all natural processes are good, and death will be but another experience of God's kindness.

The unborn baby, tucked up under its mother's heart, must feel very secure. Suppose somebody might come to him and say, "You are going to leave this place and pass into another world. In other words, you are going to die." The baby might say, "But I don't want to leave, I like it here. I am comfortable. I know this place. I am secure." So he might express his dread of what, to us, is known as birth, but to him is death, or the end of his present existence.

But there comes the day when the baby "dies" out of that prenatal world, or, as we say from our side, he is born. For him it means passing from a known form of life to an unknown and it might very well seem death, since it is the end of that existence as he knows it.

Then what happens to him? Immediately he finds himself in loving arms. Looking down at him is the kindliest and most loving face in all the world and everybody hovers around and rushes to do his bidding. Surely he must say, "What a wonderful place this is. How foolish I was to dread and fear it and to doubt God's provision."

So he begins to love this new world which he once feared. Then the years add up until he becomes an old man. One day the thought comes, "I must die and leave this world, which has been my home for so long. I love its sunlight which warms my body. I love its starlight which lifts my soul. I love its dear old human ways. I am secure here. I do not want to leave loved ones. I do not want to die out of this world into another." He resists it and again he is afraid.

Then comes that final moment when he "dies" as we call the process. But who are we to say that it is not, instead, simply another birth? What will happen to him when this change takes place? All of a sudden he is young again and surrounded by love and beauty. Twice he "died" and twice he was "born." It is all very reasonable to believe that when your time comes to die you will simply be born into a more wonderful world.

The observed experience of men and women as they pass the so-called valley of the shadow of death indicates, I believe, conclusively that the other side is a place of life and beauty. Sometimes, of course, there is pain in sickness and the passage of a human being through physical death may be a pathetic and seemingly difficult one. But at the moment of death, as a great physician described it, "A great wave of peace seems to come over one and all human suffering ends."

A nurse who told me that she had seen many people die and that never had she noted terror in any face at the moment of death, except in one woman who had cheated her sister. She died with fright written on her face. "Many patients," said this nurse, "have given expression, at the moment of death, of having 'seen' something, and often they spoke about wondrous light and music. Some spoke of seeing faces which apparently they recognized. There was often a look of incredulous wonder in their eyes."

A friend tells of a man who submitted to an operation under local anesthetic. But the strain was greater than anticipated and during the operation he sank alarmingly. Heart action practically ceased, but the patient was finally brought through the operation. Afterward, he reported that at one point he had a strange desire to go further into a state of being which gave the impression of being more appealing than anything he had ever known. The deeper he sank, the less he wanted to return. That was the moment when the physician noted a definite sinking. What he saw as he ventured farther and farther across the river, apparently was something so wonderfully beautiful that it lured him deeply.

Then there was another friend, a meteorologist or weather man. I was with him when his time came to die. As the mist of the valley came over him, suddenly he said, speaking to his son who was sitting beside him,

"Jim, I see beautiful buildings. And in one of them is a light, and the light is for me. It is very beautiful." Then he was gone.

Jim said, "My father was strictly an intellectual and in his scientific work never reported anything that was not a proven fact. The habit of years could not change. He was reporting what he saw."

I talked with the late Mrs. Thomas A. Edison about her husband's view of the after life. He was working on a project to determine the weight of the soul. He believed that the soul is an actual entity that leaves the body at death. By weighing the body before and after death he hoped to get some idea of the soul's substantiality.

Edison was one of the few greatest minds in this country. When he was close to the moment of death, the physician saw that he was attempting to say something. He bent over him and distinctly heard Edison say, "It is very beautiful over there."

When Edison invented the electric light he performed hundreds of experiments before he reported that he had an incandescent bulb. Can we believe that the habit of a lifetime of scientific exactitude would disappear at the moment of death and the man of science would suddenly begin to talk poetry? Definitely he saw something, or he would not have said that he did. He sent back to us the reassuring word . . . "It is very beautiful over there." And you can believe it is so.

I was asked to call upon a woman who was very ill in the hospital. Upon entering her room I asked her how she felt and was startled by the directness of her answer. "Mentally and spiritually I am fine. Physically I may as well tell you that I am going to die."

The level and unfrightened look in her eyes made me realize here was a person able, imperturbably, to meet that which frightens most of us. With serene objectivity she approached the event that holds terror for so many. She was like a person making ready to go on a long journey, a beautiful journey. There was no sense of fear, only sublime trust.

She said, "I wanted to see you, not because I particularly need comfort, but to urge you to keep on teaching Christ's message of hope and faith. You must continue to tell people that Jesus Christ has the truth about life and death; that He will help them throughout life and then guide them across to Heaven at the end." A lovely smile crossed her face. "As I have faced my inevitable death I lay here thinking of all the spiritual truth I had read and heard. I determined to put myself completely into God's hands. A deep conviction came that it would be all right. He is so close to me." And she added another sentence which rings like a bell in my mind. "I have no fear of life; I have no fear of death."

Before leaving, I stood at the foot of her bed and said, "I salute you as a very great lady, one of the greatest I have known. You have no fear of life; you have no fear of death. You have won the greatest of all possible victories. Wherever you go in the vastness of eternity Jesus Christ will be with you."

How good God is. The Bible, His Book, promises the most astonishing blessings. Personally, I believe the Bible makes good on every promise, as extraordinary as they are. And so superlative are these promised blessings that even the Bible sometimes runs out of words to describe them. It simply declares, . . . "Eye hath not seen, nor ear heard, neither have entered into the heart of man, [that is, even to imagine] the things which God hath prepared for them that love Him." (I Cor. 2:9) So, have no fear of life, no fear of death.

Dr. Leslie D. Weatherhead, of London says: "Let me tell you as one who has witnessed many deaths, that in my experience I have never seen one that was unhappy. Sometimes there is fear beforehand, and pain, too, but the end is either sudden and over before we can register any emotion, or else we enter the complete painlessness of sleep, or else it is one of the most joyous experiences we can undergo.

"I sat once on the bed of a man who was dying and his hand lay within my own. I must have gripped his hand more tightly than I thought, for he said a strange thing to me. 'Don't pull me back. It looks so wonderful further on.' And when my own sister was thought to be dying, she overheard the doctor say to the nurse, 'She won't get through the night.' The patient heard it as the best news in the world. When later, the nurse said, 'She is going to pull through after all,' my sister told us afterwards that she heard the words with regret."

Dr. Weatherhead also quotes Dr. William Hunter, a distinguished physician who, on his death bed said, "If I had strength enough to hold a pen I would write how easy and pleasant a thing it is to die."

Of course, the instinct to live is very strong and we resist death to the end. That is part of our human nature. Resistance to death is built into us by a wise Creator. If we did not have resistance we would often give up in the presence of life's difficulties and take the easiest way out. Therefore, we are so constructed that no man will take his own life unless reason has been, at least, temporarily disenthroned. But God who has built this resistance to death into us has also built into life another great truth in the form of instinctive faith that when we must die we go from life to life, from mortal life on earth to eternal life with God.

Since God never did anything badly, but has arranged good for his children (the bad is man-made), all evidence points to the fact that when we pass over to the other side, this death that we have feared for so long will hold no terror at all.

My father died at eighty-five years of age. I never knew a man who wanted so to live. Everytime I saw him he would say, "Norman, I am going to live to be one hundred." And the only weakness I ever saw in my father was a fear of dying. But about three months before he died I noticed that he seemed no longer afraid of it.

My stepmother, who was with him when he passed to the other side, said that as he came to the last he looked at her enquiringly (he could no longer speak), as if to say, "Is this it?"

And she said, "Yes, Clifford, this is it." She said that a wonderful smile passed over his face as if to say, "How foolish I have been."

My stepmother, Mary Peale, is a very factual, sensible woman. She is a wonderful person. Some months after my father's death she told me, "I had an experience with your father. You won't think I am foolish if I tell it to you, will you?"

"Why, of course not," I replied.

"The other night he seemed to come to me," she continued. "I seemed to hear him; there was no sound, but the hearing was by an inward ear, and it was with exactly the old time inflection and tone of his voice.

"This is what he said, 'I would be willing to die again if I could only make you understand how beautiful it all is and how all right I am.' And then he said, speaking of death, 'There's nothing to it.' "

Now that is precisely the way my father would dispose of a matter once he knew the facts. That was his characteristic way of speaking. When he reached a conclusion and saw the facts he expressed his opinion forthrightly and positively. If he found, "There's nothing to it," he would say just that and in that manner.

Of course, when he said, "There's nothing to it," he did not mean that death is not a profound experience. He did not mean that those who are left behind do not suffer great sorrow. He would not minimize it. But what he did mean was that when we come to that final moment when God receives us from one world to another, it is nothing to fear. I am sure that my father now knows what he could not know while in mortal life, that God takes us to that other side where we are reunited with loved ones and live forever in joy and peace.

In Syracuse, New York, I was told that I should talk with Dr. James H. Bennett who was selected by the Medical Society of the State of New York as the General Practitioner of the Year. Dr. Bennett who practiced for many years in Baldwinsville, New York, had contracted an inoperable disease at age forty-nine.

I was told that everyone knew about his sickness and that he would talk quite freely about it. And it was further stated that he had a wonderful philosophy of life. So, I telephoned and had a half-hour talk with him over the phone. He mentioned his illness quite naturally, and without hesitancy, telling me that his time on earth was very short.

"How do you feel about that?" I asked.

"I have learned to take things as they come," he said. "All my professional career I have been dealing with life and death."

"Are you afraid?" I asked of him.

His answer was direct and forthright. "What is there to be afraid of? My conscience is clear. And besides, God is good."

"When your time comes to die," I asked, "do you feel that you will still be in life on the other side?"

His answer was equally forthright, "I have no doubt of it," he replied.

So, neither do I and neither should you. Therefore, be glad and live with faith, as is fitting of those who never die.

Develop deep confidence in the eternal future of your own life and that of your loved ones. Keep believing until you know with certainty that you are an ever alive and deathless part of a dynamic universe. Learn to know that faith in immortality is completely reliable and absolutely true. Immerse yourself in the Bible, in the deathless faith which it teaches. Learn to know, not only by your mind, but by the intuitive perception of the spirit that the great assumptions of continuing life are true.

Life is filled with uncertainties; fogs of doubt, dismal and shadowy fears sometime obscure the landmarks of our faith. Simply put your trust in God and in the deep instincts of your own nature. Read the Bible, pray, and fill your life with love and goodness. Have faith in the accuracy and dependability of your spiritual instruments. They will guide you through the overcasts of this life to a perfect landing in that beautiful land beyond.

Some time ago I flew in a United States Navy plane with an officer who is one of the best pilots in the service, into Floyd Bennett Field, Brooklyn. He told me several hundred miles out that the ceiling at Floyd Bennett was very low. "Are we going in?" I asked.

"I think we'll go in there, but if we don't then we'll go in someplace else," he replied nonchalantly.

I do not know what the ceiling was at Floyd Bennett when we came in because the pilot did not tell me, but I knew we were descending rapidly. Down, down, down, we went, but still we did not break through the heavy overcast.

Then, peering out the window, I saw a sandy beach. I estimated we were one hundred feet above it, perhaps more; it was hard to tell. Then water. I knew there were sandy beaches and inlets around Floyd Bennett. Then another sandy beach, and then . . . out of the mist, the runway . . . lights dimly illuminating it in the fog.

When the pilot came from his cockpit I said admiringly, "That was a marvelous landing. That required skill."

"Ah, no; maybe a little experience. Really, it required faith more. I must have faith in my instruments and not deviate on my own. If I become doubtful and think 'These instruments could be wrong, they could be deflecting,' then I could go very wrong indeed. But if I put full trust in my instruments, we make good landings."

We have our instruments, too, precise, exact instruments; prayer, faith, the instinct of God and immortality. They are trustworthy and will take you through the fogs, the drifting winds, the storms, and the uncertainties of life. Trusting those instruments of faith you will come in, finally, to be welcomed by the lights on the eternal runway. And there will be your loved ones to meet you with the same old smile on their beloved faces. Believe . . . and live forever.

THE AMAZING RESULTS OF POSITIVE THINKING

TO CHERISHED ASSOCIATES

Smiley Blanton
Daniel A. Poling
Herman L. Barbery
Eugene McKinley Pierce
Donald Wayne Hoffman
Mary F. Brinig

A WORD TO THE READER

HUNDREDS OF PEOPLE wrote this book. I have simply put together the combined experiences of many men and women.

This is a result book. It is the story of thrilling things which took place in the lives of thousands of people when they applied the principles of dynamic change.

Since publication of *The Power of Positive Thinking*, a book which teaches effective living through right thinking and practical religious faith, thousands of readers have communicated with me. They told how, by the application of positive thinking principles to their own life situations, they have mastered fear, healed personal relationships, found better health, overcome inner conflicts and gained strong new confidence.

Writers of these letters invariably expressed themselves in terms of joy and faith in God. Readers repeatedly said that they started reading the Bible, and they told how it took on new meaning. Indeed, they declared that they drew from it faith and happiness they had not previously known. They discovered new values in the church, and the use of practical spiritual techniques became an exciting adventure. These letters came from Catholics, Protestants and Jews alike, and told how God had become a living reality. Many referred to experiencing Jesus Christ in their lives, and this spiritual phenomenon is described with deep feeling as being very warm, rich and personal. New potentials were found in spiritual living, especially in the power of prayer. Some who had gone regularly to church for years, but with no joy or sense of lift, spoke wonderingly of fresh discoveries in faith.

What excitement, what sense of wonder, what new life, what love of their fellow men, and of life itself, these people told about.

While readers have graciously expressed appreciation of the teachings outlined in *The Power of Positive Thinking*, many have found either new uses for the suggested methods or, in some cases, exciting new formulas for effective living, which in their enthusiasm they sent to me. These discoveries of fresh techniques should, I felt, be passed on to others for the helpfulness they are certain to bring.

So wonderful were the letters and word-of-mouth statements concerning the workability of the positive way of life that, when I gathered many of them together in book form, a natural title was *The Amazing Results of Positive Thinking*. This book is a laboratory demonstration of the real experiences of many people with formulas that actually changed lives.

Through these formulas thousands of people have discovered a way of thinking and living that changed sorrow to joy, weakness to strength, failure to success, despair to hope, and defeat to victory. This new book explains how the same principles can help you. And, after reading these results, perhaps you will want to put these powerful techniques to work in your life. Then won't you write me about your own results, that I may pass them on to encourage and help others.

To you, my reader and friend, God bless and guide you always. And He will, too.

NORMAN VINCENT PEALE

CONTENTS

1

DOES POSITIVE THINKING ALWAYS WORK?

DOES POSITIVE THINKING ALWAYS WORK? Yes.

Now, I realize this is a rather bold statement. And someone may object: "Is that so. I had lots of problems. I read positive thinking and I still have problems." Someone else may say, "Well, I had a business that was in the doldrums, and I tried positive thinking, and my business is still in the doldrums. Positive thinking didn't change the facts. Failure exists. If you deny that, you're just being an ostrich, burying your head in the sand."

So often, people don't really understand the nature of positive thinking. A positive thinker does not refuse to *recognize* the negative, he refuses to *dwell* on it. Positive thinking is a form of thought which habitually looks for the best results from the worse conditions. It is possible to look for something to build on; it is possible to expect the best for yourself even though things look bad. And the remarkable fact is that when you seek good, you are very likely to find it.

This seeking-the-positive is a deliberate process, and a matter of choice. Not long ago I received word that a friend of mine had been fired. In talking with Bill, I learned the circumstances. He had been summarily dismissed. No explanation was given except there had been a policy change, and he was no longer needed. To make matters worse, nine months earlier Bill had received a handsome offer from a competing firm, he had talked the matter over with his boss, and his boss had persuaded him to stay on, saying: "We need you here, Bill. And frankly, things look pretty good for you."

Well, of course, Bill reacted rather bitterly to all of this. He went around feeling unwanted, insecure, rejected. His ego had been hurt. He became morose and resentful, and in a state of mind like that, he wasn't in a very good condition to look for another job.

This is exactly the kind of situation where positive thinking can do its best. One day, Bill dug out an old copy of *The Power of Positive Thinking*, and read it through. What possible good was there in his condition, he wondered? He didn't know. But he could see plenty of negative factors, and he clearly realized that these negative emotions were dragging him down. If he was going to put positive thinking to work, the first thing he had to do was get rid of the negative feelings.

Here, at least, was a place he could begin. So he practiced the principle of thought replacement. That is, he deliberately filled his mind with positive affirmations and crowded out the negative thoughts. He began a systematic program of prayer and told the Lord: "I believe You have a plan for my life, so there must be some purpose in my getting fired. Instead of railing against my fate, I humbly ask You to show me the purpose in what has happened." Once he began to believe there had been a reason and some meaning behind what had happened to him, it was easier to rid himself of resentment against his former employers. And once that happened he was "employable" again.

One day, shortly after he had reached this point in his thinking, Bill met an old friend. They got to talking, and the friend asked how things were.

"Oh, I've just been fired," Bill said, casually.

The friend was surprised. "Well you're certainly honest enough about it," he said. "What happened?"

Bill told him, and he finished by saying: ". . . and I know the Lord has a job for me somewhere else."

"The *Lord!* Aren't you worried?"

"Not at all. Something better will turn up. In my philosophy, when one door shuts another will open if you just have faith and put it in God's hands."

A few days later Bill received a telephone call from his friend, saying that there was a long-unfilled opening in his company, and asking him if he wanted the job—salarywise it wasn't as good as his last position, but it had potential. Bill took it. There was no doubt about the fact that in his new job he was in a better position to be of service to people. He realized this very shortly and soon discovered that his new activity was one he had always wanted. He became stimulated and excited about his work in a way that he had almost forgotten at his previous place of employment. He would grow. This, he felt sure, was part of the plan that God had in mind.

Now the important thing to analyze here is *why* positive thinking worked. It's not that some magic entered the picture and created a job out of the ether. There was a definite scientific principle at work. When Bill had his mind filled with resentments and angers and hatreds, he was destroying his own value as an employee. He was making it impossible for himself to do his best at the business of job-seeking. On the day Bill met his friend, if he had been bitter and full of sly defenses, do you think his friend would have considered him a good person to recommend for the new job? There is no mysticism at work here. This way of thinking and of acting is, above all, down-to-earth common sense.

Positive thinking is looking at events with the knowledge that there will be both good and bad in life, but that it is better to emphasize the good. And as you do that, good seems to increase.

The other day I went out the door of my office and hailed a cab. As soon as I got in the taxi, I could tell that my driver was a happy man. He was whistling. First he whistled a tune from, "My Fair Lady," and then he launched himself into a version of "Stars and Stripes Forever." After a while I said to him, "You seem to be in a happy mood."

"Why shouldn't I be?" he said. "I've just learned something. I've learned that there's no percentage in getting excited, or in the dumps, because things average out."

And he went on to explain what he meant. Early that morning he had taken his cab out, hoping to take advantage of the morning rush hour. It was a bitterly cold day. The driver said it was ". . . the kind of temperature where, if you touch metal, your hand will stick to it." And as luck would have it, no sooner had he started his day than he had a flat tire. He was angry. Muttering, he got out his jack and lug wrench and tried to take off the tire. It was so cold he could only work for a few minutes at a time. And while he was struggling, a truck stopped. The driver jumped out and, much to the taxi-driver's surprise, began to help him. When the tire was back in place, the trucker gruffly waved off the cabby's thanks, got in his truck and drove off.

"Well, this put me in a high mood," the cabby said to me. "Already things were averaging out. First, I was angry with the flat, then I felt good because of that trucker's help and right away things started going good. Even the money had averaged out. I've never had a busier morning, one fare after another in and out of the cab. Things average out, Mister. Don't get excited when a situation gets rocky; things average out."

Here was a positive thinker, all right. He said he was never again going to let life's mishaps annoy him. He was just going to live by the theory that things average out OK. That is real positive thinking, and it will work, too, because things always come around to a brighter view when you wait them out and work them out optimistically. The law of averages is always on the positive thinker's side. A positive thinker chooses to keep his mind fixed on the bright future that is always just around the corner, and in this way he helps make the dark moments more cheerful, productive and creative. That attitude gets you around the "corner" quicker, too.

It is a fact of life that all of us will come face to face with plenty of frustration, difficulty and trouble. But there isn't one of us who needs to be defeated by these obstacles. If you face life with the sincere faith that through the aid of the Almighty you can overcome your troubles, then you will keep defeat at arm's length. And this applies in all the circumstances life can bring.

One evening in San Francisco, I had the pleasure of dining in the home of a charming lady named Elena Zelayeta. I have never attended a dinner party presided over by an individual of happier personality or more irresistible gaiety. Elena is Mexican, and the dinner she served that evening was a 17-course Mexican dinner (small courses)—the most delicious repast I could hope to experience. She cooked it herself—and she is totally blind.

Elena Zelayeta once ran a restaurant in San Francisco. It was a beautiful place, full of color and life. Then her eyesight began to fail. Soon she was blind, living in darkness. One day the telephone rang and she groped her way to answer it and received the shocking news that her husband had just been killed in an accident.

Blindness—and now her husband suddenly dead. She sat by the telephone, utterly crushed, wondering what she was going to do. She was dejected for weeks, living in helplessness. But in this most complete darkness, emotionally and physically, she perceived finally, by the help of her strong faith, that there was something positive to which she could attach herself. She did not choose to dwell on the negative, she sought the positive, and she found it in a most remarkable way. As she struggled in shock and sorrow, suddenly she felt "as if a great, strong hand gripped her and lifted her up."

Putting sincere faith and strong positive thinking against her sad conditions, she determined that she would conquer her grief, loneliness and handicap. So complete was her ultimate victory that presently she picked up her life again as a career woman. How well Elena Zelayeta succeeded is shown by the fact that in recent years she has lectured on cooking up and down the West Coast, sometimes to as many as a thousand women at a time. She has written three successful cook books and a book of inspiration. She operates a frozen food business with her two sons and goes to the office every day.

She had to cook by sense of feel and taste and smell. But these, she says with a smile, are what cooking is all about anyway. This inspiring woman is one of the most marvelous examples of positive thinking I have ever ran across. Naturally I sought for her secret of conquering adversity. While we were having dinner at her home, Mrs. Zelayeta made this powerful statement which is the guiding principle of her life. It is the formula through which she found victory. "Always act," she said, "as if it were impossible to fail and God will see you through."

Always act as if it were *impossible* to fail!

Elena Zelayeta is the type of person William James the philosopher-psychologist would call "tough minded." The world, according to this great thinker, is made up of two kinds of people—the "tough-minded" and "tender-minded." The tender-minded are the ones who wilt under obstacles and difficulties. They are cut to the quick by criticism and lose heart. They are the ones who whine and fail. But the tough-minded individuals are not like that. They are people from all walks of life, the manual workers and the merchants, the mothers and the fathers, the teachers, the old people, and the young people too, who have a strong element of toughness built into them by Almighty God. By toughness is meant the inner power to stand up to a difficulty; to have what it takes to take it.

Up in the little town of Carmel, New York, where we publish *Guideposts* magazine, lived a boy named Jim Mackey. Jim was fourteen years old; a lovable boy and real man, one of the truly tough-minded people of this world. He was a natural born athlete, one of the very best. But early in his high school career, he began to limp. It soon developed that he had a cancer. An operation was required, and Jim's leg was amputated. As soon as he was out of the hospital, he went around to the high school on his crutches, talking cheerfully about how he was going to have a wooden leg soon. "Then I'll be able to hold up my socks with a thumb tack," he said. "None of you guys can do that!"

As soon as the football season started, Jim went to the coach and asked if he could be one of the team managers. For weeks he appeared regularly for practice, carrying the coach's set of plays and infusing the team with his contagious, fiery courage. Then one afternoon he missed a practice. The coach was worried. He checked, and learned that Jim was in the hospital having another examination. Later, he learned that the examination had revealed lung cancer. "Jim will be dead," said the doctor, "within six weeks."

Jim's parents decided not to tell the boy about his death sentence; they wanted him to live as normal a life as he could for the last few weeks. So, Jim was soon back at practice again with his big smile and his offering of enthusiasm and courage. With his inspiration the team raced through the season undefeated, and to celebrate they decided to throw a banquet. Jim was to receive a victory football autographed by each member of the team. The banquet, however, was not the success it should have been. Jim was not there. He was too weak to attend.

A few weeks later, however, Jim was back again, this time at a basketball game. He was pale, very pale, but aside from that he was the same old Jim, smiling, laughing, making jokes. When, after the game, he went to the coach's office the entire football team was there. The coach scolded him gently for missing the banquet. "I'm on a diet, Coach," said Jim with a grin that covered his pain. Then one of the team members presented him with the victor's football. "We won it because of you, Jim," he said. Jim said a quiet thanks with tears in his eyes. The coach and Jim and the other boys talked about plans for the next season, and then it was time to go. Jim turned, and at the door he said, looking at the coach with a steady, level gaze:

"Good-bye, Coach."

"Don't you mean, 'so long,' Jim?" the coach asked.

Jim's eyes lighted up and his steady gaze turned into a smile. "Don't worry, Coach," he said. "I'm all set." And with that he was gone.

Two days later, he was dead.

Jim had known all along about his death sentence. But he could take it, for you see he was a tough-minded positive thinker. He made of this sad and tragic fact a creative experience. But, someone might say, he died; his positive thinking didn't get him very much. This is not true. Jim knew how to reach out for faith and how to create something warm and uplifting from the worse possible situation. He wasn't burying his head in the sand; he knew full well what was in store for him, and yet he chose not to be defeated! Jim was never defeated. He took his life, short as it was, and used it to instill courage, faith and laughter, permanently, into the lives and minds of the people who knew him. Could you, in any possible way, say that a person who succeeded in doing that with his life had been a failure?

That's what positive thinking is; it is tough-mindedness. It is refusing to be defeated. It is making the most of what you have to deal with in life. I have always been a reader of the works of the apostle of tough-mindedness: Thomas Carlyle. Recently I went up to Ecclefechan, the little Scotch village where he was born, to see if I might find there something of the strength of mind and character he possessed. Carlyle was the son of a stone mason. He started off to Edinburgh for his education with a shilling in his pocket and he walked into immortality.

Carlyle grew up in the little town of Ecclefechan, halfway between the Scottish border and the town of Dumfries. He loved Ecclefechan and Dumfrieshire. He might have been buried in Westminster Abbey but he preferred Ecclefechan. Queen Victoria once asked Carlyle what he considered the most beautiful road in Britain, and he answered, "The road from Ecclefechan to Dumfries." And then she asked him what he considered the second most beautiful road, and he answered, "Why, it's the road back to Ecclefechan."

I visited Carlyle's grave in the cemetery of his beloved Ecclefechan and sat at his graveside reading some of his words. Carlyle's message came to me anew—the essence of which is never give up; never give in; stand up to it—fight it through. God will aid you. According to Carlyle's understanding, life asks of each of us, "Will you be a hero, or will you be a coward?" It is just that direct and forthright. Where did Carlyle get such ideas? Of course, from the most rugged Book ever put together. "Be strong and of good courage; be not afraid, neither be thou dismayed; for the Lord thy God is with thee whithersoever thou goest." (Joshua 1:9)

Will you be a hero, or will you be a coward? Will you be tough-minded or tender-minded. The positive thinker will not be a coward. He believes in himself, in life, in humanity and in God. He knows his own capacity and his own ability. He is undaunted and invincible. He will draw the best from whatever comes.

The formula he uses is one by which he is changed from weakness to strength. Some time ago the Chase Manhattan Bank started excavation for a new skyscraper. Most of Manhattan Island is composed of solid bed-rock. This is the reason we can have structures that pierce the sky. But early excavations revealed that this site was not solid rock, as had been supposed, but contained a large pocket of quicksand! And of course it would be very difficult indeed to build a skyscraper on such a base.

So the bank people called in experts to suggest ways for meeting this situation constructively. One expert suggested pilings; another said to seal it off with caissons; but the cost would be prohibitive. Geologists were consulted: How long would it take to turn quicksand into sandstone? About a million years, the geologists answered. Well, the bank didn't feel they could wait that long. They then called in some soil solidification people, and this is where their search ended. These experts knew how to handle the quicksand problem. They sank pipes down into the quicksand and pumped into it a solution of sodium silicate and calcium chloride. In a few days the quicksand solidified into sandstone hard enough to permit the erection of a sixty-floor skyscraper building.

Does this seem miraculous? No, because it was done according to a sound, scientific principle; a proven, scientific formula. But I have seen "miracles" that make this achievement fade into insignificance. I have seen weak, defeated personalities who have had infused into them a special mental-spiritual formula called positive thinking, and I have seen them become as solid as rock. They have become strong people, well able to bear the weight of life most successfully.

This kind of transformation is available to all of us. It is in this sense that positive thinking always works. Positive thinking is able to transform us from cowards to heroes, from tender-minded to tough-minded individuals, from weak, negative, vacillating people to men of positive strength.

Although the life-changing power of positive thinking is available to all, some people experience difficulty in making it work. This is because of some strange psychological barrier that stands between them and the full use of positive thinking. One that keeps cropping up, is simply that they do not *want* it to work. They do not want to succeed. Actually, they are afraid to succeed. It's easier to wallow in self-pity. So, we create our own failure, and when a suggestion (such as positive thinking) comes along that will help overcome that failure, we subconsciously see to it that the suggestion doesn't work, and so we believe the principle, rather than ourselves is at fault. But when we understand such unhealthy mental reactions, then positive thinking begins to work. Recently I received this letter from a reader who lives in Petaluna, California:

For the first time in my life I can see where I have created my own bad luck by my thought pattern. Since reading your book about positive thinking and trying to clear my mind, I find little resentments cropping up I thought I'd forgotten years ago. Such silly little things to carry along with me all these years.

Certainly if you have helped me rub out these little termites, I owe you a great deal for showing me the way. I, too, have a pattern of failure and defeat. I never expected the best and I never got it, either. From here on out I'm going to go after the things I want, with confidence.

I feel God gave me a good chance and I just didn't have sense enough to use it. My faith will certainly deepen as I remove these mental blocks that I have so industriously set up. Believe me I built them strong!

This woman states that, for the first time, she sees that she has been creating her own bad luck by her thoughts. We have to stop creating our own failure. We have to stop being afraid that success will come our way.

I have a very good friend who is outstanding in the field of industrial medicine. He is the medical director of one of the nation's giant companies. He has come up from the worst kind of failure to the finest kind of success. Like the quicksand, he was made into rock, but by a spiritual formula of great strength. The other day I received a letter from him which had this paragraph in it:

I struggle constantly with success. For me, it has an insidious sweetness far more difficult to handle than the bitterness of failure, and much more uncertain as a stepping stone to spiritual progress.

I will call this man simply Dr. Tom, because he has such a spectacular story hidden in his past that I cannot name him fully. His was a dramatic struggle with success. He did not want it. It frightened him so thoroughly that he came close to killing himself rather than face it. In 1938 Dr. Tom was on the staff of a state mental hospital. Exactly ten years later he was paroled from this same hospital *as a patient!*

Dr. Tom started out in life with all the advantages. In fact, he had so many advantages that they got him in trouble. He had social position, a fine education, wealth, health and good looks. A nurse sat beside him in private school until he was nine years old; his father gave him an open checkbook when he was in high school. If Tom wanted anything, he just wrote a check; it was as simple as that. But along with this ease went trouble. People were always watching him, expecting great things from him because he came of such an outstanding family and "wonderful" environment. Nothing that Tom did seemed to live up to people's expectations. He never got any satisfaction out of success; in fact; success always seemed to get people annoyed with him: "Of course he's successful," they'd snap. "He ought to be!"

So Tom's subconscious mind did the thing that so many of our minds do. It said, "All right. If I can't get satisfaction from success, I'll get it from failure." And he proceeded to fail magnificently. When he was in college he started drinking. At medical school, his drinking became excessive. Drug addiction compounded his troubles. He married, set up a practice and had a child; the degeneration continued. In about ten years he reached the place where "just one" drink would start him off on a wild, blind drinking orgy that would last for days, even weeks. After one of his long disappearances, Dr. Tom came home to find that commitment papers had been made out against him. He was put in the violent ward of the state hospital, the same hospital where he had served as a doctor only a few years earlier.

"For forty-five days," Tom says, "I was out of my mind with D.T.'s. I was in solitary confinement, eating out of a tin plate like an animal. Then I began to come out of it and for another eighty-six days I lay in a comatose state, halfway between life and death. Surely this was as low as a man could sink. And then, suddenly—my heart still pounds when I think of it—I heard words spoken very slowly, and very distinctly. 'As far as the east is from the west, so far have I removed your transgressions from you.' (Psalm 103:12) Nothing has been the same for me since."

What had happened? Tom didn't know. He only knew that he had changed. He became calm. He was released from solitary confinement and allowed the comparative freedom of the ward. There he met two men who befriended him, and introduced him to Alcoholics Anonymous. In time, under the sponsorship of his AA friends, he was paroled from the hospital.

It was at this point that I met Tom at a religious conference where I was speaking. Scarcely have I ever known a man so thirsty for the water of life, so hungry for the bread of life. He wanted God, and God wanted him, and they found each other.

Dr. Tom did not go back to his practice right away. He felt he wasn't ready for that. He wanted to get a job on his own, one that had no relation to his childhood education. The only work he could find was a manual laboring job in the city dump. Think of that! A highly skilled, wealthy young man working as a laborer on the city dump and in the very southern community of his birth. But it was what Tom wanted. He wanted to see if he could be accepted for himself, and not for his family or his money.

One day while he was working, several of the "city fathers" came down to the dump for an inspection. Dr. Tom recognized some of his former schoolmates. He was suddenly filled with shame that they might recognize him, and he turned his back, bent down, and pretended to be working with something on the ground. A fellow-worker saw him do this, and at the same time saw the neatly dressed city fathers. He must have sized up the situation quickly because, without saying a word, he turned and did Dr. Tom's work for him until the visitors left. To my mind that is one of the greatest, kindliest acts of understanding and brotherhood that I have ever heard about. Dr. Tom and his friend never spoke about it, but it created a bond between them that was to have a wonderful effect on the young doctor. He took from it the strength that he needed.

"That man's name was Frank," Dr. Tom told me. "Frank will never know what he did for me. He accepted me. He taught me that I could be accepted for myself. First I had the acceptance of God, there in the hospital's solitary ward. Then I had the acceptance of man. It was what I needed in order to start again."

Today, Dr. Tom is again practicing medicine very successfully. He has a kind of enthusiasm about him, and a basic solidarity that comes from the new tough-mindedness that he has found. He was transformed from a "coward" to a "hero," to use Carlyle's terms. Of course, not many of us have such dramatic experiences with our fear of success, but it is nonetheless true that we often *don't want* positive thinking to work. We subconsciously see to it that our failure patterns remain intact.

But this is not the only block that can keep positive thinking from being effective. Sometimes there are strong negative elements in our lives that we refuse to clean out. We make feeble efforts to put positive forces to work, but they get stymied behind negative forces.

One night after I finished speaking at a dinner meeting in a hotel ballroom a man came up to me with the challenge: "I've been reading your stuff," he said, "I've tried it and it won't work."

"Why won't it work?" I asked him.

"That's what I'd like to know," he blustered.

Having a little time before taking a late plane I invited him to my hotel room for a talk. "I didn't mean to be impolite," he said as we sat down to chat. "But I'm trying to find out what's wrong. I seem to have lost my grip. I'm nervous and tense. I have a wonderful wife and family, a good business, a nice home, and I go to church. You'd think I'd be happy. But . . ." The recital went on and on. One trouble after another. And positive thinking, he said, did him no good at all.

After some discussion it occurred to me to throw out this question: "Are you doing anything wrong?"

"Nothing much," he muttered.

"What?" I asked.

"There's no point in going into that. I'm not doing anything that is in any way connected with my troubles. I'm only doing what everybody does."

"What does everybody else do?" I asked.

"Well," he said, "there is a little affair with a woman in Milwaukee."

"How little?" I asked.

He hesitated, "Well, maybe not so little."

"Maybe we had better face it. The plain truth is that you know you are doing something wrong, something you are ashamed of, something that could very well be the reason positive thinking isn't working for you."

"But how?" he demanded, on the defensive.

"Because guilt has a way of closing off your personality," I continued. "It sprouts fear and self-doubt; it restricts the power that gives vitality to the thought-flow. Constructive thinking becomes more difficult. Also, there is the self-punishment mechanism to deal with. When you are doing something wrong, you want to punish yourself to get relief from conscience distress. So actually, you try to make yourself fail, strange as it may sound. Of course all this blocks the positive feelings and thoughts that you do have. It's possible that all your misery and conflict stems from this sour area in your life."

"Well, what do I do about it?" he asked. Then he continued, "I guess I know the answer—stop doing it, get forgiveness—is that it?"

"That's it," I agreed. "And then you must forgive yourself. Do you want to start now?" He nodded. I could see that he was in earnest so I prayed, and he prayed. I made him pray out loud because he really had a lot to unload. And because he was sincere in his desire for change, God came into the picture and poured spiritual strength into him. Then his positive thinking really started working. Gone now is the woman in Milwaukee. Gone are the guilt and conflict feelings. As he became spiritually organized he found that it was quite possible for him to apply the principles of positive thinking with effective results. Naturally, this change did not happen all at once, but it *did* happen, and of course that's the important thing. One of the greatest facts in this world is that when a man changes, really changes in the God-centered way, everything changes.

Again, there is nothing mysterious about this. It is just common sense. We do something wrong, we feel guilty about it, and we expect punishment. If this remains uncorrected, the tendency is to punish ourselves, often through failures. That is the way the human mind is made. To correct the situation we must first clean out the wrong-doings; then the guilt feelings disappear and the need to punish ourselves with failures is thus eliminated. When this process has been completed, the principles of positive thinking can be tremendously effective.

One of the most important reasons why positive thinking seems not to work sometimes is that it has not really been put to a test. Positive thinking requires training and study and long perseverance. You have to be willing to work at it, sometimes for a long while, as was the case of a woman who spent four months of good solid, even painful effort before she got the results she sought. She wrote the following:

Dear Dr. Peale:

On the morning of January 21, 1956, I awoke with a headache. I am a registered nurse and I didn't think much of it at the time. A headache for a mother of three children is not an unheard of thing. Little did I know, as I downed a couple of aspirins, that this one was to be my constant companion for the next eight months.

Why should I have a headache? Seven doctors later, a badly depleted bank account, and a skin full of the newest drugs found me fifteen pounds lighter, an almost raving maniac, the sight badly impaired in one eye, blood pressure sky high and the headache.

My husband and I are devout Catholics. I was beyond the ability to pray so my husband prayed for both of us. He prayed God would direct him to help for me. It was in a chiropractor's office that I learned the power of positive thinking. I did not believe all this doctor told me, but when your book, *The Power of Positive Thinking*, fell into my hands I began to believe it might be so. Fortified with the spoken word of this sage doctor, plus the written material in your book, I began to apply to myself the principles.

To the degree I was able to understand and change my concepts from negative to positive—my headaches lessened. It took four months. I took no medication during this time and by September of that same year I had the last of the headaches.

I must add, our medical expenses have dropped about 80 per cent since I've changed my pattern of thinking. Do you know how a nurse thinks? Well, I'll tell you. One of the children has a running nose. Now, to the average person it is a running nose, but not to a nurse. It's pneumonia! She shoots that concept out into the air, and into the child's head. The child accepts it and puts the picture into reality.

How do I know this—because I did it. Hospital insurance records will bear me out. I was so good at it I was able to put not one of our children in the hospital, but all three of them at once, plus myself.

Now when they get a cold I look at it for what it is, a cold. And you know something—that's just as far as it goes. They throw it off in a couple of days.

Notice that it took four months of hard work to get results. This registered nurse understood the principle of positive thinking all right, but it wasn't until she was willing to put it to a test, go all out with it, make an effort really to change herself that she got rid of her headaches and experienced radical change within herself.

Ben Hogan, one of the greatest golfers of all time, practices what he calls muscle memory. He gets out on the links and swings the very same golf shot over, and over, and yet over again until his muscles "memorize" the exact pattern they have to follow. It is the same with our thinking habits. They have to be trained by a deliberate learning process to react the way we want them to react when we are faced with life's problems. Our mind has to be *trained* to think positively.

A final thing that I would like to mention has to do with belief. Positive thinking will not work unless you believe it will work. You have to bring your faith to bear on your thinking processes. The reason a lot of people do not get anywhere with positive thinking is that their faith is diluted. They water it down with timid little doubts. They do not dare to believe! But when you *do* believe, what amazing results you have.

There is D. H. Metzger, for example. But first let me refer to one of the most effective positive thinkers I have ever been privileged to know, my friend, Roger Burman, New York Sales Manager for the National Cash Register Company. Roger has a passion for helping others. He is always bringing out latent possibilities and guiding men in overcoming difficulties.

Roger Burman's teaching of positive thinking was a godsend to one of his top salesmen, D. H. Metzger, who suddenly was afflicted with a growth in the throat. During the days of crisis Dave Metzger was able to say, "My mind was alerted to think right and have faith. I knew my life was at stake, but the feeling of doing right at the right time added confidence as to my future."

Then Dave Metzger encountered an even greater crisis, learning to speak again. How could he ever sell unless he could speak? Roger Burman told him that, with God's help, he could and would; and he did, too. In fact he became a top salesman, one of the most successful in his line. In his desire to help others Dave said:

> In order that I may be helpful to others who may find themselves in a similar predicament, more or less, I would like to emphasize that I put into practice Dr. Norman Vincent Peale's philosophy as outlined in his *Power of Positive Thinking*, of getting to the point of emptying one's mind of all negative thoughts, all unhappy thoughts and all pessimistic thinking and filling that vacuum with happy thoughts, filling the mind with a determination to get well at all costs. I pictured in my mind a return of my former faculties and good health. By following the specialist's prescribed exercises, I visualized my return as a leading salesman for my company once again.
>
> "Faith power works wonders" and I quote it from Dr. Peale's book. I cannot stress the value of this philosophy, the magic power of positive thinking for anyone who has any kind of a problem.
>
> This whole new experience has renewed the statement: "Salesmen talk too much." Finding it necessary to say the "mostest" in the "leastest" number of words I have framed my word story in such a manner and in such a tone that the results have been most gratifying. I speak slower and lower, and find the customer leaning forward if he misses a word. I am not dominating the situation and giving the customer a chance to say "yes" much sooner than before. In this way I do not tax my strength. I "word plan" my sentence and now give the buyer a chance to be part of the sales. I confess I used to be part of that Etc., Etc., and Etc.

Conrad Hilton, an inspiring friend of mine for many years, magnificently demonstrated positive thinking in his victory over adversity in the building of his vast hotel empire. In his dynamic book, *Be My Guest*, he tells us that his parents gave him a two-part formula to which he owes much of his success. His mother said "pray" and his father said "work." Pray and work; how wise!

My own parents helped me similarly. My father said "think" and my mother said "believe." What power is in those four words when taken together; pray, work, think, believe!

Belief that is bold and daring—there is the formula. It carries all before it. Nothing can permanently stand against it. It magnificently focuses power. "If ye have faith . . . nothing shall be impossible unto you." (Matthew 17:20) Faith in God, faith in God's power in you, faith in life itself—that is the essence of positive thinking; not timid doubt, not weak speculation, but big, bold, daring faith—this is the victory.

Does positive thinking always work?

Of course it does; positive thinking will work if you are willing to work at it. It is not an easy discipline. It takes hard work and hard belief. It takes honest living, and a strong desire to succeed. And you will need to keep working at it constantly to achieve success in applying positive thinking. Just when you believe you have mastered it, you will have to develop it again.

My friend Justin Dart, head of Rexall Drugs, one of our greatest salesmen and business leaders said, "Positive thinking is just like golf. You get a good stroke or two, and you think you've mastered the game. But the next thing you know, you flub your shots again. So, with positive thinking you have to work at it again and then again, ever relearning it."

How right Mr. Dart is. You must do a day-to-day job on yourself, conditioning and reconditioning your thinking. But the results are really amazing. They are worth all the effort and change-in-habit that is required, as I will demonstrate in the chapters that follow.

2

PRECONDITION YOUR MIND TO SUCCESS

YOU CAN precondition your mind to success. This is a basic principle of positive thinking. You can actually forecast what your future failure or success will be by your present type of thinking.

And right here I think it is important to define what we mean by success. Naturally we do not mean mere achievement, but rather the more difficult feat of handling your life efficiently. It means to be a success as a person; controlled, organized, not part of the world's problem but part of its cure. This is the goal we should have for ourselves: the goal of successful living, of being a creative individual.

I learned a valuable lesson in successful living from a Pullman porter. I had a speaking date in Olean, New York, and my travel schedule called for an overnight trip on the Erie Railroad. My journey got off to a wonderful start the moment I stepped into the sleeping car. I was greeted by the porter, a big, genial, friendly man.

"Good evening, sir," he said. "Are you ready for a good night's sleep?"

"I sure am," I replied. "I can't wait to get into bed."

As he showed me into my compartment I saw that the bed was already made up. It was really an inviting sight. The sheets and covers were tight and neatly turned back, the bedroom was immaculate with a generous supply of towels, the temperature was exactly right. "You certainly know how to prepare an attractive room," I commented. I got into bed, read a few verses from my Bible, and then fell into a deep sleep. The next thing I knew it was nine o'clock and I usually wake up automatically at seven.

"Good morning, sir," said the porter as I was going in to breakfast. "How did you sleep?"

"Fine," I said, "just fine."

"Well, I'm not surprised; I knew you would. But you should have seen the man who got on just after you. First thing he said was, 'I know I'm not going to sleep, porter.' And then nothing was right. He wanted to be moved to the center of the car. He didn't like the way his bed was facing. The room was too cold and then it was too hot. Do you know the difference between you two gentlemen and why you slept well and he didn't?"

"No. I'm interested."

"You slept well because you had made up your mind to it. That other man had made up his mind not to sleep. A long time ago I discovered that those who ride with me sleep if they think they are going to sleep. They precondition their minds to sleep."

It was worth making the trip just to get that remark which contained such amazing insight. You can precondition your mind. You can precondition it to sleep, or to insomnia. You can precondition it to success, or to failure. In other words, that which you constantly think is going to happen, tends to happen. At this very minute, as you are reading this book, you are what your thoughts have made you over a long period of time. And it is possible to figure out, almost scientifically, what kind of person you will be ten years from now by analyzing the kind of thoughts you are now holding in your mind. Are they negative, destructive thoughts? Are you preconditioning yourself to failure? Or are they positive, healthy thoughts, so that you are forecasting your own success?

Let me tell you about a friend of mine, Norman A. McGee. Better still, here's a story from the *Savannah Morning News* about him:

> Ten years ago, the Southland Oil Corporation was just an idea in the fertile brain of Norman A. McGee. Today it is a flourishing Savannah corporation occupying 24 acres at the Georgia State Port with fixed assets topping the $2,000,000 mark.
>
> "I've been lucky many times," the 43-year-old McGee says. "On the other hand, I've resorted to prayer often, too. I believe anybody could have done it with persistence and faith—and a wife like mine."
>
> McGee had this idea about forming a corporation for the distribution of oil products and he had worked hard to interest others in it. The prospects looked good, but McGee had no income and he was down to his last $1,000 in the bank.
>
> "I asked my wife," McGee recalls, "what should I do? Keep on trying, or give up and take a job?"
>
> Her answer made Southland Oil possible. "Keep on trying," she said. "Don't ever give up!"

What is McGee's secret? He thinks, he prays, he believes, he works and he has a wife who would never let him quit. What marvelous assets! He preconditioned himself to success. And he isn't working only for himself either. He is active in the Presbyterian Church and was elected to the legislature.

Now listen, my friend. You can also gain success. Stop thinking failure. Start thinking success. Think and pray and work. Get a goal, clearly define it, and never give up. But first start working on your thoughts. Precondition them with sound positive thinking. When you precondition your mind, you are in the process of transforming your life. We transform our lives by how we think. The Bible says ". . . be ye transformed by the renewing of your mind." (Romans 12:2) Thoughts are things. Thoughts are dynamic, thoughts are vital and creative, thoughts actually change conditions. If you hold defeatist thoughts, hate thoughts, dishonest thoughts, failure thoughts—these are destructive. If you have honest thoughts, love thoughts, if you have service thoughts, success thoughts— these are creative. By the renewing of your mind you can be transformed as a person. Your condition may be transformed by the substitution of positive thinking for negative thinking. This is being done every day as my contacts reveal. The following letter is an example:

> Five years ago, right after my husband returned from the service, I had a complete physical and nervous breakdown. I was not able to face life. I became weak and nauseated after having given a simple devotional for our Sunday school class.
>
> I became panicky and made excuses when asked to do things socially. When more than one or two unusual things faced me at a time, I would go to bed with nervous chills and a real and intense sickness. Then depression would set in, and I would feel so guilty and bad about leaving my family in the lurch and at upsetting them, that I would have a long hard battle before I could again face a full day's routine. I was miserable.
>
> All this time my husband was taking his place in the community. Civic clubs, church and business were demanding more and more of his time and talent. I knew that as far as our marriage was concerned, I was being outgrown and the years would see us with nothing in common . . . he an active and happy person away from home and I more of a recluse each day.
>
> Then came help! I found out about positive thinking. My husband ordered some literature about positive thinking, and here it was! I started reading with the feeling of, "I might as well try this, too." But this was new. Real. Something definite to work with.
>
> Now time has passed. Six months ago when they asked me to be president of our Sunday school class I said no. I had no more than hung up the phone than I realized that this was God giving me a chance to overcome my sense of defeat. After a prayer, I phoned the committee and accepted the nomination. Then, until I took office, I prayed daily that God would let it be His work.
>
> I have never faced that class with anything except a perfect calm and peace of heart. I am now secretary of our School Parents; work two days a week for my husband; bowl every week and do all my own housework. I seldom have even an hour of depression. My husband loves his home and we do civic work together. Thank you, Dr. Peale, and God bless you.

Here is a woman whose life was completely changed by a change in her thought pattern. She changed the conditions of her life by changing the conditions of her mental life. Disraeli, the great English statesman, made this wise remark: "Nurture your mind with great thoughts for you will never go any higher than you think." Therefore, think big. I believe the trouble with all of us is that we have a tendency to think only little thoughts about everything: about ourselves, our family, our children, our business. So we get little results.

I really believe it is a law—you will get no bigger results than your thoughts are big. Big thoughts get big results; little thoughts get little results. One of the most successful men I have ever known was William Danforth, who headed the Purina Company. When Mr. Danforth was a boy he was puny. He would have qualified well for one of the "before" pictures in a body building advertisement. He has told me that he was small in thought, too. He did not think well of himself, and this insecurity was compounded by the slenderness of his physique.

But all this changed. William had a teacher in school who must have been one of the world's great builders of men. Privately, one day his teacher took him aside and said, "William, your thinking is all wrong. You think of yourself as a weakling and you are becoming one. But this need not be. I *dare* you to be a strong boy."

"What do you mean?" the boy asked. "You can't just dare yourself strong."

"Oh, yes, you can. Stand up here in front of me." Young Danforth stood up before the teacher. "Now take your posture, for instance. It shows that you are thinking weakness. What I want you to do is to think strength. Pull in your stomach, draw it up under your rib cage. Now. Do this. Think tall. Believe tall. Act tall. Dare tall. Stand on your own two feet and live tall like a man."

And that is what William Danforth did. The last time I saw him he was eighty-five years old. He was vigorous, healthy, active. And the last thing he said to me as we were parting was: "Remember, stand tall."

Justin Dart, head of the Rexall Drug Company, once played guard for Northwestern University. Before an important game the coach called him aside and said, "Go out there today and play as a great guard should. You can do it!"

Justin told me, "I know the coach overestimated me, but he gave me a new mental concept of myself. I shall never forget how I ran out on the field, running tall."

One of my readers describes himself as a business doctor. John, as I shall designate him, takes ailing businesses and makes them well again. And he tells me that in nine out of ten cases there is nothing much wrong with the business except the personnel. "A sick business is usually run by sick men," he says. "The trick is to get the men to thinking of themselves as successful; and then the business will be successful."

John told me about a boy he met at one of the companies he was doctoring. This boy was about as low on the totem pole of that business as he could possibly be. He was the fifth assistant to the shipping clerk; he spent his days sticking on labels. But there was something appealing about him, and one day my friend said to the boy, "I see no reason why you couldn't be a great success if you *thought* you could be. You are a bright boy. You have the brains and the personality. I hope you're not content with sticking on labels. Have you ever thought of becoming a salesman?"

"Oh no, no. I couldn't do that," the boy said quickly.

"Don't answer so fast," said John. "I think you'd make a good salesman. I'm going to speak to the front office about switching you to another job."

The boy was upset. It made him feel insecure. He was used to sticking on labels. But John had his way and in a few days the boy was out of his blue denims and into a smart suit, reporting for instructions.

"What do you want me to do?" said the boy. "I couldn't possibly sell anything."

"Well now, the first thing I want you to do is to take a good look at that door over there." The boy looked. On the glass panel were the words "Sales Manager," and under it was the name of the present sales manager, an older man who was scheduled to retire in a few years.

"Now," said our business doctor, "I want you to photograph mentally a picture of that door. Only I want you to substitute your own name for the name you see there now. Close your eyes. Can you mentally see that door? Can you see your own name on it?" The boy nodded yes. "All right, then. Here's what you do. Hold that picture firmly in your mind; then work hard, study hard all the time, believe that your name will eventually be on that door, and I know that it will."

"And was it?" I asked.

"What do *you* think? I never saw anyone work so hard and so long and so persistently. When I thought he was ready to go out and sell I went with him on his first trip. I left him at Wheeling, West Virginia. The boy looked at me and said, 'When you leave me I'm all alone, but I'll do my best.' "

"But I reminded him, 'You're not alone. Just remember that; and remember also, you know how to sell. And that Partner who is with you will help you.' "

A look of satisfaction came over John's face. "He turned out great, that boy, and finally became the best sales manager that company has ever had."

The manner in which you precondition your mind is extremely important because, whether good or bad, strong or weak, that preconditioning tends to become a reality. Whatever you picture about yourself either as a success or a failure will likely come to pass. "There is a deep tendency in human nature," said a psychologist, "to become precisely like that which we habitually imagine ourselves to be." Now imagination isn't fantasy. Imagination is the art or science of the projected image. You might call it image-ing. And the sort of image of yourself that you hold is very important—for that image may become fact.

The thought is ancestor of the deed. If you precondition your mind with thoughts of success, the deeds of success naturally tend to follow. But, notice that an important ingredient of this pattern is to ask for God's help. Let me just say that again: A very important part of the secret of using positive thinking in any form is to include the active participation of God. This is borne out time and again in our mail.

I ordered *The Power of Positive Thinking* from Montgomery Ward at Fort Worth. At that time I was out of work. I called all over the country to find work. Everything looked very black for me and my family, then one day I just happened to see this book. Well, I didn't tell anyone about it but just ordered it and when it came I got busy reading it.

In a few days I began to get some confidence in myself, which I didn't have before, and God gave me courage. So one night I read where you could take God as a partner in your business so I asked him to be my partner. I got me a welding machine for I am a welder; and then I got a contract to build some cattle guards for the county. I kept asking God to be my partner so I finally got me a truck and put my stuff on, welding machine and equipment. Everything on credit. Didn't know how I was going to come out, just kept on fighting, having faith in God and praying.

All of a sudden my prayers began to be answered. I got some oil field welding pipe and got a pipeline contract that really gave me a push. He liked my work and gave me another line.

I could write about many things, but it is getting late. I can say one thing, through this book I got to know God more and the way you can have joy out of life that I didn't know before. Now I know what you can do with faith in God. Thank God, and you, for sending me on my way to success.

And then in a completely different vein, there is this letter from a woman who faced a terrible ordeal, but who preconditioned her mind to a successful adjustment. Here, too, note the important role God played in her success.

During the last year I have had three operations for cancer, the last one involving the amputation of my right arm and shoulder. I have been so thankful for God's presence during this time.

I had quite a struggle deciding whether to let the doctors do the extensive surgery they felt was necessary. I read the chapter "How To Use Faith in Healing" in *The Power of Positive Thinking* several times and prayed for guidance. I came to the conclusion that the best thing to do was to let the doctors do all they could and trust God for the rest. Once I was able to put myself completely in His hands I found peace and was able to go to the operating room without fear.

I made a very rapid recovery and now, eight weeks after surgery, am making preparations to be fitted with an artificial arm. I have been amazed at the way I have been able to accept this handicap without bitterness and depression.

Taking the power of God into your life is one of the most essential steps in preconditioning your mind to success. Forecast that you are going to achieve a certain goal, and then move steadily toward that goal. But if you have given yourself a really difficult assignment, you cannot achieve it by yourself. You need the help of God. The pathetic fact is that many of us do not live as people who have the Kingdom of God within us. We do not really use the great forces that Almighty God has put into us. Draw fully and confidently upon the power of God that He placed within you when He created you.

These are the powers that are available to all of us on our road to success. They are available, but they are of no use unless we take advantage of them. Far too often people spend their whole lives close to these riches without ever tapping them. They are like an old man I once heard about down in Texas. He had a small ranch which never amounted to much. All his life he had scrimped for a living and eventually he grew old and died.

The property was sold. The new owner drilled a well and struck a rich deposit of oil. Of course, the oil was there all the time waiting to gush forth. Many of us are living like that: we are sitting right on top of the richest sources of power that can be imagined, and we do nothing about it at all. It is there, waiting to be tapped. But the exploitation of these resources is up to you. Precondition your thinking to this truth and successful living can be yours.

It doesn't matter who you are or how often you've failed. Neither does it matter how old you are. Successful living can always be yours. I received a letter from a woman in Georgia describing the amazing transformation in the success-pattern of her father after he discovered what God could really do with his life. Before he tapped the powers of the Almighty, this lady told me, her father was a very unsuccessful person. He lost all his money in the market and after that he became bitter and resentful. He changed his work and tried to make the climb back, by himself, but failed again. But read the daughter's letter:

. . . he was terribly unhappy. He had no belief. He didn't believe in God, he didn't even believe in himself. He shut out all friendships, and did nothing but criticize people. You can imagine the effect this had on his children. I don't remember ever having a peaceful meal at home. None of us could gain any weight because we were so tense all the time.

About eighteen months ago my mother and father moved to Florida. He wanted to start all over again. Well, as you can probably guess things didn't work out well, and he became more unbearable than he was back in the dark days. He finally became so despondent that last September he had a serious heart attack. Later it was decided that he would have to have an operation.

It was while he was waiting for the operation that God came in. First of all,

God told my sister and me at exactly the same time to send Dad some material about positive thinking. Dad read it and took God into his life.

Well now, here is your miracle, Dr. Peale. I was in Florida in February and my father looks twenty years younger. He is full of health and vitality. He keeps a Bible by his chair all the time. He loves everybody now, and he made three big sales in one day just while I was there. He constantly talks unashamedly of God and after witnessing this metamorphosis I am convinced that nothing, absolutely nothing, is impossible in this world as long as God is given half a chance.

Success is available to all of us if we will follow the basic principles of positive thinking.

You must never conclude, even though everything goes wrong, that you cannot succeed. Even at the worst there is a way out, a hidden secret that can turn failure into success and despair into happiness. No situation is so dark that there is not a ray of light. So if you face circumstances that you think are extremely difficult, if not utterly hopeless, I urge you to read and ponder the experience of Mr. and Mrs. J. P. Lingle of Missouri.

A couple of years ago Mrs. Lingle wrote me after reading *The Power of Positive Thinking* as follows:

Three years ago, after fourteen years with a national chain variety store, my husband and I had an opportunity to open a store of our own. We were quite undecided, and turned the decision over to God, asking that, if it were His will to please provide the money we would need to get started; and if it were not His will, to keep us from getting it.

Well, friends and relatives actually came and offered money to help us, and we felt that was our answer.

But it seemed to have been wrong from the beginning—we could never make ends meet and were constantly, for two and one-half years threatened with lawsuits, telegrams demanding payment, etc.

We are $10,000 in debt, and have no material assets other than a seven-year-old car and our furniture. My husband is making $310.00 a month after taxes, so that doesn't leave much to pay off debts. We refused to go into bankruptcy as too many people would have been cheated out of what we rightfully owe them, and we felt God wouldn't want us to do it that way, even though we could have, legally. It's especially hard to keep faith when we get a nasty letter from a creditor or I look at the staggering debts compared with the miniature salary.

If you would just send me a word that will help me through this, I would be deeply grateful. I'm not experienced enough to know how to handle my spiritual thinking at a time like this.

Well, I wrote the Lingles describing some steps which I thought might be helpful. But I thought that the *most* helpful thing I could do was to put them in touch with a successful positive thinker who lived near them. I asked him to talk with them. I am going to call this man simply "Mr. S." because Mr. S. believes in keeping his good works secret. He follows the spiritual principle of not letting the right hand know what the left hand is doing.

Mr. S., I knew, believed strongly in the spiritual principle of sharing, not only as a means of maintaining a successful way of life, but also as a means of obtaining it in the first place. He promptly went to see the Lingles and found that they were so deeply engrossed with their problem that they could talk of nothing but their $10,000 debt. He told them that the first step in solving their problem was to start sharing, to begin at once to give away at least 10 per cent of the little that was coming in.

"But," they protested, "we are $10,000 in debt!"

"So what," Mr. S. replied. "My wife and I went broke back in 1933. We were in your very same situation—only we were $63,000 in debt. And we tithed our way out." He explained the principle of sharing, how it stimulates and maintains success. He pointed out one of the most subtle rules of successful living; namely, that unselfish giving makes real receiving possible.

Mr. S. prayed with this couple and together they surrendered the problem into the Lord's hands, promising to follow His guidance as it would be revealed to them. They broke with their self-pity, worry and tension. They let the problem go into God's hands; they let God take over. Then they were ready to start doing business on a creative and positive spiritual level. And incidentally, as they found, this is where being practical begins. They began to tithe their time, money and effort—in other words, they began to share themselves.

The first result to be recorded was in a letter from Mrs. Lingle in August, about four months after she wrote me the first time.

> I wanted to let you know that I haven't had a single worry day. I even received a letter from a creditor and it didn't upset me in the least, which is a remarkable change in itself.

And a little later there was another report from the Lingles on the effects of tithing:

> Have you time for an "inspiration story?" I have one. Two weeks ago, we received a notice from the State Tax Department informing us we were being assessed for $90. In addition the points were worn out in our car, and our liability insurance on the car had expired.
>
> We had no more than received the assessment notice, (and had no idea where the money was to come from) when the Monroe Calculator office man here called and said he could sell our calculator (we've been trying to sell it for

five months) at a price which would cover the tax, the auto repairs and buy the necessary insurance! Isn't that wonderful? But there's more to come!

I hadn't had any luck finding work that would allow me to be home with Skippy (our little boy). But, following the principles of tithing one's self, on an impulse, I stopped by the church here and went to the office, introduced myself and told them I had a typewriter at home; and if they ever had extra work to do, I would like to take it home and do it in an effort to give some of my time to the church.

Well, they were almost stricken dumb! They explained they had lost a secretary, and were so snowed under, my offer was truly an answer to prayer! So I brought several stencils home and cut them; and then the next day ran them, and lots more, off on the mimeo for them.

That night I received a phone call from an office I had called two months ago about work and had almost forgotten about. They wondered if I would be interested in doing extra work—*cutting stencils*—at $1.25 per hour to start. There wouldn't be any regular hours for me, I could come in each day whenever I wanted and go home whenever I wanted! Don't you find that inspiring?

And so it went, blessing after blessing, guidance after guidance to these happy people. They prayed, they trusted, they gave, and they got right up on top of their difficulties. Mr. Lingle made a new business connection as a store manager and he did all right, too, as the following happy letter from Mrs. Lingle, written two years later, indicates:

I just can't wait any longer!

Here is another story for you of how God is looking after us. It happened after your last visit.

You remember we had been looking for a car since last October, when our seven-year-old Studebaker started giving us fits. We found the one we wanted then, in October, a second-hand Buick, but we felt that we didn't need such a fine one. So Jim kept looking and looking, but none came up to the Buick in price, mileage, cleanness and all things considered.

So one day he said, "Well, we know we don't need that nice a car; we know we don't have the down payment, but if that's the car we're supposed to have, the down payment will come to us, and the car will still be on the lot waiting when it does."

You know, in Jim's business, he gets a percentage on any profit made during the year, but we were only open two months in 1958 and, of course, the profit the store made was eaten up by the opening expenses.

So imagine our surprise when Jim got a note from the office saying they were going to pay him a bonus on his profit, just as if there had been no opening expenses, but they felt he had worked hard and deserved it. They just don't do things like that! And instead of the usual 10 per cent, it was 15 per cent! So there was our down payment! And after four months of waiting, the car was still there!

Remember you asked how much we had been able to repay on our $10,000 debt when we talked on the phone? Well, next month, it will have been two years and we have repaid $4,000 since then! Well, four down and six to go. What a challenge!

And here is the last report to date from the Lingles. Note in it how the Lingles have now completely absorbed the principle of sharing:

This will tell how we are doing at the present time. We are far from being out of debt, but far from out of faith, too.

As for some of the spiritual principles which have helped us, there is no doubt that *helping others who are in need* stands at the top of the list. I'm enclosing a copy of the type of note we send when we discover someone who could use a little boost. In so doing, I'm letting out our secret, but perhaps, Dr. Peale, if you desire to use the idea, other people will pick it up and it's the sort of thing that can snowball into something wonderful. Here is the note which we send:

Dear Friends:
Every week Jim and I put back an offering in a little envelope we have for "others." Then when we learn of someone who could use a little boost—as we often have—we send something to them with a note like this.

We know Stan has a job now, but Saturday you said you only had a dollar, so maybe this will help out with his lunches and carfare until his first pay check comes in.

We don't want it back for ourselves, but there are two things we would like you to do—don't tell anyone about it, and when you begin to get on your feet again, find someone who could use it, and repay us by giving it to them under the same conditions.

No one knows we do this, and it must be kept just between God and you and us. And if you want to know our reasons, I'll give you a clue. Read Matthew 6:1–4.

Well, let's run down the list of principles of successful living that we have been talking about in this chapter.

First, it is important to define what success means to you. Define your goal clearly, pinpoint it. Be sure that your goal is in harmony with God's desires for you. For example, don't make the mistake of having only material success as your goal: God wants a lot more for you than superficial material wealth. He wants real wealth for you, the wealth of life that is successful in all its aspects: economic, social, spiritual, intellectual, physical. It is His desire to give you real riches. Don't underestimate the good things that God wants for you and will give you if you will only learn to receive.

Second, study until you really grasp the life-changing power of the truth that you can precondition your own success. Paint a picture of yourself as succeeding, hold that picture ever before you, and it will materialize. With positive thinking you can actually change the conditions of your life.

Third, bring God into a central place in your thought pattern. Pray, seek His guidance, strive to bring your effort into harmony with His teachings.

Fourth, to maintain your success with poise and without tension, learn to share. Share your success liberally with others. Teach others how to think positively, how to achieve the same results with their lives that you do with yours. In this way you will be guaranteeing the continued flow of creative ideas in and around you: you will be paying the premiums on an insurance policy protecting the success you have achieved.

Use these four principles steadily and regularly in your life, and success—the true success of bountiful living—will be yours. Start now to precondition your mind to success.

3

NO MORE FAILURE FOR YOU

His NAME was Bob. He was a big man, but shy. He was a sales-man. But Bob's record was perilously near the bottom.

Yet, only a year after his superiors had decided to give Bob one last chance, he passed every other salesman to become the company's top producer. At the annual sales meeting, the manager called Bob to the platform to receive the prize as top man for the year. As the manager handed him a check he said: "Bob, you're a mystery. You've never been anywhere near the top in sales before, but now you've reached it. Besides, you came up from near the bottom. How did you do it? Tell the boys here."

Bob was embarrassed. He shifted from one foot to the other and his face turned red. "There's nothing I can tell them," he said. "I just got hold of something that changed me into a new man."

"What was that?" the manager asked curiously.

"Well, I simply found thirteen words—and those words changed every-thing. You see, when I was told you'd have to let me go if I didn't improve, I got to thinking. I went home that night and sat in my chair thinking some pretty honest thoughts with myself.

"Well, after a while, I happened to see an old Bible my mother had given me but which I hadn't looked at very often. She told me if I ever got into trouble I'd find an answer in that Book. Well, I was in real trouble. Maybe this was the time. Anyway, I took it from the shelf, blew the dust off it, and began to leaf through. But it wasn't until I was almost going to close it that I found exactly what I needed."

He hesitated in some embarrassment. Talking religion wasn't his line, but he continued doggedly. "I found these thirteen words: 'Behold, I make all things new . . . He that overcometh shall inherit all things.'

"Well, those words hit me like a ton of bricks. If anyone needed to be made new it was I.

"Right there I prayed to God to make me a new man, to help me stop being such a flop. I meant this too, and I felt much better. I had the best sleep in weeks. I felt a little confidence for the first time.

"Next morning, I said those thirteen words to myself several times. And because I made up my mind to change everything about me and make it all new like the words I said, I went downtown and shot some of my last few bucks for a new suit and tie and took them home. I undressed, got into the tub and scrubbed myself hard. It seemed like I wanted to wash all the failure off of me. Then I dressed, and before going out, knelt down and prayed to God to help me. I looked in the mirror and, believe it or not, I actually looked like a new man. I know that sounds crazy, but it's the way I felt, too.

"I said, 'God, I'm going out now to make calls and I'm a new man. I'll do better with Your help.' I found myself taking a lot more interest in the prospects I called on. I was more enthusiastic. I began to sell. I was enjoying myself, too. Everything went better. I guess that's all there is to it."

The man who told me this story said, "You could hear a pin drop. Then the boys tore off the lid with cheering like you'd never heard at a sales meeting." And why not, for they had seen actual proof that a man, with God's help, can make himself over, despite all failures.

So you do not need to put up with continued failure. I know this to be a fact and not theory. My reason for being so certain is because of the many people who have convincingly demonstrated the power to change from failure to success. Such change may not come easily, but it can and does come and that is the main thing. When you decide, really decide, that there shall be no more failure for you, and carry out the principles outlined in this chapter and book, there is no doubt there need be no more failure for you.

I base this assertion upon the many amazing results which have been reported to me by those who have practiced positive thinking.

For example, in a western state I stayed in a large and beautiful hotel. When I checked out, the manager came over to say good-bye.

"A fine hotel you have here," I said in thanking him for a pleasant stay.

He smiled and said quietly, "I owe it all to God and the help I received from positive thinking." Later he wrote me a sincere and moving statement of his dynamic change.

> I used to be the biggest worry and fear man alive. When I had nothing to worry over, I would dream one up to stay in step with all the confusion and upheaval I lived in. This was a condition dating back from early childhood.
>
> Five years ago this coming September, I came across some of your writing about positive thinking. This article aroused a tremendous amount of interest, and I knew immediately that here I had found something which could help me. I began to collect all the material you had written and listened to your Sunday radio broadcasts.
>
> Dr. Peale, it is not easy to shake off long established habits, but the one thing which helped me most was that I began to read the Bible, and in very

short order I realized that I wanted God to help me, and I received Jesus Christ.

I came across in your writing where you suggested draining out all your bad thoughts, like water out of a faucet, and replacing them with clean, healthy thoughts. I did this and had a real brain washing. Gone are the worries, fears and emotions. I might also like to mention that I gave up drinking.

Today, I am happy. I love everything I come in contact with and have acquired your habit of staying on top of every situation.

The principles of positive thinking work when applied with the honesty and sincerity this man used. Let me suggest an experiment. Take a pencil and paper and list your three chief failure areas; three points at which you are currently failing, or at least not doing as well as you desire.

It may be you do not get along too well with other people. Perhaps you are having trouble controlling desire. Is it for alcohol, sex, tobacco, or perhaps simply too much fattening food? Could be you simply cannot seem to master efficiency. Maybe you are easily discouraged, or negative. Whatever they are, big or little, list your failure areas in the order of their importance. Then let's see what to do about turning these failures into successes.

The first thing is to get an answer to that basic question, "Why do you have these failure points?"

That may be difficult to determine, and you may even require professional help to ferret out the real reasons for your failure. But actually, more often the place to look is within ourselves. And here we come upon some strange and complex facts. For one thing, psychologists tell us that there is even such a quirk as a failure wish. Success, for some psychological reason, seems too dangerous for many people. They cleverly find ways to avoid it, unconsciously, of course. They do not really want to succeed. So, when you give the reason for your failure, be sure it's the true reason.

But let us suppose that you really want to do something about failure. What corrective formula can you use? There is one simple formula that I have known to produce amazing results. It is a definite one, two, three positive-thinking procedure. If applied with maximum effort, it will almost certainly result in no more failure for you. Here's the formula:

Try, really try.
Think, really think.
Believe, really believe.

Let's take that first point; *Try, really try.* Probably this doesn't have too much appeal, because trying can be very hard, so hard, in fact, that few people will actually attempt it. Or they may attempt it, but do not have what it takes to keep on trying. Let's face it, when was the last time you tackled one of the failures on your list with the determined attitude that you were going to get in there and try, *really* try? Most failure is simply due to the fact that we take the line of least "persistence." We do not make a prodigious effort to succeed.

Eddie Arcaro, the famous jockey, says that only a few horses really try. "Seventy per cent of them don't want to win," he declares, and he ought to know. In this respect it would seem that we are like race horses; we too seldom try, really try, to win.

William James, the famous psychologist, recognized the difficulty of making a great effort. He speaks of "the first layer of fatigue." This is the tiredness that comes after a little unusual effort. You try for a short while, become fatigued then simply quit. But God built an enormous reservoir of reserve energy into your system, which is available if you will just push down to it—just give a little more effort. It is like the accelerators on some automobiles which produce a sudden burst of added energy and power whenever needed by simply pressing down harder. Personality is constructed in much the same way. Push down hard on our personality accelerator and this extra power will come surging forth. We seldom give ourselves the extra push that penetrates below the first layer of fatigue to where vast untapped power lies. But when you do, you get amazing results.

The secret is in putting your *whole* mind to it. Actually we seldom use our full mental power—certainly not our full spiritual potential. We might as well admit we do not give a problem all we've got; only in the rarest instances or in the greatest crises. If you put your whole mind to a difficulty you will be astonished at your own power over it.

Do you really want power over your failures? Do you want it enough to try, really try? You can have it if you do. This applies in any failure area. A remarkable example of the victory-producing power over sheer, dogged effort, plus faith, is described in the following letter from a reader in New York. The writer herself says she hasn't much education. Indeed, the lack of punctuation adds to the letter's charm, so I am going to copy it just as it is written.

> I'm a little old lady in my late 60's, and I would like to tell you all the ones that have no faith that with the power of faith one can achieve miracles. I'm sorry I have no education and can't even spell right, but I'm going to try and relate to you my first great problem of my life and how I did draw on the power of faith.
>
> I was born a cripple with dislocation of both my hips and doctors said I would never walk but as I grew up and looked at others walk I said to myself please God help me. I know you love me, I was six years old and my heart was broke and so one day I tryed to stand up between two chairs and down I would go but I didn't give up. Every day I'd speak to God and tryed again and

again until I held myself up for a few seconds and I can't describe to you the joy in my heart being able to stand on my feet. I gave one scream to mamma. I'm up. I can walk!

Then I went down again. I can't never forget the joy of my parents and when I tryed again my mother handed me the end of a broom stick while she held the other end and said, Give one step forward with one foot and then another and that is how my faith helped me to walk the duck walk thats what the doctors calls it but I have been so grateful ever since then.

Three years ago I had an accident and I broke my left ankle and was in the hospital and they took exrays of my legs. Then the doctors came to me and said lady how did you walk? And I said God was my doctor and they said its a miracle you have no socketts and no joints on your hips how did you stand up? And memories came back to me and I have waited 60 years to find out that I have no socketts and no joints for I never knew why.

Then the doctors were afraid that with the accident and broken ankle and my age I would not walk again but God came to my rescue again and to the surprise of all I'm walking again, and still holding my job of taking care of four children of a widow mother while she works. I'm a widow too and had to work very hard to grow my children. My husband died with the spanish flu in 1919. I had two little girls and a son was born two month later. I scrubbed floors on my knees for 17 years and never was sick in life. I don't know what an headache is.

Now here is a person who knows what it is to try, really try. "Every day I'd speak to God and tryed again and again until I held myself up," she said. And I like that advice of her mother, too: "Give one step forward with one foot and then another." That's what trying means. It means being willing to keep at your problems until they are solved. Keep at it, try, keep at it; that constant attack attitude will ultimately overcome any failure.

So with regard to your own problem area, or your own failure area, are you tackling it well, only half-well, or just well enough to get by? Are you putting an honest, all-out effort into the solution? The fact cannot be repeated too often, namely: You can eliminate your failure pattern by learning to try, really try.

Difficulties should act as a spur. Charles de Gaulle once said, "Difficulty attracts the man of character because it is in embracing it that he realizes himself." That's real stuff. Try and try and keep on trying and God will come to your aid. God is always with the man who is willing to make a gallant and repetitive effort.

I witnessed the Millrose Games in Madison Square Garden. These are great games in which the finest athletes in the country compete in various track events: running races, pole vaulting, high jumping. And I saw something that was truly wonderful, the breaking of the world's indoor high jump record by John Thomas, a seventeen-year-old freshmen from Boston University.

I saw John Thomas become the champion high jumper of the world. One month before the Millrose Games, he jumped 6'9"; two weeks before the games, he jumped 6'11¾". On the night of the games themselves, before a hushed fifteen thousand people, he broke the world's record. To quote one sports writer: "In one of the greatest moments of sports, he took off toward the ceiling and topped the bar at seven feet."

Only seventeen years old and world's champion indoor high jumper! The crowd went wild. John was immediately besieged by photographers, reporters, people hugging him and shaking his hand. But he paid scant attention to them. In fact, he waved them aside. He wasn't through trying yet. He had made one world's record. He could have rested on his laurels, but he was a boy who knows what it is to keep trying, and there was another record he wanted that night. He wanted to go after the outdoor record too. That was 7'1.2". It was a record held by a Russian. John told the officials to put the bar at 7'1.25". And once again fifteen thousand people dropped into a deep silence. One time John failed. Twice, he failed. A third time . . . he failed.

Now, I had a curious reaction to all this. At first I said to myself that John Thomas had made a mistake. He had taken the edge off his victory. But then I was ashamed of myself. When I got to thinking about what that boy had done, I saw that he was not out for the glory; he was driven by some godlike impulse to try for something always just a little bit out of his reach. Something greater.

They wouldn't let him try further that night. But I came away with the feeling that I had been watching one of the greatest athletes of all time in the making, because he knew what it was to reach up and try, and even when he had won, to try again for a higher goal. And this feeling proved itself three weeks later when, in the same Madison Square Garden, John "took off toward the ceiling" again, and this time topped the bar at 7'1.25", thus becoming the world's champion for both the indoor and the outdoor jump. He tried, really tried. And it paid off in victory.

How about your own efforts? Are you willing to stretch yourself? Have you honestly given your problem that big extra try and done it more than once? Once isn't enough. It takes many tries. And you will be surprised at what real trying will release in you. For so many people failure is simply a matter of not making the expenditure of physical and mental effort that is needed for victory. Look over your failure list. Can you say that each of these failures has been probed with an honest, all-out effort, the kind of trying that makes champions? If not, test the theory of trying, and trying some more, and see what happens.

The second part of the formula for overcoming the failure pattern is to think, really think . . . positively. I believe that the power of positive thought is so great that you can think yourself through any failure. You can think yourself out of any problem.

An illustration is the fourteen-year-old boy who read a want ad in the newspaper in which a job for a boy of his age was offered. When he arrived next morning at the appointed place, on time, he found twenty boys already in line.

This would have stumped a less forceful and resourceful boy, but this lad had what it takes to handle a situation. He thought. He made use of his head, which is a thinking machine designed by the Creator to help a person solve problems. His mind was not negative. He could think, really think, and so an idea was born. What a wonderful thing a thought-out idea is. It's powerful.

Taking a piece of paper he wrote a few lines; then, stepping out of line and asking the boy behind him to hold his place, he went over to the secretary of the man doing the hiring and said politely, "Please, Miss, will you kindly hand this note to your boss? It's important. Thank you very much."

The secretary was impressed by the boy; he was courteous, pleasant and forceful. A lesser boy she would no doubt have brushed aside, but this youngster was different. He had that attractive, indefinable quality called force. So she complied with his request and took the note in to her employer.

He read it, grinned, and handed it back to her. She read it and laughed. This is what it said:

"Dear Sir, I am the twenty-first kid in line. Please don't do anything until you see me."

Did he get the job? What do you think? A boy like that will inevitably go places and do things. He knew, though young in years, how to think, really think. He had already developed the ability to size up a problem quickly, attack it forcefully, and do the very best about it.

If the problem happens to be yourself, as actually a great many of life's problems are, solutions come more surely and even more easily when you think, really think. The *Saturday Evening Post* carried an interesting article about Tommy Bolt, who won the National Open Golf Championship in 1958. The subtitle of this article read, "It was clean, positive thinking that changed my life." It is a story of how a champion was made by positive thinking.

It seems that Mr. Bolt used to be called the "terrible tempered Mr. Bolt." He missed the championship a couple of times, due to his terrible temper. On one occasion, in a rage because he had missed a putt, he deliberately broke all of his clubs. Frequently he broke his five iron. To use his own colloquial phrase, he would just "wrap the five iron around a tree." Gradually the fans got onto this. Spectators followed Tommy Bolt around the course, and they would congregate at the greens and chant,

"Miss it, miss it!" And he would accommodate them by missing. Then he would go into one of his rages, and the spectators were delighted. Mr. Bolt, not knowing how to think properly, was emotionally unstable. Wrong thinking, expressed in temper, resulted in failure to reach his goals.

Finally Tommy Bolt read a couple of books which straightened out his thinking. One of these was by Bishop Fulton J. Sheen. Another, as I was pleasantly surprised to learn, was one of my own books. And here is some of Tommy Bolt's testimony about his experience.

"I reformed my thinking," he said. "I reconditioned my attitudes, I strengthened my faith and put my trust in Someone bigger than I was, and it worked. My new positive attitude never wavered once I started. Clean positive thinking changed my life. I wanted to keep my thinking clear and straight. The things I read put a safety valve on my temper and formed a sort of protective coating against outside influences and distractions." The last sentence is a classic, but now comes one that is even more so: "I promised the Lord I would help Him help me." That's a tremendous idea, for God needs your help with you. Tommy Bolt used his failures to spur him on to success. Failure, for him, became a challenge, and that of course is what failure should always be.

It is absolutely vital to learn to think positively if failure patterns are to be overcome. You must recondition your attitudes until you have turned negativism into positivism. In this I am always reminded of a dynamic and unforgettable schoolteacher I had when I was a boy. All of a sudden, for no apparent reason, he would stop the class, walk up to the blackboard and write in big bold letters the word, CAN'T. And then he would turn to the class and smile and chant to them:

"What do I do?"

And the kids would laugh and chant back to him, "Knock the T off the CAN'T!!!"

He whisked an eraser over the "t" and the word became CAN. That's the kind of teaching we need to give ourselves. Knock the T off the Can't, and make it Can. This is the way to think, really think yourself away from your failures. If the word Can't ever gets firmly embedded in your mind it will cause all sorts of trouble.

It is astonishing how even successful enterprises can go badly when you take on the can't attitude. Years ago I knew an old gentleman who ran a lunch counter along the highway. It was a time of depression in business. The old man was fortunate enough to be a little blind and deaf. I say fortunate, because he didn't have to read about the depression or hear the negative conversation of his friends. So, not knowing there was a depression, he had a remarkably successful business. He painted his stand, he delivered a good article; he put up bright signs along the road which almost conveyed the aroma of his sandwiches. He made his merchandise so delicious that people who "had no money," would stop and buy his food.

The old man worked hard and sent his boy to college. There the boy took courses in economics and learned how bad things were. When he came home for Christmas and noticed the thriving business, he went to his father and said, "Pop, something's wrong around here. You shouldn't be as successful as you are. Why, you act as if you didn't know there was a depression on!"

And he told his father all about the depression, and how people were retrenching everywhere. As the father began to think it over and look around him, and listen to the negative thoughts, he said to himself: "Maybe I'd better not repaint my stand this year. I'd better save my money because there's a depression. And I'd better cut down on the amount of hamburger I put in these sandwiches. And what's the use of putting out signs if nobody has any money." And so he stopped all positive efforts. The result: business soon fell off. When the boy came back for the Easter vacation the father told him, "Son, I want to thank you for the information you gave me about the depression. It's absolutely true. I feel it in my business. A college education, son, is a wonderful thing."

That is what happens when negative thinking gets lodged in our minds. Such thoughts should be drained out constantly. Dr. Sara Jordan, co-founder of Boston's Lahey Clinic, has a wonderful way of putting it. "Every day give your brain a shampoo." What a thought! Get rid of all the dust and dirt and grime of negative thinking. Start off every day with clean, sparkling thoughts that will have nothing in them to impede the flow of success to you.

Give your brain a shampoo every morning. Get your day started right mentally and it will continue right. One winter morning I had occasion to get up very early. I went into the living room and looked out at the glorious morning sky. It suddenly occurred to me that Emerson was right when he said that ". . . The sky is the daily bread of the soul." Our apartment faces west, overlooking Central Park, an area in the heart of the city, four miles long and one-half mile wide. The sky that morning was like a gigantic fireplace, with flames shooting up over the city. There was a soft blanket of broken clouds overhead and, across the park, windows were golden as they reflected the rising sun. The whole city was as still as an etching. The air was clear as crystal. The snow was clean and fresh. Suddenly I felt a strong instinct to pray and the prayer became one of joy and exhilaration. It was an unforgettable experience.

That day was a wonderful day. There were no failures in it, and I am sure it was because I had washed my mind clean before the day ever began. I felt stimulated and on a higher level of energy all day long. There is an anonymous poem that describes this type of experience graphically:

Every morning, lean thine arms awhile
Upon the window-sill of Heaven,
And gaze upon the Lord . . .
Then, with that vision in thy heart,
Turn strong to meet the day.

I have made this a kind of morning habit and can assure you of the amazing value of this technique for starting off a day—"lean upon the window-sill of heaven," leave off looking so hard at your difficulties, and instead, "gaze upon the Lord." In so doing you will have strength and peace and power. This practice has powerful revitalizing potential.

What are the things that you may wash out of your mind by a daily mental and spiritual shampoo? Resentments, of course, and fears and hatreds; also, the negative and selfish thoughts that impede the flow of power through your personality are flushed out. Such daily mental shampoo or thought cleansing re-establishes the perspective that leads to successful action.

Some years ago I was in Hollywood as technical advisor for a motion picture called "One Foot in Heaven." One of the character actors working in this picture was a man named Harry Davenport. Harry told me a story about an experience he had with right-thinking a few years earlier. It seems that, at one time, he had been in a profession slump.

"I was actually a failure," said Harry. "And when I began to analyze what had happened to me, I saw that my motives had been all wrong. Performing before an audience I would think about how great I was, and had no special interest in the people of the audience. Well, it didn't take long for that kind of self-centered thinking to transmit itself to the audience, and ultimately it threatened my whole career. For if you think only of yourself, people pick it up and don't like you. I wasn't getting good jobs. After a while I became really disturbed and began to pray about it, and the answer I got was this: Project an attitude of love to your audience and see what happens.

"I thought that was a strange idea, but I was in such desperate straits that I would have tried anything. A few days later I received a call to play a part; it was not an important role, but I took it. Before the play started, I stood off stage in the wings and looked out over the audience. I saw a business man out front who seemed very unhappy. He looked like he had been dragged there by his wife, and wanted to be elsewhere. 'Well, I will try making you happy tonight,' I said silently. 'I will project love to you, and try to give you a pleasant evening.' And do you know I have never had a better performance or felt greater happiness in my work. It was the turning point in my career. Today I wouldn't dare give a performance without first seeing to it that my thinking is in proper order."

This conversation was one of the most determinative of my own life. I decided then and there never to go on the platform to make a speech or into the pulpit to deliver a sermon without sending out genuine love thoughts to my audience or congregation. I look out at the people present and pray that through me, as a medium, God may help each one. I wouldn't think of attempting a speech without carrying through this formula.

The same principle and procedure applies to anyone in any kind of work. Jim Johnson, my friend who operates a big hotel in Harrisburg, Pennsylvania, spends a definite period each day sending out such thoughts to his employees, and has created a wonderful spirit in his organization. At night when he leaves for his home, he stops his car across the river and looks back at the towering hotel. From there he sends out thoughts of good will and prayer to all the guests behind those windows and to all the workers who staff the hotel throughout the night. As you might suspect, this kind of thinking gives one a positive and wise attitude toward life. Jim once said something I never forgot. "I never knew a storm that didn't blow itself out."

And, last of all, believe, really believe. Believe in whom? In God, in Jesus Christ, and, with real humility, believe in yourself. Believe that you are going to be victorious and that very belief will go far toward bringing you the victory you believe in. Why does the Bible talk about faith so much? Because if you really believe, you can do tremendous things. You can if you believe you can. Believing opens the channels of creative, dynamic good. It sets power to flowing in even the most difficult circumstances.

One of the world's most accomplished positive thinkers is Casey Stengel, pilot of the New York Yankees. During one World Series, when the Yankees were fighting it out with the Milwaukee Braves, positive thought power brought really spectacular results. The Yankees had had an easy year of it in the American League. They had no real competition at all, and they won the pennant so early that it worked to their disadvantage, for they played rather colorless ball toward the end of the season. The Yankee players were not really on their toes by the time the World Series started. The Yankees lost three out of the first four games. It looked like an ignominious defeat for Casey Stengel and his team. He had to win the next three games in a row if he was going to take the Series.

And that is exactly what Casey did. He got his players fired up to the point where they played super-human baseball. It was one of the most thrilling exploits I have ever witnessed, and at the time I found myself wondering what magic Casey used to turn such defeat into victory. Later I found the answer. I read an article in *Sports Illustrated* about Mr. Stengel, and in this article were two sentences that describe him perfectly. I copied them and memorized them, because to me they are really powerful sentences. "Defeat does not awe Casey, and he is on good terms with hope."

And the other was, "In the worst moment of defeat, he was looking for victory."

There you have it. Casey Stengel never once believed in defeat. He believed in victory. He "knew" he was going to win that Series, and he managed by some peculiar alchemy to transmit this belief to the Yankee ball team. And, of course, with that kind of certainty behind them, they were invincible.

I am going to close this chapter with a deeply moving letter that I received from a young mother. If you have any doubts as to the amazing results of positive thinking, you will surely lose them after reading this letter. We get thousands of letters in my office, from people in all kinds of circumstances. Some are enough to break your heart. They are filled with stories of pain, suffering, heartache, disappointment—it is most pathetic, all the troubles people have to deal with in life. But it is also inspiring to read about how tremendous people become when they develop that magic ingredient of belief. You can believe yourself to victory over the greatest obstacles in the world, as did Mrs. Harry Fike of Bexley, Ohio, who writes:

Dear Dr. Peale:

On October 30 of last year when I was pregnant five and one-half months I had an unfortunate accident—a rupture of the membrane enclosing the baby. This had happened to me in two previous pregnancies with the resulting loss of the baby. On the first two occasions the doctors told me such an accident was absolutely hopeless and I accepted their decision. I remember going to the hospital and saying on the delivery table, "It is hopeless. My baby is too small and will die," and that is what happened, exactly.

This time another doctor told me, "It's up to you and God." At first I panicked, but soon got hold of myself. My instructions were not to move. So I propped myself in an upright position in bed and vowed I would not move for at least a month—which I did not. With a four-year-old and a two-year-old this was easier to say than to do. But with the help of my husband I stayed there one month to the day, never lying down or turning to the side. Whenever the situation seemed threatening I would thank God that the baby was going to be all right. I prayed constantly for myself, but most of the time I thanked God for His blessings.

Every time someone talked discouragingly to me I simply told them that everything would be all right. One month later I went into labor, but I was not afraid. Even the resident doctor in the labor room told me that my baby would be too small. I heard him on the hall telephone telling my doctor that I thought the baby would be large enough but it was wishful thinking. I watched the baby's birth and when I saw him I almost panicked again seeing how tiny he was. But his eyes were open and he was struggling for breath. He was also deep purple. He weighed 2 lbs. 9 ozs.

My pediatrician arrived at the hospital and met me coming out of the delivery room. While all others shook their heads he smiled and said, "It is possible for him to survive." He didn't spout the discouraging statistics to me as most of the others did. On the fourth day my obstetrician came in and told me the baby was barely breathing, but I can remember saying, "But he *is* breathing." I called my pediatrician and he said the next time the obstetrician comes in and talks that way, tell him to jump out the window. So I hung on and thanked God over and over again.

After seven weeks my baby was discharged weighing 5 lbs. 3¾ ozs. He has been home a week, has a wonderful appetite and weighs 6 lbs. In four days he will be two months old and he wasn't even due until February 8th. No one will ever discourage me in believing the power of faith.

How about that for a human experience of faith over defeat? She simply determined that, with God's help she would not fail. I sent the letter back to that mother to save for her baby when he grows up. What a priceless and inspiring possession it will be to him.

So, take another look at your failures in the light of these three principles: *Try, really try. Think, really think. Believe, really believe.* Put these powerful principles to work on your failures, and they can be overcome. As you work with positive and creative ideas you can so develop yourself that there will be no more failure for you.

4

THE KIND OF PEOPLE
PEOPLE LIKE

YOU WANT to be liked. So do I. To be liked and appreciated is a deep-seated human desire. That is why Dale Carnegie sold several million copies of his book *How to Win Friends and Influence People.* That is why tooth paste and gargles and deodorants are sold by the millions from ads which promise popularity for fifty-nine cents. In poll after poll the personal wish that comes up strongest is the desire to be well liked.

And so the problem of getting along well with others is no trifling matter; it is an important skill which must be mastered if we are to be effective and happy. And how is it done?

A first answer is a simple one, but one that is extremely vital, as experts will testify. I was having lunch with two good friends of mine, C. K. Woodbridge and Carol Lyttle, Chairman of the Board and Vice President of the Dictaphone Corporation, respectively. Our conversation was concerned mainly with the techniques of effective living. Since these two men are outstanding in sales work, I asked what, in their opinion, was the basic requirement of a successful salesman. Mr. Woodbridge answered me quickly. "It's to like people. Of course a man must believe in and know his product. He must be a hard worker and a positive thinker. But first of all he must like people."

I think that is the basic ingredient of popularity, too. Essentially, popularity is a form of salesmanship in that you "sell" yourself, if I may use that concept. When a man genuinely likes other people, he himself is quite certain to be liked in return. So, a primary step in being well liked is simply to like other people and like them sincerely, not for a purpose.

Of course, this is not always easy. Some people are more difficult to like than others. But the more you practice liking people, the easier it becomes. This is not done by blithely saying, I am now going to like everybody. While, as I said, it is simple, it is not that simple. Liking other people is the *result* of a way of life. It is the result of certain disciplined thought patterns. And one of the principal thought patterns for liking other people is positive thinking. It is taking a positive and not a negative attitude toward everyone.

It amazes me how often I hear the phrase, "I began to love everybody," when people are telling about the results of positive thinking in their lives. Here are a few examples culled from letters that come from Oshkosh, Fort Worth, San Diego and Louisville.

1. And then I just began to love everybody.
2. So that is the way things stand now. I like everybody and get along fine with them.
3. Then a strange thing began to happen to me. I began loving everybody.
4. Before I read *Positive Thinking*, frankly, I loved only myself; but then I went beyond myself. Now I actually like everyone. I can in all honesty say that.

It's not hard to understand why this is true. When people get rid of fear, anxiety and self-centeredness they develop a kind of ecstatic joy and delight in living. The world seems so different and newly wonderful that they tend to love everybody and everything. And they become so warm-hearted and delightful that people take a real liking to them. They change from withdrawn, worrying persons to ones with vitality and charm. They become "out-flowing" personalities; that is, personalities which now flow outward toward others in kindness and helpfulness.

If you are primarily concerned with yourself, you really haven't much chance of being one of the people people like. To become of that enviable type you'll just have to shift your primary attention away from yourself to other people. William James said, "The deepest drive in human nature is the desire to be appreciated." That also goes for the other person; he, too, wants to be appreciated by you. If you are abnormally concerned with yourself, craving attention, but absorbed in yourself, you will have no time to appreciate others and no inclination to do so, for that matter. And the other fellow wanting attention and regard, failing to get it from you, isn't going to be too enthusiastic about you.

I have a friend who is a natural-born positive thinker, and that's a blessing, for most people have to cultivate it. His name is Charles Heydt. Charlie is one of the great "appreciators" of this world. And as a result he is very well liked by everyone. When my secretary buzzes and tells me that Charlie Heydt is on the line, my face always brightens. I am delighted to talk to him, because Charlie is a builder-upper. If he sees an article that I have written for some magazine, he will take time out to call, or even to write a letter. "Dear Norman: By golly that was a good article. Something that needed to be said, too. You sure came up with a ringer."

It is not surprising, of course, that Charlie Heydt is one of the people people like. Being a builder-upper is essentially a question of paying attention to the other person's needs and the inevitable result of this is that the builder-upper himself becomes a beloved person.

If you want to be liked and respected, get to loving other people. Really put yourself out in interest and love for them, and stimulate them to bring out their best. Then, like bread on the waters, interest and love will come back to you a hundredfold.

One of my readers told me a story about Henry Ford which I like very much. He and this friend were lunching together when suddenly Henry Ford asked this question. "Who is your best friend?"

His companion named several persons, but Ford took a pencil and wrote these words on the tablecloth: "Your best friend is he who brings out the best that is within you."

Look behind actions and see the real person. If you try to help him be his best self, you will win esteem and confidence. If, in trying situations, you show a deep understanding and patience for a person, not only he, but others also will like you very much indeed.

I received a letter from a woman in Philadelphia who works on this principle. She had a difficult office manager to deal with:

> . . . the day the office manager opened up a tirade against me, I wanted to quit. Actually I started to look for another job. Then, what I had been reading about positive thinking caught up with me. Now was the time for me to put it to work.
>
> So I took a chance. I wrote the boss a letter and told him I was very appreciative of his giving me a job and an opportunity of working in his business, but I felt that he could double his business if the atmosphere around the place was more amiable.
>
> Did he realize that every time he called his office manager, the man became paralyzed? His brain went numb, he dropped whatever was in his hand on the nearest desk; that when he lit into the office manager he, in retaliation, lit into the people in the office? I told him I wanted to be a Christian. Why can't we all start loving one another around this place?
>
> That was some weeks ago and to date I haven't been fired. The conditions are 90 per cent improved and everybody is happier. I know the boss came up the hard way and I feel sorry for him, so I am going to redouble my efforts to help him all I can.

This woman, thinking positive, reacted to a difficult situation, not emotionally, but intelligently. She looked behind the "crippled condition" of the frightened office manager and had the keen insight to see that he acted as he did because he was insecure. She lifted the situation to a higher level of understanding because she was looking behind actions to the people themselves. Naturally she was a well liked and respected person in that office. She had learned to listen with understanding to a person's troubles even when he communicated through odd behavior rather than words.

She knew that behavior often speaks as plainly as words, sometimes even more plainly. Many of us listen to words, but not to the harsher language of behavior, and therefore are blundering in our human relations.

And many of us, unfortunately, do not even know how to listen to words. The art of listening is certainly one of the great secrets of being well liked. Most of us tend to talk too much when people come to us with a problem. We try to give advice, whereas more often the thing that is needed is silence and the ability to transmit to the other person the sense of patient, understanding love.

My friend Arthur Gordon, the writer, tells a poignant story about a newspaper editor in a small town. He was often at his desk until late at night writing editorials and doing other work. One night about midnight there was a rap on his door. "Come in," he called. The door opened and there before him was the haggard face of a neighbor, a man whose little boy had recently been drowned. The editor knew the story. This man had taken his wife and son out canoeing. The canoe had overturned; the wife was saved, but the child had drowned. Ever since the tragedy the father had been beside himself. Apparently he had been walking the streets in a daze and had been drawn by the editor's light—perhaps by the editor's understanding and kindness.

"Here, Bill," said the newspaperman. "Sit down and rest yourself a while."

The broken-hearted father sat down, then slumped forward in utter dejection and silence. And here the editor did an interesting thing. Instead of filling the void with a lot of talk, he simply went back to work. He was not upset by the other man's silence. After awhile he asked, "Would you like to have a cup of coffee, Bill?" He poured Bill a steaming cupful. "Drink that, old boy. The heat inside you will do you good." They sipped their coffee. Still there was no conversation.

After quite awhile the neighbor said, "I'm not ready to talk yet, Jack."

"That's OK. Just sit there as long as you want. I'll keep on with my work."

Much later Bill said, "I'm ready to talk." Then for a solid hour he poured it all out, while Jack listened. Bill went over the tragedy in meticulous, minute detail—what actually happened, what would have happened had he done this, what would not have happened had he done that, blaming himself for everything. He talked on and on until about three o'clock in the morning. Finally he stopped talking and said, "That's all I want to say tonight."

The editor came over, put his arm around his shoulder and said, "Go home, Bill, and get some sleep."

"May I come and talk to you again?"

"Any time," the editor told him. "Whenever you want to, day or night. God bless you."

That was all the editor did; he listened quietly, sympathetically and with love in his heart. And he was beloved by everybody in his community because he had this ability to listen creatively. He stimulated people to talk out their problems and find their own solutions. They all liked him for that.

Out in Ottumwa, Iowa, there is a man by the name of Al Stevens, a good friend of mine, who also knows how to listen creatively. Al Stevens is in a business that often stirs up a good deal of ill will; he is a bill collector. He owns the Wapello Adjustment Bureau. Businessmen pay him to collect bad debts. For years Al's was like any other collection agency. He made his calls, cajoled, pleaded, and sometimes he had to be rather firm. But then one day he came across the principles of positive thinking and he decided to run his business along those lines.

"Suppose," he said to himself, "that I take a more positive approach. Suppose I try to see each of these debtors as people who are faced with serious problems that are getting them into debt. Suppose I try to help them solve their problems . . ."

So Al Stevens turned his collection agency into a human service bureau aimed at helping other people. On his first interview after he had made his decision, he met a twenty-seven-year-old housewife who owed a seven months old bill to a local merchant. Al didn't ask for money right away. Instead he said, "I know you have a problem or you wouldn't be in debt. I'm confident that we can work it out. Let's see if there isn't some solution." The kindly yet positive tone in which he spoke inspired a spirit of confidence.

He learned that a series of medical bills had consumed all the family's savings. Heavy debts had followed. Depression set in. The husband couldn't seem to hold a job and soon he and the wife were fighting all the time. Al figured out that the basic problem these people faced was the lack of a sense of organization. They couldn't seem to conquer their debts, no matter what they did. Al saw his job—he had to restore these people's confidence by showing them how to organize their way out of their difficulties. Then and there he had the young housewife write down all her family's debts in one column, and in another column, all their assets. Then, together, they worked a system of rotating payments.

"For eighty-five cents a day you can have all of your debts paid within a year. Can you manage that?" Al asked. The young woman was now sure that she could . . . and she did. Nine months later she was completely debt free, the husband had a good job, and their marital relations were on a much better footing.

Is it any wonder that Al Stevens is known as the Debt Doctor around Ottumwa? He is so beloved in his town that many of his customers send him Christmas cards. People go out of their way to cross the street and wish him a Happy New Year. Imagine that—sending cards and good wishes to your bill collector! When you start to think positively about your relations with other people, when you start to see their behavior as the result of problems which they are not handling successfully, you quickly become one of the people people like.

There is another quality that is possessed by an astounding percentage of sought-after people and it is this: they seem to know how to help their friends to accept themselves. Anyone who can do that will always gain affection. It is amazing how self-conscious people are, and it makes them most unhappy.

Self-conscious people are often those who have never learned to accept themselves. It's a very misery-producing state of mind, and self-defeating, too. Because the individual is suffering inwardly, other people unconsciously pick up tension and rigidity from his attitude and he never quite makes the grade with them. At least he thinks he doesn't and, in thinking it, he helps to create unsatisfactory relationships.

One of my readers is a writer of note and a popular public speaker. He is about 5'8" in height, which is only a shade below average. But he was very self-conscious about his height. He would never allow himself to be pictured with a group of men lest he appear dwarfed by them. He became shrinking and retiring and avoided social contacts as much as possible. He happened to read in one of my books about an old friend of mine, a rugged character who had a formula which he often gave to those who were having trouble, either with themselves or with circumstances, and it was this: Think big, pray big, believe big, act big and you'll be big.

That formula really took hold with this man and he began practicing it. It started him on the study and practice of positive thinking which led ultimately to a normalizing of his attitudes toward himself. He accepted himself. Now he has no self-consciousness at all about his height. I have heard him say that height isn't measured by the length of a man's legs or the size of his frame, but it's how tall he is above his ears that counts. Now, big men look up to him even though they have to glance down to do it. He learned to accept himself and his height and, in so doing, found his real size—which is plenty big. He often tells me that he loves me because he feels that I helped him accept himself. And I feel the same toward those who helped me accept myself.

I used to be very self-conscious of my speech because I felt that I never could get just the right words. Oftentimes I would grow hot and almost blush because of my awkwardness of expression, especially in small groups in personal conversation. Strangely enough, I was not bothered by this before an audience. If a person from a university background was present, for example, one whose use of words was exceptionally cultivated, it gave me an enormous inferiority complex and tended to cause me to close up and retreat. The inhibitions and inferiority feelings caused by this self-consciousness was one of my most painful struggles.

The man who together with the never failing support of my mother helped me conquer this sensitivity was Professor Hugh M. Tilroe, Dean of the College of Public Speaking of Syracuse University. He taught me the importance of being myself, of not trying to be like any other person or following any style or mode of speech. "Use plain, simple, every day English," he said, "words everyone understands. And just talk like yourself; you sound all right to me."

Professor Tilroe was a member of my church and I was very young. I asked him if he would criticize my sermons from the standpoint of technique. "Not on your life," he responded. "If you want instruction in public speaking, register at the University and pay your bills and I'll teach you in class. But when I come to church, you are the teacher and I am the pupil in the great school of Christ. You just be yourself and speak out of your heart."

To this day and until the end of my days, I shall love this man, for he helped me to accept myself and be myself.

If you always have a genuine interest in people and always think of them as important, if you are concerned about them, it will vastly add to your success and happiness and they will like you in return. This requires having something constructive to give to others and a skill in communicating it. Knowing how to help people is an art and the person who knows how to do it can always know that he will have the lasting affection of many.

One of my readers runs a clothing store in upstate New York. This man's business was in a run-down condition a few years ago. The store was drab and dark and unattractive. Merchandise lay on the tables in sloppy piles. The owner himself was in a state of gloom and negativism which paralleled the physical condition of his store.

One day an old friend, who was concerned about the storekeeper, came in to see him. "How's business?" the friend asked.

"Awful," was the answer. "Simply terrible."

The friend walked around studying the situation and he said, "Really, I'm not surprised. Just take a look at the condition of this place. What's eating you, Fred? You used to have the snappiest store in town."

The storekeeper said, "The trouble is I haven't enough money to freshen things up. I know how everything looks. If I could just collect my outstanding accounts I'd have enough to start fixing things the way they once were."

"You can't collect any of your debts?" asked the friend. "That's strange. Maybe I can help you. Let's just take a look. Would you mind showing me the names of those who are behind in payments?"

The storekeeper brought out his accounts and pointed to a list of some ninety-six customers who owed him money. The friend took out a pencil and pointed at random to a name. "Tell me something about this person," he said.

The storekeeper looked at him in surprise. "What do you mean?"

"You don't know this customer—anything about him, his family, his problems, his needs?"

The storekeeper was astonished. "Of course not. I haven't time for that kind of stuff. He's just an account to me and one who doesn't pay, at that."

The friend chose another name. "What about this one?" The story was the same. The storekeeper had to admit that he did not know, personally, more than ten of the ninety-six people he carried on his books as bad debts.

"All right now," the friend said, "will you try an experiment? Send out all of these bills as usual, but this time say a prayer for the person who will be receiving it. In your prayer express the desire that each person have a happy and prosperous use of the clothing which you have sold him. Pray that things will go well with him. Then at the bottom of the bill add a word of personal interest. I do not care what it is. Simply, 'I hope you are enjoying the sweater,' or 'If there is any problem with this pair of shoes, be sure to bring them in and we will see what we can do about it.' Then add a cheery word like 'Lots of luck,' or 'Hope the family is all well.'

"Then, at the first opportunity, learn something personal about each one of these people. When this customer comes to you again think of him not as a sale, but as a person you are going to help. These are not accounts—they are people. Your job is to serve human beings through your store, helping them to the best of your ability."

Well, the storekeeper was not sure this was a very businesslike approach, but he was at the point where he was willing to try anything. So, to please his friend and with a new feeling of faith, he decided to try the experiment of praying for each of the persons he was billing and adding the personal note.

And then was he surprised. Right away an amazing thing happened. Of the ninety-six people, over half promptly remitted in whole or in part. Others wrote back that they were sorry to be slow in their payments and asked if it would be all right if they paid next month. Some few even came by personally to pay their bill. The storekeeper was so impressed with the first success of the experiment that he decided to double his efforts. From that day his philosophy of business changed and today he is a very greatly liked and sought after member of his community. People think of him first as a friend and then as the man from whom they buy their clothes. Being liked is so simple; just be concerned in a helpful way about people.

I would like to mention another characteristic that almost all popular people have. It is a kind of urbane imperturbability. They are not easily irritated or annoyed. Some people seem to be able to rise above their irritations and they are fun to be with because they are poised and even-tempered. They seem to live on an upper level emotionally and are not easily riled up. They keep in a good humor and spirit.

In California I met Mrs. Sadie Bunker, a remarkable lady now over sixty-five who has come to be known as the "flying grandmother." Three years before, she had decided she would be a licensed pilot. She studied, practiced, got her license and now flies her own plane all the time. Recently she passed all the tests necessary to go on a sound-breaking flight. She told me she thought everybody ought to have a plane. When things get on her nerves she just goes to the airport, takes her plane seven thousand feet up in the air and right away everything seems different. "You look down on the earth and it looks like an awfully nice place; and the people, too, seem different from up above," she explained.

While you and I may not be able to get into a plane whenever we get irritated and go up to a higher altitude in the physical sense, anyone can, by positive thinking, take altitude in his mind and spirit. The higher your spiritual altitude the less irritated you will be and the more fun you will be as a companion. Just be sure you always stay on top of things.

Suppose, for instance, that you are being criticized. Does criticism get under your skin, hurt your feelings, make you irritable and therefore unpleasant to be around? Or are you able to handle criticism in such a way that you gain friends? Anyone can handle criticism if he tries. And the secret is to keep your thinking positive. Note the following letter:

> I am a member of our City Council. At a recent meeting one Councilman became incensed when the rest of us disagreed with him over a bill. He stalked out of the chambers in wrath and into the arms of reporters.
>
> The next day the newspapers quoted him as berating each of us for attempts to block progress. In his anger he attempted to cause sectional bitterness.
>
> Fortunately, before the news reporters interviewed me I had been doing some reading in positive thinking. I shall always be grateful for the thoughts on this subject because it gave me the power to make the right kind of reply. I answered softly and constructively. That was several weeks ago and I am still hearing approval of my kindly feelings toward the angry councilman.

People who are able to turn criticism into a positive situation are going to attract friends. One of the most beloved public figures in this country was former President Herbert Hoover. Some time ago I had a good visit with Mr. Hoover and asked him this question. "At one time," I said, "you were probably the most criticized man in the United States. Nearly everybody seemed to be against you. It was customary to sneer at you. Nowadays, of course, you are America's grand old man and everybody on both sides of the political fence admires you. But when you were being so criticized, didn't it ever get inside you and bother you?"

Mr. Hoover looked at me with genuine surprise in his penetrating eyes and said, "Of course not."

Rather amazed, I asked, "But how come?"

"All you have to do in life," he said, "is to use your head. That is what you have it for—to use. When I decided to go into politics I sat down and figured out what it would mean. I weighed the cost. One thing was sure, I would get some very hard criticism. But in spite of that I went ahead. So when I got the criticism, I wasn't surprised. I had expected it and there it was. I was, therefore, better able to handle it. You see," he smiled, "I'm a positive thinker."

He looked at me for a moment. "But that is not the whole answer. I am a Quaker." He did not amplify that remark, for he knew that I would understand. Quakers cultivate peace at the center. Irritation is simply absorbed in a deep spiritual peace in the mind and heart.

And so, being able to handle criticism, Mr. Hoover was destined to outlive the slurs of political life and become one of our best liked Americans. His philosophy is one that all of us could well follow, whether in public or private life. We are going to be criticized; you can count on that all right. This is one of the facts of living. By urbanely recognizing that fact we can develop the right spiritual attitude for handling criticism creatively. And it won't get you down when it comes if you are mentally and spiritually prepared for it.

Senator Paul Douglas of Illinois tells of a Quaker meeting where he learned a great lesson in handling criticism. As you know, the Quakers practice silence in their worship. Sometimes they sit for a long time without anybody saying anything. At this particular meeting the only person who spoke was an old man who rose and made this statement:

"Whenever a man differs with you or criticizes you, try to show him by every look, by your demeanor, and by your actions that you love him."

That was all the old man said, but Senator Douglas instantly knew that, as the Quakers phrase it, this man had "spoken to his condition."

One of the most practical anti-criticism formulas ever outlined is this: "Love your enemies, bless them that curse you, do good to them that hate you, and pray for them which despitefully use you, and persecute you." (Matthew 5:44) This is wonderful teaching when put into action, for it enables you to remain poised and confident in the face of the hostile words and actions of others. And those who watch you handling criticism in this way will instinctively be drawn to you. You will be the kind of person other persons like. As a matter of fact, people tend to like a criticized person (providing he is criticized a great deal by a great many) on the basis of the kicked dog psychology. And if the criticized person takes it quietly without rancor, not striking back but constantly loving, he will gather in friends faster than his critics can manufacture enemies.

That Scripture verse about loving enemies and treating people kindly is actually the subtlest technique ever devised for getting the love of every-one. It proves once again, if proof is needed, that Jesus Christ is the wisest of all teachers of the skill of living.

It is so easy to hate, so easy to be negative, so easy to accept defeat and live on a low level. It is easy, but it is also frustration and misery, because we never can be happy, deep in our souls, until we live according to what we are; namely, children of God with the Kingdom of God within us.

In my correspondence with those who are working with the principles of positive thinking, I have noticed something else about the kind of people people like. And it is this; those who have what you might call up-beat personalities, who inspire others, who supply courage, strength and hope are deeply appreciated. All of us need courage, we need strength and hope, sometimes we need these qualities desperately. So, when people are able to draw this strong spirit from you, the natural result is that you become important to them. You gain a place in their hearts.

I know full well the effect of such people on me, and many others also testify to the effect upon them of the inspirational personality. The man who believes in something, who has some real convictions, who lives by a strong and sturdy faith and shares it freely becomes an influence in men's lives.

For example, one of my esteemed friends, George E. Sokolsky, the famous newspaper columnist, is a strong positive thinker and the word defeat is not in his vocabulary. He experienced several illnesses and I saw little of him for quite a while as he restricted his activity. But a few days ago he telephoned me about helping some people and I noted the old time vigor and verve in his voice.

"You seem on top of things, George," I commented.

"Sure thing," he replied. "We're supposed to be on top of things."

"But you've been through so much, what is your secret?"

"Secret! It's no secret. We have Someone with us, haven't we?"

He went on to tell about going into the hospital for examination. Then the doctors came in and put the X-ray pictures up against the window. "Know how to read an X-ray?" they asked.

George took a long look and said, "Sure, I've got cancer . . . let's cut it out."

"They told me," he explained, "because they knew I could take it."

His heart doctor called to check his heart, to determine whether it could take an operation since he had experienced a coronary. He was amazed at Sokolsky's calmness. "You astonish me by your composure," the doctor said. "If I had your attitude I would live ten years longer."

"But," said George, "I have faith so I'm completely at ease. I'm in God's hands."

Following nearly five hours on the operating table, upon Sokolsky's return to consciousness, the surgeon said, "Well, you're alive."

"How do you know I'm alive?" returned his vigorous patient. "There's only one way I can know I'm alive—can I do my work. If I can't work, I am dead. Bring me a pad and pencil and I'll try writing a column. Then I'll know whether I'm alive."

The column was one of the best of his entire career.

Another up-beat personality is Colonel Frank Moore, head usher in my church in New York. Frank is a positive thinker who takes his Christian faith into business activity as well as into personal life.

In his office is a large conference table around which his executive staff of seven persons gathers regularly for important conferences. The table accommodates eight chairs. Colonel Moore at the beginning of his service in this organization commented to his staff upon the importance of the decisions they would reach in conferences and referred to the necessity for Divine guidance. In view of the fact that there was normally a vacant chair at the table, he wondered if it might not be a good idea always to leave the chair at the head of the table vacant to remind each person of a Presence who would always guide in decisions.

Slowly at first, but with growing appreciation for what it did to the meetings, the suggestion was accepted. The information regarding the vacant chair got around through the other offices and when joint meetings were held that chair was never occupied. The news spread outside the organization and a quiet but definite influence seemed to be derived.

Back of the table on the wall a prayer was reproduced on a framed mat 18 × 24 inches. It so impressed buyers and others that in one year alone over two thousand copies were requested and given away. This is the prayer:

> O Lord, grant that each one who has to do with me today may be happier for it. Let it be given me each hour today what I shall say, and grant me the wisdom of a loving heart that I may say the right thing rightly. Help me to enter into the mind of everyone who talks with me, and keep me alive to the feelings of each one present. Give me a quick eye for little kindnesses that I may be ready in doing them and gracious in receiving them. Give me a quick perception of the feelings and needs of others, and make me eager hearted in helping them. Amen.

Want to be liked? Lift people's spirit. Give them a little extra inspiration. Help build up their strength. They will like you for it. You'll have a warm place in their hearts for always.

So let's review some of the things we have been talking about in this chapter. What are the secrets of popularity? How do we go about becoming the kind of people people like?

1. In the first place, start now to like other people. How do you do this? One of the most successful ways is through positive thinking. Positive

thinkers become out-flowing personalities, they cease to be obsessively concerned about themselves, and they begin to be concerned for others. They "love everybody" as is evidenced by the many times this phrase has cropped up in the letters people write me about the results of positive thinking. Once they begin to "love everybody," they themselves become lovable. They are sought out, needed personalities.

2. Always try to bring out the best in other people and you will be welcomed wherever you go. Learn to "listen" to behavior as well as to words that are spoken. People are often trying to communicate with you, for good or bad, through the way they act as well as by what they say. When you learn to listen to the problems people have, you are in a position to help them bring out the best that is within themselves.

3. Make your friends feel comfortable with themselves. People have a hard time accepting themselves. Help them do that and everyone will enjoy having you around.

4. Be calm, poised and cheerful. Learn how to rise above the irritations that life holds for us all. Develop an ability to fly to higher "spiritual altitudes," so that criticisms and petty unpleasantnesses will no longer ruffle you. Take for its full meaning the Biblical injunction, "Love your enemies, bless them that curse you, do good to them that hate you, and pray for them which despitefully use you, and persecute you."

5. Be an up-beat personality so that people may receive inspirational support from you. You'll become very important to their lives.

Practice these principles in your daily life, and it will follow automatically that you will become one of the people people like.

5

THERE CAN BE LOTS OF FUN IN LIFE

How GOOD it is to be alive! What a glorious morning! I've really never felt better. This promises to be a wonderful day.

This may sound a bit exuberant but it's the way I feel this morning. I'm happy, I feel good. I'm getting ready to have a lot of fun today. When I walk down the street I wouldn't be surprised if I whistled, just like when I was a youngster.

Come to think of it, it's been a long time since I heard anyone whistling on the street in New York City. And this isn't just an observation of my own. I was talking to Bill Arthur, the other day. Bill is managing editor of *Look* magazine. "Have you noticed that no one ever walks down Madison Avenue whistling?" he asked. Bill was raised in Louisville, Kentucky and he remembers his childhood days as a time when people seemingly knew how to get more fun from life than they do today.

Why is this? If it is true of you, what can you do to bring the want-to-whistle back into your attitude-of-living? What can you do to gain the natural, unaffected kind of joy that comes from deep down inside? I heard recently about a well-known psychiatrist who is working on a program called Positive Mental Health. Whenever he describes the results he hopes to obtain, he talks about his dog. "I come home from work and my dog greets me with a bound and a yelp and a kind of frenzy of joy. What a contrast this is to the gloom and depression I see on human faces during the day. This animal has the secret of deep fun. *This* is the way we should be able to react to life."

Now I'm not suggesting that we start bounding all over the place. We've all known people who make themselves a little ridiculous by over-doing this kind of enthusiastic happiness. I've often suspected that such people are only feigning happiness. But all of us have also known the rare and wonderful individual who is full of *deep* fun. There's the key. It's a fun that is not on the surface, nor light or superficial but one that derives from a deep sense of happiness at being what you are and where you are and doing what you are doing. Catch such a completely well adjusted person unawares, and you are apt to find him singing or whistling.

Let me repeat. I really feel happy today. And I think I can spot the origin of this good feeling, too. Yesterday afternoon it was a bright Sunday, and my wife Ruth and I took a walk with our young daughter, Lizzie. (I can't break myself of the habit of calling her Lizzie, although her mother would much prefer Elizabeth.) We had a lot of fun together. We walked up Fifth Avenue along the park, stepping out briskly, with our heads held high and our spirits held high, too. "It's fun to walk tall," Lizzie and Ruth and I agreed.

We walked a mile or more, all of us feeling dynamic, gay and enjoying life. We passed the Frank Lloyd Wright building, the Guggenheim Museum, on upper Fifth Avenue. "Isn't that beautiful!" said Lizzie. Well, I had never thought of that building as being particularly beautiful, but through her eyes I took a second look. (I was thinking a little taller, perhaps.) And when I looked that second time, I sensed the joy that the great architect had built into this structure. It spirals upward. It really transmits an emotion of enthusiasm and happiness and vigor. For the first time I began liking that building. Perhaps it was just the way I was feeling.

But that's the point. When you feel right, you tend to be joyful, you tend to have a sense of deep fun and your appreciation of everything expands. Dr. Henry C. Link, the psychologist, would never see a patient who was in a state of depression without first sending him for a vigorous turn around the block. "Walk rapidly around the block ten times," Dr. Link would say. "This will exercise the motor centers of the brain, and the blood will flow away from the emotional-activity centers. When you come back, you will be much more rational and receptive to positive thoughts."

Your physical condition has a lot to do with your ability to enjoy life. When you are refreshed and rejuvenated, life takes on new meaning. Proper exercise and proper rest are essential ingredients of joyful emotions. Some scientists, according to an account I read, recently made some experiments with what they call "massive doses of sleep." Using drugs, they induced sleep in people who were tired and aging, and they reported a regeneration of tissues, a prolonging of life, the disappearance of disease and of course with this, the appearance of a new vitality and joy in living.

So, the first step in attaining this wonderful sense of the deep fun of life is to feel right. And treat your body right if you want your feelings to be right.

And the second step is to think right. Treat your mind right. Think positively. The positive thinker trains himself in the attitude of joy. He expects it, and then he finds it. What you look for, you will find—that is a basic law of life. Start looking for joy and you'll find it. For when you look for it, you will be able to see and recognize it. Some good friends of mine, Elsie and Otto Palmer, who live in Brooklyn, N.Y. looked for it and found it. They wrote:

It is extremely difficult to give expression to one's innermost feelings; but since we have been learning about positive thinking, we feel you should know that we, too, are experiencing that wonderful something within that makes us want to sing for joy and tell the world about it.

The application of your techniques has revolutionized our lives. While we have been brought up in a religious home, we never before understood how helpful and practical religion could and should be. It has given us a completely new and happy outlook on life to the extent that each day is begun with great expectancy and joy.

I have made it a habit to expect a pleasant surprise each day and it has never failed to come to pass with one exception; and that is, the degree of the surprise depends on the degree of faith I put into my expectancy. If I am very sure, lukewarm, or cool—to that degree will the surprise come to pass.

I like the paragraph in this letter that speaks about expecting a pleasant surprise each day. This is first-rate positive thinking. The people who look forward into the future expecting to see great things are people who are going to be happy.

The other night I was driving up Park Avenue with a wonderful man, Dr. Arthur Judson Brown. Dr. Brown is 101 years old, and he has the spirit and verve of a teenager. "Just look at that skyline," he said. "New buildings everywhere. I think it's just great the way this town is always changing, always improving itself."

That's the way a *young* person thinks. I asked Dr. Brown what he thinks of modern young people. "I thank God for them," he said. "They are really great, these youngsters. They're so much wiser and better than I was at their age. They're going to create a new world for us. There is a new day on the way, and I'm looking forward to it."

At 101 years of age, he's looking forward to a great new day! I apologized to Dr. Brown for keeping him out so late at night. It was nearly eleven, and I thought he would normally be in bed at that hour. "Oh, not at all," he said. "I'm often up until midnight. But I'll get my rest tomorrow. I've learned, long ago, not to push myself too much. You ought to learn that too, you youngsters. Tomorrow I'll get up and have a leisurely breakfast and read the paper; and if I don't see my name in the obituary column, I'll go back to bed for some extra sleep."

The thing that determines whether or not a person is happy is an *inward* state or condition. It is what goes on in the mind that tells the story of whether you are happy and positive or sad and negative. Marcus Aurelius Antonius said, "No man is happy who does not think himself so." William Lyon Phelps remarked, "The happiest person is he who thinks the most interesting thoughts."

So, if you're not happy, you can experience this deep fun in life by doing a constructive job on your thoughts. If your mind is filled with grudges, hate, selfishness or off-color thoughts, why naturally the clear light of joy cannot filter through. You'll need to shift to a different mental life, and up-beat attitude, if you want a lot of fun out of life.

A reader I have known for some years was originally one of my "miserable" friends. A miserable friend is a person who makes everybody around him unhappy because he is unhappy himself. You might come into the presence of this man in a more or less jaunty frame of mind but he was a jauntiness-extractor. In no time at all he would take the jauntiness out of you.

In the course of time this man moved away, though he remained on my mailing list for positive thinking material. Then, three or four years later, I saw him again. He was so changed it was as though he had been reborn, which is exactly what had happened to him. He had been mentally reborn and spiritually, too. He was definitely a different person. I was so impressed by his change that I asked how he had managed it.

"I went on a seven day mental diet," he replied. He explained that he had become interested in a pamphlet by Emmet Fox called, "The Seven Day Mental Diet," which I had recommended to my readers. Observing that Americans are physically diet conscious, Dr. Fox urged people to undertake a mental diet as well. He made the point that a man becomes what he thinks.

And what is the seven day mental diet? It is this: you resolve that from a given minute you will, for seven days thereafter, watch your every word. You will not say a single negative thing, or a mean thing, or a dishonest thing. You will not make a depressing remark for seven days.

Now that is, of course, a big undertaking. "I tried it one day and failed," my friend said. "I tried it again, and went two days this time before I slipped. I tried again, unsuccessfully, and then again." But this is the kind of man who, when he goes out for anything, goes all out. "I asked God to help me, for I knew I just had to change myself or else! Then finally, for a whole week I succeeded. Not once, for seven days, did I fail. Then I thought I would ease off and just slump back a little into the old ways. But do you know, I found that there was a difference within myself. Actually, I could not slip back. I was changed, not completely of course; but I was not the same person. Since then life has become different. Now my mind is free of negative thoughts and I get real fun out of living." This is one of those sound new angles on positive thinking that readers pass along.

The two most important moments in the day are when you first open your eyes, and the moment when you drop off to sleep. These are the brackets of your conscious day. If those moments are packed full of positive, joyful thoughts, your day will be full of positive, joyful living. Elbert Hubbard said, "Be pleasant until ten o'clock in the morning and the rest of the day will take care of itself." Henry David Thoreau used to give himself good news first thing in the morning. He would tell himself how lucky he was to have been born. If he had never been born, he'd never have known the crunch of snow underfoot, or the glint of starlight; he'd never have smelled the fragrance of a wood fire nor would he have seen the love light in human eyes. He started off each day with thanksgiving.

My old friend from college days, Judson S. Sayre, President of the Norge Corporation, gets up every morning, looks in the mirror and says, "I am going to make good things happen today." And sometimes when he tends to become discouraged, he stops everything and thinks of some of the happiest experiences of his life. His spirit rises again. During the forty years I've known him, I've never seen him when he didn't radiate optimism and joy.

An excellent go-to-sleep technique is suggested by J. Harvey Howells in *This Week* magazine. "When the last good night has been said and the head is on the pillow, the soul is utterly alone with its thoughts. It is then that I ask myself, 'What was the happiest thing that happened today?' "

This has a great effect not only in setting the tone for a deep and peaceful night's sleep, but also in conditioning the mind to anticipate the new day soon to dawn.

This happiest thing may be only a little experience like the aroma of a flower, golden sunlight through a soft glass curtain, a chance word of friendship, a little kindness done, a fragment of melody. But to go mentally searching through the activities and fleeting impressions of the day for that one happiest thing; this is a most rewarding adventure on the borderline of sleep.

And Emerson used to end his day in a wonderful way. He would see to it that he finished it, completely. "Finish each day and be done with it," he advised. "You have done what you could. Some blunders and absurdities no doubt crept in; forget them as soon as you can. Tomorrow is a new day; begin it well and serenely and with too high a spirit to be cumbered with your old nonsense."

He knew better than to let his day end with regrets. Emerson was a door shutter. He shut the door on the day, and forgot it. He was like Lloyd George who, one day, was taking a walk with a friend and was carefully closing every gate after him. "You don't need to close those gates," said the friend.

"Oh yes," said Lloyd George. "I've spent my life shutting gates behind me. It's necessary, you know. You shut the gate behind you and the past is held there. Then you can start again."

In becoming a joyful person, it is extremely important to clean up mistakes, sins, errors; then forget them and go forward. "Forgetting those things which are behind, and reaching forth unto those things which are before." (Philippians 3:13) This is to be smart and wise.

The kind of people to whom life with Christ has become a personal friendship are as natural as they can be in their enjoyment of religion. My friend Floyd McElroy, for example, is one. He and his wife Edith invited us to dinner with some other friends in their apartment on Fifth Avenue overlooking Central Park.

When we sat down to dinner Floyd did not call on me, his pastor, to offer thanks. I loved what he did. He offered the blessing himself and I thought it was one of the best I ever heard. Floyd said in his humble and unaffected manner, "Lord we thank You for our friends and we are happy that they are with us tonight. You have been so good to all of us and we are grateful. And now give us a gay and jovial evening in Jesus' name. Amen."

This kind of religion, in my judgment, is the real thing and it is a big natural part of life. Why do people insist upon making religion stilted and unnatural, and above all, getting pained looks on their faces when it is mentioned. When you've got the real article, you can hardly contain yourself, you're so happy. You are walking toward the sun.

The McElroys are people that I like to call "shadow leaders" rather than "shadow pushers." And what might that be? One sunny day I was standing with a friend at a window in one of New York's tall office buildings looking down on Fifth Avenue at 42nd Street near the Public Library. The friend I was with, Amos Parrish, is one of the nation's great merchandising experts and a man with a picturesque, imaginative mind. I knew that an idea was agitating him because he was scratching his chin and had a reflective look. Suddenly, pointing down at the sidewalk in front of the library he said, "A lot of those people down there are shadow pushers."

"What do you mean, shadow pushers?" I asked.

"Why don't you see," he replied. "They are walking away from the sun and their shadows go ahead of them. They are shadow pushers. Those others," he continued, pointing again, "Are shadow leaders. They are walking toward the sun, so their shadows fall behind them."

The difference is very significant, for if you are leading the shadow, you are master of life; but if you are trying to push shadows, life can be hard indeed. You can't have any real fun in life if you always have your back to the sun pushing shadows.

Another important principle in leading a happy fun-loving life is to learn to love and esteem the best in people. My father taught me the great truth that how you think about people, how you treat them and react to them is extremely important to your own happiness. "Treat each man as a child of God is the secret," he said. "Hold him in esteem and it will make both him and you happy."

On Christmas Eve, when I was very young, I was out with my father doing some late Christmas shopping in our home town of Cincinnati. My father had as big a heart of love as any man I ever knew. It made no difference who a person was, he loved and talked with them all. And he was an extremely happy man. He had respect and esteem for every person.

He saw beneath their exteriors, not as they appeared to be, but rather as they really were. And he had sharp insight, too. He knew people.

On this occasion I was loaded down with packages and felt tired and irritable. I was thinking how good it would be to get home when a beggar, a bleary-eyed, unshaved, dirty old man came up to me, touched my hand with his and asked for money. I recoiled from his soiled hand and rather impatiently brushed him aside.

"You shouldn't treat a man that way, Norman," said my father as soon as we were out of earshot.

"But, Dad, he's nothing but a bum."

"Bum?" he said. "There is no such thing as a bum. He is a child of God, my boy. Maybe he hasn't made the most of himself but he is a child of God, nonetheless. We must always look upon a man with esteem. Now, I want you to go and give him this." My father pulled out his pocketbook and handed me a dollar. That was a lot for his means. "And do exactly the way I tell you. Go up to him, hand him this dollar and speak to him with respect. Tell him you are giving him this dollar in the name of Christ."

"Oh," I objected, "I don't want to say that."

My father insisted. "Go and do as I tell you."

So I ran after the old man, caught up with him and said, "Excuse me, sir. I give you this dollar in the name of Christ."

The old man looked at me in absolute surprise. Then a wonderful smile spread over his face. A smile that made me forget he was dirty and unshaven. I could see his real face through the streaks of grime. His essential nobility came out. Graciously, with a sort of bow, he said, "I thank you, young sir, in the name of Christ."

My irritation and annoyance faded like magic. And suddenly I was happy, deeply happy. The very street seemed beautiful. In fact, I believe that in the moment I held that man in full and complete esteem, I came very close to Christ Himself. And that, of course, is one of the most joyful experiences any person can ever have. Since then I have made every effort to see people as my father saw them. And that has brought me untold satisfaction. I have often returned to the exact spot where this incident took place, on Fourth Street, Cincinnati.

Giving is another joy producer. This may mean giving money or time or interest or advice; anything that takes something out of you and transfers it to other people, helpfully. Anything that gets you out of yourself, actually helps you find yourself. It's a strange principle but it's true, nevertheless, that those who give the most have the most of whatever they give.

I recall a young businessman who was ambitious. To get money and get ahead was his idea. And there is nothing wrong with that idea if you keep yourself in the center of a sharing process at the same time. He gave to his job all he had and then some. He was not naturally selfish, but he wanted to go places and so he concentrated upon himself rather exclusively.

He read everything that had to do with self-improvement. So it was that he bought *The Power of Positive Thinking.* It was "right down his alley" he said. He put positive thinking principles into action though he had a materialistic slant on it! But he went all out with it; and as a result, he "took off like a jet for the top echelon" to quote his picturesque, though not too modest, words.

But soon he began developing tension and anxiety symptoms, the former from overdrive, the latter because he feared he couldn't sustain the fast, competitive pace he had set for himself. Then developed a pathetic reaction often experienced by those who "get ahead." Such men have a lot of fun arriving, but when they arrive there isn't as much fun in it as they expected. The top can turn out to be a rat race and ulcers, if being at the top is all you're interested in.

"Why don't I get fun out of life any more?" this man asked me. "I've hit the top through positive thinking and look—I'm still not forty. What's the matter with me? Am I stale or something?"

We checked him over for the usual causes of unhappiness. We started by looking into his participation, or lack of it, in things which wouldn't "get him something."

"Why, I can't believe it," I said. "You're not giving a thing to anyone except your family, to whom you give everything."

The church which he attended with fair regularity got exactly one big dollar a week from him—about a twentieth of what he should have been giving on his income. He gave the community chest just as little as he could get away with. It wasn't that he was tight. This dollar-pinching was rather a holdover from his old insecurity feelings when he was a poor boy starting out. As for giving of his time and thought to help others, this didn't check out at all on his personal evaluation test.

"No wonder there's no fun in life for you," I said. "You've got to get outside of yourself. You've stopped the creative process. You're run down because everything has been coming in and nothing going out. You're like the dead sea, inlets but no outlets, and that means mental and spiritual stagnation."

Now, he wasn't as bad as this sounds. The fact that he was worried about the way he felt and frankly was willing to discuss it, humbly asking for guidance, showed him to be a pretty real person. And a real person can always get answers to problems like this.

We therefore gave him a positive thinking program which he had missed by stressing the materialistic values in positive thinking. Sure you can use it to make money but if you use it only that way it will fold back on you as it did with this man. So, we stepped it up to a higher level, into a positive thinking he hadn't seen before. This was designed to release him and remake him and it did.

1. He was to increase his giving to the Lord's work to 10 per cent of his income. Some of this was to go to the church, some to individuals (for whom there would be no tax exemption claim) and some to other charitable institutions.

2. He was to look for someone who needed help outside his family and friends, someone who might never be able to help him in return. The help might be monetary or in the form of advice, or just friendly interest. Perhaps he might select a deserving boy and help him get an education or get started in business.

3. He was to stop rushing long enough to give himself to people—a few leisurely words with those who were part of his daily life: the waiter, the policeman on the corner, the news vendor, the elevator operator, or even his wife and children.

4. He was to go to his pastor and offer to help in some of the church's business problems. More than that he was to offer to call on a few people to carry the helpful ministry of the church to them, people in the hospital for example.

"Gosh that sounds like a time-consuming layout to me," he complained.

"Sure," I said, "that's exactly right. You must learn to give, not only money and good will, but time for the benefit of other people. But the pay-off will be more than worth it. You'll get back your old sense of fun if you follow this plan. It's either-or, take it or leave it." I knew my man, I knew he wouldn't leave it. He went for the businesslike approach when he knew it was sound. And this was.

To sum up this case history, which strung out over many months, he did follow the program and he did recover the ability to get a lot of fun out of life. He became an active factor in his community life. Moreover, the tension and anxiety subsided. Maybe he staved off a heart attack, who knows?

Still another element in the total joy-in-life formula is to know for a fact that you are able to meet and overcome the hardships, sorrows and tough circumstances of this world. This kind of happiness is priceless. This is that deep fun we were talking about earlier.

One thing after another happening to you can literally "knock the life out of you." The expression is realistic, life is knocked out of you, for a fact. Blow after blow can leave you pretty limp and discouraged. Ultimately you may feel so beaten that you crawl through life instead of standing up courageously and masterfully, taking things as they come and handling them with sure skill and force. There is no fun in life for the crawler-through-life. The licked are always unhappy. But those who know in their hearts that they are equal to every challenge, minor or major, are the ones who get a huge amount of fun out of life.

A man on a plane said "I'm a positive thinking Exhibit A! I don't say that boastfully, but because it's done so much for me. I was the world's worst self-defeating person. I blamed everyone for my failures—even the government. But I knew who was my worst enemy. As someone put it, 'If I could kick the pants of the man causing all my troubles I couldn't sit down for a week!' "

"And believe me it wasn't funny." Then he described a series of defeats and disappointments sufficient to take the heart out of any man. "At first I shied off positive thinking because you tied God into it and I didn't go for that religious approach. I took the psychology in the book and let the religion alone. But while I mentally agreed with the psychology, it didn't take with me. Perhaps I was too negative. But I noticed that you were always urging your readers to read and apply the Bible to problems. Frankly, I hadn't opened a Bible in years. But finally I started reading. At first I couldn't get a thing out of it and wondered why you were so keen for it. So I limited myself to looking up your references. I really tried to follow the things you suggested.

"I was reading the 84th Psalm and the eleventh verse struck me . . . 'No good thing will he withhold from them that walk uprightly.' (Psalm 84:11) 'Walk uprightly'—what did that mean? But it wasn't hard to figure out that I was crawling like a worm. I should stand up like a man and quit griping and being sorry for myself. I was full of self-pity. *Uprightly*—that was the word! Stand up to things—that was what I should be doing! And I got the idea that if I did that, God wouldn't hold back any good thing. So I started walking as sprightly as I could, not cringing like I had been doing. I also saw that *uprightly* meant no double dealing. I decided I'd straighten some things out, with God's help.

"I now see why you tie religion and practical psychology together. Religion makes it work, puts the oomph into it."

That's really an idea to get hold of. Or better still let it get hold of you. "No good thing will be withhold from them that walk uprightly." It gave this man new fun in living. He really had it.

But what about sorrow and grief? An effective demonstrator of positive thinking who achieved out of sorrow a quiet joy in life is Mrs. Anne Scherer of Switzerland. I met Mr. and Mrs. Scherer several years ago at the Beau Rivage Palace Hotel in Lausanne where he was the manager. Some months later Mr. Scherer died suddenly. Mrs. Scherer worked on, under the new manager, as hostess of the hotel. Recently when I returned to Lausanne it was evident that in her modest way Mrs. Scherer had adjusted quite well to her sorrow problem. She had achieved a quietly serene spirit that obviously derived from a deep source of strength.

"I admire the way you have managed to pull through this sad time with such fine spirit," I said. "You did the right thing by going back to work and keeping yourself busy."

Then Mrs. Scherer answered with an extraordinary philosophy of sorrow. "Actually it wasn't going back to work that did it for, you see, work is not a medicine, it is a drug. It desensitizes, but does not heal. It is only faith that heals."

That insight is a classic. Work desensitizes, but it does not heal. It is faith that heals. When we are suffering from deep emotional wounds, of course, we cannot have real happiness; not until the wounds are healed. Some of us make the mistake of thinking we can cure them with work, or perhaps with play; with drink or attempted forgetfulness. As Mrs. Scherer pointed out, these efforts only desensitize the wound for a while. But they do not cure. It is when one learns to apply faith in depth that a true curative process is begun.

A man from out West used to come to New York every now and then on business, and he would call me on the telephone. He had a deep emotional wound and his mood was invariably dejected, his thinking gloomy and somewhat cynical. This negative reaction to sorrow, negative to the point of being abnormal, went on for several years and then, all of a sudden, he wrote me a ten-page letter. I left it lying on my desk for a while before undertaking to read it. But I got into it and I was amazed; it was full of joy and hope. Here was the buoyant testimony of a man who at last had found himself and was telling me how happy he was.

What had happened? Well, this man finally decided he was on the wrong track with his gloomy attitudes and resolved to study and "try to apply" positive thinking techniques to his sorrow problem. He said, "I evolved some techniques you didn't give in your book and they worked beautifully. Perhaps you would like to pass them along to others." And I am glad to do just that for these ideas are sound. I give them to you just as I received them.

This man's "five-fold program of faith" follows:

First, I pray twenty-five times a day. Yes, I mean that; but these are fragmentary prayers as I walk or drive or work at my desk. I guarantee that if anybody will pray twenty-five times a day he will change the character of his thoughts and change his life. Perhaps this is what the Bible means when it tells us to "pray without ceasing."

Second, I soak my mind with Bible passages. I must have committed a couple of hundred texts by now. I say them over and think of them as going down and down into my subconscious.

Third, I take a piece of paper and see how many good thoughts I can write down about people I know and about situations, too. This was the toughest thing in the whole process as I had a lot of gripes about lots of people. And as to situations, I was always negative and pessimistic. However, I've found that if you think mean thoughts about people it makes you unhappy. But pleasant thoughts about people make you happy all over. And if you make yourself think that things are going to be O.K. that makes you happier too; and thinking that way often makes them turn out that way.

Fourth, I see how many times every day I can tell the Lord how much I love Him. This love-for-God feeling really does something to you. There was a time I would have ridiculed such a thing, but no more. The more I express my love for God the happier I become.

Fifth, I try to keep all sin out of my life. This is a big order, but even making the effort gives me a clean and happy feeling.

As I said, I tried this man's program on quite a few people and where they really worked at it, it proved effective. It is my belief that this spiritual formula will, as he indicates, go far toward curing anybody of unhappiness.

Who wants to live with joy? Who wants to feel like whistling on Madison Avenue or any other street? Pray twenty-five times a day. Soak the mind with Bible passages. See how many good thoughts you can think about people. Tell the Lord you love Him. Get sin out of your life. It is not easy. It takes self-discipline. It requires your doing something about yourself. But really there is no need for you to be unhappy. Simply do a rehabilitation job on your thoughts. Try spiritual living, really try it. You will discover for yourself that there's lots of fun in life.

6

THE WONDERFUL LAW OF ABUNDANCE

THERE IS a law of abundance operating in life. And this abundance is for you.

Abundance is a wonderful word. I like the sound of it; it's full and rich. The root of this word, I'm told, is the Latin *undare* which means "to rise up in waves." So actually, when you think and practice abundance you stimulate all manner of good things to rise up toward you in waves.

I received a letter from a young man in Washington, D. C. A year ago this man, Lloyd, was in all sorts of trouble. His marriage was on the rocks, he was drinking, he couldn't hold a job; he had been fired seven times from positions with the Hot Shoppes restaurant chain. Certainly Lloyd couldn't say that all manner of good things were rising up toward him in waves, or even in dribbles.

Then Lloyd began to hear about the amazing effect that positive thinking had on people's lives. He read and studied *The Power of Positive Thinking* and all the books and articles he could find on the subject, and he made up his mind to try these techniques for himself. First, he had to deal with the past. Who would hire him with his record? But that was negative thinking. Sure he had failed before, but that did not have to determine the future.

In *The Power of Positive Thinking* he had read those dynamic words from the Bible, "Forgetting those things which are behind, and reaching forth unto those things which are before; I press toward the mark . . ." (Philippians 3:13)

Lloyd went out once more and applied for a job . . . at the Hot Shoppes; right back where he had been fired seven times. With his chin held high, but scared and frightened, and saying over those words from Philippians, Lloyd walked into the office of the personnel director. His new faith enabled him to tell this man that he wanted to work again. And an amazing thing happened. The personnel director said that if he could find one manager who would take Lloyd on, he could work there again. This firm, as I have since learned, began and operates on positive spiritual principles.

"I'm thankful to say," writes Lloyd, "that I found a manager who remembered my good qualities as well as the bad, and gave me another chance." He was hired as a waiter at this drive-in restaurant. Then and there Lloyd set a new pattern for himself. His letter continues:

> I made two simple promises to God and to myself, something which I've never dared do before, for to me a promise to anyone is serious but to God it is more so.
>
> First, I promised to read my Bible and pray—really pray—every day. Second, I promised to tithe, to give a tenth of my income to God regardless of whether I had a good night as a waiter or a bad one. I decided to go for that promise in the Bible: "Bring ye all the tithes into the storehouse—and prove me now herewith, said the Lord of hosts, if I will not open you the windows of heaven, and pour you out a blessing, that there shall not be room enough to receive it." (Malachi 3:10)
>
> Now, I'm no saint and have plenty of faults but for once in my life I've found a happy, peaceful, workable relationship with my God. Often on the curb (drive-in service) when someone has failed to tip and my blood pressure starts to rise, somewhere from the Bible, or some phrase from one of your books will come to mind and I try to give that much *better* service to the next car.
>
> This morning, after I came home from work, I was reflecting on the past year, and I suddenly realized that the problems I had a year ago no longer exist.

And then Lloyd made an amazing statement. I think of it as a most constructive result of positive thinking. Remember, this statement comes from a young man whose life has been remade.

> I never thought I could afford to tithe before. But now I can't afford not to!

What dynamic thinking! The exclamation point at the end of the sentence is Lloyd's own. He felt like exclaiming to the world the power of the new idea he had uncovered. When he began to tithe, to give in earnest of himself and his money, he unleashed one of the most potent spiritual principles in the universe. He discovered a basic fact of successful living: that to receive the good things of this life you must give.

This is the secret of the law of abundance.

Let me repeat it for you, because the idea contained in that sentence is literally life changing. It will make your life full and abundant and satisfying beyond anything you have ever imagined.

To receive the good things of this life, you must first give.

Firmly imbed that idea in your consciousness. Say it over and over. Let your mind dwell on it until it becomes a fundamental part of your thought pattern. To receive the good things of this life, you must first give. I cannot over-emphasize its importance. It can change anyone's situation.

This creative law of vital living is expressed in familiar words: "He that findeth his life shall lose it: and he that loseth his life for my sake shall find it." (Matthew 10:39) And the law is again stated in a sentence which I, personally, regard as one of the most important in the entire Bible: "I am come that they might have life, and that they might have it more abundantly." (John 10:10)

Poverty-stricken and defeated living has no place in the planning of a Creator who crammed this world to overflowing with riches and blessings beyond description. It is man who has messed up the supply of good to all. By his crude interference with the laws of Divine abundance, both socially and personally, he merely exists when all around him are values, not simply in sufficient supply, but in prolific abundance. Such a simple thing as the giving of self, of thought, of money, of time, of helpfulness starts it flowing.

Sometimes the results of putting this technique into practice seem almost miraculous. I choose the following illustration from among many because it is so down-to-earth and about plain everyday people like most of us. And it's one of those situations we call "desperate." But no situation need be thought of as desperate, really; not with the law of abundance to call upon.

A few years ago a woman living in Florida was really up against it. She had moved there from Illinois with enough, she thought, for a humble but secure future; she had a small private income from investments in popular common stocks.

Well, as happens to so many people, something came along to upset all her plans. "The best laid schemes of mice and men gang aft a-gley, and leave us nought but grief and pain for promised joy," wrote Robert Burns. And it's so true.

Certainly that was true for this lady because, when the 1929 crash came, she was completely wiped out. She lost all her money. Fortunately, her home was paid for, so she had a roof over her head but no income, and naturally she was worried.

"What can I do?" she wrote to an old and invalid aunt who lived in Pennsylvania. "Actually, things are so bad that I don't know where I'm going to find enough money to buy food. Right now, believe it or not, I have only a loaf of bread and some cheese in the kitchen, but by the time I get an answer back from you even that will be gone. I'm really up against it."

Well, when the invalid aunt got that letter she sat down and wrote a reply by return mail. She didn't have any money herself but she gave her niece something better, a dynamic motivation, the idea of abundance, the concept of supply. She gave her a formula for getting out of her predicament.

"The trouble with you," wrote the aunt, "is that you are thinking of starving when God will supply abundantly. You are thinking of getting instead of giving, so the secret of your situation is to give, give, give!"

You might say that's the kind of advice you can expect from an old aunt, living in a rocking chair; but as a matter of fact, the apparently unrealistic advice showed a sharp, keen insight into the deeper nature of things.

On the day the aunt's letter arrived in Florida, her niece was almost destitute. She had exactly two slices of bread left in the house. You may not remember, but I recall very well the unbelievable condition that developed during the depression back in the thirties. This type of situation was common then.

When the postman arrived, she tore open the letter hoping, perhaps, there would be something green inside. She didn't see anything green. She turned the letter over and opened the envelope wider and searched inside, but the aunt had sent no money at all. And then she read the note.

She was annoyed. Impatiently she tossed the letter aside. And just as she did there was a knock at the door. Still somewhat annoyed, she opened it and there stood a neighbor, an old man, a dignified elderly gentleman who lived down the road a way. He was embarrassed, terribly embarrassed to come to her door this way, he said, but would she by any chance happen to have something to eat. He was on his way home from a fruitless search for work. His wife wasn't well, and he just had to have something for her to eat. He couldn't believe, he said sadly, that he would ever be in such a condition.

The words from the aunt's letter came rushing back. "The secret of your situation is give, give, give." On impulse, this lady walked back to her kitchen and picked up a piece of bread. Half of all she had. She started back with it, and then she stopped. "The secret of your situation is to give, give, give!" She thought a moment and then returned to the kitchen and got the other piece of bread too, and she wrapped them both in a piece of paper and when she handed them to the old man she did so with an apology for not having more to offer. The grateful old man never knew that she had given him every bit of food there was in the house.

Now, the things that happened next are going to sound a bit on the extravagant side. They are going to appear exaggerated. All I can do is to assure you, further, that even more exciting things are happening to people every day. The door to this lady's house had hardly closed when there came another knocking. There stood a neighbor with a whole *loaf* of bread in her hand, fresh out of the oven. And the next day an unexpected dividend check arrived for $10, which this lady quickly shared. And then, a few days thereafter, a check for $50 arrived "as a belated birthday gift" from a brother. "It just occurred to me that you might be a bit low," he wrote. This, of course, was quickly shared too, because by this time our lady had come to the same conclusion that Lloyd was going to reach years later at the Hot Shoppes. She just couldn't afford not to share.

So this is the way the law of abundance works. It is there, ready to shower you with all manner of good things. All you need to do is stimulate the flow of abundance. And that is accomplished by developing certain stimulators; that is, certain attitudes and habits which will start and maintain the flow of abundance.

One is definitely and deliberately to work with abundance thoughts. Set yourself to eliminate all lack thoughts from your mind. Practice the abundance concept until it becomes habitual. See or picture your life as full of rich values. Conceive of yourself as being a stimulating part of the flow of good, not bad, of prosperity, not poverty. Help other people to think and act similarly, for there can be no permanent abundance for one unless it spreads to many. Prosperity, widely enjoyed, always lifts the level of abundance for everyone.

And there is another significant fact: those who apply the law of abundance, right thinking, right acting, outgoing service keep the flow of values in motion. Even when men, by wrong thinking, interrupt the smooth operation of another of God's great laws, the law of economics, those who keep in harmony are still able to draw upon the vast basic prosperity of God's abundant world.

Catherine Thrower tells of a study class composed of business people who were working with the principles in Charles Fillmore's book *Prosperity*. It was in a period of business recession. Each student was asked to "pour living words of truth into their situation," believing they would be prospered in their work regardless of recession. This was a city where the psychology of lack was very strong. Each class session began with such an affirmation as the following:

> I am the rich child of a loving Father. All that the Father has is mine. Divine intelligence is now showing me how to claim my God-given blessings of wealth, health and happiness. All that is mine by Divine heritage now comes to me in abundance.

Each student was expected to pour positive thinking into the atmosphere of office, business establishment or home. He was to turn the energy of his thinking upon "plenty" ideas rather than upon "lack" ideas and thus to counter with thought-vitality the negativism expressed all around him.

These business people studied, learned and applied the simple principles of the law of abundance. They thought creatively, they helped each other, they shared with God and man, they worked creatively and thus they set the immense force of positive ideas against the dismal defeatism everyone was talking.

Results began to show. Two secretaries became so valuable to their firms that they received pay increases at a time when many salaries were being cut. A lawyer became so helpful to his clients that his receipts for professional services took a swift upturn. A steel man, whose business was supposed to be particularly affected by recession, unexpectedly received several good orders. One abundance student, a saleslady in a downtown department store, as a result of her application of abundance principles, did so much business in an organization riddled by negative thoughts that she was the only clerk to receive a commission for having sold more than her quota.

In such experiences as those mentioned, positive thinking stimulated fresh and creative ideas. Abundance begins in your thoughts, in the form of new slants, fresh insights concerning problems. These produce better results. Buried deeply in your mind are all the potential values you need for a complete life. The Bible tells us "the Kingdom of God is within you." What a promise! Think of it; all the riches of God's great Kingdom are potentially resident in your mind. It remains only to learn the method of releasing them into abundance. And by abundance, of course, is meant every good: health, well-being, sufficiency, usefulness—every creative value in life.

I have a friend in St. Joseph, Missouri, who showed me recently how right thinking can act as a stimulator of abundance. This friend's name is Jack Spratt. His first name isn't really "Jack," it's Elliott; but with a last name like Spratt it seems that no one can resist the temptation to call him Jack. And he is a living demonstration of the amazing results of positive thinking.

One day when I was visiting Mr. Spratt we got to talking about the law of abundant supply. "It's an amazing thing," Mr. Spratt said, "how a simple change in thinking can affect a man's whole career." And then he told me how, whenever he has a salesman who has begun to slow down on sales, maybe get a bit stale, he calls him into his office.

"Joe," he says, "I want you to give me your order book. I'm taking it away from you."

Well, that scares the salesman pretty badly; he thinks Mr. Spratt is discharging him. But Mr. Spratt is not; actually he is re-charging the salesman. He takes away the order book, but he gives the man an opportunity to find himself, to start abundance flowing again.

"Now Joe," says Mr. Spratt, "I want you to go out and make the rounds of your customers."

"But you've got my order book," Joe answers.

"That's because I don't want you to take a single order," says Mr. Spratt. "Don't even try to get an order. You're going out on a new angle of salesmanship. You are going to sell yourself on the law of abundance."

"What's the idea, I haven't been getting enough orders as it is, and now you want me to stop taking them entirely?"

And then Mr. Spratt says, "The trouble with you, Joe, is that you've been hoarding yourself. You've got to give yourself away. Now here's what I want you to do. Make your rounds as usual; but this time, for one week, I want you to go to each of your customers and give yourself to him. I mean, do something good for at least one of them each day this week. Help them to have something they really need, something like courage, faith, hope. Give them just plain old friendship. Think about them as people, not as customers. Then, after you've given yourself away for a week, come back and see me."

Mr. Spratt told me that usually at the end of such a week, the salesman is quite a different person. A revitalized enthusiasm shows in his voice and a kind of excitement has come into his relations with his customers. And then, in most cases, amazing things begin to happen to his sales record. Orders start to flow in. And they don't come out of gratitude, either. A man substituting a go-out-to-give system for a go-out-to-get attitude breaks down barriers with people and releases creative qualities within himself.

"The key idea, of course," said Mr. Spratt, "is the tithing of yourself and your time as well as your money. When this is done miraculous things begin to occur in you, in your job, in your family life, in everything. I've seen it work a hundred times right here in St. Jo. The more you try to keep to yourself, the less you have to keep; and the more you give yourself away, the more you have to give away."

Tithe yourself, give yourself, share yourself. What a lot of power there is in that idea, and how it stimulates the flow of abundance whether your need is for abundant material things, or ideas, or happiness. Tithing yourself means giving yourself to people and to God; doing something for your fellow man and for God's work in the world. As you do this humbly and sincerely, good things will flow back toward you. Try it for yourself. See for yourself.

At one time I received a letter from a young mother who complained that she was getting a raw deal.

> Who is it that has to do all the cooking and all the ironing and scrubbing around here? Me.
> Who is it who is scullery maid while the others play? Me!
> My lot is an unhappy one and I don't mind saying so. This house is not a place of love, Dr. Peale; it is a house where there is one overworked maid-of-all-work and that maid is me. And what do I get out of it? Nothing! Absolutely nothing, but work and more work.

Well, I wrote back that I certainly was sorry she felt that way about her home. It is sad indeed when a woman does not like her job as wife-mother-homemaker. Obviously she had developed a self-centered thought pattern that was keeping her from receiving and enjoying the flow of love that her family would want to send out to her. She was blocking it off and in so doing was making herself tired and irritable.

I suggested to this young woman that she put into effect a new philosophy; just to see what would happen. Suppose, I suggested, that instead of waiting for love and appreciation to come from others, she stimulate the flow of these healthy emotions by giving them away first.

"When you cook," I said, "you use seasonings. You use salt and pepper and spices. Why not 'season' your home life? Try, for one month, adding a generous tablespoon of love to your recipe. As you stir in the other seasonings think these words, maybe even say them aloud: 'I am now adding love. This will make the meal more enjoyable for everyone.' Try the same thing with your cleaning. Sweep out your old, injured thoughts and bring in thoughts of love. Sprinkle thoughts of appreciation over your family's clothes as you prepare them for ironing. But the important thing is this: don't wait for someone else to begin. You start the loveflow yourself, and then write me again and let me know how things are."

Well, I didn't have to wait long to find out how the experiment worked. Three weeks later I got a letter from this woman. It went, in part, like this:

> I must admit, Dr. Peale, that at first I thought your ideas were a little extreme. Imagine adding a tablespoon of love to a recipe, sweeping out negative thoughts, sprinkling clothes with affection! But frankly things were so bad around here and I was feeling so miserable that I decided to try your ideas anyway, as queer as they seemed. All I can say is, it's amazing how they did work!
>
> The very first night, for instance, my husband paid me a compliment on my cooking; it was the first he had given me in a long time, and do you know what he said? "What's your secret ingredient, Baby? This is really good!"
>
> Well, I was surprised to hear myself reply that it *was* a secret, but that I had lots more where it came from. And it's been the same way with other things around the house. Not always compliments; sometimes it's simply a look of appreciation, and sometimes it's even a helping hand. Anyway, I can see now that a whole new world lies before me.

These are but a few of the stimulators of the law of abundance. They all have one denominator in common; in each case the flow of abundance was started when a person dared to open himself up, ceased to be afraid, and believed that good things were going to flow toward him; and then underlined his belief by first giving away much of himself to others. It is a fact that negative thought will attract negative thought, and positive thought will attract positive thought. If you live on a basis of pinched, patched, poor, little thoughts, you will attract others of similar outlook. But if you make the first, bold move to get rid of your shabby thoughts, and replace them with fresh, healthy, abundance thoughts you will attract more such thoughts to yourself.

Abundance does not come by praying for things, money, possessions. Instead pray for insights and ideas. These you can turn into useful implements to enrich your life.

Actually, all values are in the mind. Creative achievement is in the mind. You have abundance within you. You can think your way to all manner of good if you will only *think: think* new thoughts.

Abundance is never likely to come to the "grooved-in thinker." That phrase was often used by the late great scientific genius Charles F. "Boss" Kettering, inventor of the automatic self-starter.

Some people, he pointed out, simply get into mental ruts and stay there. They have capacities, just as the people have who do things, but they won't ask questions and won't think, or if they do it's negative thinking. They can even defend their failures and sometimes actually call it the will of God, if they are piously disposed. In this abundant universe anyone, except the infirm and very aged perhaps, can think his way into abundance. And actually I could cite cases of people flat on their backs in bed who carry on worthwhile activities, even paying businesses.

Kettering shows how the negative or grooved-in thinker shuts off abundance and how the positive thinker stimulates it in full measure. He told the following story about his early experiences in the automobile industry.

In the early days of cars, we finished them off, like pianos, with varnish. For the cheaper cars, the job took seventeen days; more expensive ones took thirty-five. One day I called in all the paint experts and asked if we could shorten that part of automobile production. They thought maybe two days could be lopped off.

"Why can't you paint a car in one hour?" I asked.

"The paint won't dry," they said.

That was the best advice of the experts; so, with my question still in my mind I went looking. One day I saw lacquered pin trays in a jewelry store on Fifth Avenue in New York. I bought one for $11.50. The jeweler told me he bought the trays from a little laboratory over in New Jersey. So I went out there.

When I asked for a quart of his lacquer, the man was startled. He had never made a quart of it before. When I told him I wanted to use it on an automobile, he shook his head. "It won't work. Put it in your spray guns and it will dry before it hits the door."

"Can't you slow it down?"

"Nope, that's impossible!"

Of course it wasn't impossible. One question led to another, then another. Finally, by working closely with one of the paint manufacturers, we obtained a lacquer which could be sprayed on and a car completely finished in a few hours. Grooved-in thinking could have stopped us cold, back at the horse-and-carriage level.

And when we first put the self-starter in the automobile, the Detroit Edison people had a special meeting of the American Institute of Electrical

Engineers. They wanted me to explain the self-starter, which I did; but about halfway through, a dignified gentleman interrupted.

"I move this meeting come to an end," he said. "This man doesn't know what he is talking about. He has profaned every fundamental law of electrical engineering!"

He was a victim of grooved-in thinking.

So, to stimulate abundance, *think*. Really think there is a way to better conditions. And, if you can think it in your mind, your can think it into actuality. Believe, pray, think, give—these are the four horsemen of abundance. Don't be a grooved-in thinker!

In Hong Kong I met a most remarkable man named Mr. Chou, a refugee from the Chinese communists. Mr. Chou, formerly a wealthy merchant in the old China, loved freedom so much that he and his family walked out of Red China with nothing; nothing, that is, except courage and faith and love; nothing, but positive thinking. He had known what it was to live abundantly in the material sense; but in Hong Kong he also knew what it was to live on a very, very meager scale. In fact, he was in plain, miserable poverty.

When he and his family first arrived without money or any source of money, they built a shack made of a couple of packing boxes insulated with burlap bags. They did their cooking on an open fire in front of their shanty home. After Mr. Chou had been in Hong Kong for several weeks, living on this subsistence level, he managed to get a humble job. It paid ten Hong Kong dollars a month ($1.60 U.S.)!

And yet the remarkable thing is that Mr. Chou was neither bitter nor resentful. He made every effort to improve his condition; but when his efforts failed he knew how to shift gears mentally and think abundantly regardless of setbacks. He tried to arrange for living quarters for his family in a Methodist housing project nearby called Wesley Village. Mr. Chou was a Methodist and Wesley Village was a nice cottage community especially built to house refugees. The two room cottages were situated on a sunny hillside and were neat, warm and attractive; but they cost 50¢ a day (8¢ U.S.). This was much more than Mr. Chou could afford so his dream was not realized.

But even so, on the day when his friends and neighbors who could afford to live there packed up their possessions and struggled up the hill to Wesley Village, Mr. Chou was on the spot to help them. He carried the heaviest boxes. He laughed and sang as he carried in the belongings of the fortunate ones. He was happy for them. He helped the aged grandmothers and the very young children. How much he wanted to move his own family there too; but since he couldn't, he rejoiced with those who could. Mr. Chou knew how to think abundantly. Wasn't he a true follower of

Christ who promises: "I am come that they might have life, and that they might have it more abundantly." (John 10:10)

To me the wonderful point in this story is that Mr. Chou possessed abundant happiness, outgoing unselfishness, good will and cheerfulness even while his fortunes were at an extremely low ebb. But there is something about a personality such as his that attracts good will for others. You should see this man's radiant face—it warms your heart just to look at him.

Before long someone found a job for Mr. Chou that paid 35 Hong Kong dollars, more than tripling his previous wage. The law of abundant supply was working. And shortly after that a vacancy occurred in the Wesley cottage community. Is it any wonder that Mr. Chou and family were asked to take it? This Chinese man will always remain in my memory as one of the truly great souls I have met in my lifetime.

His experience clearly demonstrates that the law of abundance operates even in most desolate and desperate circumstances. It stimulates forces which result in astonishing readjustment of conditions and, what is perhaps more important, constructive attitude toward conditions. Mr. Chou gave freely (at a time when many might have said he had nothing to give) and so he received abundantly. By this law of thinking and living one can do a creative job with the toughest possible conditions.

When you are in tune with the law of abundance the good things of life shall rise up toward you in waves. You will know emotional, physical (perhaps even material) wealth far beyond your present dreams. If today you are experiencing something less than abundant living, review this chapter and select one of the abundance stimulators that applies to your situation. Give it full cooperation. Live with it, believe in it, make it part of your unconscious thought pattern. You'll know this has happened when the new technique no longer requires effort. At the end of six months I am sure your life will be enriched beyond measure.

7

WHAT TO DO ABOUT
WHAT YOU'RE AFRAID OF

YOU CAN do something about your fear. You can overcome it. And to do that, simply develop faith as did this young naval officer.

He wrote me about his victory in the same factual manner he would report an engagement with an enemy.

> I am the commanding officer of this ship, a job which carries both pleasure and responsibility in large measure. It is as fine a task as could be assigned a young officer and I am grateful for the opportunity.
>
> My problems arise from the fear of failure, from the habit of worry, and from the lack of self-confidence. An imposing array of shortcomings, I know. Of all the methods tried to overcome or alleviate these weaknesses the only one proven successful has been Faith.
>
> From this realization stems my gratitude to you, for the simple, down-to-earth, and above all, believable manner in which you picture the power of reliance on God. I have been a skeptic in the past but you make further doubt so illogical as to be impossible. The strength I gather from you has enriched my life and made possible a hitherto unknown happiness.

How much time and energy do you spend on fear?

None? When did you last knock on wood or walk around a ladder or throw a pinch of salt over your shoulder? When did you suddenly feel your heart pounding for no apparent reason? Was it when you awakened in the night, tense, mouth dry? Maybe you felt it as you went in to call on a prospective customer?

We are a curious generation when you come to think about it. We have developed the resources of the earth and advanced our scientific knowledge to a remarkable degree; we are masters in so many areas. Yet we are not really masters of our own anxieties. We still live in fear.

Actually, ours is a frightened generation. Albert Camus, the French author, called this "the century of fear." There is even a modern symphony called, "Age of Anxiety." That's something when we make music based on fear.

Not only do we have all the normal, old-fashioned fears but we now have a big fear in the nuclear bombs which can strike across oceans. And even if they never strike, we can still worry about a sinister invisible killer called "fallout" which may wreak its damage on us and future generations. A scientist recently said, "We have a free-floating anxiety induced by the atom bomb, by space missiles and every destructive device."

"Free-floating anxiety!" What an apt way to describe the fear of our time. This is not the fear which the caveman felt when he heard the growl of the saber-toothed tiger. That fear triggered the caveman to run, or (if he was inventive) to tie a piece of rock to a stick and get himself that tiger's skin for a coat. Of course, this is the basic and original purpose of fear; to impel us to action in order to save our lives. And this use of fear is as valid today as it ever was. When we check our tires because we are afraid they are wearing thin, that's healthy use of fear.

But this is not the type of fear on which most of us expend our time and strength. Today we are afflicted more often with a vague uneasy anxiety that's hard to name. We can't fight back at this fear because we don't really know what we're scared of. Or perhaps we are fearful of so many things that attacking any of them seems futile. Fear, for us, isn't always a specific pinpointed menace that we can act on and do something concrete about, but a cloud that hovers over us, just out of reach, and casts its black shadow on everything we do.

It's a hazy, pervasive apprehension. Some time ago I was lecturing in Wichita, Kansas and had to fly to Cincinnati. Mrs. Olive Ann Beech, of the Beech Aircraft Corporation kindly loaned me a plane and pilot for that seven-hundred mile flight. When we were flying over the Mississippi the weather, which was sunny, became hazy.

"We'll have to go up above the haze level," said the pilot. "Ground heat, dust and smoke often make a low-lying haze. We'll go up another thousand feet and get above it."

We emerged into an altogether different world, one that was clear and with far visibility. This is what we have to do in our thinking; lift our thoughts above the haze level of our own conflicted, fear-ridden thoughts. We need to rise above the cloud of fear, anxiety and worry into an upper level where we can think clearly and rationally.

It is most important to do something about fear. Fear is an enemy of your happiness. It affects your ability to think, thus hampering your efficiency, and poses danger to your health.

My own heart specialist and good friend Dr. Louis F. Bishop says: "It is not generally realized how many cardiovascular symptoms can be produced by tension and anxiety. Anxiety states are very common, and whereas it can be stated that a certain amount of anxiety is good for everybody, because it spurs you to get things done, at the same time it can be very crippling. It may produce symptoms affecting almost any organ of the body.

"The heart itself reacts in various ways to anxiety. The rate may be remarkably increased; the rhythm may be affected; a stressful or anxious situation may produce a serious irregularity of the heart. Anxiety may also produce, as is well known, particularly in the middle-aged, attacks of precordial pain, known as angina pectoris. Tension may play a role as a precipitating factor in the closure of one of the vessels supplying the heart with blood—the condition known as coronary thrombosis."

Dr. Leo Rangell, Clinical Professor of Psychiatry at U.C.L.A., says, according to the *Los Angeles Times:* "Bacteria and other micro-organisms find it easier to infect people who worry and fret."

But do not be alarmed. You have the power to overpower fear. It need not be allowed to harm you at all. The great fact is that you can, if you will, do something constructive about what you're afraid of. The ability to do this is one of the greatest results of positive thinking. Positive thinking presupposes a firm mind control. When you control your thoughts you will be able to control your emotions, including fear and worry.

I received a letter from a lady in Philadelphia whose little boy, named Carl, was troubled with fears. He was having nightmares; he was afraid of his playmates; he had grown thin and was constantly tired. She wanted to know if she could come to see me. Well, there is nothing sadder than a little boy full of fear and I wanted to help if possible, so we fixed an appointment.

When the time for the appointment arrived, it was a beautiful, spring-like day, which was a bit unusual as it was the fifteenth of January. When this mother walked in (she came without Carl), I made some passing remark about what a fine day it was.

"Sickness weather," said this woman. "It's not healthy to have it warm this time of year. Watch out for influenza when you get a warm stretch in January."

That was just the start. This woman was afraid of everything. Within the first five minutes of our conversation, she mentioned that she had not brought her son with her from the hotel because she was afraid of the "dirty" air in the subways. She was afraid of all the "foreigners" she saw on the streets. She was afraid to go up on the Empire State Building for fear of the pressure on her ears. This was the tone of her talk. After we had visited in this way for a while, I brought the conversation around to Carl. I mentioned to her that his problem was by no means unique.

"So many children have fears," I said. "Where do you think they come from?"

This woman didn't know. She thought perhaps children were born with their fears.

"Not at all," I said. "Most fears are acquired from the people around them, especially, of course, from their parents."

"What you're trying to say is that Carl gets his fears from me?"

"I assure you this is nothing to be ashamed of," I said. "It is the way of human nature. You probably picked up your own fear thoughts from your parents and they from their parents and so on. The important thing is to break the chain."

"And how can I do that?"

"With positive thinking. Fear is a negative thought, and one helpful way to get rid of it is to think of your mind as a scale, a balance. On one side of the scale are all of your negative thoughts. On the other side are all of your positive thoughts. Right now, your scale is pretty badly out of balance; your negative thoughts far outweigh your positive thoughts . . . and, of course, these are being reflected in your son. The solution is to outweigh your fears.

"Try this method. The next time you have a negative thought, put a positive thought in the other scale. Take, for instance, the weather. It's a beautiful day outside. When you leave here, say to yourself, 'What a health-giving day! In fact it's so unusually clear that this would be a good day to take Carl up the Empire State Building to see the view.'"

The woman laughed—but doubtfully, "Do you think it would really work?" I replied, "It will work. Stick with it until that emotional scale is completely balanced; and then stick with it some more, until your positive thoughts outweigh your negative thoughts. When you have done this for, let us say, three months, let me know how Carl's fears are coming."

It was more than three months before I heard from this woman, nearer six, actually. But she really did make the experiment. When she finally wrote me, her letter reflected a state of healthy, happy excitement. She said:

> You've no idea what an amazing effect on our lives this simple plan of outweighing your fears has had. We have had to do a lot of struggling with them, but I do believe they are under much better control. Carl is much more relaxed and has fun with his playmates. He no longer seems so afraid or tense. I like to feel that I have, at last, broken that chain of inherited fears. One of these days I hope I can report that they are conquered altogether.

The basic idea employed here is an indirect approach to the problem of handling fears. Instead of tackling the anxiety and fear directly, by which process they often refuse to budge, we tried the indirect method of floating the fears out.

This is one of the best strategies for ridding yourself of fears; much better than trying to force them out by mustering your will power, which may be weak anyway. Rather let the rising tide of faith do the job for you. Fill your mind with such a large quantity of faith that your fears will actually be floated away. By this method God's power will do for you what you cannot do for yourself. Your part is simply to believe, trust and surrender yourself to His power. Let His tremendous strength lift you above fear.

Those who have used this principle of positive thinking in dealing with fear have had amazing results. But how do you fill your mind with faith to this degree? One of the methods is what we call the practice of the presence of God.

For example, I received a letter from Mrs. Grace Lichtenstein of Oakland, California, telling how one lady used this same positive technique to handle a situation that usually arouses panic and fear.

> A woman was caught in an elevator which had stopped between floors. The manager of the building called to her and asked if she were alone. She replied, "No, not alone." He assured her the elevator would soon be repaired and urged her not to worry.
>
> When finally the elevator was repaired, and the door opened, the lady was quite alone. The man looked at her in surprise, "Lady, you said you were not alone."
>
> "No," she replied calmly, "I wasn't alone. God was with me."

How many people, who constantly live with fear thoughts, could have answered as calmly as she did? There is a profound comfort and security in believing, for a fact, that God is with you. Perhaps the greatest comfort in this world is, "I am not alone." When you know this for yourself, your fears will lose their hold upon you.

Next time you are afraid, next time your heart pounds or anxiety clutches at your mind, repeat the following eight confidence-building words from Isaiah 41:10: "Fear thou not; for I am with thee." Say them over and over to yourself, listen intently to them as if God were actually with you speaking to you. He is, of course, so try to sense His presence. When you are able to do this with a sense of conviction, then you will experience release from your fears.

In the great crises of life, when men really need to have a sense of the Lord's presence in order to endure, they can get it. In Belgium I visited what was once a notorious Nazi prison, located midway between Antwerp and Brussels and known as the Breendonk. It is now maintained by the Belgium government as a sacred place of memory, and the flag flies over it proudly.

To the Breendonk during the Occupation, the Nazis took loyal, patriotic Belgium citizens who had the audacity to oppose their tyranny, kept them like animals in miserable cells and strove by indescribable maltreatment and torture to crush their spirits; but the prisoners stood up against all this. Passing through the dark, dank, dismal passageways that have been left just as they were in those days, one gets an awful sense of the degradation of man and at the same time an uplifting sense of the greatness of man.

I said to our guide, "How could people stand up against anything so terrible?"

"I'll show you the answer," he said, and he took us back into one of the darkest of the cells. There in the corner, carved crudely in the stone, was an outline of the face of the Saviour, Jesus Christ. The guide said, "When the going got hard these men, one by one, would come in here and put their hands on His face. It was their way of remembering that they were not alone.

"One night the Nazis came to our house and took my father. We never saw him again. We heard, after the war, that he probably died here; but we cannot be sure. We were told that he was one of those who came to this very cell to feel the face of Christ. I know he would do that for he was a devout Christian. I am comforted by the thought that our Lord was with my father to make him unafraid of whatever he had to suffer."

What an answer to fear. *We are not alone!* Practice this tremendous truth until it becomes a positive conviction. I AM NOT ALONE. Make it personal. No fear on earth is greater than this thought.

This truth suggests that one big factor in doing something about fear is to keep your head and not panic. As long as you can think calmly, you can think rationally. When you can do this you will get along all right. The only way God can guide you is through your thoughts and even He cannot get through panicky thoughts to direct you. But God will help you maintain calmness as you practice positive thinking. In a radio talk describing certain aspects of positive thinking, I said: "There is a passage in the Bible, in Luke, ninth chapter, first verse, where we are told that Jesus called unto His disciples and 'gave them power and authority over all devils.' "

Now, did you ever have any idea you might have a devil in you? By devils I mean the devil of hate, the devil of sensuality, the devil of dishonesty or the devil of fear? When the Bible says men may be possessed by devils, it is of course a truth. And modern psychological medicine confirms it. I have known people who have had devils in them. In fact I have felt devils within myself: meanness, hate, fear, resentment, jealousy. These things are well named, for devils they are, considering all the misery they cause. But an enormous fact to depend upon is that Jesus gave his disciples power and authority over devils so that they may rise up in a vast strength and cast them out in His name.

A businessman in Tennessee wrote me of his experience with this truth.

> Dear Dr. Peale:
>
> About three years ago I found myself engulfed with doubts and fears. They crept in and peace crept out. For months I was swamped with a tormenting depression. I felt as if I were almost lost and there was no God. I prayed and I did everything I could think of.
>
> One day I found myself impatient, if not angry, that He would let me go on this way. I told Him I was angry and asked Him to forgive me.
>
> I found information in the writing of Reverend J. A. MacMillan of the Christian and Missionary Alliance faith about the authority of the believer. I saw I was a victim of doubts and fears which are really evil demons. I acknowledged it. I cried out to God and I asked Him for this authority.
>
> Then, as if I were in the presence of a person, I spoke to these doubts and fears and commanded them to leave me in the name of Jesus. A miracle happened. As if a light were turned on, the doubts and fears fled and my soul leaped for joy in a peace that is hard to describe.
>
> For five months now I have been getting up around five o'clock to read the Bible and to meditate and pray. Peace has so flooded my soul that it is like liquid joy.

This man learned that Christianity is not some little, nice thing, a mere intellectual system of thought. It is rather a very strong power given to those who truly accept it. It is the power of God unto salvation to all who will believe. And if you really want freedom, Jesus Christ will give you power and authority to say to these devils of fear, or hate or sensuality or whatever: I command you to leave me.

That is man-sized Christianity and its blessings are yours if you want them badly enough. But you will have to develop some very real and strong faith. Say to the Lord, "I am tired of fooling with this fear; I want peace and relief." Don't go cringing and crawling in front of life. We are supposed to be strong people of faith, filled with power. Take the Gospel of Jesus Christ, really take it in depth; and transplant it into your mind, and you can have power and authority over your fear. Stand up to your fear and in the name of God and His son Jesus Christ command it to leave you. Then believe it is gone. Repeat this process until you feel a deep sense of victory.

One thing we must watch is that a fear thought has a way of popping into your mind when you least expect it and when it can do the most damage. At such times it is particularly important, as we have said before, not to try a frontal attack against the fear, but to use the displacement and substitutionary method of eliminating it. If you constantly fill your mind with faith thoughts, the fear thoughts will be firmly and surely displaced in due course of time. Of course, no change of personality of this character may be accomplished without effort. But that it can be accomplished there is no doubt at all.

A woman wrote me in French from Switzerland to report on the remarkable effects of such thought changing and displacement.

> Dear Friend:
>
> Allow me to start my letter so. You do not know me. I know you well after reading your book.
>
> I am the daughter of a French Presbyterian minister. I have been brought up by real Christian parents, but having lived through two wars, I lived in terrible fear of the future. What would I ever do if I lost my husband? How would I ever bring up my three boys with very little money? And so on.
>
> Then I became dreadfully ill with eczema, which was real torture. It lasted, on and off, for seven years. The doctors could not find the origin of this eczema. But I found it in reading your book. Fear had actually poisoned my blood. As I was itching on the inside, so also I itched on the outside, and I assure you it was agony.
>
> So after reading your book I followed your advice. I started reading the Psalms. I copied all the verses which were helpful. I followed the way you said, of letting these verses soak into my mind. At last I fell upon the last verse of the Fourth Psalm: "I will both lay me down in peace, and sleep: for thou, Lord, only makest me dwell in safety." (Psalm 4:8) Security, that is what I needed. I can find it in God. I have found it in God.
>
> And as for money, I found these verses in Job which set me free from money worries: "Then shalt thou lay up gold as dust . . . Yea, the Almighty shall be thy defense . . ." (Job 22:24–25)
>
> So now at last I have understood, now that I am over fifty, that the spiritual reserves within me are unlimited, and I can call upon Him and be well and joyful.

This woman literally crowded out fear by crowding faith in, faith in the form of great spiritual truths which were received deeply into her mind.

Harold Medina, you recall, was the famous judge who presided over the long trial of eleven top U. S. communists who had been charged with conspiracy to overthrow the United States government by violence. This trial was an extremely difficult experience. Emotions were high; tempers were short. And a great deal of the emotion and temper was directed at the judge in person.

He soon became aware of the fact that this was not entirely an accident. Something unusual was happening. It seemed that the defendants were more interested in breaking up the trial than they were in obtaining an acquittal. They were after a mistrial. They could achieve this goal in one of two ways: either by creating a tremendous confusion, or else by putting Judge Medina himself under such a strain that he would break.

The defense worked both plans at once. Throughout the trial, there was great difficulty in keeping order. Witnesses were insolent; attorneys were devious. But the attack that came closest to breaking up the entire trial was directed against Judge Medina himself. Somehow or other the master planners for the defense found out that the judge was afraid of high places. He had what is known as acrophobia, a fear of heights.

When Harold Medina was a small boy his father took him to Niagara Falls. Harold saw the crowd of people pressing up against the railing, looking down at the falls, but he could not go near that rail. He was afraid he would jump over. Time and time again throughout his childhood and young manhood, Medina faced this fear and handled it simply by avoiding it.

But now, suddenly, he could no longer avoid it. Judge Medina's chambers were on the twenty-second floor of the skyscraper federal courthouse in New York City overlooking Foley Square. One day the judge became aware of crowds down below shouting about him. "Medina will *fall*, like Forrestal." It was just a few days after Defense Secretary James Forrestal had fallen to his death from a hospital window. Was it just his imagination, Judge Medina wondered, or were these people stressing the word "fall." Quickly he stepped back from the window.

Bit by bit, Medina became aware of the deliberateness of the campaign. The word "fall" began to be stressed all around him. He found it underlined in letters, circled in newspaper clippings; he heard it stressed in conversations. He managed to carry on, but the strain was beginning to tell. One evening as he was preparing to go to bed, his wife opened the window of their apartment to let in some air. It was a stifling night, but Judge Medina said:

"Close that window, please, Ethel."

His wife looked at him, puzzled. He had never mentioned to her the fear of falling that he had had as a child. "I'm not fooling," he said, and then he told her about the signs, the chants, the whispers and the underlinings. Mrs. Medina was convinced. After that, they slept with the window open only a crack, from the bottom.

"Now the problem was," said Judge Medina talking about the experience later, "what do you do when you cannot avoid your fears? When I was a child the solution was simple; I just shunned the things that would make me afraid. Now I couldn't do that. What could I do? How does a man face a fear he cannot avoid? I'll tell you the answer . . . prayer.

"I don't mean a prayer directed only toward my fear of falling. I didn't suddenly say, 'Now, Lord, You have got to take away my acrophobia.' I mean a whole prayer pattern that asked for strength and guidance in *all* that I was doing. It was prayer that I had been building since I was a boy, when my mother knelt with me at bedtime to read from her Episcopal Book of Common Prayer. I inherited not just a Sunday kind of prayer, but a daily, often hourly kind of prayer. I prayed constantly, on and off throughout the day, any time when I was thankful, or under stress, or when I was in any kind of trouble.

"It was prayer alone that kept me going during the sixth and seventh months of the trial. There was no visitation, no sudden apparition, but there was the slow renewal of strength. With it came the firm realization that I would be able to meet whatever lay ahead of me . . . free of my old fear."

Do you see what Judge Medina was doing? He did not try to fight this one fear; he did not struggle and strain trying to rid himself of his acrophobia. He floated his fear away with a total prayer program that acted in the same way the tide did in raising that old tanker out of the Jersey mud flat. He so completely filled his mind with faith thoughts, that there simply was no room for fear thoughts, and they were firmly and finally floated away.

Judge Medina told this story in our monthly, inspirational magazine, *Guideposts*. It illustrates how a man can use prayer to eliminate his fears, even old deep ones. But this is not the only way that prayer can be used to conquer anxiety. There is also intercessory prayer when many people pray for a given objective.

One of the editors of *Guideposts* is a man named John Sherrill. In September, 1957, John had an experience which convinced him of the power of other people's prayers to dispel fear. Right up until the morning of September 20, of that year, John was leading a fairly normal life. He was married, he and his wife (and the bank) owned a house in the suburbs of New York; they had three children and a four-year-old Ford automobile. Theirs was a happy, creative life.

Then, on this morning, John got a telephone call from his doctor. The doctor wanted to see him right away. A few days earlier, John had had a small mole removed from his left ear. Now he was told the shocking fact that it was highly malignant. Without an operation, the doctor said, his chances of being alive at the end of a year were one in nine. With an operation, he had one chance in three. Further examination by specialists at Memorial Center and Presbyterian Hospital confirmed the diagnosis. Immediate surgery was recommended by every doctor.

A few days after that operation, I received a letter from John which I would like to share, in part, with you. This is what he had to say about the fear that took hold of him when he learned about the cancer:

. . . Fear is such a devastating emotion, Dr. Peale . . . it harried us day and night. I woke up in the night and knew that I was afraid. I answered the children's questions automatically; my mind was elsewhere. I spent hours with Tibby [his wife] going over insurance, wills, finances. When I tried to force my mind to more healthy matters, I could not: I was afraid.

And then, Dr. Peale, something remarkable happened. As our friends began to hear the news of the cancer, they needed to feel they were helping and their immediate response was to pray. The first prayer that we learned about, I think, was the one that you said for us from your pulpit that Sunday. After that, prayer rose about us like a flood.

There was prayer at *Guideposts*, both in the New York and Carmel office. Did you know, Dr. Peale, that your friend, Tessie Durlac, asked her synagogue to pray for us, and that she called long distance to the Prayer Tower at Unity? Our assistant art director, Sal Lazzarotti, told me he almost drove off the road saying the rosary on his way home Friday after he heard the news. "I haven't been saying the rosary too regularly, God," he said, "but starting tonight it's going to be different."

Prayer was in the air we breathed. We were surrounded by it, submerged in it. Early the following week I was admitted to the hospital. To my amazement the atmosphere there was one of prayer, too. No sooner had I settled down in my bed in Room 609 when I heard a weird and haunting note, almost a cry, permeate the corridor. In the room next to mine an Orthodox Jewish patient was celebrating Rosh Hashana, the Jewish New Year. The nurse told me I had heard the cry of the ram's horn, which for centuries has been used to summon men to prayer.

During these days in the hospital, I was praying too. But there was something strange about my own prayers; they were not for myself, they were for others. I must emphasize, Dr. Peale, that I am trying simply to report facts. I prayed for others, not from any deliberate sense of selflessness, but because I genuinely did not feel the need to pray for myself. This struck me as odd until I realized the reason. *Suddenly, on the night before the operation, I was aware that I was free of fear!*

Was this the tangible result of all the prayers? I think it was. On the night before the operation I felt such a surge of health that it was hard to realize I was in a hospital. At six o'clock the next morning a nurse roused me and gave me a needle.

"This will make you sleepy," she said.

I laughed. "You wake me up to give me something to make me sleepy?"

They came and wheeled me into the operating room. It was as if I, and the white-masked nurses, and the doctors were in the center of a force that dispelled fear. The closest I can come to describing it is to say that I felt as if I were deeply and personally loved.

And that, of course, must be a perfect condition for healing.

The operation was over. There was a week of tortuous waiting. Then the doctor brought me his report. He did not tell me the results of the operation right away. He shined a light into my eyes, probed and thumped, and then, in a matter-of-fact voice, he said: "Your report is the best one I could possibly have for you. There is no evidence of residual melanoma."

Does this mean that there has been a cure? I am not a doctor, and I do not pretend to understand the vagaries of cancer. Has it all been removed? Will it come back? No one really knows. But I do know about another kind of cure, one that may be more important.

With as much honesty as I can possibly muster, I must say that I personally have experienced the power of prayer to heal the most devastating disease of all—the power of prayer to heal fear.

So John Sherrill's fear was healed. And of course this experience means that yours can be healed also—no matter what it is—if you will let prayer open for you the tremendous world of faith. We have God's own promise that our fears can be overcome: "For I the Lord thy God will hold thy right hand, saying unto thee, Fear not; I will help thee." (Isaiah 41:13)

And He will, too. Place your fears in God's hands and leave them there.

And now let's sum up what to do about what you're afraid of:

1. Know what it is you are afraid of. Pinpoint it. Isolate it. Set it off and see it for what it is. Know exactly what you have to deal with.

2. Study the origins and reasons for being afraid of this or that. If you are not absolutely sure that you know the reason or reasons, then you had better get some expert counseling.

3. Get the fear out into the open. Divest it of all the mystery. Get it out where you can really attack it. Often you will be surprised what a puny thing has been frightening you all this time.

4. Cram your mind full of faith thoughts, for fear cannot occupy the mind when it is full of faith. Remember always that faith is stronger than fear. So, the more faith you have the less fear you'll have. It's that simple, though this process requires some hard discipline.

5. Just do your very level best. You can do no more. Then practice until you strongly develop it, the ability to leave results calmly to the good Lord.

6. Stand up to your fear and challenge it to do its worst. Usually there will be no worse, for actually most fear is an unreal bluffing of the imagination.

7. For the real fears that have substance in fact, you have what it takes to meet them. God will help you release the necessary mental and spiritual strength. Pray.

8. Affirm always that by the grace of God you are more than equal to any fearsome situation.

9. Keep uppermost the most powerful thought and fact of all—"*I am not alone.* God is my friend, my *support.* He is always with me."

10. Finally, if you would like further help, I shall be glad to send you free upon request, my pocket-sized thirty-two page booklet entitled, *12 Steps to a Happy and Successful Life*. Write to: Peale Center for Christian Living, 66 East Main Street, Pawling, New York 12564, if you would like a copy.

8

HOW TO FEEL REAL SECURITY

A SENSE of security is one of the most priceless assets you can have. With it, you can be efficient and contented. Without it, you may not be able to function effectively at all.

I received a letter recently, a really remarkable letter, from a woman who had lost all the security props that one usually depends upon. She was fifty-four years old and had been married thirty-one years when her husband suddenly asked for a divorce. So, she lost her husband. She simultaneously lost her "home" since, for her, home meant the place where she and her family lived. She lost her son when he was killed in an automobile accident. And then her daughter married, and in a very real sense this was a loss too—as any mother knows who has ever cried at a wedding.

So where did she turn? Here is an excerpt from her letter:

> It wasn't easy to lose my son or give up my daughter in marriage, or my husband, or my home, or my friends; but I found that security is within one's self, and not in persons, places or things and we really don't possess anything except in our consciousness.

That is a philosophical classic, that sentence. She tried finding security in the three traditional ways: persons, places and things; and she came to the conclusion that she couldn't possess anything except in her own consciousness. What she meant by this is that security is a spiritual matter and not a physical one. The fact is, *only* in spirit will we ever be able to find security. In order to feel confident and secure we must have a secure spiritual life; that is, we must get close to God.

This precept has very good foundation in psychology. Victor Frankl, world-famous psychiatrist and professor at the University of Vienna, practices what he calls *Logo Therapy*, or God Therapy. It has been his observation that much of the mental trouble we experience today stems from the fact that "we have broken with the sense of the reality of God." Along with this goes a loss in the sense of life's meaning. We feel a decline in well-being; we feel hopelessness and insecurity. But when a person does establish a closeness to God, a great sense of security follows, says Dr. Frankl.

How practical a sense of God's presence can be is shown in this letter from the vice-president of an important company in the midwest:

> You have gotten me to going around talking to the Lord just like I talk to the president of this company. I do not call that praying, or what the average prayer sounds like. But in reading and following your advice these past years I have come to actually feel that the Lord is with me in my office, or when I am traveling, or walking, or in a conference. In fact, I know He is near me and I have frequent conversations with Him just as naturally as with any friend. You have taught me that the Lord is a constant companion.
>
> I can tell you that in the last six years since I have been practicing this, it does not make any difference what the problem is in this business, the Lord is with me and helping me. I do not talk to Him, perhaps, in the same way in which you do. You are working on the sacred front and I am working on the secular front, but it all comes out at the same place. You and I know that God is with us.
>
> Why did I have to be sixty years of age before I discovered the wonderful, practical value of religion in my daily life! Everything has been different since I discovered the amazing truth that God can be my constant companion.

So runs this letter from a businessman. This man's life has been revitalized and renewed, his whole outlook changed, his grip on himself strengthened, his record of achievement enhanced. He has found security in God.

So we are on very realistic grounds when we talk about getting close to God and finding security. But the big question is, how does one get close to God? Since many people ask me this question, I have worked out a formula that I have tested often and found very helpful.

1. Feel a deep need of God.
2. Have a deep desire for God.
3. Pray in depth to God.
4. Live in partnership with God.

The most difficult part of this formula, I think, is to learn how to pray in depth. When this happens, lives are really altered. It is as if you are able to focus all the strength-giving, life-changing powers of God on your soul at once. God's power is around us all the time. Occasionally we are able to focus it on our problems with definite effect. And sometimes we are able to focus it with a mighty power that shakes us to the depths of our very beings.

It is as though God's power were sunlight. The sunlight is around us daily, affecting our lives. As children we learned how to bring the rays of the sun together with a piece of glass and generate enough energy to set fire to paper. Recently, the Army engineers developed a series of lenses and mirrors which concentrate and re-concentrate the simple rays of the sun to such a degree that they could develop the thermal power of an atomic bomb! This force is so great that it can cut through a four-inch beam of steel as easily as if the beam were composed of ice. And this astonishing force is simply the concentrated rays of the sun. Similarly, the power of God through concentrated positive faith can cut through our problems with tremendous results.

This is what it is like to pray in depth.

Have you ever had that experience? You can have it, when you reach for it and pray with all your heart and soul and mind. When you really pray with powerful intensity of belief and earnestness, you can burn out your insecurity and gain new confidence in yourself and in life.

I had such an experience twenty-five years ago, which is as vivid to me now as when it occurred. Mrs. Peale and I were in England staying in the little town of Keswick, in the English Lake District. And it was there I had one of my most profound experiences of prayer. This was the situation.

I was filled with insecurity and lack of confidence. I had just become pastor of the Marble Collegiate Church, a famous and distinguished church on Fifth Avenue in New York City. I was young, had come to the big city from upstate New York; and some people said I couldn't handle the job. I became convinced they were right. I floundered and was frightened and just knew I was going to fail. That was the mental condition I was in when my wife and I took this trip to England and found ourselves in Keswick.

We were sitting on a bench in the lovely, formal garden of the Keswick Hotel. We had been married for only two years and my wife was young, but she was a forceful young girl, and a spiritual one. She said to me very plainly, "Norman, I don't know what to make of you. I listen to you preach sermons and know you are sincere; but I also know that you are thinking of yourself too much. You have ability but it will never be realized until you surrender your self-consciousness and all your insecurities to God."

She put her hand upon mine. A soft hand, but a determined one. She said, "Let us sit right here and pray this thing through. We are not going to leave this garden or this bench until you really let God take over your life." I looked into her eyes, and I knew that what she was saying to me was the truth.

So we sat there together for a long, long time. Then I started praying. And by some self-releasing I really prayed; and it was an agonizing prayer, trying to get free from myself. Finally, in the depths of that prayer, I felt a Presence giving me release. It was an amazing sense of release and from that moment my feelings of insecurity and lack of confidence had less strength. Ultimately, with God's help, I was able to break their power over me. Years later when Ralph Edwards on his "This Is Your Life" program suddenly asked me what my greatest spiritual experience had been, I unhesitatingly told him, and the millions watching, that it was this one at Keswick.

Anyone can find an answer to insecurity if he will pray with everything he has, and pray until he actually senses God's presence. This isn't easy or superficial: it is like drilling for deep water. The shaft has to sink far below the usual water levels, but once these deep-down sources of supply are tapped they will not dry up with every passing drought.

The Power of Positive Thinking has brought me many good friends. One is Elmer Cary and he has developed a very workable technique for living close to God and overcoming insecurity.

Now, Elmer has an unusual job. He sells cemetery lots. As a matter of fact, he is the world's greatest salesman of cemetery lots, having set a record during an international contest. You might think he would be a long-faced, lugubrious character, but this is not so. He has brought a warmth, a genuine naturalness and a spirit of dedicated service to his work. Elmer is really a great persuader; so much so that, although he sells lots in Houston and I live in New York City, I find it all I can do to keep from buying one of his properties whenever he unleashes his salesmanship on me.

One time we were traveling across the ocean on the *S.S. Constitution*. It was the first time Elmer had ever been overseas, but even so, he was a better sailor than I. The weather, actually, was rough and after a couple of days of being tossed about, I became slightly green around the gills. In fact, I went to bed.

Well, I'd not been in bed long when Elmer knocked on the door and came bouncing in looking unpleasantly healthy. There's nothing worse, when you're seasick, than seeing one of your shipmates feeling good.

"Well, what's the matter with you!" he asked. He seemed genuinely surprised to see me flat on my back.

"I just thought I'd lie down a while," I said wanly, trying not to show how I really felt.

"You're not sick?"

"Well, you might say I've felt better in my life. As a matter of fact, I do feel kind of woozy."

"Now look," he said, "where's your positive thinking? Let me give you a lesson in right thinking. The trouble with you is you're not in harmony with God and His wondrous works. The sea is His—He made it. God made this ship through men's hands. And here it is in its natural element, moving like a thing alive on the waves. It rides the sea with graceful and beautiful symmetry. You ought to come up on deck and feel the spume flying off the waves, and watch the great billowing clouds in the sky, and hear the whistling of the wind. It's really great! And up there you will know one of the best fellowships with God, in the wonder and glory of the elements."

"My, that's wonderful talking," I said admiringly. "Where did you get it?"

"From one of your talks," grinned Elmer.

So I got dressed and went up on deck with Elmer and we stood there facing the flying spray and spume that he had spoken of so rhetorically. After the first few wobbly moments I began to get the feel of it. We stood swaying to the ship's motion and identifying ourselves with God's ocean and His waves. And I, too, began to sense the rhythm and wonder of a ship mastering a sea. Never again on that trip did I feel the slightest edge of seasickness.

Elmer says that the secret of his confidence and security is living with God. He used to feel quite insecure. One thing, he is short of stature; and this shortness bothered him a lot, especially since he was quite slender as well. And for another thing, Elmer once told me that he never liked his name. "I didn't like 'Elmer,' " he said. "Why any mother and father ever named me 'Elmer' is something I will never know! But I discovered a long time ago that confidence doesn't come from the way you look, or from what people call you. Confidence comes from living close to God. You can't live close to God and feel insecure."

"No," I answered, "and the size of a man is not determined by the length of his legs but by what's in his head."

I think that one phrase Elmer used is worth memorizing. "You can't live close to God and feel insecure." Elmer Cary spends a lot of time at the task of living close to God. He told me once that every morning he spends more than thirty minutes, figuratively putting on the whole armor of God.

"I protect myself with 'the helmet of salvation' . . ." he says with a twinkle in his eyes. "That keeps my mind and my thoughts safe. Then I put on 'the shield of faith' to protect my heart and keep it strong. But I still have fears to live with, so I put on 'the sword of the Spirit' and with it I go out to do battle with the things that otherwise would frighten me." (Ephesians 6:13–17)

Is it any wonder that Elmer Cary is full of self-confidence? "You can't live close to God and feel insecure," he says. That, my friends, is it! The Bible puts it another way: "In the fear of the Lord is strong confidence." (Proverbs 14:26) What does "fear of the Lord" mean? I never did like that phrase too well because I feel certain the word "fear" conveys the wrong concept. Either "awe" or "respect," I think, would be closer to the intended meaning. In respect of the Lord there is strong confidence. When an individual is close to God, in harmony with God, then his weaknesses, his self-doubts, his shyness, his bashfulness disintegrate.

I know another man who spends a particular time every day getting close to God, and in this way achieves a strong confidence. He is the well-known writer, Roy L. Smith. Not long ago he suggested that instead of having the usual "coffee break" we should have a "Bible break." "Why, wouldn't that be a good idea?" he suggested. "Well, as a matter of fact, we could have a Bible break right along with the coffee break."

This idea impressed me as unique and sound and I advocated it in my own writings and speeches. One reader became particularly interested in the idea and decided to try it. So, five days a week he read the Bible while having coffee in his office. He began with the New Testament. He read it through and then went back and read it through again, for it had gripped him. Then things began to occur that had life-changing potentialities. "I found things were beginning to happen to me. For one thing, surprisingly, I wasn't as nervous. I didn't feel so negative about things. Then I discovered that people were more friendly. There were some curious situations which could only be ascribed to God's guidance. All in all, the Bible breaks gave me a new insight into the nature of security and confidence."

This is a wonderful confidence-producing technique. I am absolutely convinced that if a man were to carry out such a program faithfully, five days a week, for one year, he would be an altogether different person. Nothing would floor him. The reason I am so sure of this is that I have seen it work; not only with a Bible break explicitly, but with a little booklet called *Thought Conditioners* that we wrote and published back in 1951. In a small footnote at the bottom of page 109 in *The Power of Positive Thinking*, I offered a free copy of *Thought Conditioners* to anyone who would like to have one. As a result we have given away well over one million copies of this forty-page booklet.*

The ideas we worked out in *Thought Conditioners* seem to have caught on. Time after time people have told me that these powerful nuggets of scriptural thought have altered their lives. Since this volume you are reading is a book about the amazing results of positive thinking, I would like to mention two ideas from this booklet.

Thought Conditioners is a pocket-sized booklet containing forty creative and dynamic Scripture passages. The idea is this: As you can air-condition a room, so you can thought-condition your mind. First of all, you must be willing to go into the program with the idea that you are about to perform a major operation on your thoughts. You are definitely going to get rid of all those old insecure thoughts. In their place you are going to substitute real faith and security thoughts. It will be an operation by displacement. One way in which this is done is by a simple memorization of each and every one of the texts suggested in *Thought Conditioners*. Take one example:

---

* Readers may still obtain a copy of *Thought Conditioners*, free of charge, by writing to Peale Center for Christian Living, Pawling, New York 12564.

What things soever ye desire, when ye pray, believe that ye receive them, and ye shall have them. (Mark 11:24)

Next you meditate briefly on the technique for using this Thought Conditioner. For this one the explanation reads:

> To pray successfully you must employ affirmation and visualization. From a picture in your mind, not of lack or denial or frustration or illness, but of prosperity, abundance, attainment, health. Always remember you will receive, as a result of prayer, exactly what you think, not what you say. If you pray for achievement but think defeat, your words are idle because your heart has already accepted defeat.
>
> Therefore practice believing that even as you pray you are receiving God's boundless blessings and they will come to you.

Throughout the day refer to the Scripture passage and repeat it until it is thoroughly memorized. Then, on the second day, select another Thought Conditioner, and *add it to the first*. This is the way thought-conditioning works. As you repeat one right after the other, the second will "hammer and drive" the first deeply into your mind. The next day a third is added, then another and another on successive days. This will strongly displace any negative thoughts that are now resident there. Keep this process up steadily for forty days, each day saying all the verses you have learned before until finally you have committed to memory all forty and know them so well you can repeat them in your sleep. The effect upon you will astonish you. Thousands of people bear testimony to the powerful results of this method.

I will defy anybody to remain insecure, or to lack confidence, if he will deeply saturate his mind, and keep it saturated, with these creative thoughts. How well thought-conditioning works was illustrated by a man I met at a luncheon meeting of a state association of businessmen. A diamond-in-the-rough type of man walked up to the head table where I was sitting and said, "Doctor, I just wanted you to know that I am in the state legislature today because I read *The Power of Positive Thinking* and sent for that *Thought Conditioners* booklet of yours. They mean so much to me that I couldn't carry on without them. They turned me from a person full of insecurity into a man of real confidence. Through following the plan of using those Scripture texts, I was able to overcome my fears and inferiority so much that I went into politics which, as you know, means liking and working with people. By thought-conditioning my mind I emptied out my insecurity. No, I didn't do it," he corrected himself, "God did it for me. Now I am trying to do something for God and my country." The man seated beside me at the table overhearing this conversation said, "I've seldom seen such a change in anyone as in Jack. So it was thought-conditioning that did it!" He asked for the booklet to work the plan on himself.

A few months later I stopped at a motel out West. The manager came up and handed me an old, dirty, battered copy of *Thought Conditioners*. "I just wanted you to know, Dr. Peale, that this little book is the reason I'm successful in this business today. I used it to pull myself out of a very bad debt situation, and now I'm doing right well."

I suggested to him that he get a fresh copy. His copy looked pretty dog-eared. "Let me send you one when I get back to New York," I said.

"No, sir," he said. "This is the one that did it. I've got sentiment for this particular copy and I wouldn't exchange it for anything." Then he went on to say, "At first I thought the idea of merely committing Bible verses to memory was too simple, and that your idea of reconditioning your thoughts was sort of on the queer side. I'd never heard anything like that before. But then, from somewhere I found the will actually to do the memorizing. It was so helpful that I kept on doing it and all I can say is that this simple practice has changed my life. It burned out all the old negative, defeatist thoughts and substituted more confidence than I've had in years."

A man from Connecticut who experienced some pretty bad times tells in the following letter how he found security and a new business career. His is another demonstration of the amazing power of positive thinking:

> While going through a very trying period of losing my business about five years ago, a friend suggested *The Power of Positive Thinking* and I became a disciple of your teachings from the first chapter. I also sent for a copy of *Thought Conditioners* and followed instructions to the letter, working, studying and praying for a way out of my difficulty. I know that you won't be surprised to hear that the way out appeared before I had committed all the verses in *Thought Conditioners* to memory. I was led to close the business and talked to each of my creditors in person and was surprised at the way my fear of them was suddenly taken away. I found them all very agreeable to give me a chance to see what I could work out without having to resort to bankruptcy. I was led to talk with my banker and was able to arrange a mortgage loan of $3500 on my home and was able to pay all my debts in full. I just can't put into words the relief I experienced in clearing this mountain of despair up in such a short time, truly proving "The things which are impossible with men are possible with God," and your words in *Thought Conditioners:* "Keep relaxed. Don't worry. Avoid getting panicky . . ."
>
> The very next day after this demonstration of the power of prayer I landed a job with an aircraft company as an aircraft mechanic, after having been away from that field for over ten years, and have rapidly risen to my present position where I am trusted with the most difficult repair jobs on the aircraft in the factory. Another proof of God's POWER.
>
> A few months later I formed my own band with a group of dedicated

musicians. This was the first time I had fronted a band in fifteen years and we were a success from the first date we played, and new fields are opening for us all the time.

So to develop more confidence within yourself, try using *Thought Conditioners.* Saturate your mind with them. Let these dynamic principles work for you, and I am sure you will have a deeper feeling of security than you have ever enjoyed. Actually, you do not need the booklet, though I will be glad to send you a copy. You can go through the Bible taking out your own texts which speak of faith, and peace and strength. But insert at least one every day deeply into your mind until it really takes hold of you.

There is one last thing which is quite important in living confidently. And that is the values which the church affords you. A church is a wonderful source of security because this is where people, for generations, have congregated in an effort to bring the health-producing, life-changing laws of God together in a single concentrated experience. Church worship is much more than a formal duty to perform. It is your exposure to the greatest of all power. In fact, a vital church is the greatest power relay station in existence. Through it flows the vibrant life-changing energy of Almighty God Himself.

The church has probably produced more real, sensible and effective positive thinkers than any institution in the world. And that is because it reaches the power of faith. It provides peace of mind and heart, and these qualities are very essential to efficient mental processes. The church puts hope and love and confidence into men's minds. True, you will find some gloomy, depressive, negative, even mean people in churches. There are two things that may be said about this phenomenon: First, the exposure just hasn't taken; and second, it's good that such people are in the church, for it means there is still hope of doing something with them. Of course the basic reason the church produces positive thinkers is due to the life-changing force in Christianity, the basic genius of which is that, when taken into one's life, it can dramatically eliminate weaknesses and add strength. Christianity can literally make a new person of anyone who wills it so.

In *The Power of Positive Thinking* the reader was constantly urged to practice the teachings of Jesus Christ, or if not of the Christian faith to practice the laws of God as he has been taught. Church worship was advocated as an invaluable aid in solving personal problems, of contributing to human welfare and helping one to know God.

One of my readers, a man who had no church contact whatsoever, resisted that particular emphasis in the book. He said, "I took the common sense of the book but skipped the religion. As a matter of fact, I thought you just brought that in because you happen to be a minister."

However, he became convinced by my insistence, and one Sunday he attended a neighborhood church. Unfortunately, the minister devoted his sermon to a denunciation of businessmen, strangely seeming to regard them all as evil influences. The church was only partially filled and the spirit was without lift or enthusiasm. This man did not sense or note the spiritual power I had promised he would find.

My reader was so incensed that he sat down and wrote me a rather sharp letter and ended by saying that this finished him with the church. However, he did admit that he felt a real sense of need and would continue to work with the book—but no church, that was "out, period!" for him.

I wrote back suggesting that it was hardly fair to judge a minister by one sermon or to dismiss such a great and vast institution as the church because of one unfortunate contact. I gave him the name of a church not too far from his home where I knew the minister to be a pastor of radiant spirit and infectious faith.

My friend, a bit mollified, went to this church. He found it filled with a great congregation of eager people.

> They all struck me as happy and everyone was so friendly. The minister was obviously a man of conviction. He was so sincere and kindly and down-to-earth that he got to me. I kept on going.
>
> The minister called on me and invited me to join a group of fellows who met for lunch once a week. To my astonishment they actually had a good time together talking about religion and how they were applying it to personal and business problems. I was amazed by all this and continued attending these luncheons. I soon realized that you were right in your book; Christianity is actually a way of life. At least it was for these guys. One day one fellow told how insecure he had been, how he had suffered all his life from feelings of inadequacy and inferiority.
>
> Well, that was me all over, and I listened carefully as he told how, through this fellowship of spiritually-minded men, he had found peace and a new strength to solve his own problems. So I decided that this was for me if I could only get it.
>
> On Sunday in church we have a quiet period and the big congregation silently prays. Some real power is developed—there's no doubt about that. Suddenly, one Sunday, I felt a wonderful sense of peace. It wasn't like me, or at least like I thought I was, but tears came to my eyes. I actually felt God's presence. It had to be that, for all that old insecurity seemed gone. It was simply wonderful, the greatest thing that ever happened to me.

So ends the letter of a man who found security through spiritual fellowship.

Finally, to sum up, I recommend the use of the following formula for gaining a sense of security and confidence:

1. Study yourself to discover where *your* real security lies. Check over the things upon which you are now depending for security. Persons? Places? Things? Are they really satisfactory? Or do you need to look for a more basic security in the spiritual realm by getting close to God?
2. For getting close to God, practice the following:

> *First, feel a deep need of God.*
> *Second, have a deep desire for God.*
> *Third, pray in depth to God.*
> *And fourth, live in partnership with God.*

3. Take God as your actual working partner. Let God guide your thoughts and actions.
4. Practice systematic thought displacement to dislodge your insecure thoughts and replace them by confidence thoughts.
5. Associate with people of a confident and secure frame of mind. These feelings are contagious.
6. Read and implement positive ideas about everything in your life.
7. Find a positive, dynamic church where victorious living is taught and practiced. Become a vital part of such a creative spiritual community. Give to it. Draw from it. Believe, share and practice a power-packed faith.

Do the above and a strong confidence will displace your insecurity.

9

HOW TO HANDLE YOUR DIFFICULTY

A DIFFICULTY can break you, or it can make you. It all depends on how you take hold of it, and what you do with it. "Mishaps are like knives, that either serve us or cut us, as we grasp them by the blade or the handle," said James Russell Lowell.

Grasp a difficulty by the "blade" and it cuts; grasp it by the "handle" and you can use it constructively. It may be hard to get hold of that handle but it can be done—that's for sure. And there are some practical techniques for so doing that have been tried and tested.

But before we get to them let me say that actually you ought to be glad you have some difficulties; life would not be worth living without them. While this element in life may have its unpleasant aspects, difficulty is still essential to growth and direction.

Recently on a flight from New York to Los Angeles on a Boeing Jet 707 airplane, I noticed a line of small blades midway down the wing surface and also on the tail. These blades I was told are called vortex generators. Their function is to cause the air flow to swirl as it passes over the rear wing area. Engineers tell me that the rear assembly of these big planes does not steer truly if the air situation is too smooth, so vortexes must be generated. The element of roughness must be inserted to attain precise directional accuracy. God's wisdom is demonstrated by the fact that He installed vortex generators in our human experience.

Many people write to me complaining about the problems they have. "Why must there be so many problems?" they ask.

Actually, problems are a sign of life! In fact the more problems, the more you are a part of life. The only place I've ever been where people have no problems is a cemetery and there they are all dead. Be glad that God trusts you with some problems. Thank Him for the compliment. He believes you have what it takes to handle them.

In this chapter we shall outline a technique for handling difficulty and this can be very important to you for, as Confucius says, "Settle one difficulty and you keep a hundred away."

In handling difficulty, first of all, get yourself as quiet, calm and composed as you can. You can never competently handle a difficulty unless you are quiet mentally. It is so very important to think calmly. When a difficulty arises, the first tendency is to become upset, even panicky. Nervously we assume that the problem has to be solved right away, quick; that something must be done immediately.

When you are mentally hectic, rational answers to difficulties tend to elude you; but when you become quiet your mind gets down to its real business, which is rational thinking.

So I must stress the importance of learning the use of silence in meeting life's difficult problems. "Silence is the element in which great things fashion themselves," said Carlyle. Silence conditions the mind to those sharper illuminations which surely come from God working in your thoughts. Divine guidance is always spoken in a still, small voice. You can scarcely hear it in confusion—certainly not in excited panic, nor when your mind is filled with anxiety. You cannot perceive God's will or receive His guidance in the midst of noise, especially noise within. So, the technique is to let yourself down into the relaxed and deep quietness of faith and confidence in which clear thinking is possible. Then a sense of direction will be opened to you for dealing with your difficulties.

The Japanese seem to practice quietness to a high degree of efficiency. It is one of their characteristics that I admire most—their ability to be quiet, composed and unruffled in the face of difficulty. Recently when I was in Japan, I spent some time studying quietness techniques. The practice of quietness is actually an important ritual in Japan; sometimes it is called *Ryōmi*. In English perhaps the nearest meaning of the word is "the taste of coolness" or "a refreshing." What a wonderful idea! When you have a problem, get "the taste of coolness." We put it another way, "keep cool." But to keep cool you must first get cool. In Japan this is done in an unusual but effective manner.

Let us say it is a pleasant summer evening. The first thing is to sit in a hot Japanese bath and reflectively soak yourself. A bath is frequently more like a pool—a hot thermal pool. Everybody goes into the same bath together. Most Westerners balk at this beyond the family group. You relax, become quiet, and after awhile you feel like philosophizing.

Then you come out of the bath and put on a *yukata*, the name for a cotton kimono. You proceed into a cool room which is without furniture and sit on the floor on a soft straw matting called *tatami*. You sit quietly, listening to the wind bells tinkling in the gentle breeze and watching the *gifu* lanterns swaying overhead.

Then you are brought a little bowl of amber tea. You don't gulp the tea down hurriedly in American style; rather you savor it thoughtfully, even commune with it. The Japanese linger long over a cup of tea, making of it an act of serenity. The idea is to induce quiet reflection; to relax and grow still, thus entering into the essence of peacefulness. You talk very little but rather meditate in an effort to cultivate the creative values of silence. In this way your mind brings the scattered ends of life together, the heat goes out of your thinking, and you get the taste of coolness. The effect of this practice on problem solving is amazing. Problems seem the more readily to dissolve. And they are resolved. This is a most effective method for perceiving difficulties clearly in their deeper implications. It is extraordinarily helpful in arriving at sound solutions.

Since you and I don't live in Japan, we have to develop our own kind of *Ryōmi*. Actually, one already exists in our own religious tradition. Christianity and Judaism are basically Oriental faiths and the value of quietness and meditation is emphasized in the Bible. "Come ye yourselves apart into a desert place and rest a while." (Mark 6:31)

Indeed, one of the best places to find creative quietness in our country is in a church. If you have a problem that you have difficulty in solving and wish to find a quiet place for meditation, I suggest that you go into an empty church when no service is in progress. Sit quietly in a pew and think of your mind, and then of your muscles, as letting go their tension. Let down and down, until you are relaxed.

Then practice consciously sensing God's presence. Say the following affirmative prayer, repeating it several times slowly: "You are here, Lord . . . You are now touching me with Your healing peace . . . My mind is becoming quiet. You are now giving me the answer . . . Your answer . . . The right answer to my problem." Then empty out any wrong thinking which you may be holding. Forgive everyone. Quietly say, "I forgive ——— (mention name)." Enumerate a few things for which you are thankful and others for which you ought to be thankful. Don't hurry, but rest quietly in the Lord. Try this experiment in creative quietness. It's really a wonderful method for handling difficulty.

Another method is to associate yourself with spiritually-minded people who have developed some skill in the use of creative quietness. I once had a very perplexing personal difficulty and had not been able to get an answer. While I was struggling with it I attended a Quaker Meeting. In a Quaker Meeting the practice of silence is a well-developed spiritual skill. It is a practical demonstration of the principle suggested in two Scripture passages: "Be still, and know that I am God." (Psalm 46:10) and "In quietness and in confidence shall be your strength." (Isaiah 30:15) Even to the unpracticed, the deep and vital silence-power of a Quaker Meeting has a way of getting through to you.

Before the silence period began, a man said something which was most enlightening: "If anyone here has a problem, drop it now into the deep pool of spiritual quietness."

It was an apt description, for the silence that followed was indeed like a deep pool. I took that problem, which had been baffling me, and said, "All right. We'll see what happens." And I let it drop into that pool of spiritual quietness. We continued to sit and wait and pray and listen to the silence and to the Reality within the silence. I don't know how long we sat there, for the passing of time was not important; but suddenly as clear as crystal, came the answer to my problem. And it proved to be so right an answer. I saw that I had been thinking and searching in wrong directions. But intuitively I now recognized this solution for what it was: God's answer.

It is always very important to find God's answer, and then to follow it. Mencius (second only to Confucius among the sages of China) says: "To follow the will of God is to prosper; to rebel against the will of God is to be destroyed."

One of the greatest people I ever knew for handling problems through mind-power plus Divine guidance was a wonderful old man, Harlow B. Andrews, who lived in Syracuse, New York. "Brother" Andrews we all called him. Brother Andrews is said to have operated the first supermarket in the United States. Years ago he brought in perishable goods from California by fast express trains and sold them in his big Andrews Brothers store. He is credited with developing the first dishwasher. He was a highly effective businessman.

Brother Andrews had only three years of schooling, but his was a great mind and he used it to the maximum. His method of thinking through a problem was an amazing combination of common sense, scientific analysis, intuition and prayer. I had a chance, once, to see his mind at work on a tough problem of my own about which I had asked Brother Andrews' help. As I outlined my problem I paced nervously up and down in front of his desk.

"Wait a minute, hold your horses, don't pace around so much," said Brother Andrews. "Sit down and get relaxed. Let's get that mind of yours untensed. How do you expect to think when your mind is so tied up."

After he had me sitting relaxed and laughing a bit with him, he said, "Now let's examine this difficulty." He began talking the problem through, step by step, detail by detail, with consummate exactitude. He really took it apart and studied every aspect. He gave me the impression of walking around the difficulty, poking at it here and there with his gnarled old finger saying: "Let's see if we can find a soft spot." Or, "Let's chip a little off here, a little there and get it down to size where you can handle it, son."

He walked around it mentally, and I walked around with him. "Every problem has a soft spot," he declared. "But we don't know enough. What are our little minds compared to the great mind of God. Let's take it up with God." So saying, he prayed, outlining the problem in detail. The prayer itself was a process of thinking it through, of analyzing it. He knew God so well that he talked to God as though He was right there with us. (I believe He was, too.) And as Brother Andrews talked to the Lord about my problem it began to clarify in my thinking. It was remarkable how my nervousness passed off and suddenly I just knew the solution would come.

Brother Andrews' advice came to mind recently when I had a phone call from a well-known figure in baseball. He told me about a difficult decision he had to face. "I'd like you to pray with me about this matter. Will you?"

I told him I would, and advised him, "Don't worry. You'll get the right answer. Don't push it."

He answered, "I'm not worrying, nor am I tense. It's only that I have to have the answer by tomorrow, that's all. But I know I'll get the answer that God wants me to have." Then he used a phrase which I liked very much. He said, "I'm walking around this problem with prayerful thought." That really is an interesting idea: "I'm walking around the problem with prayerful thought."

Later I learned that my friend had made the choice that had seemed to him the more difficult of two alternatives which he described at the time he talked with me. In explaining his decision he said, "I took the job I thought the Lord wanted me to take." That had been the outcome of walking around the problem with prayerful thought. Incidentally, it turned out very well indeed.

Use the power of your human mind fortified with Divine guidance to organize the attack against a difficulty. No matter what your situation or however difficult the nature of your problem, or how hopeless it seems, this organized, analytical-spiritual attack will get results, and right results, too.

Another very good technique for handling a problem is just to stay with it; in other words, don't give up. It's amazing what simple *persistence* will do where you use it intelligently on your difficulties.

When everything goes wrong and you seem particularly inadequate, what shall you do? Just keep on pitching. And tenaciously hold a positive picture of the outcome. Put your faith in God . . . all your faith. You will get through if you persevere.

That's the way the great men of history handled their problems. It is a good idea to read about those men and get acquainted with the inspiring persons of all time who didn't know how to quit.

There is another element in winning victory, and that is the element of belief. "Believe you can, and you can." Belief is one of the most powerful of all problem dissolvers. When you believe that a difficulty can be overcome, you are more than halfway to victory over it already. One of the greatest of all principles is that men can do what they think they can do.

For example, it was generally accepted for a great many years that it was impossible to run a mile in four minutes. But then along came a lanky, frail-looking English physician named Roger Bannister who didn't look like he had the strength to run a mile at all. But one fine day, back in 1954, Roger Bannister ran the mile in four minutes flat.

Why had no one ever run the mile so fast before? Bannister feels it was because people didn't think it could be done, and that seems to be a very reasonable conclusion. Back in 1886, a man named Walker ran the mile in 4:12³/₄, a world record. And thirty-seven years later Paavo Nurmi ran it in 4:10³/₄ shaving two seconds off the earlier record. That was a wonderful achievement. I remember reading about it in the papers at Boston where I was living at the time. The fastest man on earth—Nurmi! Nobody, they said, will be able to beat his record!

But thirty-one years later Roger Bannister broke it. For the first time in history a man ran a mile in four minutes flat.

And now what has happened? Since Bannister's feat no less than twenty-three other runners have run the mile in *less* than four minutes. When asked whether this is due to scientific improvements in the style of running, Bannister says that it cannot be explained that way. He believes it is due to a change in psychology. Once the mile had been run in four minutes, the mental conception was accepted that it could be run in less, and this belief in the runner's mind was responsible for its being done.

This, of course, is positive thinking in its purest form. And the use of positive thinking in overcoming difficulties is becoming more and more widespread. I can tell this from my mail. Letters come in by the hundreds, even by the thousands, telling how faith thoughts and positive thinking attitudes have helped in surmounting difficulties.

For instance, one man says that he keeps a card index of every passage in the Bible dealing with faith. He commits these to memory. One text among hundreds which he has collected is this one: "I can do all things through Christ which strengtheneth me." (Philippians 4:13) Another text is: "If God be for us, who can be against us?" (Romans 8:31) He substitutes the pronoun "me" for "us" in the latter text.

Read the Bible regularly and when you come to a passage that states positive thinking in a fresh new way that appeals to you, put it in your collection of faith ideas. As you fill your mind with these great thoughts your own attitudes will become more positive and more vitally strong.

So keep positive thoughts from the Bible at your fingertips or more properly your "mindtips" throughout the day—thoughts that will be ready to help you meet any new difficulty that may arise. This method is a practical one and we recommend it.

In this connection I am reminded of my friend Arthur D. Rodenbeck of Dayton, Ohio. When I spoke to the National Home Builders great convention in Chicago, I had a very unique and dramatic introduction. The stage was set, special lighting arranged and dialogue prepared and rehearsed. The "star" of the cast was Art Rodenbeck, a successful home builder who told how positive thinking had pulled him through some difficult experiences.

To that big hushed audience Art Rodenbeck gave the healing potency of God's Word in practical human problems. He said:

I had plenty of problems, not financial, but with people. You know, people in the office, salesmen, foremen, mechanics—a big turnover—and nothing seemed to go right. Well, I was getting nervous and irritable and it began to affect my health. I was in pretty bad shape and actually on the verge of a crack-up. I read *The Power of Positive Thinking* by Dr. Peale and it helped. But then I went further. I got one of his pamphlets called *Spirit Lifters*, and I memorized thirty-two verses from the Bible. Everytime things were going bad, I'd mentally recite one of those verses. It did the trick; saved my mind and maybe my life.

Later I went to New York and I found out about his Foundation, The American Foundation of Religion and Psychiatry, where people are helped by a permanent staff of specially trained pastors, psychologists and some top psychiatrists.

Well, just a year ago I was having the same trouble and the *Spirit Lifters* saved me again. I was in deep trouble, financially this time, and I couldn't see my way out. But I drew all the strength I needed from those Bible verses just as you'd draw money from the bank, and it worked again. Right now, I'm sold out in Dayton and in Florida and my lumber company is doing fine. And I know that nothing can ever get me down again.

And here is a letter from a family in Massachusetts who describe another type of satisfying experience with positive thinking:

None of the letters that you receive can be more inspired by a deeper gratitude than that which is in our hearts. My husband (an engineer) and I sincerely feel that our seventeen-year-old boy would have lost the opportunity of a lifetime if it had not been for our daily letters based on your book, *The Power of Positive Thinking for Young People*.

After high school graduation this spring, our son received a full scholarship to a famous school in New York. This is a specialized, completely endowed college, necessarily very small. Candidates are carefully screened and admitted by their standing on the Board Exams. Only twenty are taken each year from all over the United States. The course is extremely tough, and a test of character as well as brains.

The first six weeks were a severe strain on our son who concluded from the evidence available that he was flunking. It would have been the first failure of his life; he was so upset we feared for a complete nervous breakdown.

I wrote him every day, and his father wrote as often as possible—the gist of our letters being to think positively. He began to do this, and also to pray seriously, from his heart, for the first time in his life.

As a result, he kept plugging instead of just giving up! And he has passed his mid-terms this month with an average of 84 per cent, standing seventh in his class. Only seventeen of the boys are left now, as three freshmen did flunk out! After questioning our son, we have concluded that their failure was due more to attitude than to lack of ability or intelligence. I just felt that I should let you know this story.

A chief reason that people are beaten down by difficulties is simply that they allow themselves to think they can be beaten. And one of the greatest techniques for overcoming difficulty, as we have said, is to learn to believe that they can be overcome; and that you can do the overcoming with God's help. In order to accomplish this you may have to do considerable growing, both mentally and spiritually; but that can be done also. It is possible to grow tall in the mind, taller than any problem. This is another way of saying that you are bigger than any difficulty.

I had lunch recently with a friend, John Powers, president of Prentice-Hall, Inc., my publishers. He makes interesting use of diagrams to illustrate his ideas. He draws them all over the paper at hand, and then perhaps over the tablecloth as well. On this particular day he drew a picture of a huge mountain, and next to it a small man. "This mountain symbolizes a difficulty," said John. "Now how is this little man going to get on the other side?"

"That's easy," I said. "He will go around the end."

"Too wide, he can't do that."

"Well then, he will skirt the other end," I said.

But John shook his head, "That's just as wide."

"He will crawl over the top."

But John replied, "That won't work either for it's too high."

I thought and then said, "He will burrow under it."

"Too deep," he replied.

"O.K. then," I declared, "he will just haul off and plow right through it."

"That's out too," said John. "It's much too thick and he would only break himself."

"Well," I said, "it looks like an impasse; though I'm sure there is a way."

"There is indeed," said John Powers. "The answer is in your power of positive thinking. Rise over the difficulty by the enlargement of your thoughts. The man will grow tall in his thoughts until he is taller than the difficulty."

Of course that is the secret. There is apparently an unlimited extension facility in the human mind. Physically a man's height is limited. I once saw a man 7'6" tall; but I presume the average height for man is from 5'8" to 5'10". But man has the unique mental ability to extend far beyond those limits. In his mind he developed the ladder which made him, let us say, about twenty feet high. His brain produced the elevator which made him, perhaps, two hundred to three hundred feet high; and the jet airplane which raised his height to thirty thousand feet. You have a tremendous extension power within yourself.

"You teach that fact in positive thinking," John declared.

So here is our little man apparently blocked and baffled by the big mountainous difficulty confronting him. This is how he meets this seeming impasse. He starts thinking pure, unadulterated, positive thoughts. He explores the matter from every angle. He affirms that with God's help and his own creative powers he will get the answer. Then he prays and this prayer takes the form of affirmation, the expression of the belief that he can rise above even this huge difficulty. In his prayer he receives guidance about how to do it. Through prayer, also, comes the inspiration and motivating force which supplies lifting power. As a result he begins to grow in mind and spirit until he is taller than the problem and looks down upon it.

You are indeed greater than any difficulty—always remember that. Grow until you're bigger than your difficulty. That's really a power-packed idea, and the way to achieve this growth is through understanding of yourself, and through prayer and spiritual development. You can grow bigger than any difficulty you may face.

One of the great things that positive thinking does for people is that it teaches them to stop working against themselves. So many people actually practice self-defeat. By their thoughts they actually convince themselves that they can not handle their difficulties. They are defeated in their minds. And since you are intended to be master of your thoughts, if you have used your thinking negatively you are responsible for your own inability to deal successfully with your difficult problems.

One of the greatest blessings of my life is the association I have had through the years with laymen in the church. As a pastor I was supposed to be their guide and teacher but it's a two-way street; and I can never pay the debt I owe to them for their guidance and inspiration to me.

In my first church in Berkeley, Rhode Island, I formed a lifetime friendship with Rob Rowbottom. When I recently went back to Berkeley to speak at the dedication of the remodeled church, I had an interview with reporters from Pawtucket, Providence and Woonsocket newspapers. I was asked if I had learned the idea of positive thinking from Mr. Rowbottom.

I replied that many had contributed to my thinking but to Rob I owe the conviction that sound thinking and prayer to God will take you successfully through any difficulty. In my young and acutely impressionable years I watched him meet up with some very difficult problems. Nothing ever floored him. He would say, "Well, now let's see, let's pray and think and we'll come through this all right." Then he would chuckle and keep on hacking away at the difficulty, always with good spirit and always believing. It was marvelous the way things worked out. This quiet but determined man was actually an indomitable personality.

We discussed the principle of positive thinking after the reporter had raised the question. "Tell me your secret, Rob," I said.

His reply was priceless, one of the wisest statements I have ever heard. "When a problem arises, I think it through patiently and carefully. I analyze it and analyze it some more. Sometimes, in doing so, I go off alone where I can talk to myself. I can understand better by talking out loud." Then he added, and this I hope you will never forget, *"I never build a case against myself."*

That is so very important. Stop working against yourself down in that mind of yours. God, your creator, is not a poor workman. He made you and He never intended that life should defeat you. He made life hard, to be sure, but He wants you to know that He will help you. "Hope thou in God: for I shall yet praise Him . . ." (Psalm 42:11) is one of the great words from His book. And another is, "God is our refuge and strength, a very present help in trouble." (Psalm 46:1)

So, with faith in that help, print those words of my friend Rob Rowbottom indelibly upon your mind: *I never build a case against myself.*

What thrilling victories people have who practice these principles of positive thinking. I have before me a letter from a man who was faced by one of the toughest kinds of problems. This is what he has to say about his difficulty:

> For twenty-five years I had been progressing from a heavy drinker to a hopeless alcoholic. I had lost position after position; had been locked up for common drunkenness; had been confined to alcoholic wards; spent many weeks in mental wards where alcoholics were confined while being given treatment. I spent a year and a half a hopeless drunk on skid row in Philadelphia.
>
> For years I was completely out of touch with my family. My marriage, never a happy one, dissolved. I am a photographer. At one time I had two portrait studios. These I lost. About 1950 I heard about Alcoholics Anonymous and attended some meetings. I tried to work the program but had too many reservations. Then, in a Jacksonville, Florida AA I met a fine woman and a year later we were married. However, not long afterward we both began drinking again and things went from bad to worse. Hospital after hospital.
>
> One day I took to my bed with a bottle—my usual routine when a difficult problem arose—and passed out. My wife, to pass the time, went downtown to the library. Somehow she stumbled across a book of yours, *The Power of Positive Thinking.* She glanced through it and as she later told me, rushed home and put it on my night table. When I came to in my drinking bouts I usually liked to read something, as it seemed to calm me down.
>
> So I reached out and picked up this book and began reading it. At first, of course, none of it made much sense. I remember closing it and placing it on the table. But a phrase I read made its way through my muddled thoughts. "If God be for us, who can be against us?" I tried visualizing Him there beside me and immediately felt assured and stronger. I then picked up the book again and commenced reading it from the beginning, feeling better as I went along. During the next days, reading a little each day, I could feel a resolve within me becoming stronger and stronger to regain and keep my sobriety.
>
> My wife and I celebrated our fourth anniversary the other day. Four years without a drink. We don't have too much in the way of worldly goods, but we

are very happy. I manage a portrait studio in a small town in Massachusetts. We have nice clothes, our own car, attend the Episcopal church, and hope to build our own home next year.

Here is a man who grew. He grew over his difficulties through the power of that one phrase, "If God be for us, who can be against us?" Completely defeated, he got hold of this tremendous force, the power of the Almighty, and with this he began to grow. And he built a case not against, but for himself!

There is a corollary to this idea. If it is true that by growing you can overcome your difficulties, it is also true that your difficulties can help you grow. Difficulties are growth stimulators. The Russians have a proverb which I find interesting in this connection: "The hammer shatters glass but forges steel." If you are like steel, if you have good, malleable stuff in you the difficulties of life will forge you in strength and power.

It is interesting how many of our outstanding leaders have had this philosophy. President Eisenhower told me one day about an early memory he had of his mother as one of the wisest persons he had ever known. And her wisdom came from her religion. She created a wonderful spirit in the home, and she herself was the center of it.

He recalled one evening playing some kind of game with cards and complaining about the bad hands he was getting. Suddenly, his mother stopped the game and told him that when you play a game you have to take the cards as they come, and play them! She reminded him that life is like that. God deals the cards in life, and you've just got to play your best with what you have.

The President said he had never forgotten that advice and follows it to this day.

Thomas A. Edison took life in this same man-sized manner He too was a tough, positive thinker. Former Governor of New Jersey, Charles Edison, his son, told me this fascinating story about his father. On the night of December 9, 1914, the great Edison industries of West Orange were practically destroyed by fire. Mr. Edison lost two million dollars that night and much of his life's work went up in flames. He was insured for only ten cents on the dollar because the buildings had been made of concrete, at that time supposed to be fireproof.

Young Edison was twenty-four, his father was sixty-seven. The young man ran about frantically, trying to find his father. Finally he came upon him, standing near the fire, his face ruddy in the glow, his white hair blown by the winter winds. "My heart ached for him," Charles Edison told me. "He was no longer young and everything was going up in flames. He spotted me. 'Charles,' he shouted, 'where's your mother?' "

" 'I don't know, Dad,' I answered."

" 'Find her!' he bade me. 'Bring her here. She will never see anything like this again as long as she lives.' "

The next morning, walking about the charred embers of all his hopes and dreams, Thomas A. Edison said, "There is great value in disaster. All our mistakes are burned up! Thank God we can start anew." And three weeks later, just twenty-one days after that disastrous fire, his firm delivered the first phonograph.

To sum up, I recommend the following:

1. Thank God you have difficulties. It's a sign you are alive.
2. Learn to stand back from your troubles and take a calm survey of them. The best way to do this is through the practice of quietness. In quietness and peace, take a level look at your problems.
3. Use your full mind power to analyze your difficulty. Then systematically chip away at it, bit by bit.
4. Think positively about your difficulty. Believe that you can overcome it. Do this and you are already well on the way to victory.
5. Learn the spiritual-practical method for handling a difficulty.
6. Let persistence work for you. Keep everlastingly at it, and you eventually will be victorious.
7. Grow to the high point where you can look down on your problem, and then use your problem to help you grow.
8. Calmly take life as it comes. Deal with your difficulties with controlled emotion and steadily keep on working for victory.
9. Never build a case against yourself.
10. Make use of the available power of the Almighty. Troubles will defeat you without God, but with His help you can handle any difficulty.

10

DON'T LET PRESSURE
PRESSURE YOU

IT IS a generally recognized fact that we live in a world that is full of tension. Tension surrounds us. It is in the rhythm of our cities and of our machines. It is in our talk and on our faces and in our bearing. It is built into our society. Certainly it shows in our work. Believe it or not, in New York City you can get the correct time by dialing N-E-R-V-O-U-S!

Fortunate indeed are those who do not let tension push them around; who do not let pressure pressure them. One evening, not long ago, when I was out on the West Coast, I had a very interesting talk on the subject of tension with Desi Arnaz. Desi and Lucy had just finished a hectic week at the studio, where they were filming scenes for a new show. But when I saw them in the living room of their country home, they were both as calm and cool as if they had just finished a refreshing week on vacation rather than on location.

"I've read that book of yours about positive thinking," Desi said suddenly. He has a way of fixing you with those wide-open, deep brown eyes of his when he talks. "You know," he said, "there're some pretty good parts in it."

Lucy laughed. "Just pretty good?" she asked.

"Especially that part, there, where you talk about tensions," he went on. "I really liked that part because we're in the business of tension, Lucy and me."

"You know what I did after I finished your book?" Desi said. And then he came up with a unique result of positive thinking. He leaned forward and pulled back his sleeve to show a bare wrist. "I threw away my watch."

I was a little startled. This wasn't exactly the kind of effect I had expected when I wrote *The Power of Positive Thinking*. But I felt better when I got the whole picture, because it turned out that although Desi does throw his watch away, he does it for just a few hours.

During the week, Desi's time is very tightly scheduled. At 8:05 in the morning he must do this; at 11:40 he must do that. Commercials must fit smoothly into the program, timed down to the exact second. And, of course, there are always delays and last minute changes to gum up plans and create tensions that mount higher and higher.

But always, after a while there comes a breather. Maybe it's a break in the production schedule. Or just a weekend, or a holiday. On these occasions, if it's winter, Desi and Lucy drive out to their house at Palm Springs, or if summer, to one they own on the ocean. Both are beautiful places. The desert home is rimmed around by glorious mountains. The seashore home sits right on the edge of the Pacific. Out there in the desert and mountains, or next to the surf, they are far away from deadlines and appointment pads. But this is not enough. Just to make sure they won't be hounded by time, Desi throws away his watch.

He literally takes his watch off as soon as he walks into the house, tosses it into the dresser drawer and closes the drawer with a bang.

"After that," he said—and then he came up with a wonderful phrase— "I take a vacation from tension."

Isn't that a great idea! Take a vacation from tension. Desi does it by ignoring time. "I go down to the beach," he said. "And I lie down and let my mind and body relax. Then if someone calls me and says that it's time to eat, I tell them it isn't time to eat because I'm not hungry. If they come and say it's time for bed, I tell them the stars are out and the moon has just come up. It'll be time for bed when I get sleepy."

Later, of course, after the little vacation-from-tension is over, Desi has to go back to the dresser drawer and put the watch back on again. But he does it with a new sense of vitality; he is refreshed and ready to get back to work.

It isn't the Desi Arnazes of this world who need to learn how to handle tensions. Almost everyone these days faces the same problem. Thousands of children no longer stroll out the door and walk leisurely off to school, thumping picket fences and breaking the ice that has formed on puddles along the way; they must hurry to catch the bus at the corner—it leaves precisely at 8:12 A.M.

Even the routine business of getting to work has become a tightly scheduled affair. I know one pathetic fellow who has to meet three deadlines before he can sit down at his desk in the morning. He must get up in time to catch the 7:28 bus that takes him to the railroad station. He must be at the station in time to catch the 7:43 train to New York. He must arrive in the city in time to catch a car pool that takes him fifty blocks uptown. The schedule is so tight that at every stoplight he wonders if he's going to be at his desk by the time the 9 o'clock "starting bell" rings.

I once asked this man what time he had to set the alarm in order to make that series of deadlines. His answer was a classic. I think about it whenever I think about twentieth century man and the way he is pushed around by time.

"Oh," he said casually, "I usually set it for approximately 6:32."

Approximately 6:32!

This is symbolic of a problem that thousands upon thousands of men and women face daily. How to handle unwanted tension.

Notice that word "unwanted." A certain amount of tension is a good thing. Normal tension keys you up, it stimulates you and keeps your creative processes operating at top efficiency. But perhaps it would be a good thing if we learned how to turn tension off and on as we turn off the energy that flows through an electric wire. We would then be able to use tension when it served our purposes, and stop it when it begins to over-pressure us. When it came time to relax, all the pressures could be drained off with little vacations from tensions.

Actually, that turning off of pressurized tension can be done. Here's one way to do it. First, consciously tense up your whole body. Start with your eyebrows. Draw them together into a frown. Now move on down to your jaw muscles and your lip muscles and your throat muscles. Tense them without relaxing. Hold the tension in all these muscles and move on down to your shoulders; tighten the muscles there and clench your fists. Con-tract the muscles in your stomach and press your knees together. Finally, push your feet down against the floor.

If you have done this as outlined, just about every muscle in your body is now tight. Hold that for a minute. Note the amount of energy that it takes to keep yourself tense!

I suggest this experiment to demonstrate what we are doing to our-selves, for many of us go through life pretty much tightened up like this twenty-four hours a day. Not every muscle at once, perhaps. Maybe it's just the throat muscles, or the shoulder muscles. For a great many people it's the stomach muscles. But the point is that because of such tension much energy is being wasted. It is being dissipated through effort that shows no results except fatigue and irritability.

Now, go on with the experiment; let the tension relax. Reverse the process described above. This time consciously relax every muscle. Carry this relaxing through your eyebrows, your jaw muscles, lip muscles, throat muscles. Now your shoulders and your fists. Your stomach. Your legs. Think of yourself as letting go. Relax all muscles and sink back in your chair until you feel limp all over. Imagine that the chair is carrying every ounce of your weight. There is nothing for your muscles to do—you are relaxed, completely relaxed.

I have a friend who works in a health club in a large city. George gets his clients to try this experiment of tensing all the body muscles and then relaxing them. He may sometimes use an additional relaxing method. With the muscle tensions eased, George tells them to bring the thought of God to mind.

"You are now perfectly relaxed," George says. "The tensions are leav-ing your body. In place of the tension, healing thoughts are coming into your mind and into your body. Now, let's go deeper. Say to yourself, 'God is in me. God is in my whole being. Just a moment ago I was rushed and anxious. I was tense, but now I am released from tension. My energies are now operating in a normal and creative way.' "

And then George asks, "Do you notice anything different about your-self?"

And one does indeed. I have tried the exercise myself many times, and know that something very different is present. I feel refreshed, invigo-rated, a new sense of control, as if I had the power to tackle the most difficult problem.

"That's relaxed power," says George. "You can now take that power back with you to the office, or back into your home. You can take relaxed power into the most tensed-up situation and the pressures won't bother you at all."

This is an excellent technique for handling the physical tensions that have a way of seizing us and not letting go. But I am of the opinion that most physical tension is really mental tension that has been translated into a new dimension. Our minds get to racing with a problem; pretty soon our bodies get to racing too. Even when seated in a chair our bodies can race. The muscles tense up as if they were in motion, and before we know it, we find ourselves knotted up. You must find ways and means to keep pressure under control, to keep the great quality of relaxed quietness.

Some years ago my wife and I bought a farm about seventy-five miles north of New York City. While the chief purpose in getting the place was to give our children the benefit of country life, I also wanted that farm to try an experiment on myself. I had a theory that everyone should have a private retreat where he can retire from the hurrying, scurrying, tension-filled world, and renew his spirit. My theory was based on the words: "In quietness and in confidence shall be your strength." (Isaiah 30:15)

I was born a country boy and they say you may take the boy out of the country, but you can never take the country out of the boy. At any rate, I wanted an actual place away from the city where I could retire at times and give God a chance to re-create in me a quiet mind. I wanted to see if this return to the country had a noticeable effect on the mental and mus-cular tensions that I was feeling.

Out back of the old farmhouse, on the place we finally bought, there is an orchard. To reach it you walk past the barn and follow a little path over a small stream, then through a corn patch and along an old stone wall. Finally you come to a little hill hard by a woods. You are completely alone up there. If you strain your ears, you can hear the wind in the trees, or the far-off whistle of a New York Central train working its way up the valley. Occasionally, you might hear the lonesome barking of a dog.

Nothing happens to you right away, up there on that windswept hilltop. You have to give God a chance to reach into your soul with His healing power. It requires a sort of settling down. But after a while you become aware that there is a certain rhythm in nature, a rhythm you had not been conscious of before. You look around you. It is autumn, say. The world is slowly going to sleep. A squirrel chatters to himself as he gathers nuts for the winter. A leaf falls; its very fall is lazy and relaxed. Down in the valley the corn is standing in shocks; the harvest is in, the fields are asleep, not to awaken for months. The entire world, as you see it from up there on the hilltop, has a rhythm of its own.

And it is a slow, relaxed rhythm. It is not the hurried pace that you brought with you from the city. You came racing up the hill with your mind running to keep pace with your body. But up there on that elevation, if you sit back and let the rhythm of the universe seep into your bones, or more importantly, into your thought processes, you find that your mind has slowed down; you simply are not in the same rush you were before. You find yourself repeating, with a new sense of meaning, the words: "In quietness and in confidence shall be your strength." God has heard your prayer. You feel less tension, more peace, and greater strength.

Once recently, when I was telling this story to a tired and harassed business executive who had come to me for help, I had it pointed out that not everyone has a convenient, lonely hill to which he can retire. "No," I said, "but anyone can find a quiet place if he really wants one."

On a recent trip to the Orient I noticed that the Japanese have beautiful, small gardens scattered throughout their cities. Maybe it's a garden of stones or of sand or of moss; it doesn't matter. They can retire to their gardens for a few minutes of contemplation. And it is a most effective practice, as I myself discovered.

During the weeks I was in Japan I made good use of the quieting and relaxing qualities of those unique Japanese gardens. Two in particular were so unforgettable that I often find myself returning to them in memory to experience anew their healing touch.

A moss garden in Kyoto was the scene of frequent relaxing meditations. There, where the sun falls gently through lacy-leafed trees onto a soft floor of moss and gleams on little lily pads in miniature ponds, the confusing world retreats and peace abounds. One is supposed to sit as immobile as possible, letting the eyes rest upon this beauty and permitting the mind to open wider and even wider to receive peaceful impressions. The effect, when you have learned to yield to it, is amazing in its ability to heal tension.

The stone garden of Kyoto will ever remain a significant spot in my long study of the techniques for reducing tension. Located within the confines of a Buddhist temple, the garden is an area perhaps 75×40 feet. It consists only of sand in which are set fifteen stones of varying size and shape. Sand and stones, that is all. The stones, according to one theory, are supposed to represent the fifteen basic problems of human existence.

They are so placed that only part of them are in your line of vision, on the theory that it is too much for the mind to consider all human problems at one time.

One is supposed to become physically and mentally still and, without being conscious of time, to contemplate life's deepest meaning.

On my last visit, the Japanese taxi-driver volunteered, "Do not hurry from Stone Garden. I will wait. No charge. If you worry about time you will miss what Garden has to say." I was the only Westerner in the Stone Garden at the time. Two venerable men in kimonos, a woman of uncertain age in Japanese dress, and a young couple in western clothes, holding hands but not speaking: these were my companions in meditation.

We all sat quietly, each thinking his own thoughts. Deep stillness prevailed, but I recall thinking that it was an alert stillness, full of dynamic force but no tension. Suddenly a phrase came to my mind: "Motion in stillness." I realized again that out of quietness comes vitality and force. Tension swirls one apart, but motion in stillness puts one together again. Quietness does not curtail, but stimulates drive; however, it is a drive that is organized and controlled.

The experience gave me an extraordinarily acute awareness of God. "In him we live, and move, and have our being," (Acts 17:28) was a Scripture passage I found myself repeating.

Later I addressed the Kyoto Rotary Club on "How to Live and Work Without Worry and Tension." In replying to my talk the club president said it was, "very appropriate since Japanese businessmen are Far Eastern Yankees, full of stress." I suggested that they visit their own shrines of healing quietness, just as I advise Americans to seek "the peace of God, which passeth all understanding." (Philippians 4:7) So, find your place of quietness for the practice of meditation, contemplation and prayer. It is one effective answer to tension.

A good friend of mine, Jesse L. Lasky, one of the founders of Hollywood as a motion-picture center, did this most impressively. In his house Mr. Lasky had a special room set aside which he called his Silence Room. It was simply furnished with a table, one stiff-backed chair, and a picture of the Matterhorn on the wall. On the table was a Bible.

Whenever Jesse became tense or found that pressure was mounting in him he would go into his Silence Room, shut the door and just sit for a while gazing at the picture of the majestic Matterhorn. "I will lift up mine eyes unto the hills," (Psalm 121:1) he would say to himself. Then he would open his Bible at random and read.

Jesse Lasky told me that he never failed to come out of his Silence Room refreshed and renewed in spirit. Anyone can find a quiet place of his own, if he really wants to. It is significant that a good many people nowadays are arranging, if not a room, at least a little spiritual meditation nook in the home. Islands of spiritual quietness, you might call them, in a time of tension.

Actually, a quiet place doesn't have to be a physical place; it can be in the thoughts. Years ago I developed a technique of my own for storing up peaceful experiences in my mind. I have used this technique literally hundreds of times, and can personally guarantee its effectiveness. It has done much in helping me master tension.

Here is what you do. Let's imagine that you are standing alone on a beach. The rest of the world has gone to sleep, but you were restless, so you got up, dressed, and took this walk on the beach. All of a sudden you find your eyes rising to the heavens. For the briefest moment you throw your soul out into the universe. You consciously expand yourself into an identification with the great God and His vast creation. You stand there and become at one with the pounding surf and the infinity of the skies.

Then you memorize the experience. It is like memorizing a poem. First you start with the things you can hear: the ocean and the wind and the sound of the beach grass rustling. Then you memorize the things you can feel; the spray in your face, the bite of the cool night air. And taste? There is salt in the air; if you run your tongue over your lips you can actually taste the ocean. Down your five senses you go, memorizing each one so that as you stand there you can bring it back at will.

And then the next time you find yourself tense, close your eyes and bring the scene back by conscious memory recreation. Run down each of the senses and re-create the peaceful experience. In just a few moments you will bring back into your mind the feeling of harmony and of relaxation that you knew that night on that vast and empty beach.

One night at Pensacola a high-ranking naval officer told a group of us a wonderful story illustrating the importance of calm, emotional control in doing a vital job.

> The aircraft carrier *Essex* was entering Pearl Harbor, the first of her class, loaded with planes and gear from San Francisco, including five thousand Marines. All officers and men in Pearl were eager to see the first of the replacement ships, and her arrival was a significant event in the war.
>
> As she entered the channel a fire broke out on the hangar deck. Simultaneously a merchant ship was sighted coming out. The channel at Pearl was not wide enough for two ships under normal conditions and the situation was critical. Word of the fire was passed to the bridge and the officer of the deck called to the captain, "Fire on the hangar deck!"
>
> Every captain is seriously concerned about a fire on the hangar deck because of the many gasoline filled aircraft always present there, and because of the proximity of fuel and ammunition stowage.
>
> The captain was closely watching the approaching ship and did not appear to have heard, so the officer of the deck repeated his report more loudly.

Without turning his head the Captain, who was noted for his imperturbability, said quietly, "Put it out."

The two ships passed safely, and the fire was put out with little damage.

But some people are always telling me that the times are so filled with tension! Tension, they complain, is all around, so how can you keep from being tense. I repeat—tension exists in the mind, in your attitude toward confusion, noise and problems.

How do successful positive thinkers keep their lives poised and relaxed? There seems to be a definite pattern that they follow. For one thing, they do what Bernard Haldane suggests. They "study their successes." Some people keep poking around among their failures for know-how. There's not much wisdom in a failure, otherwise it wouldn't have been a failure. It's really only good as a reminder how not to do something.

But when you have succeeded, study how you did it, and see if you can apply the technique to the next job. You will then know that you know, and that you can, and your tension and nervousness will give way to the calmness of the man who knows that he can, and does it.

The successful person has had to learn how to organize, so that he is free from those swamped feelings that cause pressure to rise.

A great many of the successful positive thinkers with whom I have talked, or who have written me, are men who were thoughtful enough to realize they couldn't handle everything on their own. They were part of a team in which many others were important. They learned to train and encourage others, and trust them to do their part.

And, finally, men of this caliber know the real source of strength and peace. Having big minds, they are able to comprehend the importance of spiritual values in life. The bigger they are, the humbler they are.

And now, what about the times when it is *necessary* to live with tension. I guess one of the most confusion-ridden, ten-square-feet of real estate in the whole world must be the area under the information sign on the upper level of Grand Central Station, New York. I went there one day to ask a question. Out of the surging crowds there was constantly a little knot of people clustered up against the booth, each with a burning question that had to be answered right *now!*

I watched the man behind the desk handle people. And he showed no signs of tension. It was fascinating. Here was a small, bespectacled man, subjected to heavy pressures, trying to answer the questions of impatient and confused travelers. And yet he was one of the calmest people I have ever seen.

The next passenger to get his attention was a short, plump woman, a shawl tied over her head. I remember that she had little whiskers growing from her chin.

The information man leaned forward so he could single out her voice from all the noise around him. "Yes, madam?"

The information man looked up slowly and focused his eyes on this woman through the bottom lenses of his bifocals. "Let's see . . . where was it you were going?"

A smartly dressed man with a briefcase in one hand and an expensive hat in the other tried to break in with a question. The information man just kept on talking to the woman in front of him. "Where was it you were going?"

"Springfield."

"And that was Springfield, Ohio?"

"Massachusetts."

Without looking at his timetable he gave her the answer. "That train leaves on Track 25 in just ten minutes. You don't need to run; you have plenty of time."

"Did you say Track 25?"

"Yes, ma'am."

"Twenty-five?"

"Twenty-five."

The woman turned to leave and the information man focused his attention on the man with the expensive hat. But once again the woman asked him the track number. "Did you say it was Track 25?" she asked. This time, however, the man behind the desk was giving his attention to his new passenger, and he would no longer listen to the little woman with the shawl tied over her head.

Finally, there was a momentary lull, and I took the opportunity to ask the information man a question. "I've been admiring the way you handle the public," I said. "Tell me, how can you do it and keep so calm?"

And then this man raised his head and looked at me through his bifocals. "I don't deal with the public," he said. "I deal with one passenger. And then with another passenger. It's just one person at a time right on through the day. Now where was it you were going?"

I've never forgotten that phrase: one person at a time right on through the day. And I don't intend that I ever shall, for it is too important in the proper regulation of factors that make for tension. It's been a great help to me when many multiplying problems compete for my attention at once. When things start coming at me from every direction I remind myself: "One thing at a time." That's it. That policy can undercut tension and keep your emotions under good control.

"This one thing I do," said St. Paul. (Philippians 3:13) There is magic in that phrase. If life is crowding you, if pressures are mounting inside you and tensions are leaving you high-strung and irritable, memorize that phrase. "This one thing I do." Refer to it before you start to work, and then determine to live by it. Develop the habit of saying, "Just a minute please" to interruptions, whether they come in the form of people, ideas or noise. As you perfect the technique of doing only one thing at a time you will find that much of the tension has been eased away, and in its place has come a smooth power-flow.

If you learn to think in terms of peacefulness then, no matter how hectic your circumstances, you can live with calmness and peace of mind.

I saw this demonstrated in the case of a man I met one winter morning. To begin with, I make it a practice in my morning prayers to ask the Lord to guide me to anyone He wishes me to help during the day. I recommend this practice. It will lead you to many exciting adventures.

Well, on this particular day the telephone rang and a tense voice reminded me of a meeting I was supposed to attend in midtown Manhattan. I got the impression from the tense person who was calling that if I failed to show up or was late, civilization would fall. I dashed out of my apartment building urging Mike, our genial doorman, to get me a taxicab. But it was the morning rush hour and none was readily available. I live on upper Fifth Avenue and, failing to note a cab in sight, started walking rather rapidly toward Madison Avenue, a block away, where I felt the chances for getting a cab might be better.

Then I decided to practice the tension-free control which I advocate for others. I slowed down to a relaxed pace and humbly suggested to the Lord that if He wanted me at that meeting He would just have to make a cab available. And that is exactly what happened, for there at the corner was an empty taxi. And, as I soon discovered, my earlier prayer was answered, for this driver was certainly a man who needed help.

He was extraordinarily tense, gripping the wheel so tightly his knuckles showed white. He talked ceaselessly in a nervous manner, complaining about all the other drivers thronging the avenue. Pushing through the maelstrom of traffic, listening to him, I got the naïve idea that he alone, of all the drivers on Madison Avenue, knew how to drive. He leaned out of the window and instructed the others vociferously. In fact, he communicated with them in theological terminology.

He created a very tense atmosphere despite the fact that a sign in the cab urged his passengers to "Sit back, enjoy the ride." I really felt very sorry for this high-strung, nervous man and employed a spiritual technique I have often used of sending out quieting prayers toward him. I tried to surround him with God's peace as we pushed on down the jampacked thoroughfare.

Then I noticed something that explained much. It was a printed sign, not hand-lettered, but apparently done by a printer. It was appended with Scotch tape to the instrument panel at eye level where one could easily see it. I became quite amused by this sign which read: "If you can keep your head amidst all this confusion—you don't understand the situation."

I asked the taxi-driver what it meant and he said he didn't know but it comforted him. Well, of course, we are not likely to escape from the confusion of this world. We have to live in it and we must understand the situation. And that is just the point; we *can* understand and adjust to outward tension, living in it successfully, because we have the secret of peace of mind.

When we reached our destination I said to the driver that I was sorry he was so nervous, that unless he conquered it he might become ill. He assumed from my remarks that I might be a physician and anxiously asked me how a nervous, tense condition might be cured.

I told him that I was not a medical doctor, but could recommend a Doctor who could heal him. In fact, I knew that Doctor's methods, and could give him a prescription. It would not be a liquid in a bottle or a pill, but a healing thought which, lodged in his mind, could fill him with peace and strength. Whereupon, I took a sheet of paper and lettered the following words; "The peace of God, which passeth all understanding." (Phillippians 4:7)

"Put that up alongside your other sign," I said. "Keep looking at it until those eight words are printed upon your mind so deeply that they sink into your consciousness. They have healing power. They can draw off your tension."

The man looked long and intently at what I had written. That the words impressed him was evident. "Guess that's what I need," he said. "I'll try taking your prescription."

I could have given him other tension-healing words, but this seemed sufficient for the time.

But for you who may work with the teaching of this book, I shall add others. The procedure is to cancel out your tension thoughts by the systematic and deliberate use of more powerful thoughts of peace. Inject into the mass of tension thinking which fills your mind with some really potent and healing thoughts that have the power to change the condition. Physicians tell us that certain thoughts can make you sick, actually physically sick. Such thoughts are hate, fear and tension, to mention only three. Alexis Carrel says: "Envy, hate, fear, when these sentiments are habitual, are capable of starting organic changes and genuine diseases." And other thoughts can make you well; such long-held thoughts as love, faith and peace.

But they must be directed and systematic thoughts, taken regularly into the thought stream. In due time they will change its essential character. Then the tension which has agitated you, which has perhaps even affected your blood pressure, your heart and certainly your disposition, will subside and you will return to a normal and satisfying condition of mental, emotional and physical well-being.

For one week "take" the following thoughts daily. Read each one thoughtfully several times to perceive its deeper meaning and to get the feel of the words. Then commit each to memory. Keep saying it until it is firmly lodged in your conscious mind. Then conceive of it as sinking steadily and deeply into your subconscious, there to do its healing work.

Proceed similarly each day with each one. After these seven have been fully integrated into the thought stream, go through the Bible on your own, culling out the many texts that are especially designed for tension curing. Saturate your mind with them, "soak" them deeply into the inner consciousness.

This may seem a strange and curious method, but it will work miracles, so what else matters? Hundreds, maybe thousands of people tell me the great things this procedure has done for them; how finally it has freed them from tension. It is truly one of the most amazing results of positive thinking thoughts:

Monday	"Peace I leave with you, my peace I give unto you . . . Let your heart not be troubled, neither let it be afraid." (John 14:27) (Where it says you or your, use your own name.)
Tuesday	"Thou wilt keep him in perfect peace, whose mind is stayed on thee; because he trusteth in thee." (Isaiah 26:3)
Wednesday	"My presence shall go with thee, and I will give thee rest." (Exodus 33:14)
Thursday	"Rest in the Lord, and wait patiently for him; fret not thyself." (Psalm 37:7)
Friday	"Come unto me, all ye that labour and are heavy laden, and I will give you rest." (Matthew 11:28)
Saturday	"Let the peace of God rule in your hearts." (Colossians 3:15)
Sunday	"He maketh me to lie down in green pastures: he leadeth me beside the still waters. He restoreth my soul." (Psalm 23:2,3)

Another point at which to attack tension is in your conversation or talk. Actually, you can easily talk yourself into being tense. A verbal statement is simply an articulated thought. So, when you talk tension you are thinking tension; and as you think tension you develop a tense state which results in high-tempo talk. Manifestly then, if you stop making tense and nervous remarks you will in time starve the thought that produces tense talking. The process can be encouraged by speaking calmly and by reducing the tempo of speech, using quiet, composed tones and words.

Take it slow and easy when you speak. Watch the elevation of the voice, keep a curb on its intensity. If someone breaks in before you are finished, just realize that maybe they are tense, so let them break in. If you want to resume your line of thought later, very well. But maybe you'll just let it slide. It's a kind of nervous habit nowadays just to jabber, whether anything is said or not.

Easy does it in speech as in all human activity.

There is one final technique that I would like to tell you about. It is a technique that is always used by the men and women who have learned to live successfully with pressure. Sometimes it is used instinctively; sometimes, as in the case of the business executive I am about to tell you of, it is used with planned deliberation.

I met this man on a railroad train and he taught me a good technique for reducing tension. A distinguished looking gentleman, he was headed for a business convention in the South. He settled down in his roomette across from me, pulled out a small briefcase and proceeded to surround himself with various stacks of paper. He had brought his office with him, and he was getting ready to go to work right there on the train.

But before starting, he did a strange thing. From his briefcase he pulled a black enamel plaque about the size of a postcard. Written on the plaque in large white letters were two words: PLAN BACKWARD. The man propped these words on the table before him and went to work.

Curiosity finally got the better of me, and I leaned across the aisle and said, "Pardon me, I hope you don't mind if I ask you a question?"

The gentleman took off his glasses and looked at me and said that he didn't mind at all: what could he do for me?

"Well," I continued, "I've seen a lot of these signs that say PLAN AHEAD. But I've never seen one that says PLAN BACKWARD."

He laughed. "All it is," he said, "is a reminder to myself that I've got to organize my time."

"But why the backward? Why not ahead?"

"Because," he said, "planning backward contains the idea of a specific goal. You choose a goal, picture yourself accomplishing it, then plan backward until you know exactly where and when you must start."

What a clever idea that is, really. Plan backward! I have tried it and it works. The big thing it helps you do is to organize yourself so that you start a project in time. I am a firm believer in the idea that every program has an ideal, intrinsic time-value of its own. To allow less time produces tension; to allow more time produces waste.

Try to discover this intrinsic time-value for the tasks that make up your day. How long does it really take you to handle your correspondence thoughtfully? How long does it really take you to prepare breakfast, walk to the bus stop, get the children off to school? Plan backward from these goals, and you will know when you have to *start* in order to reach them effortlessly, efficiently and without rush. This really cuts down tension. Simply start in time.

Of course, as previously suggested, the basic cure of tension and pressure is through God's peace. "Peace I give unto you: not as the world giveth, give I unto you. Let not your heart be troubled . . ." (John 14:27)

Knowing that modern people need the peace of God, I introduced a period of creative spiritual quietness into the services of worship in Marble Collegiate Church. Everyone is urged to let the body relax and to think only of God and Jesus Christ. A deep, a very deep silence settles over the large congregation. The only sounds are those on Fifth Avenue, but they are muffled by the thick marble walls of the ancient church.

When all is still I suggest quietly that everyone "drop" his problems, fears, tensions into the "deep pool of quietness" which has been created. The effect is deeply moving. The peace of God does indeed move over the people, taking life's fitful fever from minds and hearts.

And, as an illustration of how we all need the peace of God, I want to close this chapter with a touching letter from a young woman:

> First of all, I'll tell you that I'm twenty years old and a Roman Catholic. I've been brought up to practice my religion faithfully, and I have always done so. But lately, I had begun noticing that my faith in God, and His powers, was leaving my thinking more and more. I knew my faith was slipping away, and so I prayed that my faith and belief in God be renewed and strengthened. God, through your book, has done just that for me.
>
> I cannot tell you how much happier I am . . . how much peace of mind I now have, and how much more I love life. As I read your book, I practiced every suggestion you gave with all my heart, and so I will continue practicing those suggestions until they become so much a part of me that I will do them naturally.
>
> The other day, I had a rather upsetting experience. I have, for about a year, lived with an acute guilt complex about something I did. This feeling kept me from being happy, and in fact, kept me constantly nervous and miserable. I have confessed this sin to God many months ago, and have received absolution. Yet, in my mind, this wasn't enough. I let it eat at me, and imagined all sorts of terrible things that could result from it. Just the other day, reminders of this sin, and memories were brought back to me, and my guilt feeling kept telling me that I might some day do these things again, thus falling back into sin. The whole day I was a case of nerves, and even though I kept trying to apply your suggestions of relaxation, etc., to myself, I was still very upset. That night, in bed, I couldn't sleep, but suddenly I thought that by my talking it over with God, He would give me peace and relief. I told Him I knew He had forgiven me, and that He knew how sincere I now was to better myself. I asked Him to let the guilt feelings leave me. Instantly they did, and I fell into a peaceful sleep. These feelings have never again haunted me, and I know that they never will.
>
> In your book, I felt, as I read it, that you were sincerely trying to help me personally. And so you have.

Take a vacation from tension when you can. Throw away your watch temporarily; build little islands of peace into your day; learn the art of storing up relaxed power. But for those times when you must live with tension, learn the art of saying, "Just a minute, please . . ." Cram the mind full of peace producing thoughts. Keep the speech tempo down. And avoid getting tense in reaching objectives. Plan backward; allow yourself enough time for the jobs you have to do. And, finally, and most important of all, practice the peace of God every day.

Follow these simple rules regularly, and there is no reason why your life cannot become one of peace, tranquility and poise. You don't need to allow pressures to pressure you.

11

BETTER HEALTH THROUGH POSITIVE THINKING

IN MY OFFICE at Marble Collegiate Church is a small, toy coal bucket containing miniature lumps of real coal. I think I shall always keep that bucket, because it symbolizes an effective secret of health through positive thinking.

It happened in this way. A well known political personality asked me to call upon his wife's aunt who was in the hospital. This woman proved to be an amazingly interesting and able person. "I'm already getting better," she said. "It's my coal bucket that's doing it."

"Your coal bucket," I repeated. "I never knew coal buckets had healing properties. Besides, who has coal buckets in this era of better heating."

Then I saw it. There she was, propped up in her hospital bed, surrounded by the usual bottles and buzzers and vases of flowers; and on her bedside table, right in the middle of it all, was a miniature coal bucket, an exact replica of the black, old-fashioned kind our grandparents used.

"Well," I said, "this is certainly the most unusual piece of hospital equipment I've ever seen. Does it have something to do with how well you're looking?" And she did look very well, sitting straight up in bed, her eyes sparkling.

"It does indeed," she said. "It is my symbol of victory. Let me tell you about it. Here I was in the hospital, sick in body and despondent in mind. One dark trouble after another went through my thoughts. Then someone gave me a copy of your book about positive thinking. I was particularly struck with the idea that negative thoughts can do damage to our bodies. So I decided I would get all the old, black thoughts out of my mind and put bright, hopeful thoughts in their place.

"I started praying and reading the Bible as you suggested, but the black thoughts continued. Then one day I got to thinking that a black thought was something like an ugly black lump of coal. Strange the ideas we get, but I believe God gave me this one. So I sent out and got this little bucket of coal. Now, when a black thought comes, I pick up a lump of coal and say, "With the help of God I now cast this thought out of my mind and I toss the coal into that receptacle over there. I'm sure my nurse thought I was going daft; but then she saw how much my spirits were improving.

This simple technique has helped me no end, and I thank God for the bright thoughts that have come to take the place of the dark old thoughts which had so much to do with making me ill. You have no idea, Dr. Peale, how much this silly, little coal bucket has had to do with my recovery."

When she left the hospital she sent the miniature coal bucket to me and there it stands atop a bookshelf to remind me of an important truth about well being—get rid of black thoughts.

I have been impressed many times by the effect of positive thinking on health and how dark negative thoughts tend to induce illness. Holding negative thoughts is very dangerous. Job said, "The thing I greatly feared is come upon me." (Job 3:35) And Job was not the last to find that you can bring catastrophe upon yourself by unhealthy thinking.

Occasionally one comes across some dramatically clearcut example of this fact. In England I read a story in the *London Daily Mail* describing the curious death of Gem Gilbert, a British tennis star. She had died as a dentist was about to extract a tooth.

Years before, when Gem Gilbert was a small girl, she had gone to the dentist where her mother was to have a tooth pulled. And a most unusual and tragic thing happened. The little girl, terrified, watched her mother die in the dentist's chair. So what happened? Her mind painted an indelible picture of herself dying in the same way. The picture became a mental reality. Gem Gilbert carried it in her mind for thirty years. This fear was so real that she would never go to a dentist, no matter how badly she needed treatment.

But finally there came a time when she was suffering such acute pain that she agreed to have a dentist come to her house at a seacoast place in Sussex to extract a tooth. She had her medical doctor and her pastor with her. She sat in the chair. The dentist put a bib around her. He took out his instruments and at the sight of them—she died.

The writer in the *Daily Mail* remarked that Gem Gilbert had been killed by "thirty years of thought." It is an extreme case, of course, but everywhere there are people who are doing great damage to themselves just as surely, if more slowly, by sickness-producing attitudes compounded of defeat, hate, fear, guilt. Obviously, then a most important technique of good health is ridding the mind of all unhealthy thoughts. It is important to have regular mind cleansings. We must get rid of mental infection in order to have healthy bodies.

It is astounding how often the pattern of resentment causing illness is repeated. Bernard Baruch says, "Two things are bad for the heart: running up stairs and running down people." It's true not only of the heart but of the entire physical being. And forgiveness has an amazingly therapeutic effect. I received a letter from a woman who had suffered an accident, while hunting with her husband, which bears this out:

I had an accident in 1946, when a gun I was firing gave a hard recoil and injured my right shoulder. Great pain ensued, and some time later I went to an orthopedic specialist. X-rays revealed a bony spur, with a great amount of calcium, and a nerve spasm was also present over the site of injury.

I was given an injection of procane into the nerve spasm and put on cortisone. But the pain came back again and I was unable to lift the arm beyond a certain degree in motion. I had made an appointment with my orthopedic surgeon to begin X-ray treatments when he returned from a trip.

Then I started reading *The Power of Positive Thinking.* After reading about resentments and their effect on physical conditions, I put the book down and did some thinking. I had had some trouble over family affairs with my only sister, and we were not on good terms, though we observed the amenities when meeting. We had not visited nor made personal calls for over four months, and had not been truly friendly for a number of years.

After a great deal of thinking I called her on the phone, had a pleasant talk with her, which was a great surprise, and I found myself offering to help her, if I could, in any way. When I laid down the phone I was weeping silently.

Then, much to my astonishment, I had a burning sensation on the inside of my forearm. It's hard to explain the sensation only to say it felt as if the glands were secreting backwards, with a warm burning sensation. So intense was this sensation that I just looked at the spot on my forearm expecting to see it break out in some rash. It lasted for a few seconds only, and the pain went.

I then, gingerly at first, began putting my arm through motions and found I could move it freely, in flexion, extension, supination. Since then I have had complete free motion of the arm without soreness or pain.

Resentment! What is this powerful emotion that wreaks so much havoc with our bodies? Apparently what happens is that we make ourselves feel painful experiences over and over again. "Resent" is an interesting word: it comes from the Latin words meaning "to feel again." It operates in the following manner. We have an experience that is full of hurt to the personality. We resent it and so make ourselves miserable and sick by constantly re-feeling it. But finally the conscious mind may refuse to relive the actual painful memory. However, instead of forgiving and forgetting, it forces the memory down into the subconscious and then the smothered, emotional reaction may break out in the form of physical pain or sickness.

A physician told me about a woman of fifty who kept coming to him with various kinds of sores on her body. He would cure the sores with local applications, but sooner or later they would reappear and so would she. Finally, the doctor began to suspect that his patient's trouble was more spiritual than physical, and he decided to make an experiment.

"Do you know," he told her the next time she came for treatment, "I believe you are terribly afraid of something or else you are holding some deep resentment. I don't know what it is, and unless I do know I'm not going to be of much help to you."

There followed a prolonged counseling session in which it became obvious that the doctor's suspicion was well founded. This patient, as a child, had suffered a shocking traumatic experience. She had a beautiful sister, while she herself was always considered a homely child. When they were both still very young, the pretty sister died. Alongside the casket, the mother stood weeping. Suddenly she whirled around on the homely daughter and cried, "Why wasn't it you!"

This was such an extremely painful experience for the girl that her mind tried to avoid accepting it. How incredible that her own mother did not love her! But she did not want to remember that. So she managed to bury it in the unconscious, but still it remained very active in total consciousness. She developed a hatred for her mother and this, too, was an emotion that she could not accept and would not admit. She also buried that in the subconscious. So these unhealthy emotions were driven deep underground and there they festered, sending off ill health.

Things would go all right until for some reason (perhaps it was a telephone call from her mother, or maybe she saw someone on the street who reminded her vividly of her mother) the old resentments were stimulated again. She resisted the painful, remembered emotions, but they came out anyhow, in the form of another *kind* of pain. But once she recognized the real source of her physical troubles, she was able to empty out her resentments to her doctor. When she utilized the therapy of forgiveness she finally was rid of hate. The spiritual health she achieved led to mental and physical health. Thereafter she was also rid of the constantly recurring sores.

This patient had buried her feelings of ill will for many years before they erupted into ill health, but sometimes the effects of such feelings are much more immediate. Just the normal frictions of day-to-day life can result in headaches, back troubles, aching joints, and that "gray sickness." A case of this kind came to my attention recently in a rather amusing way. An old friend blurted out that he was "feeling lousy" and that he "hated his mother-in-law." He, himself, saw the connection between the unwell feeling and the cause.

"Let me tell you about her, Norman," he said. "If you want to hear about witches, listen to this one. I have to get up early each morning, earlier than my wife; and while I'm getting breakfast in comes the mother-in-law. She's a hag. Underneath a frayed kimono she wears a sloppy old nightgown that's dragging along the floor, and she shuffles along in dirty carpet slippers that keep kicking off and on. Her hair is never combed and it falls down in front of her eyes. But the thing that I hate worst of all is the way she grinds her toast. She puts it between her false teeth and grinds it back and forth like a horse. I set there every morning, just waiting for her to start grinding the toast."

Well, it's no wonder my friend was having stomach troubles, starting his day off with such emotions. I suggested a simple solution. "You're not distinguishing between your mother-in-law as a mother-in-law and as a woman," I said.

"She's no woman," my friend said firmly. "That's all she is, a mother-in-law."

"Well now, that just isn't so. She was a woman before she was a mother-in-law; and if you want to find a solution to your problem, I suggest you start treating her like a woman. Some morning soon, when she comes to breakfast, why not invite her out to lunch. That will surprise her. She won't know what to do with that one, and she'll at least be so surprised she'll stop grinding her toast for a couple of minutes.

"Invite her to lunch in a nice place. Say to her, 'I'm going to take you to a swank spot that I know, so you'll want to dress your best.' And when she meets you at the restaurant, usher her in like you were proud of her. Buy her a corsage, and pin it on her. Compliment her on her hair-do, and on her dress. And then, say this: 'I never realized how pretty you were, just seeing you at breakfast and all. My, but you are really a pretty woman.' Then drop it. Have a good meal, be full of fun, give her a good time and see what happens."

It worked like a charm. The morning after that luncheon the mother-in-law came down with her hair combed and as soon as she had the opportunity she purchased some new slippers and a bright, pretty house-coat to replace the shabby old kimono. In time the two became as thick as thieves, and all the old symptoms of tension and stomach distress disappeared.

But you may say, "Dr. Peale, your ideas are all very well for the person who has an emotionally induced illness. But not all illness is caused by the emotions."

This is very true. But in one important way, it makes no difference whether the disability is functional or organic. In either case, the patient's spirit can be healed. And that is a large element in healing, even if the physical disability remains.

In fact I believe that, whatever your problem—it can be solved. I make that statement with complete awareness of all the terrible, heartrending problems to which human nature is subject.

I preach no easy philosophy because we do not live in an easy world. But neither do we live in an impossible world. Never forget that fact. We have available the help of Almighty God in the problems of this life. And underscore that word *Almighty*. The help we get from God is tremendous help. We all know of the astonishing victories which are achieved in the lives of human beings through that vast Power. For example, take this letter from a woman in Wisconsin:

My husband was a strong, healthy man until, in his early forties, he was stricken with arthritis. Many days of suffering extreme pain followed, but after the first bout was over he continued to travel his sixteen states as a salesman.

Finally he had to use a cane. The joints on his feet and fingers became horrible knobs. I was with him on one of his trips. It was so pathetic to see this once strong man hobbling along the streets, complaining about his inability to take a step without pain.

Suddenly a young man in his thirties passed us, whistling merrily. As he went by, to my dismay, I noticed that he had only hooks for hands. I called this to my husband's attention. It suddenly presented a picture of a young man with a lifetime ahead of him, having hooks for hands. And yet he was happy.

So my husband braced himself and said, "I'll never complain again." He never has. He has had phlebitis, gangrene, and lost the sight of one eye. Three weeks ago he had an operation for a ruptured gall bladder, has an eneurysm of the lower aorta, and the liver growing around the gall bladder. His fingers are so bent he cannot button his shirt.

But he is happy, victorious. He never complains. He is grateful for all small or large favors. When the ambulance man deposited him in his chair, he turned to me and said, "I've come through this just great. God has been so good to me."

This man's problem was not removed from him, but he solved it. There are many situations like this, where problems are not eliminated, no matter what one does. But the person who has faith in God, even though his problem remains unchanged, shall indeed gain victory over it. This arthritic man emptied himself of his negative and self-pity thoughts, and while his arthritis was not cured, his spirit was healed. He is not an unhappy man today. He is not victimized by his condition. And as a result, he has the blessings of mental and spiritual health despite his physical handicaps. So it is possible for us to improve our spirits even though, occasionally, we may not be able to improve our physical condition. Many times our physical condition is beyond control. We inherit our health from our parents and from our grandparents. Frequently, fortunately, it is good health we inherit. Sometime ago I had a letter from President Harry S. Truman in which he pointed out this fact:

I have always been of the opinion that to live a long, healthy and happy life, you must be careful to pick the right grandparents on both sides of the house. Apparently, that is what I did. Of course, I have obeyed the rules the best I could about the forms of exercise best suited to my age and about eating habits. I eat what I want when I want it, but not as much as I would like.

Mr. Truman, however, does go on to say that living by spiritual principles has effected his health:

One of the principal contributions to good health is a moral code that considers the welfare of the people around you as well as your own. I have found the 20th Chapter of Exodus and the 5th, 6th and 7th Chapters of the Gospel according to St. Matthew to be nearly perfect guides by which to live. The 10th Chapter of St. Luke also has a wonderful effect upon people who are trying to find the true definition of a good neighbor.

Dr. George W. Crane says, "In modern medicine we are beginning to realize that positive thinking seems to exert a beneficial tonic to many of the internal organs. On the other hand, negative thinking can throw a monkey wrench into the smooth functioning of those inner organs and glands. Drugs and chemicals can influence glands, but the mind can do so too."

Ronald J. Smith discovered that fact. The *S.S. Homeric* was moving slowly up the St. Lawrence River and Ronald Smith, who had long been plagued with a nervous disorder that affected his stomach bringing the chances of an ulcer within distance, was standing in his cabin looking at a large jar of stomach tablets in one hand and a copy of *The Power of Positive Thinking* in the other.

Ronald Smith's cabin companion ventured: "You have been reading that book for five days now. Are you going to ignore what you have learned from it? Go ahead and throw the tablets out the porthole." After a brief hesitation, Smith gave one throw and the jar of stomach tablets splashed out of sight.

Smith has never again had need to revert to the habit of taking tablets. He learned the amazing power of positive thinking to heal. Let me repeat. The technique is to believe that you are going to be better, believe that positive thinking is going to work for you, and remedial forces actually will tend to be set in motion.

The newspapers carried a story about a man who was hit by a truck while crossing a street and was killed. An autopsy established that he had lesions from tuberculosis, ulcers, bad kidneys and heart trouble. Yet he had lived a vigorous life to the age of 84. The doctor performing the autopsy said, "This man should have been dead thirty years ago." The widow, when she was asked how he had lived so long, answered, "My husband always *believed* he would feel better tomorrow."

One definite step that some have found helpful in applying positive attitudes to physical well-being is that of affirmation or the use of definite positive statements. Words are dynamite. If you constantly use negative words concerning your health, you may stimulate negative forces that can adversely affect you. Words, habitually used, are reflections of strongly held thought, and thoughts can affect internal organs negatively or positively. But this fact also works to your advantage in that forces favorable to well-being may be stimulated by the constant use of positive words of affirmations. And it is a fact that positive thinking is stronger than negative thinking as faith is stronger than fear.

Alfred J. Cantor, M.D., former President of the Academy of Psychosomatic Medicine, in speaking of the effect of affirmations on health cautions against even such qualified statements as, "I am not going to be ill today." That is a half-positive assertion. Use instead, "I am going to be better today," which is a wholly positive statement and therefore much healthier. "Affirmations," says Dr. Cantor, "are based upon proved, scientific facts—the facts of biology, chemistry and medicine. Properly employed, such affirmations will improve your health, lengthen your life, rejuvenate your body, increase your happiness, give you success and guarantee for you the most important gift of all—peace of mind."

Here are some examples of health affirmations which have been used successfully by many persons. Try them for yourself, but be sure to use them daily, thus training the mind to think in positive concepts.

> I see myself as whole—every organ of my body operating perfectly in harmony with God's perfect laws.
> My whole being is fulfilled with health, I think health, feel health, practice health.
> The healing grace of the great physician Jesus Christ is flooding my life. In Him was life. His life is in me.
> I am a child of God. In Him I live and move and have my being. I am strong, vital, joyous. The kingdom of God is within me and I am grateful to God.

Here is a prominent medical doctor who recognizes the role of affirmed belief in health and who recommends affirmation as a road to well-being.

Actually, making affirmative statements and holding affirmative thoughts is a major first step toward causing the affirmed belief to be actualized. A second step is to put the affirmations into action. And to do that, act as if the thing affirmed is already true. As you think, affirm and act; just so will you strongly tend to feel. Act vigorously and energetically and you will be amazed at the new energy and vigor you will enjoy.

Recently I sat beside James A. Farley at a luncheon. I marveled at his obvious good health and vigor. He seemed to be in the very best of condition and didn't appear any older than he had twenty years ago when I first knew him.

"Jim, don't you ever intend to get old?" I asked admiringly.

"No, sir!" he answered, smiling at me broadly, "not on your life."

"Well, I can believe it," I said. "But what's your secret?"

"I never think any old thoughts," he declared.

Jim Farley by thinking and living on that positive basis is actually demonstrating the power of positive affirmations.

Sessue Hayakawa, the Japanese actor who played the role of the prison camp commander in the film "Bridge on the River Kwai," is often mistaken for a man in his forties, although he is seventy. How does he accomplish this? By acting quietly and sincerely as though he were in his forties. "I stopped counting the years when I became 45," he said recently. "Aging is often a matter of the spirit. It exists in the imagination before it exists in the body. It is in the mind. It does not matter how long I sleep or what I eat. When a person gets little sleep one night, he usually says to himself, 'I didn't get enough sleep last night, I must be tired.' And so he is tired. His body did not need the sleep. Only his imagination did."

What sound insight! Our bodies do not need to become tired, sick, exhausted and old. Change your "image" of yourself; see yourself well, of course observing and practicing all the rules of health, and you will tend to be that which you visualize and practice.

This has long been a personal theory of mine, one that I have applied to myself through actual personal demonstration. I am humbly grateful to God that through the practice of His mental, physical and spiritual laws I have, in sixty years, been inside a hospital, as a patient, exactly twice. Once was when I was still a youngster and had a slight ear operation. The second time was when I was twenty and had my tonsils and adenoids out.

I am not a strapping athlete but have been fortunate in having good health. In twenty-eight years at the Marble Collegiate Church I have missed just one Sunday due to illness, and that was because of a cold that settled in my vocal cords and I couldn't speak. Since then I have discovered principles of relaxation and right thinking that would have overcome such a voice difficulty. What are the principles I use? Simply those I have advocated in previous books which many have applied effectively.

They are all sound principles, adapted from a lifetime of observation and experiment, not merely by myself, but in the "laboratory" demonstration of thousands of people who have shared their practice with me. They will work. I know that they will work because they have worked for me, and for the many others with whom I have shared them. They are part of the amazing results of positive thinking.

1. Affirm that you are healthy. Say to yourself, "I feel well today. God created my body, mind and soul; so today, I feel as God intended, healthy and vigorous."

2. Hold constantly before your mind a clear picture of yourself as a well person.

3. Thank God frequently, every day, for the wonderful feeling of vitality. I asked Dr. John Riley who, at 91, was the oldest practicing physician in the state of New York the secret of his good health to ninety plus. He said, "Every day I thank God for the amazing organs of my body. I name them over and

say, 'Thank you God, for my excellent stomach; thank you God, for my wonderful heart; thank you God for my marvelous blood stream.'"

That this rather unique procedure added to his life of health and longevity Dr. Riley had no doubt. In daily thanksgiving he was firmly establishing the image of good health in consciousness and it demonstrated itself in fact.

4. Make every effort to keep your mind free of unhealthy thoughts. Flush out negative thoughts such as antagonisms, regrets, mean or vindictive images, disappointments. Replace them with healthy, kindly, positive thoughts. Did you ever hear the Balinese proverb, "If you get angry you will quickly get old"? I am told that in Bali there is less heart trouble than anywhere in the world.

5. Take nothing into the system that debilitates.

6. Keep your weight down. Find out what the doctors think your weight should be and keep it there. The solution of the weight problem requires a kind of strength that is essentially spiritual in nature. Control of extreme appetite whether for drink, for power, or for food is a problem of character. And character, of course, is spiritually conditioned.

A few years ago I became increasingly concerned about my own weight. It was far beyond the point at which I should have tipped the scales. Still, I kept on eating. I wasn't cutting down and realized that fact all too well. I began to wonder if I really could. It became an issue with me, actually a moral problem; was I defeated by a food appetite?

So I went on a diet that took off thirty-five pounds. Several years later, having re-added some fifteen of the lost poundage, I repeated the process—thirty pounds this time—to reduce to a level that has seemingly become a permanent weight. To accomplish this desired weight reduction, I employed certain spiritual and mental procedures.

7. Regular daily exercise is essential to good health. I prefer push-ups, calisthenics and swimming, sometimes a little golf, and hiking. It is important to choose a form of exercise that you enjoy enough to keep up regularly without its becoming a bore.

Personally I walk at least a mile every day, usually just before retiring. And when I am at my farm, I follow Dr. Paul Dudley White's advice to ride a bicycle.

Dr. White says, "A long brisk walk in the evening may help more to induce sleep than any medication. Nervous stress and strain can be counteracted and even prevented by regular, vigorous exercise. It is the best antidote I know."

Dr. White further points out that "good muscle tone in the arms and particularly in the legs resulting from regular exercise maintains an improved circulation in the veins. Since the veins have valves which, when in good condition prevent the blood from going the wrong way, the compression of the veins by the skeletal muscles helps to pump the blood back to the heart. Soft unused muscles do not accomplish the job as well and also make clotting in the veins more likely. And," adds Dr. White, "deep breathing exercises several times a day are of definite value." I have added this latter to my own exercise program with excellent results.

8. Have regular examinations by a doctor. Prompt attention to any imbalance helps restore the proper health conditions.

9. The greatest point of all, in my opinion, and this is based on personal experience, is to open one's life to the inflow of God's renewing power. The words "meditate" and "medicate" are almost identical in root meaning. Right thinking is medicinal. God creates good health, and He re-creates it as well. The word health comes from the Anglo-Saxon word "wholth," which is also the root of the word "wholeness," and of the word "holy." Thus health is directly related to the idea of wholeness, and to the idea of holiness. In fact, holiness means to be a whole person, not a disorganized one; more than it means to be pious.

This brings to mind Plato's famous statement, "So neither ought you to attempt to cure the body without the soul." Indeed the whole man must be well, body and soul, if health is to be sound. So I keep in mind always that to be a healthy person it is important to be spiritually vital. When one becomes filled with positive thoughts and God thoughts there is no room for negative, unhealthy thoughts that are so often at the root of ill health.

12

HOW TO BE MARRIED AND ENJOY IT

Do YOU WANT a successful and happy marriage? Of course, everyone does. And many couples have learned through positive thinking how to be married and enjoy it.

Take, for example, that cynical young man who sneered, "Me marry—nothing doing. I'm too smart for that." He began attending the Young Adult activities at our church shortly after the last war. He went out on dates, but made it clear that he wasn't going to marry. That was that!

Eventually we discovered the reason for his cynicism about marriage. In the first place he had come from a broken home. Then, he had seen too many unhappy marriages among the couples he knew. When he was overseas with the Navy as a pharmacist's mate on a small ship, he got the idea that "not one of the married men aboard was faithful to his wife." As soon as the ship pulled into port, the married men, it seemed, were the first ashore, "running to cavort" with whatever women they could find.

The result of such negative experiences was that this young man firmly decided that marriage was not for him. He had kept his eyes open. He knew the score and he was going to steer clear of it. That was for sure.

Well, it happens that in our church there is a wonderful couple, the Merle Wicks. The Wicks are happily married. It was arranged for the young man to visit the Wicks in their home. He spent several days with them. He watched them laugh and play and pray, and even argue, disagree and make up. He saw them in a variety of moods and situations, handling a variety of problems; and what he observed proved to be a revelation.

"Do you know," he said later, his face animated with a new discovery, "these people actually know how to be married and enjoy it!"

I've always liked that phrase: "How to be married and enjoy it!" This is a vitally important factor in successful living. When people know how to "enjoy" such a close relationship it means that they have a healthy, creative marriage in which both partners are encouraged, helped, built up.

Each bolsters the other. It is a relationship in which the children know genuine warmth and affection. It produces a home that radiates happiness and emanates well-being.

The National Education Association held a meeting at which the presidents of practically every important university in the country were present. The purpose of the meeting was to discuss what education could do about the country's most pressing need. And what was the most pressing need? More scientific education to compete with the Russians? More space education? Better training in economics? Not at all; these educators felt that the most pressing need of today is happy and substantial home and family life. The happy, healthy home is the cornerstone of a healthy society. Create health in the home and that health will radiate outward, touching business, industry, education, government, all phases of society.

So, how to have a successful marriage is a vital matter, a top concern of our time.

In collecting material for this book, I have separated my correspondence according to categories, and one of the thickest folders is marked "Marriage Problems." Week after week the letters pour in:

> I have been married fourteen years and not at all happily, though I do have three wonderful healthy daughters for whom I thank the good Lord. My husband, age forty-nine, treats me shabbily. Sometimes he strikes me so hard with his fists. I think the real trouble is that he needs rest and relaxation. He doesn't take his vacation. He'd rather have double pay, though we don't need it. He makes good money. He owns his home. And we have never been in debt. Well, I wonder what should be done tactfully about him. Can you give me any suggestions?

> We have a daughter who is married to a man who does not work steadily and is otherwise very irresponsible. They have three young children. She has made regular trips for a long time to a guidance center, as the pressures were affecting her nerves and mind. Her condition is better, but she has been advised that her only hope of complete recovery is divorce.

> There is always a lot of talk and advice about the "little woman" keeping herself attractive, not to let herself show the effects of child bearing, housework and worry; keep herself as pretty as the office secretary. How about the husband; a paunchy, bald male is no longer a jaunty Romeo. How about a bit of advice to him?

> I have a problem in my marriage, and I don't know what to do. I left my husband nine months ago, one month before our wonderful little son was born to us. I haven't been happy since I left him. The reason for leaving my husband was that he started running around with single men and drank an awful lot. Also, he would never let me have any money in my purse. Just

enough to pay the rent and get groceries with. You see my real problem is that I live with my parents and they want me to get a divorce and they are planning on it very much. I'm afraid of losing their love if I go back to him, and I still love him very much. He has told me of the mistake he has done and wishes me to come back to him. What should I do?

It seems the thing that disturbs me most of the time is my relationship with my wife. I never know how to take her. We have been married eighteen years and I love her very much, but she, being the type she is, quiet, self-sufficient, and satisfied to be by herself, I find it difficult to feel that she needs me for anything. Sometimes she volunteers some affection, but seldom cares for me to go any further. When I try to tell her how I feel she simply won't listen. Can you help me?

And so it goes, on and on, week after week the letters pouring in, giving intimate glimpses into problems people face in their married life.

One of the outstanding results of positive thinking has been its effectiveness in difficult marital situations. When people who are having trouble with their marriages begin to apply positive attitudes to their situation, the marriage almost always strengthens. New appreciation, esteem and regard come into the relationship. When two people begin to think constructively about marriage they get constructive results.

Not long ago I was making a speech on the West Coast. When the talk was over a man came up to me and said he wanted to tell me how positive thinking had affected his life.

He said that he had been married for nine years. Two weeks after his wedding he began to realize that he had not chosen his mate wisely.

"That marriage was a mistake," he said. "Right away both of us knew it. It had been a case of physical attraction, but my wife turned out to be just plain dumb. She was selfish, too. I had to face the fact that I wasn't ever going to get along with her, and I had to make up my mind whether or not to stick it out."

This man chose to stay with his wife. He told me that he decided to make the best of a bad situation and endure the marriage. He said that as soon as he made this decision he stopped griping and tried to get along as well as he could with a woman he did not love.

Things went along this unhappy course for five years and then this man read *The Power of Positive Thinking*. He began to use the principles outlined in this book in his business life. They worked very well. One day it occurred to him that if the principles of positive thinking worked in business, perhaps they would also work in his personal life.

"What would happen," he asked himself, "if I applied *The Power of Positive Thinking*, chapter by chapter, idea by idea, to my own home situation."

He began to do this. He began to analyze his wife, asking himself why she was selfish and why she appeared to be stupid. The thought came that perhaps his marriage had been a form of guidance. He started to picture his wife as an entirely different sort of person: as a stimulating, attractive life partner. He began to pray for her and eventually even out loud with her. Simultaneously he examined his own personality objectively and honestly for the flaws which were making his wife unhappy. This was important to the process for he, too, had not a little selfishness and self-centeredness, as he readily admitted.

This process lasted for four years, but "the results were very good," he declared. And it was evident how sincerely he meant that. From a marriage which was simply endured, the relationship between these two people became a warm partnership in which each tried to give more than he received.

"Positive thinking," this man told me, "was directly responsible for the remaking of our marriage."

Now the fact of the matter is that the married relationship is one of the most touchy and difficult of all human relationships requiring, as it does, the adjustment of two different personalities in intimate association. Making a marriage succeed cannot be left up to chance, or even to hope. A definite, practical program needs to be established so that each party to the marriage may grow and mature; so that the children may have full, rounded, happy, creative lives. These are the purposes of marriage and should always be held firmly in mind. A happy marriage, let me repeat, is one in which all parties concerned—husband, wife and children—are fulfilled to the maximum.

Let us examine a few of the problems that arise in marriage and see how they have been met successfully.

Some years ago I had a rather amusing example of conflicting interests when a member of our church told me that he and his wife had begun to argue over who was going to watch television. This was back in the days when TV was new and most people could afford only one set. So there they were sitting in the living room each night, the husband wanting to watch fights, sports programs and westerns, and the wife wanting to see programs on the cultural side. They began to argue over the television. They said cutting, mean things to each other, and while the marriage never came close to divorce, things definitely were not smooth.

This problem may seem too petty to bring to a pastor, but what seems petty can be a symptom of a deeper problem, or it can work up into a major cleavage. The husband could not understand his wife's dumb interests, and the wife could not understand her husband's stupid interests. Well, this went on for quite a while until both husband and wife decided they would have to do something about the situation, so they came to see me. After talking with them I decided upon a little strategy. Privately I made an arrangement with the husband, then later with the wife, on the basis of the principle of ". . . in honor preferring one another." (Romans 12:10)

"Now what this means," I said, "is that you should prefer each other: by that I mean that you insist that the *other* party shall have the preferred treatment. I want you to apply this Bible principle to your problem with the television. When you get back home tonight," I said to the husband, "you insist that you both see her cultural program, and really get something out of it." A little later the same day, I said to the wife, "When you go home, you insist that you and your husband watch the ball game. See if you can't enjoy it yourself."

At first this had a rather unhappy turn. That night the wife turned on the TV—to the ball game.

"Oh no you don't!" said the husband. "I *insist* that you listen to the Philharmonic tonight."

"Not at all," said the wife. "We are going to watch the ball game, whether you like it or not."

So that first night, believe it, they got into a terrific argument trying to follow the Biblical injunction, ". . . in honor preferring one another."

Later, when they came back to my office to complain, they saw the humor of the situation, and after that we got down to the more serious question involved. Actually, their problem was only a lack of common interest. Their lives were too narrow. They were living by themselves, for themselves. They needed to find outside activities which would take them together, away from their television set into the great world outside.

Since then this couple has become so active in community and church activities that they seldom watch television. Together they have achieved the goal of finding mutual interest. They are one of the happiest married couples of my acquaintance.

The matter of common interest raises the question of marriage with a member of another faith. I have received hundreds of questions dealing with the problem of whether a Protestant should marry a Catholic, or a Christian marry a Jew. Few questions so agitate families as this one.

If people truly practice positive thinking they can work out an interfaith marriage successfully. But it involves complete mutual respect for each other's faith, and an equal balance of every factor relating to the marriage. However, on the basis of considerable experience, I strongly urge young people to marry within their own religious group: Protestants with Protestants, Catholics with Catholics, Jews with Jews. Many hazards are eliminated by selecting a life partner from your own background. Marriage has many problems of adjustment as it is, and it's wiser not to add a difference of religion.

But a mixed marriage, as indeed any marriage, can rise to high levels of happiness if the home is packed full of love and faith and esteem for personality. Fill any household full of a love of God and of each other that transcends theological differences, and men and women and children can dwell together in peace and joy.

One of the really major steps that a couple needs to take in developing a successful marriage is to become mature individuals. Perhaps this is the most difficult assignment that life gives us. Dr. Smiley Blanton, the psychiatrist who heads The American Foundation of Religion and Psychiatry, with the assistance of Dr. Irwin Smalheiser, psychologist, has worked out a Maturity Score. This simple test will give some clues as to whether or not you need to work on the question of maturity in your own married life or in your life generally, for that matter.

Maturity Score

Yes   *No*

1. Do you lose your temper, stamp your feet, throw or kick things?
2. Do you always give the other person equal consideration with yourself?
3. Do you criticize your wife or husband in the presence of other people?
4. Are you insistent upon always having your own way, and sulk if you don't get it?
5. Are you a chronic worrier?
6. Do you put your trust in God and then just do your best?
7. Do you accept the ups and downs, and things that are inevitable, with serenity of spirit?
8. Do you have a positive conviction that you can meet and solve your problems?

Yes to questions one, three, four and five indicates immaturity.

Yes to questions two, six, seven and eight is a sign of a mature personality.

With the results of this test as a guide you will be able to know whether you need development of your emotional maturity. Certainly a major difficulty is that many people have an immature concept of love. A great deal of damage has been done to marriage by our Hollywoodish ideas of love. We seem to feel that "love" has got to be one prolonged moonlight and roses thrill.

Just the other day a young wife came to my office complaining that there was no thrill left in her marriage. She had been married nine months and now her husband's touch ceased to start her heart pounding.

She had, however, found another boy who did give her this Hollywoodish sense of excitement. She wanted my advice about divorcing her husband to find married happiness with the second boy. She "simply must recapture the thrill of romance," she said.

"Well, young lady," I said, "suppose this new excitement lasts, as did the first, for only nine months; then what? In fact, the next might last only five months, for thrills tend to diminish with repetition. You need to realize that this thrill you seek is something special that belongs to a certain stage in your development, but to expect it to last at high intensity is pure Hollywood hokum. It won't do that and it should not. It is against all the facts of human psychology that it should."

This young lady had never been apprised of the fact that sexual excitement is only one facet of a successful and enjoyable marriage. My father, who was first a physician and later a minister, and always a wise man, used to say that thrill-love was nothing but a biological trick on the part of nature for the simple purpose of perpetuating the race.

Far too many young couples think that as soon as sexual excitement begins to wear thin, they are falling out of love. They haven't adjusted to each other on any other basis than sex, and in their immaturity they do not want to work at marriage in all of its many aspects. The physical, while it is important, is certainly not the whole by any means.

In a newspaper I saw the results of a survey in which some four hundred happily married couples were interviewed. This survey indicated that the *average* time needed for two people to adjust to each other was six years! Note the fact that this is the average length of time; for many people it must have taken considerably longer. So when a young couple tries marriage for a few months, or even for a few years, and finds that the sense of excitement has abated somewhat, they should not become discouraged. Learning to be happily married takes time and patience. It is a mistake, indeed it is preposterous to think that as soon as the first flush of romance passes, it is time to seek another partner.

Now I do not want to indicate that sexual enjoyment should be confined to the first, few, pink-cloud months. Sexual adjustment is vital to a mature marriage. And in the overwhelming majority of successful marriages, sexual interest and capacity lasts into old age. Certainly sexual maladjustment can cause deep problems as many letters indicate:

> You have said many wise things about sex, so I turn to you with a serious problem.
> I have a perfectly good relationship with my wife in everything but the sexual area. She is about one-third as needful as I am. What should I do with my psycho-sexual difference? I don't want to express myself with another woman, yet my wife, whom I love, does not fulfill me.

My wife is a dream girl, very attractive. She has the personality that attracts friends, especially children, who love her. It is her dream to have a child. I love her very much, and she is everything in the world to me. My problem is that we have been married two years and I have not been able to have sexual intercourse with my wife.

I have been to one doctor after another, and all they tell me is that there is nothing wrong with me physically. Finally, one doctor told me that it was a combination of emotions, nerves and subconscious mind that was blocking off any successful attempts.

Do you think I have the right to ask her to spend the rest of her life with me when I cannot fulfill the part of the husband and man to make a happy home and marriage? Is there anything you could suggest that might help me?

My husband and I have been married a year and one month. I haven't enjoyed our sexual relations at all, don't get any pleasure in love making, and dread even kissing him for fear it will lead to intercourse. I have never actually wanted intercourse and my life would be perfectly happy without it. I've explained this to my husband. It disgusts him, which I suppose, is normal. Should I divorce my husband and let him have another chance at happiness, or should we go through life like this?

My daughter was married last July. I tried to prepare her adequately for the physical side of marriage. I felt that she was quite mature and ready. She seems to be having trouble adjusting—wonders if, after all, she is "frigid." I wonder sometimes if we read too much and become completely confused. Would you have a word of some sort that might help her?

I have been married eighteen years and have a wonderful husband and four children. But, Dr. Peale, I still have an indifferent attitude toward sex relations. Possibly it is because I was led as a child to look at it as a vulgar act. Does the Lord look at it that way? Is it to be entered into only for conception's sake and the bringing of babies into the world?

So very often this question of vulgarity comes up. Apparently our Puritan backgrounds have left an indelible mark on our attitudes toward sex. I think it is important to state firmly that a full, natural enjoyment of sex is normal and right, else God would never have created people as He did. Love is both physical and spiritual. Therefore, a complete enjoyment of the physical senses within a spiritual marriage is never an expression of vulgarity.

The sexual act is a sacred expression of love between two people who have spiritually become one through marriage. "The twain shall be one flesh," the Bible says. While sexual union itself is physical in nature, it is also a fundamental expression of the highest and purest emotions in love. To regard it as vulgar indicates a warped concept, probably originating in childhood when, to make you moral, a dirty connotation was put upon God's principle.

Notice, however, that while we have been talking about the physical aspects of love, we have consistently brought the spiritual side of married life into focus. The spiritual element is where its real strength lies, and this is one of the areas where positive thinking becomes most important. Positive thinking says that through the proper mental and spiritual attitudes we are able to overcome our difficulties, whether they are marital or otherwise.

One of the most effective aspects of positive thinking is positive prayer. I am a firm believer in a statement originally made, I believe, by Father Patrick J. Peyton, "The family that prays together stays together."

A young couple told me they happened to be walking on Fifth Avenue in New York City at the moment the boy asked the girl if she would marry him. She said, "Yes." These two youngsters were both religiously inclined. Their first impulse was to drop into church and dedicate their engagement to God.

The nearest church happened to be St. Patrick's Cathedral, and although they were both Protestants, they entered the church, knelt, and prayed together. They felt that their forthcoming marriage was thus spiritually consecrated to God long before it was officially sanctified at the altar. It isn't surprising that their marriage turned out to be highly successful. That is really a valuable thought; consecrate your engagement to God. Thus, from the very beginning the relationship is based on an enduring spiritual foundation.

Far too many young people actually leave God at the marriage altar. They do not take Him into their homes. I was talking recently with one very troubled woman named Sally whose marriage, she said, was about to dissolve. In the course of our conversation, I spoke about my belief that a praying family will stay together. "Is God ever mentioned in your home?" I asked her.

"Oh yes," she said, "but not in the way you mean."

"Have you ever considered praying aloud with your husband?" I asked, and to this the woman gave a short but conclusive little laugh. "You just don't know my husband!" said Sally.

"Well now," I said, "I have known many men who give that impression. They say they will never pray. But that's an act, I've found, in a great many cases. I want you to try something tonight. At the table before dinner is served tell your husband that you would like to say a blessing. Use that as an opening wedge to bring a spiritual note and then, bit by bit, see if you can't bring additional prayer into your home."

I could see that this lady felt it was a useless experiment, but she agreed to try it, even so. As she reported later the experiment worked. That evening when her husband came home even more morose and grumpy than usual, he buried himself behind his newspaper and refused to talk, except to mumble, "About time!" when the wife finally announced that dinner was ready.

When they were seated at the table she said, "It may surprise you, but I feel like saying a blessing. Do you mind?"

"Well, go on," growled the husband. "It's a free country."

So a little embarrassed, the wife did say the blessing. And at breakfast she said one again. She kept this up for several days until one evening, still in a rough manner, the husband said, "Hold your horses, Sally. You've been saying the blessing at every meal. Who's the head of this house? I'll say the blessing around here." With that he searched his memory and drew out one of the old family blessings that he had heard as a child and, stumbling, he got it off successfully.

This couple had never before heard each other's voice in prayer. As time went on, it became easier to pray together. Eventually they began to say a prayer at bedtime. The last time I spoke with Sally she was able to report that a remarkable new spirit of cooperation and affection had come into their marriage.

Having a prayer centered home is one of the best of all techniques for a happy marriage. I have known couples who have made God central in their home life in a variety of very interesting ways. One woman was having a great deal of trouble with her housekeeping. "I decided that the only way for me to handle my attitude toward my house," she told me, "was to dedicate my housekeeping to God. The Bible says, 'Let all things be done decently and in order.' (I Corinthians 14:40) This became my housekeeping motto, and the results were really quite pleasing."

Another wife who has tried this technique successfully gets up earlier than her family and "fills her house full of positive affirmations." She stands in the middle of her living room and faces, in sequence, every corner of her house. As she does this she affirms aloud that "this house is a place where God dwells; it is a home full of peace, love and joy." She declares, "The result is really marvelous." Such affirmations become a reality; any home can become a happy place; the toilsome part of housekeeping can be transformed into meaningful purpose.

My own mother had a remarkable ability to turn the chores of housekeeping into creative family experiences. Our house was always full of fun and happy excitement. Mother was a real strategist. No one was aware, for instance, of the fact that the dishes were being washed. Mother's trick was to start a discussion on some lively subject just at the moment that the unpleasant job of dish washing had to be done. Automatic dish washers were away off in the future. We were the dish washers of that generation, and we were not automatic.

When the meal was over, my mother would throw some highly controversial subject into the conversation. In no time, we would all take sides. As soon as the argument had reached a certain crescendo, mother would quietly hand a dish to my father, another one to me, and others to my brothers. She herself would rise and walk out into the kitchen carrying some dishes, all the while constantly stimulating the discussion. Before we knew what was happening we were all out there with her, washing and wiping dishes, and still arguing at full tilt, and having a wonderful time.

In any chapter on successful married life, a discussion of the selection of your mate is important. This is, of course, one of the most important decisions that a person will have to make in his life. Sometimes the decision is wrong, and a lifetime of misery follows. Therefore, I am a firm believer in an engagement of adequate length. A couple has so much to learn about each other. Can they really communicate with each other? Are they interested in many of the same things? Do their family backgrounds mesh gears?

A good friend of mine, Mr. M., a very prominent man, told me that his son Jim came home with the announcement that he was in love. He had fallen head over heels for a "fabulous" girl and was going to marry her right off, just as soon as commencement was over. The boy's family met this young girl and immediately sensed that she was not right for Jim. But to say so would have been wasted energy.

Wisely, the M's decided to let their son discover for himself how he really felt; so at the first opportunity they invited the girl to spend a week with them in their home. Almost immediately it became clear that the girl was not fitting in. She was quite a bit on the sloppy side. She did not get up when the rest of the family did. She would not help with the household chores. She obviously considered herself intellectually superior to the rest of the family, and in general succeeded in keeping herself apart from the rest of the group.

The boy was somewhat disillusioned, but was not ready to admit that he had made a mistake. Then, at Christmas time, Jim's parents strategically insisted that he spend the whole vacation at this young lady's home. They packed him off to her home, not expecting to see him until New Year's Day. But three days later he was back. Bit by bit the story came out. Jim was particularly disturbed by the way his fiancée yelled at her parents. She was difficult around the house and refused to participate in normal household activities. She acted sullen and spoiled.

The parents themselves seemed "neurotic" and were slovenly. Jim said the bathroom soap dish looked as if it had not been cleaned since Hector was a pup. The result of these two visits was that Jim's ardor cooled off entirely. Suppose, however, that Jim had not discovered these facts about his "true love" until after they had been married. Suppose he had insisted

upon haste in marrying the girl, only to have his education in her qualities when it was too late to retreat. Love at first sight may have its place,
but that doesn't go for marriage at first sight. There are far too many
problems to be ironed out before marriage to risk a hasty wedding.

13

LEARN TO LIVE WITH THE SPIRITUAL FORCES AROUND YOU

WHAT WONDERS there are in your mind!

A woman says, "I saw in the paper that so-and-so died of a heart attack."

"What paper?" she is asked.

"I don't know just what paper, but I saw it in the paper." She quotes the item verbatim.

A search of the files of newspapers discloses no such item. Inquiry establishes that the person in question has not had a heart attack. But, three days later, that person dies of heart failure and the newspaper story reads exactly as the woman had quoted it in advance.

And what is this strange power? Precognition.

A little four-year-old girl, during World War I, calls to her mother: "Mommy, Daddy is choking to death! He is down a deep hole!"

Later investigation ascertains that the child's father, at that exact moment, had been down in a cellar under gas attack.

And this is an equally strange power—clairvoyance.

A middle-aged man is driving his car along a New Jersey highway when he feels a terrible pain in his chest. It is so excruciating that he stops his car, thinking he is suffering a heart attack, but eventually it passes.

A few hours later, he learns that his son, driving in Colorado, had been killed at that exact moment, his chest crushed by the wheel of his car.

And this mystic force? Telepathy.

Such phenomena as the foregoing are being investigated by Dr. J. B. Rhine of Duke University, leader in the science of parapsychology, the systematic study of mental activity by means other than the physical senses. What are these things that he describes as precognition, clairvoyance, telepathy? What could they prove? Well, Dr. Rhine believes that these are only some of the powers of the human mind ranging the universe without obstruction of space and time. We mention them here as further evidence of greater capacity within yourself, a capacity that can aid you in living a stronger more effective life.

Now, of course, there are always people who will respond to such phenomena with the flat assertion, "It's impossible." Yet their only reason for saying so is that they have never heard of it before. I met the man who developed the automobile radio. The banker he asked for a loan to finance production told him: "I never heard of such a preposterous idea! There will never be radios in automobiles!" That is how an unimaginative mind often responds to anything that is new.

This author is convinced there is something very great in man that is beyond the physical, beyond the material. We need to see ourselves in vaster relationships in God's great plan. A prominent scientist told me that in higher mathematics if they introduce infinity into the formula it works.

This emphasis on infinity will bring you into closer contact with great forces around you and within you. As you tap these deeper powers you will gain greater victories over the defeated elements in your life.

For example, I have before me a remarkable letter which illustrates graphically what happens to some people when, through positive thinking they make contact with the spiritual forces around them.

> I was forty-four years old in June. I have been a professional jockey since 1930. The reason for this letter is an incident that happened to me in October, 1956.
>
> I had been a heavy drinker since 1934. In April, 1955, a copy of your book, *The Power of Positive Thinking*, came into my possession. Incidentally, the man who owned the bar where I drank gave the book to me.
>
> I had practically lost my power of concentration, though I had always been able to keep in shape fairly well physically—had to, to ride. It took me three weeks to memorize the 23rd Psalm—so you can see I was pretty far gone.
>
> I bought a Bible and put your theories to work. It was slow work. I couldn't remember what I read, but I kept on reading and praying. Even memorized a few short psalms.
>
> In the meantime, I had practically cut out hard liquor, but hit the beer pretty hard. I didn't get drunk as often, but I still got drunk, and I kept on reading my Bible, drunk, or sober, and praying, too.
>
> By fall of 1956 I had made some progress—nothing startling, but noticeable. This brings me up to the point.
>
> I was riding in a race meeting at Spokane, Washington at the time. I lived in a motel a few miles from the track. One night I went to sleep early. I was awakened by a strange feeling starting in the vicinity of my heart, gradually spreading over my entire body. First, all the tension that had accumulated inside me over the years passed, and was replaced by a great feeling of love. My whole body was aglow. I could see my father and mother beside me. They faded away, and I saw many things. I shed tears of joy and tears of sorrow. I prayed for many people who floated through my mind one after another.
>
> I got up and turned on the light so I could look in the mirror. My skin felt like smooth warm satin. I was shedding tears of ecstasy and then of great sorrow.
>
> When we went to work at the track next morning, people would look at me

real puzzled. A few said, "What in the world happened to you?" Most of them were good friends of mine so they didn't say anything more. I felt that I could heal any crippled or lame person by touching them. I stayed in this state of illumination about two weeks, then it diminished and would come and go for short periods at a time. It has never gone away altogether.

Now, here's where you come in. The next day I didn't ride any races, so I stayed at the boss's house and mowed the lawn. Everyone had gone to the races. I went by the side of the garage and sat in the sun. A donkey they had there that I could never get close to at all, walked right up to me and stood there and looked at me a long time. I began to cry, and after awhile I got up and cranked the mower and went to work.

All the time I was in this condition there was great emphasis on the most minute details. After I had finished the lawn, I went in the house and took a bath, and lay down on the sofa. I didn't sleep, but seemed to be in a sort of trance of prayer. There were running through my mind many things. Finally your name came to me. It hit me with great force, not once, but many times, one right after the other, with great emphasis upon each one of your names.

Then a little later I was reciting the 23rd Psalm, and when I would come to the last verse, "Surely goodness and mercy shall follow me all the days of my life; and I shall dwell in the house of the Lord forever," a wondrous burst of happiness came over me, with great emphasis on each and every word. I quit smoking in about ten days. By the first of January I had lost all desire to drink. I haven't smoked or taken a drink of any kind since.

I have met this man personally and found him a quiet and intelligent person. He shows a strong desire to help people and seems to go about doing so in a sensible and creative manner.

What a fabulous world we live in! We are surrounded by strange mystic forces which we have only barely begun to understand, let alone use. This jockey was privileged to know a mystical force, the like of which few experience, especially in such a dramatic form, and his life was remade thereby.

But to some degree, everyone of us may identify ourselves with these tremendous forces. In this chapter I am going to share with you some of the remarkable letters I have received dealing with these great matters. I shall not attempt to interpret these letters, but quote them for you to reflect upon. Those who have had these mystical powers touch their lives have many times found an amazing remedy for frustration, hates, weaknesses, sin, even physical ills. Perhaps the experience of others will be of comfort and strength to you.

The following experience was sent me by a professor at a famous New England College:

In my student days, I was bothered by occasional headaches which were always relieved when my grandmother, who made her home with my parents, would place her hand on my forehead. Later, when I began teaching at Amherst College, these peculiar headaches continued to trouble me.

One night, in December of my first year there, the pain obliged me to retire earlier than usual. Toward midnight I suddenly felt my grandmother standing beside my bed. She placed her hand on my head and the pain ceased, *never to return*.

There had been no recent letter from my parents so I had not been told of grandmother's sudden illness. It was not until the following day that word was received saying that she had passed on at the very hour when I felt her hand on my head. I am sure that she thus took the first opportunity to bring me the relief she alone could give.

In a letter written by a reader who lives in Inman, Kansas we are told of an experience that tended to diminish the fear of death.

This past November 18th, I was stricken by an illness and was taken to the hospital in an unconscious state.

The ambulance driver, afterwards, told me it was a miracle I was still alive as he thought that he hadn't gotten me to the hospital in time.

I experienced a wondrous thing. I saw a bright light and as I came nearer and nearer to it, it was like a beautiful sunrise close by, and as I advanced I saw a wide expanse of water and I stood by the edge of the water, finally just looking across at this beautiful light. Then I turned and saw it was such a long way back to the place where I had started.

Is this type of experience unique? By no means. In my files are scores of similar accounts, all pointing to the possibility that death is not the dread terror we think it is. It, too, is surely governed by the amazing forces all around us.

A national magazine ran a remarkable article called, "How Does it Feel to Die?" The article consists of a series of nine statements by eminent doctors on the nature of death. Sir William Osler, the famous physician, once made the statement, "Most human beings not only die like heroes, but in my wide clinical experience, die really without pain or fear. There is as much oblivion about the last hours as about the first and therefore people fill their minds with spectres that have no reality."

Kate Holliday, the author of this article, asked the nine doctors whether they agreed with Sir William's statement and the amazing thing is that not one of the doctors disagreed. "Nature is good to the human race," said Dr. Frank Adair, Associate Professor of Clinical Surgery, Cornell University Medical College. "The haunting fear which the average person carries all through life is dissipated by the approach of death."

And Dr. H. D. Van Fleet, President of the Los Angeles Academy of Medicine, says, "I have sat with dying men of every race and creed—Hindus, Shintoists, Catholics, Protestants, Jews and Muslins. They die in peace and I have found that the sweetness of death is intensified in all men by a childlike faith in their religion. Except for their own interpretation of religion, what men cling to is the same throughout the world."

Dr. Johannes Neilsen, Associate Clinical Professor of Medicine at the University of Southern California says, "People who dread death do so because they imagine they're going to be snuffed out of life suddenly. That isn't the way it is at all. As you become more and more ill, whether it is from anemia or cancer or even accident, you become more and more absorbed with the problem of the moment, the condition of your own body. Even doctors who are dying experience this. Their circle of interest grows smaller until they are concerned only with the immediate challenge, until life at last is merely a question of whether or not they will breathe again. And when the circle becomes too small, they go to heaven . . . The circle, in other words, has drawn in to such a degree that even fear is shut out. When you meet eternity all trivialities, even fear, fade into nothing."

So, it would seem from Kate Holliday's research that the fear of death is not as realistic as we have supposed. It is acute to us in the fullness of life, but in sickness and disability the world recedes and God provides a blessed anesthetic for the mind and spirit. The final end is not a painful experience, nor a frightening one, though the illnesses preceding death may be painful indeed. The fears which we attach to death are strongest while we are still very much alive and healthy. But when people approach the experience itself and are weak and ill, it seems that life constricts, ordinary concerns lose their value and death itself becomes so natural that it no longer frightens.

Who knows how near those on the other side may be to us. Readers almost shyly tell how departed loved ones seem to brush their lives for what reason we cannot know. But it does suggest that great and good forces are around us. Some years ago I was driving with my wife from Asbury Park, New Jersey to New York City. At Asbury Park I had attended an auction of household furnishings from an estate called Shadow Lawn, made famous as the summer White House of President Woodrow Wilson. I purchased a pair of beautiful hurricane lamps. While I got them at a bargain price, still I paid a rather good sum for them and perhaps felt a bit guilty. But since they were intended as a birthday gift for my wife, Ruth, I thought the expenditure justified. They were packed and put into the luggage compartment of the car and we started for home.

Midway on the trip we stopped at a Howard Johnson roadside restaurant for lunch. The place was crowded but we got two stools at the counter. I finished first and to give someone else a seat, I told Ruth I would wait for her at the car.

As I stepped into the brilliant sunshine outside, I suddenly had an overwhelming sense of my mother's presence. She had crossed to the other side several years before. I felt rather than saw her smile, and sensed her warm loving personality as distinctly as any feeling I have ever had. Then came the sound of her voice with all the old time familiarity and strength. She said something about Ruth being a wonderful girl and that she deserved those beautiful hurricane lamps and not to worry about things, but be happy and keep on doing good. Then it all faded but I was stirred and moved to the depths of my being. I stood speechless and totally unconscious of surroundings except for a sharp clear beauty in every-thing.

I wept and believe me I am not the weeping kind. I hurried to the car and when Ruth found me, she was shocked to find me weeping and unable to talk. We drove for several miles before I recovered myself and told her the story. Why should my mother have contacted me at such a time and place and about a seemingly trivial matter? Who knows the logic of the amazing forces around us. That we were together in that vibrant moment, personally I have no doubt, and from this meeting I have drawn a strange peace and strength.

Such things are not uncommon and there is certainly no need to be reticent about relating these experiences. I had a letter from Mrs. Mark Clark, the wife of the famous World War II general. In part it read:

> On many occasions I have heard my grandmother and mother relate the story of the death of the former's twenty-five year old son, Elmer.
>
> Elmer had typhoid fever and in 1900 that was often fatal. A twin sister, Eva, to whom Elmer was devoted, had died two years previously with the same disease.
>
> For many days my uncle had been in a coma, too weak to move. Suddenly he sat up straight in bed with arms extended to the heavens, his face radiant with happiness and cried out in a firm clear voice, "Eva"—then he died.

Cecil B. DeMille told a wonderful little story of an experience which gave him insight into the nature of life and death and life again. "I was up on a lake in the Maine woods. The canoe was drifting. I was reading, resting, searching for an idea. I looked down in the water, for my little craft had drifted where the lake was only about four-inches deep. There in a world of mud and wet, were water beetles.

"One crawled up on the gunwale, stuck the talons on his legs into the woodwork and died. I let it alone and turned to my reading. The sun was hot. In about three hours I noticed my water beetle again. He was parched. His back was cracking open. I watched, and out of the back of that dead beetle I saw crawling a new form—a moist head—then wings. A most beautiful dragonfly. It scintillated all the colors of the rainbow. As I sat watching, it flew. It flew farther in a second than the water beetle had crawled in days. It hovered above the surface, just a few inches from the water beetles beneath. They did not know it was there.

"I took my fingertips and moved the shriveled water beetle husk from the canoe's gunwale. It fell back into the lake and sank down to the mud-covered bottom.

"The other water beetles crawled awkwardly to see what it was.

"It was a dead body. They backed away from it.

"If God does that for a water beetle, don't you believe He will do it for me?" asked Cecil B. DeMille.

This is a sound description, to my way of thinking, of the nature of death. Death is simply a change, not an ending, and that we shall emerge into a better form of life it seems logical to assume.

All of the experiences related to me, dealing with extra sensory phenomena, seem to stress continuity.

On May 2, 1914, our beloved mother was dying. She was in a weakened physical condition due to diabetes. She had not gotten up since May 1st and gradually sank into a coma.

Father was sitting at the head of the bed, holding his opened-face watch in one hand, his fingers on mother's pulse with the other. I was gone from the room for a few minutes, leaving my sister standing at the foot of mother's bed. As I came from the hallway to the open doorway, facing the foot of the bed, I stopped suddenly, in astonishment at what I saw—then I slowly walked to the bed and stood silently beside my sister at its foot—to the end. I never mentioned to her what I had seen lest she imagine she saw the same thing. I wanted her to tell *me*.

Two weeks after mother was buried, my sister and I were quietly sitting on the porch, occasionally speaking. After some time she spoke, saying: "I saw the strangest, most unusual thing as we stood at the foot of mother's bed shortly before the end came." I did not interrupt her. When she had finished I said: "Yes, I saw the same. I have waited for you to tell me." The following is what we saw:

Directly over and about nine or so inches above mother was a thin sheet of grayish-blue mist, the color one sometimes sees at twilight in the mountains. This mist, side edges blending into the air like a water color painting, was very slowly moving from foot to head; as it moved upward, the bottom edge was even—straight as this paper's edge.

Mother's gown was open carelessly at the neck to several inches on her chest. The flesh seen *through* the mist was the color of life, but as the mist passed upward, over her flesh, the color was of death, both colors visible in passing.

Just as the mist passed over her head, father, eyes never raised from his watch, fingers yet on her pulse, said sadly: "Mother has gone." The mist vanished immediately into the atmosphere of the room. No outside door nor window was open. We two saw her life pass from her visibly.

These two women believe that they "saw her life pass from her visibly," as if the life itself were a separate entity that continued outside of the body. The incident seems to indicate that death is a passing of the personality or soul from one state into another.

The scores of experiences which have been told to me indicate further that the change in life called death is not without beauty. Always the spiritual forces around us seem to be concerned for us.

A reader from Stratford, Connecticut, wrote me about an incident related by a medical doctor. A woman had been hit by a car and lay by the roadside. Those who gathered thought she was dead. When the ambulance came bringing the doctor, he knelt and lifted the woman's head. She opened her eyes and asked if he was the doctor. When he replied that he was she said, "Well, I want to tell you to tell all my friends; if this is dying, it is the most beautiful experience I ever went through," and with that she dropped her head back and she died.

God has built into us the will to live and the love of life. It is our nature to resist the death of the body to the very last. But can we not believe that God has also arranged our lives so that when they are finished in this world, they shall pass into a better place. Those who live with God in this life need have no fear of the next one. This is the testimony of the hundreds of sincere people who have described their experiences, in one form or another, as to the spiritual forces around us.

Such experiences are related to me with great frequency and they invariably are reported as having aspects of beauty. For instance here is a letter from a lady who lives in Hamilton, Ohio.

> When I was twelve, a simple tonsil operation touched off terrible hemorrhages. In those days transfusions were seldom given and I was already home from the clinic. My mind was clear; and since children seem singularly unafraid of such occasions, I only wished the ordeal were over.
>
> I saw that my mother's face was gray as she brought more basins; the doors of my bedroom were filling up with people, even Grandma had managed to get up the stairs. . . . Suddenly they were all gone, and I was alone. I was standing in a dark corridor, unafraid, just hesitating. In the darkness of it, at times, people would brush against me, rushing forward, together, to the end of the corridor, where shone a wondrous light, more bright than any I had ever known. They were all happy people.
>
> I went forward a little, until I could see "outside." No crowds, only a beautiful field of great white daisies, shining under a radiant sky, and in the field a little girl, smaller than I, was sitting and picking the flowers.
>
> All my short life, since a visit to an uncle's farm, I, a city girl, had always thought a field of daisies shimmering on a breeze-swept hill under a bright sky was the most beautiful thing I had ever seen. I knew for certain the daisies were for me; and the brightness of all that lay beyond that corridor, beyond that hill, was mine.

Then, like a curtain dropped against the light, the words came: "Mama needs me." I shall not trouble you with why I believed this, but it was so. . . . I woke, to find my head cradled on my mother's breast; she was softly calling me, over and over again. In the ensuing days, I alone was sure that I would get well.

Such experiences may offer some hint of the nature of life on the other side. And note that they are vivid and bright and joyous experiences without exception. Do they provide a glimpse of reality that is usually known only after death?

Extra-sensory perception must be another of God's kindly gifts supplying occasional glimpses into the true nature of reality. There is something extra wonderful that is just beyond our usual mortal reach but which can effect our lives even so. It is given to us only in flashes and in fragments of insight to remind us that while we are physical beings in a mortal world, we are also part of a greater world.

Do we understand these mystic laws? Not as yet. We do not even understand to any great extent the physical laws which surround us, much less these profounder spiritual laws. C. B. Colby writing in the White Plains *Reporter Dispatch* posed the following question:

Have you ever wondered what ultimately becomes of the waves that radio and TV stations send out into space twenty-four hours a day? Do they fade and vanish, or do they keep going forever? We do know that sometimes pictures appear mysteriously, long after a program has finished. One of the most famous of all such weird happenings was in England in September, 1953.

Suddenly in many parts of England television screens blossomed out with the identification card and call letters of TV station KLEE in Houston, Texas. Even today transatlantic programming is but a dream, so several viewers took pictures of the image to prove the happening.

What really startled the TV world was the fact that when British broadcasting engineers advised KLEE in Houston of the unusual event, they were told that the station had been off the air since 1950. No KLEE identification card had been shown for the past three years.

Where had that picture been for three years? Why did it appear only in England and how did it get back from wherever it had been? Does make you wonder, doesn't it?

We are surrounded by phenomena—even physical phenomena—which we cannot easily explain. And strange happenings give hints of a fantastic world of spirit in which we are doubtless nearer to the true realities of our universe and which also defy explanation. What, for example, is the relationship of those on the other side to our lives? Do they sometimes draw near in strange and wonderful ways to help us?

Over the years many instances have been reported which suggest the protecting and supporting aid of the strange forces about us. From a practical point of view it bears out our conviction that the broader life in which we dwell will undergird us with extra power if we go confidently about our duty.

Dr. Smiley Blanton gave me a letter from an enthusiastic reader of his fascinating new book *Now or Never*. This reader tells of a controversy in a community meeting years ago in which the local Episcopal minister opposed an action which was violently advocated by a rough sort of man named Sam———. When the vote was taken the minister's position was sustained. Enraged, Sam shouted, "I'll kill you for this!"

Since this man's character was known to be violent, some men said to the minister, "We will walk home with you for you have to pass that lonely wood lot and we aren't too sure Sam won't try to carry out his threat."

But the minister said no, he would go without them as he was never alone . . . there was Someone who would watch over him.

A number of years later the minister was called to Sam's deathbed. He said, "Reverend, there is something I must confess before I die. You remember the night I swore I'd kill you? Well, I intended to and I waited for you in the wood lot with a bar in my hand."

The minister asked, "Why didn't you, Sam?"

Sam looked at the pastor in surprise, "How could I with those two big men on each side of you?"

There is no magic in the universe. But God is there and His powers are vast indeed. We have long since learned and accepted that fact in the world of materiality. What men once called "Miracles" are now everyday facts. No wonders of any kind astonish us, for so many wonders occur almost daily in the realm of science.

Why, then, should we doubt the workings of a whole world of phenomena in the psychic sphere? That isn't miraculous either, for without doubt it will be found to be operating according to law. This is a law abiding universe. We call a phenomenon a miracle until we understand its relationship to law. Instances such as I cite are not presented as bizarre curiosities but are given to indicate that, as spiritual beings in a spiritual universe, we are related to immense forces which we do not comprehend. Their meaning is that, if we live normal humble lives, walking by faith, living in unbroken contact with God, we shall be strangely supported all our days.

Then, by the same forces, we shall enter into that even larger life, which impinges on this one so closely, which we call the eternal. We cannot separate mortal life from eternal life. Eternity means all of time. We are in eternity now. When mortality ends, immortality begins; but there is no break in the flow of time.

The mortal is only an aspect of the spiritual. The body is but a temporary tool of the real person, who is spirit.

Dr. J. B. Rhine cites many cases of physical phenomena bearing on this matter, for example, this from a school teacher:

> It occurred in the first school where I taught. I was then just eighteen and doing my practice teaching. There was a young lad (he was fourteen) who insisted on knowing where I was going to teach. I didn't know at the time. He made it very emphatic on several occasions that no matter where I taught, he was going to my school and no other.
>
> I was seated at my desk shortly after our afternoon studies began when a voice said "Hello, Miss Long." Glancing up, I saw him standing there, smiling at me, hat in hand, holding onto the door. "I told you that no matter where you taught I was going to your school and here I am." Pleased as well as startled I smiled back, exclaiming, "Truman, how did you get here?" He replied, "Oh, I just came. Where can I sit?"
>
> I was aware of the dead silence in the room and every pupil seemed frozen in their places, mingled emotions stamped on their faces, all eyes watching me. Ready to reply I noticed that instead of a solid substance, as he had first appeared, the figure was fading and I could see the details of the room through him. Shaken, I, who hadn't thought of him before, couldn't get this out of my mind.
>
> A few days later a letter from my mother telling of Truman's sudden death made me have the creeps. He had been only slightly ill for a few days and his mother was planning on sending him to school the next day. He had been downstairs eating his noon lunch. At 1:30, the time I saw his apparition, as he started to go back upstairs he collapsed and died, hanging on the stair post.

Such phenomena are remarkable in that they are repeated with frequency and similarity of detail. That they indicate a world beyond our senses seems not unreasonable. And since every phenomenon in God's created universe is intelligent and purposive we cannot but feel that we are related to these amazing powers, that their values may contribute to man's well-being.

Dr. Rhine, in his collection of experiences of pre-recognition, tells the startling story of a Los Angeles streetcar motorman who dreamed one night that he was driving over a new route. As he passed a streetcar coming from the opposite direction, a green truck shot across the tracks. In his dream, his streetcar struck the truck; two men were killed instantly and a woman was badly injured. "You could have prevented it!" the woman screamed at him. He saw that her eyes were bright blue.

The next morning the motorman reported for work, still musing over his dream. "I'm giving you Jim's route this morning," the dispatcher said to him. "He's just phoned in sick." As the motorman drove over the new route he suddenly became aware that it was the very route of his dream.

He broke out in a cold sweat. Then he saw a streetcar coming toward him. Instinctively, he slammed on his brakes. At that moment a green truck shot from a side street and darted across the tracks. The streetcar squealed to a halt, missing the truck by inches. In it were two men and a woman. As they passed close to him, the woman's bright blue eyes caught his. She said nothing, but slowly closed her thumb and forefinger in the familiar gesture of "okay."

These experiences would seem to indicate that our usual concepts of time and place are not based on total reality. There are, apparently, other ways of receiving knowledge than through ordinary sensory reactions. One of the top technical experts in the United States, Charles F. Kettering, said that a great mistake of education today is that it does not place sufficient emphasis upon intuitive knowledge. He cited the case of a professor of organic chemistry at Darmstadt about one hundred years ago. This professor had a dream or vision in which he saw the complete atomic structure of a molecule of hexametabenzene. He wrote it down, but he died with people still ridiculing it.

In a research laboratory only recently, a scientist took a picture of a molecule of hexametabenzene. And there, precisely as the professor had seen it by pre-cognitive insight one hundred years ago, to the exact detail, was the outline of its atomic structure!

We seem to be part of some immense spiritual mechanism which, occasionally, in spite of ourselves, we grapple with. A practicing neuropsychiatrist in New York City, Dr. Russell G. MacRobert, wrote an article called, "Science Studies Intuition," for *Tomorrow* magazine. In it Dr. MacRobert said:

> The following experience occurred to a woman in April, 1949, while she was being given gas anesthesia in the office of a prominent New York dentist. The patient had a dream under the anesthetic and when she awakened she was very upset. In her dream she saw her friend, Mrs. Manuel Quezon, widow of the first President of the Philippines, ambushed and murdered on a lonely mountain road near Manila, halfway around the world. Allowing for the difference in time between New York and Manila, the dream occurred ten hours before the same crime was actually committed—a very ample margin of knowing beforehand as well as seeing something true at a distance without the eyes.
>
> Weird [concluded the dentist's report to me] especially coming from a very intelligent, two-feet-on-the-ground type of person.

That's the kind of report that makes one pause. And note, these experiences do not necessarily come to the spiritualist; often as not they are experienced by the most conservative personalities. And sometimes they are extremely well documented. One of the editors of our own

Guideposts magazine happened to be in Boston a few hours after the occurrence of an amazing example of mental telepathy. This editor himself interviewed the people involved, cross-examining them carefully for any possibility of intentional or accidental "exaggeration," and came away convinced that he had just seen a genuine illustration of the fact that the human mind is capable of mysterious extensions of itself. This is the story:

On the afternoon of June 14, 1955, Thomas Whittaker, a welder from Boston, got a sudden and strong hunch. He had the feeling that something was wrong. He didn't know what it was, but he sensed it so strongly that he quit work and got into his car and just started driving. At various stoplights along the way, he tried to turn his car toward his own home, but the intuition kept him from doing so. Time after time instead of turning toward home, he turned toward Washington Street where his company was also doing some work.

"This is ridiculous," he kept telling himself. "That Washington Street job has been suspended." But he kept edging toward the area just the same.

It's a good thing that he did. When he finally got there, he looked down into a fourteen-foot deep trench that had been dug down the center of the street, and there in the bottom, he saw a cave-in. The sides of the trench had collapsed. And projecting out of the tons of dirt, sand and debris, was a human hand!

Whittaker jumped down into the trench and tried to claw away the dirt with his own hands. He dug down deep enough to uncover a wrist watch, and immediately he recognized it as belonging to his best friend and boss, John H. Sullivan, owner of the Stoneham Welding Service. The hand moved. Frantic now, Whittaker scrambled to the top of the trench and called for the fire and police to help dig Sullivan out of the hole.

Several hours later, safe, if not entirely sound after his ordeal of being buried alive, John Sullivan told the *Guidepost* editor how he had decided to go, alone, to the Washington Street job to finish up some work, and how the sides of the trench had suddenly given way. He was buried. The only thing that saved him from immediate suffocation was the fact that he had on his welder's mask, and inside of it there had been captured enough air to keep him alive until help came.

Had he called for help? Indeed he had. At first he called out loud, and then, when it became clear that that would do no good, he began sending out mental distress signals like an S.O.S. "God send someone," he prayed. "God send someone. God send someone." Over and over again he said these words. And it was while he was thus praying that Tommy Whittaker began to get his strong urge to visit the Washington Street scene. It seems logical to assume that John Sullivan called Tommy Whittaker to his aid by means that are not usually available.

What has all this got to do with everyday life?

Perhaps some day it will be possible for us to bring these spiritual processes under control for the use of mankind, just as we have controlled natural processes the very thought of which our forefathers regarded as miraculous, even ridiculous. Whoever thought that man would fly or send pictures through the air? The Creator placed these powers in the world for man to find and use for his betterment.

Apparently these strange forces around us have been known and used for centuries. For example, in the writings of the early Spanish explorers and adventurers who fought the South American Inca Indians, there are strange reports that indicate the Incas knew the secret of controlling mental telepathy. The Spanish armies would move out on a secret expedition only to discover that the Incas knew exactly when they were leaving, with how many troops, and with what intent. It drove the Spanish mad. There was no evidence of drums, or smoke signaling or of any other form of physical transmission of information. The Spanish concluded that the Incas had the secret of passing information to each other through a form of telepathy.

But even if the day of our practical use of such phenomena should be far off, we cannot avoid the belief that man will become ultimately master of forces in the psychic realm as he is in the material. This is an amazing world God has set us in. It is a world that is ruled by physical laws which are being used in ways almost incredible, as for example outer space exploration. But also around us and within us are spiritual laws which are hardly being used at all in comparison with potential possibility.

We are part of an alive, vibrant universe where the true reality is spirit. When we learn to live in harmony with this spirit, and catch its rhythm, then we will be in tune with power as never before. The end result will be to bring us closer to God and to the exciting knowledge that our existence with Him is not tied to the physical world but to a far greater spiritual world. We shall find that we are part of His immortal spirit and thus are greater and more important than we think. It will make us know that the Lord does not intend us to be weak or little or defeated but to walk the earth in the power of God's great spirit.

You and I have the power to live truly great lives. The strange and powerful forces all about us and within us were surely designed by God to enable His children to master life rather than to be mastered by it. And these forces are infinitely greater than all our weaknesses and sins, our fears, hates and inferiorities.

The power to live with joy and victory is available to you and to me. This power can lead you to a solution of your problems, help you to meet your difficulties successfully and fill your mind and heart with peace and contentment.

The life which the Good God created for us is not little and mean and limited. It is big and beautiful and unlimited. Its possibilities are boundless.

14

YOU CAN BECOME STRONGEST IN YOUR WEAKEST PLACE

Y̲OU CAN become strongest in your weakest place. That is a fact of vast importance to you, to me, to everyone. Repeat that amazing statement aloud, allowing it to sink deeply into consciousness. It is absolutely true—you can become strongest in your weakest place.

That people can become altogether different—strong where they were weak, right where they were wrong, is demonstrated by the experience of a twenty-year-old boy. From his letter it seems he had been a "delinquent," but he is certainly that no longer. Read his letter:

> I have just read your book *The Power of Positive Thinking*. It has made a new man out of me. I am only twenty years old, but I never realized how badly I have wasted those years. All I have ever done with my life is try to be bad, such as fighting, drinking and swearing, because all my friends did it. But I see now how mistaken I have been and I have really been trying your ideas. They have done wonders for me. I have quit smoking and drinking and looking for fights. I have stopped hanging around with people that do those things. I have turned to sports which I greatly enjoy, but best of all I have started going to church again because I have learned to believe in God.
>
> I have found a girl friend that really loves me and we believe in the same things. She is a good girl, not like the girls I have known before. I have learned love and respect with her help, which is something I never had much of, for anyone but myself, before. And I am making more and more friends because I am using your ideas. Truly I have never been happier in my whole life than I have been since reading your book.

Many people have demonstrated in various ways how you can become strongest in your weakest place. There was Glenn Cunningham, whose legs were so badly burned as a child that he was told he would not walk again. But he became one of the fastest Olympic milers in history.

Glenn Cunningham told me that faith and positive thinking are 85 per cent of an athlete's success; in other words, believing that you can do it. "You have to perform on three levels," he explained, "physical, mental and spiritual. And the spiritual helps you to draw on power from the

Master to help pull you through. And," he added, "I don't believe there is such a thing as an impossibility."

Paul Anderson was a sickly, puny weakling. In back of his house in Tacoma, Georgia, he constructed a homemade weight-lifting outfit. It consisted of blacksmith weights tied on the end of a stick. Paul Anderson became the strongest man in the world, breaking strength records that had stood for decades.

Positive thinking looks upon weak places in people as challenging opportunities. You can turn them into your strongest points. The process of so doing is somewhat like that of welding. If a piece of metal breaks and is welded together, the weld is stronger than the metal which surrounds it. At the point of intense heat the molecular structure of the metal flows together.

A cabinet maker once told me that when two pieces of wood are reversed and glued together under heat, the wood will crack elsewhere before it will break at the glued point. This same process can, and often does, take place in personality. Through the intense application of right thinking and strong faith, a weakness can actually become one's strongest point.

Well then, how do we go about turning a weak point into a strong point? The following six-point formula has been used most successfully.

1. Isolate your weakness; then study and know it thoroughly. Plan a real campaign against it.
2. Precisely specify the strength results you wish to attain.
3. Picture or visualize yourself as becoming strongest at your weakest point.
4. Immediately start *becoming* the strong person you wish to be.
5. Act as though you are strongest where you have been weakest.
6. Ask God to help you and believe that He does.

This formula was developed by H. C. Mattern, one of the most thoroughgoing positive thinkers I have known. H. C. Mattern himself is an example of how a man can change a serious weakness into real strength. He was thoroughly negative, in fact so negative that on a balmy night some years ago he walked into a lonely meadow on Long Island and tried to commit suicide. Life was worthless. There was no hope left. He had with him a vial of poison. He lifted it to his lips, drank it and slumped to the ground.

The next thing he knew he was opening his eyes and staring with astonishment into a moonlit sky. At first he wondered whether he were dead. He never did know why he did not die. He always believed, simply, that God wanted him to do a job in life. When he realized that he was still alive, suddenly he wanted very much to live. He thanked God for having spared him and dedicated himself to a life of helping other people.

Mattern became a unique positive thinker. He made it his whole mission in life to encourage others.

What weakness do *you* want to conquer? Is it fear? Anger? Hurt feelings? Inferiority? Disappointment? Is liquor your weakness? Or woman? Whatever it may be, one thing is sure, it does not need to keep on defeating you. Remember this powerful fact; you can become strongest in your weakest place.

Let us look at some examples of people who have turned weakness into strength.

This letter is from a young man who lives in New Mexico.

Dear Dr. Peale:
I don't know how to start this letter. I live on a ranch here in New Mex. For the last ten years I have spent most of my time in bars and night spots. And I was getting in bad shape. I have tried three times to kill myself. I had no friends of my own. And no girl would have anything to do with me. And I don't blame them. I have no one to blame but myself.

But things have changed for me now. I was in Lubbock, Texas, to see my brother. Him and his wife left me there one night to take care of their kids so they could go to the show.

While the kids were asleep, I went into the bedroom to see how they were. On the floor was two of your books about positive thinking. I picked them up and looked at them. I went back in the living room and sat down.

Began reading them. I had found what I was looking for. A new life. I have been without God for a long time. I have now been going to church every Sunday and Bible Class every Wednesday night. The people here in town sure have changed toward me now. I have lots of friends, new ones. But I lost a lot of my old bar buddies. They think I've lost my mind. I just wish and pray that they could follow me and find what I have—a new life. Without God's help I could not have done it. And I have you to thank, too.

I still don't have a girl friend, but I understand that now. Because here in the Southwest a ranch hand or cowboy isn't too well liked. I don't have too much school, but I am not going to let it get me down. If I live by God's way, which I will, there will be a home for me up there if I cannot have it here on earth—because I have faith and believe and have confidence in myself and God. Be content with what you have, for he has said, "I will never fail you nor forsake you." I carry these books with me all the time. Never a day goes by that I do not learn a verse from one of them.

I am thirty-two years old. I am sending a picture of me taken here on the ranch last summer. I am so happy I had to write this letter to let you know what your books have done for me. I will close this letter. And pray for me.

P.S. Please overlook my writing. I don't know how to spell very good. I have to write with pencil. I make mistakes. I have to cross out a lot.

The life of this young man was transformed by a sudden exposure of his mind to the power of God through positive, creative ideas. If a person has a weakness which he wants to get under control and seemingly cannot, but is willing to take into his mind the best positive ideas, he will find that the power of such ideas to affect his life is amazing indeed. This explains many of the dramatic changes that happen to people through religious faith. A new and powerful thought has burst into the mind, shattering old weaknesses, breaking them to bits. It is in the mental processes that all motivation changes take place. The phrase "a change of heart" really means a profound change of mind. The heart is only a muscle to pump blood. It is the mind that accepts the new concept that changes. And faith is an idea so powerful that it can set the entire life going in a new direction with new and amazingly increased strength.

This is why you should read the Bible, the most powerful accumulation of life changing thoughts ever assembled. This is why you should go regularly to church and hear the great words, the words of God which, if received deeply into your mind, have the power to change your life. Dynamic, powerful, positive thoughts take a bold step forward in the conquering of an individual weakness.

Some time ago I was lecturing in Los Angeles when I ran across a most interesting example of a young lady who was ruining her life by the use of the wrong kind of words—words as symbols of a destructive idea. If you constantly use negative or deprecatory words about yourself, you are implanting equivalent destructive concepts in your mind.

On this particular day, after my lecture, I was at the front of the auditorium greeting quite a number of people. In this line was an attractive young lady who took my hand with a timid little shake and greeted me with this shocking sentence. "I so much wanted to speak to you," she said. "But of course I'm a nobody. You wouldn't know me. I don't amount to anything, but I have read your books and I just wanted to shake your hand."

I say this statement was shocking, for it minimized and depreciated God's highest form of creation, a human being.

I was a little tired of hearing so many people say they were "nobodies." It happens time and again across the country that people speak this way of themselves. So I stopped this young lady and said, "Miss Nobody, will you do me a favor? Will you please wait until I am through here . . . I'd like to talk with you." A little later I turned and found that sure enough she was there waiting.

"Now, Miss Nobody," I said. "I'd like a few words with you."

The girl laughed. "What did you call me?" she asked

"Miss Nobody," I said. "Because that is what you called yourself. Do you have some other name?"

She said yes and gave me her proper name.

"Just why did you tell me you are a Nobody?" I continued. "You say you've read about positive thinking, but you evidently haven't gotten very much out of it, else you'd never think of yourself as Miss Nobody. These books are designed to make people realize who and what they really are. Now, obviously, you have been telling not only others, but what is more serious, you tell yourself that you do not amount to much of anything. But I can see that you are wrong for, obviously, you have many qualities which are admirable. Certainly you are attractive. You have a good, clear eye. You know how to dress well. You have a charming smile. I think you are a very fine person and I don't think you should be carrying around a 'nobody' complex."

This young lady and I talked for some time about her ambitions and hopes and about the fact that it is very important not to weight these hopes down with negative thoughts. Her weak spot was a deep-seated "nobody complex" and she was compounding the difficulty with negative words. The cure for her situation was a reversal of the concept of herself.

I gave her the formula for overcoming her weakness and told her how to apply. I also suggested that she use the following affirmation: "I am the temple of God. In God I live and move and have my being. I am a child of God. I will think and act like a child of God."

She agreed to say this affirmation a dozen times every day and at the same time to visualize herself as being as the words describe. Months later, when I was again in California on a speaking engagement, an attractive young lady appeared before me and said, "You used to know me, but you don't now." That was an unusual thing to say and I turned to look carefully. To my astonishment who should it be but "Miss Nobody." "I have found that I can do things," she continued. "I have gotten out of that awful habit of thinking of myself as a Nobody and I just wanted to thank you for helping me change my identity."

As we talked it became very clear that she had, indeed, changed noticeably. Here was a girl who overcame a weakness through the use of positive ideas. She had become strongest in her weakest place; she had had a depreciatory and inferior attitude toward herself.

This self-depreciatory weakness is one that a great many face under the name of inferiority. Such feelings of inferiority can be extremely painful and self-defeating. Believe me, I know from hard, personal experience. When I was a boy I was what they used to call "bashful." That word isn't used much any more, but under whatever name, the feeling of being abashed by life is certainly painful. And the trouble is very widespread judging from the number of letters I receive on this subject. Here is one, for example:

Dear Dr. Peale,

I have been wanting to write to you for a long time. I surely do need help, but do not know if anyone can help me or not.

This is my problem. My husband is custodian of our church and I assist him, but I do not feel accepted among the women. Many times when I go to church I sit alone. The women will come in and sit in front of me or behind, but not in the pew with me unless all the others are filled up.

We do not dress as well as they do and I think the main reason is because I am not as bright as they are. I am quiet and sometimes say things that I should not and I do not mean it the way it sounded.

The women do not have me work with them in sewing or anything they do in groups. I have volunteered my services, but they say they are saving me for a time when I am needed. Still I hear them asking others to help.

My relatives seem to be ashamed of me or something. They do not introduce me to their friends or do not care to have me go to church with them. We have lived here in this community for a year and only one neighbor has been in.

I surely would appreciate it if I could learn how to be accepted among the women and have friends.

This is a typical letter showing tragic glimpses into the suffering of men and women who have become victims of the feelings of inadequacy. Very often (and I think this was true of the custodian's wife) these painful weaknesses are self-imposed. Notice in the above letter that this woman puts herself into a position where she asks to be hurt. She deliberately arrives in the church early, sits in the pew where people will either have to say to her, symbolically, "I like you" or "I do not like you." Now, the mathematics of the situation are very much against her. If one hundred people came to the church, only two can sit next to her and ninety-eight have to sit somewhere else. But she interprets the action of each of the ninety-eight as being against her.

Why is it that so many people actually seek out this feeling of inferiority? Psychologists tell me that one of the most common weaknesses of personality is that people often *do not want to succeed!* Somewhere along the line they have learned that it is a dangerous thing to succeed as it imposes upon them the burden of responsibility to live up to a success status. So they deliberately, though unconsciously, seek ways to keep themselves inferior by emphasizing their weaknesses.

Now it is a fact of life that each person is made up of stronger and weaker areas of personality. The question is, which are you going to dwell on? Which are you going to emphasize? If you specialize on the weaker areas in your personality you will become weak; if you stress the stronger areas you will become strong. It is as simple and certain as that.

But we must be careful not to confuse real weaknesses with self-assumed ones. Learning to accept ourselves is the first step in overcoming the weakness of inadequacy. Most of us, at least those of us who are troubled with the inferiority complex, pay far too much attention to ourselves, to our self-assumed weaknesses and drawbacks. We become self-conscious about things which are not important. We feel that everyone is noticing them when in reality they are not.

Not long ago I had an unusual opportunity to test this theory. I had been receiving a great deal of mail from people all saying the same, pathetically inferior thing: "No one likes me because of this or that."

One girl was ashamed because she was too fat; another because she was too thin. One boy felt that his ears were too big; another that his ears hugged his head too closely. Still another boy was self-conscious because he was too tall and another had painful inferiority feelings because he was short. I even recall one letter from a young girl who complained that she was too pretty. Nobody liked her for herself, but only for her body.

Now it happened that one of these typical complaints came to me from a young boy in our city. "Dr. Peale," he said, "nobody likes me because my nose is too big."

I had heard so much of this sort of thing that I decided then and there to make an experiment. "Name six of your acquaintances who do not like you because your nose is too big," I said to this boy. He gave me six names and a little later I took the time to place a call to each of these young people. As soon as I got them on the phone I asked them to name the outstanding characteristic of this young man's personality. Each one had to think a while, but this was the result of my inquiry. One told it was his friendliness; another that he was unusually good in arithmetic. A girl said he was a marvelous dancer. And so it went. Not *one* of these people signaled out this boy's nose as his outstanding characteristic. Apparently no one but he himself had any consciousness of that nose.

So it is true that many of us pick out some little characteristic which we consider to be a weakness and spend a great deal of effort convincing ourselves that *because of this weakness we cannot succeed.* The solution of the problem lies in realizing that God intends you to be a happy, successful, strong person. You must decide whether you will emphasize your weak points or your strong points, for you have both. The choice is up to you. Just as soon as you start emphasizing your strengths, your inferiority will diminish and a new sense of capacity will replace your old weakness and inadequacy.

Let us take a look at another common weakness and at solutions that were found; and this weakness is that of discouragement. So many times discouragement spells the difference between success and failure. If only you had carried on a little bit longer! Or harder! But discouragement made you give up just short of something really great. How tragic to quit when one more extra push would have brought success.

The fact of ups and downs is something we have to deal with in life. But positive thinking handles that problem. My friend Frank W. Kridel, General Manager of the great Manhattan and Astor hotels in New York, is a good example of the power of positive thinking in meeting potential discouragement. Referring to the helpfulness of prayer and guidance in practical problems, he said, "It is terrific how the whole pattern has worked out. And we've had some tough problems too, but it's a fact that when you trust God and keep plugging, while you have your ups and downs, with positive thinking you can turn your downs into ups." What a tremendous truth: "You can turn your downs into ups." That is to say, we must know how to turn our negatives into positives.

It is in problems of difficulty and discouragement that positive thinking has had some of its most amazing results. Another friend of mine, Ruth Hardy, also a hotel proprietor, runs the Ingleside Inn in Palm Springs, California. This is a little gem of a place set amidst lush gardens of bougainvillea, orchid bushes, palm and orange trees. Nestling in the lee of towering San Jacinto, it basks in the golden sun and balmy desert air. At night, when a silvery moon rises over the mountains, the place is almost ethereal in charm and peacefulness. It is one of my favorite spots.

But there has been struggle here as well as beauty. Indeed, how can there be any real beauty without struggle?

This charming Inn came into being through faith and positive thinking. Mrs. Hardy had plenty of troubles before making a success of her enterprise. She knew that she needed spiritual strength to do it and searched everywhere for guidance. She found help through Ernest Holmes and others.

To a friend, who passed the letter along to me, she writes:

It is strange how Norman's teachings came to me. Away back in 1942, when I was left alone, I decided I had to have some plan of living or something to go by. I have read everything that I could find in metaphysics that seemed to have some of the answers. Then along in the 40's someone sent me some of the literature from the Marble Collegiate Church. To me it made sense, and I thought that if this theory that I believed in really works then I should depend on it. And from that time on I have attempted as near as possible to run Ingleside along the plan for living that Norman advocates. Norman has told me many times that his theory is in the proving stage. He believes it and he knows it works, and he is always looking for evidence and proof that it *is* the way of life.

You know, by all the rules of aerodynamics, the bumblebee cannot fly! But the bumblebee doesn't know it and just keeps on flying! He is too fat, too big, and his wings are too short, but he just keeps going. In all the hotel books it says that any American Plan hotel under fifty rooms cannot exist, as there is not enough income to make it survive, as it is too small an operation with a dining room. Yet for twenty-six years I have run a small American Plan hotel, and it has worked. And the more I go along the lines of Norman's teachings, the better it works. I find I don't have to hurry and strain and be tense—I find that it is a very relaxing, happy life, all because I ask God for guidance and get it. I read my Bible and my books and apply the theory. The greatest thing that ever happened to me was to have Norman's literature fall into my hands.

Positive thinking has been responsible for many a successful battle against failure by turning another prevalent kind of weakness into strength. One man, today a successful and respected executive, had to battle a dull sense of inferiority. When I first met him he seemed an extremely retiring young man. In fact, he was retiring to the point of shrinking. It was a real weakness which hampered him greatly. By it he minimized himself and gave the impression that he lacked force and ability.

He was with a large business organization in the personnel department. One day he was notified that his services were no longer required—this after eight years with the company. He was crushed and dazed. He had accumulated very little money, the future was dark, he was keenly discouraged. But then a strange thing happened; now that he had to depend upon himself, now that he was faced with a real crisis, he turned his weakness into strength. He remembered some of the things we had been saying about positive thinking, and he resolved to put these theories to work.

I heard of his difficulty and said, "I want to help you. I have some contacts and maybe we can do something."

But to my surprise he replied, "I do not want you to do a thing, not a thing. I am going to put your principles of positive thinking into effect. You just forget me except to pray for me; that is all. If these principles are workable, they will work whether you help me or not, and if they will not work, then your help will not do me much good." I liked that as it showed strength coming up.

A few months later he told me of the results of his experiment. He said, "For the first time in my life I was forced to do some real creative thinking. Here I was, no job, none in sight and a family to support. But I visualized that somewhere was a future for me. Indeed, I intended to find it. I had to use my brain and my faith to do it."

So what did he do? Simply this; he secured the names of the presidents of one hundred firms. He read *Who's Who* and other types of directories in order to form an insight into the thinking of each executive whom he wanted to contact. He studied what type of businessmen they were. He investigated their personal attitudes, their likes and dislikes. He developed a comprehensive analysis of the mental slant of each man.

To each of them he then wrote a personal letter saying that he was trained for personnel work and outlining his experience. He told the prospective employer, modestly but specifically, what he had to offer. He outlined how he felt he could help that employer. He slanted his sales presentation of his own services to the employer's self-interest. He was not bold, but neither was he shrinking. He presented his qualifications objectively. And he received a number of replies expressing interest.

He held on to his mental picture of the work he wanted, continuing to think positively, and his contacts produced a choice between two good positions. He accepted a job at twelve hundred dollars more a year than he had received in the business he had left. After he started his new job I said to him, "It is really a miracle, the thing that happened to you."

"Miracle, not at all. It's merely a demonstration of the power of positive thinking which you teach. I've discovered by the acid test of personal experience that positive thinking is practically and scientifically sound. I know now why the Bible tells us to have faith, for when you believe, really believe, your mind becomes clear and then you can think your way through your difficulties. And besides," he added, "an experience like this isn't all bad. Maybe I needed something to shake me out of the mouse-like, half-scared rabbit that I was. I feel more self-confidence now." He had, in fact, become strongest where previously he had been weakest.

The most effective way for developing strength from weakness is through the life changing process of a positive faith. Evidences of this fact are multiplied daily; so much so, that selection among illustrations is most difficult. Dramatic demonstrations of people who out of weakness were made strong seem to be without limit.

Oftentimes I have mentioned this process of change to people struggling with a weakness and they say to me, "But I go to church, I contribute to charities and read my Bible. It seems to me that I am living with an active faith and it doesn't help at all." But, you see, the really important thing is a spiritual experience of God's power. It requires much more than religious formality to do the powerful job necessary in building real strength out of weakness.

Take the case of Bill Carter. I will call him that though Carter is not his name. Bill was having a great deal of trouble with alcohol. He tried every known method of curing himself of this weakness, with no results at all. One day his physician told him rather bluntly, "Bill, I am sorry but there is nothing more that I can do for you."

"You mean my case is hopeless?"

"Yes, unless you get top expert help."

"But, Doctor, who knows more about alcoholism than you?"

"Well," said the doctor, "I know of one specialist who might be able to help you. He is very high priced, however, and you'll have to be willing to pay. He takes everything you've got, but He can cure you for sure."

Bill sat straight up in his chair. "Who is this specialist? I will pay whatever is necessary if I can just get a hold on myself and solve this drinking problem."

"Bill," said the physician, "this specialist I'm talking about keeps office in the New Testament. You know who He is. And I doubt very much that you are willing to pay the price He asks. I know that you go to church, say your prayers; you even read your Bible, but you are not paying the price required for change. And what does this Doctor charge? Yourself, your whole self. You're holding out, that's why we can't get a cure in your case. You won't let go of that last 5 per cent of yourself. I've got the alcohol boiled out of you, but that area of 5 per cent of your brain, that I cannot reach. Only the Great Physician can get in there and cure the weakness that licks you and will continue to lick you.

"You see, you have to go all out, give all of yourself. Do that and you will really get strength."

He was a doctor! He was a doctor of the mind and soul as well as body. It is true that a great many of us actually are giving just a part of ourselves to our faith. It takes the whole man, the whole heart and soul, to make religious faith effective in this deeper sense. Bill Carter finally took his doctor's advice. He said a simple prayer which, however, was a prayer he had never before been able to say. Here is what he said—and meant:

"Lord, I am no longer going to hold on to this 5 per cent of resistance. I am going to give You the whole of myself. You take charge. I no longer belong to me. Do with me what You will. Amen."

As a result, spiritual power began to come. In time Bill's ability to cope with the problem of alcohol strengthened. Today he is a sober and effective person because he learned how to give all of himself to God's will. "When I let God take over," he said, "I could actually feel that old weakness being burned out of me." It is a basic fact about faith that it will work with power when you give *all* of yourself to what you believe. Withhold nothing. Have no reservations. Believe *positively* with all your heart, all your mind, all your spirit and no weakness can be too great for you to master.

In this chapter we have been looking at the methods used by actual people to transform weakness into strength through positive thinking. We have paid particular attention to anger, inferiority, discouragement, moral defeat.

The same principles can be applied to any weakness, whatever it is. Bring your own particular problem into the patterns suggested by this chapter. First, get your problem into a clear focus so that you know specifically what weakness it is you are trying to combat. Then focus on the results you wish to attain; specifically, what is it that you wish to accomplish? Start right away to become the person you wish to be. Practice expecting to be strongest in your weakest place. And you will be. Always persevere in your efforts to attain this goal. Don't give up. Continue—continue—continue.

If you feel your energies flagging, reread this chapter; notice in particular how others who have faced similar weaknesses have carried on to victory. And, finally, keep forever before you the firm belief that God does not intend you to be victimized by weaknesses. Believe this, for it is true. Believe that the natural way for you to face life is with courage and strength. Believe that God built potential strength into you which you have not been using. But now you are going to start using it.

Isolate your weak spot, specify the results you wish to attain, picture yourself becoming strong, start being the strong person you wish to be. Act as though you are now changing into strength, believe you can attain the results you seek, humbly trusting in God to help you. This is the pattern, the tremendous pattern of deep personality change. Apply it to your own particular problem and you, too, can become strongest in your weakest place.

In fact your whole life can become stronger and happier in every particular. As you study and apply the teachings of this book, great things will happen to you because something great will have happened within you. Your stronger faith, deeper understanding and greater dedications will open up a wonderful new life for you. You will become a vital personality well able to handle all your own problems. And you will have enough extra strength and insight to be a creative influence in the lives of many others.

No more defeat, no more failure, no more dull hopelessness. Life won't suddenly become easy or superficial—not at all. Life is real. Life is earnest and it is full of problems. But thank God it now becomes full of the overcoming of problems. Through the formulas of thinking and acting outlined in this book you need no longer be mastered by your difficulties. You can now master them. The difference is due to that Master who has entered into your life to make you a very different person. So to you, as to the others, will come the amazing results of positive thinking.

EPILOGUE

I COULD GO ON and on telling of the amazing results of positive thinking. So many others than those mentioned in this book have experienced great personal victories. And I would like to tell you about all of them. But there is a limit to the length of a book. And we must close.

But before doing so there is just one final thing I want to say: Never become discouraged with yourself or with your life. Never give in to defeat, never lose heart.

There is a way out, there is a way around, there is a way through any problem, any difficulty. And that way is by positive thinking and positive action. It is accomplished by spiritual motivation.

What others have done—with the help of God—you also can do. And how to do it has been stated with sincerity, and, I hope, with clarity in this book. On page after page are formulas and techniques used by others to turn defeat into victory.

Now that you have read the book go back and practice it. This, unlike most books, is not merely a reading book. It's a practicing manual. It will work, but only when you work it. For best results disciplined and prayerful perseverance is required.

I dedicated this book in sincere prayer. I dedicated it to God with a prayer that it might help you. And the book *can* help you as others have been helped. Faithfully practice its teachings as suggested and you too can have the amazing results of positive thinking.

With friendly good wishes and a sincere God bless you, I am

Cordially Yours,
NORMAN VINCENT PEALE

ABOUT THE AUTHOR

Dr. Norman Vincent Peale was once called "the most widely read inspirational author of a generation." He was a renowned lecturer, author of over 46 books, cofounder of the Institutes of Religion and Health, and founder and copublisher of *Guideposts* magazine. He passed away in 1993.